THE DECLINE AND FALL OF THE ROMAN EMPIRE

THE DECLINE AND FALL OF THE ROMAN EMPIRE

By EDWARD GIBBON

CONDENSED FOR MODERN READING

It was among the ruins of the Capitol that I first conceived the idea of a work which has amused and exercised nearly twenty years of my life, and which, however inadequate to my own wishes, I finally deliver to the curiosity and candour of the public.

EDWARD GIBBON

LAUSANNE,
June 27, 1787.

WISE & CO.

New York

PRINTED IN THE UNITED STATES OF AMERICA

CONTENTS

INTRODUCTION

In 1776, when America was ceasing to be a colony of England, an Englishman wrote of the time when England was a colony of Rome. As a member of Parliament, Edward Gibbon voted against American liberties. As a historian, the author of *The Decline and Fall of the Roman Empire* reluctantly testified to the temporal nature of imperialism.

His book was severely criticized, but not on political grounds. Seething as it was with political revolutions, the eighteenth century had time for religious debate; and Gibbon was challenged by bishops, deans and dons for the chapters in which he showed that the fall of Rome was hastened by the rise of Christianity. It was rightly suspected that Gibbon's sympathy for the ancient world made him unsympathetic to the new. He was attacked unfairly as an atheist, more fairly as a pagan. Devout ladies tore from Volume One of his book the controversial 15th and 16th chapters.* James Boswell, calling the author an "infidel wasp," expressed the irritation felt by right-minded people for one who clearly preferred the character of Marcus Aurelius to that of Constantine.

Gibbon could take care of himself; of his most vociferous clerical critic, he wrote "If he will take the trouble of calling at my house any afternoon when I am *not* at home, my servant shall show him my library." No one could disprove Gibbon's basic facts, and today the religious controversy as such has lost its point. Gibbon himself was converted to Roman Catholicism at sixteen, re-converted to Protestantism six months later, and thereafter professed Church of England orthodoxy with that acquiescence in authority which made him jilt his first love when his father forbade the bans. This detachment from religious fervor he admired in his Roman heroes; it is generally practiced in our own period. Even in the still devout nineteenth century, Gibbon was re-admitted to respectable religious society; Sir James MacIntosh observed that his views "might all safely be adopted by a Christian writer, with some change in the language and manner"; a doctor of divinity in Princeton, N. J., wrote a pamphlet noting that Gibbon read the Greek testament on Sundays and never rejected Christianity; and Cardinal Newman admitted that Gibbon was "the chief, perhaps the only English writer who has any claim to be considered an ecclesiastical historian."

Today the only one of Gibbon's critics to strike a modern note (and the only one Gibbon chose to answer) is that Bishop of Landaff who, as Regius Professor of Divinity at Cambridge, wrote *Two Apologies*—open letters to Edward Gibbon and to Thomas Paine. Remonstrating with both, the bishop managed to couple the names of two men whose political views were diametrically opposed. Our present concern is not with the Gibbon who joined

*Renumbered in this edition as Chapters X and XI.

with Tom Paine in questioning church authority, but with the Gibbon who differed with Paine about the American Revolution, the French Revolution and the whole question of the rights of man.

In his lifetime it was said of Gibbon that he thought he was the Roman Empire. There is no doubt that he admired the empire as he admired his own monumental work and, perhaps, his portly person. In our own time, which questions imperial aims and values, there is no book as pertinent to the discussion as *The Decline and Fall.* The author of *Mein Kampf* exposed, while advocating, a system so simple and dreadful that no sane reader could be converted to it. Gibbon reveals the vices and the virtues of an infinitely more complex society which, over the centuries, more nearly resembles our own.

Most of us are familiar with the obvious physical parallels between our civilization and that of Rome. We know that the Romans had firstrate plumbing, with hot and cold running water in their baths; that they built good roads, loved the theater, assembled by thousands for sporting events, and suffered long speeches in their Senate. But Gibbon discovered a thousand further parallels in event, in attitude, in problem and policy, and above all in the conduct of defensive war.

The characteristic Roman attitude was the complacent superiority of established civilization confronted with change. When they met the barbarians with too little, too late, they said Rome might lose a battle but she always won the war. It was the barbarians who tried new methods–Commando tactics, raiding at night with blackened faces; heavy new weapons and armor–mechanization; swift movement–the blitz; destruction of a country–"scorched earth." After Hadrian's wall, their Maginot line, failed to protect, a Roman general argued that nothing could reconcile the barbarians to peace until they experienced in their own country the calamities of war; and Probus, crossing the Rhine into Germany, as well as Julian, who won his German war before he sent food from Britain into the Rhineland, succeeded for a time by determined action. But mainly the Romans relied on simple, craven appeasement, and it failed. They tried it with the Germans and on the African coast; they tried it again and again, with large bribes and bright hopes. Always it failed.

Roman policy also included corruption of enemy leaders, and setting opponents at loggerheads. These methods met with varying success but in the end they too failed. One reason is perhaps that the Romans chose to deal with native princes in Persia and Egypt, and exiled nobles from Poland; there is no record of their considering the common people anywhere.

Domestic problems are familiar. Abandoned farms turned to wasteland, hard-up tenant farmers, miners who welcomed the Gothic invaders because their own lot could not be worsened, starving city dwellers in tall tenements –all these were problems of home administration. They were met by all varieties of appeasement rather than reform–by tariffs and taxes, by price-fixing (under Diocletian), state medical care (under Valentinian), and the ever-necessary dole.

As for the barbarians, the troublesome Germans are the first to claim that they have changed little since first they emerged from obscurity to war on the civilized world. According to Gibbon, they were ignorant, drunken, stupid, and proud of it; their sole virtue was bravery in war and their sole enterprise adoption of effective arms. Winning, they used techniques which repetition has made familiar: they took hostages to hold ravaged territory, rated their own lives higher than those of civilized persons tried in the same courts and punished the liberal-minded for harboring dangerous thoughts.

If it is easy to identify German faults, it is more difficult to say with certainty who are the Romans of today. Disregarding Il Duce's bid, Americans note an obvious correlation with the British Empire, summarized long ago in the play song English children chant:

"Oh yes, we will have two cups full, for we are the Romans!
"Oh no, you won't have two cups full, for we are the English soldiers!"

But among the English-speaking peoples it is not the English alone who have far-flung territories and some unrest at home.

In the realm of ideas, an obvious parallel can be drawn between the rise of Christianity as described by Gibbon, and the spread of communism as seen or feared today. Gibbon outraged the Christians of his era by suggesting "human" reasons for the success of Christianity, then considered to have been established by divine fiat. Among these reasons he noted that Christianity released the suppressed energies of the Jews, that it attracted to its "common tables" slaves, women, reformed criminals, and other persons of small importance—in short that Christianity was a "people's movement" of low social origin, rising as the people rose.

Many persons today, and most of all the orthodox Communists, are shocked by the suggestion that communism possesses a religious appeal. Yet observers as far apart as the Dean of Canterbury and Mr. Max Eastman have remarked on it; and Gibbon supplies the historic background when he dwells on the social significance of the primitive church. Although he neglects specific mention of the Catacombs, he describes an underground movement impossible to extirpate by burning books or bodies, or by placing the blame for the burning of public buildings on an innocent but unpopular minority. He shows how, even after Christianity was established as a successful social force, some converts became fanatics, submitting to a hard discipline and bitterly denouncing heretics in their own ranks—for the Arian controversy, read Trotsky vs. Stalin party division. He presents the early Christians as conscientious objectors to war and eager watchers for a millennium.

The conversion of Constantine as Gibbon describes it has further present-day application. For the same year, Constantine ordered consultation of the ancient haruspices, and celebration of the new Christian Sunday. It is not difficult to find among us politicians who favor both the elder Capitoline gods and the new five-day week.

There is, of course, a fatal implication in these parallels. We do as the Romans do; but Rome fell. . . .

This fearful application of the cycle theory has been made by the famous archeologist Flinders Petrie, by the famous psychopath Oswald Spengler, and by others. In 1926, the Right Honorable Stanley Baldwin said "Who in Europe does not know that one more war in the West, and the civilization of the ages will fall with as great a shock as that of Rome?" This fear explains the Baldwin policies while suggesting that the prime minister overlooked Gibbon on appeasement.

Henry Wallace, writing eight years later in *New Frontiers*, took note of the cycle theory and agreed with its premise: "There is sufficient likeness between the Graeco-Roman civilization and our own to make us consider to what extent we are in a period somewhat similar to that of Augustus Caesar." But he denied the necessity for decline. "With modern machinery, modern science, and the insight obtainable in our modern universities, there is no necessary compulsion for this civilization to follow the rhythms of the past."

More, Mr. Wallace found a hopeful difference to help break the cycle: "Did Roman leaders in the time of the Caesars speculate on the causes of the decline of the ancient Egyptian and Persian civilizations? Probably not—and to that extent we may have a decided and determining advantage over the Romans."

Such speculation was no part of Gibbon's task; his consideration of causes omits the one which many people would now put first, the institution of slavery throughout the Roman Empire. Today, with slavery illegal even in recaptured Ethiopia, some say that American Negroes were better off as slaves than as sharecroppers or migrants, and argue that modern civilization moves on rubber harvested by near-slaves in the tropic outposts of empire now in barbarian hands. Yet there is still hope that Judeo-Christian democracy, breaking through the slave civilization of Rome, helped establish a basis for resisting the recurrent decline. At least our machine civilization is mainly dependent on semi-skilled labor that is semi-free; and though rulers remain, never did so few owe so much to so many.

Gibbon had no room for speculation because he furnished such extensive grounds for it. "Another damned thick book! Always scribble, scribble! Eh, Mr. Gibbon?" said the Duke of Gloucester, presented with the third volume of *The Decline and Fall*. Three more were to come, and other than royal readers were to find the six "thick, fat, square" volumes too much. Charles Lamb put them among the books unread; Walter Bagehot suggested that the way to reverence Gibbon was to look at him in the bookcase; and only last year Lord Elton told the National Book Council, meeting in bombed London, that to live in the same room with an unread set of Gibbon was a liberal education.

This comfortable conclusion is dangerous if Gibbon, finishing his sixth volume in Geneva in 1787, had something to say which concerns a world subject to bombs over bookstalls and peace palaces. The obvious remedy is to reprint, that he may run who reads, those parts of the great work applicable to present crisis. For such rude handling of his lifework Gibbon affords a precedent. Quoting from one of his Latin sources, he confesses: "It is incumbent on me to explain the liberties which I have taken with the text of Ammianus. 1. I have melted down into one piece the sixth chapter of the fourteenth and the fourth of the twenty-eighth book. 2. I have given order and connection to the confused mass of materials. 3. I have softened *some* extravagant hyperboles and pared away some superfluities of the original. 4. I have developed some observations which were insinuated rather than expressed. With these allowances my version will be found, not literal indeed, but faithful and exact."

Fewer liberties have here been taken with Gibbon than he took with Ammianus. One large simplification omits the descriptions of the eastern empire and of mediaeval Europe which fill the later volumes, on the theory that Mohammed and Charlemagne and that Holy Roman Empire which was "neither holy, nor Roman, nor an empire" belong to a later world. It is true that Rome fell, as Mr. Shaw said of Adam, not by one step only but down a whole flight. Nevertheless, for most of us the date of the fall is approximately 476 A.D., and here this edition stops, with no more about Justinian than belongs to the chapter on Roman law.

Much theology has been cut, but all of Gibbon on imperialism–Empire politics and administration–is here. Editing has been a job of thinning the trees that the wood may be seen.

And what a wood it is–that dark forest from which the barbarians came, into which the Roman ruins lapsed, which waits still for any empire unable to escape. Gibbon has told the story of the last imperial cycle before our own. Our best chance to break the cycle may be, as Mr. Wallace suggests, to profit by the mistakes of the Romans.

WILLSON WHITMAN

New York, March 15, 1943.

CHAPTER I

The Extent and Military Force of the Empire in the Age of the Antonines

In the second century of the Christian era, the Empire of Rome comprehended the fairest part of the earth, and the most civilised portion of mankind. The frontiers of that extensive monarchy were guarded by ancient renown and disciplined valour. The gentle but powerful influence of laws and manners had gradually cemented the union of the provinces. Their peaceful inhabitants enjoyed and abused the advantages of wealth and luxury. The image of a free constitution was preserved with decent reverence: the Roman senate appeared to possess the sovereign authority, and devolved on the emperors all the executive powers of government. During a happy period (A.D. 98–180) of more than fourscore years, the public administration was conducted by the virtue and abilities of Nerva, Trajan, Hadrian, and the two Antonines. It is the design of this, and of the two succeeding chapters, to describe the prosperous condition of their empire; and afterwards, from the death of Marcus Antoninus, to deduce the most important circumstances of its decline and fall; a revolution which will ever be remembered, and is still felt by the nations of the earth.

The principal conquests of the Romans were achieved under the republic; and the emperors, for the most part, were satisfied with preserving those dominions which had been acquired by the policy of the senate, the active emulation of the consuls, and the martial enthusiasm of the people. The seven first centuries were filled with a rapid succession of triumphs; but it was reserved for Augustus to relinquish the ambitious design of subduing the whole earth, and to introduce a spirit of moderation into the public councils. Inclined to peace by his temper and situation, it was easy for him to discover that Rome, in her present exalted situation, had much less to hope than to fear from the chance of arms; and that, in the prosecution of remote wars, the undertaking became every day more difficult, the event more doubtful, and the possession more precarious, and less beneficial. The experience of Augustus added weight to these salutary reflections, and effectually convinced him that, by the prudent vigour of his counsels, it would be easy to secure every concession which the safety or the dignity of Rome might require from the most formidable barbarians. Instead of exposing his person and his legions to the arrows of the Parthians, he obtained, by an honourable treaty, the restitution of the standards and prisoners which had been taken in the defeat of Crassus.

His generals, in the early part of his reign, attempted the reduction of Æthiopia and Arabia Felix. They marched near a thousand miles to the south of the tropic; but the heat of the climate soon repelled the invaders, and protected the unwarlike natives of those sequestered regions. The northern countries of Europe scarcely deserved the expense and labour of conquest. The forests and morasses of Germany were filled with a hardy race of barbarians, who despised life when it was separated from freedom; and though, on the first attack, they seemed to yield to the weight of the Roman power, they soon, by a signal act of despair, regained their independence, and reminded Augustus of the vicissitude of fortune. On the death of that emperor, his testament was publicly read in the senate. He bequeathed, as a valuable legacy to his successors, the advice of confining the empire within those limits which nature seemed to have placed as its permanent bulwarks and boundaries: on the west the Atlantic Ocean; the Rhine and Danube on the North; the Euphrates on the East; and towards the South, the sandy deserts of Arabia and Africa.

Happily for the repose of mankind, the moderate system recommended by the wisdom of Augustus was adopted by the fears and vices of his immediate successors. Engaged in the pursuit of pleasure, or in the exercise of tyranny, the first Cæsars seldom showed themselves to the armies, or to the provinces; nor were they disposed to suffer that those triumphs which *their* indolence neglected should be usurped by the conduct and valour of their lieutenants. The military fame of a subject was considered as an insolent invasion of the Imperial prerogative; and it became the duty, as well as interest, of every Roman general to guard the frontiers entrusted to his care, without aspiring to conquests which might have proved no less fatal to himself than to the vanquished barbarians.

The only accession which the Roman empire received, during the first century of the Christian era, was the province of Britain. In this single instance the successors of Cæsar and Augustus were persuaded to follow the example of the former, rather than the precept of the latter. The proximity of its situation to the coast of Gaul seemed to invite their arms; the pleasing, though doubtful, intelligence of a pearl fishery attracted their avarice; and as Britain was viewed in the light of a distinct and insulated world, the conquest scarcely formed any exception to the general system of continental measures. After a war of about forty years, undertaken by the most stupid, maintained by the most dissolute, and terminated by the most timid of all the emperors, the far greater part of the island submitted to the Roman yoke.[1] The various tribes of Britons possessed valour without conduct, and the love of freedom without the spirit of union. They took up arms with savage fierceness; they laid them down, or turned them against each other with wild inconstancy; and while they fought singly, they were successively subdued. Neither the fortitude of Caractacus, nor

[1]Claudius, Nero, and Domitian. A hope is expressed by Pomponius Mela, I. iii. c. 6. (he wrote under Claudius) that, by the success of the Roman arms, the island and its savage inhabitants would soon be better known.

the despair of Boadicea, nor the fanaticism of the Druids, could avert the slavery of their country, or resist the steady progress of the Imperial generals, who maintained the national glory when the throne was disgraced by the weakest or the most vicious of mankind. At the very time when Domitian, confined to his palace, felt the terrors which he inspired, his legions under the command of the virtuous Agricola defeated the collected force of the Caledonians at the foot of the Grampian hills; and his fleets, venturing to explore an unknown and dangerous navigation, displayed the Roman arms round every part of the island. The conquest of Britain was considered as already achieved; and it was the design of Agricola to complete and ensure his success by the easy reduction of Ireland, for which in his opinion, one legion and a few auxiliaries were sufficient. The western isle might be improved into a valuable possession, and the Britons would wear their chains with the less reluctance, if the prospect and example of freedom were on every side removed from before their eyes.

But the superior merit of Agricola soon occasioned his removal from the government of Britain; and for ever disappointed this rational though extensive scheme of conquest. Before his departure, the prudent general had provided for security as well as for dominion. He had observed that the island is almost divided into two unequal parts by the opposite gulfs, or, as they are now called, the Firths of Scotland. Across the narrow interval of about forty miles, he had drawn a line of military stations, which was afterwards fortified, in the reign of Antoninus Pius, by a turf rampart erected on foundations of stone. This wall of Antoninus, at a small distance beyond the modern cities of Edinburgh and Glasgow, was fixed as the limit of the Roman province. The native Caledonians preserved in the northern extremity of the island their wild independence, for which they were not less indebted to their poverty than to their valour. Their incursions were frequently repelled and chastised; but their country was never subdued. The masters of the fairest and most wealthy climates of the globe turned with contempt from gloomy hills assailed by the winter tempest, from lakes concealed in a blue mist, and from cold and lonely heaths, over which the deer of the forest were chased by a troop of naked barbarians.

Such was the state of the Roman frontiers, and such the maxims of Imperial policy, from the death of Augustus to the accession of Trajan. That virtuous and active prince had received the education of a soldier, and possessed the talents of a general. The peaceful system of his predecessors was interrupted by scenes of war and conquest; and the legions, after a long interval, beheld a military emperor at their head. The first exploits of Trajan were against the Dacians, the most warlike of men, who dwelt beyond the Danube, and who, during the reign of Domitian, had insulted with impunity the majesty of Rome. To the strength and fierceness of barbarians, they added a contempt for life, which was derived from a warm persuasion of the immortality and transmigration of the soul. Decebalus, the Dacian king, approved himself a rival not unworthy of

Trajan; nor did he despair of his own and the public fortune, till, by the confession of his enemies, he had exhausted every resource both of valour and policy. This memorable war, with a very short suspension of hostilities, lasted five years; and as the emperor could exert, without control, the whole force of the state, it was terminated by an absolute submission of the barbarians. The new province of Dacia, which formed a second exception to the precept of Augustus, was about 1300 miles in circumference. Its natural boundaries were the Dniester, the Teyss [Theiss modern form], or Tibiscus, the Lower Danube, and the Euxine Sea. The vestiges of a military road may still be traced from the banks of the Danube to the neighbourhood of Bender, a place famous in modern history, and the actual frontier of the Turkish and Russian empires.

Trajan was ambitious of fame; and as long as mankind shall continue to bestow more liberal applause on their destroyers than on their benefactors, the thirst of military glory will ever be the vice of the most exalted characters. The praises of Alexander, transmitted by a succession of poets and historians, had kindled a dangerous emulation in the mind of Trajan. Like him the Roman emperor undertook an expedition against the nations of the East, but he lamented with a sigh, that his advanced age scarcely left him any hopes of equalling the renown of the son of Philip. Yet the success of Trajan, however transient, was rapid and specious. The degenerate Parthians, broken by intestine discord, fled before his arms. He descended the river Tigris in triumph, from the mountains of Armenia to the Persian gulf. He enjoyed the honour of being the first, as he was the last, of the Roman generals who ever navigated that remote sea. His fleets ravaged the coasts of Arabia; and Trajan vainly flattered himself that he was approaching towards the confines of India. Every day the astonished senate received the intelligence of new names and new nations that acknowledged his sway. They were informed that the kings of Bosphorus, Colchos, Iberia, Albania, Osrhoene, and even the Parthian monarch himself, had accepted their diadems from the hands of the emperor; that the independent tribes of the Median and Carduchian hills had implored his protection; and that the rich countries of Armenia, Mesopotamia, and Assyria, were reduced into the state of provinces. But the death of Trajan soon clouded the splendid prospect; and it was justly to be dreaded, that so many distant nations would throw off the unaccustomed yoke, when they were no longer restrained by the powerful hand which had imposed it.

It was an ancient tradition, that when the Capitol was founded by one of the Roman kings, the god Terminus (who presided over boundaries, and was represented according to the fashion of that age by a large stone) alone, among all the inferior deities, refused to yield his place to Jupiter himself. A favourable inference was drawn from his obstinacy, which was interpreted by the augurs as a sure presage that the boundaries of the Roman power would never recede. During many ages, the prediction, as it is usual, contributed to its own accomplishment. But though Terminus had resisted the majesty of Jupiter, he submitted to the authority of the emperor Hadrian. The resignation of all the eastern conquests of Trajan was the first measure of his reign. He restored to the Parthians the election of an independent sovereign, withdrew the Roman garrisons from the provinces of Armenia, Mesopotamia, and Assyria, and, in compliance with the precept of Augustus, once more established the Euphrates as the frontier of the empire.

The martial and ambitious spirit of Trajan formed a very singular contrast with the moderation of his successor. The restless activity of Hadrian was not less remarkable, when compared with the gentle repose of Antoninus Pius. The life of the former was almost a perpetual journey; and as he possessed the various talents of the soldier, the statesman, and the scholar, he gratified his curiosity in the discharge of his duty. Careless of the difference of seasons and of climates, he marched on foot, and bareheaded, over the snows of Caledonia, and the sultry plains of the Upper Egypt; nor was there a province of the empire which, in the course of his reign, was not honoured with the presence of the monarch. But the tranquil life of Antoninus Pius was spent in the bosom of Italy; and, during the twenty-three years that he directed the public administration, the longest journeys of that amiable prince extended no farther than from his palace in Rome to the retirement of his Lanuvian villa.

The general system of Augustus was equally adopted and uniformly pursued by Hadrian and by the two Antonines. They persisted in the design of maintaining the dignity of the empire, without attempting to enlarge its limits. By every honourable expedient they invited the friendship of the barbarians, and endeavoured to convince mankind that the Roman power, raised above the temptation of conquest, was actuated only by the love of order and justice. During a long period of forty-three years their virtuous labours were crowned with success; and if we except a few slight hostilities that served to exercise the legions of the frontier, the reigns of Hadrian and Antoninus Pius offer the fair prospect of universal peace. The Roman name was revered among the most remote nations of the earth. The fiercest barbarians frequently submitted their differences to the arbitration of the emperor; and we are informed by a contemporary historian that he had seen ambassadors refused the honour, which they came to solicit, of being admitted into the rank of subjects.

The terror of the Roman arms added weight and dignity to the moderation of the emperors. They preserved peace by a constant preparation for war; and while justice regulated their conduct, they announced to the nations on their confines that they were as little disposed to endure as to offer an injury. The military strength, which it had been sufficient for Hadrian and the elder Antoninus to display, was exerted against the Parthians and the Germans by the emperor Marcus. The hostilities of the barbarians provoked the resentment of that philosophic monarch, and, in the prosecution of a just defence, Marcus and his generals obtained many signal victories, both on the Euphrates and on the Danube.

The safety and honour of the empire were principally entrusted to the legions, but the policy of Rome condescended to adopt every useful instrument of war. Considerable levies were regularly made among the provincials, who had not yet deserved the honourable distinction of Romans. Many dependent princes and communities dispersed round the frontiers were permitted, for a while, to hold their freedom and security by the tenure of military service. Even select troops of hostile barbarians were frequently compelled or persuaded to consume their dangerous valour in remote climates, and for the benefit of the state. All these were included under the general name of auxiliaries; and howsoever they might vary according to the difference of times and circumstances, their numbers were seldom much inferior to those of the legions themselves.

Among the auxiliaries, the bravest and most faithful bands were placed under the command of præfects and centurions, and severely trained in the arts of Roman discipline; but the far greater part retained those arms to which the nature of their country, or their early habits of life, more peculiarly adapted them. By this institution each legion, to whom a certain proportion of auxiliaries was allotted, contained within itself every species of lighter troops, and of missile weapons; and was capable of encountering every nation with the advantages of its respective arms and discipline.

Such were the arts of war by which the Roman emperors defended their extensive conquests, and preserved a military spirit, at a time when every other virtue was oppressed by luxury and despotism. If, in the consideration of their armies, we pass from their discipline to their numbers, we shall not find it easy to define them with any tolerable accuracy. We may compute, however, that the legion, which was itself a body of six thousand eight hundred and thirty-one Romans, might, with its attendant auxiliaries, amount to about twelve thousand five hundred men. The peace establishment of Hadrian and his successors was composed of no less than thirty of these formidable brigades; and most probably formed a standing force of three hundred and seventy-five thousand men. Instead of being confined within the walls of fortified cities, which the Romans considered as the refuge of weakness or pusillanimity, the legions were encamped on the banks of the great rivers, and along the frontiers of the barbarians. As their stations, for the most part, remained fixed and permanent, we may venture to describe the distribution of the troops. Three legions were sufficient for Britain. The principal strength lay upon the Rhine and Danube, and consisted of sixteen legions, in the following proportions: two in the Lower and three in the Upper Germany; one in Rhætia, one in Noricum, four in Pannonia, three in Mæsia, and two in Dacia. The defence of the Euphrates was entrusted to eight legions, six of whom were planted in Syria, and the other two in Cappadocia. With regard to Egypt, Africa, and Spain, as they were far removed from any important scene of war, a single legion maintained the domestic tranquillity of each of those great provinces. Even Italy was not left destitute of a military force. Above twenty thousand chosen soldiers, distinguished by the titles of City Cohorts and Prætorian Guards, watched over the safety of the monarch and the capital. As the authors of almost every revolution that distracted the empire, the Prætorians will, very soon, and very loudly, demand our attention; but in their arms and institution, we cannot find any circumstance which discriminated them from the legions, unless it were a more splendid appearance, and a less rigid discipline.

The navy maintained by the emperors might seem inadequate to their greatness; but it was fully sufficient for every useful purpose of government. The ambition of the Romans was confined to the land; nor was that warlike people ever actuated by the enterprising spirit which had prompted the navigators of Tyre, of Carthage, and even of Marseilles, to enlarge the bounds of the world, and to explore the most remote coasts of the ocean.

If we review this general state of the Imperial forces, of the cavalry as well as infantry, of the legions, the auxiliaries, the guards, and the navy, the most liberal computation will not allow us to fix the entire establishment by sea and by land at more than four hundred and fifty thousand men; a military power, which, however formidable it may seem, was equalled by a monarch of the last century, whose kingdom was confined within a single province of the Roman empire.

We have attempted to explain the spirit which moderated, and the strength which supported, the power of Hadrian and the Antonines. We shall now endeavour, with clearness and precision, to describe the provinces once united under their sway, but, at present, divided into so many independent and hostile states.

Spain, the western extremity of the empire, of Europe, and of the ancient world, has in every age preserved the same natural limits: the Pyrenæan mountains, the Mediterranean, and the Atlantic Ocean. That great peninsula, at present so unequally divided between two sovereigns, was distributed by Augustus into three provinces, Lusitania, Bætica, and Tarraconensis. The kingdom of Portugal now fills the place of the warlike country of the Lusitanians; and the loss sustained by the former, on the side of the East, is compensated by an accession of territory towards the North. The confines of Grenada and Andalusia correspond with those of ancient Bætica. The remainder of Spain, Gallicia and the Asturias, Biscay and Navarre, Leon and the two Castilles, Murcia, Valencia, Catalonia, and Aragon, all contributed to form the third and most considerable of the Roman governments, which, from the name of its capital, was styled the province of Tarragona. Of the native barbarians, the Celtiberians were the most powerful, as the Cantabrians and Asturians proved the most obstinate. Confident in the strength of their mountains, they were the last who submitted to the arms of Rome, and the first who threw off the yoke of the Arabs.

Ancient Gaul, as it contained the whole country between the Pyrenees, the Alps, the Rhine, and the Ocean, was of greater extent than modern France. To the dominions of that powerful monarchy, with its recent acquisitions of Alsace and Lorraine, we must add the duchy of Savoy, the cantons of Switzerland, the four electorates of the Rhine, and the territories of Liege, Luxemburg, Hainault, Flanders, and Brabant. When Augustus gave laws to the conquests of his father, he introduced a division of Gaul equally adapted to the progress of the legions, to the course of the rivers, and to the principal national distinctions which had comprehended above an hundred independent states. The sea-coast of the Mediterranean, Languedoc, Provence, and Dauphiné, received their provincial appellation from the colony of Narbonne. The government of Aquitaine was extended from the Pyrenees to the Loire. The country between the Loire and the Seine was styled the Celtic Gaul, and soon borrowed a new denomination from the celebrated colony of Lugdunum, or Lyons. The Belgic lay beyond the Seine, and in more ancient times had been bounded only by the Rhine; but a little before the age of Cæsar the Germans, abusing their superiority of valour, had occupied a considerable portion of the Belgic territory. The Roman conquerors very eagerly embraced so flattering a circumstance, and the Gallic frontier of the Rhine, from Basil to Leyden, received the pompous names of the Upper and the Lower Germany. Such, under the reign of the Antonines, were the six provinces of Gaul; the Narbonnese, Aquitaine, the Celtic, or Lyonnese, the Belgic, and the two Germanies.

We have already had occasion to mention the conquest of Britain, and to fix the boundary of the Roman province in this island. It comprehended all England, Wales, and the Lowlands of Scotland, as far as Dumbarton and Edinburgh. Before Britain lost her freedom, the country was irregularly divided between thirty tribes of barbarians, of whom the most considerable were the Belgæ in the West, the Brigantes in the North, the Silures in South Wales, and the Iceni in Norfolk and Suffolk. As far as we can either trace or credit the resemblance of manners and language, Spain, Gaul, and Britain were peopled by the same hardy race of savages. Before they yielded to the Roman arms, they often disputed the field, and often renewed the contest. After their submission they constituted the western division of the European provinces, which extended from the columns of Hercules to the wall of Antoninus and from the mouth of the Tagus to the sources of the Rhine and Danube.

Before the Roman conquest, the country which is now called Lombardy was not considered as a part of Italy. It had been occupied by a powerful colony of Gauls, who, settling themselves along the banks of the Po, from Piedmont to Romagna, carried their arms and diffused their name from the Alps to the Apennine. The Ligurians dwelt on the rocky coast, which now forms the republic of Genoa. Venice was yet unborn; but the territories of that state, which lie to the east of the Adige, were inhabited by the Venetians. The middle part of the peninsula that now composes the duchy of Tuscany and the ecclesiastical state was the ancient seat of the Etruscans and Umbrians, to the former of whom Italy was indebted for the first rudiments of civilised life. The Tiber rolled at the foot of the seven hills of Rome, and the country of the Sabines, the Latins, and the Volsci, from that river to the frontiers of Naples, was the theatre of her infant victories. On that celebrated ground the first consuls deserved triumphs; their successors adorned villas, and *their* posterity have erected convents. Capua and Campania possessed the immediate territory of Naples; the rest of the kingdom was inhabited by many warlike nations, the Marsi, the Samnites, the Apulians, and the Lucanians; and the sea-coasts had been covered by the flourishing colonies of the Greeks. We may remark that when Augustus divided Italy into eleven regions, the little province of Istria was annexed to that seat of Roman sovereignty.

The European provinces of Rome were protected by the course of the Rhine and the Danube. The latter of those mighty streams, which rises at the distance of only thirty miles from the former, flows above thirteen hundred miles, for the most part to the south-east, collects the tribute of sixty navigable rivers, and is, at length, through six mouths, received into the Euxine, which appears scarcely equal to such an accession of waters. The provinces of the Danube soon acquired the general appellation of Illyricum, or the Illyrian frontier, and were esteemed the most warlike of the empire; but they deserve to be more particularly considered under the names of Rhætia, Noricum, Pannonia, Dalmatia, Dacia, Mæsia, Thrace, Macedonia, and Greece.

The province of Rhætia, which soon extinguished the name of the Vindelicians, extended from the summit of the Alps to the banks of the Danube; from its source, as far as its conflux with the Inn. The greatest part of the flat country is subject to the elector of Bavaria; the city of Augsburg is protected by the constitution of the German empire; the Grisons are safe in their mountains, and the country of Tyrol is ranked among the numerous provinces of the house of Austria.

The wide extent of territory, which is included between the Inn, the Danube, and the Save; Austria, Styria, Carinthia, Carniola, the Lower Hungary, and Sclavonia, was known to the ancients under the names of Noricum and Pannonia. In their original state of independence, their fierce inhabitants were intimately connected. Under the Roman government they were frequently united, and they still remain the patrimony of a single family. They now contain the residence of a German prince, who styles himself Emperor of the Romans, and form the centre, as well as strength, of the Austrian power. It may not be improper to observe, that if we except Bohemia, Moravia, the northern skirts of Austria, and a part of Hungary, between the Theiss and the Danube, all the other dominions of the house of Austria were comprised within the limits of the Roman empire.

Dalmatia, to which the name of Illyricum more properly belonged, was a long but narrow tract between the Save and the Adriatic. The best part of the sea-coast, which still retains its ancient appellation, is a province of the Venetian state, and the seat of the little republic of Ragusa. The inland parts have assumed the Sclavonian names of Croatia and Bosnia; the former obeys an Austrian governor, the latter a Turkish pasha; but the whole country is still infested by tribes of barbarians, whose savage independence irregularly marks the doubtful limit of the Christian and Mahometan power.

After the Danube had received the waters of the Theiss and the Save, it acquired, at least among the Greeks, the name of Ister. It formerly divided Mæsia and Dacia, the latter of which, as we have already seen, was a conquest of Trajan, and the only province beyond the river. If we inquire into the present state of those countries, we shall find that, on the left hand of the Danube, Temeswar and Transylvania have been annexed, after many revolutions, to the crown of Hungary; whilst the principalities of Moldavia and Wallachia acknowledge the supremacy of the Ottoman Porte. On the right hand of the Danube, Mæsia, which, during the Middle Ages, was broken into the barbarian kingdoms of Servia and Bulgaria, is again united in Turkish slavery.

The appellation of Roumelia, which is still bestowed by the Turks on the extensive countries of Thrace, Macedonia, and Greece, preserves the memory of their ancient state under the Roman empire. In the time of the Antonines, the martial regions of Thrace, from the mountains of Hæmus and Rhodope, to the Bosphorus and the Hellespont, had assumed the form of a province. Notwithstanding the change of masters and of religion, the new city of Rome, founded by Constantine on the banks of the Bosphorus, has ever since remained the capital of a great monarchy. The kingdom of Macedonia, which, under the reign of Alexander, gave laws to Asia, derived more solid advantages from the policy of the two Philips; and with its dependencies of Epirus and Thessaly, extended from the Ægean to the Ionian Sea. When we reflect on the fame of Thebes and Argos, of Sparta and Athens, we can scarcely persuade ourselves that so many immortal republics of ancient Greece were lost in a single province of the Roman empire, which, from the superior influence of the Achæan league, was usually denominated the province of Achaia.

Such was the state of Europe under the Roman emperors. The provinces of Asia, without excepting the transient conquests of Trajan, are all comprehended within the limits of the Turkish power. But, instead of following the arbitrary divisions of despotism and ignorance, it will be safer for us, as well as more agreeable, to observe the indelible characters of nature. The name of Asia Minor is attributed with some propriety to the peninsula which, confined betwixt the Euxine and the Mediterranean, advances from the Euphrates towards Europe. The most extensive and flourishing district, westward of Mount Taurus and the river Halys, was dignified by the Romans with the exclusive title of Asia. The jurisdiction of that province extended over the ancient monarchies of Troy, Lydia, and Phrygia, the maritime countries of the Pamphylians, Lycians, and Carians, and the Grecian colonies of Ionia, which equalled in arts, though not in arms, the glory of their parent. The kingdoms of Bithynia and Pontus possessed the northern side of the peninsula from Constantinople to Trebizond. On the opposite side, the province of Cilicia was terminated by the mountains of Syria: the inland country, separated from the Roman Asia by the river Halys, and from Armenia by the Euphrates, had once formed the independent kingdom of Cappadocia. In this place we may observe that the northern shores of the Euxine, beyond Trebizond in Asia, and beyond the Danube in Europe, acknowledged the sovereignty of the emperors, and received at their hands either tributary princes or Roman garrisons.

Under the successors of Alexander, Syria was the seat of the Seleucidæ, who reigned over Upper Asia, till the successful revolt of the Parthians confined their dominions between the Euphrates and the Mediterranean. When Syria became subject to the Romans, it formed the eastern frontier of their empire; nor did that province, in its utmost latitude, know any other bounds than the mountains of Cappadocia to the North, and towards the South the confines of Egypt, and the Red Sea. Phœnicia and Palestine were sometimes annexed to, and sometimes separated from, the jurisdiction of Syria. The former of these was a narrow and rocky coast; the latter was a territory scarcely superior to Wales, either in fertility or extent. Yet Phœnicia and Palestine will for ever live in the memory of mankind, since America, as well as Europe, has received letters from the one and religion from the other. A sandy desert alike destitute of wood and water skirts along the doubtful confine of Syria, from the Euphrates to the Red Sea. The wandering life of the Arabs was inseparably connected with their independence; and wherever, on some spots less barren than the rest, they ventured to form any settled habitation, they soon became subjects to the Roman empire.

The geographers of antiquity have frequently hesitated to what portion of the globe they should ascribe Egypt. By its situation that celebrated kingdom is included within the immense peninsula of Africa; but it is accessible only on the side of Asia, whose revolutions, in almost every period of history, Egypt has humbly obeyed. A Roman præfect was seated on the splendid throne of the Ptolemies; and the iron sceptre of the Mamalukes is now in the hands of a Turkish pasha. The Nile flows down the country, above five hundred miles from the tropic of Cancer to the Mediterranean, and marks, on either side, the extent of fertility by the measure of its inundations. Cyrene, situate towards the west, and along the sea-coast, was first a Greek colony, afterwards a province of Egypt, and is now lost in the desert of Barca.

From Cyrene to the ocean, the coast of Africa extends above fifteen hundred miles; yet so closely is it pressed between the Mediterranean and the Sahara, or sandy desert, that its breadth seldom exceeds fourscore or an hundred miles. The eastern division was considered by the Romans as the more peculiar and proper province of Africa. Till the arrival of the Phœnician colonies, that fertile country was inhabited by the Libyans, the most savage of mankind. Under the immediate jurisdiction of Carthage, it became the centre of commerce and empire; but the republic of Carthage is now degenerated into the feeble and disorderly states of Tripoli and Tunis. The military government of Algiers oppresses the wide extent of Numidia, as it was once united under Massinissa and Jugurtha: but in the time of Augustus, the limits of Numidia were contracted; and at least two-thirds of the country acquiesced in the name of Mauritania, with the epithet of Cæsariensis. The genuine Mauritania, or country of the Moors, which, from the ancient city of Tingi, or Tangier, was distinguished by the appellation of Tingitana, is represented by the modern kingdom of Fez. Sallè, on the ocean, long infamous for its piratical depredations, was noticed by the Romans, as the extreme object of their power, and almost of their geography. A city of their foundation may still be discovered near Mequinez, the residence of the barbarian whom we condescend to style the Emperor of Morocco; but it does not appear that his more southern dominions, Morocco itself, and Segelmessa, were ever comprehended within the Roman province.

Having now finished the circuit of the Roman empire, we may observe that Africa is divided from Spain by a narrow strait of about twelve miles, through which the Atlantic flows into the Mediterranean. The columns of Hercules, so famous among the ancients, were two mountains which seemed to have been torn asunder by some convulsion of the elements; and at the foot of the European mountain the fortress of Gibraltar is now seated. The whole extent of the Mediterranean Sea, its coasts, and its islands, were comprised within the Roman dominion. Of the larger islands, the two Baleares, which derive their name of Majorca and Minorca from their respective size, are subject at present, the former to Spain, the latter to Great Britain. It is easier to deplore the fate than to describe the actual condition of Corsica. Two Italian sovereigns assume a regal title from Sardinia and Sicily. Crete, or Candia, with Cyprus, and most of the smaller islands of Greece and Asia, have been subdued by the Turkish arms; whilst the little rock of Malta defies their power, and has emerged, under the government of its military Order, into fame and opulence.

This long enumeration of provinces, whose broken fragments have formed so many powerful kingdoms, might almost induce us to forgive the vanity or ignorance of the ancients. Dazzled with the extensive sway, the irresistible strength, and the real or affected moderation of the emperors, they permitted themselves to despise, and sometimes to forget, the outlying countries which had been left in the enjoyment of a barbarous independence; and they gradually usurped the licence of confounding the Roman monarchy with the globe of the earth. But the temper, as well as knowledge, of a modern historian requires a more sober and accurate language. He may impress a juster image of the greatness of Rome, by observing that the empire was above two thousand miles in breadth, from the wall of Antoninus and the northern limits of Dacia, to Mount Atlas and the tropic of Cancer; that it extended, in length, more than three thousand miles from the Western Ocean to the Euphrates; that it was situated in the finest part of the Temperate Zone, between the twenty-fourth and fifty-sixth degrees of northern latitude; and that it was supposed to contain above sixteen hundred thousand square miles, for the most part of fertile and well-cultivated land.

CHAPTER II

Of the Union and Internal Prosperity of the Roman Empire, in the Age of the Antonines

It is not alone by the rapidity, or extent of conquest, that we should estimate the greatness of Rome. The sovereign of the Russian deserts commands a larger portion of the globe. In the seventh summer after his passage of the Hellespont, Alexander erected the Macedonian trophies on the banks of the Hyphasis. Within less than a century, the irresistible Zingis, and the Mogul princes of his race, spread their cruel devastations and transient empire from the sea of China to the confines of Egypt and Germany. But the firm edifice of Roman power was raised and preserved by the wisdom of ages. The obedient provinces of Trajan and the Antonines were united by laws and adorned by arts. They might occasionally suffer from the partial abuse of delegated authority; but the general principle of government was wise, simple, and beneficent. They enjoyed the religion of their ancestors, whilst in civil honours and advantages they were exalted, by just degrees, to an equality with their conquerors.

The policy of the emperors and the senate, as far as it concerned religion, was happily seconded by the reflections of the enlightened, and by the habits of the superstitious, part of their subjects. The various modes of worship which prevailed in the Roman world were all considered, by the people, as equally true; by the philosopher, as equally false; and by the magistrate, as equally useful. And thus toleration produced not only mutual indulgence, but even religious concord.

The superstition of the people was not embittered by any mixture of theological rancour; nor was it confined by the chains of any speculative system. The devout polytheist, though fondly attached to his national rites, admitted with implicit faith the different religions of the earth. Fear, gratitude, and curiosity, a dream or an omen, a singular disorder, or a distant journey, perpetually disposed him to multiply the articles of his belief, and to enlarge the list of his protectors. The thin texture of the Pagan mythology was interwoven with various but not discordant materials. As soon as it was allowed that sages and heroes who had lived or died for the benefit of their country were exalted to a state of power and immortality, it was universally confessed that they deserved, if not the adoration, at least the reverence of all mankind. The deities of a thousand groves and a thousand streams possessed, in peace, their local and respective influence; nor could the Roman who deprecated the wrath of the Tiber, deride the Egyptian who presented his offering to the beneficent genius of the Nile. The visible powers of Nature, the planets, and the elements, were the same throughout the universe. The invisible governors of the moral world were inevitably cast in a similar mould of fiction and allegory. Every virtue, and even vice, acquired its divine representative; every art and profession its patron, whose attributes, in the most distant ages and countries, were uniformly derived from the character of their peculiar votaries. A republic of gods of such opposite tempers and interest required, in every system, the moderating hand of a supreme magistrate, who, by the progress of knowledge and flattery, was gradually invested with the sublime perfections of an Eternal Parent, and an Omnipotent Monarch. Such was the mild spirit of antiquity, that the nations were less attentive to the difference than to the resemblance of their religious worship. The Greek, the Roman, and the Barbarian, as they met before their respective altars, easily persuaded themselves, that under various names, and with various ceremonies, they adored the same deities. The elegant mythology of Homer gave a beautiful, and almost a regular form, to the polytheism of the ancient world.

The philosophers of Greece deduced their morals from the nature of man, rather than from that of God. They meditated, however, on the Divine Nature, as a very curious and important speculation; and in the profound inquiry, they displayed the strength and weakness of the human understanding. Of the four most celebrated schools, the Stoics and the Platonists endeavoured to reconcile the jarring interests of reason and piety. They have left us the most sublime proofs of the existence and perfections of the first cause; but, as it was impossible for them to conceive the creation of matter, the workman in the Stoic philosophy was not sufficiently distinguished from the work; whilst, on the contrary, the spiritual God of Plato and his disciples resembled an idea rather than a substance. The opinions of the Academics and Epicureans were of a less religious cast; but whilst the modest science of the former induced them to doubt, the positive ignorance of the latter urged them to deny, the providence of a Supreme Ruler. The spirit of inquiry, prompted by emulation, and supported by freedom, had divided the public teachers of philosophy into a variety of contending sects; but the ingenuous youth who, from every part, resorted to Athens, and the other seats of learning in the Roman empire, were alike instructed in every school to reject and to despise the religion of the multitude. How, indeed, was it possible, that a philosopher should accept, as divine truths, the idle tales of the poets, and the incoherent traditions of antiquity; or, that he should adore as gods those imperfect beings whom he must have despised as men! Against such unworthy adversaries, Cicero condescended to employ the arms of reason and eloquence; but the satire of Lucian was a much more adequate, as well as more efficacious weapon. We may be well assured, that a writer conversant with the world would never have ventured to expose the gods of his country to public ridicule, had they not already been the objects of secret contempt among the polished and enlightened orders of society.

Notwithstanding the fashionable irreligion which prevailed in the age of the Antonines, both the interests of the priests and the credulity of the people were sufficiently respected. In their writings and conversation, the philosophers of antiquity asserted the independent dignity of reason; but they resigned their actions to the commands of law and of custom. Viewing with a smile of pity and indulgence the various errors of the vulgar, they diligently practised the ceremonies of their fathers, devoutly frequented the temples of the gods; and sometimes condescending to act a part on the theatre of superstition, they concealed the sentiments of an atheist under the sacerdotal robes. Reasoners of such a temper were scarcely inclined to wrangle about their respective modes of faith or of worship. It was indifferent to them what shape the folly of the multitude might choose to assume; and they approached, with the same inward contempt, and the same external reverence, the altars of the Libyan, the Olympian, or the Capitoline Jupiter.

It is not easy to conceive from what motives a spirit of persecution could introduce itself into the Roman councils. The magistrates could not be actuated by a blind, though honest bigotry, since the magistrates were themselves philosophers; and the schools of Athens had given laws to the senate. They could not be impelled by ambition or avarice, as the temporal and ecclesiastical powers were united in the same hands. The pontiffs were chosen among the most illustrious of the senators; and the office of Supreme Pontiff was constantly exercised by the emperors themselves. They knew and valued the advantages of religion, as it is connected with civil government. They encouraged the public festivals which humanise the manners of the people. They managed the arts of divination as a convenient instrument of policy; and they respected as the firmest bond of society the useful persuasion that, either in this or in a future life, the crime of perjury is most assuredly punished by the avenging gods. But whilst they acknowledged the general advantages of religion, they were convinced that the various modes of worship contributed alike to the same salutary purposes; and that, in every country, the form of superstition which had received the sanction of time and experience was the best adapted to the climate and to its inhabitants. Avarice and taste very frequently despoiled the vanquished nations of the elegant statues of their gods, and the rich ornaments of their temples; but, in the exercise of the religion which they derived from their ancestors, they uniformly experienced the indulgence, and even protection, of the Roman conquerors. The province of Gaul seems, and indeed only seems, an exception to this universal toleration. Under the specious pretext of abolishing human sacrifices, the emperors Tiberius and Claudius suppressed the dangerous power of the Druids; but the priests themselves, their gods and their altars, subsisted in peaceful obscurity till the final destruction of Paganism.

Rome, the capital of a great monarchy, was incessantly filled with subjects and strangers from every part of the world, who all introduced and enjoyed the favourite superstitions of their native country. Every city in the empire was justified in maintaining the purity of its ancient ceremonies; and the Roman senate, using the common privilege, sometimes interposed, to check this inundation of foreign rites. The Egyptian superstition, of all the most contemptible and abject, was frequently prohibited; the temples of Serapis and Isis demolished and their worshippers banished from Rome and Italy. But the zeal of fanaticism prevailed over the cold and feeble efforts of policy. The exiles returned, the proselytes multiplied, the temples were restored with increasing splendour, and Isis and Serapis at length assumed their place among the Roman deities. Nor was this indulgence a departure from the old maxims of government. In the purest ages of the commonwealth, Cybele and Æsculapius had been invited by solemn embassies; and it was customary to tempt the protectors of besieged cities, by the promise of more distinguished honours than they possessed in their native country. Rome gradually became the common temple of her subjects; and the freedom of the city was bestowed on all the gods of mankind.

The narrow policy of preserving, without any foreign mixture, the pure blood of the ancient citizens, had checked the fortune and hastened the ruin of Athens and Sparta. The aspiring genius of Rome sacrificed vanity to ambition, and deemed it more prudent, as well as honourable, to adopt virtue and merit for her own wheresoever they were found, among slaves or strangers, enemies or barbarians. During the most flourishing era of the Athenian commonwealth, the number of citizens gradually decreased from about thirty to twenty-one thousand. If, on the contrary, we study the growth of the Roman republic, we may discover, that, notwithstanding the incessant demands of wars and colonies, the citizens, who, in the first census of Servius Tullius, amounted to no more than eighty-three thousand, were multiplied, before the commencement of the social war, to the number of four hundred and sixty-three thousand men, able to bear arms in the service of their country.

Till the privileges of Romans had been progressively extended to all the inhabitants of the empire, an important distinction was preserved between Italy and the provinces. The former was esteemed the centre of public unity, and the firm basis of the constitution. Italy claimed the birth, or at least the residence, of the emperors and the senate. The estates of the Italians were exempt from taxes, their persons from the arbitrary jurisdiction of governors. Their municipal corporations, formed after the perfect model of the capital, were entrusted, under the immediate eye of the supreme power, with the execution of the laws. From the foot of the Alps to the extremity of Calabria, all the natives of Italy were born citizens of Rome. Their partial distinctions were obliterated, and they insensibly coalesced into one great nation, united by language, manners, and civil institutions, and equal to the weight of a powerful empire. The republic gloried in her generous policy, and was frequently rewarded by the merit and services of her adopted sons. Had she always confined the distinction of Romans to the ancient families within the walls of the city, that immortal name would have been deprived of some of its noblest ornaments. Virgil was a native of

Mantua; Horace was inclined to doubt whether he should call himself an Apulian or a Lucanian: it was in Padua that an historian was found worthy to record the majestic series of Roman victories. The patriot family of the Catos emerged from Tusculum; and the little town of Arpinum claimed the double honour of producing Marius and Cicero, the former of whom deserved, after Romulus and Camillus, to be styled the Third Founder of Rome; and the latter, after saving his country from the designs of Catiline, enabled her to contend with Athens for the palm of eloquence.

The provinces of the empire (as they have been described in the preceding chapter) were destitute of any public force, or constitutional freedom. In Etruria, in Greece, and in Gaul, it was the first care of the senate to dissolve those dangerous confederacies which taught mankind that as the Roman arts prevailed by division, they might be resisted by union. Those princes, whom the ostentation of gratitude or generosity permitted for a while to hold a precarious sceptre, were dismissed from their thrones as soon as they had performed their appointed task of fashioning to the yoke the vanquished nations. The free states and cities which had embraced the cause of Rome were rewarded with a nominal alliance, and insensibly sunk into real servitude. The public authority was everywhere exercised by the ministers of the senate and of the emperors, and that authority was absolute, and without control. But the same salutary maxims of government, which had secured the peace and obedience of Italy, were extended to the most distant conquests. A nation of Romans was gradually formed in the provinces, by the double expedient of introducing colonies, and of admitting the most faithful and deserving of the provincials to the freedom of Rome.

"Wheresoever the Roman conquers, he inhabits," is a very just observation of Seneca, confirmed by history and experience. The natives of Italy, allured by pleasure or by interest, hastened to enjoy the advantages of victory; and we may remark, that about forty years after the reduction of Asia, eighty thousand Romans were massacred in one day, by the cruel orders of Mithridates. These voluntary exiles were engaged, for the most part, in the occupations of commerce, agriculture, and the farm of the revenue. But after the legions were rendered permanent by the emperors, the provinces were peopled by a race of soldiers; and the veterans, whether they received the reward of their service in land or in money, usually settled with their families in the country where they had honourably spent their youth. Throughout the empire, but more particularly in the western parts, the most fertile districts and the most convenient situations were reserved for the establishment of colonies, some of which were of a civil and others of a military nature. In their manners and internal policy, the colonies formed a perfect representation of their great parent; and they were soon endeared to the natives by the ties of friendship and alliance, they effectually diffused a reverence for the Roman name, and a desire, which was seldom disappointed, of sharing, in due time, its honours and advantages.

The municipal cities insensibly equalled the rank and splendour of the colonies; and in the reign of Hadrian it was disputed which was the preferable condition, of those societies which had issued from, or those which had been received into the bosom of Rome. The right of Latium, as it was called, conferred on the cities to which it had been granted a more partial favour. The magistrates only, at the expiration of their office, assumed the quality of Roman citizens; but as those offices were annual, in a few years they circulated round the principal families. Those of the provincials who were permitted to bear arms in the legions, those who exercised any civil employment, all, in a word, who performed any public service, or displayed any personal talents, were rewarded with a present whose value was continually diminished by the increasing liberality of the emperors. Yet even in the age of the Antonines, when the freedom of the city had been bestowed on the greater number of their subjects, it was still accompanied with very solid advantages. The bulk of the people acquired, with that title, the benefit of the Roman laws, particularly in the interesting articles of marriage, testaments, and inheritances; and the road of fortune was open to those whose pretensions were seconded by favour or merit. The grandsons of the Gauls who had besieged Julius Cæsar in Alesia commanded legions, governed provinces, and were admitted into the senate of Rome. Their ambition, instead of disturbing the tranquillity of the state, was intimately connected with its safety and greatness.

So sensible were the Romans of the influence of language over national manners, that it was their most serious care to extend, with the progress of their arms, the use of the Latin tongue. The ancient dialects of Italy, the Sabine, the Etruscan, and the Venetian, sank into oblivion; but in the provinces, the East was less docile than the West to the voice of its victorious preceptors. This obvious difference marked the two portions of the empire with a distinction of colours, which, though it was in some degree concealed during the meridian splendour of prosperity, became gradually more visible as the shades of night descended upon the Roman world. The western countries were civilised by the same hands which subdued them. As soon as the barbarians were reconciled to obedience, their minds were opened to any new impressions of knowledge and politeness. The language of Virgil and Cicero, though with some inevitable mixture of corruption, was so universally adopted in Africa, Spain, Gaul, Britain, and Pannonia, that the faint traces of the Punic or Celtic idioms were preserved only in the mountains, or among the peasants. Education and study insensibly inspired the natives of those countries with the sentiments of Romans; and Italy gave fashions as well as laws to her Latin provincials. They solicited with more ardour, and obtained with more facility, the freedom and honours of the state; supported the national dignity in letters and in arms; and, at length, in the person of Trajan, produced an emperor whom the Scipios would not have disowned for their countryman.

The situation of the Greeks was very different from that of the Barbarians. The former had been long since civilised and corrupted. They had too much taste to relinquish their language, and too much vanity to adopt any foreign institutions. Still preserving the prejudices after they had lost the virtues of their ancestors, they affected to despise the unpolished manners of the Roman conquerors, whilst they were compelled to respect their superior wisdom and power. Nor was the influence of the Grecian language and sentiments confined to the narrow limits of that once celebrated country. Their empire, by the progress of colonies and conquest, had been diffused from the Hadriatic to the Euphrates and the Nile. Asia was covered with Greek cities, and the long reign of the Macedonian kings had introduced a silent revolution into Syria and Egypt. In their pompous courts those princes united the elegance of Athens with the luxury of the East, and the example of the court was imitated, at an humble distance, by the higher ranks of their subjects.

Such was the general division of the Roman empire into the Latin and Greek languages. To these we may add a third distinction for the body of the natives in Syria, and especially in Egypt. The use of their ancient dialects, by secluding them from the commerce of mankind, checked the improvements of those barbarians. The slothful effeminacy of the former exposed them to the contempt, the sullen ferociousness of the latter excited the aversion of the conquerors. Those nations had submitted to the Roman power, but they seldom desired or deserved the freedom of the city; and it was remarked that more than two hundred and thirty years elapsed after the ruin of the Ptolemies before an Egyptian was admitted into the senate of Rome.

It is a just though trite observation, that victorious Rome was herself subdued by the arts of Greece. Those immortal writers who still command the admiration of modern Europe, soon became the favourite object of study and imitation in Italy and the western provinces. But the elegant amusements of the Romans were not suffered to interfere with their sound maxims of policy. Whilst they acknowledged the charms of the Greek, they asserted the dignity of the Latin tongue, and the exclusive use of the latter was inflexibly maintained in the administration of civil as well as military government. The two languages exercised at the same time their separate jurisdiction throughout the empire: the former as the natural idiom of science, the latter as the legal dialect of public transactions. Those who united letters with business were equally conversant with both; and it was almost impossible, in any province, to find a Roman subject of a liberal education who was at once a stranger to the Greek and to the Latin language.

It was by such institutions that the nations of the empire insensibly melted away into the Roman name and people. But there still remained, in the centre of every province and of every family, an unhappy condition of men who endured the weight, without sharing the benefits, of society. In the free states of antiquity the domestic slaves were exposed to the wanton rigour of despotism. The perfect settlement of the Roman empire was preceded by ages of violence and rapine. The slaves consisted, for the most part, of barbarian captives, taken in thousands by the chance of war, purchased at a vile price, accustomed to a life of independence, and impatient to break and to revenge their fetters. Against such internal enemies, whose desperate insurrections had more than once reduced the republic to the brink of destruction, the most severe regulations and the most cruel treatment seemed almost justified by the great law of self-preservation. But when the principal nations of Europe, Asia, and Africa were united under the laws of one sovereign, the source of foreign supplies flowed with much less abundance, and the Romans were reduced to the milder but more tedious method of propagation. In their numerous families, and particularly in their country estates, they encouraged the marriage of their slaves. The sentiments of nature, the habits of education, and the possession of a dependent species of property, contributed to alleviate the hardships of servitude. The existence of a slave became an object of greater value, and though his happiness still depended on the temper and circumstances of the master, the humanity of the latter, instead of being restrained by fear, was encouraged by the sense of his own interest.

The progress of manners was accelerated by the virtue or policy of the emperors; and by the edicts of Hadrian and the Antonines, the protection of the laws was extended to the most abject part of mankind. The jurisdiction of life and death over the slaves, a power long exercised and often abused, was taken out of private hands, and reserved to the magistrates alone. The subterraneous prisons were abolished; and, upon a just complaint of intolerable treatment, the injured slave obtained either his deliverance, or a less cruel master.

Hope, the best comfort of our imperfect condition, was not denied to the Roman slave; and if he had any opportunity of rendering himself either useful or agreeable, he might very naturally expect that the diligence and fidelity of a few years would be rewarded with the inestimable gift of freedom. The benevolence of the master was so frequently prompted by the meaner suggestions of vanity and avarice, that the laws found it more necessary to restrain than to encourage a profuse and undistinguishing liberality, which might degenerate into a very dangerous abuse. It was a maxim of ancient jurisprudence that a slave had not any country of his own; he acquired with his liberty an admission into the political society of which his patron was a member. The consequences of this maxim would have prostituted the privileges of the Roman city to a mean and promiscuous multitude. Some seasonable exceptions were therefore provided; and the honourable distinction was confined to such slaves only, as for just causes, and with the approbation of the magistrate, should receive a solemn and legal manumission. Even these chosen freedmen obtained no more than the private rights of citizens, and were rigorously excluded from civil or military honours. Whatever might be the merit or fortune of their sons, *they* likewise were esteemed unworthy of a seat in the senate; nor were the traces of a servile origin allowed to be completely obliterated till the third or fourth generation. Without destroying the distinction of ranks, a distant prospect of freedom and honours was presented, even to those whom pride and prejudice almost disdained to number among the human species.

It was once proposed to discriminate the slaves by a peculiar habit; but it was justly apprehended that there might be some danger in acquainting them with their own numbers. Without interpreting, in their utmost strictness, the liberal appellations of legions and myriads, we may venture to pronounce, that the proportion of slaves who were valued as property was more considerable than that of servants, who can be computed only as an expense. The youths of a promising genius were instructed in the arts and sciences, and their price was ascertained by the degree of their skill and talents. Almost every profession, either liberal or mechanical, might be found in the household of an opulent senator. The ministers of pomp and sensuality were multiplied beyond the conception of modern luxury. It was more for the interest of the merchant or manufacturer to purchase than to hire his workmen; and in the country, slaves were employed as the cheapest and most laborious instruments of agriculture. To confirm the general observation, and to display the multitude of slaves, we might allege a variety of particular instances. It was discovered, on a very melancholy occasion, that four hundred slaves were maintained in a single palace of Rome. The same number of four hundred belonged to an estate which an African widow, of a very private condition, resigned to her son, whilst she reserved for herself a much larger share of her property. A freedman, under the reign of Augustus, though his fortune had suffered great losses in the civil wars, left behind him three thousand six hundred yoke of oxen, two hundred and fifty thousand head of smaller cattle, and, what was almost included in the description of cattle, four thousand one hundred and sixteen slaves.

The number of subjects who acknowledged the laws of Rome, of citizens, of provincials, and of slaves, cannot now be fixed with such a degree of accuracy, as the importance of the object would deserve. We are informed that when the emperor Claudius exercised the office of censor, he took an account of six million nine hundred and forty-five thousand Roman citizens, who, with the proportion of women and children, must have amounted to about twenty millions of souls. The multitude of subjects of an inferior rank was uncertain and fluctuating. But, after weighing with attention every circumstance which could influence the balance, it seems probable that there existed, in the time of Claudius, about twice as many provincials as there were citizens, of either sex, and of every age; and that the slaves were at least equal in number to the free inhabitants of the Roman world. The total amount of this imperfect calculation would rise to about one hundred and twenty millions of persons, a degree of population which possibly exceeds that of modern Europe, and forms the most numerous society that has ever been united under the same system of government.

Domestic peace and union were the natural consequences of the moderate and comprehensive policy embraced by the Romans. If we turn our eyes towards the monarchies of Asia, we shall behold despotism in the centre, and weakness in the extremities; the collection of the revenue, or the administration of justice, enforced by the presence of an army; hostile barbarians established in the heart of the country, hereditary satraps usurping the dominion of the provinces, and subjects inclined to rebellion, though incapable of freedom. But the obedience of the Roman world was uniform, voluntary, and permanent. The vanquished nations, blended into one great people, resigned the hope, nay even the wish, of resuming their independence, and scarcely considered their own existence as distinct from the existence of Rome. The established authority of the emperors pervaded without an effort the wide extent of their dominions, and was exercised with the same facility on the banks of the Thames, or of the Nile, as on those of the Tiber. The legions were destined to serve against the public enemy, and the civil magistrate seldom required the aid of a military force. In this state of general security, the leisure as well as opulence both of the prince and people were devoted to improve and to adorn the Roman empire.

Among the innumerable monuments of architecture constructed by the Romans, how many have escaped the notice of history, how few have resisted the ravages of time and barbarism! And yet even the majestic ruins that are still scattered over Italy and the provinces would be sufficient to prove that those countries were once the seat of a polite and powerful empire. Their greatness alone, or their beauty, might deserve our attention; but they are rendered more interesting by two important circumstances, which connect the agreeable history of the arts with the more useful history of human manners. Many of those works were erected at private expense, and almost all were intended for public benefit.

It is natural to suppose that the greatest number, as well as the most considerable of the Roman edifices, were raised by the emperors, who possessed so unbounded a command both of men and money. Augustus was accustomed to boast that he had found his capital of brick, and that he had left it of marble. The strict economy of Vespasian was the source of his magnificence. The works of Trajan bear the stamp of his genius. The public monuments with which Hadrian adorned every province of the empire, were executed not only by his orders, but under his immediate inspection. He was himself an artist; and he loved the arts, as they conduced to the glory of the monarch. They were encouraged by the Antonines, as they contributed to the happiness of the people. But if the emperors were the first, they were not the only architects of their dominions. Their example was universally imitated by their principal subjects, who were not afraid of declaring to the world that they had spirit to conceive, and wealth to accomplish, the noblest undertakings. Scarcely had the proud structure of the Coliseum been dedicated at Rome, before the edifices of a smaller scale indeed, but of the same design and materials, were erected for the use and at the expense, of the cities of Capua and Verona. The inscription of the stupendous bridge of Alcantara attests that it was thrown over the Tagus by the contribution of a few Lusitanian communities. When Pliny was entrusted with the government of Bithynia and Pontus, provinces by no means the richest or most considerable of the empire, he found the cities within his jurisdiction striving with each other in every useful and ornamental work, that might deserve the curiosity of strangers, or the gratitude of their citizens.

In the commonwealths of Athens and Rome, the modest simplicity of private houses announced the equal condition of freedom; whilst the sovereignty of the people was represented in the majestic edifices destined to the public use; nor was this republican spirit totally extinguished by the introduction of wealth and monarchy. It was in works of national honour and benefit that the most virtuous of the emperors affected to display their magnificence. The golden palace of Nero excited a just indignation, but the vast extent of ground which had been usurped by his selfish luxury was more nobly filled under the succeeding reigns by the Coliseum, the baths of Titus, the Claudian portico, and the temples dedicated to the goddess of Peace and to the genius of Rome. These monuments of architecture, the property of the Roman people, were adorned with the most beautiful productions of Grecian painting and sculpture; and in the temple of Peace a very curious library was open to the curiosity of the learned. At a small distance from thence was situated the Forum of Trajan. It was surrounded with a lofty portico, in the form of a quadrangle, into which four triumphal arches opened a noble and spacious entrance: in the centre arose a column of marble, whose height of one hundred and ten feet denoted the elevation of the hill that had been cut away. This column, which still subsists in its ancient beauty, exhibited an exact representation of the Dacian victories of its founder. The veteran soldier contemplated the story of his own campaigns, and by an easy illusion of national vanity, the peaceful citizen associated himself to the honours of the triumph.

All the other quarters of the capital, and all the provinces of the empire, were embellished by the same liberal spirit of public magnificence, and were filled with amphitheatres, theatres, temples, porticos, triumphal arches, baths, and aqueducts, all variously conducive to the health, the devotion, and the pleasures of the meanest citizen. The last mentioned of those edifices deserve our peculiar attention. The boldness of the enterprise, the solidity of the execution, and the uses to which they were subservient, rank the aqueducts among the noblest monuments of Roman genius and power. The aqueducts of the capital claim a just pre-eminence; but the curious traveller, who, without the light of history, should examine those of Spoleto, of Metz, or of Segovia, would very naturally conclude that those provincial towns had formerly been the residence of some potent monarch. The solitudes of Asia and Africa were once covered with flourishing cities, whose populousness, and even whose existence, was derived from such artificial supplies of a perennial stream of fresh water.

Ancient Italy is said to have contained eleven hundred and ninety-seven cities; and for whatsoever era of antiquity the expression might be intended, there is not any reason to believe the country less populous in the age of the Antonines than in that of Romulus. The splendour of Verona may be traced in its remains: yet Verona was less celebrated than Aquileia or Padua, Milan or Ravenna.

The spirit of improvement had passed the Alps, and been felt even in the woods of Britain, which were gradually cleared away to open a free space for convenient and elegant habitations. York was the seat of government; London was already enriched by commerce; and Bath was celebrated for the salutary effects of its medicinal waters. Gaul could boast of her twelve hundred cities; and though in the northern parts many of them, without excepting Paris itself, were little more than the rude and imperfect townships of a rising people, the southern provinces imitated the wealth and elegance of Italy. Many were the cities of Gaul, Marseilles, Arles, Nismes, Narbonne, Thoulouse, Bourdeaux, Autun, Vienna, Lyons, Langres, and Treves, whose ancient condition might sustain an equal, and perhaps advantageous comparison with their present state.

With regard to Spain, that country flourished as a province, and has declined as a kingdom. Exhausted by the abuse of her strength, by America, and by superstition, her pride might possibly be confounded if we required such a list of three hundred and sixty cities, as Pliny has exhibited under the reign of Vespasian.

Three hundred African cities had once acknowledged the authority of Carthage, nor is it likely that their numbers diminished under the administration of the emperors: Carthage itself rose with new splendour from its ashes; and that capital, as well as Capua and Corinth, soon recovered all the advantages which can be separated from independent sovereignty.

The provinces of the East present the contrast of Roman magnificence with Turkish barbarism. The ruins of antiquity, scattered over uncultivated fields, and ascribed by ignorance to the power of magic, scarcely afford a shelter to the oppressed peasant or wandering Arab. Under the reign of the Cæsars, the proper Asia alone contained five hundred populous cities, enriched with all the gifts of nature, and adorned with all the refinements of art. Eleven cities of Asia had once disputed the honour of dedicating a temple to Tiberius, and their respective merits were examined by the senate. Four of them were immediately rejected as unequal to the burden; and among these was Laodicea, whose splendour is still displayed in its ruins. Laodicea collected a very considerable revenue from its flocks of sheep, celebrated for the fineness of their wool, and had received, a little before the contest, a legacy of above four hundred thousand pounds by the testament of a generous citizen. If such was the poverty of Laodicea, what must have been the wealth of those cities, whose claim appeared preferable, and particularly of Pergamus, of Smyrna, and of Ephesus, who so long disputed with each other over the titular primacy of Asia. The capitals of Syria and Egypt held a still superior rank in the empire: Antioch and Alexandria looked down with disdain on a crowd of dependent cities, and yielded, with reluctance, to the majesty of Rome itself.

All these cities were connected with each other, and with the capital, by the public highways, which issuing from the Forum of Rome, traversed Italy, pervaded the provinces, and were terminated only by the frontiers of the empire. If we carefully trace the distance from the wall of Antoninus to Rome, and from thence to Jerusalem, it will be found that the great chain of communication, from the north-west to the south-east point of the empire, was drawn out to the length of four thousand and eighty Roman miles. The public roads were accurately divided by mile-stones, and ran in a direct line from one city to another, with very little respect for the obstacles either of nature or private property. Mountains were perforated, and bold arches thrown over the broadest and most rapid streams. The middle part of the road was raised into a terrace which commanded the adjacent country, consisted of several strata of sand, gravel, and cement, and was paved with large stones, or in some places, near the capital, with granite. Such was the solid construction of the Roman highways, whose firmness has not entirely yielded to the effort of fifteen centuries. They united the subjects of the most distant provinces by an easy and familiar intercourse; but their primary object had been to facilitate the marches of the legions; nor was any country considered as completely subdued, till it had been rendered, in all its parts, pervious to the arms and authority of the conqueror.

The advantage of receiving the earliest intelligence, and of conveying their orders with celerity, induced the emperors to establish throughout their extensive dominions, the regular institution of posts. Houses were everywhere erected at the distance only of five or six miles; each of them was constantly provided with forty horses, and by the help of these relays it was easy to travel an hundred miles in a day along the Roman roads. The use of the posts was allowed to those who claimed it by an Imperial mandate; but though originally intended for the public service, it was sometimes indulged to the business or conveniency of private citizens. Nor was the communication of the Roman empire less free and open by sea than it was by land. The provinces surrounded and inclosed the Mediterranean; and Italy, in the shape of an immense promontory, advanced into the midst of that great lake. The coasts of Italy are, in general, destitute of safe harbours; but human industry had corrected the deficiencies of nature; and the artificial port of Ostia, in particular, situate at the mouth of the Tiber, and formed by the emperor Claudius, was a useful monument of Roman greatness. From this port, which was only sixteen miles from the capital, a favourable breeze frequently carried vessels in seven days to the columns of Hercules, and in nine or ten, to Alexandria in Egypt.

Whatever evils either reason or declamation have imputed to extensive empire, the power of Rome was attended with some beneficial consequences to mankind; and the same freedom of intercourse which extended the vices, diffused likewise the improvements of social life. In the more remote ages of antiquity, the world was unequally divided. The East was in the immemorial possession of arts and luxury; whilst the West was inhabited by rude and warlike barbarians, who either disdained agriculture, or to whom it was totally unknown. Under the protection of an established government, the productions of happier climates, and the industry of more civilised nations, were gradually introduced into the western countries of Europe; and the natives were encouraged, by an open and profitable commerce, to multiply the former, as well as to improve the latter. It would be almost impossible to enumerate all the articles, either of the animal or the vegetable reign, which were successively imported into Europe, from Asia and Egypt; but it will not be unworthy of the dignity, and much less of the utility, of an historical work, slightly to touch on a few of the principal heads. Almost all the flowers, the herbs, and the fruits, that grow in our European gardens, are of foreign extraction, which, in many cases, is betrayed even by their names: the apple was a native of Italy, and when the Romans had tasted the richer flavour of the apricot, the peach, the pomegranate, the citron, and the orange, they contented themselves with applying to all these new fruits the common denomination of apple, discriminating them from each other by the additional epithet of their country.

In the time of Homer, the vine grew wild in the island of Sicily, and most probably in the adjacent continent; but it was not improved by the skill, nor did it afford a liquor grateful to the taste, of the savage inhabitants. A thousand years afterwards, Italy could boast, that of the fourscore most generous and celebrated wines, more than two-thirds were produced from her soil. The blessing was soon communicated to the Narbonnese province of Gaul; but so intense was the cold to the north of the Cevennes, that, in the time of Strabo, it was thought impossible to ripen the grapes in those parts of Gaul. This difficulty, however, was gradually vanquished; and there is some reason to believe, that the vineyards of Burgundy are as old as the age of the Antonines.

The olive, in the western world, followed the progress of peace, of which it was considered as the symbol. Two centuries after the foundation of Rome, both Italy and Africa were strangers to that useful plant; it was naturalised in those countries; and at length carried into the heart of Spain and Gaul. The timid errors of the ancients, that it required a certain degree of heat, and could only flourish in the neighbourhood of the sea, were insensibly exploded by industry and experience.

The cultivation of flax was transported from Egypt to Gaul, and enriched the whole country, however it might impoverish the particular lands on which it was sown. The use of artificial grasses became familiar to the farmers both of Italy and the provinces, particularly the Lucerne, which derived its name and origin from Media. The assured supply of wholesome and plentiful food for the cattle during winter, multiplied the number of the flocks and herds, which in their turn contributed to the fertility of the soil.

To all these improvements may be added an assiduous attention to mines and fisheries, which, by employing a multitude of laborious hands, serve to increase the pleasures of the rich, and the subsistence of the poor. The elegant treatise of Columella describes the advanced state of the Spanish husbandry under the reign of Tiberius; and it may be observed, that those famines which so frequently afflicted the infant republic were seldom or never experienced by the extensive empire of Rome. The accidental scarcity in any single province was immediately relieved by the plenty of its more fortunate neighbours.

Agriculture is the foundation of manufactures, since the productions of nature are the materials of art. Under the Roman empire, the labour of an industrious and ingenious people was variously, but incessantly employed, in the service of the rich. In their dress, their table, their houses, and their furniture, the favourites of fortune united every refinement of conveniency, of elegance, and of splendour, whatever could soothe their pride or gratify their sensuality. Such refinements, under the odious name of luxury, have been severely arraigned by the moralists of every age; and it might perhaps be more conducive to the virtue, as well as happiness, of mankind, if all possessed the necessities, and none of the superfluities, of life. But in the present imperfect condition of society, luxury, though it may proceed from vice or folly, seems to be the only means that can correct the unequal distribution of property. The diligent mechanic, and the skilful artist, who have obtained no share in the division of the earth, receive a voluntary tax from the possessors of land; and the latter are prompted, by a sense of interest, to improve those estates with whose produce they may purchase additional pleasures. This operation, the particular effects of which are felt in every society, acted with much more diffusive energy in the Roman world. The provinces would soon have been exhausted of their wealth, if the manufactures and commerce of luxury had not insensibly restored to the industrious subjects the sums which were exacted from them by the arms and authority of Rome. As long as the circulation was confined within the bounds of the empire, it impressed the political machine with a new degree of activity, and its consequences, sometimes beneficial, could never become pernicious.

But it is no easy task to confine luxury within the limits of an empire. The most remote countries of the ancient world were ransacked to supply the pomp and delicacy of Rome. The forests of Scythia afforded some valuable furs. Amber was brought over land from the shores of the Baltic to the Danube; and the barbarians were astonished at the price which they received in exchange for so useless a commodity. There was a considerable demand for Babylonian carpets and other manufactures of the East; but the most important and unpopular branch of foreign trade was carried on with Arabia and India. Every year, about the time of the summer solstice, a fleet of an hundred and twenty vessels sailed from Myos-hormos, a port of Egypt, on the Red Sea. By the periodical assistance of the Monsoons, they traversed the ocean in about forty days. The coast of Malabar, or the island of Ceylon, was the usual term of their navigation, and it was in those markets that the merchants from the more remote countries of Asia expected their arrival. The return of the fleet of Egypt was fixed to the months of December or January; and as soon as their rich cargo had been transported on the backs of camels, from the Red Sea to the Nile, and had descended that river as far as Alexandria, it was poured, without delay, into the capital of the empire. The objects of oriental traffic were splendid and trifling; silk, a pound of which was esteemed not inferior in value to a pound of gold; precious stones, among which the pearl claimed the first rank after the diamond; and a variety of aromatics, that were consumed in religious worship and the pomp of funerals. The labour and risk of the voyage was rewarded with almost incredible profit; but the profit was made upon Roman subjects, and a few individuals were enriched at the expense of the public. As the natives of Arabia and India were contented with the productions and manufactures of their own country, silver, on the side of the Romans, was the principal, if not the only instrument of commerce. It was a complaint worthy of the gravity of the senate, that in the purchase of female ornaments, the wealth of the state was irrevocably given away to foreign and hostile nations. The annual loss is computed, by a writer of an inquisitive but censorious temper, at upwards of eight hundred thousand pounds sterling. Such was the style of discontent, brooding over the dark prospect of approaching poverty. And yet, if we compare the proportion between gold and silver, as it stood in the time of Pliny, and as it was fixed in the reign of Constantine, we shall discover within that period a very considerable increase. There is not the least reason to suppose that gold was become more scarce; it is therefore evident that silver was grown more common; that whatever might be the amount of the Indian and Arabian exports, they were far from exhausting the wealth of the Roman world; and that the produce of the mines abundantly supplied the demands of commerce.

Notwithstanding the propensity of mankind to exalt the past, and to depreciate the present, the tranquil and prosperous state of the empire was warmly felt, and honestly confessed, by the provincials as well as Romans. "They acknowledged that the true principles of social life, laws, agriculture, and science, which had been first invented by the wisdom of Athens, were now firmly established by the power of Rome, under whose auspicious influence the fiercest barbarians were united by an equal government and common language. They affirm, that with the improvement of arts, the human species was visibly multiplied. They celebrate the increasing splendour of the cities, the beautiful face of the country, cultivated and adorned like an immense garden; and the long festival of peace, which was enjoyed by so many nations, forgetful of their ancient animosities, and delivered from the apprehension of future danger."[1] Whatever suspicions may be suggested by the air of rhetoric and declamation which seems to prevail in these passages, the substance of them is perfectly agreeable to historic truth.

It was scarcely possible that the eyes of contemporaries should discover in the public felicity the latent causes of decay and corruption. This long peace, and the uniform government of the Romans, introduced a slow and

[1]Among many other passages, see Pliny (Hist. Natur. iii. 5), Aristides (de Urbe Romá), and Tertullian (de Animâ, c. 30).

secret poison into the vitals of the empire. The minds of men were gradually reduced to the same level, the fire of genius was extinguished, and even the military spirit evaporated. The natives of Europe were brave and robust, Spain, Gaul, Britain, and Illyricum supplied the legions with excellent soldiers, and constituted the real strength of the monarchy. Their personal valour remained, but they no longer possessed that public courage which is nourished by the love of independence, the sense of national honour, the presence of danger, and the habit of command. They received laws and governors from the will of their sovereign, and trusted for their defence to a mercenary army. The posterity of their boldest leaders was contented with the rank of citizens and subjects. The most aspiring spirits resorted to the court or standard of the emperors; and the deserted provinces, deprived of political strength or union, insensibly sank into the languid indifference of private life.

The love of letters, almost inseparable from peace and refinement, was fashionable among the subjects of Hadrian and the Antonines, who were themselves men of learning and curiosity. It was diffused over the whole extent of their empire; the most northern tribes of Britons had acquired a taste for rhetoric; Homer as well as Virgil was transcribed and studied on the banks of the Rhine and Danube; and the most liberal rewards sought out the faintest glimmerings of literary merit.[2] The sciences of physic and astronomy were successfully cultivated by the Greeks; the observations of Ptolemy and the writings of Galen are studied by those who have improved their discoveries and corrected their errors; but if we except the inimitable Lucian, this age of indolence passed away without having produced a single writer of original genius, or who excelled in the arts of elegant composition. The authority of Plato and Aristotle, of Zeno and Epicurus, still reigned in the schools; and their systems, transmitted with blind deference from one generation of disciples to another, precluded every generous attempt to exercise the powers, or enlarge the limits, of the human mind. The beauties of the poets and orators, instead of kindling a fire like their own, inspired only cold and servile imitations: or if any ventured to deviate from those models, they deviated at the same time from good sense and propriety. On the revival of letters, the youthful vigour of the imagination, after a long repose, national emulation, a new religion, new languages, and a new world, called forth the genius of Europe. But the provincials of Rome, trained by a uniform artificial foreign education, were engaged in a very unequal competition with those bold ancients, who, by expressing their genuine feelings in their native tongue, had already occupied every place of honour. The

[2]Herodes Atticus gave the sophist Polemo above eight thousand pounds for three declamations. Philostrat. 1. i. p. 558 [vita Herodes, cap. 7]. The Antonines founded a school at Athens, in which professors of grammar, rhetoric, politics, and the four great sects of philosophy, were maintained at the public expense for the instruction of youth. The salary of a philosopher was ten thousand drachmæ, between three and four hundred pounds a year. Similar establishments were formed in the other great cities of the empire.

name of Poet was almost forgotten; that of Orator was usurped by the sophists. A cloud of critics, of compilers, of commentators, darkened the face of learning, and the decline of genius was soon followed by the corruption of taste.

The sublime Longinus, who in somewhat a later period, and in the court of a Syrian queen, preserved the spirit of ancient Athens, observes and laments this degeneracy of his contemporaries, which debased their sentiments, enervated their courage, and depressed their talents. "In the same manner," says he, "as some children always remain pigmies, whose infant limbs have been too closely confined; thus our tender minds, fettered by the prejudices and habits of a just servitude, are unable to expand themselves, or to attain that well-proportioned greatness which we admire in the ancients; who living under a popular government, wrote with the same freedom as they acted." This diminutive stature of mankind, if we pursue the metaphor, was daily sinking below the old standard, and the Roman world was indeed peopled by a race of pigmies, when the fierce giants of the North broke in, and mended the puny breed. They restored a manly spirit of freedom; and after the revolution of ten centuries, freedom became the happy parent of taste and science.

CHAPTER III

Of the Constitution of the Roman Empire in the Age of the Antonines

The obvious definition of a monarchy seems to be that of a state in which a single person, by whatsoever name he may be distinguished, is entrusted with the execution of the laws, the management of the revenue, and the command of the army. But, unless public liberty is protected by intrepid and vigilant guardians, the authority of so formidable a magistrate will soon degenerate into despotism.

After the victory of Actium, the fate of the Roman world depended on the will of Octavianus, surnamed Cæsar, by his uncle's adoption, and afterwards Augustus, by the flattery of the senate. The conqueror was at the head of forty-four veteran legions, conscious of their own strength and of the weakness of the constitution; habituated, during twenty years' civil war, to every act of blood and violence; and passionately devoted to the house of Cæsar, from whence alone they had received, and expected, the most lavish rewards. The provinces, long oppressed by the ministers of the republic, sighed for the government of a single person, who would be the master, not the accomplice, of those petty tyrants. The people of Rome, viewing, with a secret pleasure, the humiliation of the aristocracy, demanded only bread and public shows; and were supplied with both by the liberal hand of Augustus. The rich and polite Italians, who had almost universally embraced the philosophy of Epicurus, enjoyed the present blessings of ease and tranquillity, and suffered not the pleasing dream to be interrupted by the memory of their old tumultuous freedom. With its power, the senate had lost its dignity; many of the most noble families were extinct. The republicans of spirit and ability had perished in the field of battle, or in the proscription. The door of the assembly had been designedly left open for a mixed multitude of more than a thousand persons, who reflected disgrace upon their rank instead of deriving honour from it.

The reformation of the senate was one of the first steps in which Augustus laid aside the tyrant, and professed himself the father of his country. He was elected censor; and, in concert with his faithful Agrippa, he examined the list of the senators, expelled a few members whose vices or whose obstinacy required a public example, persuaded near two hundred to prevent the shame of an expulsion by a voluntary retreat, raised the qualification of a senator to about ten thousand pounds, created a sufficient number of Patrician families, and accepted for himself the honourable title of Prince of the Senate, which had always been bestowed by the censors on the citizen the most eminent for his honours and services. But whilst he thus restored the dignity, he destroyed the independence of the senate. They refused to accept the resignation of Augustus; they conjured him not to desert the republic, which he had saved. After a decent resistance, the crafty tyrant submitted to the orders of the senate; and consented to receive the government of the provinces, and the general command of the Roman armies, under the well-known names of PROCONSUL and IMPERATOR.

Without any violation of the principles of the constitution, the general of the Roman armies might receive and exercise an authority almost despotic over the soldiers, the enemies, and the subjects of the republic. With regard to the soldiers, the jealousy of freedom had, even from the earliest ages of Rome, given way to the hopes of conquest, and a just sense of military discipline. The dictator, or consul, had a right to command the service of the Roman youth; and to punish an obstinate or cowardly disobedience by the most severe and ignominious penalties, by striking the offender out of the list of citizens, by confiscating his property, and by selling his person into slavery. The most sacred rights of freedom, confirmed by the Porcian and Sempronian laws, were suspended by the military engagement. In his camp the general exercised an absolute power of life and death; his jurisdiction was not confined by any forms of trial or rules of proceeding, and the execution of the sentence was immediate and without appeal.

The choice of the enemies of Rome was regularly decided by the legislative authority. The most important resolutions of peace and war were seriously debated in the senate, and solemnly ratified by the people. But when the arms of the legions were carried to a great distance from Italy, the generals assumed the liberty of directing them against whatever people, and in whatever manner, they judged most advantageous for the public service. It was from the success, not from the justice, of their enterprises, that they expected the honours of a triumph. In the use of victory, especially after they were no longer controlled by the commissioners of the senate, they exercised the most unbounded despotism. When Pompey commanded in the East, he rewarded his soldiers and allies, dethroned princes, divided kingdoms, founded colonies, and distributed the treasures of Mithridates. On his return to Rome, he obtained, by a single act of the senate and people, the universal ratification of all his proceedings. Such was the power over the soldiers, and over the enemies of Rome, which was either granted to, or assumed by, the generals of the republic. They were, at the same time, the governors, or rather monarchs, of the conquered provinces, united the civil with the military character, administered justice as well as the finances, and exercised both the executive and legislative power of the state.

From what has been already observed in the first chapter of this work, some notion may be formed of the armies and provinces thus entrusted to the ruling hand of Augustus. But as it was impossible that he could personally command the legions of so many distant frontiers, he was indulged by the senate, as Pompey had already been, in the permission of devolving the execution of his great office on a sufficient number of lieutenants. In rank and authority these officers seemed not inferior to the ancient proconsuls; but their station was dependent and precarious. They received and held their commissions at the will of a superior, to whose *auspicious* influence the merit of their action was legally attributed. They were the representatives of the emperor. The emperor alone was the general of the republic, and his jurisdiction, civil as well as military, extended over all the conquests of Rome. It was some satisfaction, however, to the senate, that he always delegated his power to the members of their body. The Imperial lieutenants were of consular or prætorian dignity; the legions were commanded by senators, and the præfecture of Egypt was the only important trust committed to a Roman knight.

Within six days after Augustus had been compelled to accept so very liberal a grant, he resolved to gratify the pride of the senate by an easy sacrifice. He represented to them that they had enlarged his powers, even beyond that degree which might be required by the melancholy condition of the times. They had not permitted him to refuse the laborious command of the armies and the frontiers; but he must insist on being allowed to restore the more peaceful and secure provinces, to the mild administration of the civil magistrate. In the division of the provinces, Augustus provided for his own power, and for the dignity of the republic. The proconsuls of the senate, particularly those of Asia, Greece, and Africa, enjoyed a more honourable character than the lieutenants of the emperor, who commanded in Gaul or Syria. The former were attended by lictors, the latter by soldiers. A law was passed that wherever the emperor was present, his extraordinary commission should supersede the ordinary jurisdiction of the governor; a custom was introduced, that the new conquest belonged to the Imperial portion; and it was soon discovered that the authority of the *Prince*, the favourite epithet of Augustus, was the same in every part of the empire.

In return for this imaginary concession, Augustus obtained an important privilege, which rendered him master of Rome and Italy. By a dangerous exception to the ancient maxims, he was authorised to preserve his military command, supported by a numerous body of guards, even in time of peace, and in the heart of the capital. His command, indeed, was confined to those citizens who were engaged in the service by the military oath; but such was the propensity of the Romans to servitude, that the oath was voluntarily taken by the magistrates, the senators, and the equestrian order, till the homage of flattery was insensibly converted into an annual and solemn protestation of fidelity.

Although Augustus considered a military force as the firmest foundation, he wisely rejected it as a very odious instrument of government. It was more agreeable to his temper, as well as to his policy, to reign under the venerable names of ancient magistracy, and artfully to collect, in his own person, all the scattered rays of civil jurisdiction. With this view, he permitted the senate to confer upon him, for his life, the powers of the consular and tribunitian offices, which were, in the same manner, continued to all his successors. The consuls had succeeded to the kings of Rome, and represented the dignity of the state. They superintended the ceremonies of religion, levied and commanded the legions, gave audience to foreign ambassadors, and presided in the assemblies both of the senate and people. The general control of the finances was entrusted to their care; and though they seldom had leisure to administer justice in person, they were considered as the supreme guardians of law, equity, and the public peace. Such was their ordinary jurisdiction; but whenever the senate empowered the first magistrate to consult the safety of the commonwealth, he was raised by that degree above the laws, and exercised, in the defence of liberty, a temporary despotism.

The character of the tribunes was, in every respect, different from that of the consuls. The appearance of the former was modest and humble; but their persons were sacred and inviolable. Their force was suited rather for opposition than for action. They were instituted to defend the oppressed, to pardon offences, to arraign the enemies of the people, and, when they judged it necessary, to stop, by a single word, the whole machine of government. As long as the republic subsisted, the dangerous influence which either the consul or the tribune might derive from their respective jurisdiction was diminished by several important restrictions. Their authority expired with the year in which they were elected; the former office was divided between two, the latter among ten persons; and, as both in their private and public interest they were averse to each other, their mutual conflicts contributed, for the most part, to strengthen rather than to destroy the balance of the constitution. But when the consular and tribunitian powers were united, when they were vested for life in a single person, when the general of the army was, at the same time, the minister of the senate, and the representative of the Roman people, it was impossible to resist the exercise, nor was it easy to define the limits, of his Imperial prerogative.

To these accumulated honours, the policy of Augustus soon added the splendid as well as important dignities of Supreme Pontiff, and of censor. By the former he acquired the management of the religion, and by the latter a legal inspection over the manners and fortunes, of the Roman people. If so many distinct and independent powers did not exactly unite with each other, the complaisance of the senate was prepared to supply every deficiency by the most ample and extraordinary concessions. The emperors, as the first ministers of the republic, were exempted from the obligation and penalty of many inconvenient laws: they were authorised to convoke the senate, to make several motions in the same day, to recommend candidates for the honours of the state, to enlarge the bounds of the city, to employ the revenue at their discretion, to declare peace and war, to ratify treaties; and by a most comprehensive clause, they were empowered to execute whatsoever they should judge advantageous to the empire, and agreeable to the majesty of things private or public, human or divine.

When all the various powers of executive government were committed to the *Imperial magistrate*, the ordinary magistrates of the commonwealth languished in obscurity, without vigour, and almost without business. The names and forms of the ancient administration were preserved by Augustus with the most anxious care. The usual number of consuls, prætors, and tribunes were annually invested with their respective ensigns of office, and continued to discharge some of their least important functions. Those honours still attracted the vain ambition of the Romans; and the emperors themselves, though invested for life with the powers of the consulship, frequently aspired to the title of that annual dignity, which they condescended to share with the most illustrious of their fellow-citizens. In the election of these magistrates, the people, during the reign of Augustus, were permitted to expose all the inconveniences of a wild democracy. That artful prince, instead of discovering the least symptom of impatience, humbly solicited their suffrages for himself or his friends, and scrupulously practised all the duties of an ordinary candidate. But we may venture to ascribe to his councils the first measure of the succeeding reign, by which the elections were transferred to the senate. The assemblies of the people were for ever abolished, and the emperors were delivered from a dangerous multitude, who, without restoring liberty, might have disturbed, and perhaps endangered, the established government.

By declaring themselves the protectors of the people, Marius and Cæsar had subverted the constitution of their country. But as soon as the senate had been humbled and disarmed, such an assembly, consisting of five or six hundred persons, was found a much more tractable and useful instrument of dominion. It was on the dignity of the senate that Augustus and his successors founded their new empire; and they affected, on every occasion, to adopt the language and principles of Patricians. In the administration of their own powers they frequently consulted the great national council, and *seemed* to refer to its decision the most important concerns of peace and war. Rome, Italy, and the internal provinces, were subject to the immediate jurisdiction of the senate. With regard to civil objects, it was the supreme court of appeal; with regard to criminal matters, a tribunal constituted for the trial of all offences that were committed by men in any public station, or that affected the peace and majesty of the Roman people. The exercise of the judicial power became the most frequent and serious occupation of the senate; and the important causes that were pleaded before them afforded a last refuge to the spirit of ancient eloquence.

As a council of state, and as a court of justice, the senate possessed very considerable prerogatives; but in its legislative capacity, in which it was supposed virtually to represent the people, the rights of sovereignty were acknowledged to reside in that assembly. Every power was derived from their authority, every law was ratified by their sanction. Their regular meetings were held on three stated days in every month, the Calends, the Nones, and the Ides. The debates were conducted with decent freedom; and the emperors themselves, who glorified in the name of senators, sat, voted, and divided with their equals.

To resume, in a few words, the system of the Imperial government, as it was instituted by Augustus, and maintained by those princes who understood their own interest and that of the people, it may be defined an absolute monarchy disguised by the forms of a commonwealth. The masters of the Roman world surrounded their throne with darkness, concealed their irresistible strength, and humbly professed themselves the accountable ministers of the senate, whose supreme decrees they dictated and obeyed.

The face of the court corresponded with the forms of the administration. The emperors, if we except those tyrants whose capricious folly violated every law of nature and decency, disdained that pomp and ceremony which might offend their countrymen, but could add nothing to their real power. In all the offices of life they affected to confound themselves with their subjects, and maintained with them an equal intercourse of visits and entertainments. Their habit, their palace, their table, were suited only to the rank of an opulent senator. Their family, however numerous or splendid, was composed entirely of their domestic slaves and freedmen. Augustus or Trajan would have blushed at employing the meanest of the Romans in those menial offices which, in the household and bed-chamber of a limited monarch, are so eagerly solicited by the proudest nobles of Britain.

The deification of the emperors is the only instance in which they departed from their accustomed prudence and modesty. The Asiatic Greeks were the first inventors, the successors of Alexander the first objects, of this servile and impious mode of adulation. It was easily transferred from the kings to the governors of Asia; and the Roman magistrates very frequently were adored as provincial deities, with the pomp of altars and temples, of festivals and sacrifices. It was natural that the emperors should not refuse what the proconsuls had accepted; and the divine honours which both the one and the other received from the provinces, attested rather the despotism than the servitude of Rome. But the conquerors soon imitated the vanquished nations in the arts of flattery, and the imperious spirit of the first Cæsar too easily consented to assume, during his lifetime, a place among the tutelar deities of Rome. The milder temper of his successor declined so dangerous an ambition, which was never afterwards revived, except by the madness of Caligula and Domitian.

Augustus permitted indeed some of the provincial cities to erect temples to his honour, on condition that they should associate the worship of Rome with that of the sovereign; he tolerated private superstition, of which he might be the object; but he contented himself with being revered by the senate and people in his human character, and wisely left to his successor the care of his public deification. A regular custom was introduced, that on the decease of every emperor who had neither lived nor died like a tyrant, the senate by a solemn decree should place him in the number of the gods: and the ceremonies of his Apotheosis were blended with those of his funeral. This legal, and, as it should seem, injudicious profanation, so abhorrent to our stricter principles, was received with a faint murmur, by the easy nature of polytheism; but it was received as an institution, not of religion, but of policy. We should disgrace the virtues of the Antonines, by comparing them with the vices of Hercules or Jupiter. Even the character of Cæsar or Augustus was far superior to those of the popular deities. But it was the misfortune of the former to live in an enlightened age, and their actions were too faithfully recorded to admit of such a mixture of fable and mystery, as the devotion of the vulgar requires. As soon as their divinity was established by law, it sank into oblivion, without contributing either to their own fame, or to the dignity of succeeding princes.

The tender respect of Augustus for a free constitution which he had destroyed, can only be explained by an attentive consideration of the character of that subtle tyrant. A cool head, an unfeeling heart, and a cowardly disposition prompted him, at the age of nineteen, to assume the mask of hypocrisy which he never afterwards laid aside. With the same hand, and probably with the same temper, he signed the proscription of Cicero, and the pardon of Cinna. His virtues, and even his vices, were artificial; and according to the various dictates of his interest, he was at first the enemy, and at last the father, of the Roman world. When he framed the artful system of the Imperial authority, his moderation was inspired by his fears. He wished to deceive the people by an image of civil liberty, and the armies by an image of civil government. The death of Cæsar was ever before his eyes; the title of king had armed the Romans against his life. Augustus was sensible that mankind is governed by names; nor was he deceived in his expectation that the senate and people would submit to slavery, provided they were respectfully assured that they still enjoyed their ancient freedom.

During a long period of two hundred and twenty years, from the establishment of this artful system to the death of Commodus, the dangers inherent to a military government were, in a great measure, suspended. The soldiers were seldom roused to that fatal sense of their own strength, and of the weakness of the civil authority, which was, before and afterwards, productive of such dreadful calamities. Caligula and Domitian were assassinated in their palace by their own domestics; the convulsions which agitated Rome on the death of the former were confined to the walls of the city. But Nero involved the whole empire in his ruin. In the space of eighteen months, four princes perished by the sword; and the Roman world was shaken by the fury of the contending armies. Excepting only this short, though violent, eruption of military licence, the two centuries from Augustus to Commodus passed away unstained with civil blood, and undisturbed by revolutions. The emperor was elected by *the authority of the senate*, and *the consent of the soldiers*.

Antoninus diffused order and tranquillity over the greatest part of the earth. His reign is marked by the rare advantage of furnishing very few materials for history; which is, indeed, little more than the register of the crimes, follies, and misfortunes of mankind. In private life, he was an amiable as well as a good man. The native simplicity of his virtue was a stranger to vanity or affectation. He enjoyed with moderation the conveniencies of his fortune, and the innocent pleasures of society; and the benevolence of his soul displayed itself in a cheerful serenity of temper.

The virtue of Marcus Aurelius Antoninus was of a severer and more laborious kind. It was the well-earned harvest of many a learned conference, of many a patient lecture, and many a midnight lucubration. At the age of twelve years he embraced the rigid system of the Stoics, which taught him to submit his body to his mind, his passions to his reason; to consider virtue as the only good, vice as the only evil, all things external as things indifferent. His meditations, composed in the tumult of a camp, are still extant; and he even condescended to give lessons of philosophy in a more public manner than was perhaps consistent with the modesty of a sage, or the dignity of an emperor. But his life was the noblest commentary on the precepts of Zeno. He was severe to himself, indulgent to the imperfections of others, just and beneficent to all mankind. He regretted that Avidius Cassius, who excited a rebellion in Syria, had disappointed him, by a voluntary death, of the pleasure of converting an enemy into a friend; and he justified the sincerity of that sentiment, by moderating the zeal of the senate against the adherents of the traitor. War he detested as the disgrace and calamity of human nature; but when the necessity of a just defence called upon him to take up arms, he readily exposed his person to eight winter campaigns on the frozen banks of the Danube, the severity of which was at last fatal.

If a man were called to fix the period in the history of the world, during which the condition of the human race was most happy and prosperous, he would, without hesitation, name that which elapsed from the death of Domitian to the accession of Commodus. The vast extent of the Roman empire was governed by absolute power, under the guidance of virtue and wisdom. The armies were restrained by the firm but gentle hand of five successive emperors, whose characters and authority commanded involuntary respect. The forms of the civil administration were carefully preserved by Nerva, Trajan, Hadrian, and the Antonines, who delighted in the image of liberty, and were pleased with considering themselves as the accountable ministers of the laws.

The labours of these monarchs were overpaid by the immense reward that inseparably waited on their success; by the honest pride of virtue, and by the exquisite delight of beholding the general happiness of which they were the authors. A just, but melancholy reflection embittered, however, the noblest of human enjoyments. They must often have recollected the instability of a happiness which depended on the character of a single man. The fatal moment was perhaps approaching, when some licentious youth, or some jealous tyrant, would abuse, to the destruction, that absolute power which they had exerted for the benefit of their people.

These gloomy apprehensions had been already justified by the experience of the Romans. The annals of the emperors exhibit a strong and various picture of human nature, which we should vainly seek among the mixed and doubtful characters of modern history. In the conduct of those monarchs we may trace the utmost lines of vice and virtue; the most exalted perfection, and the meanest degeneracy of our own species. The golden age of Trajan and the Antonines had been preceded by an age of iron. It is almost superfluous to enumerate the unworthy successors of Augustus. Their unparalleled vices, and the splendid theatre on which they were acted, have saved them from oblivion. The dark unrelenting Tiberius, the furious Caligula, the feeble Claudius, the profligate and cruel Nero, the beastly Vitellius, and the timid inhuman Domitian, are condemned to everlasting infamy. During fourscore years (excepting only the short and doubtful respite of Vespasian's reign) Rome groaned beneath an unremitting tyranny, which exterminated the ancient families of the republic, and was fatal to almost every virtue, and every talent, that arose in that unhappy period.

Oppressed beneath the weight of their own corruption and of military violence, the Romans for a long while preserved the sentiments, or at least the ideas, of their free-born ancestors. The education of Helvidius and Thrasea, of Tacitus and Pliny, was the same as that of Cato and Cicero. From Grecian philosophy they had imbibed the justest and most liberal notions of the dignity of human nature, and the origin of civil society. The history of their own country had taught them to revere a free, a virtuous, and a victorious commonwealth; to abhor the successful crimes of Cæsar and Augustus; and inwardly to despise those tyrants whom they adored with the most abject flattery. As magistrates and senators, they were admitted into the great council which had once dictated laws to the earth, whose name still gave a sanction to the acts of the monarch, and whose authority was so often prostituted to the vilest purposes of tyranny. Tiberius, and those emperors who adopted his maxims, attempted to disguise their murders by the formalities of justice, and perhaps enjoyed a secret pleasure in rendering the senate their accomplice as well as their victim. By this assembly the last of the Romans were condemned for imaginary crimes and real virtues. Their infamous accusers assumed the language of independent patriots, who arraigned a dangerous citizen before the tribunal of his country.

The division of Europe into a number of independent states, connected, however, with each other, by the general resemblance of religion, language, and manners, is productive of the most beneficial consequences to the liberty of mankind. A modern tyrant, who should find no resistance either in his own breast, or in his people, would soon experience a gentle restraint from the example of his equals, the dread of present censure, the advice of his allies, and the apprehension of his enemies. The object of his displeasure, escaping from the narrow limits of his dominions, would easily obtain, in a happier climate, a secure refuge, a new fortune adequate to his merit, the freedom of complaint, and perhaps the means of revenge. But the empire of the Romans filled the world, and when that empire fell into the hands of a single person, the world became a safe and dreary prison for his enemies. "Wherever you are," said Cicero to the exiled Marcellus, "remember that you are equally within the power of the conqueror."

CHAPTER IV

The Cruelty, Follies, and Murder of Commodus—Public Sale of the Empire by the Prætorian Guards

The mildness of Marcus, which the rigid discipline of the Stoics was unable to eradicate, formed, at the same time, the most amiable, and the only defective, part of his character. His excellent understanding was often deceived by the unsuspecting goodness of his heart. Artful men, who study the passions of princes and conceal their own, approached his person in the disguise of philosophic sanctity, and acquired riches and honours by affecting to despise them. His excessive indulgence to his brother, his wife, and his son, exceeded the bounds of private virtue and became a public injury, by the example and consequences of their vices.

Commodus, the beloved son of Marcus, succeeded (A.D. 180) to his father, amidst the acclamations of the senate and armies, and when he ascended the throne the happy youth saw round him neither competitor to remove nor enemies to punish. In this calm elevated station it was surely natural that he should prefer the love of mankind to their detestation, the mild glories of his five predecessors, to the ignominious fate of Nero and Domitian.

Yet Commodus was not, as he has been represented, a tiger born with an insatiate thirst of human blood, and capable, from his infancy, of the most inhuman actions. Nature had formed him of a weak, rather than a wicked, disposition. His simplicity and timidity rendered him the slave of his attendants, who gradually corrupted his mind. His cruelty, which at first obeyed the dictates of others, degenerated into habit, and at length became the ruling passion of his soul.

Whilst he abandoned the reins of empire to unworthy favourites, he valued nothing in sovereign power, except the unbounded licence of indulging his sensual appetites. His hours were spent in a seraglio of three hundred beautiful women, and as many boys, of every rank, and of every province; and, wherever the arts of seduction proved ineffectual, the brutal lover had recourse to violence. The ancient historians have expatiated on these abandoned scenes of prostitution, which scorned every restraint of nature or modesty; but it would not be easy to translate their too faithful descriptions. The intervals of lust were filled up with the basest amusements. The influence of a polite age, and the labour of an attentive education, had never been able to infuse into his rude and brutish mind the least tincture of learning; and he was the first of the Roman emperors totally devoid of taste for the pleasures of the understanding. Nero himself excelled, or affected to excel, in the elegant arts of music and poetry; nor should we despise his pursuits had he not converted the pleasing relaxation of a leisure hour into the serious business and ambition of his life. But Commodus, from his earliest infancy, discovered an aversion to whatever was rational or liberal, and a fond attachment to the amusements of the populace: the sports of the circus and amphitheatre, the combats of gladiators, and the hunting of wild beasts. The masters in every branch of learning whom Marcus provided for his son were heard with inattention and disgust.

Pestilence and famine contributed to fill up the measure of the calamities of Rome. The first could be only imputed to the just indignation of the gods; but (A.D. 189) a monopoly of corn, supported by the riches and power of the minister, was considered as the immediate cause of the second. The popular discontent, after it had long circulated in whispers, broke out in the assembled circus. The people quitted their favourite amusements for the more delicious pleasure of revenge, rushed in crowds towards a palace in the suburbs, one of the emperor's retirements, and demanded, with angry clamours, the head of the public enemy. Cleander, who commanded the Prætorian guards, ordered a body of cavalry to sally forth and disperse the seditious multitude. The multitude fled with precipitation towards the city; several were slain, and many more were trampled to death: but when the cavalry entered the streets, their pursuit was checked by a shower of stones and darts from the roofs and windows of the houses. The foot guards who had been long jealous of the prerogatives and insolence of the Prætorian cavalry, embraced the party of the people. The tumult became a regular engagement, and threatened a general massacre. The Prætorians, at length, gave way, oppressed with numbers; and the tide of popular fury returned with redoubled violence against the gates of the palace, where Commodus lay, dissolved in luxury, and alone unconscious of the civil war. It was death to approach his person with the unwelcome news. He would have perished in this supine security, had not two women, his elder sister Fadilla, and Marcia, the most favoured of his concubines, ventured to break into his presence. Bathed in tears, and with dishevelled hair, they threw themselves at his feet; and with all the pressing eloquence of fear, discovered to the affrighted emperor, the crimes of the minister, the rage of the people, and the impending ruin, which, in a few minutes, would burst over his palace and person. Commodus started from his dream of pleasure, and commanded that the head of Cleander should be thrown out to the people.

Commodus attained the summit of vice and infamy. Amidst the acclamations of a flattering court, he was unable to disguise, from himself, that he had deserved the contempt and hatred of every man of sense and virtue in his empire. His ferocious spirit was irritated by the consciousness of that hatred, by the envy of every kind of merit, by the just apprehension of danger, and by the habit of slaughter, which he contracted in his daily amusements. History has preserved a long list of consular senators sacrificed to his wanton suspicion. His cruelty proved at last fatal to himself. He had shed with impunity the noblest blood of Rome: he perished as soon as he was dreaded by his own domestics. Marcia his favourite concubine, Eclectus his chamberlain, and Lætus his Prætorian præfect, alarmed by the fate of their companions and predecessors, resolved to prevent the destruction which every hour hung over their heads, either from the mad caprice of the tyrant, or the sudden indignation of the people. Marcia seized the occasion of presenting a draught of wine to her lover, after he had fatigued himself with hunting some wild beasts. Commodus retired to sleep; but whilst he was labouring with the effects of poison and drunkenness, a robust youth, by profession a wrestler, entered his chamber, and strangled him without resistance. The body was secretly conveyed out of the palace, before the least suspicion was entertained in the city, or even in the court, of the emperor's death. Such was the fate of the son of Marcus, and so easy was it to destroy a hated tyrant, who, by the artificial powers of government, had oppressed, during thirteen years, so many millions of subjects, each of whom was equal to their master in personal strength and personal abilities.

The measures of the conspirators were conducted with the deliberate coolness and celerity which the greatness of the occasion required. They resolved instantly to fill the vacant throne with an emperor whose character would justify and maintain the action that had been committed. They fixed on Pertinax, præfect of the city, an ancient senator of consular rank, whose conspicuous merit had broke through the obscurity of his birth, and raised him to the first honours of the state. He had successively governed most of the provinces of the empire; and in all his great employments, military as well as civil, he had uniformly distinguished himself by the firmness, the prudence, and the integrity of his conduct. He now remained almost alone of the friends and ministers of Marcus; and when, at a late hour of the night, he was awakened with the news, that the chamberlain and the præfect were at his door, he received them with intrepid resignation, and desired they would execute their master's orders. Instead of death, they offered him the throne of the Roman world. During some moments he distrusted their intentions and assurances. Convinced at length of the death of Commodus, he accepted the purple with a sincere reluctance, the natural effect of his knowledge both of the duties and of the dangers of the supreme rank.

Pertinax resigned over to his wife and son his whole private fortune, that they might have no pretence to solicit favours at the expense of the state. He had the generous firmness to remit all the oppressive taxes invented by Commodus, and to cancel all the unjust claims of the treasury; declaring, in a decree of the senate, "that he was better satisfied to administer a poor republic with innocence, than to acquire riches by the ways of tyranny and dishonour." The expense of the household was immediately reduced to one half. All the instruments of luxury Pertinax exposed to public auction, gold and silver plate, chariots of a singular construction, a superfluous wardrobe of silk and embroidery, and a great number of beautiful slaves.

Amidst the general joy, the sullen and angry countenance of the Prætorian guards betrayed their inward dissatisfaction. They had reluctantly submitted to Pertinax; they dreaded the strictness of the ancient discipline which he was preparing to restore; and they regretted the licence of the former reign. Their discontents were secretly fomented by Lætus their præfect, who found, when it was too late, that his new emperor would reward a servant, but would not be ruled by a favourite. On the third day of his reign the soldiers seized on a noble senator, with a design to carry him to the camp, and to invest him with the Imperial purple. Instead of being dazzled by the dangerous honour, the affrighted victim escaped from their violence, and took refuge at the feet of Pertinax. A short time afterwards Sosius Falco, one of the consuls of the year, a rash youth, but of an ancient and opulent family, listened to the voice of ambition; and a conspiracy was formed during a short absence of Pertinax, which was crushed by his sudden return to Rome, and his resolute behaviour. Falco was on the point of being justly condemned to death as a public enemy, had he not been saved by the earnest and sincere entreaties of the injured emperor, who conjured the senate that the purity of his reign might not be stained by the blood even of a guilty senator.

These disappointments served only to irritate the rage of the Prætorian guards. On the twenty-eighth of March, eighty-six days only after the death of Commodus, a general sedition broke out in the camp, which the officers wanted either power or inclination to suppress. Two or three hundred of the most desperate soldiers marched at noon-day, with arms in their hands and fury in their looks, towards the Imperial palace. The gates were thrown open by their companions upon guard and Pertinax was dispatched with a multitude of wounds. His head, placed on a lance, was carried in triumph to the Prætorian camp.

The power of the sword is more sensibly felt in an extensive monarchy than in a small community. It has been calculated by the ablest politicians that no state, without being soon exhausted, can maintain above the hundredth part of its members in arms and idleness. But there is no superiority of natural strength, artificial weapons, or acquired skill, which could enable one man to keep in constant subjection one hundred of his fellow-creatures: the tyrant of a single town, or a small district, would soon discover that an hundred armed followers were a weak defence against ten thousand peasants or citizens; but an hundred thousand well-disciplined soldiers will command, with despotic sway, ten millions of subjects; and a body of ten or fifteen thousand guards will strike terror into the most numerous populace that ever crowded the streets of an immense capital.

The Prætorian bands, whose licentious fury was the first symptom and cause of the decline of the Roman empire, scarcely amounted to the last-mentioned number. They derived their institution from Augustus. That crafty tyrant, sensible that laws might colour, but that arms alone could maintain, his usurped dominion, had gradually formed this powerful body of guards in constant readiness to protect his person, to awe the senate, and either to prevent or to crush the first motions of rebellion. He distinguished these favoured troops by a double pay and superior privileges; but as their formidable aspect would at once have alarmed and irritated the Roman people, three cohorts only were stationed in the capital, whilst the remainder was dispersed in the adjacent towns of Italy. But after fifty years of peace and servitude, Tiberius ventured on a decisive measure, which for ever riveted the fetters of his country. Under the fair pretences of relieving Italy from the heavy burthen of military quarters, and of introducing a stricter discipline among the guards, he assembled them at Rome in a permanent camp, which was fortified with skilful care and placed on a commanding situation.

Such formidable servants are always necessary, but often fatal to the throne of despotism. By thus introducing the Prætorian guards, as it were, into the palace and the senate, the emperors taught them to perceive their own strength and the weakness of the civil government; to view the vices of their masters with familiar contempt, and to lay aside that reverential awe, which distance only, and mystery, can preserve towards an imaginary power. In the luxurious idleness of an opulent city, their pride was nourished by the sense of their irresistible weight; nor was it possible to conceal from them that the person of the sovereign, the authority of the senate, the public treasure, and the seat of empire, were all in their hands. To divert the Prætorian bands from these dangerous reflections, the firmest and best established princes were obliged to mix blandishments with commands, rewards with punishments, to flatter their pride, indulge their pleasures, connive at their irregularities, and to purchase their precarious faith by a liberal donative; which, since the elevation of Claudius, was exacted as a legal claim on the accession of every new emperor.

The advocates of the guards endeavoured to justify by arguments, the power which they asserted by arms; and to maintain that, according to the purest principles of the constitution, *their* consent was essentially necessary in the appointment of an emperor. The election of consuls, of generals, and of magistrates, however it had been recently usurped by the senate, was the ancient and undoubted right of the Roman people. But where was the Roman people to be found? Not surely amongst the mixed multitude of slaves and strangers that filled the streets of Rome; a servile populace, as devoid of spirit as destitute of property. The defenders of the state, selected from the flower of the Italian youth, and trained in the exercise of arms and virtue, were the genuine representatives of the people, and the best entitled to elect the military chief of the republic. These assertions, however defective in reason, became unanswerable when the fierce Prætorians increased their weight by throwing, like the barbarian conqueror of Rome, their swords into the scale.

The Prætorians violated the sanctity of the throne by the atrocious murder of Pertinax; they dishonoured the majesty of it by their subsequent conduct. The more prudent of the Prætorians, apprehensive that they should not obtain a just price for so valuable a commodity, ran out upon the ramparts; and, with a loud voice, proclaimed that the Roman world was to be disposed of to the best bidder by public auction.

This infamous offer, the most insolent excess of military licence, diffused an universal grief, shame, and indignation throughout the city. It reached at length the ears of Didius Julianus, a wealthy senator, who, regardless of the public calamities, was indulging himself in the luxury of the table. His wife and his daughter, his freedmen and his parasites, easily convinced him that he deserved the throne, and earnestly conjured him to embrace so fortunate an opportunity. The vain old man (A.D. 193, March 28th) hastened to the Prætorian camp, and began to bid. The unworthy negotiation was transacted by faithful emissaries, who passed alternately from one candidate to the other, and acquainted each of them with the offers of his rival. Julian, eager for the prize, rose at once to the sum of six thousand two hundred and fifty drachms, or upwards of two hundred pounds sterling. The gates of the camp were instantly thrown open to the purchaser; he was declared emperor, and received an oath of allegiance from the soldiers.

It was now incumbent on the Prætorians to fulfil the conditions of the sale. They placed their new sovereign, whom they served and despised, in the centre of their ranks, surrounded him on every side with their shields, and conducted him in close order of battle through the deserted streets of the city. The senate was commanded to assemble; and those who had been the distinguished friends of Pertinax, or the personal enemies of Julian, found it necessary to affect a more than common share of satisfaction at this happy revolution. After Julian had filled the senate-house with armed soldiers, he expatiated on the freedom of his election, his own eminent virtues, and his full assurance of the affections of the senate. The obsequious assembly congratulated their own and the public felicity; engaged their allegiance, and conferred on him all the several branches of the Imperial power. Yet it was observed, that after the crowd of flatterers dispersed, and left him to darkness, solitude, and terrible reflection, he passed a sleepless night; revolving most probably in his mind his own rash folly, the fate of his virtuous predecessor, and the doubtful and dangerous tenure of an empire which had not been acquired by merit, but purchased by money.

He had reason to tremble. On the throne of the world he found himself without a friend, and even without an adherent. The guards themselves were ashamed of the prince whom their avarice had persuaded them to accept; nor was there a citizen who did not consider his elevation with horror, as the last insult on the Roman name. The nobility, whose conspicuous station and ample possessions exacted the strictest caution, dissembled their sentiments and met the affected civility of the emperor with smiles of complacency and professions of duty. But the people, secure in their numbers and obscurity, gave a free vent to their passions. The streets and public places of Rome resounded with clamours and imprecations. The enraged multitude affronted the person of Julian, rejected his liberality, and conscious of the impotence of their own resentment, they called aloud on the legions of the frontiers to assert the violated majesty of the Roman empire.

The public discontent was soon diffused from the centre to the frontiers of the empire. The armies of Britain, of Syria, and of Illyricum lamented the death of Pertinax, in whose company, or under whose command, they had so often fought and conquered. They received with surprise, with indignation, and perhaps with envy, the extraordinary intelligence that the Prætorians had disposed of the empire by public auction; and they sternly refused to ratify the ignominious bargain. Their immediate and unanimous revolt was fatal to Julian, but it was fatal at the same time to the public peace; as the generals of the respective armies, Clodius Albinus, Pescennius Niger, and Septimius Severus, were still more anxious to succeed than to revenge the murdered Pertinax. Their forces were exactly balanced. Each of them was at the head of three legions, with a numerous train of auxiliaries; and however different in their characters, they were all soldiers of experience and capacity.

Clodius Albinus, governor of Britain, surpassed both his competitors in the nobility of his extraction, which he derived from some of the most illustrious names of the old republic. But the branch from whence he claimed his descent was sunk into mean circumstances, and transplanted into a remote province. It is difficult to form a just idea of his true character. Under the philosophic cloak of austerity, he stands accused of concealing most of the vices which degrade human nature. But his accusers are those venal writers who adored the fortune of Severus, and trampled on the ashes of an unsuccessful rival. He was employed in a distant honourable command, when he received a confidential letter from the emperor, acquainting him of the treasonable designs of some discontented generals, and authorising him to declare himself the guardian and successor of the throne, by assuming the title and ensigns of Cæsar. The governor of Britain wisely declined the dangerous honour, which would have marked him for the jealousy, or involved him in the approaching ruin, of Commodus. He courted power by nobler, or, at least, by more specious arts. On a premature report of the death of the emperor, he assembled his troops; and, in an eloquent discourse, deplored the inevitable mischiefs of despotism, described the happiness and glory which their ancestors had enjoyed under the consular government, and declared his firm resolution to reinstate the senate and people in their legal authority. This popular harangue was answered by the loud acclamations of the British legions, and received at Rome with a secret murmur of applause.

Personal merit alone had raised Pescennius Niger from an obscure birth and station to the government of Syria; a lucrative and important command, which in times of civil confusion gave him a near prospect of the throne. Yet his parts seem to have been better suited to the second than to the first rank; he was an unequal rival, though he might have approved himself an excellent lieutenant, to Severus, who afterwards displayed the greatness of his mind by adopting several useful institutions from a vanquished enemy. In his government, Niger acquired the esteem of the soldiers, and the love of the provincials. His rigid discipline fortified the valour and confirmed the obedience of the former, whilst the voluptuous Syrians were less delighted with the mild firmness of his administration than with the affability of his manners, and the apparent pleasure with which he attended their frequent and pompous festivals. As soon as the intelligence of the atrocious murder of Pertinax had reached Antioch, the wishes of Asia invited Niger to assume the Imperial purple and revenge his death. The legions of the eastern frontier embraced his cause; the opulent but unarmed provinces from the frontiers of Æthiopia to the Hadriatic cheerfully submitted to his power; and the kings beyond the Tigris and the Euphrates congratulated his election, and offered him their homage and services. The mind of Niger was not capable of receiving this sudden tide of fortune; he flattered himself that his accession would be undisturbed by competition, and unstained by civil blood; and whilst he enjoyed the vain pomp of triumph, he neglected to secure the means of victory. Instead of entering into an effectual negotiation with the powerful armies of the West, instead of advancing without delay towards Rome and Italy, Niger trifled away in the luxury of Antioch those irretrievable moments which were diligently improved by the decisive activity of Severus.

The country of Pannonia and Dalmatia, which occupied the space between the Danube and the Hadriatic, was one of the last and most difficult conquests of the Romans. In the defence of national freedom, two hundred thousand of these barbarians had once appeared in the field, alarmed the declining age of Augustus, and exercised the vigilant prudence of Tiberius at the head of the collected force of the empire. The Pannonians yielded at length to the arms and institutions of Rome. Their recent subjection, however, the neighbourhood, and even the mixture, of the unconquered tribes, and perhaps the climate, adapted, as it has been observed, to the production of great bodies and slow minds, all contributed to preserve some remains of their original ferocity, and under the tame and uniform countenance of Roman provincials, the hardy features of the natives were still to be discerned. Their warlike youth afforded an inexhaustible supply of recruits to the legions stationed on the banks of the Danube, which, from a perpetual warfare against the Germans and Sarmatians, were deservedly esteemed the best troops in the service.

The Pannonian army was at this time commanded by Septimius Severus, a native of Africa, who, in the gradual ascent of private honours, had concealed his daring ambition, which was never diverted from its steady course by the allurements of pleasure, the apprehension of danger, or the feelings of humanity. On the first news of the murder of Pertinax, he assembled his troops, painted in the most lively colours the crime, the insolence, and the weakness of the Prætorian guards, and animated the legions to arms and to revenge. He concluded (and the peroration was thought extremely eloquent) with promising every soldier about four hundred pounds; an honourable donative, double in value to the infamous bribe with which Julian had purchased the empire. The acclamations of the army immediately saluted Severus with the names of Augustus, Pertinax, and Emperor; and he

(A.D. 193, April 13th) thus attained the lofty station to which he was invited, by conscious merit and a long train of dreams and omens, the fruitful offspring either of his superstition or policy.

The new candidate for empire saw and improved the peculiar advantage of his situation. His province extended to the Julian Alps, which gave an easy access into Italy; and he remembered the saying of Augustus, that a Pannonian army might in ten days appear in sight of Rome.

The wretched Julian had expected, and thought himself prepared, to dispute the empire with the governor of Syria; but in the invincible and rapid approach of the Pannonian legions he saw his inevitable ruin. The hasty arrival of every messenger increased his just apprehensions. He was successively informed that Severus had passed the Alps; that the Italian cities, unwilling or unable to oppose his progress, had received him with the warmest professions of joy and duty; that the important place of Ravenna had surrendered without resistance, and that the Hadriatic fleet was in the hands of the conqueror. The enemy was now within two hundred and fifty miles of Rome; and every moment diminished the narrow span of life and empire allotted to Julian.

Every motion of Julian betrayed his trembling perplexity. He insisted that Severus should be declared a public enemy by the senate. He entreated that the Pannonian general might be associated to the empire. He sent public ambassadors of consular rank to negotiate with his rival; he dispatched private assassins to take away his life.

Severus had the laudable ambition of ascending the throne without drawing the sword. His emissaries, dispersed in the capital, assured the guards that provided they would abandon their worthless prince and the perpetrators of the murder of Pertinax to the justice of the conqueror, he would no longer consider that melancholy event as the act of the whole body. The faithless Prætorians, whose resistance was supported only by sullen obstinacy, gladly complied with the easy conditions, seized the greatest part of the assassins, and signified to the senate that they no longer defended the cause of Julian. That assembly, convoked by the consul, unanimously acknowledged Severus as lawful emperor, decreed divine honours to Pertinax, and pronounced a sentence of deposition and death against his unfortunate successor. Julian was conducted into a private apartment of the baths of the palace, and (A.D. 193, June 2) beheaded as a common criminal, after having purchased, with an immense treasure, an anxious and precarious reign of only sixty-six days. The almost incredible expedition of Severus, who in so short a space of time conducted a numerous army from the banks of the Danube to those of the Tiber, proves at once the plenty of provisions produced by agriculture and commerce, the goodness of the roads, the discipline of the legions, and the indolent subdued temper of the provinces.

If his two competitors, reconciled by their common danger, had advanced upon him without delay, perhaps Severus would have sunk under their united effort. Had they even attacked him, at the same time, with separate views and separate armies, the contest might have been long and doubtful.

But they fell, singly and successively, an easy prey to the arts as well as arms of their subtle enemy, lulled into security by the moderation of his professions, and overwhelmed by the rapidity of his action.

The civil wars of modern Europe have been distinguished, not only by the fierce animosity, but likewise by the obstinate perseverance, of the contending factions. They have generally been justified by some principle, or at least coloured by some pretext, of religion, freedom, or loyalty. The leaders were nobles of independent property and hereditary influence. The troops fought like men interested in a decision of the quarrel; and as military spirit and party zeal were strongly diffused throughout the whole community, a vanquished chief was immediately supplied with new adherents, eager to shed their blood in the same cause. But the Romans, after the fall of the republic, combated only for the choice of masters. Under the standard of a popular candidate for empire, a few enlisted from affection, some from fear, many from interest, none from principle. The legions, uninflamed by party zeal, were allured into civil war by liberal donatives and still more liberal promises. A defeat, by disabling the chief from the performance of his engagements, dissolved the mercenary allegiance of his followers and left them to consult their own safety by a timely desertion of an unsuccessful cause. In the vast extent of the Roman empire, there were few fortified cities capable of protecting a routed army; nor was there any person, or family, or order of men, whose natural interest, unsupported by the powers of government, was capable of restoring the cause of a sinking party.

Severus considered the Roman empire as his property, and had no sooner secured the possession, than he bestowed his care on the cultivation and improvement of so valuable an acquisition. Salutary laws, executed with inflexible firmness, soon corrected most of the abuses with which, since the death of Marcus, every part of the government had been infected. In the administration of justice, the judgments of the emperor were characterised by attention, discernment, and impartiality. Whenever he deviated from the strict line of equity, it was generally in favour of the poor and oppressed; not so much indeed from any sense of humanity, as from the natural propensity of a despot, to humble the pride of greatness, and to sink all his subjects to the same common level of absolute dependence. His expensive taste for building, magnificent shows, and above all a constant and liberal distribution of corn and provisions, were the surest means of captivating the affection of the Roman people. The misfortunes of civil discord were obliterated. The calm of peace and prosperity was once more experienced in the provinces; and many cities, restored by the munificence of Severus, assumed the title of his colonies, and attested by public monuments their gratitude and felicity. The fame of the Roman arms was revived by that warlike and successful emperor, and he boasted with a just pride, that, having received the empire oppressed with foreign and domestic wars, he left it established in profound, universal, and honourable peace.

Till the reign of Severus, the virtue and even the good sense of the emperors had been distinguished by their zeal or affected reverence for the senate, and by a tender regard to the nice frame of civil policy instituted by Augustus. But the youth of Severus had been trained in the implicit obedience of camps, and his riper years spent in the despotism of military command. His haughty and inflexible spirit could not discover, or would not acknowledge, the advantage of preserving an intermediate power, however imaginary, between the emperor and the army. He disdained to profess himself the servant of an assembly that detested his person and trembled at his frown; he issued his commands, where his request would have proved as effectual; assumed the conduct and style of a sovereign and a conqueror, and exercised, without disguise, the whole legislative as well as the executive power.

The victory over the senate was easy and inglorious. Every eye and every passion was directed to the supreme magistrate, who possessed the arms and treasure of the state; whilst the senate, neither elected by the people, nor guarded by military force, nor animated by public spirit, rested its declining authority on the frail and crumbling basis of ancient opinion. The fine theory of a republic insensibly vanished, and made way for the more natural and substantial feelings of monarchy. As the freedom and honours of Rome were successively communicated to the provinces, in which the old government had been either unknown, or was remembered with abhorrence, the tradition of republican maxims was gradually obliterated. The Greek historians of the age of the Antonines observe with a malicious pleasure that although the sovereign of Rome, in compliance with an obsolete prejudice, abstained from the name of king, he possessed the full measure of regal power. In the reign of Severus, the senate was filled with polished and eloquent slaves from the eastern provinces, who justified personal flattery by speculative principles of servitude. These new advocates of prerogative were heard with pleasure by the court, and with patience by the people, when they inculcated the duty of passive obedience, and descanted on the inevitable mischiefs of freedom. The lawyers and the historians concurred in teaching, that the Imperial authority was held, not by the delegated commission, but by the irrevocable resignation of the senate; that the emperor was freed from the restraint of civil laws, could command by his arbitrary will the lives and fortunes of his subjects, and might dispose of the empire as of his private patrimony. The most eminent of the civil lawyers flourished under the house of Severus; and the Roman jurisprudence, having closely united itself with the system of monarchy, was supposed to have attained its full maturity and perfection.

The contemporaries of Severus, in the enjoyment of the peace and glory of his reign, forgave the cruelties by which it had been introduced. Posterity, who experienced the fatal effects of his maxims and example, justly considered him as the principal author of the decline of the Roman empire.

CHAPTER V

Tyranny of Caracalla—Licentiousness of the Army—General State of the Roman Finances

The dissolute tyranny of Commodus, the civil wars occasioned by his death, and the new maxims of policy introduced by the house of Severus, all contributed to increase the dangerous power of the army, and to obliterate the faint image of laws and liberty that was still impressed on the minds of the Romans. The personal characters of the emperors, their victories, laws, follies, and fortunes, can interest us no farther than as they are connected with the general history of the decline and fall of the monarchy. Our constant attention to that great object will not suffer us to overlook a most important edict of Antoninus Caracalla, which communicated to all the free inhabitants of the empire the name and privileges of Roman citizens. His unbounded liberality flowed not, however, from the sentiments of a generous mind; it was the sordid result of avarice, and will naturally be illustrated by some observations on the finances of that state, from the victorious ages of the commonwealth to the reign of Alexander Severus.

The siege of Veii in Tuscany, the first considerable enterprise of the Romans, was protracted to the tenth year, much less by the strength of the place than by the unskilfulness of the besiegers. The unaccustomed hardships of so many winter campaigns, at the distance of near twenty miles from home, required more than common encouragements; and the senate wisely prevented the clamours of the people, by the institution of a regular pay for the soldiers, which was levied by a general tribute, assessed according to an equitable proportion on the property of the citizens. During more than two hundred years after the conquest of Veii, the victories of the republic added less to the wealth than to the power of Rome. The states of Italy paid their tribute in military service only, and the vast force both by sea and land, which was exerted in the Punic wars, was maintained at the expense of the Romans themselves. That high-spirited people cheerfully submitted to the most excessive but voluntary burdens, in the just confidence that they should speedily enjoy the rich harvest of their labours. Their expectations were not disappointed. In the course of a few years, the riches of Syracuse, of Carthage, of Macedonia, and of Asia, were brought in triumph to Rome. The treasures of Perseus alone amounted to near two millions sterling, and the Roman people, the sovereign of so many nations, was for ever delivered from the weight of taxes. The increasing revenue of the provinces was found sufficient to defray the ordinary establishment of war and government, and the superfluous mass of gold and silver was deposited in the temple of Saturn, and reserved for any unforeseen emergency of the state.

History has never perhaps suffered a greater or more irreparable injury than in the loss of the curious register bequeathed by Augustus to the senate, in which that experienced prince so accurately balanced the revenues and expenses of the Roman empire. Deprived of this clear and comprehensive estimate, we are reduced to collect a few imperfect hints from such of the ancients as have accidentally turned aside from the splendid to the more useful parts of history. We are informed that, by the conquests of Pompey, the tributes of Asia were raised from fifty to one hundred and thirty-five millions of drachms, or about four millions and a half sterling. Under the last and most indolent of the Ptolemies, the revenue of Egypt is said to have amounted to twelve thousand five hundred talents; a sum equivalent to more than two millions and a half of our money, but which was afterwards considerably improved by the more exact economy of the Romans, and the increase of the trade of Æthiopia and India. Gaul was enriched by rapine, as Egypt was by commerce, and the tributes of those two great provinces have been compared as nearly equal to each other in value. The ten thousand Euboic or Phœnician talents, about four millions sterling, which vanquished Carthage was condemned to pay within the term of fifty years, were a slight acknowledgment of the superiority of Rome, and cannot bear the least proportion with the taxes afterwards raised both on the lands and on the persons of the inhabitants, when the fertile coast of Africa was reduced into a province.

Spain, by a very singular fatality, was the Peru and Mexico of the old world. The discovery of the rich western continent by the Phœnicians, and the oppression of the simple natives, who were compelled to labour in their own mines for the benefit of strangers, form an exact type of the more recent history of Spanish America. The Phœnicians were acquainted only with the sea-coast of Spain; avarice, as well as ambition, carried the arms of Rome and Carthage into the heart of the country, and almost every part of the soil was found pregnant with copper, silver, and gold. Mention is made of a mine near Carthagena which yielded every day twenty-five thousand drachms of silver, or about three hundred thousand pounds a year. Twenty thousand pound weight of gold was annually received from the provinces of Asturia, Gallicia, and Lusitania.

We want both leisure and materials to pursue this curious inquiry through the many potent states that were annihilated in the Roman empire. Some notion, however, may be formed of the revenue of the provinces where considerable wealth had been deposited by nature, or collected by man, if we observe the severe attention that was directed to the abodes of solitude and sterility. Augustus once received a petition from the inhabitants of Gyarus, humbly praying that they might be relieved from one-third of their excessive impositions. Their whole tax amounted indeed to no more than one hundred and fifty drachms, or about five pounds; but Gyarus was a little island, or rather a rock, of the Ægean Sea, destitute of fresh water and every necessary of life, and inhabited only by a few wretched fishermen.

From the faint glimmerings of such doubtful and scattered lights we should be inclined to believe, 1st, that (with every fair allowance for the difference of times and circumstances) the general income of the Roman provinces could seldom amount to less than fifteen or twenty millions of our money; and, 2ndly, that so ample a revenue must have been fully adequate to all the expenses of the moderate government instituted by Augustus, whose court was the modest family of a private senator, and whose military establishment was calculated for the defence of the frontiers, without any aspiring views of conquest, or any serious apprehension of a foreign invasion.

Notwithstanding the seeming probability of both these conclusions, the latter of them at least is positively disowned by the language and conduct of Augustus. It is not easy to determine whether, on this occasion, he acted as the common father of the Roman world, or as the oppressor of liberty; whether he wished to relieve the provinces, or to impoverish the senate and the equestrian order. But no sooner had he assumed the reins of government than he frequently intimated the insufficiency of the tributes, and the necessity of throwing an equitable proportion of the public burden upon Rome and Italy. In the prosecution of this unpopular design, he advanced, however, by cautious and well-weighed steps. The introduction of customs was followed by the establishment of an excise, and the scheme of taxation was completed by an artful assessment on the real and personal property of the Roman citizens, who had been exempted from any kind of contribution above a century and a half.

In a great empire like that of Rome, a natural balance of money must have gradually established itself. It has been already observed, that as the wealth of the provinces was attracted to the capital by the strong hand of conquest and power, so a considerable part of it was restored to the industrious provinces by the gentle influence of commerce and arts. In the reign of Augustus and his successors, duties were imposed on every kind of merchandise, which through a thousand channels flowed to the great centre of opulence and luxury; and in whatsoever manner the law was expressed, it was the Roman purchaser, and not the provincial merchant, who paid the tax. The rate of the customs varied from the eighth to the fortieth part of the value of the commodity; and we have a right to suppose that the variation was directed by the unalterable maxims of policy: that a higher duty was fixed on the articles of luxury than on those of necessity, and that the productions raised or manufactured by the labour of the subjects of the empire, were treated with more indulgence than was shown to the pernicious, or at least the unpopular, commerce of Arabia and India.[1] There is still extant a long but imperfect catalogue of

[1]Pliny (Hist. Natur. 1. vi. c. 28 [s. 32]; 1. xii. c. 18). His observation that the Indian commodities were sold at Rome at a hundred times their original price may give us some notion of the produce of the customs, since that original price amounted to more than eight hundred thousand pounds.

Eastern commodities, which about the time of Alexander Severus were subject to the payment of duties: cinnamon, myrrh, pepper, ginger, and the whole tribe of aromatics, a great variety of precious stones, among which the diamond was the most remarkable for its price, and the emerald for its beauty, Parthian and Babylonian leather, cottons, silks, both raw and manufactured, ebony, ivory, and eunuchs. We may observe that the use and value of those effeminate slaves gradually rose with the decline of the empire.

The excise, introduced by Augustus after the civil wars, was extremely moderate, but it was general. It seldom exceeded one per cent.; but it comprehended whatever was sold in the markets or by public auction, from the most considerable purchases of lands and houses to those minute objects which can only derive a value from their infinite multitude and daily consumption. Such a tax, as it affects the body of the people, has ever been the occasion of clamour and discontent. An emperor well acquainted with the wants and resources of the state was obliged to declare by a public edict that the support of the army depended in a great measure on the produce of the excise.

When Augustus resolved to establish a permanent military force for the defence of his government against foreign and domestic enemies, he instituted a peculiar treasury for the pay of the soldiers, the rewards of the veterans, and the extraordinary expenses of war. The ample revenue of the excise, though peculiarly appropriated to those uses, was found inadequate. To supply the deficiency, the emperor suggested a new tax of five per cent. on all legacies and inheritances. But the nobles of Rome were more tenacious of property than of freedom. Their indignant murmurs were received by Augustus with his usual temper. He candidly referred the whole business to the senate, and exhorted them to provide for the public service by some other expedient of a less odious nature. They were divided and perplexed. He insinuated to them that their obstinacy would oblige him to *propose* a general land-tax and capitation. They acquiesced in silence. The new imposition on legacies and inheritances was however mitigated by some restrictions. It did not take place unless the object was of a certain value, most probably of fifty or an hundred pieces of gold, nor could it be exacted from the nearest of kin on the father's side. When the rights of nature and poverty were thus secured, it seemed reasonable that a stranger or a distant relation who acquired an unexpected accession of fortune should cheerfully resign a twentieth part of it for the benefit of the state.

Such a tax, plentiful as it must prove in every wealthy community, was most happily suited to the situation of the Romans, who could frame their arbitrary wills, according to the dictates of reason or caprice, without any restraint from the modern fetters of entails and settlements. From various causes the partiality of paternal affection often lost its influence over the stern patriots of the commonwealth and the dissolute nobles of the empire; and if the father bequeathed to his son the fourth part of his estate, he removed all ground of legal complaint. But a rich childless old man was a domestic tyrant, and his power increased with his years and infirmities. A servile crowd, in which he frequently reckoned prætors and consuls, courted his smiles, pampered his avarice, applauded his follies, served his passions, and waited with impatience for his death. The arts of attendance and flattery were formed into a most lucrative science; those who professed it acquired a peculiar appellation; and the whole city, according to the lively descriptions of satire, was divided between two parties, the hunters and their game. Yet, while so many unjust and extravagant wills were every day dictated by cunning, and subscribed by folly, a few were the result of rational esteem and virtuous gratitude. Cicero, who had so often defended the lives and fortunes of his fellow-citizens, was rewarded with legacies to the amount of an hundred and seventy thousand pounds; nor do the friends of the younger Pliny seem to have been less generous to that amiable orator. Whatever was the motive of the testator, the treasury claimed, without distinction, the twentieth part of his estate; and in the course of two or three generations, the whole property of the subject must have gradually passed through the coffers of the state.

In the first and golden years of the reign of Nero, that prince, from a desire of popularity, and perhaps from a blind impulse of benevolence, conceived a wish of abolishing the oppression of the customs and excise. The wisest senators applauded his magnanimity; but they diverted him from the execution of a design which would have dissolved the strength and resources of the republic. Had it indeed been possible to realise this dream of fancy, such princes as Trajan and the Antonines would surely have embraced with ardour the glorious opportunity of conferring so signal an obligation on mankind. Satisfied, however, with alleviating the public burden, they attempted not to remove it. The mildness and precision of their laws ascertained the rule and measure of taxation, and protected the subject of every rank against arbitrary interpretations, antiquated claims, and the insolent vexation of the farmers of the revenue. For it is somewhat singular that, in every age, the best and wisest of the Roman governors persevered in this pernicious method of collecting the principal branches at least of the excise and customs.

The sentiments, and, indeed, the situation of Caracalla, were very different from those of the Antonines. Inattentive, or rather averse, to the welfare of his people, he found himself under the necessity of gratifying the insatiate avarice which he had excited in the army. Of the several impositions introduced by Augustus, the twentieth on inheritances and legacies was the most fruitful, as well as the most comprehensive. As its influence was not confined to Rome or Italy, the produce continually increased with the gradual extension of the ROMAN CITY. The new citizen, though charged, on equal terms with the payment of new taxes which had not affected them as subjects, derived an ample compensation from the rank they obtained, the privileges they acquired, and the fair prospect of honours and fortune that was thrown open to their ambition. But the favour which implied a distinction was lost in the prodigality of Caracalla, and the reluctant provincials were compelled to assume the vain title, and the real obligations, of Roman citizens. Nor was the rapacious son of Severus contented with such a measure of taxation as had appeared sufficient to his moderate predecessors. Instead of a twentieth, he exacted a tenth of all legacies and inheritances; and during his reign (for the ancient proportion was restored after his death) he crushed alike every part of the empire under the weight of his iron sceptre.

When all the provincials became liable to the peculiar impositions of Roman citizens, they seemed to acquire a legal exemption from the tributes which they had paid in their former condition of subjects. Such were not the maxims of government adopted by Caracalla and his pretended son. The old as well as the new taxes were, at the same time, levied in the provinces. It was reserved for the virtue of Alexander to relieve them in a great measure from this intolerable grievance, by reducing the tributes to a thirtieth part of the sum exacted at the time of his accession. It is impossible to conjecture the motive that engaged him to spare so trifling a remnant of the public evil; but the noxious weed, which had not been totally eradicated, again sprang up with the most luxuriant growth, and in the succeeding age darkened the Roman world with its deadly shade. In the course of this history we shall be too often summoned to explain the land-tax, the capitation, and the heavy contributions of corn, wine, oil, and meat, which were exacted from the provinces for the use of the court, the army, and the capital.

As long as Rome and Italy were respected as the centre of government, a national spirit was preserved by the ancient, and insensibly imbibed by the adopted, citizens. The principal commands of the army were filled by men who had received a liberal education, were well instructed in the advantages of laws and letters, and who had risen, by equal steps, through the regular succession of civil and military honours. To their influence and example we may partly ascribe the modest obedience of the legions during the two first centuries of the Imperial history.

But when the last enclosure of the Roman constitution was trampled down by Caracalla, the separation of professions gradually succeeded to the distinction of ranks. The more polished citizens of the internal provinces were alone qualified to act as lawyers and magistrates. The rougher trade of arms was abandoned to the peasants and barbarians of the frontiers, who knew no country but their camp, no science but that of war, no civil laws, and scarcely those of military discipline. With bloody hands, savage manners, and desperate resolutions, they sometimes guarded, but much oftener subverted, the throne of the emperors.

CHAPTER VI

The State of Germany Till the Invasion of the Barbarians

Whenever Tacitus indulges himself in those beautiful episodes in which he relates some domestic transaction of the Germans or of the Parthians, his principal object is to relieve the attention of the reader from a uniform scene of vice and misery. From the reign of Augustus to the time of Alexander Severus, the enemies of Rome were in her bosom; the tyrants, and the soldiers; and her prosperity had a very distant and feeble interest in the revolutions that might happen beyond the Rhine and the Euphrates. But when the military order had levelled, in wild anarchy, the power of the prince, the laws of the senate, and even the discipline of the camp, the barbarians of the North and of the East, who had long hovered on the frontier, boldly attacked the provinces of a declining monarchy. Their vexatious inroads were changed into formidable irruptions, and, after a long vicissitude of mutual calamities, many tribes of the victorious invaders established themselves in the provinces of the Roman empire.

The government and religion of Persia have deserved some notice from their connection with the decline and fall of the Roman empire. We shall occasionally mention the Scythian or Sarmatian tribes, which, with their arms and horses, their flocks and herbs, their wives and families, wandered over the immense plains which spread themselves from the Caspian Sea to the Vistula, from the confines of Persia to those of Germany. But the warlike Germans, who first resisted, then invaded, and at length overturned, the western monarchy of Rome, will occupy a much more important place in this history, and possess a stronger, and, if we may use the expression, a more domestic, claim to our attention and regard. The most civilised nations of modern Europe issued from the woods of Germany, and in the rude institutions of those barbarians we may still distinguish the original principles of our present laws and manners. In their primitive state of simplicity and independence the Germans were surveyed by the discerning eye, and delineated by the masterly pencil, of Tacitus, the first of historians who applied the science of philosophy to the study of facts. The expressive conciseness of his descriptions has deserved to exercise the diligence of innumerable antiquarians, and to excite the genius and penetration of the philosophic historians of our own times. The subject, however various and important, has already been so frequently, so ably, and so successfully discussed, that it is now grown familiar to the reader, and difficult to the writer. We shall therefore content ourselves with observing, and indeed with repeating, some of the most important circumstances of climate, of manners, and of institutions, which rendered the wild barbarians of Germany such formidable enemies to the Roman power.

Ancient Germany, excluding from its independent limits the province westward of the Rhine, which had submitted to the Roman yoke, extended itself over a third part of Europe. Almost the whole of modern Germany, Denmark, Norway, Sweden, Finland, Livonia, Prussia, and the greater part of Poland, were peopled by the various tribes of one great nation, whose complexion, manners, and language denoted a common origin and preserved a striking resemblance. On the west, ancient Germany was divided by the Rhine from the Gallic, and on the south by the Danube from the Illyrian, provinces of the empire. A ridge of hills, rising from the Danube, and called the Carpathian mountains, covered Germany on the side of Dacia or Hungary. The eastern frontier was faintly marked by the mutual fears of the Germans and the Sarmatians, and was often confounded by the mixture of warring and confederating tribes of the two nations. In the remote darkness of the North, the ancients imperfectly descried a frozen ocean that lay beyond the Baltic Sea, and beyond the Peninsula, or islands, of Scandinavia.

Some ingenious writers have suspected that Europe was much colder formerly than it is at present; and the most ancient descriptions of the climate of Germany tend exceedingly to confirm their theory. The general complaints of intense frost, and eternal winter, are perhaps little to be regarded, since we have no method of reducing to the accurate standard of the thermometer the feelings or the expressions of an orator, born in the happier regions of Greece or Asia. But I shall select two remarkable circumstances of a less equivocal nature. 1. The great rivers which covered the Roman provinces, the Rhine and the Danube, were frequently frozen over, and capable of supporting the most enormous weights. The barbarians, who often chose that severe season for their inroads, transported, without apprehension or danger, their numerous armies, their cavalry, and their heavy wagons, over a vast and solid bridge of ice. Modern ages have not presented an instance of a like phenomenon. 2. The reindeer, that useful animal, from whom the savage of the North derives the best comforts of his dreary life, is of a constitution that supports, and even requires, the most intense cold. He is found on the rock of Spitzberg, within ten degrees of the Pole; he seems to delight in the snows of Lapland and Siberia; but at present he cannot subsist, much less multiply, in any country to the south of the Baltic. In the time of Cæsar, the reindeer, as well as the elk and the wild bull, was a native of the Hercynian forest, which then overshadowed a great part of Germany and Poland. The modern improvements sufficiently explain the causes of the diminution of the cold. These immense woods have been gradually cleared, which intercepted from the earth the rays of the sun. The morasses have been drained, and, in proportion as the soil has been cultivated, the air has become more temperate. Canada, at this day, is an exact picture of ancient Germany. Although situated in the same parallel with the finest provinces of France and England, that country experiences the most rigorous cold. The reindeer are very numerous, the ground is covered with deep and lasting snow, and the great river of St. Lawrence is regularly frozen, in a season when the waters of the Seine and the Thames are usually free from ice.

It is difficult to ascertain, and easy to exaggerate, the influence of the climate of ancient Germany over the minds and bodies of the natives. Many writers have supposed, and most have allowed, though, as it should seem, without any adequate proof, that the rigorous cold of the North was favorable to long life and generative vigour, that the women were more fruitful, and the human species more prolific, than in warmer or more temperate climates. We may assert, with greater confidence, that the keen air of Germany formed the large and masculine limbs of the natives, who were, in general, of a more lofty stature than the people of the South, gave them a kind of strength better adapted to violent exertions than to patient labour, and inspired them with constitutional bravery, which is the result of nerves and spirits. The severity of a winter campaign, that chilled the courage of the Roman troops, was scarcely felt by these hardy children of the North, who in their turn were unable to resist the summer heats, and dissolved away in languor and sickness under the beams of an Italian sun.[1]

There is not anywhere upon the globe a large tract of country which we have discovered destitute of inhabitants, or whose first population can be fixed with any degree of historical certainty. And yet, as the most philosophic minds can seldom refrain from investigating the infancy of great nations, our curiosity consumes itself in toilsome and disappointed efforts. When Tacitus considered the purity of the German blood, and the forbidding aspect of the country, he was disposed to pronounce those barbarians *Indigenæ*, or natives of the soil. We may allow with safety, and perhaps with truth, that ancient Germany was not originally peopled by any foreign colonies already formed into a political society; but that the name and nation received their existence from the gradual union of some wandering savages of the Hercynian woods. To assert those savages to have been the spontaneous production of the earth which they inhabited would be a rash inference, condemned by religion and unwarranted by reason.

Such rational doubt is but ill-suited with the genius of popular vanity. Among the nations who have adopted the Mosaic history of the world, the ark of Noah has been of the same use as was formerly to the Greeks and Romans the siege of Troy. On a narrow basis of acknowledged truth

[1]The Romans made war in all climates, and by their excellent discipline were in a great measure preserved in health and vigour. It may be remarked, that man is the only animal which can live and multiply in every country from the equator to the Poles. The hog seems to approach the nearest to our species in that privilege.

an immense but rude superstructure of fable has been erected, and the "Wild Irishman," as well as the Wild Tartar, could point out the individual son of Japhet, from whose loins his ancestors were lineally descended. The last century abounded with antiquarians of profound learning and easy faith, who by the dim light of legends and traditions, of conjectures and etymologies, conducted the great-grandchildren of Noah from the tower of Babel to the extremities of the globe. Of these judicious critics, one of the most entertaining was Olaus Rudbeck, professor in the University of Upsal. Whatever is celebrated, either in history or fable, this zealous patriot ascribes to his country. From Sweden (which formed so considerable a part of ancient Germany) the Greeks themselves derived their alphabetical characters, their astronomy, and their religion. Of that delightful region (for such it appeared to the eyes of a native) the Atlantis of Plato, the country of the Hyperboreans, the gardens of the Hesperides, the Fortunate Islands, and even the Elysian Fields, were all but faint and imperfect transcripts. A clime so profusely favoured by Nature could not long remain desert after the flood. The learned Rudbeck allows the family of Noah a few years to multiply from eight to about twenty thousand persons. He then disperses them into small colonies to replenish the earth and to propagate the human species. The German or Swedish detachment (which marched, if I am not mistaken, under the command of Askenaz, the son of Gomer, the son of Japhet) distinguished itself by a more than common diligence in the prosecution of this great work. The northern hive cast its swarms over the greatest part of Europe, Africa, and Asia; and (to use the author's metaphor) the blood circulated from the extremities to the heart.

But all this well-laboured system of German antiquities is annihilated by a single fact, too well attested to admit of any doubt, and of too decisive a nature to leave room for any reply. The Germans, in the age of Tacitus, were unacquainted with the use of letters; and the use of letters is the principal circumstance that distinguishes a civilised people from a herd of savages incapable of knowledge or reflection. Without that artificial help, the human memory soon dissipates or corrupts the ideas entrusted to her charge; and the nobler faculties of the mind, no longer supplied with models or with materials, gradually forget their powers; the judgment becomes feeble and lethargic, the imagination languid or irregular. Fully to apprehend this important truth, let us attempt, in an improved society, to calculate the immense distance between the man of learning and the *illiterate* peasant. The former, by reading and reflection, multiplies his own experience, and lives in distant ages and remote countries; whilst the latter, rooted to a single spot, and confined to a few years of existence, surpasses, but very little, his fellow-labourer the ox in the exercise of his mental faculties. The same, and even a greater, difference will be found between nations than between individuals; and we may safely pronounce that, without some species of writing, no people has ever preserved the faithful annals of their history, ever made any considerable progress in the abstract sciences, or ever possessed, in any tolerable degree of perfection, the useful and agreeable arts of life.

Of these arts, the ancient Germans were wretchedly destitute. They passed their lives in a state of ignorance and poverty, which it has pleased some declaimers to dignify with the appellation of virtuous simplicity. Modern Germany is said to contain about two thousand three hundred walled towns. In a much wider extent of country, the geographer Ptolemy could discover no more than ninety places, which he decorates with the name of cities; though, according to our ideas, they would but ill deserve that splendid title. We can only suppose them to have been rude fortifications, constructed in the centre of the woods, and designed to secure the women, children, and cattle, whilst the warriors of the tribe marched out to repel a sudden invasion. But Tacitus asserts, as a well-known fact, that the Germans, in his time, had *no* cities; and that they affected to despise the works of Roman industry as places of confinement rather than of security. Their edifices were not even contiguous, or formed into regular villas; each barbarian fixed his independent dwelling on the spot to which a plain, a wood, or a stream of fresh water had induced him to give the preference. Neither stone, nor brick, nor tiles, were employed in these slight habitations. They were indeed no more than low huts of a circular figure, built of rough timber, thatched with straw, and pierced at the top to leave a free passage for the smoke. In the most inclement winter, the hardy German was satisfied with a scanty garment made of the skin of some animal. The nations who dwelt towards the North clothed themselves in furs; and the women manufactured for their own use a coarse kind of linen. The game of various sorts, with which the forests of Germany were plentifully stocked, supplied its inhabitants with food and exercise. Their monstrous herds of cattle, less remarkable indeed for their beauty than for their utility, formed the principal object of their wealth. A small quantity of corn was the only produce exacted from the earth: the use of orchards or artificial meadows was unknown to the Germans; nor can we expect any improvements in agriculture from a people whose property every year experienced a general change by a new division of the arable lands, and who, in that strange operation, avoided disputes by suffering a great part of their territory to lie waste and without tillage.

Gold, silver, and iron were extremely scarce in Germany. Its barbarous inhabitants wanted both skill and patience to investigate those rich veins of silver, which have so liberally rewarded the attention of the princes of Brunswick and Saxony. Sweden, which now supplies Europe with iron, was equally ignorant of its own riches; and the appearance of the arms of the Germans furnished a sufficient proof how little iron they were able to bestow on what they must have deemed the noblest use of that metal. The various transactions of peace and war had introduced some Roman coins (chiefly silver) among the borderers of the Rhine and Danube; but the more distant tribes were absolutely unacquainted with the use of money, carried on their confined traffic by the exchange of commodities, and prized their rude earthen vessels as of equal value with the silver vases, the presents of Rome to their princes and ambassadors. To a mind capable of reflection, such leading facts convey more instruction than a tedious detail of subordinate circumstances. The value of money has been settled by general consent to express our wants and our property, as letters were invented to express our ideas; and both these institutions, by giving a more active energy to the powers and passions of human nature, have contributed to multiply the objects they were designed to represent. The use of gold and silver is in a great measure fictitious; but it would be impossible to enumerate the important and various services which agriculture, and all the arts, have received from iron, when tempered and fashioned by the operation of fire and the dexterous hand of man. Money, in a word, is the most universal incitement, iron the most powerful instrument, of human industry; and it is very difficult to conceive by what means a people, neither actuated by the one nor seconded by the other, could emerge from the grossest barbarism.

If we contemplate a savage nation in any part of the globe, a supine indolence and a carelessness of futurity will be found to constitute their general character. In a civilised state, every faculty of man is expanded and exercised; and the great chain of mutual dependence connects and embraces the several members of society. The most numerous portion of it is employed in constant and useful labour. The select few, placed by fortune above that necessity, can, however, fill up their time by the pursuits of interest or glory, by the improvement of their estate or of their understanding, by the duties, the pleasures, and even the follies of social life. The Germans were not possessed of their varied resources. The care of the house and family, the management of the land and cattle, were delegated to the old and the infirm, to women and slaves. The lazy warrior, destitute of every art that might employ his leisure hours, consumed his days and nights in the animal gratifications of sleep and food. And yet, by a wonderful diversity of nature (according to the remark of a writer who had pierced into its darkest recesses), the same barbarians are by turns the most indolent and the most restless of mankind. They delight in sloth, they detest tranquillity. The languid soul, oppressed with its own weight, anxiously required some new and powerful sensation; and war and danger were the only amusements adequate to its fierce temper. The sound that summoned the German to arms was grateful to his ear. It roused him from his uncomfortable lethargy, gave him an active pursuit, and, by strong exercise of the body, and violent emotions of the mind, restored him to a more lively sense of his existence. In the dull intervals of peace, these barbarians were immoderately addicted to deep gaming and excessive drinking; both of which, by different means, the one by inflaming their passions, the other by extinguishing their reason, alike relieved them from the pain of thinking. They gloried in passing whole days and nights at table; and the blood of friends and relations often stained their numerous and drunken assemblies.

Strong beer, a liquor extracted with very little art from wheat or barley, and *corrupted* (as it is strongly expressed by Tacitus) into a certain semblance of wine, was sufficient for the gross purposes of German debauchery. But those who had tasted the rich wines of Italy, and afterwards of Gaul, sighed for that more delicious species of intoxication. They attempted not, however (as has since been executed with so much success), to naturalise the vine on the banks of the Rhine and Danube; nor did they endeavour to procure by industry the materials of an advantageous commerce. To solicit by labour what might be ravished by arms was esteemed unworthy of the German spirit. The intemperate thirst of strong liquors often urged the barbarians to invade the provinces on which art or nature had bestowed those much envied presents. The Tuscan who betrayed his country to the Celtic nations attracted them into Italy by the prospect of the rich fruits and delicious wines, the productions of a happier climate. And in the same manner the German auxiliaries, invited into France during the civil wars of the sixteenth century, were allured by the promise of plenteous quarters in the provinces of Champagne and Burgundy. Drunkenness, the most illiberal, but not the most dangerous, of *our* vices, was sometimes capable, in a less civilised state of mankind, of occasioning a battle, a war, or a revolution.

The climate of ancient Germany has been mollified, and the soil fertilised, by the labour of ten centuries from the time of Charlemagne. The same extent of ground which at present maintains, in ease and plenty, a million of husbandmen and artificers, was unable to supply an hundred thousand lazy warriors with the simple necessaries of life. The Germans abandoned their immense forests to the exercise of hunting, employed in pasturage the most considerable part of their lands, bestowed on the small remainder a rude and careless cultivation, and then accused the scantiness and sterility of a country that refused to maintain the multitude of its inhabitants. When the return of famine severely admonished them of the importance of the arts, the national distress was sometimes alleviated by the emigration of a third, perhaps, or a fourth part of their youth. The possession and the enjoyment of property are the pledges which bind a civilised people to an improved country. But the Germans, who carried with them what they most valued, their arms, their cattle, and their women, cheerfully abandoned the vast silence of their woods for the unbounded hopes of plunder and conquest. The innumerable swarms that issued, or seemed to issue, from the great storehouse of nations, were multiplied by the fears of the vanquished and by the credulity of succeeding ages. And from facts thus exaggerated, an opinion was gradually established, and has been supported by writers of distinguished reputation, that, in the age of Cæsar and Tacitus, the inhabitants of the North were far more numerous than they are in our days. A more serious inquiry into the causes of population seems to have convinced modern philosophers of the falsehood, and indeed the impossibility, of the supposition.

A warlike nation like the Germans, without either cities, letters, arts, or money, found some compensation for this savage state in the enjoyment of liberty. Their poverty secured their freedom, since our desires and our possessions are the strongest fetters of despotism. "Among the Suiones (says Tacitus), riches are held in honour. They are *therefore* subject to an absolute monarch, who, instead of entrusting his people with the free use of arms, as is practised in the rest of Germany, commits them to the safe custody not of a citizen, or even of a freedman, but of a slave. The neighbours of the Suiones, the Sitones, are sunk even below servitude; they obey a woman." In the mention of these exceptions, the great historian sufficiently acknowledges the general theory of government. We are only at a loss to conceive by what means riches and despotism could penetrate into a remote corner of the North, and extinguish the generous flame that blazed with such fierceness on the frontier of the Roman provinces: or how the ancestors of those Danes and Norwegians, so distinguished in latter ages by their unconquered spirit, could thus tamely resign the great character of German liberty. Some tribes, however, on the coast of the Baltic, acknowledged the authority of kings, though without relinquishing the rights of men; but in the far greater part of Germany, the form of government was a democracy tempered indeed, and controlled, not so much by general and positive laws, as by the occasional ascendant of birth or valour, of eloquence or superstition.

Civil governments, in their first institutions, are voluntary associations for mutual defence. To obtain the desired end, it is absolutely necessary that each individual should conceive himself obliged to submit his private opinion and actions to the judgment of the greater number of his associates. The German tribes were contented with this rude but liberal outline of political society. As soon as a youth, born of free parents, had attained the age of manhood, he was introduced into the general council of his countrymen, solemnly invested with a shield and spear, and adopted as an equal and worthy member of the military commonwealth. The assembly of the warriors of the tribe was convened at stated seasons or on sudden emergencies. The trial of public offences, the election of magistrates, and the great business of peace and war, were determined by its independent voice. Sometimes, indeed, these important questions were previously considered and prepared in a more select council of the principal chieftains. The magistrates might deliberate and persuade, the people only could resolve and execute; and the resolutions of the Germans were for the most part hasty and violent. Barbarians accustomed to place their freedom in gratifying the present passion, and their courage in overlooking all future consequences, turned away with indignant contempt from the remonstrance of justice and policy, and it was the practice to signify by a hollow murmur their dislike of such timid counsels. But whenever a more popular orator proposed to vindicate the meanest citizen from either foreign or domestic injury, whenever he called upon his fellow-countrymen to assert the national honour, or to pursue some enterprise full of danger and glory, a loud clashing of shields and spears expressed the eager applause of the assembly. For the Germans always met in arms, and it was constantly to be dreaded lest an irregular multitude, inflamed with faction and strong liquors, should use those arms to enforce, as well as to declare, their furious resolves. We may recollect how often the diets of Poland have been polluted with blood, and the more numerous party has been compelled to yield to the more violent and seditious.[2]

A general of the tribe was elected on occasions of danger; and, if the danger was pressing and extensive, several tribes concurred in the choice of the same general. The bravest warrior was named to lead his countrymen into the field, by his example rather than by his commands. But this power, however limited, was still invidious. It expired with the war, and in time of peace the German tribes acknowledged not any supreme chief. *Princes* were, however, appointed in the general assembly, to administer justice, or rather to compose differences, in their respective districts. In the choice of these magistrates as much regard was shown to birth as to merit. To each was assigned, by the public, a guard and a council of an hundred persons; and the first of the princes appears to have enjoyed a pre-eminence of rank and honour which sometimes tempted the Romans to compliment him with the regal title.

The comparative view of the powers of the magistrates, in two remarkable instances, is alone sufficient to represent the whole system of German manners. The disposal of the landed property within their district was absolutely vested in their hands, and they distributed it every year according to a new division. At the same time they were not authorised to punish with death, to imprison, or even to strike, a private citizen. A people thus jealous of their persons, and careless of their possessions, must have been totally destitute of industry and the arts, but animated with a high sense of honour and independence.

The Germans respected only those duties which they imposed on themselves. The most obscure soldier resisted with disdain the authority of the magistrates. "The noblest youths blushed not to be numbered among the faithful companions of some renowned chief, to whom they devoted their arms and service. A noble emulation prevailed among the companions to obtain the first place in the esteem of their chief; amongst the chiefs, to acquire the greatest number of valiant companions. To be ever surrounded by a band of select youths was the pride and strength of the chiefs, their ornament in peace, their defence in war. The glory of such distinguished heroes diffused itself beyond the narrow limits of their own tribe. Presents and embassies solicited their friendship, and the fame of their arms often ensured victory to the party which they espoused. In the hour of danger it was shameful for the chief to be surpassed in valour by his companions; shameful for the companions not to equal the valour of their chief. To survive his fall in battle was indelible infamy. To protect his person and to adorn his glory with the trophies of their own exploits

[2]Even in *our* ancient parliament, the barons often carried a question, not so much by the number of votes, as by that of their armed followers.

were the most sacred of their duties. The chiefs combated for victory, the companions for the chief. The noblest warriors, whenever their native country was sunk in the laziness of peace, maintained their numerous bands in some distant scene of action, to exercise their restless spirit and to acquire renown by voluntary dangers. Gifts worthy of soldiers, the warlike steed, the bloody and ever victorious lance, were the rewards which the companions claimed from the liberality of their chief. The rude plenty of his hospitable board was the only pay that *he* could bestow or *they* would accept. War, rapine, and the free-will offerings of his friends, supplied the materials of this munificence." This institution, however it might accidentally weaken the several republics, invigorated the general character of the Germans, and even ripened amongst them all the virtues of which barbarians are susceptible; the faith and valour, the hospitality and the courtesy, so conspicuous long afterwards in the ages of chivalry. The honourable gifts, bestowed by the chief on his brave companions, have been supposed, by an ingenious writer, to contain the first rudiments of the fiefs distributed, after the conquest of the Roman provinces, by the barbarian lords among their vassals, with a similar duty of homage and military service.

"In the days of chivalry, or more properly of romance, all the men were brave, and all the women were chaste;" and notwithstanding the latter of these virtues is acquired and preserved with much more difficulty than the former, it is ascribed, almost without exception, to the wives of the ancient Germans. Polygamy was not in use, except among the princes, and among them only for the sake of multiplying their alliances. Divorces were prohibited by manners rather than by laws. Adulteries were punished as rare and inexpiable crimes; nor was seduction justified by example and fashion.[3] We may easily discover that Tacitus indulges an honest pleasure in the contrast of barbarian virtue with the dissolute conduct of the Roman ladies; yet there are some striking circumstances that give an air of truth, or at least of probability, to the conjugal faith and chastity of the Germans.

Although the progress of civilisation has undoubtedly contributed to assuage the fiercer passions of human nature, it seems to have been less favourable to the virtue of chastity, whose most dangerous enemy is the softness of the mind. The refinements of life corrupt while they polish the intercourse of the sexes. The gross appetite of love becomes most dangerous when it is elevated, or rather, indeed, disguised by sentimental passion. The elegance of dress, of motion, and of manners gives a lustre to beauty, and inflames the senses through the imagination. Luxurious entertainments, midnight dances, and licentious spectacles, present at once temptation and opportunity to female frailty. From such dangers the unpolished wives of the barbarians were secured by poverty, solitude, and the painful cares of a domestic life. The German huts, open on every side to the eye of indiscretion or jealousy, were a better safeguard of conjugal fidelity

[3]The adulteress was whipped through the village. Neither wealth nor beauty could inspire compassion, or procure her a second husband. Germ. c. 18, 19.

than the walls, the bolts, and the eunuchs of a Persian harem. To this reason, another may be added of a more honourable nature. The Germans treated their women with esteem and confidence, consulted them on every occasion of importance, and fondly believed that in their breasts resided a sanctity and wisdom more than human. Some of these interpreters of fate, such as Velleda, in the Batavian war, governed, in the name of the deity, the fiercest nations of Germany. The rest of the sex, without being adored as goddesses, were respected as the free and equal companions of soldiers; associated even by the marriage ceremony to a life of toil, of danger, and of glory. In their great invasions, the camps of the barbarians were filled with a multitude of women who remained firm and undaunted amidst the sound of arms, the various forms of destruction, and the honourable wounds of their sons and husbands. Fainting armies of Germans have more than once been driven back upon the enemy by the generous despair of the women who dreaded death much less than servitude. If the day was irrecoverably lost, they well knew how to deliver themselves and their children, with their own hands, from an insulting victor.

The religious system of the Germans (if the wild opinions of savages can deserve that name) was dictated by their wants, their fears, and their ignorance. They adored the great visible objects and agents of nature, the Sun and the Moon, the Fire and the Earth, together with those imaginary deities, who were supposed to preside over the most important occupations of human life. They were persuaded that, by some ridiculous arts of divination, they could discover the will of the superior beings, and that human sacrifices were the most precious and acceptable offering to their altars. Some applause has been hastily bestowed on the sublime notion entertained by that people of the Deity[4] whom they neither confined within the walls of a temple, nor represented by any human figure; but when we recollect that the Germans were unskilled in architecture, and totally unacquainted with the art of sculpture, we shall readily assign the true reason of a scruple which arose not so much from a superiority of reason as from a want of ingenuity. The only temples in Germany were dark and ancient groves, consecrated by the reverence of succeeding generations. Their secret gloom, the imagined residence of an invisible power, by presenting no distinct object of fear or worship, impressed the mind with a still deeper sense of religious horror; and the priests, rude and illiterate as they were, had been taught by experience the use of every artifice that could preserve and fortify impressions so well suited to their own interest.

The same ignorance which renders barbarians incapable of conceiving or embracing the useful restraints of laws exposes them naked and unarmed to the blind terrors of superstition. The German priests, improving

[4]Tacitus has employed a few lines, and Cluverius one hundred and twenty-four pages, on this obscure subject. The former discovers in Germany the gods of Greece and Rome. The latter is positive, that under the emblems of the sun, the moon, and the fire, his pious ancestors worshipped the Trinity in unity.

this favourable temper of their countrymen, had assumed a jurisdiction, even in temporal concerns, which the magistrate could not venture to exercise; and the haughty warrior patiently submitted to the lash of correction, when it was inflicted, not by any human power, but by the immediate order of the god of war. The defects of civil policy were sometimes supplied by the interposition of ecclesiastical authority. The latter was constantly exerted to maintain silence and decency in the popular assemblies, and was sometimes extended to a more enlarged concern for the national welfare. A solemn procession was occasionally celebrated in the present countries of Mecklenburg and Pomerania. The unknown symbol of the *Earth,* covered with a thick veil, was placed on a carriage drawn by cows; and in this manner the goddess, whose common residence was in the isle of Rugen, visited several adjacent tribes of her worshippers. During her progress the sound of war was hushed, quarrels were suspended, arms laid aside, and the restless Germans had an opportunity of tasting the blessings of peace and harmony. The *truce of God*, so often and so ineffectually proclaimed by the clergy of the eleventh century, was an obvious imitation of this ancient custom.

But the influence of religion was far more powerful to inflame than to moderate the fierce passions of the Germans. Interest and fanaticism often prompted its ministers to sanctify the most daring and the most unjust enterprises, by the approbation of Heaven, and full assurances of success. The consecrated standards, long revered in the groves of superstition, were placed in the front of the battle; and the hostile army was devoted with dire execrations to the gods of war and of thunder. In the faith of soldiers (and such were the Germans) cowardice is the most unpardonable of sins. A brave man was the worthy favourite of their martial deities; the wretch who had lost his shield was alike banished from the religious and the civil assemblies of his countrymen. Some tribes of the North seem to have embraced the doctrine of transmigration, others imagined a gross paradise of immortal drunkenness. All agreed that a life spent in arms, and a glorious death in battle, were the best preparations for a happy futurity either in this or in another world.

The immortality so vainly promised by the priests was in some degree conferred by the bards. That singular order of men has most deservedly attracted the notice of all who have attempted to investigate the antiquities of the Celts, the Scandinavians, and the Germans. Their genius and character, as well as the reverence paid to that important office, have been sufficiently illustrated. But we cannot so easily express, or even conceive, the enthusiasm of arms and glory, which they kindled in the breast of their audience. The view of arms and of danger heightened the effect of the military song; and the passions which it tended to excite, the desire of fame and the contempt of death, were the habitual sentiments of a German mind.

Such was the situation, and such were the manners, of the ancient Germans. Their climate, their want of learning, of arts, and of laws, their notions of honour, of gallantry, and of religion, their sense of freedom, impatience of peace, and thirst of enterprise, all contributed to form a people of military heroes. And yet we find that, during more than two hundred and fifty years that elapsed from the defeat of Varus to the reign of Decius, these formidable barbarians made few considerable attempts, and not any material impression on the luxurious and enslaved provinces of the empire. Their progress was checked by their want of arms and discipline, and their fury was diverted by the intestine divisions of ancient Germany.

It has been observed, with ingenuity, and not without truth, that the command of iron soon gives a nation the command of gold. But the rude tribes of Germany, alike destitute of both those valuable metals, were reduced slowly to acquire, by their unassisted strength, the possession of the one as well as the other. The face of a German army displayed their poverty of iron. Swords, and the longer kind of lances, they could seldom use. Their *frameæ* (as they called them in their own language) were long spears headed with a sharp but narrow iron point, and which, as occasion required, they either darted from a distance or pushed in close onset. With this spear, and with a shield, their cavalry was contented. A multitude of darts, scattered with incredible force, were an additional resource of the infantry. Their military dress, when they wore any, was nothing more than a loose mantle. A variety of colours was the only ornament of their wooden or osier shields. Few of the chiefs were distinguished by cuirasses, scarce any by helmets. Though the horses of Germany were neither beautiful, swift, nor practised in the skilful evolutions of the Roman manege, several of the nations obtained renown by their cavalry; but in general the principal strength of the Germans consisted in their infantry, which was drawn up in several deep columns, according to the distinction of tribes and families. Impatient of fatigue or delay, these half-armed warriors rushed to battle with dissonant shouts and disordered ranks; and sometimes, by the effort of native valour, prevailed over the constrained and more artificial bravery of the Roman mercenaries. But as the barbarians poured forth their whole souls on the first onset, they knew not how to rally or to retire. A repulse was a sure defeat; and a defeat was most commonly total destruction.

When we recollect the complete armour of the Roman soldiers, their discipline, exercises, evolutions, fortified camps, and military engines, it appears a just matter of surprise how the naked and unassisted valour of the barbarians could dare to encounter in the field the strength of the legions, and the various troops of the auxiliaries which seconded their operations. The contest was too unequal, till the introduction of luxury had enervated the vigour, and a spirit of disobedience and sedition had relaxed the discipline, of the Roman armies. The introduction of barbarian auxiliaries into those armies was a measure attended with very obvious dangers, as it might gradually instruct the Germans in the arts of war and of policy.

The strength of ancient Germany appears formidable when we consider the effects that might have been produced by its united effort. The wide extent of country might very possibly contain a million of warriors, as all who were of age to bear arms were of a temper to use them. But this fierce multitude, incapable of concerting or executing any plan of national greatness, was agitated by various and often hostile intentions. Germany was divided into more than forty independent states; and even in each state the union of the several tribes was extremely loose and precarious. The barbarians were easily provoked; they knew not how to forgive an injury, much less an insult; their resentments were bloody and implacable. The casual disputes that so frequently happened in their tumultuous parties of hunting or drinking were sufficient to inflame the minds of whole nations; the private feud of any considerable chieftains diffused itself among their followers and allies.

"The Bructeri (it is Tacitus who now speaks) were totally exterminated by the neighbouring tribes, provoked by their insolence, allured by the hopes of spoil, and perhaps inspired by the tutelar deities of the empire. Above sixty thousand barbarians were destroyed; not by the Roman arms, but in our sight, and for our entertainment. May the nations, enemies of Rome, ever preserve this enmity to each other! We have now attained the utmost verge of prosperity, and have nothing left to demand of Fortune, except the discord of these barbarians." These sentiments, less worthy of the humanity than of the patriotism of Tacitus, express the invariable maxims of the policy of his countrymen. They deemed it a much safer expedient to divide than to combat the barbarians, from whose defeat they could derive neither honour nor advantage. The money and negotiations of Rome insinuated themselves into the heart of Germany; and every art of seduction was used with dignity to conciliate those nations whom their proximity to the Rhine or Danube might render the most useful friends as well as the most troublesome enemies. Chiefs of renown and power were flattered by the most trifling presents, which they received either as marks of distinction, or as the instruments of luxury. In civil dissensions, the weaker faction endeavoured to strengthen its interest by entering into secret connections with the governors of the frontier provinces. Every quarrel among the Germans was fomented by the intrigues of Rome; and every plan of union and public good was defeated by the stronger bias of private jealousy and interest.[5]

[5]cf. Theodoric to his Gothic followers:

"Are you ignorant," exclaimed the son of Triarius, "that it is the constant policy of the Romans to destroy the Goths by each other's swords?"

CHAPTER VII

The General Irruption of the Barbarians

From the great secular games celebrated by Philip to the death of the emperor Gallienus there elapsed (A.D. 248–268) twenty years of shame and misfortune. During that calamitous period every instant of time was marked, every province of the Roman world was afflicted by barbarous invaders and military tyrants, and the ruined empire seemed to approach the last and fatal moment of its dissolution.

The emperor Decius had employed a few months in the works of peace and the administration of justice, when (A.D. 250) he was summoned to the banks of the Danube by the invasion of the Goths. This is the first considerable occasion in which history mentions that great people, who afterwards broke the Roman power, sacked the Capitol, and reigned in Gaul, Spain, and Italy. So memorable was the part which they acted in the subversion of the Western empire that the name of Goths is frequently but improperly used as a general appellation of rude and warlike barbarism.

In the beginning of the sixth century, and after the conquest of Italy, the Goths, in possession of present greatness, very naturally indulged themselves in the prospect of past and of future glory. They wished to preserve the memory of their ancestors, and to transmit to posterity their own achievements. On the faith of ancient songs, the uncertain, but the only, memorials of barbarians, they deduced the first origin of the Goths from the vast island, or peninsula, of Scandinavia. Many vestiges attest the ancient residence of the Goths in the countries beyond the Baltic. From the time of the geographer Ptolemy, the southern part of Sweden seems to have continued in the possession of the less enterprising remnant of the nation, and a large territory is even at present divided into east and west Gothland. During the middle ages (from the ninth to the twelfth century), whilst Christianity was advancing with a slow progress into the North, the Goths and the Swedes composed two distinct and sometimes hostile members of the same monarchy. The latter of these two names has prevailed without extinguishing the former. The Swedes, who might well be satisfied with their own fame in arms, have in every age claimed the kindred glory of the Goths. In a moment of discontent against the court of Rome, Charles the Twelfth insinuated that his victorious troops were not degenerated from their brave ancestors who had already subdued the mistress of the world.

Till the end of the eleventh century, a celebrated temple subsisted at

Upsal, the most considerable town of the Swedes and Goths. It was enriched with the gold which the Scandinavians had acquired in their piratical adventures, and sanctified by the uncouth representations of the three principal deities, the god of war, the goddess of generation, and the god of thunder. In the general festival that was solemnised every ninth year, nine animals of every species (without excepting the human) were sacrificed, and their bleeding bodies suspended in the sacred grove adjacent to the temple. The only traces that now subsist of this barbaric superstition are contained in the Edda, a system of mythology compiled in Iceland about the thirteenth century, and studied by the learned of Denmark and Sweden as the most valuable remains of their ancient traditions.

Nothwithstanding the mysterious obscurity of the Edda, we can easily distinguish two persons confounded under the name of Odin, the god of war, and the great legislator of Scandinavia. The latter, the Mahomet of the North, instituted a religion adapted to the climate and to the people. Numerous tribes on either side of the Baltic were subdued by the invincible valour of Odin, by his persuasive eloquence, and by the fame which he acquired of a most skilful magician. The faith that he had propagated during a long and prosperous life he confirmed by a voluntary death. Apprehensive of the ignominious approach of disease and infirmity, he resolved to expire as became a warrior. In a solemn assembly of the Swedes and Goths, he wounded himself in nine mortal places, hastening away (as he asserted with his dying voice) to prepare the feast of heroes in the palace of the god of war.

It is supposed that Odin was the chief of a tribe of barbarians which dwelt on the banks of the lake Mætois, till the fall of Mithridates and the arms of Pompey menaced the North with servitude; that Odin, yielding with indignant fury to a power which he was unable to resist, conducted his tribe from the frontiers of the Asiatic Sarmatia into Sweden, with the great design of forming, in that inaccessible retreat of freedom, a religion and a people which, armed with martial fanaticism, should issue in numerous swarms from the neighbourhood of the Polar circle to chastise the oppressors of mankind.

If so many successive generations of Goths were capable of preserving a faint tradition of their Scandinavian origin, we must not expect, from such unlettered barbarians, any distinct account of the time and circumstances of their emigration. To cross the Baltic was an easy and natural attempt. The inhabitants of Sweden were masters of a sufficient number of large vessels, with oars, and the distance is little more than one hundred miles from Carlscrona to the nearest ports of Pomerania and Prussia. Here, at length, we land on firm and historic ground. At least as early as the Christian era, and as late as the age of the Antonines, the Goths were established towards the mouth of the Vistula in that fertile province where the commercial cities of Thorn, Elbing, Koningsberg, and Dantzic were long afterwards founded. Westward of the Goths, the numerous tribes of the Vandals were spread along the banks of the Oder, and the sea-coast of Pomerania and Mecklenburg. A striking resemblance of manners, complexion, religion, and language seemed to indicate that the Vandals and the Goths were originally one great people. The latter appear to have been subdivided into Ostrogoths, Visigoths, and Gepidæ. The distinction among the Vandals was more strongly marked by the independent names of Heruli, Burgundians, Lombards, and a variety of other petty states, many of which, in a future age, expanded themselves into powerful monarchies.

In the age of the Antonines, the Goths were still seated in Prussia. About the reign of Alexander Severus, the Roman province of Dacia had already experienced their proximity by frequent and destructive inroads. In this interval, therefore, of about seventy years, we must place the second migration of the Goths from the Baltic to the Euxine; but the cause that produced it lies concealed among the various motives which actuate the conduct of unsettled barbarians. Either a pestilence or a famine, a victory or a defeat, an oracle of the gods or the eloquence of a daring leader, were sufficient to impel the Gothic arms on the milder climates of the South.

The fame of a great enterprise excited the bravest warriors from all the Vandalic states of Germany, many of whom are seen a few years afterwards combating under the common standard of the Goths. The first motions of the emigrants carried them to the banks of the Prypec, a river universally conceived by the ancients to be the southern branch of the Borysthenes. The windings of that great stream through the plains of Poland and Russia gave a direction to their line of march, and a constant supply of fresh water and pasturage to their numerous herds of cattle. They followed the unknown course of the river, confident in their valour, and careless of whatever power might oppose their progress.

The Goths were now in possession of the Ukraine, a country of considerable extent and uncommon fertility, intersected with navigable rivers which, from either side, discharge themselves into the Borysthenes; and interspersed with large and lofty forests of oaks. The plenty of game and fish, the innumerable bee-hives, deposited in the hollows of old trees and in the cavities of rocks, and forming even in that rude age a valuable branch of commerce, the size of the cattle, the temperature of the air, the aptness of the soil for every species of grain, and the luxuriancy of the vegetation all displayed the liberality of Nature, and tempted the industry of man. But the Goths withstood all these temptations, and still adhered to a life of idleness, of poverty, and of rapine.

The Scythian hordes which, towards the East bordered on the new settlements of the Goths presented nothing to their arms except the doubtful chance of an unprofitable victory. But the prospect of the Roman territories was far more alluring; and the fields of Dacia were covered with rich harvests, sown by the hands of an industrious, and exposed to be gathered by those of a warlike, people. It is probable that the conquests of Trajan maintained by his successors, less for any real advantage than for ideal dignity, had contributed to weaken the empire on that side. The new and unsettled province of Dacia was neither strong enough to resist, nor rich enough to satiate, the rapaciousness of the barbarians. As long as the remote banks of the Dniester were considered as the boundary of the Roman power, the fortifications of the Lower Danube were more carelessly guarded, and the inhabitants of Mæsia lived in supine security, fondly conceiving themselves at an inaccessible distance from any barbarian invaders. The irruptions of the Goths, under the reign of Philip, fatally convinced them of their mistake. The king, or leader, of that fierce nation traversed with contempt the province of Dacia, and passed both the Dniester and the Danube without encountering any opposition capable of retarding his progress. The relaxed discipline of the Roman troops betrayed the most important posts where they were stationed, and the fear of deserved punishment induced great numbers of them to enlist under the Gothic standard. The various multitude of barbarians appeared, at length, under the walls of Marcianopolis, a city built by Trajan in honour of his sister, and at that time the capital of the second Mæsia. The inhabitants consented to ransom their lives and property by the payment of a large sum of money, and the invaders retreated back into their deserts, animated, rather than satisfied, with the first success of their arms against an opulent but feeble country. Intelligence was soon transmitted to the emperor Decius that Cniva, king of the Goths, had passed the Danube a second time, with more considerable forces; that his numerous detachments scattered devastation over the province of Mæsia, whilst the main body of the army, consisting of seventy thousand Germans and Sarmatians, a force equal to the most daring achievements, required the presence of the Roman monarch and the exertion of his military power.

Decius found (A.D. 250) the Goths engaged before Nicopolis, on the Jatrus, one of the many monuments of Trajan's victories. On his approach they raised the siege, but with a design only of marching away to a conquest of greater importance, the siege of Philippopolis, a city of Thrace founded by the father of Alexander. The camp of the Romans was surprised and pillaged, and, for the first time, their emperor fled in disorder before a troop of half-armed barbarians. After a long resistance, Philippopolis, destitute of succour, was taken by storm. A hundred thousand persons are reported to have been massacred in the sack of that great city. Many prisoners of consequence became a valuable accession to the spoil; and Priscus, a brother of the late emperor Philip, blushed not to assume the purple under the protection of the barbarous enemies of Rome. The time, however, consumed in that tedious siege enabled Decius to revive the courage, restore the discipline, and recruit the numbers of his troops. He repaired and strengthened the fortifications of the Danube, and anxiously waited for an opportunity to retrieve, by a great and decisive blow, his own glory and that of the Roman arms.

The flower of their troops had perished in the long siege of Philippopolis, and the Goths would gladly have purchased, by the surrender of all their booty and prisoners, the permission of an undisturbed retreat. But the emperor, confident of victory, and resolving by the chastisement of these invaders to strike a salutary terror into the nations of the North, refused to listen to any terms of accommodation.

The Gothic army was drawn up in three lines, and, either from choice or accident, the front of the third line was covered by a morass. In the morass the Roman army, after an ineffectual struggle, was irrecoverably lost; nor could the body of the emperor ever be found.

From a just regard for the memory of Decius, the Imperial title was (A.D. 251, Dec.) conferred on Hostilianus, his only surviving son; but an equal rank, with more effectual power, was granted to Gallus, whose experience and ability seemed equal to the great trust of guardian to the young prince and the distressed empire. The first care of the new emperor was to deliver the Illyrian provinces from the intolerable weight of the victorious Goths. He (A.D. 252) consented to leave in their hands the rich fruits of their invasion, an immense booty, and, what was still more disgraceful, a great number of prisoners of the highest merit and quality. He plentifully supplied their camp with every conveniency that could assuage their angry spirits, or facilitate their so much wished-for departure; and he even promised to pay them annually a large sum of gold, on condition they should never afterwards infest the Roman territories by their incursions.

In the age of the Scipios, the most opulent kings of the earth, who courted the protection of the victorious commonwealth, were gratified with such trifling presents as could only derive a value from the hand that bestowed them; an ivory chair, a coarse garment of purple, an inconsiderable piece of plate, or a quantity of copper coin. After the wealth of nations had centred in Rome, the emperors displayed their greatness, and even their policy, by the regular exercise of a steady and moderate liberality towards the allies of the state. They relieved the poverty of the barbarians, honoured their merit, and recompensed their fidelity. These voluntary marks of bounty were understood to flow not from the fears, but merely from the generosity or the gratitude of the Romans; and whilst presents and subsidies were liberally distributed among friends and suppliants, they were sternly refused to such as claimed them as a debt. But this stipulation of an annual payment to a victorious enemy appeared without disguise in the light of an ignominious tribute; the minds of the Romans were not yet accustomed to accept such unequal laws from a tribe of barbarians; and the prince who by a necessary concession had probably saved his country became the object of the general contempt and aversion.

But the Romans were irritated to a still higher degree when they discovered that they had not even secured their repose, though at the expense of their honour. The dangerous secret of the wealth and weakness of the empire had been revealed to the world. New swarms of barbarians, encouraged (A.D. 253) by the success, and not conceiving themselves bound by the obligation, of their brethren, spread devastation through the Illyrian provinces, and terror as far as the gates of Rome.

As the Roman empire was at the same time, and on every side, attacked by the blind fury of foreign invaders, and the wild ambition of domestic usurpers, we shall consult order and perspicuity by pursuing not so much the doubtful arrangement of dates as the more natural distribution of subjects. The most dangerous enemies of Rome, during the reigns of Valerian and Gallienus, were, 1. The Franks; 2. The Alemanni; 3. The Goths; and 4. The Persians. Under these general appellations we may comprehend the adventures of less considerable tribes, whose obscure and uncouth names would only serve to oppress the memory and perplex the attention of the reader.

I. As the posterity of the Franks compose one of the greatest and most enlightened nations of Europe, the powers of learning and ingenuity have been exhausted in the discovery of their unlettered ancestors. To the tales of credulity have succeeded the systems of fancy. Every passage has been sifted, every spot has been surveyed, that might possibly reveal some faint traces of their origin. It has been supposed that Pannonia, that Gaul, that the northern parts of Germany, gave birth to that celebrated colony of warriors. At length the most rational critics, rejecting the fictitious emigrations of ideal conquerors, have acquiesced in a sentiment whose simplicity persuades us of its truth. They suppose that, about the year two hundred and forty, a new confederacy was formed under the name of Franks, by the old inhabitants of the Lower Rhine and the Weser. The present circle of Westphalia, the Landgraviate of Hesse, and the duchies of Brunswick and Luneburg, were the ancient seat of the Chauci, who, in their inaccessible morasses, defied the Roman arms; of the Cherusci, proud of the fame of Arminius; of the Catti, formidable by their firm and intrepid infantry; and of several other tribes of inferior power and renown. The love of liberty was the ruling passion of these Germans; the enjoyment of it their best treasure; the word that expressed that enjoyment the most pleasing to their ear. They deserved, they assumed, they maintained the honourable epithet of Franks or Freemen, which concealed though it did not extinguish the peculiar names of the several states of the confederacy. Tacit consent, and mutual advantage, dictated the first laws of the union; it was gradually cemented by habit and experience. The league of the Franks may admit of some comparison with the Helvetic body, in which every canton, retaining its independent sovereignty, consults with its brethren in the common cause, without acknowledging the authority of any supreme head or representative assembly. But the principles of the two confederacies were extremely different. A peace of two hundred years has rewarded the wise and honest policy of the Swiss. An inconstant spirit, the thirst of rapine, and a disregard to the most solemn treaties, disgraced the character of the Franks.

The Rhine, though dignified with the title of Safeguard of the provinces, was an imperfect barrier against the daring spirit of enterprise with which the Franks were actuated. Their rapid devastations stretched from the river to the foot of the Pyrenees: nor were they stopped by those mountains. Spain, which had never dreaded, was unable to resist the inroads of the Germans. During twelve years, the greatest part of the reign of Gallienus, that opulent country was the theatre of unequal and destructive hostilities. Tarragona, the flourishing capital of a peaceful province, was sacked and almost destroyed, and so late as the days of Orosius, who wrote in the fifth century, wretched cottages, scattered amidst the ruins of magnificent cities, still recorded the rage of the barbarians. When the exhausted country no longer supplied a variety of plunder, the Franks seized on some vessels in the ports of Spain, and transported themselves into Mauritania. The distant province was astonished with the fury of these barbarians, who seemed to fall from a new world, as their name, manners, and complexion were equally unknown on the coast of Africa.

II. In that part of Upper Saxony beyond the Elbe, which is at present called the Marquisate of Lusace, there existed in ancient times a sacred wood, the awful seat of the superstition of the Suevi. None were permitted to enter the holy precincts without confessing, by their servile bonds and suppliant posture, the immediate presence of the sovereign Deity. Patriotism contributed as well as devotion to consecrate the Sonnenwald, or wood of the Semnones. It was universally believed that the nation had received its first existence on that sacred spot. At stated periods, the numerous tribes who gloried in the Suevic blood resorted thither by their ambassadors; and the memory of their common extraction was perpetuated by barbaric rites and human sacrifices. The wide extended name of Suevi filled the interior countries of Germany from the banks of the Oder to those of the Danube. They were distinguished from the other Germans by their peculiar mode of dressing their long hair, which they gathered into a rude knot on the crown of the head; and they delighted in an ornament that showed their ranks more lofty and terrible in the eyes of the enemy. Jealous as the Germans were of military renown, they all confessed the superior valour of the Suevi; and the tribes of the Usipetes and Tencteri, who, with a vast army, encountered the dictator Cæsar, declared that they esteemed it not a disgrace to have fled before a people to whose arms the immortal gods themselves were unequal.

In the reign of the emperor Caracalla, an innumerable swarm of Suevi appeared on the banks of the Mein, and in the neighbourhood of the Roman provinces, in quest either of food, of plunder, or of glory. The hasty army of volunteers gradually coalesced into a great and permanent nation, and as it was composed from so many different tribes, assumed the name of Alemanni, or *All-men,* to denote at once their various lineage and their common bravery. The latter was soon felt by the Romans in many a hostile inroad. The Alemanni fought chiefly on horseback; but their cavalry was rendered still more formidable by a mixture of light infantry, selected from the bravest and most active of the youth, whom frequent exercise had inured to accompany the horsemen in the longest march, the most rapid charge, or the most precipitate retreat.

This warlike people of Germans had been astonished by the immense preparations of Alexander Severus, they were dismayed by the arms of his successor, a barbarian equal in valour and fierceness to themselves. But still hovering on the frontiers of the empire, they increased the general disorder that ensued after the death of Decius. They inflicted severe wounds on the rich provinces of Gaul; they were the first who removed the veil that covered the feeble majesty of Italy. A numerous body of the Alemanni penetrated across the Danube, and through the Rhætian Alps, into the plains of Lombardy, advanced as far as Ravenna, and displayed the victorious banners of barbarians almost in sight of Rome. The insult and the danger rekindled in the senate some sparks of their ancient virtue. Both the emperors were engaged in far distant wars, Valerian in the East and Gallienus on the Rhine. All the hopes and resources of the Romans were in themselves. In this emergency, the senators resumed the defence of the republic, drew out the Prætorian guards, who had been left to garrison the capital, and filled up their numbers by enlisting into the public service the stoutest and most willing of the Plebeians. The Alemanni, astonished with the sudden appearance of an army more numerous than their own, retired into Germany laden with spoil; and their retreat was esteemed as a victory by the unwarlike Romans.

III. We have already traced the emigration of the Goths from Scandinavia, or at least from Prussia, to the mouth of the Borysthenes, and have followed their victorious arms from the Borysthenes to the Danube. Under the reigns of Valerian and Gallienus, the frontier of the last-mentioned river was perpetually infested by the inroads of Germans and Sarmatians but it was defended by the Romans with more than usual firmness and success. The provinces that were the seat of war recruited the armies of Rome with an inexhaustible supply of hardy soldiers; and more than one of these Illyrian peasants attained the station and displayed the abilities of a general. Though flying parties of the barbarians, who incessantly hovered on the banks of the Danube, penetrated sometimes to the confines of Italy and Macedonia; their progress was commonly checked or their return intercepted, by the Imperial lieutenants. But the great stream of the Gothic hostilities was diverted into a very different channel. The Goths, in their new settlement of the Ukraine, soon became masters of the northern coast of the Euxine: to the south of that inland sea were situated the soft and wealthy provinces of Asia Minor, which possessed all that could attract, and nothing that could resist, a barbarian conqueror.

The little kingdom of Bosphorus, whose capital was situated on the Straits through which the Mæotis communicates itself to the Euxine, was composed of degenerate Greeks and half-civilised barbarians. It subsisted, as an independent state, from the time of the Peloponnesian war, was at last swallowed up by the ambition of Mithridates, and, with the rest of his dominions, sunk under the weight of the Roman arms. From the reign of Augustus, the kings of Bosphorus were the humble, but not useless, allies of the empire. By presents, by arms, and by a slight fortification drawn across the Isthmus, they effectually guarded against the roving plunderers of Sarmatia the access of a country which, from its peculiar situation and convenient harbours, commanded the Euxine Sea and Asia Minor. As long as the sceptre was possessed by a lineal succession of kings, they acquitted themselves of their important charge with vigilance and success. Domestic factions, and the fears or private interest of obscure usurpers who seized on the vacant throne, admitted the Goths into the heart of Bosphorus. With the acquisition of a superfluous waste of fertile soil, the conquerors obtained the command of a naval force sufficient to transport their armies to the coast of Asia.

The ships used in the navigation of the Euxine were of a very singular construction. They were slight flat-bottomed barks framed of timber only, without the least mixture of iron, and occasionally covered with a shelving roof on the appearance of a tempest. In these floating houses, the Goths carelessly trusted themselves to the mercy of an unknown sea, under the conduct of sailors pressed into the service, and whose skill and fidelity were equally suspicious. But the hopes of plunder had banished every idea of danger, and a natural fearlessness of temper supplied in their minds the more rational confidence which is the just result of knowledge and experience.

The fleet of the Goths, leaving the coast of Circassia on the left hand, first appeared before Pityus, the utmost limits of the Roman provinces; a city provided with a convenient port and fortified with a strong wall. Here they met with a resistance more obstinate than they had reason to expect from the feeble garrison of a distant fortress.

Circling round the eastern extremity of the Euxine Sea, they even attempted, though without success, to pillage a rich temple at the mouth of the river Phasis. Trebizond, celebrated in the retreat of the Ten Thousand as an ancient colony of Greeks, derived its wealth and splendour from the munificence of the emperor Hadrian, who had constructed an artificial port on a coast left destitute by nature of secure harbours. The city was large and populous; a double enclosure of walls seemed to defy the fury of the Goths, and the usual garrison had been strengthened by a reinforcement of ten thousand men. But there are not any advantages capable of supplying the absence of discipline and vigilance. The numerous garrison of Trebizond, dissolved in riot and luxury, disdained to guard their impregnable fortifications. The Goths soon discovered the supine negligence of the besieged, erected a lofty pile of fascines, ascended the walls in the silence of the night, and entered the defenceless city sword in hand. A general massacre of the people ensued, whilst the affrighted soldiers escaped through the opposite gates of the town. The most holy temples, and the most splendid edifices, were involved in a common destruction. The booty that fell into the hands of the Goths was immense: the wealth of the adjacent countries had been deposited in Trebizond, as in a secure place of refuge. The number of captives was incredible, as the victorious barbarians ranged without opposition through the extensive province of Pontus. The rich spoils of Trebizond filled a great fleet of ships that had been found in the port. The robust youth of the sea-coast were chained to the oar; and the Goths, satisfied with the success of their first naval expedition, returned in triumph to their new establishments in the kingdom of Bosphorus.

The second expedition of the Goths was undertaken with greater powers of men and ships; but they steered a different course, and disdaining the exhausted provinces of Pontus, followed the western coast of the Euxine, passed before the wide mouths of the Borysthenes, the Dniester, and the Danube. Increasing their fleet by the capture of a great number of fishing barks, they approached the narrow outlet through which the Euxine Sea pours its waters into the Mediterranean, and divides the continents of Europe and Asia. The garrison of Chalcedon was encamped near the temple of Jupiter Urius, on a promontory that commanded the entrance of the Straits; and so dreaded were the invasions of the barbarians that this body of troops surpassed in number the Gothic army. But it was in numbers alone that they surpassed it. They deserted with precipitation their advantageous post, and abandoned the town of Chalcedon, most plentifully stored with arms and money, to the discretion of the conquerors. Nice, Prusa, Apamæa, Cius, cities that had sometimes rivalled, or imitated, the splendour of Nicomedia, were involved in the same calamity, which, in a few weeks, raged without control through the whole province of Bithynia. Three hundred years of peace, enjoyed by the soft inhabitants of Asia, had abolished the exercise of arms and removed the apprehension of danger. The ancient walls were suffered to moulder away, and all the revenue of the most opulent cities was reserved for the construction of baths, temples, and theatres.

The season was rainy, and the lake Apolloniates, the reservoir of all the springs of Mount Olympus, rose to an uncommon height. The little river of Rhyndacus, which issues from the lake, swelled into a broad and rapid stream, and stopped the progress of the Goths. Their retreat to the maritime city of Heraclea, where the fleet had probably been stationed, was attended by a long train of waggons, laden with the spoils of Bithynia, and was marked by the flames of Nice and Nicomedia, which they wantonly burnt. Approach of the autumnal equinox summoned them to hasten their return.

The third fleet steered from the Cimmerian to the Thracian Bosphorus. When they had almost gained the middle of the Straits, they were suddenly driven back to the entrance of them, till a favourable wind springing up the next day carried them in a few hours into the placid sea, or rather lake, of the Propontis. Their landing on the little island of Cyzicus was attended with the ruin of that ancient and noble city. From thence issuing again through the narrow passage of the Hellespont, they pursued their winding navigation amidst the numerous islands scattered over the Archipelago, or the Ægean Sea. The assistance of captives and deserters must have been very necessary to pilot their vessels and to direct their various incursions, as well on the coast of Greece as on that of Asia. At length the Gothic fleet anchored in the port of Piræus, five miles distant from Athens, which had attempted to make some preparations for a vigorous defence. Cleodamus, one of the engineers employed by the emperor's orders to fortify the maritime cities against the Goths, had already begun to repair the ancient walls fallen to decay since the time of Sylla. The efforts of his skill were ineffectual, and the barbarians became masters of the native seat of the muses and the arts.

A general conflagration blazed out at the same time in every district of Greece. Thebes and Argos, Corinth and Sparta, which had formerly waged such memorable wars against each other, were now unable to bring an army into the field, or even to defend their ruined fortifications. The rage of war, both by land and by sea, spread within sight of Italy.

The temple of Diana at Ephesus, after having risen with increasing splendour from seven repeated misfortunes, was finally burnt by the Goths in their third naval invasion. The arts of Greece, and the wealth of Asia, had conspired to erect that sacred and magnificent structure. Successive empires, the Persian, the Macedonian, and the Roman, had revered its sanctity and enriched its splendour. But the rude savages of the Baltic were destitute of a taste for the elegant arts, and they despised the ideal terrors of a foreign superstition.

Another circumstance is related of these invasions, which might deserve our notice, were it not justly to be suspected as the fanciful conceit of a recent sophist. We are told that in the sack of Athens the Goths had collected all the libraries, and were on the point of setting fire to this funeral pile of Grecian learning, had not one of their chiefs, of more refined policy than his brethren, dissuaded them from the design by the profound observation that as long as the Greeks were addicted to the study of books, they would never apply themselves to the exercise of arms. The sagacious counsellor (should the truth of the fact be admitted) reasoned like an ignorant barbarian. In the most polite and powerful nations, genius of every kind has displayed itself about the same period; and the age of science has generally been the age of military virtue and success.

IV. The new sovereigns of Persia, Artaxerxes and his son Sapor, had triumphed over the house of Arsaces. Of the many princes of that ancient race, Chosroes, king of Armenia, had alone preserved both his life and his independence. He defended himself by the natural strength of his country; by the perpetual resort of fugitives and malcontents; by the alliance of the Romans, and, above all, by his own courage. Invincible in arms, during a thirty years' war, he was at length assassinated by the emissaries of Sapor, king of Persia. The patriotic satraps of Armenia, who asserted the freedom and dignity of the crown, implored the protection of Rome in favour of Tiridates the lawful heir. But the son of Chosroes was an infant, the allies were at a distance, and the Persian monarch advanced towards the frontier at the head of an irresistible force. Young Tiridates, the future hope of his country, was saved by the fidelity of a servant, and Armenia continued above twenty-seven years a reluctant province of the great monarchy of Persia. Elated with this easy conquest, and presuming on the distresses or the degeneracy of the Romans, Sapor obliged the strong garrisons of Carrhæ and Nisibis to surrender, and spread devastation and terror on either side of the Euphrates.

The loss of an important frontier, the ruin of a faithful and natural ally, and the rapid success of Sapor's ambition, affected Rome with a deep sense of the insult as well as of the danger. Valerian flattered himself that the vigilance of his lieutenants would sufficiently provide for the safety of the Rhine and of the Danube; but he resolved, notwithstanding his advanced age, to march in person to the defence of the Euphrates. He passed the Euphrates, encountered the Persian monarch near the walls of Edessa, was (A.D. 260) vanquished and taken prisoner by Sapor. We are told that Valerian, in chains, but invested with the Imperial purple, was exposed to the multitude, a constant spectacle of fallen greatness; and that whenever the Persian monarch mounted on horseback, he placed his foot on the neck of a Roman emperor. Notwithstanding all the remonstrances of his allies, who repeatedly advised him to remember the vicissitude of fortune, to dread the returning power of Rome, and to make his illustrious captive the pledge of peace, not the object of insult, Sapor still remained inflexible. When Valerian sunk under the weight of shame and grief, his skin, stuffed with straw, and formed into the likeness of a human figure, was preserved for ages in the most celebrated temple of Persia; a more real monument of triumph than the fancied trophies of brass and marble so often erected by Roman vanity. The tale is moral and pathetic, but the truth of it may very fairly be called in question. Whatever treatment the unfortunate Valerian might experience in Persia, it is at least certain that the only emperor of Rome who had ever fallen into the hands of the enemy languished away his life in hopeless captivity.

So rapid were the motions of the Persian cavalry that, if we may credit a very judicious historian, the city of Antioch was surprised when the idle multitude was fondly gazing on the amusements of the theatre. The splendid buildings of Antioch, private as well as public, were either pillaged or destroyed; and the numerous inhabitants were put to the sword, or led away into captivity. The ruin of Tarsus, and many other cities, furnishes a melancholy proof that, except in this single instance, the conquest of Syria and Cilicia scarcely interrupted the progress of the Persian arms. The advantages of the narrow passes of Mount Taurus were abandoned, in which an invader, whose principal force consisted in his cavalry, would have been engaged in a very unequal combat: and Sapor was permitted to form the siege of Cæsarea, the capital of Cappadocia; a city, though of the second rank, which was supposed to contain four hundred thousand inhabitants.

It is difficult to paint the light, the various, the inconstant character of Gallienus, which he displayed without constraint, as soon as he became sole possessor of the empire. In every art that he attempted his lively genius enabled him to succeed; and as his genius was destitute of judgment, he attempted every art except the important ones of war and government. He was a master of several curious but useless sciences, a ready orator and elegant poet, a skilful gardener, an excellent cook, and most contemptible prince. When the great emergencies of the state required his presence and attention, he was engaged in conversation with the philosopher Plotinus, wasting his time in trifling or licentious pleasures, preparing his initiation to the Grecian mysteries, or soliciting a place in the Areopagus of Athens. His profuse magnificence insulted the general poverty; the solemn ridicule of his triumphs impressed a deeper sense of the public disgrace. The repeated intelligence of invasions, defeats, and rebellions he received with a careless smile; and singling out, with affected contempt, some particular production of the lost province, he carelessly asked whether Rome must be ruined unless it was supplied with linen from Egypt and Arras cloth from Gaul?

At a time when the reins of government were held with so loose a hand, it is not surprising that a crowd of usurpers should start up in every province of the empire against the son of Valerian. Of the nineteen tyrants who started up under the reign of Gallienus, there was not one who enjoyed a life of peace or a natural death. As soon as they were invested with the bloody purple, they inspired their adherents with the same fears and ambition which had occasioned their own revolt. Encompassed with domestic conspiracy, military sedition, and civil war, they trembled on the edge of precipices, in which, after a longer or shorter term of anxiety, they were inevitably lost.

Whilst the public forces of the state were dissipated in private quarrels, the defenceless provinces lay exposed to every invader. The bravest usurpers were compelled, by the perplexity of their situation, to conclude ignominious treaties with the common enemy, to purchase with oppressive tributes the neutrality or services of the barbarians, and to introduce hostile and independent nations into the heart of the Roman monarchy.

CHAPTER VIII

Reign of Claudius—Victories of Aurelian—Conduct of the Army and Senate

Under the deplorable reigns of Valerian and Gallienus the empire was oppressed and almost destroyed by the soldiers, the tyrants, and the barbarians. It was saved by a series of great princes, who derived their obscure origin from the martial provinces of Illyricum. Within a period of about thirty years, Claudius, Aurelian, Probus, Diocletian and his colleagues triumphed over the foreign and domestic enemies of the state, re-established, with the military discipline, the strength of the frontiers, and deserved the glorious title of restorers of the Roman world.

The virtues of Claudius, his valour, affability, justice, and temperance, his love of fame and of his country, place him in that short list of emperors who added lustre to the Roman purple. In his last illness he convened the principal officers of the state and army, and in their presence recommended Aurelian, one of his generals, as the most deserving of the throne, and the best qualified to execute the great design which he himself had been permitted only to undertake.

The death of Claudius had revived the fainting spirit of the Goths. The troops which guarded the passes of Mount Hæmus and the banks of the Danube had been drawn away by the apprehension of a civil war; and it seems probable that the remaining body of the Gothic and Vandalic tribes embraced the favourable opportunity, abandoned their settlements of the Ukraine, traversed the rivers, and swelled with new multitudes the destroying host of their countrymen. Their united numbers were at length encountered by Aurelian, and the bloody and doubtful conflict ended only with the approach of night. Exhausted by so many calamities, which they had mutually endured and inflicted during a twenty years' war, the Goths and the Romans consented to a lasting and beneficial treaty. It was earnestly solicited by the barbarians, and cheerfully ratified by the legions, to whose suffrage the prudence of Aurelian referred the decision of that important question.

The Gothic nation engaged to supply the armies of Rome with a body of two thousand auxiliaries, consisting entirely of cavalry, and stipulated in return an undisturbed retreat, with a regular market as far as the Danube, provided by the emperor's care, but at their own expense. The treaty was observed with such religious fidelity that when a party of five hundred men straggled from the camp in quest of plunder, the king or general of the barbarians commanded that the guilty leader should be apprehended and shot to death with darts, as a victim devoted to the sanctity of their engagements. It is, however, not unlikely that the precaution of Aurelian, who had exacted as hostages the sons and daughters of the Gothic chiefs, contributed something to this pacific temper. The youths he trained in the exercise of arms, and near his own person; to the damsels he gave a liberal and Roman education, and, by bestowing them in marriage on some of his principal officers, gradually introduced between the two nations the closest and most endearing connections.

But the most important condition of peace was understood rather than expressed in the treaty. Aurelian withdrew the Roman forces from Dacia, and tacitly relinquished that great province to the Goths and Vandals. His manly judgment convinced him of the solid advantages, and taught him to despise the seeming disgrace, of thus contracting the frontiers of the monarchy. The Dacian subjects, removed from those distant possessions which they were unable to cultivate or defend, added strength and populousness to the southern side of the Danube. A fertile territory, which the repetition of barbarous inroads had changed into a desert, was yielded to their industry, and a new province of Dacia still preserved the memory of Trajan's conquests. The old country of that name detained, however, a considerable number of its inhabitants, who dreaded exile more than a Gothic master. These degenerate Romans continued to serve the empire whose allegiance they had renounced, by introducing among their conquerors the first notions of agriculture, the useful arts, and the conveniences of civilised life. An intercourse of commerce and language was gradually established between the opposite banks of the Danube; and, after Dacia became an independent state, it often proved the firmest barrier of the empire against the invasions of the savages of the North.

As the light troops of the Alemanni had spread themselves from the Alps to the Apennine, the incessant vigilance of Aurelian and his officers was exercised in the discovery, the attack, and the pursuit of the numerous detachments. Notwithstanding this desultory war, three considerable battles are mentioned, in which the principal force of both armies was obstinately engaged. Thus far the successful Germans had advanced along the Æmilian and Flaminian way, with a design of sacking the defenceless mistress of the world. But Aurelian, who, watchful for the safety of Rome, still hung on their rear, found the decisive moment of giving them a total and irretrievable defeat. The flying remnant of their host was exterminated in a third and last battle near Pavia; and Italy was delivered from the inroads of the Alemanni.

Though the best hope of the republic was in the valour and conduct of Aurelian, yet such was the public consternation when the barbarians were hourly expected at the gates of Rome that, by a decree of the senate, the Sibylline books were consulted. Even the emperor himself, from a motive either of religion or of policy, recommended this salutary measure, chided the tardiness of the senate, and offered to supply whatever expense, whatever animals, whatever captives of any nation, the gods should require. Notwithstanding this liberal offer, it does not appear that any human victims expiated with their blood the sins of the Roman people. The Sibylline books enjoined ceremonies of a more harmless nature—processions of priests in white robes, attended by a chorus of youths and virgins; lustrations of the city and adjacent country; and sacrifices, whose powerful influence disabled the barbarians from passing the mystic ground on which they had been celebrated.

But whatever confidence might be placed in ideal ramparts, the experience of the past and the dread of the future induced the Romans to construct fortifications of a grosser and more substantial kind. The seven hills of Rome had been surrounded, by the successors of Romulus, with an ancient wall of more than thirteen miles. The vast enclosure may seem disproportioned to the strength and numbers of the infant state. But it was necessary to secure an ample extent of pasture and arable land against the frequent and sudden incursions of the tribes of Latium, the perpetual enemies of the republic. With the progress of Roman greatness, the city and its inhabitants gradually increased, filled up the vacant space, pierced through the useless walls, covered the field of Mars, and, on every side, followed the public highways in long and beautiful suburbs. The extent of the new walls, erected by Aurelian, and finished in the reign of Probus, was magnified by popular estimation to near fifty, but is reduced by accurate measurement to about twenty-one miles. It was a great but a melancholy labour, since the defence of the capital betrayed the decline of the monarchy. The Romans of a more prosperous age, who trusted to the arms of the legions the safety of the frontier camps, were very far from entertaining a suspicion that it would ever become necessary to fortify the seat of empire against the inroads of the barbarians.

The victory of Claudius over the Goths, and the success of Aurelian against the Alemanni, had already restored to the arms of Rome their ancient superiority over the barbarous nations of the North. To chastise domestic tyrants, and to reunite the dismembered parts of the empire, was a task reserved for the second of those warlike emperors. Though he was acknowledged by the senate and people, the frontiers of Italy, Africa, Illyricum, and Thrace, confined the limits of his reign. Gaul, Spain, and Britain, Egypt, Syria, and Asia Minor, were still possessed by two rebels who alone, out of so numerous a list, had hitherto escaped the dangers of their situation; and to complete the ignominy of Rome, these rival thrones had been usurped by women.

A rapid succession of monarchs had arisen and fallen in the provinces of Gaul. After the murder of so many valiant princes, it is somewhat remarkable that a female for a long time controlled the fierce legions of Gaul, and still more singular that she was the mother of the unfortunate Victorinus. The arts and treasures of Victoria enabled her successively to place Marius and Tetricus on the throne, and to reign with a manly vigour under the name of those dependent emperors. Money of copper, of silver, and of gold, was coined in her name.

Aurelian had no sooner secured the person and provinces of Tetricus than he turned his arms against Zenobia, the celebrated queen of Palmyra and the East. Modern Europe has produced several illustrious women who have sustained with glory the weight of empire; nor is our own age destitute of such distinguished characters. But if we except the doubtful achievements of Semiramis, Zenobia is perhaps the only female whose superior genius broke through the servile indolence imposed on her sex by the climate and manners of Asia. She claimed her descent from the Macedonian kings of Egypt, equalled in beauty her ancestor Cleopatra, and far surpassed that princess in chastity and valour. Zenobia was esteemed the most lovely as well as the most heroic of her sex. She was of a dark complexion (for in speaking of a lady these trifles become important). Her teeth were of a pearly whiteness, and her large black eyes sparkled with uncommon fire, tempered by the most attractive sweetness. Her voice was strong and harmonius. Her manly understanding was strengthened and adorned by study. She was not ignorant of the Latin tongue, but possessed in equal perfection the Greek, the Syriac, and the Egyptian languages. She had drawn up for her own use an epitome of oriental history, and familiarly compared the beauties of Homer and Plato under the tuition of the sublime Longinus.

This accomplished woman gave her hand to Odenathus, who, from a private station, raised himself to the dominion of the East. She soon became the friend and companion of a hero. In the intervals of war Odenathus passionately delighted in the exercise of hunting; he pursued with ardour the wild beasts of the desert, lions, panthers, and bears; and the ardour of Zenobia in that dangerous amusement was not inferior to his own. She had inured her constitution to fatigue, disdained the use of a covered carriage, generally appeared on horseback in a military habit, and sometimes marched several miles on foot at the head of the troops. The success of Odenathus was in a great measure ascribed to her incomparable prudence and fortitude.

By the death of Odenathus, that authority was at an end which the senate had granted him only as a personal distinction; but his martial widow, disdaining both the senate and Gallienus, obliged one of the Roman generals who was sent against her to retreat into Europe, with the loss of his army and his reputation. Instead of the little passions which so frequently perplex a female reign, the steady administration of Zenobia was guided by the most judicious maxims of policy. If it was expedient to pardon, she could calm her resentment; if it was necessary to punish, she could impose silence on the voice of pity. Her strict economy was accused of avarice; yet on every proper occasion she appeared magnificent and liberal. The neighbouring states of Arabia, Armenia, and Persia, dreaded her enmity, and solicited her alliance. To the dominions of Odenathus, which extended from the Euphrates to the frontiers of Bithynia, his widow added the inheritance of her ancestors, the populous and fertile kingdom of Egypt.

The fate of the East was decided in two great battles; so similar in almost every circumstance, that we can scarcely distinguish them from each other, except by observing that the first was fought near Antioch, and the second near Emesa. In both the queen of Palmyra animated the armies by her presence.

In his march over the sandy desert between Emesa and Palmyra, the emperor Aurelian was perpetually harassed by the Arabs; nor could he always defend his army, and especially his baggage, from those flying troops of active and daring robbers, who watched the moment of surprise, and eluded the slow pursuit of the legions. The siege of Palmyra was an object far more difficult and important, and the emperor, who, with incessant vigour, pressed the attacks in person, was himself wounded with a dart. "The Roman people," says Aurelian, in an original letter, "speak with contempt of the war which I am waging against a woman. They are ignorant both of the character and of the power of Zenobia. It is impossible to enumerate her warlike preparations, of stones, of arrows, and of every species of missile weapons. Every part of the walls is provided with two or three *balistœ*, and artificial fires are thrown from her military engines. The fear of punishment has armed her with a desperate courage. Yet still I trust in the protecting deities of Rome, who have hitherto been favourable to all my undertakings."

Doubtful, however, of the protection of the gods, and of the event of the siege, Aurelian judged it more prudent to offer terms of an advantageous capitulation; to the queen, a splendid retreat; to the citizens, their ancient privileges. His proposals were obstinately rejected, and the refusal was accompanied with insult.

The firmness of Zenobia was supported by the hope that in a very short time famine would compel the Roman army to repass the desert; and by the reasonable expectation that the kings of the East, and particularly the Persian monarch, would arm in the defence of their most natural ally. But fortune and the perseverance of Aurelian overcame every obstacle.

Zenobia resolved to fly. She mounted the fleetest of her dromedaries, and had already reached the banks of the Euphrates, about sixty miles from Palmyra, when she was overtaken by the pursuit of Aurelian's light horse, seized and brought back a captive to the feet of the emperor. Her capital soon afterwards surrendered, and was treated with unexpected lenity. The arms, horses, and camels, with an immense treasure of gold, silver, silk, and precious stones, were all delivered to the conqueror, who, leaving only a garrison of six hundred archers, returned to Emesa, and employed some time in the distribution of rewards and punishments at the end of so memorable a war, which restored to the obedience of Rome those provinces that had renounced their allegiance since the captivity of Valerian.

Aurelian might now congratulate the senate, the people, and himself, that, in little more than three years, he had restored universal peace and order to the Roman world. Since the foundation of Rome no general had more nobly deserved a triumph than Aurelian; nor was a triumph ever celebrated with superior pride and magnificence. The pomp was opened by twenty elephants, four royal tigers, and above two hundred of the most curious animals from every climate of the North, the East, and the South. They were followed by sixteen hundred gladiators, devoted to the cruel amusement of the amphitheatre. The wealth of Asia, the arms and ensigns of so many conquered nations, and the magnificent plate and wardrobe of the Syrian queen, were disposed in exact symmetry or artful disorder. The ambassadors of the most remote parts of the earth, of Æthiopia, Arabia, Persia, Bactriana, India, and China, all remarkable by their rich or singular dresses, displayed the fame and power of the Roman emperor, who exposed likewise to the public view the presents that he had received, and particularly a great number of crowns of gold, the offerings of grateful cities.

The victories of Aurelian were attested by the long train of captives who reluctantly attended his triumph—Goths, Vandals, Sarmatians, Alemanni, Franks, Gauls, Syrians, and Egyptians. Each people was distinguished by its peculiar inscription, and the title of Amazons was bestowed on ten martial heroines of the Gothic nation who had been taken in arms. The beauteous figure of Zenobia was confined by fetters of gold; a slave supported the gold chain which encircled her neck, and she almost fainted under the intolerable weight of jewels. She preceded on foot the magnificent chariot in which she once hoped to enter the gates of Rome. The triumphal car of Aurelian (it had formerly been used by a Gothic king) was drawn, on this memorable occasion, either by four stags or by four elephants. The most illustrious of the senate, the people, and the army closed the solemn procession.

So long and so various was the pomp of Aurelian's triumph, that, although it opened with the dawn of day, the slow majesty of the procession ascended not the Capitol before the ninth hour; and it was already dark when the emperor returned to the palace. The festival was protracted by theatrical representations, the games of the circus, the hunting of wild beasts, combats of gladiators, and naval engagements. Liberal donatives were distributed to the army and people, and several institutions, agreeable or beneficial to the city, contributed to perpetuate the glory of Aurelian. A considerable portion of his oriental spoils was consecrated to the gods of Rome; the Capitol, and every other temple, glittered with the offerings of his ostentatious piety; and the temple of the Sun alone received above fifteen thousand pounds of gold.

The arms of Aurelian had vanquished the foreign and domestic foes of the republic. We are assured that, by his salutary rigour, crimes and factions, mischievous arts and pernicious connivance, the luxuriant growth of a feeble and oppressive government, were eradicated throughout the Roman world. But if we attentively reflect how much swifter is the progress of corruption than its cure, and if we remember that the years abandoned to public disorders exceeded the months allotted to the martial reign of Aurelian, we must confess that a few short intervals of peace were insufficient for the arduous work of reformation.

Rome, though deprived of freedom, was distracted by faction. The people, towards whom the emperor, himself a Plebeian, always expressed a peculiar fondness, lived in perpetual dissension with the senate, the equestrian order, and the Prætorian guards.

Such was the unhappy condition of the Roman emperors, that, whatever might be their conduct, their fate was commonly the same. A life of pleasure or virtue, of severity or mildness, of indolence or glory, alike led to an untimely grave; and almost every reign is closed by the same disgusting repetition of treason and murder. The death of Aurelian, however, is remarkable by its extraordinary consequences. The legions admired, lamented, and revenged their victorious chief. The discipline and memory of Aurelian still restrained the seditious temper of the troops, as well as the fatal ambition of their leaders. The flower of the legions maintained their stations on the banks of the Bosphorus, and the Imperial standard awed the less powerful camps of Rome and of the provinces. A generous though transient enthusiasm seemed to animate the military order; and we may hope that a few real patriots cultivated the returning friendship of the army and the senate whilst eight months insensibly elapsed; an amazing period of tranquil anarchy, during which the Roman world remained without a sovereign, without an usurper, and without a sedition. The generals and magistrates appointed by Aurelian continued to execute their ordinary functions; and it is observed that a proconsul of Asia was the only considerable person removed from his office in the whole course of the interregnum.

The administration of Tacitus was not unworthy of his life and principles. A grateful servant of the senate, he considered that national council as the author, and himself as the subject, of the laws. He studied to heal the wounds which Imperial pride, civil discord, and military violence had inflicted on the constitution, and to restore, at least, the image of the ancient republic as it had been preserved by the policy of Augustus and the virtues of Trajan and the Antonines.

Circular epistles were sent, without delay, to all the principal cities of the empire—Treves, Milan, Aquileia, Thessalonica, Corinth, Athens, Antioch, Alexandria, and Carthage—to claim their obedience, and to inform them of the happy revolution which had restored the Roman senate to its ancient dignity. Two of these epistles are still extant. We likewise possess two very singular fragments of the private correspondence of the senators on this occasion. They discover the most excessive joy and the most unbounded hopes. "Cast away your indolence," it is thus that one of the senators addresses his friend, "emerge from your retirements of Baiæ and Puteoli. Give yourself to the city, to the senate. Rome flourishes, the whole republic flourishes. Thanks to the Roman army, to an army truly Roman, at length we have recovered our just authority, the end of all our desires. We hear appeals, we appoint proconsuls, we create emperors; perhaps, too, we may restrain them—to the wise a word is sufficient." These lofty expectations were, however, soon disappointed; nor, indeed, was it possible that the armies and the provinces should long obey the luxurious and unwarlike nobles of Rome. On the slightest touch the unsupported fabric of their pride and power fell to the ground. The expiring senate displayed a sudden lustre, blazed for a moment, and was extinguished for ever.

All that had yet passed at Rome was no more than a theatrical representation, unless it was ratified by the more substantial power of the legions. Whatever flattering expectations he had conceived of reconciling the public disorders, Tacitus soon was convinced that the licentiousness of the army disdained the feeble restraint of laws, and his last hour was hastened by anguish and disappointment.

The eyes of Tacitus were scarcely closed before his brother Florianus showed himself unworthy to reign by the hasty usurpation of the purple, without expecting the approbation of the senate. The reverence for the Roman constitution, which yet influenced the camp and the provinces, was sufficiently strong to dispose them to censure, but not to provoke them to oppose, the precipitate ambition of Florianus. The discontent would have evaporated in idle murmurs, had not the general of the East, the heroic Probus, boldly declared himself the avenger of the senate.

The strength of Aurelian had crushed on every side the enemies of Rome. After his death they seemed to revive with an increase of fury and of numbers. They were again vanquished by the active vigour of Probus, who, in a short reign of about six years, equalled the fame of ancient heroes, and restored peace and order to every province of the Roman world.

The most important service which Probus rendered to the republic was the deliverance of Gaul, and the recovery of seventy flourishing cities oppressed by the barbarians of Germany, who, since the death of Aurelian, had ravaged that great province with impunity. Among the various multitude of those fierce invaders, we may distinguish, with some degree of clearness, three great armies, or rather nations, successively vanquished by the valour of Probus. He drove back the Franks into their morasses; a descriptive circumstance from whence we may infer that the confederacy known by the manly appellation of *Free* already occupied the flat maritime country, intersected and almost overflowed by the stagnating waters of the Rhine, and that several tribes of the Frisians and Batavians had acceded to their alliance. He vanquished the Burgundians, a considerable people of the Vandalic race. They had wandered in quest of booty from the banks of the Oder to those of the Seine. They esteemed themselves sufficiently fortunate to purchase, by the restitution of all their booty, the permission of an undisturbed retreat. They attempted to elude that article of the treaty. Their punishment was immediate and terrible.

But of all the invaders of Gaul, the most formidable were the Lygians, a distant people who reigned over a wide domain on the frontiers of Poland and Silesia. In the Lygian nation the Arii held the first rank by their numbers and fierceness. "The Arii" (it is thus that they are described by the energy of Tacitus) "study to improve by art and circumstances the innate terrors of their barbarism. Their shields are black, their bodies are painted black. They choose for the combat the darkest hour of the night. Their host advances, covered as it were with a funeral shade; nor do they often find an enemy capable of sustaining so strange and infernal an aspect. Of all our senses, the eyes are the first vanquished in battle." Yet the arms and discipline of the Romans easily discomfited these horrid phantoms.

Since the expedition of Maximin, the Roman generals had confined their ambition to a defensive war against the nations of Germany, who perpetually pressed on the frontiers of the empire. The more daring Probus pursued his Gallic victories, passed the Rhine, and displayed his invincible eagles on the banks of the Elbe and the Neckar. He was fully convinced that nothing could reconcile the minds of the barbarians to peace, unless they experienced in their own country the calamities of war. Germany, exhausted by the ill success of the last emigration, was astonished by his presence. Nine of the most considerable princes repaired to his camp, and fell prostrate at his feet. Such a treaty was humbly received by the Germans as it pleased the conqueror to dictate. He exacted a strict restitution of the effects and captives which they had carried away from the provinces; and obliged their own magistrates to punish the more obstinate robbers who presumed to detain any part of the spoil. A considerable tribute of corn, cattle, and horses, the only wealth of barbarians, was reserved for the use of the garrisons which Probus established on the limits of their territory. He even entertained some thoughts of compelling the Germans to relinquish the exercise of arms, and to trust their differences to the justice, their safety to the power, of Rome. To accomplish these salutary ends, the constant residence of an Imperial governor, supported by a numerous army, was indispensably requisite. Probus therefore judged it more expedient to defer the execution of so great a design; which was indeed rather of specious than solid utility. Had Germany been reduced into the state of a province, the Romans, with immense labour and expense, would have acquired only a more extensive boundary to defend against the fiercer and more active barbarians of Scythia.

Instead of reducing the warlike natives of Germany to the condition of subjects, Probus contented himself with the humble expedient of raising a bulwark against their inroads. The country which now forms the circle of Swabia had been left desert in the age of Augustus by the emigration of its ancient inhabitants. The fertility of the soil soon attracted a new colony from the adjacent provinces of Gaul. Crowds of adventurers, of a roving temper and of desperate fortunes, occupied the doubtful possession, and acknowledged, by the payment of tithes, the majesty of the empire. To protect these new subjects, a line of frontier garrisons was gradually extended from the Rhine to the Danube. About the reign of Hadrian, when that mode of defence began to be practised, these garrisons were connected and covered by a strong entrenchment of trees and palisades. In the place of so rude a bulwark, the emperor Probus constructed a stone wall of a considerable height and strengthened it by towers at convenient distances. From the neighbourhood of Neustadt and Ratisbon on the Danube, it stretched across hills, valleys, rivers, and morasses, as far as Wimpfen on the Neckar, and at length terminated on the banks of the Rhine, after a winding course of near two hundred miles. This important barrier, uniting the two mighty streams that protected the provinces of Europe, seemed to fill up the vacant space through which the barbarians, and particularly the Alemanni, could penetrate with the greatest facility into the heart of the empire. But the experience of the world, from China to Britain, has exposed the vain attempt of fortifying any extensive tract of country. An active enemy, who can select and vary his points of attack, must in the end discover some feeble spot, or some unguarded moment. The strength, as well as the attention, of the defenders is divided; and such are the blind effects of terror on the firmest troops that a line broken in a single place is almost instantly deserted. The fate of the wall which Probus erected may confirm the general observation. Within a few years after his death it was overthrown by the Alemanni. Its scattered ruins, universally ascribed to the power of the Dæmon, now serve only to excite the wonder of the Swabian peasant.

Among the useful conditions of peace imposed by Probus on the vanquished nations of Germany was the obligation of supplying the Roman army with sixteen thousand recruits, the bravest and most robust of their youth. The emperor dispersed them through all the provinces, and distributed this dangerous reinforcement, in small bands of fifty or sixty each, among the national troops; judiciously observing that the aid which the republic derived from the barbarians should be felt but not seen. Their aid was now become necessary. The feeble elegance of Italy and the internal provinces could no longer support the weight of arms. The hardy frontier of the Rhine and Danube still produced minds and bodies equal to the labours of the camp; but a perpetual series of wars had gradually diminished their numbers. The infrequency of marriage, and the ruin of agriculture, affected the principles of population, and not only destroyed the strength of the present, but intercepted the hope of future generations. The wisdom of Probus embraced a great and beneficial plan of replenishing the exhausted frontiers by new colonies of captive or fugitive barbarians, on whom he bestowed lands, cattle, instruments of husbandry, and every encouragement that might engage them to educate a race of soldiers for the service of the republic.

Into Britain, and most probably into Cambridgeshire, he transported a considerable body of Vandals. The impossibility of an escape reconciled them to their situation, and in the subsequent troubles of that island they approved themselves the most faithful servants of the state. Great numbers of Franks and Gepidæ were settled on the banks of the Danube and the Rhine. An hundred thousand Bastarnæ, expelled from their own country, cheerfully accepted an establishment in Thrace, and soon imbibed the manners and sentiments of Roman subjects. But the expectations of Probus were too often disappointed. The impatience and idleness of the barbarians could ill brook the slow labours of agriculture. Their unconquerable love of freedom, rising against despotism, provoked them into hasty rebellions, alike fatal to themselves and to the provinces, nor could these artificial supplies, however repeated by succeeding emperors, restore the important limit of Gaul and Illyricum to its ancient and native vigour.

Of all the barbarians who abandoned their new settlements, and disturbed the public tranquillity, a very small number returned to their own country. For a short season they might wander in arms through the empire, but in the end they were surely destroyed by the power of a warlike emperor. The successful rashness of a party of Franks was attended, however, with such memorable consequences that it ought not to be passed unnoticed. They had been established by Probus on the sea-coast of Pontus, with a view of strengthening the frontier against the inroads of the Alani. A fleet stationed in one of the harbours of the Euxine fell into the hands of the Franks; and they resolved, through unknown seas, to explore their way from the mouth of the Phasis to that of the Rhine. They easily escaped through the Bosphorus and the Hellespont, and, cruising along the Mediterranean, indulged their appetite for revenge and plunder by frequent descents on the unsuspecting shores of Asia, Greece, and Africa. The opulent city of Syracuse, in whose port the navies of Athens and Carthage had formerly been sunk, was sacked by a handful of barbarians, who massacred the greatest part of the trembling inhabitants. From the island of Sicily the Franks proceeded to the Columns of Hercules, trusted themselves to the ocean, coasted round Spain and Gaul, and, steering their triumphant course through the British Channel, at length finished their surprising voyage by landing in safety on the Batavian or Frisian shores. The example of their success, instructing their countrymen to conceive the advantages and to despise the dangers of the sea, pointed out to their enterprising spirit a new road to wealth and glory.

The arms of Probus had now suppressed all the foreign and domestic enemies of the state. His mild but steady administration confirmed the re-establishment of the public tranquillity; nor was there left in the provinces a hostile barbarian, a tyrant, or even a robber, to revive the memory of past disorders. It was time that the emperor should revisit Rome, and celebrate his own glory and the general happiness. The triumph due to the valour of Probus was conducted with a magnificence suitable to his fortune; and the people, who had so lately admired the trophies of Aurelian, gazed with equal pleasure on those of his heroic successor.

We cannot on this occasion forget the desperate courage of about four-score gladiators, reserved, with near six hundred others, for the inhuman sports of the amphitheatre. Disdaining to shed their blood for the amusement of the populace, they killed their keepers, broke from the place of their confinement, and filled the streets of Rome with blood and confusion. After an obstinate resistance, they were overpowered and cut in pieces by the regular forces; but they obtained at least an honourable death, and the satisfaction of a just revenge.

The military discipline which reigned in the camps of Probus was less cruel than that of Aurelian, but it was equally rigid and exact. The latter had punished the irregularities of the soldiers with unrelenting severity, the former prevented them by employing the legions in constant and useful labours. When Probus commanded in Egypt, he executed many considerable works for the splendour and benefit of that rich country. The navigation of the Nile, so important to Rome itself, was improved; and temples, bridges, porticoes, and palaces, were constructed by the hands of the soldiers, who acted by turns as architects, as engineers, and as husbandmen. It was reported of Hannibal that, in order to preserve his troops from the dangerous temptations of idleness, he had obliged them to form large plantations of olive-trees along the coast of Africa. From a similar principle, Probus exercised his legions in covering with rich vineyards the hills of Gaul and Pannonia, and two considerable spots are described which were entirely dug and planted by military labour. An army thus employed constituted perhaps the most useful as well as the bravest portion of Roman subjects.

But, in the prosecution of a favourite scheme, the best of men, satisfied with the rectitude of their intentions, are subject to forget the bounds of moderation; nor did Probus himself sufficiently consult the patience and disposition of his fierce legionaries. The imprudence of Probus is said to have inflamed the discontent of his troops. More attentive to the interests of mankind than to those of the army, he expressed the vain hope that, by the establishment of universal peace, he should soon abolish the necessity of a standing and mercenary force. The unguarded expression proved fatal to him. In one of the hottest days of summer, as he severely urged the unwholesome labour of draining the marshes of Sirmium, the soldiers, impatient of fatigue, on a sudden threw down their tools, grasped their arms, and broke out into a furious mutiny. The emperor, conscious of his danger, took refuge in a lofty tower constructed for the purpose of surveying the progress of the work. The tower was instantly forced, and a thousand swords were plunged at once into the bosom of the unfortunate Probus.

The authority of the senate expired with Probus; nor was the repentance of the soldiers displayed by the same dutiful regard for the civil power which they had testified after the unfortunate death of Aurelian. The election of Carus was decided without expecting the approbation of the senate; the new emperor, a veteran general, was preparing to execute the long-suspended design of the Persian war.

The successor of Artaxerxes, Varanes, or Bahram, though he had subdued the Segestans, one of the most warlike nations of Upper Asia, was alarmed at the approach of the Romans, and endeavoured to retard their progress by a negotiation of peace. His ambassadors entered the camp about sunset, at the time when the troops were satisfying their hunger with a frugal repast. The Persians expressed their desire of being introduced to the presence of the Roman emperor. They were at length conducted to a soldier who was seated on the grass. A piece of stale bacon and a few hard peas composed his supper. A coarse woollen garment of purple was the only circumstance that announced his dignity. The conference was conducted with the same disregard of courtly elegance. Carus, taking off a cap which he wore to conceal his baldness, assured the ambassadors that, unless their master acknowledged the superiority of Rome, he would speedily render Persia as naked of trees as his own head was destitute of hair. Notwithstanding some traces of art and preparation, we may discover in this scene the manners of Carus, and the severe simplicity which the martial princes who succeeded Gallienus had already restored in the Roman camps. The ministers of the Great King trembled and retired.

The threats of Carus were not without effect. He ravaged Mesopotamia, cut in pieces whatever opposed his passage, made himself master of the great cities of Seleucia and Ctesiphon (which seem to have surrendered without resistance), and carried his victorious arms beyond the Tigris. He had seized the favourable moment for an invasion. The Persian councils were distracted by domestic factions, and the greater part of their forces were detained on the frontiers of India. Rome and the East received with transport the news of such important advantages. Flattery and hope painted in the most lively colours the fall of Persia, the conquest of Arabia, the submission of Egypt, and a lasting deliverance from the inroads of the Scythian nations. But the reign of Carus was destined to expose the vanity of predictions. They were scarcely uttered before they were contradicted by his death; an event attended with such ambiguous circumstances that it may be related in a letter from his own secretary to the præfect of the city. "Carus," says he, "our dearest emperor, was confined by sickness to his bed, when a furious tempest arose in the camp. The darkness which overspread the sky was so thick that we could no longer distinguish each other; and the incessant flashes of lightning took from us the knowledge of all that passed in the general confusion. Immediately after the most violent clap of thunder we heard a sudden cry that the emperor was dead; and it soon appeared that his chamberlains, in a rage of grief, had set fire to the royal pavilion, a circumstance which gave rise to the report that Carus was killed by lightning. But, as far as we have been able to investigate the truth, his death was the natural effect of his disorder."

The intelligence of the mysterious fate of the late emperor was soon carried from the frontiers of Persia to Rome; and the senate, as well as the provinces, congratulated the accession of the sons of Carus.

But the only merit of the administration of Carinus that history could record, or poetry celebrate, was the uncommon splendour with which, in his own and his brother's name, he exhibited the Roman games of the theatre, the circus, and the amphitheatre. More than twenty years afterwards, when the courtiers of Diocletian represented to their frugal sovereign the fame and popularity of his munificent predecessor, he acknowledged that the reign of Carinus had indeed been a reign of pleasure. But this vain prodigality, which the prudence of Diocletian might justly despise, was enjoyed with surprise and transport by the Roman people. The oldest of the citizens, recollecting the spectacles of former days, the triumphal pomp of Probus or Aurelian, and the secular games of the emperor Philip, acknowledged that they were all surpassed by the superior magnificence of Carinus.

The spectacles of Carinus may therefore be best illustrated by the observation of some particulars which history has condescended to relate concerning those of his predecessors. If we confine ourselves solely to the hunting of wild beasts, however we may censure the vanity of the design or the cruelty of the execution, we are obliged to confess that neither before nor since the time of the Romans so much art and expense have ever been lavished for the amusement of the people. By the order of Probus, a great quantity of large trees, torn up by the roots, were transplanted into the midst of the circus. The spacious and shady forest was immediately filled with a thousand ostriches, a thousand stags, a thousand fallow-deer, and a thousand wild boars; and all this variety of game was abandoned to the riotous impetuosity of the multitude. The tragedy of the succeeding day consisted in the massacre of an hundred lions, an equal number of lionesses, two hundred leopards, and three hundred bears.

The collection prepared by the younger Gordian for his triumph, and which his successor exhibited in the secular games, was less remarkable by the number than by the singularity of the animals. Twenty zebras displayed their elegant forms and variegated beauty to the eyes of the Roman people. Ten elks, and as many camelopards, the loftiest and most harmless creatures that wander over the plain of Sarmatia and Æthiopia, were contrasted with thirty African hyænas and ten Indian tigers, the most implacable savages of the torrid zone. The unoffending strength with which Nature has endowed the greater quadrupeds was admired in the rhinoceros, the hippopotamus of the Nile, and a majestic troop of twenty-two elephants. While the populace gazed with stupid wonder on the splendid show, the naturalist might indeed observe the figure and properties of so many different species, transported from every part of the ancient world into the amphitheatre of Rome. But this accidental benefit which science might derive from folly is surely insufficient to justify such a wanton abuse of the public riches.

The hunting or exhibition of wild beasts was conducted with a magnificence suitable to a people who styled themselves the masters of the world; nor was the edifice appropriated to that entertainment less expensive of Roman greatness. Posterity admires, and will long admire, the awful remains of the amphitheatre of Titus, who so well deserved the epithet of Colossal. It was a building of an elliptic figure, five hundred and sixty-four feet in length, and four hundred and sixty-seven in breadth, founded on fourscore arches, and rising, with four successive orders of architecture, to the height of one hundred and forty feet. The outside of the edifice was encrusted with marble and decorated with statues. The slopes of the vast concave, which formed the inside, were filled and surrounded with sixty or eighty rows of seats, of marble likewise, covered with cushions, and capable of receiving with ease above four-score thousand spectators. Sixty-four doors poured forth the immense multitude; and the entrances, passages, and staircases were contrived with such exquisite skill, that each person, whether of the senatorial, the equestrian, or the plebeian order, arrived at his destined place without trouble or confusion. Nothing was omitted which, in any respect, could be subservient to the convenience and pleasure of the spectators. They were protected from the sun and rain by an ample canopy, occasionally drawn over their heads. The air was continually refreshed by the playing of fountains, and profusely impregnated by the grateful scent of aromatics. In the centre of the edifice, the *arena*, or stage, was strewed with the finest sand, and successively assumed the most different forms. At one moment it seemed to rise out of the earth, like the garden of the Hesperides, and was afterwards broken into the rocks and caverns of Thrace. The subterraneous pipes conveyed an inexhaustible supply of water; and what had just before appeared a level plain might be suddenly converted into a wide lake, covered with armed vessels, and replenished with the monsters of the deep. In the decoration of these scenes the Roman emperors displayed their wealth and liberality; and we read on various occasions that the whole furniture of the amphitheatre consisted either of silver, or of gold, or of amber. The poet who describes the games of Carinus, in the character of a shepherd attracted to the capital by the fame of their magnificence, affirms that the nets designed as a defence against the wild beasts were of gold wire; that the porticoes were gilded; and that the *belt* or circle which divided the several ranks of spectators from each other was studded with a precious mosaic of beautiful stones.

In the midst of this glittering pageantry, the emperor Carinus, secure of his fortune, enjoyed the acclamations of the people, the flattery of his courtiers, and the songs of the poets who, for want of a more essential merit, were reduced to celebrate the divine graces of his person. In the same hour, but at the distance of nine hundred miles from Rome, his brother expired; and a sudden revolution transferred into the hands of a stranger the sceptre of the house of Carus.

CHAPTER IX

The Reign of Diocletian—General Re-establishment of Order and Tranquillity—The New Form of Administration

As the reign of diocletian was more illustrious than that of any of his predecessors, so was his birth more abject and obscure. The strong claims of merit and of violence had frequently superseded the ideal prerogatives of nobility; but a distinct line of separation was hitherto preserved between the free and the servile part of mankind. The parents of Diocletian had been slaves in the house of Anulinus, a Roman senator; nor was he himself distinguished by any other name than that which he derived from a small town in Dalmatia, from whence his mother deduced her origin. It is, however, probable that his father obtained the freedom of the family, and that he soon acquired an office of scribe, which was commonly exercised by persons of his condition.

Diocletian gave himself a colleague in the person of Maximian, on whom he bestowed at first the title of Cæsar, and afterwards that of Augustus. By associating a friend and a fellow-soldier to the favours of government, he provided for the defence both of the East and of the West.

Maximian was born a peasant and, like Aurelian, in the territory of Sirmium. Ignorant of letters, careless of laws, the rusticity of his appearance and manners still betrayed in the most elevated fortune the meanness of his extraction. War was the only art which he professed. In a long course of service he had distinguished himself on every frontier of the empire; and though his military talents were formed to obey rather than to command, though perhaps he never attained the skill of a consummate general, he was capable, by his valour, constancy, and experience, of executing the most arduous undertakings. Nor were the vices of Maximian less useful to his benefactor.

The first exploit of Maximian, though it is mentioned in a few words by our imperfect writers, deserves, from its singularity, to be recorded in a history of human manners. He suppressed the peasants of Gaul, who, under the appellation of Bagaudæ, had risen in a general insurrection; very similar to those which in the fourteenth century successively afflicted both France and England. It should seem that very many of those institutions, referred by an easy solution to the feudal system, are derived from the Celtic barbarians. When Cæsar subdued the Gauls, that great nation was already divided into three orders of men; the clergy, the nobility, and the common people. The first governed by superstition, the second by arms, but the third and last was not of any weight or account in their public councils. It was very natural for the plebeians, oppressed by debt or apprehensive of injuries, to implore the protection of some powerful chief, who acquired over their persons and property the same absolute rights as, among the Greeks and Romans, a master exercised over his slaves. The greatest part of the nation was gradually reduced in a state of servitude, compelled to perpetual labour on the estates of the Gallic nobles, and confined to the soil, either by the real weight of fetters, or by the no less cruel and forcible restraints of the laws. During the long series of troubles which agitated Gaul, from the reign of Gallienus to that of Diocletian, the condition of those servile peasants was peculiarly miserable; and they experienced at once the complicated tyranny of their masters, of the barbarians, of the soldiers, and of the officers of the revenue.

Their patience was at last provoked into despair. On every side they rose in multitudes, armed with rustic weapons, and with irresistible fury. The ploughman became a foot soldier, the shepherd mounted on horseback, the deserted villages and open towns were abandoned to the flames, and the ravages of the peasants equalled those of the fiercest barbarians. They asserted the natural rights of men, but they asserted those rights with the most savage cruelty. The Gallic nobles, justly dreading their revenge, either took refuge in the fortified cities, or fled from the wild scene of anarchy. The peasants reigned without control; and two of their most daring leaders had the folly and rashness to assume the Imperial ornaments. Their power soon expired at the approach of the legions. The strength of union and discipline obtained an easy victory over a licentious and divided multitude. A severe retaliation was inflicted on the peasants who were found in arms: the affrighted remnant returned to their respective habitations, and their unsuccessful effort for freedom served only to confirm their slavery. So strong and uniform is the current of popular passions, that we might almost venture, from very scanty materials, to relate the particulars of this war; but we are not disposed to believe that the principal leaders, Ælianus and Amandus, were Christians, or to insinuate that the rebellion in the time of Luther was occasioned by the abuse of those benevolent principles of Christianity which inculcate the natural freedom of mankind.

Maximian had no sooner recovered Gaul from the hands of the peasants, than he lost Britain by the usurpation of Carausius. Ever since the rash but successful enterprise of the Franks under the reign of Probus, their daring countrymen had constructed squadrons of light brigantines, in which they incessantly ravaged the provinces adjacent to the ocean. To repel their desultory incursions, it was found necessary to create a naval power; and the judicious measure was prosecuted with prudence and vigour. Gessoriacum, or Boulogne, in the straits of the British Channel, was chosen by the emperor for the station of the Roman fleet; and the command of it was entrusted to Carausius, a Menapian of the meanest origin, but who had long signalised his skill as a pilot and his valour as a soldier. The integrity of the new admiral corresponded not with his abilities. When the German pirates sailed from their own harbours he connived at their passage, but he diligently intercepted their return, and appropriated to his own use an ample share of the spoil which they had acquired. The wealth of Carausius was, on this occasion, very justly considered as an evidence of his guilt; and Maximian had already given orders for his death. But the crafty Menapian foresaw and prevented the severity of the emperor. By his liberality he had attached to his fortunes the fleet which he commanded, and secured the barbarians in his interest. From the port of Boulogne he sailed over to Britain, persuaded the legions and the auxiliaries which guarded that island to embrace his party, and boldly assuming, with the Imperial purple, the title of Augustus, defied the justice and the arms of his injured sovereign.

When Britain was thus dismembered from the empire its importance was sensibly felt and its loss sincerely lamented. The Romans celebrated, and perhaps magnified, the extent of that noble island, provided on every side with convenient harbours; the temperature of the climate, and the fertility of the soil, alike adapted for the production of corn or of vines; the valuable minerals with which it abounded; its rich pastures covered with innumerable flocks, and its woods free from wild beasts or venomous serpents. Above all, they regretted the large amount of the revenue of Britain, whilst they confessed that such a province well deserved to become the seat of an independent monarchy.

During the space of seven years it was possessed by Carausius; and fortune continued propitious to a rebellion supported with courage and ability. The British emperor defended the frontiers of his dominions against the Caledonians of the North, invited from the continent a great number of skilful artists, and displayed, on a variety of coins that are still extant, his taste and opulence. Born on the confines of the Franks, he courted the friendship of that formidable people by the flattering imitation of their dress and manners. The bravest of their youths he enlisted among his land or sea forces; and, in return for their useful alliance, he communicated to the barbarians the dangerous knowledge of military and naval arts. Carausius still preserved the possession of Boulogne and the adjacent country. His fleets rode triumphant in the channel, commanded the mouths of the Seine and of the Rhine, ravaged the coasts of the ocean, and diffused beyond the Columns of Hercules the terror of his name. Under his command, Britain, destined in a future age to obtain the empire of the sea, already assumed its natural and respectable station of a maritime power.

By seizing the fleet of Boulogne, Carausius had deprived his master of the means of pursuit and revenge. And when, after a vast expense of time and labour, a new armament was launched into the water, the Imperial troops, unaccustomed to that element, were easily baffled and defeated by the veteran sailors of the usurper. This disappointed effort was soon productive of a treaty of peace. Diocletian and his colleague, who justly dreaded the enterprising spirit of Carausius, resigned to him the sovereignty of

Britain, and reluctantly admitted their perfidious servant to a participation of the Imperial honours. But a revolution, after a separation of ten years, restored Britain to the body of the Roman empire.

Britain had none but domestic enemies to dread; and as long as the governors preserved their fidelity, and the troops their discipline, the incursions of the naked savages of Scotland or Ireland could never materially affect the safety of the province. The peace of the continent, and the defence of the principal rivers which bounded the empire, were objects of far greater difficulty and importance. The policy of Diocletian, which inspired the councils of his associates, provided for the public tranquillity by encouraging a spirit of dissension among the barbarians, and by strengthening the fortifications of the Roman limit. In the East he fixed a line of camps from Egypt to the Persian dominions, and for every camp he instituted an adequate number of stationary troops, commanded by their respective officers, and supplied with every kind of arms from the new arsenals which he had formed at Antioch, Emesa, and Damascus.

Nor was the precaution of the emperor less watchful against the well-known valour of the barbarians of Europe. From the mouth of the Rhine to that of the Danube, the ancient camps, towns, and citadel were diligently re-established, and, in the most exposed places, new ones were skilfully constructed; the strictest vigilance was introduced among the garrisons of the frontier, and every expedient was practised that could render the long chain of fortifications firm and impenetrable. A barrier so respectable was seldom violated, and the barbarians often turned against each other their disappointed rage. The Goths, the Vandals, the Gepidæ, the Burgundians, the Alemanni, wasted each other's strength by destructive hostilities: and whosoever vanquished, they vanquished the enemies of Rome.

The conduct which the emperor Probus had adopted in the disposal of the vanquished was imitated by Diocletian and his associates. The captive barbarians, exchanging death for slavery, were distributed among the provincials, and assigned to those districts (in Gaul, the territories of Amiens, Beauvais, Cambray, Treves, Langres, and Troyes, are particularly specified) which had been depopulated by the calamities of war. They were usefully employed as shepherds and husbandmen, but were denied the exercise of arms, except when it was found expedient to enrol them in the military service. Nor did the emperors refuse the property of lands, with a less servile tenure, to such of the barbarians as solicited the protection of Rome.

Among the provincials it was a subject of flattering exultation that the barbarian, so lately an object of terror, now cultivated their lands, drove their cattle to the neighbouring fair, and contributed by his labour to the public plenty. They congratulated their masters on the powerful accession of subjects and soldiers; but they forgot to observe that multitudes of secret enemies, insolent from favour, or desperate from oppression, were introduced into the heart of the empire.

The arduous work of rescuing the distressed empire from tyrants and barbarians had now been completely achieved by a succession of Illyrian peasants. As soon as Diocletian entered into the twentieth year of his reign, he celebrated that memorable era, as well as the success of his arms, by the pomp of a Roman triumph. Maximian, the equal partner of his power, was his only companion in the glory of that day. The two Cæsars had fought and conquered, but the merit of their exploits was ascribed, according to the rigour of ancient maxims, to the auspicious influence ot their fathers and emperors. The triumph of Diocletian and Maximian was less magnificent, perhaps, than those of Aurelian and Probus, but it was dignified by several circumstances of superior fame and good fortune. Africa and Britain, the Rhine, the Danube, and the Nile, furnished their respective trophies; but the most distinguished ornament was of a more singular nature, a Persian victory followed by an important conquest. The representations of rivers, mountains, and provinces were carried before the Imperial car. The images of the captive wives, the sisters, and the children of the Great King afforded a new and grateful spectacle to the vanity of the people.

In the eyes of posterity this triumph is remarkable by a distinction of a less honourable kind. It was the last that Rome ever beheld. Soon after this period the emperors ceased to vanquish, and Rome ceased to be the capital of the empire.

The spot on which Rome was founded had been consecrated by ancient ceremonies and imaginary miracles. The presence of some god, or the memory of some hero, seemed to animate every part of the city, and the empire of the world had been promised to the Capitol. The native Romans felt and confessed the power of this agreeable illusion. It was derived from their ancestors, had grown up with their earliest habits of life, and was protected, in some measure, by the opinion of political utility. The form and the seat of government were intimately blended together, nor was it esteemed possible to transport the one without destroying the other. But the sovereignty of the capital was gradually annihilated in the extent of conquest; the provinces rose to the same level, and the vanquished nations acquired the name and privileges, without imbibing the partial affections, of Romans.

During a long period, however, the remains of the ancient constitution and the influence of custom preserved the dignity of Rome. The emperors, though perhaps of African or Illyrian extraction, respected their adopted country as the seat of their power and the centre of their extensive dominions. The emergencies of war very frequently required their presence on the frontiers; but Diocletian and Maximian were the first Roman princes who fixed, in time of peace, their ordinary residence in the provinces.

The court of the emperor of the West was, for the most part, established at Milan, whose situation at the foot of the Alps appeared far more convenient than that of Rome for the important purpose of watching the motions of the barbarians of Germany. Milan soon assumed the splendour of an Imperial city. The houses are described as numerous and well built;

the manners of the people as polished and liberal. A circus, a theatre, a mint, a palace, baths, which bore the name of their founder Maximian; porticoes adorned with statues, and a double circumference of walls, contributed to the beauty of the new capital; nor did it seem oppressed even by the proximity of Rome. Till Diocletian, in the twentieth year of his reign, celebrated his Roman triumph, it is extremely doubtful whether he ever visited the ancient capital of the empire. Even on that memorable occasion his stay did not exceed two months. Disgusted with the licentious familiarity of the people, he quitted Rome with precipitation thirteen days before it was expected that he should have appeared in the senate invested with the ensigns of the consular dignity.

The dislike expressed by Diocletian towards Rome and Roman freedom was not the effect of momentary caprice, but the result of the most artful policy. The crafty prince had framed a new system of Imperial government, which was afterwards completed by the family of Constantine; and as the image of the old constitution was religiously preserved in the senate, he resolved to deprive that order of its small remains of power and consideration.

The camp of the Prætorians, which had so long oppressed, began to protect the majesty of Rome; and as those haughty troops were conscious of the decline of their power, they were naturally disposed to unite their strength with the authority of the senate. By the prudent measures of Diocletian, the numbers of the Prætorians were insensibly reduced, their privileges abolished, and their place supplied by two faithful legions of Illyricum, who, under the new titles of Jovians and Herculians, were appointed to perform the service of the Imperial guards. But the most fatal though secret wound which the senate received from the hands of Diocletian and Maximian was inflicted by the inevitable operation of their absence. As long as the emperors resided at Rome, that assembly might be oppressed, but it could scarcely be neglected. The successors of Augustus exercised the power of dictating whatever laws their wisdom or caprice might suggest; but those laws were ratified by the sanction of the senate. The model of ancient freedom was preserved in its deliberations and decrees; and wise princes, who respected the prejudices of the Roman people, were in some measure obliged to assume the language and behaviour suitable to the general and first magistrate of the republic. In the armies and in the provinces they displayed the dignity of monarchs; and when they fixed their residence at a distance from the capital, they for ever laid aside the dissimulation which Augustus had recommended to his successors. In the exercise of the legislative as well as the executive power, the sovereign advised with his ministers, instead of consulting the great council of the nation. The name of the senate was mentioned with honour till the last period of the empire; the vanity of its members was still flattered with honorary distinctions; but the assembly which had so long been the source, and so long the instrument of power, was respectfully suffered to sink into oblivion. The senate of Rome, losing all connection with the Imperial court and the actual constitution, was left a venerable but useless monument of antiquity on the Capitoline hill.

When the Roman princes had lost sight of the senate and of their ancient capital, they easily forgot the origin and nature of their legal power. The civil offices of consul, of proconsul, of censor, and of tribune, by the union of which it had been formed, betrayed to the people its republican extraction. Those modest titles were laid aside; and if they still distinguished their high station by the appellation of Emperor, or IMPERATOR, that word was understood in a new and more dignified sense, and no longer denoted the general of the Roman armies, but the sovereign of the Roman world.

The name of Emperor, which was at first of a military nature, was associated with another of a more servile kind. The epithet of DOMINUS, or Lord, in its primitive signification, was expressive not of the authority of a prince over his subjects, or of a commander over his soldiers, but of the despotic power of a master over his domestic slaves. Viewing it in that odious light, it had been rejected with abhorrence by the first Cæsars. But the sentiments of the East were very different from those of the West. From the earliest period of history, the sovereigns of Asia had been celebrated in the Greek language by the title of BASILEUS, or King; and since it was considered as the first distinction among men, it was soon employed by the servile provincials of the East in their humble addresses to the Roman throne. At length the style of *our Lord and Emperor* was not only bestowed by flattery, but was regularly admitted into the laws and public monuments.

From the time of Augustus to that of Diocletian, the Roman princes, conversing in a familiar manner among their fellow-citizens, were saluted only with the same respect that was usually paid to senators and magistrates. Their principal distinction was the Imperial or military robe of purple; whilst the senatorial garment was marked by a broad, and the equestrian by a narrow, band or stripe of the same honourable colour. The pride, or rather the policy, of Diocletian, engaged that artful prince to introduce the stately magnificence of the court of Persia. He ventured to assume the diadem, an ornament detested by the Romans as the odious ensign of royalty, and the use of which had been considered as the most desperate act of the madness of Caligula. It was no more than a broad white fillet set with pearls, which encircled the emperor's head. The sumptuous robes of Diocletian and his successors were of silk and gold; and it is remarked with indignation that even their shoes were studded with the most precious gems. The access to their sacred person was every day rendered more difficult by the institution of new forms and ceremonies. The avenues of the palace were strictly guarded by the various *schools*, as they began to be called, of domestic officers. The interior apartments were entrusted to the jealous vigilance of the eunuchs, the increase of whose numbers and influence was the most infallible symptom of the progress of despotism. When a subject was at length admitted to the Imperial presence, he was obliged, whatever might be his rank, to fall prostrate on the ground, and to adore, according to the Eastern fashion, the divinity of his lord and master.

Diocletian was a man of sense, who, in the course of private as well as public life, had formed a just estimate both of himself and of mankind: nor is it easy to conceive that in substituting the manners of Persia to those of Rome he was seriously actuated by so mean a principle as that of vanity. He flattered himself that an ostentation of splendour and luxury would subdue the imagination of the multitude; that the monarch would be less exposed to the rude licence of the people and the soldiers, as his person was secluded from the public view; and that habits of submission would insensibly be productive of sentiments of veneration. Like the modesty affected by Augustus, the state maintained by Diocletian was a theatrical representation; but it must be confessed that, of the two comedies, the former was of a much more liberal and manly character than the latter. It was the aim of the one to disguise, and the object of the other to display, the unbounded power which the emperors possessed over the Roman world.

Ostentation was the first principle of the new system instituted by Diocletian. The second was division. The empire was divided into four parts. The East and Italy were the most honourable, the Danube and the Rhine the most laborious stations. The former claimed the presence of the *Augusti*, the latter were entrusted to the administration of two Cæsars. The strength of the legions was in the hands of the four partners of sovereignty, and the despair of successively vanquishing four formidable rivals might intimidate the ambition of an aspiring general. In their civil government the emperors were supposed to exercise the undivided power of the monarch, and their edicts, inscribed with their joint names, were received in all the provinces as promulgated by their mutual councils and authority. Notwithstanding these precautions, the political union of the Roman world was gradually dissolved, and a principle of division was introduced, which, in the course of a few years, occasioned the perpetual separation of the Eastern and Western empires.

The system of Diocletian was accompanied with another very material disadvantage, which cannot even at present be totally overlooked: a more expensive establishment, and consequently an increase of taxes and the oppression of the people. Instead of a modest family of slaves and freedmen, such as had contented the simple greatness of Augustus and Trajan, three or four magnificent courts were established in the various parts of the empire, and as many Roman *kings* contended with each other and with the Persian monarch for the vain superiority of pomp and luxury. The number of ministers, of magistrates, of officers, and of servants who filled the different departments of the state was multiplied beyond the example of former times; and (if we may borrow the warm expression of a contemporary), "when the proportion of those who received exceeded the proportion of those who contributed, the provinces were oppressed by the weight of tributes."

From this period to the extinction of the empire, it would be easy to deduce an uninterrupted series of clamours and complaints. According to his religion and situation, each writer chooses either Diocletian, or Constantine, or Valens, or Theodosius, for the object of his invectives; but they unanimously agree in representing the burden of the public impositions, and particularly the land-tax and capitation, as the intolerable and increasing grievance of their own times. From such a concurrence, an impartial historian, who is obliged to extract truth from satire, as well as from panegyric, will be inclined to divide the blame among the princes whom they accuse, and to ascribe their exactions much less to their personal vices than to the uniform system of their administration. The emperor Diocletian was indeed the author of that system; but during his reign the growing evil was confined within the bounds of modesty and discretion, and he deserves the reproach of establishing pernicious precedents, rather than of exercising actual oppression. It may be added, that his revenues were managed with prudent economy.[1]

It was in the twenty-first year of his reign that Diocletian executed his memorable resolution of abdicating the empire; an action more naturally to have been expected from the elder or the younger Antoninus than from a prince who had never practised the lessons of philosophy either in the attainment or in the use of supreme power. Diocletian acquired the glory of giving to the world the first example of a resignation, which has not been very frequently imitated by succeeding monarchs.

The amusements of letters and of devotion, which afford so many resources in solitude, were incapable of fixing the attention of Diocletian; but he had preserved, or at least he soon recovered, a taste for the most innocent as well as natural pleasures, and his leisure hours were sufficiently employed in building, planting, and gardening. His answer to Maximian is deservedly celebrated. He was solicited by that restless old man to reassume the reins of government and the Imperial purple. He rejected the temptation with a smile of pity, calmly observing that, if he could show Maximian the cabbages which he had planted with his own hands at Salona, he should no longer be urged to relinquish the enjoyment of happiness for the pursuit of power.

Before we dismiss the consideration of the life and character of Diocletian, we may for a moment direct our view to the place of his retirement. Salona, a principal city of his native province of Dalmatia, was near two hundred Roman miles (according to the measurement of the public highways) from Aquileia and the confines of Italy, and about two hundred

[1]An edict of Diocletian, according to Milman, fixed a maximum of prices throughout the empire for all the necessaries and commodities of life. The preamble insists with great vehemence on the extortion and inhumanity of the merchants and vendors. Among the articles of which the maximum value is assessed are oil, salt, honey, butchers' meat, poultry, game, fish, vegetables, fruit, the wages of labourers and artisans, schoolmasters and orators, clothes, skins, boots and shoes, harness, timber, corn, wine, and beer.

and seventy from Sirmium, the usual residence of the emperors whenever they visited the Illyrian frontier. About six or seven miles from the city Diocletian constructed a magnificent palace.[2] It covered an extent of ground consisting of between nine and ten English acres. The form was quadrangular, flanked with sixteen towers. Two of the sides were near six hundred, and the other two near seven hundred, feet in length. The whole was constructed of a beautiful free-stone, extracted from the neighbouring quarries of Trau, or Tragutium, and very little inferior to marble itself. Four streets, intersecting each other at right angles, divided the several parts of this great edifice, and the approach to the principal apartment was from a very stately entrance, which is still denominated the Golden Gate. The several parts of the building, the baths, bedchamber, the *atrium*, the *basilica*, and the Cyzicene, Corinthian, and Egyptian halls have been described with some degree of precision, or at least of probability. Their forms were various, their proportions just, but they were all attended with two imperfections, very repugnant to our modern notions of taste and conveniency. These stately rooms had neither windows nor chimneys. They were lighted from the top (for the building seems to have consisted of no more than one story), and they received their heat by the help of pipes that were conveyed along the walls. The range of principal apartments was protected towards the south-west by a portico five hundred and seventeen feet long, which must have formed a very noble and delightful walk, when the beauties of painting and sculpture were added to those of the prospect. During the summer months, this country seldom feels those sultry and noxious winds to which the coasts of Istria and some parts of Italy are exposed. The views from the palace are no less beautiful than the soil and climate were inviting. Towards the west lies the fertile shore that stretches along the Adriatic, in which a number of small islands are scattered in such a manner as to give this part of the sea the appearance of a great lake. On the north side lies the bay, which led to the ancient city of Salona; and the country beyond it, appearing in sight, forms a proper contrast to that more extensive prospect of water which the Adriatic presents both to the south and to the east. Towards the north the view is terminated by high and irregular mountains, situated at a proper distance, and in many places covered with villages, woods, and vineyards.

Had this magnificent edifice remained in a solitary country, it would have been exposed to the ravages of time, but it might, perhaps, have escaped the rapacious industry of man. The village of Aspalathus, and, long afterwards, the provincial town of Spalato, have grown out of its ruins. The Golden Gate now opens into the market-place.

[2]We may add a circumstance: the little stream of the Hyader, mentioned by Lucian, produces most exquisite trout, which a sagacious writer, perhaps a monk, supposes to have been one of the principal reasons that determined Diocletian in the choice of his retirement.

CHAPTER X

The Progress of the Christian Religion

A candid but rational inquiry into the progress and establishment of Christianity may be considered as a very essential part of the history of the Roman empire. While that great body was invaded by open violence, or undermined by slow decay, a pure and humble religion gently insinuated itself into the minds of men, grew up in silence and obscurity, derived new vigour from opposition, and finally erected the triumphant banner of the Cross on the ruins of the Capitol. Nor was the influence of Christianity confined to the period or to the limits of the Roman empire. After a revolution of thirteen or fourteen centuries, that religion is still professed by the nations of Europe, the most distinguished portion of human kind in arts and learning as well as in arms. By the industry and zeal of the Europeans it has been widely diffused to the most distant shores of Asia and Africa; and by the means of their colonies has been firmly established from Canada to Chile, in a world unknown to the ancients.

But this inquiry, however useful or entertaining, is attended with two peculiar difficulties. The scanty and suspicious materials of ecclesiastical history seldom enable us to dispel the dark cloud that hangs over the first age of the church. The great law of impartiality too often obliges us to reveal the imperfections of the uninspired teachers and believers of the Gospel; and, to a careless observer, *their* faults may seem to cast a shade on the faith which they professed. But the scandal of the pious Christian, and the fallacious triumph of the Infidel, should cease as soon as they recollect not only *by whom*, but likewise *to whom*, the Divine Revelation was given. The theologian may indulge the pleasing task of describing Religion as she descended from Heaven, arrayed in her native purity. A more melancholy duty is imposed on the historian. He must discover the inevitable mixture of error and corruption which she contracted in a long residence upon earth, among a weak and degenerate race of beings.

Our curiosity is naturally prompted to inquire by what means the Christian faith obtained so remarkable a victory over the established religions of the earth. To this inquiry an obvious but satisfactory answer may be returned: that it was owing to the convincing evidence of the doctrine itself, and to the ruling providence of its great Author. But as truth and reason seldom find so favourable a reception in the world, and as the wisdom of Providence frequently condescends to use the passions of the human heart, and the general circumstances of mankind, as instruments to execute its purpose, we may still be permitted, though with becoming submission, to ask, not indeed what were the first, but what were the secondary causes of the rapid growth of the Christian church? It will, perhaps, appear that it was most effectually favoured and assisted by the five following causes:—I. The inflexible, and, if we may use the expression, the intolerant zeal of the Christians, derived, it is true, from the Jewish religion, but purified from the narrow and unsocial spirit which, instead of inviting, had deterred the Gentiles from embracing the law of Moses. II. The doctrine of a future life, improved by every additional circumstance which could give weight and efficacy to that important truth. III. The miraculous powers ascribed to the primitive church. IV. The pure and austere morals of the Christians. V. The union and discipline of the Christian republic, which gradually formed an independent and increasing state in the heart of the Roman empire.

I. We have already described the religious harmony of the ancient world, and the facility with which the most different and even hostile nations embraced, or at least respected, each other's superstitions. A single people refused to join in the common intercourse of mankind. The Jews, who had languished for many ages the most despised slaves under the Assyrian and Persian monarchies, emerged from obscurity under the successors of Alexander; and as they multiplied to a surprising degree in the East, and afterwards in the West, they soon excited the curiosity and wonder of other nations.

The polite Augustus condescended to give orders that sacrifices should be offered for his prosperity in the temple of Jerusalem; while the meanest of the posterity of Abraham, who should have paid the same homage to the Jupiter of the Capitol, would have been an object of abhorrence to himself and to his brethren. The mad attempt of Caligula to place his own statue in the temple of Jerusalem was defeated by the unanimous resolution of a people who dreaded death much less than such an idolatrous profanation. Their attachment to the law of Moses was equal to their detestation of foreign religions. The current of zeal and devotion, as it was contracted into a narrow channel, ran with the strength, and sometimes with the fury, of a torrent.

The Jewish religion was admirably fitted for defence, but it was never designed for conquest; and it seems probable that the number of proselytes was never much superior to that of apostates. The divine promises were originally made, and the distinguishing rite of circumcision was enjoined, to a single family. When the posterity of Abraham had multiplied like the sands of the sea, the Deity, from whose mouth they received a system of laws and ceremonies, declared himself the proper and as it were the national God of Israel; and with the most jealous care separated his favourite people from the rest of mankind. The obligation of preaching to the Gentiles the faith of Moses had never been inculcated as a precept of the law, nor were the Jews inclined to impose it on themselves as a voluntary duty. The descendants of Abraham were flattered by the opinion that they alone were the heirs of the covenant, and they were apprehensive of diminishing the value of their inheritance by sharing it too easily with the strangers of the earth. A larger acquaintance with mankind extended their knowledge without correcting their prejudices; and whenever the God of Israel acquired any new votaries, he was much more indebted to the inconstant humour of polytheism than to the active zeal of his own missionaries. The religion of Moses seems to be instituted for a particular country as well as for a single nation; and if a strict obedience had been paid to the order that every male, three times in the year, should present himself before the Lord Jehovah, it would have been impossible that the Jews could ever have spread themselves beyond the narrow limits of the promised land. That obstacle was indeed removed by the destruction of the temple of Jerusalem; but even in their fallen state, the Jews, still asserting their lofty and exclusive privileges, shunned, instead of courting, the society of strangers. They still insisted with inflexible rigour on those parts of the law which it was in their power to practise. Their peculiar distinctions of days, of meats, and a variety of trivial though burdensome observances, were so many objects of disgust and aversion for the other nations, to whose habits and prejudices they were diametrically opposite. The painful and even dangerous rite of circumcision was alone capable of repelling a willing proselyte from the door of the synagogue.

Under these circumstances, Christianity offered itself to the world, armed with the strength of the Mosaic law, and delivered from the weight of its fetters. An exclusive zeal for the truth of religion and the unity of God was as carefully inculcated in the new as in the ancient system: and whatever was now revealed to mankind concerning the nature and designs of the Supreme Being was fitted to increase their reverence for that mysterious doctrine. The divine authority of Moses and the prophets was admitted, and even established, as the firmest basis of Christianity. The ceremonial law, which consisted only of types and figures, was succeeded by a pure and spiritual worship, equally adapted to all climates, as well as to every condition of mankind; and to the initiation of blood was substituted a more harmless initiation of water. The promise of divine favour, instead of being partially confined to the posterity of Abraham, was universally proposed to the freeman and the slave, to the Greek and to the barbarian, to the Jew and to the Gentile. It became the most sacred duty of a new convert to diffuse among his friends and relations the inestimable blessing which he had received.

The enfranchisement of the church from the bonds of the synagogue was a work, however, of some time and of some difficulty. The Jewish converts, who acknowledged Jesus in the character of the Messiah foretold by their ancient oracles, respected him as a prophetic teacher of virtue and religion; but they obstinately adhered to the ceremonies of their ancestors, and were desirous of imposing them on the Gentiles, who continually augmented the number of believers. These Judaising Christians seem to have argued with some degree of plausibility from the Divine origin of the Mosaic law, and from the immutable perfections of its great Author. They affirmed, *that*, if the Being who is the same through all eternity had designed to abolish those sacred rites which had served to distinguish his chosen people, the repeal of them would have been no less clear and solemn than their first promulgation: *that*, instead of those frequent declarations which either suppose or assert the perpetuity of the Mosaic religion, it would have been represented as a provisionary scheme intended to last only till the coming of the Messiah, who should instruct mankind in a more perfect mode of faith and of worship: *that* the Messiah himself, and his disciples who conversed with him on earth, instead of authorising by their example the most minute observances of the Mosaic law, would have published to the world the abolition of those useless and obsolete ceremonies, without suffering Christianity to remain during so many years obscurely confounded among the sects of the Jewish church.

The first fifteen bishops of Jerusalem were all circumcised Jews; and the congregation over which they presided united the law of Moses with the doctrine of Christ. It was natural that the primitive tradition of a church which was founded only forty days after the death of Christ, and was governed almost as many years under the immediate inspection of his apostle, should be received as the standard of orthodoxy. The distant churches very frequently appealed to the authority of their venerable Parent, and relieved her distresses by a liberal contribution of alms.

But when numerous and opulent societies were established in the great cities of the empire, in Antioch, Alexandria, Ephesus, Corinth, and Rome, the reverence which Jerusalem had inspired to all the Christian colonies insensibly diminished. The Jewish converts, or, as they were afterwards called, the Nazarenes, who had laid the foundations of the church, soon found themselves overwhelmed by the increasing multitudes that from all the various religions of polytheism enlisted under the banner of Christ. The Gentiles who, with the approbation of their peculiar apostle, had rejected the intolerable weight of Mosaic ceremonies, at length refused to their more scrupulous brethren the same toleration which at first they had humbly solicited for their own practice. The ruin of the temple, of the city, and of the public religion of the Jews was severely felt by the Nazarenes, as in their manners, though not in their faith, they maintained so intimate a connection with their impious countrymen.

The Nazarenes still enjoyed the comfort of making frequent and devout visits to the *Holy City*, and the hope of being one day restored to those seats which both nature and religion taught them to love as well as to revere. But at length, under the reign of Hadrian, the Romans exercised the rights of victory with unusual rigour. The emperor founded, under the name of Ælia Capitolina, a new city on Mount Sion to which he gave the privileges of a colony; and denouncing the severest penalties against any of the Jewish people who should dare to approach its precincts, he fixed a vigilant garrison of a Roman cohort to enforce the execution of his orders.

The Nazarenes had only one way left to escape the common proscription. They elected Marcus for their bishop, a prelate of the race of the Gentiles, and most probably a native either of Italy or of some of the Latin provinces. At his persuasion the most considerable part of the congregation renounced the Mosaic law, in the practice of which they had persevered above a century. By this sacrifice of their habits and prejudices they purchased a free admission into the colony of Hadrian, and more firmly cemented their union with the Catholic church.

When the name and honours of the church of Jerusalem had been restored to Mount Sion, the crimes of heresy and schism were imputed to the obscure remnant of the Nazarenes which refused to accompany their Latin bishop. They spread themselves into the villages adjacent to Damascus, and formed an inconsiderable church in the city of Berœa, or, as it is now called, of Aleppo, in Syria. The name of Nazarenes was deemed too honourable for those Christian Jews, and they soon received, from the supposed poverty of their understanding, as well as of their condition, the contemptuous epithet of Ebionites. In a few years after the return of the church of Jerusalem, it became a matter of doubt and controversy whether a man who sincerely acknowledged Jesus as the Messiah, but who still continued to observe the law of Moses, could possibly hope for salvation. There were very many among the orthodox Christians who not only excluded their Judaising brethren from the hope of salvation, but who declined any intercourse with them in the common offices of friendship, hospitality, and social life. The more rigorous opinion prevailed, as it was natural to expect, over the milder; and an eternal bar of separation was fixed between the disciples of Moses and those of Christ. The unfortunate Ebionites, rejected from one religion as apostates, and from the other as heretics, found themselves compelled to assume a more decided character; and although some traces of that obsolete sect may be discovered as late as the fourth century, they insensibly melted away either into the church or the synagogue.[1]

It has been remarked with more ingenuity than truth that the virgin purity of the church was never violated by schism or heresy before the reign of Trajan or Hadrian, about one hundred years after the death of Christ. We may observe with much more propriety that, during that period, the disciples of the Messiah were indulged in a freer latitude both of faith and practice than has ever been allowed in succeeding ages. As the terms of communion were insensibly narrowed, and the spiritual authority of the prevailing party was exercised with increasing severity, many of its most respectable adherents, who were called upon to renounce, were provoked to assert their private opinions, to pursue the consequences of their

[1]Of all the systems of Christianity, that of Abyssinia is the only one which still adheres to the Mosaic rites (Geddes's Church History of Æthiopia).

mistaken principles, and openly to erect the standard of rebellion against the unity of the church.

But whatever difference of opinion might subsist between the Orthodox, the Ebionites, and the Gnostics, concerning the divinity or the obligation of the Mosaic law, they were all equally animated by the same exclusive zeal, and by the same abhorrence for idolatry, which had distinguished the Jews from the other nations of the ancient world. The philosopher, who considered the system of polytheism as a composition of human fraud and error, could disguise a smile of contempt under the mask of devotion, without apprehending that either the mockery or the compliance would expose him to the resentment of any invisible, or, as he conceived them, imaginary powers. But the established religions of Paganism were seen by the primitive Christian in a much more odious and formidable light. The most trifling mark of respect to the national worship he considered an act of rebellion against the majesty of God. It was the first but arduous duty of a Christian to preserve himself pure and undefiled by the practice of idolatry.

The religion of the nations was not merely a speculative doctrine professed in the schools or preached in the temples. The innumerable deities and rites of polytheism were closely interwoven with every circumstance of business or pleasure, of public or of private life; and it seemed impossible to escape the observance of them, without, at the same time, renouncing the commerce of mankind, and all the offices and amusements of society. The important transactions of peace and war were prepared or concluded by solemn sacrifices, in which the magistrate, the senator, and the soldier were obliged to preside or to participate. The public spectacles were an essential part of the cheerful devotion of the Pagans, and the gods were supposed to accept, as the most grateful offering, the games that the prince and people celebrated in honour of their peculiar festivals. The Christian who with pious horror avoided the abomination of the circus or the theatre found himself encompassed with infernal snares in every convivial entertainment, as often as his friends, invoking the hospitable deities, poured out libations to each other's happiness. When the bride, struggling with well-affected reluctance, was forced in hymenæal pomp over the threshold of her new habitation, or when the sad procession of the dead slowly moved towards the funeral pile, the Christian was compelled to desert the persons who were the dearest to him, rather than contract the guilt inherent to those impious ceremonies. Every art and every trade that was in the least concerned in the framing or adorning of idols was polluted by the stain of idolatry; a severe sentence, since it devoted to eternal misery the far greater part of the community which is employed in the exercise of liberal or mechanic professions.

If we cast our eyes over the numerous remains of antiquity, we shall perceive that, besides the immediate representations of the gods and the holy instruments of their worship, the elegant forms and agreeable fictions consecrated by the imagination of the Greeks were introduced as the richest ornaments of the houses, the dress, and the furniture of the Pagans. Even the arts of music and painting, of eloquence and poetry, flowed from the same impure origin. The common language of Greece and Rome abounded with familiar but impious expressions, which the imprudent Christian might too carelessly utter, or too patiently hear.[2]

The dangerous temptations which on every side lurked in ambush to surprise the unguarded believer assailed him with redoubled violence on the days of solemn festivals. So artfully were they framed and disposed throughout the year, that superstition always wore the appearance of pleasure, and often of virtue. Some of the most sacred festivals in the Roman ritual were destined to salute the new calends of January with vows of public and private felicity; to indulge the pious remembrance of the dead and living; to ascertain the inviolable bounds of property; to hail, on the return of spring, the genial powers of fecundity; to perpetuate the two memorable eras of Rome, the foundation of the city, and that of the republic; and to restore, during the humane licence of the Saturnalia, the primitive equality of mankind. Some idea may be conceived of the abhorrence of the Christians for such impious ceremonies, by the scrupulous delicacy which they displayed on a much less alarming occasion. On days of general festivity it was the custom of the ancients to adorn their doors with lamps and with branches of laurel, and to crown their heads with a garland of flowers. This innocent and elegant practice might perhaps have been tolerated as a mere civil institution. But it most unluckily happened that the doors were under the protection of the household gods, that the laurel was sacred to the lover of Daphne, and that garlands of flowers, though frequently worn as a symbol either of joy or mourning, had been dedicated in their first origin to the service of superstition. The trembling Christians who were persuaded to comply with the fashion of their country and the commands of the magistrate laboured under the most gloomy apprehensions, from the reproaches of their own conscience, the censures of the church, and the denunciations of divine vengeance.

II. The writings of Cicero represent in the most lively colours the ignorance, the errors, and the uncertainty of the ancient philosophers with regard to the immortality of the soul. When they are desirous of arming their disciples against the fear of death, they inculcate, as an obvious though melancholy position, that the fatal stroke of our dissolution releases us from the calamities of life; and that those can no longer suffer who no longer exist. Yet there were a few sages of Greece and Rome who had conceived a more exalted, and, in some respects, a juster idea of human nature, though it must be confessed that, in the sublime inquiry, their reason had been often guided by their imagination, and that their imagination had been prompted by their vanity. When they viewed with complacency the extent of their own mental powers, when they exercised the

[2]Tertullian de Idololatria, c. 20, 21, 22. If a Pagan friend (on the occasion perhaps of sneezing) used the familiar expression "Jupiter bless you," the Christian was obliged to protest against the divinity of Jupiter.

various faculties of memory, of fancy, and of judgment, in the most profound speculations or the most important labours, and when they reflected on the desire of fame, which transported them into future ages, far beyond the bounds of death and of the grave, they were unwilling to confound themselves with the beasts of the field, or to suppose that a being, for whose dignity they entertained the most sincere admiration, could be limited to a spot of earth, and to a few years of duration. With this favourable prepossession they summoned to their aid the science, or rather the language, of Metaphysics. They soon discovered that, as none of the properties of matter will apply to the operations of the mind, the human soul must consequently be a substance distinct from the body, pure, simple, and spiritual, incapable of dissolution, and susceptible of a much higher degree of virtue and happiness after the release from its corporeal prison. The philosophers who trod in the footsteps of Plato asserted, not only the future immortality, but the past eternity of the human soul, which they were too apt to consider as a portion of the infinite and self-existing spirit which pervades and sustains the universe.[3]

A doctrine thus removed beyond the senses and the experience of mankind might serve to amuse the leisure of a philosophic mind; or, in the silence of solitude, it might sometimes impart a ray of comfort to desponding virtue; but the faint impression which had been received in the schools was soon obliterated by the commerce and business of active life. We are sufficiently acquainted with the eminent persons who flourished in the age of Cicero and of the first Cæsars, with their actions, their characters, and their motives, to be assured that their conduct in this life was never regulated by any serious conviction of the rewards or punishments of a future state. At the bar and in the senate of Rome the ablest orators were not apprehensive of giving offence to their hearers by exposing that doctrine as an idle and extravagant opinion, which was rejected with contempt by every man of a liberal education and understanding.

Since therefore the most sublime efforts of philosophy can extend no farther than feebly to point out the desire, the hope, or, at most, the probability of a future state, there is nothing except a divine revelation that can ascertain the existence and describe the condition of the invisible country which is destined to receive the souls of men after their separation from the body. But we may perceive several defects inherent to the popular religions of Greece and Rome which rendered them very unequal to so arduous a task. 1. The general system of their mythology was unsupported by any solid proofs; and the wisest among the Pagans had already disclaimed its usurped authority. 2. The description of the infernal regions had been abandoned to the fancy of painters and of poets, who peopled them with so many phantoms and monsters who dispensed their rewards and punishments with so little equity, that a solemn truth, the most con-

[3]The pre-existence of human souls, so far at least as that doctrine is compatible with religion, was adopted by many of the Greek and Latin fathers. See Beausobre, Hist. du Manichéisme, l. vi. c. 4.

genial to the human heart, was oppressed and disgraced by the absurd mixture of the wildest fictions. 3. The doctrine of a future state was scarcely considered among the devout polytheists of Greece and Rome as a fundamental article of faith. The providence of the gods, as it related to public communities rather than to private individuals, was principally displayed on the visible theatre of the present world. The petitions which were offered on the altars of Jupiter or Apollo expressed the anxiety of their worshippers for temporal happiness, and their ignorance or indifference concerning a future life. The important truth of the immortality of the soul was inculcated with more diligence as well as success in India, in Assyria, in Egypt, and in Gaul; and since we cannot attribute such a difference to the superior knowledge of the barbarians, we must ascribe it to the influence of an established priesthood, which employed the motives of virtue as the instrument of ambition.

We might naturally expect that a principle so essential to religion would have been revealed in the clearest terms to the chosen people of Palestine, and that it might safely have been entrusted to the hereditary priesthood of Aaron. It is incumbent on us to adore the mysterious dispensations of Providence, when we discover that the doctrine of the immortality of the soul is omitted in the law of Moses; it is darkly insinuated by the prophets; and during the long period which elapsed between the Egyptian and the Babylonian servitudes, the hopes as well as fears of the Jews appear to have been confined within the narrow compass of the present life.

After Cyrus had permitted the exiled nation to return into the promised land, and after Ezra had restored the ancient records of their religion, two celebrated sects, the Sadducees and the Pharisees, insensibly arose at Jerusalem. The former, selected from the more opulent and distinguished ranks of society, were strictly attached to the literal sense of the Mosaic law, and they piously rejected the immortality of the soul as an opinion that received no countenance from the divine book which they revered as the only rule of their faith.

To the authority of Scripture the Pharisees added that of tradition, and they accepted, under the name of traditions, several speculative tenets from the philosophy or religion of the Eastern nations. The doctrines of fate or predestination, of angels and spirits, and of a future state of rewards and punishments, were in the number of these new articles of belief; and as the Pharisees, by the austerity of their manners, had drawn into their party the body of the Jewish people, the immortality of the soul became the prevailing sentiment of the synagogue under the reign of the Asmonæan princes and pontiffs. The temper of the Jews was incapable of contenting itself with such a cold and languid assent as might satisfy the mind of a Polytheist; and as soon as they admitted the idea of a future state, they embraced it with the zeal which has always formed the characteristic of the nation. Their zeal, however, added nothing to its evidence, or even probability; and it was still necessary that the doctrine of life and immortality, which had been dictated by nature, approved by reason, and received by superstition, should obtain the sanction of divine truth from the authority and example of Christ.

When the promise of eternal happiness was proposed to mankind on condition of adopting the faith, and of observing the precepts, of the Gospel, it is no wonder that so advantageous an offer should have been accepted by great numbers of every religion, of every rank, and of every province in the Roman empire. The ancient Christians were animated by a contempt for their present existence, and by a just confidence of immortality, of which the doubtful and imperfect faith of modern ages cannot give us any adequate notion. In the primitive church the influence of truth was very powerfully strengthened by an opinion which, however it may deserve respect for its usefulness and antiquity, has not been found agreeable to experience. It was universally believed that the end of the world, and the kingdom of heaven, were at hand. The near approach of this wonderful event had been predicted by the apostles; the tradition of it was preserved by their earliest disciples, and those who understood in their literal sense the discourses of Christ himself were obliged to expect the second and glorious coming of the Son of Man in the clouds, before that generation was totally extinguished which had beheld his humble condition upon earth, and which might still be witness of the calamities of the Jews under Vespasian or Hadrian.

The revolution of seventeen centuries has instructed us not to press too closely the mysterious language of prophecy and revelation; but as long as, for wise purposes, this error was permitted to subsist in the church, it was productive of the most salutary effects on the faith and practice of Christians, who lived in the awful expectation of that moment when the globe itself, and all the various races of mankind, should tremble at the appearance of their divine Judge.

The ancient and popular doctrine of the Millennium was intimately connected with the second coming of Christ. As the works of the creation had been finished in six days, their duration in their present state, according to a tradition which was attributed to the prophet Elijah, was fixed to six thousand years. By the same analogy it was inferred that this long period of labour and contention, which was now almost elapsed, would be succeeded by a joyful Sabbath of a thousand years; and that Christ, with the triumphant band of the saints and the elect who had escaped death, or who had been miraculously revived, would reign upon earth till the time appointed for the last and general resurrection. So pleasing was this hope to the mind of believers that the *New Jerusalem*, the seat of this blissful kingdom, was quickly adorned with all the gayest colours of the imagination. A felicity consisting only of pure and spiritual pleasure would have appeared too refined for its inhabitants, who were still supposed to possess their human nature and senses. A garden of Eden, with the amusements of the pastoral life, was no longer suited to the advanced state of society which prevailed under the Roman empire. A city was therefore erected of gold and precious stones, and a supernatural plenty of corn and wine was bestowed on the adjacent territory, in the free enjoyment of whose spontaneous productions the happy and benevolent people was never to be restrained by any jealous laws of exclusive property.

The assurance of such a Millennium was carefully inculcated by a succession of fathers from Justin Martyr and Irenæus, who conversed with the immediate disciples of the apostles, down to Lactantius, who was preceptor to the son of Constantine. Though it might not be universally received, it appears to have been the reigning sentiment of the orthodox believers; and it seems so well adapted to the desires and apprehensions of mankind, that it must have contributed in a very considerable degree to the progress of the Christian faith.

Whilst the happiness and glory of a temporal reign were promised to the disciples of Christ, the most dreadful calamities were denounced against an unbelieving world. The edification of the new Jerusalem was to advance by equal steps with the destruction of the mystic Babylon; and as long as the emperors who reigned before Constantine persisted in the profession of idolatry, the epithet of Babylon was applied to the city and to the empire of Rome. A regular series was prepared of all the moral and physical evils which can afflict a flourishing nation; intestine discord, and the invasion of the fiercest barbarians from the unknown regions of the North; pestilence and famine, comets and eclipses, earthquakes and inundations. All these were only so many preparatory and alarming signs of the great catastrophe of Rome, when the country of the Scipios and Cæsars should be consumed by a flame from Heaven, and the city of the seven hills, with her palaces, her temples, and her triumphal arches, should be buried in a vast lake of fire and brimstone. It might, however, afford some consolation to Roman vanity, that the period of their empire would be that of the world itself; which, as it had once perished by the element of water, was destined to experience a second and a speedy destruction from the element of fire.

In the opinion of a general conflagration the faith of the Christian very happily coincided with the tradition of the East, the philosophy of the Stoics, and the analogy of Nature; and even the country which, from religious motives, had been chosen for the origin and principal scene of the conflagration, was the best adapted for that purpose by natural and physical causes—by its deep caverns, beds of sulphur, and numerous volcanoes, of which those of Ætna, of Vesuvius, and of Lipari exhibit a very imperfect representation. The calmest and most intrepid sceptic could not refuse to acknowledge that the destruction of the present system of the world by fire was in itself extremely probable. The Christian, who founded his belief much less on the fallacious arguments of reason than on the authority of tradition and the interpretation of Scripture, expected it with terror and confidence as a certain and approaching event; and as his mind was perpetually filled with the solemn idea, he considered every disaster that happened to the empire as an infallible symptom of an expiring world.

The condemnation of the wisest and most virtuous of the Pagans, on account of their ignorance or disbelief of the divine truth, seems to offend the reason and the humanity of the present age. But the primitive church, whose faith was of a much firmer consistence, delivered over, without hesitation, to eternal torture the far greater part of the human species. A charitable hope might perhaps be indulged in favour of Socrates, or some other sages of antiquity, who had consulted the light of reason before that of the Gospel had arisen. But it was unanimously affirmed that those who, since the birth or the death of Christ, had obstinately persisted in the worship of dæmons, neither deserved nor could expect a pardon from the irritated justice of the Deity.

These rigid sentiments, which had been unknown to the ancient world, appear to have infused a spirit of bitterness into a system of love and harmony. The ties of blood and friendship were frequently torn asunder by the difference of religious faith; and the Christians who, in this world, found themselves oppressed by the power of the Pagans were sometimes seduced by resentment and spiritual pride to delight in the prospect of their future triumph. "You are fond of spectacles," exclaims the stern Tertullian, "expect the greatest of all spectacles, the last and eternal judgment of the universe. How shall I admire, how laugh, how rejoice, how exult, when I behold so many proud monarchs, and fancied gods, groaning in the lowest abyss of darkness; so many magistrates, who persecuted the name of the Lord, liquefying in fiercer fires than they ever kindled against the Christians; so many sage philosophers blushing in red-hot flames with their deluded scholars; so many celebrated poets trembling before the tribunal, not of Minos, but of Christ; so many tragedians, more tuneful in the expression of their own sufferings; so many dancers–" But the humanity of the reader will permit me to draw a veil over the rest of this infernal description.

Doubtless there were many among the primitive Christians of a temper more suitable to the meekness and charity of their profession. There were many who felt a sincere compassion for the danger of their friends and countrymen, and who exerted the most benevolent zeal to save them from the impending destruction.

III. The supernatural gifts, which even in this life were ascribed to the Christians above the rest of mankind, must have conduced to their own comfort, and very frequently to the conviction of infidels. Besides the occasional prodigies which might sometimes be effected by the immediate interposition of the Deity when he suspended the laws of Nature for the service of religion, the Christian church, from the time of the apostles and their first disciples, has claimed an uninterrupted succession of miraculous powers, the gift of tongues, of vision, and of prophecy, the power of expelling dæmons, of healing the sick, and of raising the dead. The knowledge of foreign languages was frequently communicated to the contemporaries of Irenæus, though Irenæus himself was left to struggle with the difficulties of a barbarous dialect whilst he preached the Gospel to the natives of Gaul. The divine inspiration, whether it was conveyed in the form of a waking or of a sleeping vision, is described as a favour very liberally bestowed on all ranks of the faithful, on women as on elders, on boys as well as upon bishops.

In modern times, a latent and even involuntary scepticism adheres to the most pious dispositions. Their admission of supernatural truths is much less an active consent than a cold and passive acquiescence. Accustomed long since to observe and to respect the invariable order of Nature, our reason, or at least our imagination, is not sufficiently prepared to sustain the visible action of the Deity. But in the first ages of Christianity the situation of mankind was extremely different. The most curious, or the most credulous, among the Pagans were often persuaded to enter into a society which asserted an actual claim of miraculous powers. The primitive Christians perpetually trod on mystic ground, and their minds were exercised by the habits of believing the most extraordinary events. They felt, or they fancied, that on every side they were incessantly assaulted by dæmons, comforted by visions, instructed by prophecy, and surprisingly delivered from danger, sickness, and from death itself, by the supplications of the church. The real or imaginary prodigies, of which they so frequently conceived themselves to be the objects, the instruments, or the spectators, very happily disposed them to adopt with the same ease, but with far greater justice, the authentic wonders of the evangelic history; and thus miracles that exceeded not the measure of their own experience inspired them with the most lively assurance of mysteries which were acknowledged to surpass the limits of their understanding. It is this deep impression of supernatural truths which has been so much celebrated under the name of faith.

IV. But the primitive Christian demonstrated his faith by his virtues; and it was very justly supposed that the Divine persuasion, which enlightened or subdued the understanding, must at the same time purify the heart and direct the actions of the believer. The first apologists of Christianity who justify the innocence of their brethren, and the writers of a later period who celebrate the sanctity of their ancestors, display, in the most lively colours, the reformation of manners which was introduced into the world by the preaching of the Gospel. As it is my intention to remark only such human causes as were permitted to second the influence of revelation, I shall slightly mention two motives which might naturally render the lives of the primitive Christians much purer and more austere than those of their Pagan contemporaries or their degenerate successors—repentance for their past sins, and the laudable desire of supporting the reputation of the society in which they were engaged.

It is a very ancient reproach that the Christians allured into their party the most atrocious criminals, who, as soon as they were touched by a sense of remorse, were easily persuaded to wash away in the water of baptism the guilt of their past conduct, for which the temples of the gods refused to grant them any expiation. But this reproach, when it is cleared from misrepresentation, contributes as much to the honour as it did to the increase of the church. The friends of Christianity may acknowledge without a blush that many of the most eminent saints had been before their baptism the most abandoned sinners. Those persons who in the world had followed, though in an imperfect manner, the dictates of benevolence and propriety, derived such a calm satisfaction from the opinion of their own rectitude as rendered them much less susceptible of the sudden emotions of shame, of grief, and of terror, which have given birth to so many wonderful conversions. After the example of their Divine Master, the missionaries of the Gospel disdained not the society of men, and especially of women, oppressed by the consciousness, and very often by the effects, of their vices. As they emerged from sin and superstition to the glorious hope of immortality, they resolved to devote themselves to a life, not only of virtue, but of penitence. The desire of perfection became the ruling passion of their soul; and it is well known that, while reason embraces a cold mediocrity, our passions hurry us with rapid violence over the space which lies between the most opposite extremes.

When the new converts had been enrolled in the number of the faithful, and were admitted to the sacraments of the church, they found themselves restrained from relapsing into their past disorders by another consideration of a less spiritual but of a very innocent and respectable nature. Any particular society that has departed from the great body of the nation, or the religion to which it belonged, immediately becomes the object of universal as well as invidious observation. In proportion to the smallness of its numbers, the character of the society may be affected by the virtue and vices of the persons who compose it; and every member is engaged to watch with the most vigilant attention over his own behaviour, and over that of his brethren, since, as he must expect to incur a part of the common disgrace, he may hope to enjoy a share of the common reputation.

When the Christians of Bithynia were brought before the tribunal of the younger Pliny, they assured the proconsul that, far from being engaged in any unlawful conspiracy, they were bound by a solemn obligation to abstain from the commission of those crimes which disturb the private or public peace of society, from theft, robbery, adultery, perjury, and fraud. Near a century afterwards, Tertullian with an honest pride could boast that very few Christians had suffered by the hand of the executioner, except on account of their religion. Their serious and sequestered life, averse to the gay luxury of the age, inured them to chastity, temperance, economy, and all the sober and domestic virtues. As the greater number were of some trade or profession, it was incumbent on them, by the strictest integrity and the fairest dealing, to remove the suspicions which the profane are too apt to conceive against the appearances of sanctity. The contempt of the world exercised them in the habits of humility, meekness, and patience. The more they were persecuted, the more closely they adhered to each other. Their mutual charity and unsuspecting confidence has been remarked by infidels, and was too often abused by perfidious friends.

It is a very honourable circumstance for the morals of the primitive Christians, that even their faults, or rather errors, were derived from an excess of virtue. The bishops and doctors of the church, whose evidence attests, and whose authority might influence, the professions, the principles, and even the practice of their contemporaries, had studied the Scriptures with less skill than devotion; and they often received in the most literal sense those rigid precepts of Christ and the apostles to which the prudence of succeeding commentators has applied a looser and more figurative mode of interpretation. Ambitious to exalt the perfection of the Gospel above the wisdom of philosophy, the zealous fathers have carried the duties of self-mortification, of purity, and of patience, to a height which it is scarcely possible to attain, and much less to preserve, in our present state of weakness and corruption.

A doctrine so extraordinary and so sublime must inevitably command the veneration of the people; but it was ill calculated to obtain the suffrage of worldly philosophers. Gay apparel, magnificent houses, and elegant furniture were supposed to unite the double guilt of pride and of sensuality: a simple and mortified appearance was more suitable to the Christian who was certain of his sins and doubtful of his salvation. In their censures of luxury the fathers are extremely minute and circumstantial; among the various articles which excite their pious indignation, we may enumerate false hair, garments of any colour except white, instruments of music, vases of gold or silver, downy pillows (as Jacob reposed his head on a stone), white bread, foreign wines, public salutations, the use of warm baths, and the practice of shaving the beard, which, according to the expression of Tertullian, is a lie against our own faces, and an impious attempt to improve the works of the Creator. When Christianity was introduced among the rich and the polite, the observation of these singular laws was left, as it would be at present, to the few who were ambitious of superior sanctity. But it is always easy, as well as agreeable, for the inferior ranks of mankind to claim a merit from the contempt of that pomp and pleasure which fortune has placed beyond their reach. The virtue of the primitive Christians, like that of the first Romans, was very frequently guarded by poverty and ignorance.

The chaste severity of the fathers in whatever related to the commerce of the two sexes flowed from the same principle—their abhorrence of every enjoyment which might gratify the sensual and degrade the spiritual nature of man. It was their favourite opinion, that if Adam had preserved his obedience to the Creator, he would have lived for ever in a state of virgin purity, and that some harmless mode of vegetation might have peopled paradise with a race of innocent and immortal beings. The use of marriage was permitted only to his fallen posterity, as a necessary expedient to continue the human species, and as a restraint, however imperfect, on the natural licentiousness of desire. The hesitation of the orthodox casuists on this interesting subject betrays the perplexity of men unwilling to approve an institution which they were compelled to tolerate. The enumeration of the very whimsical laws which they most circumstantially imposed on the marriage-bed would force a smile from the young and a blush from the fair. It was their unanimous sentiment that a first marriage was adequate to all the purposes of nature and of society. The sensual connection was refined into a resemblance of the mystic union of Christ with his church, and was pronounced to be indissoluble either by divorce or by death. The practice of second nuptials was branded with the name of a legal adultery; and the persons who were guilty of so scandalous an offence against Christian purity were soon excluded from the honours, and even from the arms, of the church. Since desire was imputed as a crime, and marriage was tolerated as a defect, it was consistent with the same principles to consider a state of celibacy as the nearest approach to the Divine perfection. It was with the utmost difficulty that ancient Rome could support the institution of six vestals; but the primitive church was filled with a great number of persons of either sex who had devoted themselves to the profession of perpetual chastity.

The Christians were not less adverse to the business than to the pleasures of this world. The defence of our persons and property they knew not how to reconcile with the patient doctrine which enjoined an unlimited forgiveness of past injuries, and commanded them to invite the repetition of fresh insults. Their simplicity was offended by the use of oaths, by the pomp of magistracy, and by the active contention of public life; nor could their humane ignorance be convinced that it was lawful on any occasion to shed the blood of our fellow-creatures, either by the sword of justice or by that of war, even though their criminal or hostile attempts should threaten the peace and safety of the whole community.

It was acknowledged that, under a less perfect law, the powers of the Jewish constitution had been exercised, with the approbation of Heaven, by inspired prophets and by anointed kings. The Christians felt and confessed that such institutions might be necessary for the present system of the world, and they cheerfully submitted to the authority of their Pagan governors. But while they inculcated the maxims of passive obedience, they refused to take any active part in the civil administration or the military defence of the empire. Some indulgence might perhaps be allowed to those persons who, before their conversion, were already engaged in such violent and sanguinary occupations; but it was impossible that the Christians, without renouncing a more sacred duty, could assume the character of soldiers, of magistrates, or of princes. This indolent, or even criminal disregard to the public welfare, exposed them to the contempt and reproaches of the Pagans, who very frequently asked, what must be the fate of the empire, attacked on every side by the barbarians, if all mankind should adopt the pusillanimous sentiments of the new sect? To this insulting question the Christian apologists returned obscure and ambiguous answers, as they were unwilling to reveal the secret cause of their security; the expectation that, before the conversion of mankind was accomplished, war, government, the Roman empire, and the world itself, would be no more.

V. But the human character, however it may be exalted or depressed by a temporary enthusiasm, will return by degrees to its proper and natural level, and will resume those passions that seem the most adapted to its present condition. The primitive Christians were dead to the business and pleasures of the world; but their love of action, which could never be entirely extinguished, soon revived, and found a new occupation in the government of the church.

A separate society which attacked the established religion of the empire was obliged to adopt some form of internal policy, and to appoint a sufficient number of ministers, entrusted not only with the spiritual functions but even with the temporal direction of the Christian commonwealth. The safety of the society, its honour, its aggrandizement, were productive, even in the most pious minds, of a spirit of patriotism, such as the first of the Romans had felt for the republic, and sometimes of a similar indifference in the use of whatever means might probably conduce to so desirable an end.

The ambition of raising themselves or their friends to the honours and offices of the church was disguised by the laudable intention of devoting to the public benefit the power and consideration which, for that purpose only, it became their duty to solicit. In the exercise of their functions they were frequently called upon to detect the errors of heresy or the arts of faction, to oppose the designs of perfidious brethren, to stigmatise their characters with deserved infamy, and to expel them from the bosom of a society whose peace and happiness they had attempted to disturb. The ecclesiastical governors of the Christians were taught to unite the wisdom of the serpent with the innocence of the dove; but as the former was refined, so the latter was insensibly corrupted, by the habits of government. In the church as well as in the world, the persons who were placed in any public station rendered themselves considerable by their eloquence and firmness, by their knowledge of mankind, and by their dexterity in business.

From every cause, either of a civil or of an ecclesiastical nature, it was easy to foresee that Rome must enjoy the respect, and would soon claim the obedience, of the provinces. The society of the faithful bore a just proportion to the capital of the empire; and the Roman church was the greatest, the most numerous, and, in regard to the West, the most ancient of all the Christian establishments, many of which had received their religion from the pious labours of her missionaries. Instead of *one* apostolic founder, the utmost boast of Antioch, of Ephesus, or of Corinth, the banks of the Tiber were supposed to have been honoured with the preaching and martyrdom of the *two* most eminent among the apostles; and the bishops of Rome very prudently claimed the inheritance of whatsoever prerogatives were attributed either to the person or to the office of St. Peter. The bishops of Italy and of the provinces were disposed to allow them a primacy of order and association (such was their very accurate expression) in the Christian aristocracy. But the power of a monarch was rejected with abhorrence, and the aspiring genius of Rome experienced from the nations of Asia and Africa a more vigorous resistance to her spiritual than she had formerly done to her temporal dominion.

The progress of the ecclesiastical authority gave birth to the memorable distinction of the laity and of the clergy, which had been unknown to the Greeks and Romans. The former of these appellations comprehended the body of the Christian people; the latter, according to the signification of the word, was appropriated to the chosen portion that had been set apart for the service of religion; a celebrated order of men which has furnished the most important, though not always the most edifying, subjects for modern history. Their mutual hostilities sometimes disturbed the peace of the infant church, but their zeal and activity were united in the common cause, and the love of power, which (under the most artful disguises) could insinuate itself into the breasts of bishops and martyrs, animated them to increase the number of their subjects and to enlarge the limits of the Christian empire. They were destitute of any temporal force, and they were for a long time discouraged and oppressed, rather than assisted, by the civil magistrate; but they had acquired, and they employed within their own society, the two most efficacious instruments of government, rewards and punishments; the former derived from the pious liberality, the latter from the devout apprehensions, of the faithful.

I. The community of goods, which had so agreeably amused the imagination of Plato, and which subsisted in some degree among the austere sect of the Essenians, was adopted for a short time in the primitive church. The fervour of the first proselytes prompted them to sell those worldly possessions which they despised, to lay the price of them at the feet of the apostles, and to content themselves with receiving an equal share out of the general distribution. The progress of the Christian religion relaxed, and gradually abolished, this generous institution, which, in hands less pure than those of the apostles, would too soon have been corrupted and abused by the returning selfishness of human nature; and the converts who embraced the new religion were permitted to retain the possession of their patrimony, to receive legacies and inheritances, and to increase their separate property by all the lawful means of trade and industry. Instead of an absolute sacrifice, a moderate proportion was accepted by the ministers of the Gospel; and in their weekly or monthly assemblies every believer, according to the exigency of the occasion, and the measure of his wealth and piety, presented his voluntary offering for the use of the common fund. Nothing, however inconsiderable, was refused; but it was diligently inculcated that, in the article of tithes, the Mosaic law was still of divine obligation; and that, since the Jews, under a less perfect discipline, had been commanded to pay a tenth part of all that they possessed, it would become the disciples of Christ to distinguish themselves by a superior degree of liberality, and to acquire some merit by resigning a superfluous treasure which must so soon be annihilated with the world itself.

It is almost unnecessary to observe that the revenue of each particular church, which was of so uncertain and fluctuating a nature, must have varied with the poverty or the opulence of the faithful, as they were dispersed in obscure villages, or collected in the great cities of the empire. In the time of the emperor Decius it was the opinion of the magistrates that the Christians of Rome were possessed of very considerable wealth, that vessels of gold and silver were used in their religious worship, and that many among their proselytes had sold their lands and houses to increase the public riches of the sect, at the expense, indeed, of their unfortunate children, who found themselves beggars because their parents had been saints. We should listen with distrust to the suspicions of strangers and enemies; on this occasion, however, they receive a very specious and probable colour from the two following circumstances, the only ones that have reached our knowledge which define any precise sums or convey any distinct idea. Almost at the same period the bishop of Carthage, from a society less opulent than that of Rome, collected an hundred thousand sesterces (above eight hundred and fifty pounds sterling), on a sudden call of charity to redeem the brethren of Numidia, who had been carried away captives by the barbarians of the desert. About an hundred years before the reign of Decius the Roman church had received, in a single donation, the sum of two hundred thousand sesterces from a stranger of Pontus, who proposed to fix his residence in the capital.

These oblations, for the most part, were made in money; nor was the society of Christians either desirous or capable of acquiring, to any considerable degree, the incumbrance of landed property. It had been provided by several laws, which were enacted with the same design as our statutes of mortmain, that no real estates should be given or bequeathed to any corporate body without a special privilege or a particular dispensation from the emperor or from the senate, who were seldom disposed to grant either in favour of a sect, at first the object of their contempt, and at last of their fears and jealousy. A transaction, however, is related under the reign of Alexander Severus, which discovers that the restraint was sometimes eluded or suspended, and that the Christians were permitted to claim and to possess lands within the limits of Rome itself.[4] The progress of Christianity, and the civil confusion of the empire, contributed to relax the severity of the laws; and, before the close of the third century, many considerable estates were bestowed on the opulent churches of Rome, Milan, Carthage, Antioch, Alexandria, and the other great cities of Italy and the provinces.

The bishop was the natural steward of the church; the public stock was entrusted to his care without account or control; the presbyters were confined to their spiritual functions, and the more dependent order of deacons was solely employed in the management and distribution of the ecclesiastical revenue. If we may give credit to the vehement declamations of Cyprian, there were too many among his African brethren who, in the execution of their charge, violated every precept, not only of evangelic perfection, but even of moral virtue. By some of these unfaithful stewards the riches of the church were lavished in sensual pleasures; by others they were perverted to the purposes of private gain, of fraudulent purchases, and of rapacious

[4] Hist. August. p. 131. [Lampr. Alex. Sever. c. 49.] The ground had been public; and was now disputed between the society of Christians and that of butchers.

usury. But as long as the contributions of the Christian people were free and unconstrained, the abuse of their confidence could not be very frequent, and the general uses to which their liberality was applied reflected honour on the religious society. A decent portion was reserved for the maintenance of the bishop and his clergy; a sufficient sum was allotted for the expenses of the public worship, of which the feasts of love, the *agapæ*, as they were called, constituted a very pleasing part. The whole remainder was the sacred patrimony of the poor. According to the discretion of the bishop, it was distributed to support widows and orphans, the lame, the sick, and the aged of the community; to comfort strangers and pilgrims, and to alleviate the misfortunes of prisoners and captives, more especially when their sufferings had been occasioned by their firm attachment to the cause of religion. A generous intercourse of charity united the most distant provinces, and the smaller congregations were cheerfully assisted by the alms of their more opulent brethren.

Such an institution, which paid less regard to the merit than to the distress of the object, very materially conduced to the progress of Christianity. The Pagans, who were actuated by a sense of humanity, while they derided the doctrines, acknowledged the benevolence, of the new sect. The prospect of immediate relief and of future protection allured into its hospitable bosom many of those unhappy persons whom the neglect of the world would have abandoned to the miseries of want, of sickness, and of old age. There is some reason likewise to believe that great numbers of infants who, according to the inhuman practice of the times, had been exposed by their parents, were frequently rescued from death, baptised, educated, and maintained by the piety of the Christians, and at the expense of the public treasure.[5]

II. It is the undoubted right of every society to exclude from its communion and benefits such among its members as reject or violate those regulations which have been established by general consent. In the exercise of this power the censures of the Christian church were chiefly directed against scandalous sinners, and particularly those who were guilty of murder, of fraud, or of incontinence; against the authors, or the followers, of any heretical opinions. If the fault was of a very heinous nature, whole years of penance were esteemed an inadequate satisfaction to the Divine justice; and it was always by slow and painful gradations that the sinner, the heretic, or the apostate was readmitted into the bosom of the church. A sentence of perpetual excommunication was reserved for some crimes of an extraordinary magnitude, and particularly for the inexcusable relapses of those penitents who had already experienced and abused the clemency of their ecclesiastical superiors.

The well-tempered mixture of liberality and rigour, the judicious dispensation of rewards and punishments, according to the maxims of policy as well as justice, constituted the *human* strength of the church.

[5]See Lucian in Peregrin. [c. 13.] Julian (Epist. 49) seems mortified that the Christian charity maintains not only their own, but likewise the heathen poor.

It was by the aid of these causes—exclusive zeal, the immediate expectation of another world, the claim of miracles, the practice of rigid virtue, and the constitution of the primitive church—that Christianity spread itself with so much success in the Roman empire. To the first of these the Christians were indebted for their invincible valour, which disdained to capitulate with the enemy whom they were resolved to vanquish. The three succeeding causes supplied their valour with the most formidable arms. The last of these causes united their courage, directed their arms, and gave their efforts that irresistible weight which even a small band of well-trained and intrepid volunteers has so often possessed over an undisciplined multitude, ignorant of the subject and careless of the event of the war.

In the various religions of Polytheism, some wandering fanatics of Egypt and Syria, who addressed themselves to the credulous superstition of the populace, were perhaps the only order of priests that derived their whole support and credit from their sacerdotal profession, and were very deeply affected by a personal concern for the safety or prosperity of their tutelar deities. The ministers of Polytheism, both in Rome and in the provinces, were, for the most part, men of a noble birth and of an affluent fortune, who received, as an honourable distinction, the care of a celebrated temple or of a public sacrifice, exhibited, very frequently at their own expense, the sacred games, and with cold indifference performed the ancient rites according to the laws and fashion of their country. As they were engaged in the ordinary occupations of life, their zeal and devotion were seldom animated by a sense of interest, or by the habits of an ecclesiastical character. Confined to their respective temples and cities, they remained without any connection of discipline or government; and whilst they acknowledged the supreme jurisdiction of the senate, of the college of pontiffs, and of the emperor, those civil magistrates contented themselves with the easy task of maintaining in peace and dignity the general worship of mankind. We have already seen how various, how loose, and how uncertain were the religious sentiments of Polytheists. They were abandoned, almost without control, to the natural workings of a superstitious fancy. The accidental circumstances of their life and situation determined the object as well as the degree of their devotion; and as long as their adoration was successively prostituted to a thousand deities, it was scarcely possible that their hearts could be susceptible of a very sincere or lively passion for any of them.

When Christianity appeared in the world, even these faint and imperfect impressions had lost much of their original power. Human reason had already obtained an easy triumph over the folly of Paganism; and when Tertullian or Lactantius employ their labours in exposing its falsehood and extravagance, they are obliged to transcribe the eloquence of Cicero or the wit of Lucian. The contagion of these sceptical writings had been diffused far beyond the number of their readers. The fashion of incredulity was communicated from the philosopher to the man of pleasure or business, from the noble to the plebeian, and from the master to the menial slave who waited at his table, and who eagerly listened to the freedom of his conversation. On public occasions the philosophic part of mankind affected to treat with respect and decency the religious institutions of their country, but their secret contempt penetrated through the thin and awkward disguise; and even the people, when they discovered that their deities were rejected and derided by those whose rank or understanding they were accustomed to reverence, were filled with doubts and apprehensions concerning the truth of those doctrines to which they had yielded the most implicit belief. The decline of ancient prejudice exposed a very numerous portion of human kind to the danger of a painful and comfortless situation.

It has been observed, with truth as well as propriety, that the conquests of Rome prepared and facilitated those of Christianity. In the second chapter of this work we have attempted to explain in what manner the most civilised provinces of Europe, Asia, and Africa were united under the dominion of one sovereign, and gradually connected by the most intimate ties of laws, of manners, and of language. The authentic histories of the actions of Christ were composed in the Greek language. As soon as those histories were translated into the Latin tongue they were perfectly intelligible to all the subjects of Rome, excepting only to the peasants of Syria and Egypt, for whose benefit particular versions were afterwards made. The public highways, which had been constructed for the use of the legions, opened an easy passage for the Christian missionaries from Damascus to Corinth, and from Italy to the extremity of Spain or Britain; nor did those spiritual conquerors encounter any of the obstacles which usually retard or prevent the introduction of a foreign religion into a distant country. There is the strongest reason to believe that before the reigns of Diocletian and Constantine the faith of Christ had been preached in every province, and in all the great cities of the empire.

The rich provinces that extend from the Euphrates to the Ionian Sea were the principal theatre on which the apostle of the Gentiles displayed his zeal and piety. The seeds of the Gospel, which he had scattered in a fertile soil, were diligently cultivated by his disciples; and it should seem that, during the two first centuries, the most considerable body of Christians was contained within those limits. Among the societies which were instituted in Syria, none were more ancient or more illustrious than those of Damascus, of Berœa or Aleppo, and of Antioch. The prophetic introduction of the Apocalypse had described and immortalised the seven churches of Asia–Ephesus, Smyrna, Pergamus, Thyatira, Sardes, Laodicea, and Philadelphia; and their colonies were soon diffused over that populous country.

In a very early period, the islands of Cyprus and Crete, the provinces of Thrace and Macedonia, gave a favourable reception to the new religion; and Christian republics were soon founded in the cities of Corinth, of Sparta, and of Athens. The antiquity of the Greek and Asiatic churches allowed a sufficient space of time for their increase and multiplication; and even the swarms of Gnostics and other heretics serve to display the flourishing condition of the orthodox church, since the appellation of heretics has always been applied to the less numerous party. To these domestic testimonies we may add the confession, the complaints, and the apprehensions of the Gentiles themselves. From the writings of Lucian, a philosopher who had studied mankind, and who describes their manners in the most lively colours, we may learn that, under the reign of Commodus, his native country of Pontus was filled with Epicureans and *Christians*. Within fourscore years after the death of Christ, the humane Pliny laments the magnitude of the evil which he vainly attempted to eradicate. In his very curious epistle to the emperor Trajan he affirms that the temples were almost deserted, that the sacred victims scarcely found any purchasers, and that the superstition had not only infected the cities, but had even spread itself into the villages and the open country of Pontus and Bithynia.

Without descending into a minute scrutiny of the expressions or of the motives of those writers who either celebrate or lament the progress of Christianity in the East, it may in general be observed that none of them have left us any grounds from whence a just estimate might be formed of the real numbers of the faithful in those provinces. One circumstance, however, has been fortunately preserved, which seems to cast a more distinct light on this obscure but interesting subject. Under the reign of Theodosius, after Christianity had enjoyed, during more than sixty years, the sunshine of Imperial favour, the ancient and illustrious church of Antioch consisted of one hundred thousand persons, three thousand of whom were supported out of the public oblations. The splendour and dignity of the queen of the East, the acknowledged populousness of Cæsarea, Seleucia, and Alexandria, and the destruction of two hundred and fifty thousand souls in the earthquake which afflicted Antioch under the elder Justin, are so many convincing proofs that the whole number of its inhabitants was not less than half a million, and that the Christians, however multiplied by zeal and power, did not exceed a fifth part of that great city. How different a proportion must we adopt when we compare the persecuted with the triumphant church, the West with the East, remote villages with populous towns, and countries recently converted to the faith with the place where the believers first received the appellation of Christians! Chrysostom computes the multitude of the faithful as even superior to that of the Jews and Pagans, but the solution of this apparent difficulty is easy and obvious. The eloquent preacher draws a parallel between the civil and the ecclesiastical constitution of Antioch; between the list of Christians who had acquired heaven by baptism, and the list of citizens who had a right to share the public liberality. Slaves, strangers, and infants were comprised in the former; they were excluded from the latter.

The extensive commerce of Alexandria, and its proximity to Palestine, gave an easy entrance to the new religion. It was at first embraced by great numbers of the Therapeutæ, or Essenians, of the lake Mareotis, a Jewish sect which had abated much of its reverence for the Mosaic ceremonies. The austere life of the Essenians, their fasts and excommunications, the community of goods, the love of celibacy, their zeal for martyrdom, and the warmth though not the purity of their faith, already offered a very lively image of the primitive discipline. It was in the school of Alexandria that the Christian theology appears to have assumed a regular and scientifical form.

A perpetual stream of strangers and provincials flowed into the capacious bosom of Rome. Whatever was strange or odious, whoever was guilty or suspected, might hope, in the obscurity of that immense capital, to elude the vigilance of the law. In such a various conflux of nations, every teacher, either of truth or of falsehood, every founder, whether of a virtuous or a criminal association, might easily multiply his disciples or accomplices. The Christians of Rome, at the time of the accidental persecution of Nero, are represented by Tacitus as already amounting to a very great multitude, and the language of that great historian is almost similar to the style employed by Livy, when he relates the introduction and the suppression of the rites of Bacchus. After the Bacchanals had awakened the severity of the senate, it was likewise apprehended that a very great multitude, as it were *another people,* had been initiated into those abhorred mysteries.

A more careful inquiry soon demonstrated that the offenders did not exceed seven thousand; a number indeed sufficiently alarming when considered as the object of public justice. It is with the same candid allowance that we should interpret the vague expressions of Tacitus, and in a former instance of Pliny, when they exaggerate the crowds of deluded fanatics who had forsaken the established worship of the gods. The church of Rome was undoubtedly the first and most populous of the empire; and we are possessed of an authentic record which attests the state of religion in that city about the middle of the third century, and after a peace of thirty-eight years. The clergy, at that time, consisted of a bishop, forty-six presbyters, seven deacons, as many sub-deacons, forty-two acolytes, and fifty readers, exorcists, and porters. The number of widows, of the infirm, and of the poor, who were maintained by the oblations of the faithful, amounted to fifteen hundred. From reason, as well as from the analogy of Antioch, we may venture to estimate the Christians of Rome at about fifty thousand. The populousness of that great capital cannot perhaps be exactly ascertained; but the most modest calculation will not surely reduce it lower than a million of inhabitants, of whom the Christians might constitute at the most a twentieth part.

The western provincials appeared to have derived the knowledge of Christianity from the same source which had diffused among them the language, the sentiments, and the manners of Rome. In this more important circumstance, Africa, as well as Gaul, was gradually fashioned to the imitation of the capital. Yet notwithstanding the many favourable occasions which might invite the Roman missionaries to visit their Latin provinces, it was late before they passed either the sea or the Alps; nor can we discover in those great countries any assured traces either of faith or of persecution that ascend higher than the reign of the Antonines. The slow progress of the Gospel in the cold climate of Gaul was extremely different from the eagerness with which it seems to have been received on the burning sands of Africa. The African Christians soon formed one of the principal members of the primitive church. The practice introduced into that province of appointing bishops to the most inconsiderable towns, and very frequently to the most obscure villages, contributed to multiply the splendour and importance of their religious societies, which during the course of the third century were animated by the zeal of Tertullian, directed by the abilities of Cyprian, and adorned by the eloquence of Lactantius.

But if, on the contrary, we turn our eyes towards Gaul, we must content ourselves with discovering, in the time of Marcus Antoninus, the feeble and united congregations of Lyons and Vienne; and even as late as the reign of Decius we are assured that in a few cities only—Arles, Narbonne, Toulouse, Limoges, Clermont, Tours, and Paris—some scattered churches were supported by the devotion of a small number of Christians. Silence is indeed very consistent with devotion; but as it is seldom compatible with zeal we may perceive and lament the languid state of Christianity in those provinces which had exchanged the Celtic for the Latin tongue, since they did not, during the three first centuries, give birth to a single ecclesiastical writer. From Gaul, which claimed a just pre-eminence of learning and authority over all the countries on this side of the Alps, the light of the Gospel was more faintly reflected on the remote provinces of Spain and Britain.

The progress of Christianity was not confined to the Roman empire; and, according to the primitive fathers, who interpret facts by prophecy, the new religion, within a century after the death of its Divine Author, had already visited every part of the globe. "There exists not," says Justin Martyr, "a people, whether Greek or barbarian, or any other race of men, by whatsoever appellation or manners they may be distinguished, however ignorant of arts or agriculture, whether they dwell under tents, or wander about in covered waggons, among whom prayers are not offered up in the name of a crucified Jesus to the Father and Creator of all things." But this splendid exaggeration, which even at present it would be extremely difficult to reconcile with the real state of mankind, can be considered only as the rash sally of a devout but careless writer, the measure of whose belief was regulated by that of his wishes. It will still remain an undoubted fact that the barbarians of Scythia and Germany, who afterwards subverted the Roman monarchy, were involved in the darkness of Paganism; and that even the conversion of Iberia, of Armenia, or of Æthiopia, was not attempted with any degree of success till the sceptre was in the hands of an orthodox emperor.

From this impartial though imperfect survey of the progress of Christianity, it may perhaps seem probable that the number of its proselytes has been excessively magnified by fear on the one side, and by devotion on the other. According to the irreproachable testimony of Origen, the proportion of the faithful was very inconsiderable, when compared with the multitude of an unbelieving world; but, as we are left without any distinct information, it is impossible to determine, and it is difficult even to conjecture, the real numbers of the primitive Christians. The most favourable calculation, however, that can be deduced from the examples of Antioch and of Rome will not permit us to imagine that more than a twentieth part of the subjects of the empire had enlisted themselves under the banner of the Cross before the important conversion of Constantine. But their habits of faith, of zeal, and of union, seemed to multiply their numbers; and the same causes which contributed to their future increase served to render their actual strength more apparent and more formidable.

Such is the constitution of civil society, that, whilst a few persons are distinguished by riches, by honours, and by knowledge, the body of the people is condemned to obscurity, ignorance, and poverty. The Christian religion, which addressed itself to the whole human race, must consequently collect a far greater number of proselytes from the lower than from the superior ranks of life. This innocent and natural circumstance has been improved into a very odious imputation, which seems to be less strenuously denied by the apologists than it is urged by the adversaries of the faith: that the new sect of Christians was almost entirely composed of the dregs of the populace, of peasants and mechanics, of boys and women, of beggars and slaves, the last of whom might sometimes introduce the missionaries into the rich and noble families to which they belonged.

This unfavourable picture, though not devoid of a faint resemblance, betrays, by its dark colouring and distorted features, the pencil of an enemy. As the humble faith of Christ diffused itself through the world, it was embraced by several persons who derived some consequence from the advantages of nature or fortune. Aristides, who presented an eloquent apology to the emperor Hadrian, was an Athenian philosopher. Justin Martyr had sought divine knowledge in the schools of Zeno, of Aristotle, of Pythagoras, and of Plato, before he fortunately was accosted by the old man, or rather the angel, who turned his attention to the study of the Jewish prophets. Clemens of Alexandria had acquired much various reading in the Greek, and Tertullian in the Latin, language. Julius Africanus and Origen possessed a very considerable share of the learning of their times; and although the style of Cyprian is very different from that of Lactantius, we might almost discover that both those writers had been public teachers of rhetoric. Even the study of philosophy was at length introduced among the Christians.

Nor can it be affirmed with truth that the advantages of birth and fortune were always separated from the profession of Christianity. Several Roman citizens were brought before the tribunal of Pliny, and he soon discovered that a great number of persons of *every order* of men in Bithynia had deserted the religion of their ancestors. His unsuspected testimony may, in this instance, obtain more credit than the bold challenge of Tertullian, when he addresses himself to the fears as well as to the humanity of the proconsul of Africa, by assuring him that if he persists in his cruel intentions he must decimate Carthage, and that he will find among the guilty many persons of his own rank, senators and matrons of noblest extraction, and the friends or relations of his most intimate friends. It appears, however, that about forty years afterwards the emperor Valerian was persuaded of the truth of this assertion, since in one of his rescripts he evidently supposes that senators, Roman knights, and ladies of quality, were engaged in the Christian sect. The church still continued to increase its outward splendour as it lost its internal purity; and, in the reign of Diocletian, the palace, the courts of justice, and even the army, concealed a multitude of Christians who endeavoured to reconcile the interests of the present with those of a future life.

And yet these exceptions are either too few in number, or too recent in time, entirely to remove the imputation of ignorance and obscurity which has been so arrogantly cast on the first proselytes of Christianity. Instead of employing in our defence the fictions of later ages, it will be more prudent to convert the occasion of scandal into a subject of edification. Our serious thoughts will suggest to us that the apostles themselves were chosen by Providence among the fishermen of Galilee, and that, the lower we depress the temporal condition of the first Christians, the more reason we shall find to admire their merit and success. It is incumbent on us diligently to remember that the kingdom of heaven was promised to the poor in spirit, and that minds afflicted by calamity and the contempt of mankind cheerfully listen to the divine promise of future happiness; while, on the contrary, the fortunate are satisfied with the possession of this world, and the wise abuse in doubt and dispute their vain superiority of reason and knowledge.

We stand in need of such reflections to comfort us for the loss of some illustrious characters, which in our eyes might have seemed the most worthy of the heavenly present. The names of Seneca, of the elder and the younger Pliny, of Tacitus, of Plutarch, of Galen, of the slave Epictetus, and of the emperor Marcus Antoninus, adorn the age in which they flourished, and exalt the dignity of human nature. They filled with glory their respective stations, either in active or contemplative life; their excellent understandings were improved by study; philosophy had purified their minds from the prejudices of the popular superstition; and their days were spent in the pursuit of truth and the practice of virtue. Yet all these sages (it is no less an object of surprise than of concern) overlooked or rejected the perfection of the Christian system. Their language or their silence equally discover their contempt for the growing sect which in their time had diffused itself over the Roman empire. Those among them who condescend to mention the Christians consider them only as obstinate and perverse enthusiasts, who exacted an implicit submission to their mysterious doctrines, without being able to produce a single argument that could engage the attention of men of sense and learning.

It is at least doubtful whether any of these philosophers perused the apologies which the primitive Christians repeatedly published in behalf of themselves and of their religion; but it is much to be lamented that such a cause was not defended by abler advocates. They expose with superfluous wit and eloquence the extravagance of Polytheism. They interest our compassion by displaying the innocence and sufferings of their injured brethren. But when they would demonstrate the divine origin of Christianity, they insist much more strongly on the predictions which announced, than on the miracles which accompanied, the appearance of the Messiah. Their favourite argument might serve to edify a Christian or to convert a Jew, since both the one and the other acknowledge the authority of those prophecies, and both are obliged, with devout reverence, to search for their sense and their accomplishment. But this mode of persuasion loses much of its weight and influence when it is addressed to those who neither understand nor respect the Mosaic dispensation and the prophetic style.

But how shall we excuse the supine inattention of the Pagan and philosophic world to those evidences which were presented by the hand of Omnipotence, not to their reason, but to their senses? During the age of Christ, of his apostles, and of their first disciples, the doctrine which they preached was confirmed by innumerable prodigies. The lame walked, the blind saw, the sick were healed, the dead were raised, dæmons were expelled, and the laws of Nature were frequently suspended for the benefit of the church. But the sages of Greece and Rome turned aside from the awful spectacle, and, pursuing the ordinary occupations of life and study, appeared unconscious of any alterations in the moral or physical government of the world.

CHAPTER XI

The Conduct of the Roman Government towards the Christians, from the Reign of Nero to That of Constantine

If we seriously consider the purity of the Christian religion, the sanctity of its moral precepts, and the innocent as well as austere lives of the greater number of those who during the first ages embraced the faith of the Gospel, we should naturally suppose that so benevolent a doctrine would have been received with due reverence even by the unbelieving world; that the learned and the polite, however they might deride the miracles, would have esteemed the virtues of the new sect; and that the magistrates, instead of persecuting, would have protected an order of men who yielded the most passive obedience to the laws, though they declined the active cares of war and government.

If, on the other hand, we recollect the universal toleration of Polytheism, as it was invariably maintained by the faith of the people, the incredulity of philosophers, and the policy of the Roman senate and emperors, we are at a loss to discover what new offence the Christians had committed, what new provocation could exasperate the mild indifference of antiquity, and what new motives could urge the Roman princes, who beheld without concern a thousand forms of religion subsisting in peace under their gentle sway, to inflict a severe punishment on any part of their subjects who had chosen for themselves a singular but an inoffensive mode of faith and worship.

The religious policy of the ancient world seems to have assumed a more stern and intolerant character to oppose the progress of Christianity. About fourscore years after the death of Christ, his innocent disciples were punished with death by the sentence of a proconsul of the most amiable and philosophic character, and according to the laws of an emperor distinguished by the wisdom and justice of his general administration. The apologies which were repeatedly addressed to the successors of Trajan are filled with the most pathetic complaints that the Christians, who obeyed the dictates and solicited the liberty of conscience, were alone, among all the subjects of the Roman empire, excluded from the common benefits of their auspicious government.

It has already been observed that the religious concord of the world was principally supported by the implicit assent and reverence which the nations of antiquity expressed for their respective traditions and ceremonies. It might therefore be expected that they would unite with indignation against any sect or people which should separate itself from the communion of mankind, and, claiming the exclusive possession of divine knowledge, should disdain every form of worship except its own as impious and idolatrous. The rights of toleration were held by mutual indulgence; they were justly forfeited by a refusal of the accustomed tribute. As the payment of this tribute was inflexibly refused by the Jews, and by them alone, the consideration of the treatment which they experienced from the Roman magistrates will serve to explain how far these speculations are justified by facts, and will lead us to discover the true causes of the persecution of Christianity.

Without repeating what has been already mentioned of the reverence of the Roman princes and governors for the temple of Jerusalem, we shall only observe that the destruction of the temple and city was accompanied and followed by every circumstance that could exasperate the minds of the conquerors, and authorise religious persecutions by the most specious arguments of political justice and the public safety. From the reign of Nero to that of Antoninus Pius, the Jews discovered a fierce impatience of the dominion of Rome. The enthusiasm of the Jews was supported by the opinion that it was unlawful for them to pay taxes to an idolatrous master, and by the flattering promise which they derived from their ancient oracles, that a conquering Messiah would soon arise, destined to break their fetters, and to invest the favourites of heaven with the empire of the earth. It was by announcing himself as their long-expected deliverer, and by calling on all the descendants of Abraham to assert the hope of Israel, that the famous Barchochebas collected a formidable army, with which he resisted during two years the power of the emperor Hadrian.

Notwithstanding these repeated provocations, the resentment of the Roman princes expired after the victory, nor were their apprehensions continued beyond the period of war and danger. By the general indulgence of Polytheism, and by the mild temper of Antoninus Pius, the Jews were restored to their ancient privileges, and once more obtained the permission of circumcising their children, with the easy restraint that they should never confer on any foreign proselyte that distinguishing mark of the Hebrew race. The numerous remains of that people, though they were still excluded from the precincts of Jerusalem, were permitted to form and to maintain considerable establishments both in Italy and in the provinces, to acquire the freedom of Rome, to enjoy municipal honours, and to obtain at the same time an exemption from the burdensome and expensive offices of society. The moderation or the contempt of the Romans gave a legal sanction to the form of ecclesiastical police which was instituted by the vanquished sect. The patriarch, who had fixed his residence at Tiberias, was empowered to appoint his subordinate ministers and apostles, to exercise a domestic jurisdiction, and to receive from his dispersed brethren an annual contribution. New synagogues were frequently erected in the principal cities of the empire; and the sabbaths, the fasts, and the festivals, which were either commanded by the Mosaic law or enjoined by the traditions of the Rabbis, were celebrated in the most solemn and public manner.

Since the Jews, who rejected with abhorrence the deities adored by their sovereign and by their fellow-subjects, enjoyed the free exercise of their unsocial religion, there must have existed some other cause which exposed the disciples of Christ to those severities from which the posterity of Abraham was exempt. The difference between them is simple and obvious, but, according to the sentiments of antiquity, it was of the highest importance. The Jews were a *nation,* the Christians were a *sect:* and if it was natural for every community to respect the sacred institutions of their neighbours, it was incumbent on them to persevere in those of their ancestors. The voice of oracles, the precepts of philosophers, and the authority of the laws, unanimously enforced this national obligation. By their lofty claim of superior sanctity the Jews might provoke the Polytheists to consider them as an odious and impure race. By disdaining the intercourse of other nations they might deserve their contempt. The laws of Moses might be for the most part frivolous or absurd; yet, since they had been received during many ages by a large society, his followers were justified by the example of mankind, and it was universally acknowledged that they had a right to practise what it would have been criminal in them to neglect.

But this principle which protected the Jewish synagogue afforded no favour or security to the primitive church. By embracing the faith of the Gospel the Christians incurred the supposed guilt of an unnatural and unpardonable offence. They dissolved the sacred ties of custom and education, violated the religious institutions of their country, and presumptuously despised whatever their fathers had believed as true or had reverenced as sacred. Nor was this apostacy (if we may use the expression) merely of a partial or local kind, since the pious deserter who withdrew himself from the temples of Egypt or Syria would equally disdain to seek an asylum in those of Athens or Carthage. Every Christian rejected with contempt the superstitions of his family, his city, and his province. The whole body of Christians unanimously refused to hold any communion with the gods of Rome, of the empire, and of mankind. It was in vain that the oppressed believer asserted the inalienable rights of conscience and private judgment. Though his situation might excite the pity, his arguments could never reach the understanding, either of the philosophic or of the believing part of the Pagan world.

The surprise of the Pagans was soon succeeded by resentment, and the most pious of men were exposed to the unjust but dangerous imputation of impiety. Malice and prejudice concurred in representing the Christians as a society of atheists, who, by the most daring attack on the religious constitution of the empire, had merited the severest animadversion of the civil magistrate. They had separated themselves (they gloried in the confession) from every mode of superstition which was received in any part of the globe by the various temper of Polytheism: but it was not altogether so evident what deity, or what form of worship, they had substituted to the gods and temples of antiquity. The pure and sublime idea which they entertained of the Supreme Being escaped the gross conception of the Pagan multitude, who were at a loss to discover a spiritual and solitary God, that was neither represented under any corporeal figure or visible symbol, nor was adored with the accustomed pomp of libations and festivals, of altars and sacrifices.

The sages of Greece and Rome, who had elevated their minds to the contemplation of the existence and attributes of the First Cause, were induced by reason or by vanity to reserve for themselves and their chosen disciples the privilege of this philosophical devotion. They were far from admitting the prejudices of mankind as the standard of truth, but they considered them as flowing from the original disposition of human nature; and they supposed that any popular mode of faith and worship which presumed to disclaim the assistance of the senses would, in proportion as it receded from superstition, find itself incapable of restraining the wonderings of the fancy and the visions of fanaticism. The careless glance which men of wit and learning condescended to cast on the Christian revelation served only to confirm their hasty opinion, and to persuade them that the principle which they might have revered, of the Divine Unity, was defaced by the wild enthusiasm, and annihilated by the airy speculations, of the new sectaries.[1]

It might appear less surprising that the founder of Christianity should not only be revered by his disciples as a sage and a prophet, but that he should be adored as a God. The Polytheists were disposed to adopt every article of faith which seemed to offer any resemblance, however distant or imperfect, with the popular mythology; and the legends of Bacchus, of Hercules, and of Æsculapius had, in some measure, prepared their imagination for the appearance of the Son of God under a human form. But they were astonished that the Christians should abandon the temples of those ancient heroes who, in the infancy of the world, had invented arts, instituted laws, and vanquished the tyrants or monsters who infested the earth, in order to choose for the exclusive object of their religious worship an obscure teacher, who, in a recent age, and among a barbarous people, had fallen a sacrifice either to the malice of his own countrymen or to the jealousy of the Roman government. The Pagan multitude, reserving their gratitude for temporal benefits alone, rejected the inestimable present of life and immortality which was offered to mankind by Jesus of Nazareth. His mild constancy in the midst of cruel and voluntary sufferings, his universal benevolence, and the sublime simplicity of his actions and character, were insufficient, in the opinion of those carnal men, to compensate for the want of fame, of empire, and of success; and whilst they refused to acknowledge his stupendous triumph over the powers of darkness and of the grave, they misrepresented, or they insulted, the equivocal birth, wandering life, and ignominious death, of the divine Author of Christianity.

The personal guilt which every Christian had contracted, in thus preferring his private sentiment to the national religion, was aggravated in a very

[1]The author of the Philopatris perpetually treats the Christians as a company of dreaming enthusiasts.

high degree by the number and union of the criminals. It is well known, and has been already observed, that Roman policy viewed with the utmost jealousy and distrust any association among its subjects; and that the privileges of private corporations, though formed for the most harmless or beneficial purposes, were bestowed with a very sparing hand. The religious assemblies of the Christians, who had separated themselves from the public worship, appeared of a much less innocent nature: they were illegal in their principle, and in their consequences might become dangerous; nor were the emperors conscious that they violated the laws of justice, when, for the peace of society, they prohibited those secret and sometimes nocturnal meetings. The pious disobedience of the Christians made their conduct, or perhaps their designs, appear in a much more serious and criminal light; and the Roman princes, who might perhaps have suffered themselves to be disarmed by a ready submission, deeming their honour concerned in the execution of their commands, sometimes attempted by rigorous punishments to subdue this independent spirit, which boldly acknowledged an authority superior to that of the magistrate.

The extent and duration of this spiritual conspiracy seemed to render it every day more deserving of his animadversion. We have already seen that the active and successful zeal of the Christians had insensibly diffused them through every province and almost every city of the empire. The new converts seemed to renounce their family and country, that they might connect themselves in an indissoluble band of union with a peculiar society, which everywhere assumed a different character from the rest of mankind. Their gloomy and austere aspect, their abhorrence of the common business and pleasures of life, and their frequent predictions of impending calamities, inspired the Pagans with the apprehension of some danger which would arise from the new sect, the more alarming as it was the more obscure. "Whatever," says Pliny, "may be the principle of their conduct, their inflexible obstinacy appeared deserving of punishment."

The precautions with which the disciples of Christ performed the offices of religion were at first dictated by fear and necessity; but they were continued from choice. By imitating the awful secrecy which reigned in the Eleusinian mysteries, the Christians had flattered themselves that they should render their sacred institutions more respectable in the eyes of the Pagan world. But it was concluded that they only concealed what they would have blushed to disclose. Their mistaken prudence afforded an opportunity for malice to invent, and for suspicious credulity to believe, the horrid tales which described the Christians as the most wicked of human kind, who practised in their dark recesses every abomination that a depraved fancy could suggest, and who solicited the favour of their unknown God by the sacrifice of every moral virtue. There were many who pretended to confess or to relate the ceremonies of this abhorred society. It was asserted "that a new-born infant, entirely covered over with flour, was presented, like some mystic symbol of initiation, to the knife of the proselyte, who unknowingly inflicted many a secret and mortal wound on the innocent victim of his error; that as soon as the cruel deed was perpetrated, the sectaries drank up the blood, greedily tore asunder the quivering members, and pledged themselves to eternal secrecy, by a mutual consciousness of guilt. It was as confidently affirmed that this inhuman sacrifice was succeeded by a suitable entertainment, in which intemperance served as a provocative to brutal lust; till, at the appointed moment, the lights were suddenly extinguished, shame was banished, nature was forgotten; and, as accident might direct, the darkness of the night was polluted by the incestuous commerce of sisters and brothers, of sons and of mothers."

But the perusal of the ancient apologies was sufficient to remove even the slightest suspicion from the mind of a candid adversary. The Christians, with the intrepid security of innocence, appeal from the voice of rumour to the equity of the magistrates. They acknowledge that, if any proof can be produced of the crimes which calumny has imputed to them, they are worthy of the most severe punishment. They provoke the punishment, and they challenge the proof. At the same time they urge, with equal truth and propriety, that the charge is not less devoid of probability than it is destitute of evidence; they ask whether any one can seriously believe that the pure and holy precepts of the Gospel, which so frequently restrain the use of the most lawful enjoyments, should inculcate the practice of the most abominable crimes; that a large society should resolve to dishonour itself in the eyes of its own members; and that a great number of persons, of either sex, and every age and character, insensible to the fear of death or infamy, should consent to violate those principles which nature and education had imprinted most deeply in their minds.

Nothing, it should seem, could weaken the force or destroy the effect of so unanswerable a justification, unless it were the injudicious conduct of the apologists themselves, who betrayed the common cause of religion to gratify their devout hatred to the domestic enemies of the church. It was sometimes faintly insinuated, and sometimes boldly asserted, that the same bloody sacrifices, and the same incestuous festivals which were so falsely ascribed to the orthodox believers, were in reality celebrated by the Marcionites, by the Carpocratians, and by several other sects of the Gnostics, who, notwithstanding they might deviate into the paths of heresy, were still actuated by the sentiments of men, and still governed by the precepts of Christianity. Accusations of a similar kind were retorted upon the church by the schismatics who had departed from its communion, and it was confessed on all sides that the most scandalous licentiousness of manners prevailed among great numbers of those who affected the name of Christians. A Pagan magistrate, who possessed neither leisure nor abilities to discern the almost imperceptible line which divides the orthodox faith from heretical pravity, might easily have imagined that their mutual animosity had extorted the discovery of their common guilt. It was fortunate for the repose, or at least for the reputation of the first Christians, that the magistrates sometimes proceeded with more temper and moderation than is usually consistent with religious zeal, and that they reported, as the impartial result of their judicial inquiry, that the sectaries who had deserted the established worship appeared to them sincere in their professions and blameless in their manners, however they might incur, by their absurd and excessive superstition, the censure of the laws.

History, which undertakes to record the transactions of the past, for the instruction of future ages, would ill deserve that honourable office if she condescended to plead the cause of tyrants, or to justify the maxims of persecution. It must, however, be acknowledged that the conduct of the emperors who appeared the least favourable to the primitive church is by no means so criminal as that of modern sovereigns who have employed the arm of violence and terror against the religious opinions of any part of their subjects. From their reflections, or even from their own feelings, a Charles V. or a Louis XIV. might have acquired a just knowledge of the rights of conscience, of the obligation of faith, and of the innocence of error. But the princes and magistrates of ancient Rome were strangers to those principles which inspired and authorised the inflexible obstinacy of the Christians in the cause of truth, nor could they themselves discover in their own breasts any motives which would have prompted them to refuse a legal, and as it were a natural, submission to the sacred institutions of their country. The same reason which contributes to alleviate the guilt must have tended to abate the rigour of their persecutions. As they were actuated, not by the furious zeal of bigots, but by the temperate policy of legislators, contempt must often have relaxed, and humanity must frequently have suspended, the execution of those laws which they enacted against the humble and obscure followers of Christ. From the general view of their character and motives we might naturally conclude: I. That a considerable time elapsed before they considered the new sectaries as an object deserving of the attention of government. II. That in the conviction of any of their subjects who were accused of so very singular a crime, they proceeded with caution and reluctance. III. That they were moderate in the use of punishments; and IV. That the afflicted church enjoyed many intervals of peace and tranquillity. Notwithstanding the careless indifference which the most copious and the most minute of the Pagan writers have shown to the affairs of the Christians, it may still be in our power to confirm each of these probable suppositions by the evidence of authentic facts.

I. By the wise dispensation of Providence a mysterious veil was cast over the infancy of the church, which, till the faith of the Christians was matured, and their numbers were multiplied, served to protect them not only from the malice but even from the knowledge of the Pagan world. The slow and gradual abolition of the Mosaic ceremonies afforded a safe and innocent disguise to the more early proselytes of the Gospel. As they were for the greater part of the race of Abraham, they were distinguished by the peculiar mark of circumcision, offered up their devotions in the temple of Jerusalem till its final destruction, and received both the Law and the Prophets as the genuine inspirations of the Deity. The Gentile converts who by a spiritual adoption had been associated to the hope of Israel, were likewise confounded under the garb and appearance of Jews; and as the Polytheists paid less regard to articles of faith than to the external worship, the new sect, which carefully concealed or faintly announced its future greatness and ambition, was permitted to shelter itself under the general toleration which was granted to an ancient and celebrated people in the Roman empire. It was not long, perhaps, before the Jews themselves, animated with a fiercer zeal and a more jealous faith, perceived the gradual separation of their Nazarene brethren from the doctrine of the synagogue: and they would gladly have extinguished the dangerous heresy in the blood of its adherents. But they no longer possessed the administration of criminal justice; nor did they find it easy to infuse into the calm breast of a Roman magistrate the rancour of their own zeal and prejudice. The provincial governors declared themselves ready to listen to any accusation that might affect the public safety; but as soon as they were informed that it was a question not of facts but of words, a dispute relating only to the interpretation of the Jewish laws and prophecies, they deemed it unworthy of the majesty of Rome seriously to discuss the obscure differences which might arise among a barbarous and superstitious people. The innocence of the first Christians was protected by ignorance and contempt.[2]

If, indeed, we were disposed to adopt the traditions of a too credulous antiquity, we might relate the distant peregrinations, the wonderful achievements, and the various deaths of the twelve apostles: but a more accurate inquiry will induce us to doubt whether any of those persons who had been witnesses to the miracles of Christ were permitted, beyond the limits of Palestine, to seal with their blood the truth of their testimony. From the ordinary term of human life, it may very naturally be presumed that most of them were deceased before the discontent of the Jews broke out into that furious war which was terminated only by the ruin of Jerusalem. During a long period, from the death of Christ to that memorable rebellion, we cannot discover any traces of Roman intolerance, unless they are to be found in the sudden, the transient, but the cruel persecution, which was exercised by Nero against the Christians of the capital, thirty-five years after the former, and only two years before the latter, of those great events.

In the tenth year of the reign of Nero the capital of the empire was afflicted by a fire which raged beyond the memory or example of former ages. The monuments of Grecian art and of Roman virtue, the trophies of the Punic and Gallic wars, the most holy temples, and the most splendid palaces were involved in one common destruction. Of the fourteen regions or quarters into which Rome was divided, four only subsisted entire, three were levelled with the ground, and the remaining seven, which had experienced the fury of the flames, displayed a melancholy prospect of ruin and desolation. The vigilance of government appears not to have neglected any of the precautions which might alleviate the sense of so dreadful a calamity. The Imperial gardens were thrown open to the distressed multitude, tem-

[2]An obscure passage of Suetonius (in Claud. c. 25) may seem to offer a proof how strangely the Jews and Christians of Rome were confounded with each other.

porary buildings were erected for their accommodation, and a plentiful supply of corn and provisions was distributed at a very moderate price. The most generous policy seemed to have dictated the edicts which regulated the disposition of the streets and the construction of private houses; and, as it usually happens in an age of prosperity, the conflagration of Rome, in the course of a few years, produced a new city, more regular and more beautiful than the former. But all the prudence and humanity affected by Nero on this occasion were insufficient to preserve him from the popular suspicion. Every crime might be imputed to the assassin of his wife and mother. The voice of rumour accused the emperor as the incendiary of his own capital; and, as the most incredible stories are the best adapted to the genius of an enraged people, it was gravely reported, and firmly believed, that Nero, enjoying the calamity which he had occasioned, amused himself with singing to his lyre the destruction of ancient Troy.

To divert a suspicion which the power of despotism was unable to suppress, the emperor resolved to substitute in his own place some fictitious criminals. "With this view (continues Tacitus) he inflicted the most exquisite tortures on those men who, under the vulgar appellation of Christians, were already branded with deserved infamy. They derived their name and origin from Christ, who, in the reign of Tiberius, had suffered death by the sentence of the procurator Pontius Pilate. For a while this dire superstition was checked, but it again burst forth; and not only spread itself over Judæa, the first seat of this mischievous sect, but was even introduced into Rome, the common asylum which receives and protects whatever is impure, whatever is atrocious. The confessions of those who were seized discovered a great multitude of their accomplices, and they were all convicted, not so much for the crime of setting fire to the city as for their hatred of human kind.[3] They died in torments, and their torments were embittered by insult and derision. Some were nailed on crosses; others sewn up in the skins of wild beasts, and exposed to the fury of dogs; others again, smeared over with combustible materials, were used as torches to illuminate the darkness of the night. The gardens of Nero were destined for the melancholy spectacle, which was accompanied with a horse-race, and honoured with the presence of the emperor, who mingled with the populace in the dress and attitude of a charioteer. The guilt of the Christians deserved indeed the most exemplary punishment, but the public abhorrence was changed into commiseration, from the opinion that those unhappy wretches were sacrificed, not so much to the public welfare as to the cruelty of a jealous tyrant."

Those who survey with a curious eye the revolutions of mankind may observe that the gardens and circus of Nero on the Vatican, which were polluted with the blood of the first Christians, have been rendered still more famous by the triumph and by the abuse of the persecuted religion. On the same spot a temple which far surpasses the ancient glories of the Capitol

[3]*Odio humani generis convicti.* These words may either signify the hatred of mankind towards the Christians, or the hatred of the Christians towards mankind.

has been since erected by the Christian Pontiffs, who, deriving their claim of universal dominion from an humble fisherman of Galilee, have succeeded to the throne of the Cæsars, given laws to the barbarian conquerors of Rome, and extended their spiritual jurisdiction from the coast of the Baltic to the shores of the Pacific Ocean.

It is somewhat remarkable that the flames of war consumed almost at the same time the Temple of Jerusalem and the Capitol of Rome; and it appears no less singular that the tribute which devotion had destined to the former should have been converted by the power of an assaulting victor to restore and adorn the splendour of the latter. The emperors levied a general capitation tax on the Jewish people; and although the sum assessed on the head of each individual was inconsiderable, the use for which it was designed, and the severity with which it was exacted, were considered as an intolerable grievance.

Since the officers of the revenue extended their unjust claim to many persons who were strangers to the blood or religion of the Jews, it was impossible that the Christians, who had so often sheltered themselves under the shade of the synagogue, should now escape this rapacious persecution. Anxious as they were to avoid the slightest infection of idolatry, their conscience forbade them to contribute to the honour of that dæmon who had assumed the character of the Capitoline Jupiter. As a very numerous though declining party among the Christians still adhered to the law of Moses, their efforts to dissemble their Jewish origin were detected by the decisive test of circumcision; nor were the Roman magistrates at leisure to inquire into the difference of their religious tenets. Among the Christians who were brought before the tribunal of the emperor, or, as it seems more probable, before that of the procurator of Judæa, two persons are said to have appeared, distinguished by their extraction, which was more truly noble than that of the greatest monarchs. These were the grandsons of St. Jude the apostle, who himself was the brother of Jesus Christ. Their natural pretensions to the throne of David might perhaps attract the respect of the people, and excite the jealousy of the governor; but the meanness of their garb and the simplicity of their answers soon convinced him that they were neither desirous nor capable of disturbing the peace of the Roman empire. They frankly confessed their royal origin, and their near relation to the Messiah, but they disclaimed any temporal views, and professed that his kingdom, which they devoutly expected, was purely of a spiritual and angelic nature. When they were examined concerning their fortune and occupation, they showed their hands hardened with daily labour, and declared that they derived their whole subsistence from the cultivation of a farm near the village of Cocaba, of the extent of about twenty-four English acres, and of the value of nine thousand drachms, or three hundred pounds sterling. The grandsons of St. Jude were dismissed with compassion and contempt.

But although the obscurity of the house of David might protect them from the suspicions of a tyrant, the present greatness of his own family alarmed the pusillanimous temper of Domitian, which could only be appeased by the blood of those Romans whom he either feared, or hated, or esteemed. Of the two sons of his uncle Flavius Sabinus, the elder was soon convicted of treasonable intentions, and the younger, who bore the name of Flavius Clemens, was indebted for his safety to his want of courage and ability. The emperor for a long time distinguished so harmless a kinsman by his favour and protection, bestowed on him his own niece Domitilla, adopted the children of that marriage to the hope of the succession, and invested their father with the honours of the consulship. But he had scarcely finished the term of his annual magistracy, when on a slight pretence he was condemned and executed; Domitilla was banished to a desolate island on the coast of Campania; and sentences either of death or of confiscation were pronounced against a great number of persons who were involved in the same accusation. The guilt imputed to their charge was that of *Atheism and Jewish manners;* a singular association of ideas, which cannot with any propriety be applied except to the Christians, as they were obscurely and imperfectly viewed by the magistrates and by the writers of that period. On the strength of so probable an interpretation, and too eagerly admitting the suspicions of a tyrant as an evidence of their honourable crime, the church has placed both Clemens and Domitilla among its first martyrs, and has branded the cruelty of Domitian with the name of the second persecution.

But this persecution (if it deserves that epithet) was of no long duration. A few months after the death of Clemens and the banishment of Domitilla, Stephen, a freedman belonging to the latter, who had enjoyed the favour, but who had not surely embraced the faith, of his mistress, assassinated the emperor in his palace. The memory of Domitian was condemned by the senate; his acts were rescinded; his exiles recalled; and under the gentle administration of Nerva, while the innocent were restored to their rank and fortunes, even the most guilty either obtained pardon or escaped punishment.

About ten years afterwards, under the reign of Trajan, the younger Pliny was entrusted by his friend and master with the government of Bithynia and Pontus. He soon found himself at a loss to determine by what rule of justice or of law he should direct his conduct in the execution of an office the most repugnant to his humanity. Pliny had never assisted at any judicial proceedings against the Christians, with whose name alone he seems to be acquainted; and he was totally uninformed with regard to the nature of their guilt, the method of their conviction, and the degree of their punishment. In this perplexity he had recourse to his usual expedient, of submitting to the wisdom of Trajan an impartial, and, in some respects, a favourable account of the new superstition, requesting the emperor that he would condescend to resolve his doubts and to instruct his ignorance.

The life of Pliny had been employed in the acquisition of learning, and in the business of the world. Since the age of nineteen he had pleaded with distinction in the tribunals of Rome, filled a place in the senate, had been invested with the honours of the consulship, and had formed very numerous connections with every order of men, both in Italy and in the provinces. From *his* ignorance therefore we may derive some useful information. We may assure ourselves that when he accepted the government of Bithynia there were no general laws or decrees of the senate in force against the Christians; that neither Trajan nor any of his virtuous predecessors, whose edicts were received into the civil and criminal jurisprudence, had publicly declared their intentions concerning the new sect; and that, whatever proceedings had been carried on against the Christians, there were none of sufficient weight and authority to establish a precedent for the conduct of a Roman magistrate.

The answer of Trajan, to which the Christians of the succeeding age have frequently appealed, discovers as much regard for justice and humanity as could be reconciled with his mistaken notions of religious policy. Instead of displaying the implacable zeal of an Inquisitor, anxious to discover the most minute particles of heresy, and exulting in the number of his victims, the emperor expresses much more solicitude to protect the security of the innocent than to prevent the escape of the guilty. He acknowledges the difficulty of fixing any general plan; but he lays down two salutary rules, which often afforded relief and support to the distressed Christians. Though he directs the magistrates to punish such persons as are legally convicted, he prohibits them, with a very humane inconsistency, from making any inquiries concerning the supposed criminals. Nor was the magistrate allowed to proceed on every kind of information. Anonymous charges the emperor rejects, as too repugnant to the equity of his government; and he strictly requires, for the conviction of those to whom the guilt of Christianity is imputed, the positive evidence of a fair and open accuser. It is likewise probable that the persons who assumed so invidious an office were obliged to declare the grounds of their suspicions, to specify (both in respect to time and place) the secret assemblies which their Christian adversary had frequented, and to disclose a great number of circumstances which were concealed with the most vigilant jealousy from the eye of the profane. If they succeeded in their prosecution, they were exposed to the resentment of a considerable and active party, to the censure of the more liberal portion of mankind, and to the ignominy which, in every age and country, has attended the character of an informer. If, on the contrary, they failed in their proofs, they incurred the severe and perhaps capital penalty, which, according to a law published by the emperor Hadrian, was inflicted on those who falsely attributed to their fellow-citizens the crime of Christianity. The violence of personal or superstitious animosity might sometimes prevail over the most natural apprehensions of disgrace and danger; but it cannot surely be imagined that accusations of so unpromising an appearance were either lightly or frequently undertaken by the Pagan subjects of the Roman empire.

The pious Christian, as he was desirous to obtain or to escape the glory of martyrdom, expected either with impatience or with terror the stated returns of the public games and festivals. On those occasions the inhabitants of the great cities of the empire were collected in the circus or the theatre, where every circumstance of the place, as well as of the ceremony, contributed to kindle their devotion and to extinguish their humanity. Whilst the numerous spectators, crowned with garlands, perfumed with incense, purified with the blood of victims, and surrounded with the altars and statues of their tutelar deities, resigned themselves to the enjoyment of pleasures which they considered as an essential part of their religious worship, they recollected that the Christians alone abhorred the gods of mankind, and, by their absence and melancholy on these solemn festivals, seemed to insult or to lament the public felicity. If the empire had been afflicted by any recent calamity, by a plague, a famine, or an unsuccessful war; if the Tiber had, or if the Nile had not, risen beyond its banks; if the earth had shaken, or if the temperate order of the seasons had been interrupted, the superstitious Pagans were convinced that the crimes and the impiety of the Christians, who were spared by the excessive lenity of the government, had at length provoked the Divine justice. It was not among a licentious and exasperated populace that the forms of legal proceedings could be observed; it was not in an amphitheatre, stained with the blood of wild beasts and gladiators, that the voice of compassion could be heard. The impatient clamours of the multitude denounced the Christians as the enemies of gods and men, doomed them to the severest tortures, and, venturing to accuse by names some of the most distinguished of the new sectaries, required with irresistible vehemence that they should be instantly apprehended and cast to the lions. The provincial governors and magistrates who presided in the public spectacles were usually inclined to gratify the inclinations, and to appease the rage of the people, by the sacrifice of a few obnoxious victims. But the edicts of Hadrian and of Antoninus Pius expressly declared that the voice of the multitude should never be admitted as legal evidence to convict or to punish those unfortunate persons who had embraced the enthusiasm of the Christians.

Punishment was not the inevitable consequence of conviction, and the Christians whose guilt was the most clearly proved by the testimony of witnesses, or even by their voluntary confession, still retained in their own power the alternative of life or death. It was not so much the past offence, as the actual resistance, which excited the indignation of the magistrate. He was persuaded that he offered them an easy pardon, since, if they consented to cast a few grains of incense upon the altar, they were dismissed from the tribunal in safety and with applause.

It was esteemed the duty of a humane judge to endeavour to reclaim, rather than to punish, those deluded enthusiasts. Varying his tone according to the age, the sex, or the situation of the prisoners, he frequently condescended to set before their eyes every circumstance which could render life more pleasing, or death more terrible; and to solicit, nay to entreat them, that they would show some compassion to themselves, to their families, and to their friends. If threats and persuasions proved ineffectual, he had often recourse to violence; the scourge and the rack were called in to supply the deficiency of argument, and every art of cruelty was employed to subdue such inflexible, and, as it appeared to the Pagans, such criminal obstinacy. The ancient apologists of Christianity have censured, with equal truth and severity, the irregular conduct of their persecutors who, contrary to every principle of judicial proceeding, admitted the use of torture in order to obtain, not a confession, but a denial of the crime which was the object of their inquiry.

The martyrs devoted to immediate execution by the Roman magistrates appear to have been selected from the most opposite extremes. They were either bishops and presbyters, the persons the most distinguished among the Christians by their rank and influence, whose example might strike terror into the whole sect; or else they were the meanest and most abject among them, particularly those of the servile condition, whose lives were esteemed of little value, and whose sufferings were viewed by the ancients with too careless an indifference. The learned Origen, who, from his experience as well as readings, was intimately acquainted with the history of the Christians, declares, in the most express terms, that the number of martyrs was very inconsiderable. His authority would alone be sufficient to annihilate that formidable army of martyrs, whose relics, drawn for the most part from the catacombs of Rome, have replenished so many churches, and whose marvellous achievements have been the subject of so many volumes of holy romance. But the general assertion of Origen may be explained and confirmed by the particular testimony of his friend Dionysius, who, in the immense city of Alexandria, and under the rigorous persecution of Decius, reckons only ten men and seven women who suffered for the profession of the Christian name.

During the same period of persecution, the zealous, the eloquent, the ambitious Cyprian governed the church, not only of Carthage, but even of Africa. He possessed every quality which could engage the reverence of the faithful, or provoke the suspicions and resentment of the Pagan magistrates. His character as well as his station seemed to mark out that holy prelate as the most distinguished object of envy and of danger. The experience, however, of the life of Cyprian is sufficient to prove that our fancy has exaggerated the perilous situation of a Christian bishop; and that the dangers to which he was exposed were less imminent than those which temporal ambition is always prepared to encounter in the pursuit of honours. Four Roman emperors, with their families, their favourites, and their adherents, perished by the sword in the space of ten years, during which the bishop of Carthage guided by his authority and eloquence the councils of the African church. It was only in the third year of his administration that he had reason, during a few months, to apprehend the severe edicts of Decius, the vigilance of the magistrate, and the clamours of the multitude, who loudly demanded that Cyprian, the leader of the Christians, should be thrown to the lions. Prudence suggested the necessity of a temporary retreat, and the voice of prudence was obeyed. He withdrew himself into an obscure solitude, from whence he could maintain a constant correspondence with the clergy and people of Carthage; and, concealing himself till the tempest was past, he preserved his life, without relinquishing either his power or his reputation. His extreme caution did not escape the censure of the more rigid Christians, who lamented, or the reproaches of his personal enemies, who insulted, a conduct which they considered as a pusillanimous and criminal desertion of the most sacred duty. But his best apology may be found in the cheerful resolution with which, about eight years afterwards, he suffered death in the cause of religion.

When Valerian was consul for the third, and Gallienus for the fourth time, Paternus, proconsul of Africa, summoned Cyprian to appear in his private council-chamber. He there acquainted him with the Imperial mandate which he had just received, that those who had abandoned the Roman religion should immediately return to the practice of the ceremonies of their ancestors. Cyprian replied without hesitation that he was a Christian and a bishop, devoted to the worship of the true and only Deity, to whom he offered up his daily supplications for the safety and prosperity of the two emperors, his lawful sovereigns. With modest confidence he pleaded the privilege of a citizen in refusing to give any answer to some invidious and indeed illegal questions which the proconsul had proposed. A sentence of banishment was pronounced as the penalty of Cyprian's disobedience; and he was conducted without delay to Curubis, a free and maritime city of Zeugitana, in a pleasant situation, a fertile territory, and at the distance of about forty miles from Carthage.

The exiled bishop enjoyed the conveniences of life and the consciousness of virtue. His reputation was diffused over Africa and Italy; an account of his behaviour was published for the edification of the Christian world; and his solitude was frequently interrupted by the letters, the visits, and the congratulations of the faithful. On the arrival of a new proconsul in the province the fortune of Cyprian appeared for some time to wear a still more favourable aspect. He was recalled from banishment, and, though not yet permitted to return to Carthage, his own gardens in the neighbourhood of the capital were assigned for the place of his residence.

At length, exactly one year after Cyprian was first apprehended, Galerius Maximus, proconsul of Africa, received the Imperial warrant for the execution of the Christian teachers. The bishop of Carthage was sensible that he should be singled out for one of the first victims, and the frailty of nature tempted him to withdraw himself, by a secret flight, from the danger and the honour of martyrdom; but, soon recovering that fortitude which his character required, he returned to his gardens, and patiently expected the ministers of death. Two officers of rank, who were entrusted with that commission, placed Cyprian between them in a chariot, and, as the proconsul was not then at leisure, they conducted him, not to a prison, but to a private house in Carthage, which belonged to one of them. An elegant supper was provided for the entertainment of the bishop, and his Christian friends were permitted for the last time to enjoy his society, whilst the streets were filled with a multitude of the faithful, anxious and alarmed at the approaching fate of their spiritual father. In the morning he appeared before the tribunal of the proconsul, who, after informing himself of the name and situation of Cyprian, commanded him to offer sacrifice, and pressed him to reflect on the consequences of his disobedience. The refusal of Cyprian was firm and decisive, and the magistrate, when he had taken the opinion of his council, pronounced, with some reluctance, the sentence of death. It was conceived in the following terms: "That Thascius Cyprianus should be immediately beheaded, as the enemy of the gods of Rome, and as the chief and ringleader of a criminal association, which he had seduced into an impious resistance against the laws of the most holy emperors Valerian and Gallienus." The manner of his execution was the mildest and least painful that could be inflicted on a person convicted of any capital offence: nor was the use of torture admitted to obtain from the bishop of Carthage either the recantation of his principles or the discovery of his accomplices.

As soon as the sentence was proclaimed, a general cry of "We will die with him" arose at once among the listening multitude of Christians who waited before the palace gates. The generous effusions of their zeal and affection were neither serviceable to Cyprian nor dangerous to themselves. He was led away under a guard of tribunes and centurions, without resistance and without insult, to the place of his execution, a spacious and level plain near the city, which was already filled with great numbers of spectators. His faithful presbyters and deacons were permitted to accompany their holy bishop. They assisted him in laying aside his upper garment, spread linen on the ground to catch the precious relics of his blood, and received his orders to bestow five-and-twenty pieces of gold on the executioner. The martyr then covered his face with his hands, and at one blow his head was separated from his body. His corpse remained during some hours exposed to the curiosity of the Gentiles, but in the night it was removed, and transported, in a triumphal procession and with a splendid illumination, to the burial-place of the Christians. The funeral of Cyprian was publicly celebrated without receiving any interruption from the Roman magistrates; and those among the faithful who had performed the last offices to his person and his memory were secure from the danger of inquiry or of punishment. It is remarkable that, of so great a multitude of bishops in the province of Africa, Cyprian was the first who was esteemed worthy to obtain the crown of martyrdom.

The sober discretion of the present age will more readily censure than admire, but can more easily admire than imitate, the fervour of the first Christians, who, according to the lively expression of Sulpicius Severus, desired martyrdom with more eagerness than his own contemporaries solicited a bishopric. The epistles which Ignatius composed as he was carried in chains through the cities of Asia breathe sentiments the most repugnant to the ordinary feelings of human nature. He earnestly beseeches the Romans that, when he should be exposed in the amphitheatre, they would not, by their kind but unseasonable intercession, deprive him of the crown of glory; and he declares his resolution to provoke and irritate the wild beasts which might be employed as the instruments of his death. Some stories are related of the courage of martyrs who actually performed what Ignatius had intended, who exasperated the fury of the lions, pressed the executioner to hasten his office, cheerfully leaped into the fires which were kindled to consume them, and discovered a sensation of joy and pleasure in the midst of the most exquisite tortures.

Several examples have been preserved of a zeal impatient of those restraints which the emperors had provided for the security of the church. The Christians sometimes supplied by their voluntary declaration the want of an accuser, rudely disturbed the public service of paganism, and, rushing in crowds round the tribunal of the magistrates, called upon them to pronounce and to inflict the sentence of the law. The behaviour of the Christians was too remarkable to escape the notice of the ancient philosophers, but they seem to have considered it with much less admiration than astonishment. Incapable of conceiving the motives which sometimes transported the fortitude of believers beyond the bounds of prudence or reason, they treated such an eagerness to die as the strange result of obstinate despair, of stupid insensibility, or of superstitious frenzy. "Unhappy men!" exclaimed the proconsul Antoninus to the Christians of Asia, "unhappy men! if you are thus weary of your lives, is it so difficult for you to find ropes and precipices?"

Notwithstanding this real or affected disdain, the intrepid constancy of the faithful was productive of salutary effects on those which nature or grace had disposed for the easy reception of religious truth. On these melancholy occasions there were many among the Gentiles who pitied, who admired, and who were converted. The blood of martyrs, according to a well-known observation, became the seed of the church.

But although devotion had raised, and eloquence continued to inflame, this fever of the mind, it insensibly gave way to the more natural hopes and fears of the human heart, to the love of life, the apprehension of pain, and the horror of dissolution. The more prudent rulers of the church found themselves obliged to restrain the indiscreet ardour of their followers, and to distrust a constancy which too often abandoned them in the hour of trial. As the lives of the faithful became less mortified and austere, they were every day less ambitious of the honours of martyrdom; and the soldiers of Christ, instead of distinguishing themselves by voluntary deeds of heroism, frequently deserted their post, and fled in confusion before the enemy whom it was their duty to resist. There were three methods of escaping the flames of persecution, which were not attended with an equal degree of guilt: the first indeed was generally allowed to be innocent; the second was of a doubtful, or at least of a venial, nature; but the third implied a direct and criminal apostacy from the Christian faith.

I. A modern Inquisitor would hear with surprise, that, whenever an information was given to a Roman magistrate of any person within his jurisdiction who had embraced the sect of the Christians, the charge was communicated to the party accused, and that a convenient time was allowed him to settle his domestic concerns, and to prepare an answer to the crime which was imputed to him. If he entertained any doubt of his own constancy, such a delay afforded him the opportunity of preserving his life and honour by flight, of withdrawing himself into some obscure retirement or some distant province, and of patiently expecting the return of peace and security.

II. The provincial governors, whose zeal was less prevalent than their avarice, had countenanced the practice of selling certificates (or libels as they were called), which attested that the persons therein mentioned had complied with the laws, and sacrificed to the Roman deities. By producing these false declarations, the opulent and timid Christians were enabled to silence the malice of an informer, and to reconcile in some measure their safety with their religion. A slight penance atoned for this profane dissimulation.

III. In every persecution there were great numbers of unworthy Christians who publicly disowned or renounced the faith which they had professed; and who confirmed the sincerity of their abjuration by the legal acts of burning incense or of offering sacrifices. Some of these apostates had yielded on the first menace or exhortation of the magistrate; whilst the patience of others had been subdued by the length and repetition of tortures. The affrighted countenances of some betrayed their inward remorse, while others advanced with confidence and alacrity to the altars of the gods. But the disguise which fear had imposed subsisted no longer than the present danger. As soon as the severity of the persecution was abated, the doors of the churches were assailed by the returning multitude of penitents, who detested their idolatrous submission, and who solicited with equal ardour, but with various success, their readmission into the society of Christians.

A variety of motives might dispose the provincial governors either to enforce or to relax the execution of the laws; and of these motives the most forcible was their regard not only for the public edicts, but for the secret intentions of the emperor, a glance from whose eye was sufficient to kindle or to extinguish the flames of persecution.

During the whole course of his reign Marcus despised the Christians as a philosopher, and punished them as a sovereign. But by a singular fatality, the hardships which they had endured under the government of a virtuous prince immediately ceased on the accession of a tyrant; and as none except themselves had experienced the injustice of Marcus, so they alone were protected by the lenity of Commodus. The celebrated Marcia, the most favoured of his concubines, who at length contrived the murder of her Imperial lover, entertained a singular affection for the oppressed church; and though it was impossible that she could reconcile the practice of vice with the precepts of the Gospel, she might hope to atone for the frailties of her sex and profession by declaring herself the patroness of the Christians. Under the gracious protection of Marcia they passed in safety the thirteen years of a cruel tyranny; and when the empire was established in the house of Severus, they formed a domestic but more honourable connection with the new court. The emperor was persuaded that, in a dangerous sickness, he had derived some benefit, either spiritual or physical, from the holy oil with which one of his slaves had anointed him. He always treated with peculiar distinction several persons of both sexes who had embraced the new religion. The nurse as well as the preceptor of Caracalla were Christians; and if that young prince ever betrayed a sentiment of humanity, it was occasioned by an incident which, however trifling, bore some relation to the cause of Christianity.

Under the reign of Severus the fury of the populace was checked; the rigour of ancient laws was for some time suspended; and the provincial governors were satisfied with receiving an annual present from the churches within their jurisdiction, as the price, or as the reward, of their moderation. The controversy concerning the precise time of the celebration of Easter armed the bishops of Asia and Italy against each other, and was considered as the most important business of this period of leisure and tranquillity. Nor was the peace of the church interrupted till the increasing numbers of proselytes seem at length to have attracted the attention, and to have alienated the mind, of Severus. With the design of restraining the progress of Christianity, he published an edict, which, though it was designed to affect only the new converts, could not be carried into strict execution without exposing to danger and punishment the most zealous of their teachers and missionaries.

But the laws which Severus had enacted soon expired with the authority of that emperor; and the Christians, after this accidental tempest, enjoyed a calm of thirty-eight years. Till this period they had usually held their assemblies in private houses and sequestered places. They were now permitted to erect and consecrate convenient edifices for the purpose of religious worship; to purchase lands, even at Rome itself, for the use of the community; and to conduct the elections of their ecclesiastical ministers in so public, but at the same time in so exemplary a manner, as to deserve the respectful attention of the Gentiles. This long repose of the church was accompanied with dignity. The reigns of those princes who derived their extraction from the Asiatic provinces proved the most favourable to the Christians; the eminent persons of the sect, instead of being reduced to implore the protection of a slave or concubine, were admitted into the palace in the honourable characters of priests and philosophers; and their mysterious doctrines, which were already diffused among the people, insensibly attracted the curiosity of their sovereign.

When the empress Mamæa passed through Antioch, she expressed a desire of conversing with the celebrated Origen, the fame of whose piety and learning was spread over the East. Origen obeyed so flattering an invitation, and, though he could not expect to succeed in the conversion of an artful and ambitious woman, she listened with pleasure to his eloquent exhortations, and honourably dismissed him to his retirement in Palestine. The sentiments of Mamæa were adopted by her son Alexander, and the philosophic devotion of that emperor was marked by a singular but injudicious regard for the Christian religion. In his domestic chapel he placed the statues of Abraham, of Orpheus, of Apollonius, and of Christ, as an honour justly due to those respectable sages who had instructed mankind in the various modes of addressing their homage to the supreme and universal Deity. A purer faith, as well as worship, was openly professed and practised among his household. Bishops, perhaps for the first time, were seen at court; and, after the death of Alexander, when the inhuman Maximin discharged his fury on the favourites and servants of his unfortunate benefactor, a great number of Christians, of every rank, and of both sexes, were involved in the promiscuous massacre which, on their account, has improperly received the name of Persecution.

Notwithstanding the cruel disposition of Maximin, the effects of his resentment against the Christians were of a very local and temporary nature, and the pious Origen, who had been proscribed as a devoted victim, was still reserved to convey the truths of the Gospel to the ear of monarchs. He addressed several edifying letters to the emperor Philip, to his wife, and to his mother, and as soon as that prince, who was born in the neighbourhood of Palestine, had usurped the Imperial sceptre, the Christians acquired a friend and a protector. The public and even partial favour of Philip towards the sectaries of the new religion, and his constant reverence for the ministers of the church, gave some colour to the suspicion, which prevailed in his own times, that the emperor himself was become a convert to the faith; and afforded some grounds for a fable which was afterwards invented, that he had been purified by confession and penance from the guilt contracted by the murder of his innocent predecessor.

The fall of Philip introduced, with the change of masters, a new system of government so oppressive to the Christians that their former condition, ever since the time of Domitian, was represented as a state of perfect freedom and security if compared with the rigorous treatment which they experienced under the short reign of Decius. The virtues of that prince will scarcely allow us to suspect that he was actuated by a mean resentment against the favourites of his predecessor; and it is more reasonable to believe that, in the prosecution of his general design to restore the purity of Roman manners, he was desirous of delivering the empire from what he condemned as a recent and criminal superstition. The bishops of the most considerable cities were removed by exile or death: the vigilance of the magistrates prevented the clergy of Rome during sixteen months from proceeding to a new election; and it was the opinion of the Christians that the emperor would more patiently endure a competitor for the purple than a bishop in the capital. Were it possible to suppose that the penetration of Decius had discovered pride under the disguise of humility, or that he could foresee the temporal dominion which might insensibly arise from the claims of spiritual authority, we might be less surprised that he should consider the successors of St. Peter as the most formidable rivals to those of Augustus.

The administration of Valerian was distinguished by a levity and inconstancy ill suited to the gravity of the *Roman Censor*. In the first part of his reign he surpassed in clemency those princes who had been suspected of an attachment to the Christian faith. In the last three years and a half, listening to the insinuations of a minister addicted to the superstitions of Egypt, he adopted the maxims, and imitated the severity, of his predecessor Decius. The accession of Gallienus, which increased the calamities of the empire, restored peace to the church; and the Christians obtained the free exercise of their religion by an edict addressed to the bishops, and conceived in such terms as seemed to acknowledge their office and public character. The ancient laws, without being formally repealed, were suffered to sink into oblivion; and (excepting only some hostile intentions which are attributed to the emperor Aurelian) the disciples of Christ passed above forty years in a state of prosperity far more dangerous to their virtue than the severest trials of persecution.

The story of Paul of Samosata, who filled the metropolitan see of Antioch while the East was in the hands of Odenathus and Zenobia, may serve to illustrate the condition and character of the times. The wealth of that prelate was a sufficient evidence of his guilt, since it was neither derived from the inheritance of his fathers, nor acquired by the arts of honest industry. But Paul considered the service of the church as a very lucrative profession. His ecclesiastical jurisdiction was venal and rapacious; he extorted frequent contributions from the most opulent of the faithful, and converted to his own use a considerable part of the public revenue. By his pride and luxury the Christian religion was rendered odious in the eyes of the Gentiles. His council chamber and his throne, the splendour with which he appeared in public, the suppliant crowd who solicited his attention, the multitude of letters and petitions to which he dictated his answers, and the perpetual hurry of business in which he was involved, were circumstances much better suited to the state of a civil magistrate than to the humility of a primitive bishop. When he harangued his people from the pulpit, Paul affected the figurative style and the theatrical gestures of an Asiatic sophist, while the cathedral resounded with the loudest and most extravagant acclamations in the praise of his divine eloquence. Against those who resisted his power, or refused to flatter his vanity, the prelate of Antioch was arrogant, rigid, and inexorable; but he relaxed the discipline, and lavished the treasures of the church on his dependent clergy, who were permitted to imitate their master in the gratification of every sensual appetite. For Paul indulged himself very freely in the pleasures of the table, and he had received into the episcopal palace two young and beautiful women, as the constant companions of his leisure moments.[4]

Notwithstanding these scandalous vices, if Paul of Samosata had preserved the purity of the orthodox faith, his reign over the capital of Syria would have ended only with his life; and had a reasonable persecution intervened,

[4]If we are desirous of extenuating the vices of Paul, we must suspect the assembled bishops of the East of publishing the most malicious calumnies in circular epistles addressed to all the churches of the empire (ap. Euseb. 1. vii. c. 30).

an effort of court might perhaps have placed him in the rank of saints and martyrs. Some nice and subtle errors which he imprudently adopted and obstinately maintained, concerning the doctrine of the Trinity, excited the zeal and indignation of the Eastern churches. From Egypt to the Euxine Sea, the bishops were in arms and in motion. Several councils were held, confutations were published, excommunications were pronounced, ambiguous explanations were by turns accepted and refused, treaties were concluded and violated, and at length Paul of Samosata was degraded from his episcopal character by the sentence of seventy or eighty bishops who assembled for that purpose at Antioch, and who, without consulting the rights of the clergy or people, appointed a successor by their own authority. The manifest irregularity of this proceeding increased the numbers of the discontented faction; and as Paul, who was no stranger to the arts of courts, had insinuated himself into the favour of Zenobia, he maintained above four years the possession of the episcopal house and office.

The victory of Aurelian changed the face of the East, and the two contending parties, who applied to each other the epithets of schism and heresy, were either commanded or permitted to plead their cause before the tribunal of the conqueror. This public and very singular trial affords a convincing proof that the existence, the property, the privileges, and the internal policy of the Christians, were acknowledged, if not by the laws, at least by the magistrates of the empire.

As a Pagan and as a soldier, it could scarcely be expected that Aurelian should enter into the discussion, whether the sentiments of Paul or those of his adversaries were most agreeable to the true standard of the orthodox faith. His determination, however, was founded on the general principles of equity and reason. He considered the bishops of Italy as the most impartial and respectable judges among the Christians, and, as soon as he was informed that they had unanimously approved the sentence of the council, he acquiesced in their opinion, and immediately gave orders that Paul should be compelled to relinquish the temporal possessions belonging to an office of which, in the judgment of his brethren, he had been regularly deprived. But while we applaud the justice, we should not overlook the policy of Aurelian, who was desirous of restoring and cementing the dependence of the provinces of the capital, by every means which could bind the interest or prejudices of any part of his subjects.

Amidst the frequent revolutions of the empire the Christians still flourished in peace and prosperity; and notwithstanding a celebrated era of martyrs has been deduced from the accession of Diocletian, the new system of policy, introduced and maintained by the wisdom of that prince, continued, during more than eighteen years, to breathe the mildest and most liberal spirit of religious toleration.

The mind of Diocletian himself was less adapted indeed to speculative inquiries than to the active labours of war and government. His prudence rendered him averse to any great innovation, and, though his temper was not very susceptible of zeal or enthusiasm, he always maintained an habitual regard for the ancient deities of the empire. But the leisure of the two empresses, of his wife Prisca, and of Valeria his daughter, permitted them to listen with more attention and respect to the truths of Christianity, which in every age has acknowledged its important obligations to female devotion. The principal eunuchs, Lucian and Dorotheus, Gorgonius and Andrew, who attended the person, possessed the favour, and governed the household of Diocletian, protected by their powerful influence the faith which they had embraced. Their example was imitated by many of the most considerable officers of the palace, who, in their respective stations, had the care of the Imperial ornaments, of the robes, of the furniture, of the jewels, and even of the private treasury; and, though it might sometimes be incumbent on them to accompany the emperor when he sacrificed in the temple, they enjoyed, with their wives, their children, and their slaves, the free exercise of the Christian religion. Diocletian and his colleagues frequently conferred the most important offices on those persons who avowed their abhorrence for the worship of the gods, but who had displayed abilities proper for the service of the state.

The bishops held an honourable rank in their respective provinces, and were treated with distinction and respect, not only by the people, but by the magistrates themselves. Almost in every city the ancient churches were found insufficient to contain the increasing multitude of proselytes; and in their place more stately and capacious edifices were erected for the public worship of the faithful. The corruption of manners and principles so forcibly lamented by Eusebius may be considered, not only as a consequence, but as a proof, of the liberty which the Christians enjoyed.

Notwithstanding this seeming security, an attentive observer might discern some symptoms that threatened the church with a more violent persecution than any which she had yet endured. The zeal and rapid progress of the Christians awakened the Polytheists from their supine indifference in the cause of those deities whom custom and education had taught them to revere. The mutual provocations of a religious war, which had already continued above two hundred years, exasperated the animosity of the contending parties. The Pagans were incensed at the rashness of a recent and obscure sect, which presumed to accuse their countrymen of error, and to devote their ancestors to eternal misery. The habits of justifying the popular mythology against the invectives of an implacable enemy produced in their minds some sentiments of faith and reverence for a system which they had been accustomed to consider with the most careless levity.

Although the policy of Diocletian and humanity of Constantius inclined them to preserve inviolate the maxims of toleration, it was soon discovered that their two associates, Maximian and Galerius, entertained the most implacable aversion for the name and religion of the Christians. The minds of those princes had never been enlightened by science; education had never softened their temper. They owed their greatness to their swords, and in their most elevated fortune they still retained their superstitious prejudices of soldiers and peasants. In the general administration of the provinces they obeyed the laws which their benefactor had established; but they frequently found occasions of exercising within their camp and palaces a secret persecution, for which the imprudent zeal of the Christians sometimes offered the most specious pretences.

A sentence of death was executed upon Maximilianus, an African youth who had been produced by his own father before the magistrate as a sufficient and legal recruit, but who obstinately persisted in declaring that his conscience would not permit him to embrace the profession of a soldier. It could scarcely be expected that any government should suffer the action of Marcellus the centurion to pass with impunity. On the day of a public festival, that officer threw away his belt, his arms, and the ensigns of his office, and exclaimed with a loud voice that he would obey none but Jesus Christ the eternal King, and that he renounced for ever the use of carnal weapons, and the service of an idolatrous master. The soldiers, as soon as they recovered from their astonishment, secured the person of Marcellus. He was examined in the city of Tingi by the president of that part of Mauritania; and as he was convicted by his own confession, he was condemned and beheaded for the crime of desertion.

Examples of such a nature savour much less of religious persecution than of martial or even civil law: but they served to alienate the mind of the emperors, to justify the severity of Galerius, who dismissed a great number of Christian officers from their employments; and to authorise the opinion that a sect of enthusiasts which avowed principles so repugnant to the public safety must either remain useless, or would soon become dangerous subjects of the empire.

After the success of the Persian war had raised the hopes and the reputation of Galerius, he passed a winter with Diocletian in the palace of Nicomedia; and the fate of Christianity became the object of their secret consultations. The experienced emperor was still inclined to pursue measures of lenity; and though he readily consented to exclude the Christians from holding any employments in the household or the army, he urged in the strongest terms the danger as well as cruelty of shedding the blood of those deluded fanatics. Galerius at length extorted from him the permission of summoning a council, composed of a few persons the most distinguished in the civil and military departments of the state. The important question was agitated in their presence, and those ambitious courtiers easily discerned that it was incumbent on them to second, by their own eloquence, the importunate violence of the Cæsar. It may be presumed that they insisted on every topic which might interest the pride, the piety, or the fears, of their sovereign in the destruction of Christianity. Perhaps they represented that the glorious work of the deliverance of the empire was left imperfect, as long as an independent people was permitted to subsist and multiply in the heart of the provinces. The Christians (it might speciously be alleged), renouncing the gods and the institutions of Rome, had constituted a distinct republic, which might yet be suppressed before it had acquired any military force; but which was already governed by its own laws and magistrates, was possessed of a public treasure, and was intimately connected in all its parts by the frequent assemblies of the bishops, to whose decrees their numerous and opulent congregations yielded an implicit obedience. Arguments like these may seem to have determined the reluctant mind of Diocletian to embrace a new system of persecution: but though we may suspect, it is not in our power to relate, the secret intrigues of the palace, the private views and resentments, the jealousy of women or eunuchs, and all those trifling but decisive causes which so often influence the fate of empires and the councils of the wisest monarchs.[5]

The pleasure of the emperors was at length signified to the Christians, who, during the course of this melancholy winter, had expected with anxiety the result of so many secret consultations. The twenty-third of February, which coincided with the Roman festival of the Terminalia, was appointed (whether from accident or design) to set bounds to the progress of Christianity. At the earliest dawn of day the Prætorian præfect, accompanied by several generals, tribunes, and officers of the revenue, repaired to the principal church of Nicomedia, which was situated on an eminence in the most populous and beautiful part of the city. The doors were instantly broken open; they rushed into the sanctuary; and as they searched in vain for some visible object of worship, they were obliged to content themselves with committing to the flames the volumes of Holy Scripture. The ministers of Diocletian were followed by a numerous body of guards and pioneers, who marched in order of battle, and were provided with all the instruments used in the destruction of fortified cities. By their incessant labour, a sacred edifice, which towered above the Imperial palace, and had long excited the indignation and envy of the Gentiles, was in a few hours levelled with the ground.

The next day the general edict of persecution was published; and though Diocletian, still averse to the effusion of blood, had moderated the fury of Galerius, who proposed that every one refusing to offer sacrifice should immediately be burnt alive, the penalties inflicted on the obstinacy of the Christians might be deemed sufficiently rigorous and effectual. It was enacted that their churches, in all the provinces of the empire, should be demolished to their foundations; and the punishment of death was denounced against all who should presume to hold any secret assemblies for the purpose of religious worship.

The philosophers, who now assumed the unworthy office of directing the blind zeal of persecution, had diligently studied the nature and genius of the Christian religion; and as they were not ignorant that the speculative doctrines of the faith were supposed to be contained in the writings of the prophets, of the evangelists, and of the apostles, they most probably suggested the order that the bishops and presbyters should deliver all their sacred books into the hands of the magistrates, who were commanded,

[5] The only circumstance which we can discover is the devotion and jealousy of the mother of Galerius. She had a great influence over her son, and was offended by the disregard of some of her Christian servants.

under the severest penalties, to burn them in a public and solemn manner. By the same edict, the property of the church was at once confiscated; and the several parts of which it might consist were either sold to the highest bidder, united to the Imperial domain, bestowed on the cities and corporations, or granted to the solicitations of rapacious courtiers.

After taking such effectual measures to abolish the worship and to dissolve the government of the Christians, it was thought necessary to subject to the most intolerable hardships the condition of those perverse individuals who should still reject the religion of nature, of Rome, and of their ancestors. Persons of a liberal birth were declared incapable of holding any honours or employments; slaves were for ever deprived of the hopes of freedom; and the whole body of the people were put out of the protection of the law. The judges were authorised to hear and to determine every action that was brought against a Christian. But the Christians were not permitted to complain of any injury which they themselves had suffered; and thus those unfortunate sectaries were exposed to the severity, while they were excluded from the benefits, of public justice.

This new species of martyrdom, so painful and lingering, so obscure and ignominious, was, perhaps, the most proper to weary the constancy of the faithful: nor can it be doubted that the passions and interest of mankind were disposed on this occasion to second the designs of the emperors.

This edict was scarcely exhibited to the public view, in the most conspicuous place of Nicomedia, before it was torn down by the hands of a Christian who expressed at the same time, by the bitterest invectives, his contempt as well as abhorrence for such impious and tyrannical governors. His offense, according to the mildest laws, amounted to treason and deserved death. And if it be true that he was a person of rank and education, those circumstances could serve only to aggravate his guilt. He was burnt, or rather roasted, by a slow fire; and his executioners, zealous to revenge the personal insult which had been offered to the emperors, exhausted every refinement of cruelty, without being able to subdue his patience, or to alter the steady and insulting smile which, in his dying agonies, he still preserved in his countenance. The Christians, though they confessed that his conduct had not been strictly conformable to the laws of prudence, admired the divine fervour of his zeal; and the excessive commendations which they lavished on the memory of their hero and martyr contributed to fix a deep impression of terror and hatred in the mind of Diocletian.[6]

His fears were soon alarmed by the view of a danger from which he very narrowly escaped. Within fifteen days the palace of Nicomedia, and even the bedchamber of Diocletian, were twice in flames; and though both times they were extinguished without any material damage, the singular repetition of the fire was justly considered as an evident proof that it had not been the

[6]Lactantius only calls him quidam, etsi non recte, magno tamen animo, etc., M. P. c. 13. Eusebius (1. viii. c. 5) adorns him with secular honours. Neither have condescended to mention his name; but the Greeks celebrate his memory under that of John. See Tillemont, Mémoires Ecclésiastiques, tom. v. part ii. p. 320.

effect of chance or negligence. The suspicion naturally fell on the Christians; and it was suggested, with some degree of probability, that those desperate fanatics, provoked by their present sufferings, and apprehensive of impending calamities, had entered into a conspiracy with their faithful brethren, the eunuchs of the palace, against the lives of two emperors whom they detested as the irreconcilable enemies of the church of God. Jealousy and resentment prevailed in every breast, but especially in that of Diocletian. A great number of persons, distinguished either by the offices which they had filled or by the favour which they had enjoyed, were thrown into prison. Every mode of torture was put in practice, and the court, as well as city, was polluted with many bloody executions. But as it was found impossible to extort any discovery of this mysterious transaction, it seems incumbent on us either to presume the innocence, or to admire the resolution, of the sufferers. A few days afterwards Galerius hastily withdrew himself from Nicomedia, declaring that if he delayed his departure from that devoted palace, he should fall a sacrifice to the rage of the Christians. The ecclesiastical historians, from whom alone we derive a partial and imperfect knowledge of this persecution, are at a loss how to account for the fears and danger of the emperors. Two of these writers, a prince and a rhetorician, were eye-witnesses of the fire of Nicomedia. The one ascribes it to lightning and the divine wrath, the other affirms that it was kindled by the malice of Galerius himself.

As the edict against the Christians was designed for a general law of the whole empire, and as Diocletian and Galerius, though they might not wait for the consent, were assured of the concurrence of the Western princes, it would appear more consonant to our ideas of policy that the governors of all the provinces should have received secret instructions to publish, on one and the same day, this declaration of war within their respective departments. It was at least to be expected that the convenience of the public highways and established posts would have enabled the emperors to transmit their orders with the utmost despatch from the palace of Nicomedia to the extremities of the Roman world; and that they would not have suffered fifty days to elapse before the edict was published in Syria, and near four months before it was signified to the cities of Africa. This delay may perhaps be imputed to the cautious temper of Diocletian, who had yielded a reluctant consent to the measures of persecution, and who was desirous of trying the experiment under his more immediate eye before he gave way to the disorders and discontent which it must inevitably occasion in the distant provinces. At first, indeed, the magistrates were restrained from the effusion of blood; but the use of every other severity was permitted, and even recommended to their zeal; nor could the Christians, though they cheerfully resigned the ornaments of their churches, resolve to interrupt their religious assemblies, or to deliver their sacred books to the flames. The pious obstinacy of Felix, an African bishop, appears to have embarrassed the subordinate ministers of the government. The curator of his city sent him in chains to the proconsul. The proconsul transmitted him to the Prætorian præfect of Italy; and Felix, who disdained even to give an evasive answer, was at length beheaded at Venusia, in Lucania, a place on which the birth of Horace has conferred fame. This precedent, and perhaps some Imperial rescript, which was issued in consequence of it, appeared to authorise the governors of provinces in punishing with death the refusal of the Christians to deliver up their sacred books.

The copies as well as the versions of Scripture were already so multiplied in the empire, that the most severe inquisition could no longer be attended with any fatal consequences. But the ruin of the churches was easily effected by the authority of the government and by the labour of the Pagans. In some provinces the magistrates contented themselves with shutting up the places of religious worship. In others they more literally complied with the terms of the edict; and, after taking away the doors, the benches, and the pulpit, which they burnt as it were in a funeral pile, they completely demolished the remainder of the edifice.

It is perhaps to this melancholy occasion that we should apply a very remarkable story, which is related with so many circumstances of variety and improbability that it serves rather to excite than to satisfy our curiosity. In a small town in Phrygia, of whose name as well as situation we are left ignorant, it should seem that the magistrates and the body of the people had embraced the Christian faith; and as some resistance might be apprehended to the execution of the edict, the governor of the province was supported by a numerous detachment of legionaries. On their approach the citizens threw themselves into the church, with the resolution either of defending by arms that sacred edifice or of perishing in its ruins. They indignantly rejected the notice and permission which was given them to retire, till the soldiers, provoked by their obstinate refusal, set fire to the building on all sides, and consumed, by this extraordinary kind of martyrdom, a great number of Phrygians, with their wives and children.

Some slight disturbances, though they were suppressed almost as soon as excited, in Syria and the frontiers of Armenia, afforded the enemies of the church a very plausible occasion to insinuate that those troubles had been secretly fomented by the intrigues of the bishops, who had already forgotten their ostentatious professions of passive and unlimited obedience. The resentment, or the fears, of Diocletian at length transported him beyond the bounds of moderation which he had hitherto preserved, and he declared, in a series of cruel edicts, his intention of abolishing the Christian name.

By the first of these edicts the governors of the provinces were directed to apprehend all persons of the ecclesiastical order; and the prisons destined for the vilest criminals were soon filled with a multitude of bishops, presbyters, deacons, readers, and exorcists. By a second edict the magistrates were commanded to employ every method of severity which might reclaim them from their odious superstition, and oblige them to return to the established worship of the gods. This rigorous order was extended, by a subsequent edict, to the whole body of Christians, who were exposed to a violent and general persecution. Instead of those salutary restraints which had required the direct and solemn testimony of an accuser, it became the duty as well as the interest of the Imperial officers to discover, to pursue, and to torment the most obnoxious among the faithful. Heavy penalties were denounced against all who should presume to save a proscribed sectary from the just indignation of the gods and of the emperors. Yet, notwithstanding the severity of this law, the virtuous courage of many of the Pagans, in concealing their friends or relations, affords an honourable proof that the rage of superstition had not extinguished in their minds the sentiments of nature and humanity.

Diocletian had no sooner published his edicts against the Christians than, as if he had been desirous of committing to other hands the work of persecution, he divested himself of the Imperial purple. The character and situation of his colleagues and successors sometimes urged them to enforce, and sometimes inclined them to suspend, the execution of these rigorous laws; nor can we acquire a just and distinct idea of this important period of ecclesiastical history unless we separately consider the state of Christianity, in the different parts of the empire, during the space of ten years which elapsed between the first edicts of Diocletian and the final peace of the church.

The mild and humane temper of Constantius was averse to the oppression of any part of his subjects. The principal offices of his palace were exercised by Christians. He loved their persons, esteemed their fidelity, and entertained not any dislike to their religious principles. But as long as Constantius remained in the subordinate station of Cæsar, it was not in his power openly to reject the edicts of Diocletian, or to disobey the commands of Maximian. His authority contributed, however, to alleviate the sufferings which he pitied and abhorred. He consented with reluctance to the ruin of the churches, but he ventured to protect the Christians themselves from the fury of the populace and from the rigour of the laws. The provinces of Gaul (under which we may probably include those of Britain) were indebted for the singular tranquillity which they enjoyed to the gentle interposition of their sovereign. But Datianus, the president or governor of Spain, actuated either by zeal or policy, chose rather to execute the public edicts of the emperors than to understand the secret intentions of Constantius; and it can scarcely be doubted that his provincial administration was stained with the blood of a few martyrs.

The elevation of Constantius to the supreme and independent dignity of Augustus gave a free scope to the exercise of his virtues, and the shortness of his reign did not prevent him from establishing a system of toleration of which he left the precept and the example to his son Constantine. His fortunate son, from the first moment of his accession declaring himself the protector of the church, at length deserved the appellation of the first emperor who publicly professed and established the Christian religion. The motives of his conversion, as they may variously be deduced from benevolence, from policy, from conviction, or from remorse, and the progress of the revolution which, under his powerful influence and that of his sons, rendered Christianity the reigning religion of the Roman empire, will form a very interesting and important chapter. At present it may be sufficient to observe that every victory of Constantine was productive of some relief or benefit to the church.

The provinces of Italy and Africa experienced a short but violent persecution. The rigorous edicts of Diocletian were strictly and cheerfully executed by his associate Maximian, who had long hated the Christians, and who delighted in acts of blood and violence. In the autumn of the first year of the persecution the two emperors met at Rome to celebrate their triumph; several oppressive laws appear to have issued from their secret consultations, and the diligence of the magistrates was animated by the presence of their sovereigns. After Diocletian had divested himself of the purple, Italy and Africa were administered under the name of Severus, and were exposed, without defence, to the implacable resentment of his master Galerius.

When Galerius had obtained the supreme power and the government of the East, he indulged in their fullest extent his zeal and cruelty, not only in the provinces of Thrace and Asia, which acknowledged his immediate jurisdiction, but in those of Syria, Palestine, and Egypt. But the frequent disappointments of his ambitious views, the experience of six years of persecution, and the salutary reflections which a lingering and painful distemper suggested to the mind of Galerius, at length convinced him that the most violent efforts of despotism are insufficient to extirpate a whole people, or to subdue their religious prejudices. Desirous of repairing the mischief that he had occasioned, he published in his own name, and in those of Licinius and Constantine, a general edict, which, after a pompous recital of the Imperial titles, proceeded in the following manner:

"Among the important cares which have occupied our mind for the utility and preservation of the empire, it was our intention to correct and re-establish all things according to the ancient laws and public discipline of the Romans. We were particularly desirous of reclaiming into the way of reason and nature the deluded Christians who had renounced the religion and ceremonies instituted by their fathers, and, presumptuously despising the practice of antiquity, had invented extravagant laws and opinions according to the dictates of their fancy, and had collected a various society from the different provinces of our empire. The edicts which we have published to enforce the worship of the gods having exposed many of the Christians to danger and distress, many having suffered death, and many more, who still persist in their impious folly, being left destitute of *any* public exercise of religion, we are disposed to extend to those unhappy men the effects of our wonted clemency. We permit them, therefore, freely to profess their private opinions, and to assemble in their conventicles without fear or molestation, provided always that they preserve a due respect to the established laws and government. By another rescript we shall signify our intentions to the judges and magistrates, and we hope that our indulgence will engage the Christians to offer up their prayers to the Deity whom they adore for our safety and prosperity, for their own, and for that of the republic." It is not usually in the language of edicts and manifestoes that we should search for the real character of the secret motives of princes; but as these were the words of a dying emperor, his situation, perhaps, may be admitted as a pledge of his sincerity.

When Galerius subscribed this edict of toleration, he was well assured that any measures in favour of the Christians would obtain the approbation of Constantine. But the emperor would not venture to insert in the preamble the name of Maximin, whose consent was of the greatest importance, and who succeeded a few days afterwards to the provinces of Asia. Cruelty and superstition were the ruling passions of the soul of Maximin. The former suggested the means, the latter pointed out the objects, of persecution. The emperor was devoted to the worship of the gods, to the study of magic, and to the belief of oracles. The prophets or philosophers whom he revered as the favourites of Heaven were frequently raised to the government of provinces, and admitted into his most secret councils. They easily convinced him that the Christians had been indebted for their victories to their regular discipline, and that the weakness of Polytheism had principally flowed from a want of union and subordination among the ministers of religion. A system of government was therefore instituted, which was evidently copied from the policy of the church. In all the great cities of the empire, the temples were repaired and beautified by the order of Maximin, and the officiating priests of the various deities were subjected to the authority of a superior pontiff destined to oppose the bishop, and to promote the cause of Paganism. These pontiffs acknowledged, in their turn, the supreme jurisdiction of the metropolitans or high priests of the province, who acted as the immediate vicegerents of the emperor himself. A white robe was the ensign of their dignity; and these new prelates were carefully selected from the most noble and opulent families.

By the influence of the magistrates, and of the sacerdotal order, a great number of dutiful addresses were obtained, particularly from the cities of Nicomedia, Antioch, and Tyre, which artfully represented the well-known intentions of the court as the general sense of the people; solicited the emperor to consult the laws of justice rather than the dictates of his clemency; expressed their abhorrence of the Christians, and humbly prayed that those impious sectaries might at least be excluded from the limits of their respective territories. The answer of Maximin to the address which he obtained from the citizens of Tyre is still extant. He praises their zeal and devotion in terms of the highest satisfaction, descants on the obstinate impiety of the Christians, and betrays, by the readiness with which he consents to their banishment, that he considered himself as receiving, rather than as conferring an obligation. The priests as well as the magistrates were empowered to enforce the execution of his edicts, which were engraved on tables of brass; and though it was recommended to them to avoid the effusion of blood, the most cruel and ignominious punishments were inflicted on the refractory Christians.

The Christians had everything to dread from the severity of a bigoted monarch who prepared his measures of violence with such deliberate policy. But two circumstances insinuate that the general treatment of the Christians who had been apprehended by the officers of justice was less intolerable than it is usually imagined to have been. 1. The confessors who were condemned to work in the mines were permitted by the humanity or the negligence of their keepers to build chapels, and freely to profess their religion in the midst of those dreary habitations. 2. The bishops were obliged to check and to censure the forward zeal of the Christians, who voluntarily threw themselves into the hands of the magistrates. Some of these were persons oppressed by poverty and debts, who blindly sought to terminate a miserable existence by a glorious death. Others were allured by the hope that a short confinement would expiate the sins of a whole life; and others again were actuated by the less honourable motive of deriving a plentiful subsistence, and perhaps a considerable profit, from the alms which the charity of the faithful bestowed on the prisoners.

The vague descriptions of exile and imprisonment, of pain and torture, are so easily exaggerated or softened by the pencil of an artful orator, that we are naturally induced to inquire into a fact of a more distinct and stubborn kind; the number of persons who suffered death in consequence of the edicts published by Diocletian, his associates, and his successors. From the history of Eusebius it may be collected that only nine bishops were punished with death; and we are assured, by his particular enumeration of the martyrs of Palestine, that no more than ninety-two Christians were entitled to that honourable appellation. As we are unacquainted with the degree of episcopal zeal and courage which prevailed at that time, it is not in our power to draw any useful inferences from the former of these facts: but the latter may serve to justify a very important and probable conclusion. According to the distribution of Roman provinces, Palestine may be considered as the sixteenth part of the Eastern empire: and since there were some governors who, from a real or affected clemency, had preserved their hands unstained with the blood of the faithful, it is reasonable to believe that the country which had given birth to Christianity produced at least the sixteenth part of the martyrs who suffered death within the dominions of Galerius and Maximin; the whole might consequently amount to about fifteen hundred, a number which, if it is equally divided between the ten years of the persecution, will allow an annual consumption of one hundred and fifty martyrs. Allotting the same proportion to the provinces of Italy, Africa, and perhaps Spain, where, at the end of two or three years, the rigour of the penal laws was either suspended or abolished, the multitude of Christians in the Roman empire, on whom a capital punishment was inflicted by a judicial sentence, will be reduced to somewhat less than two thousand persons. Since it cannot be doubted that the Christians were more numerous, and their enemies more exasperated, in the time of Diocletian than they had ever been in any former persecution, this probable and moderate computation may teach us to estimate the number of primitive saints and martyrs who sacrificed their lives for the important purpose of introducing Christianity into the world.

We shall conclude this chapter by a melancholy truth which obtrudes itself on the reluctant mind; that, even admitting, without hesitation or inquiry, all that history has recorded, or devotion has feigned, on the subject of martyrdoms, it must still be acknowledged that the Christians, in the course of their intestine dissensions, have inflicted far greater severities on each other than they had experienced from the zeal of infidels.

CHAPTER XII

Troubles after the Abdication of Diocletian—Reunion of the Empire under the Authority of Constantine

The balance of power established by Diocletian subsisted no longer than while it was sustained by the firm and dexterous hand of the founder. It required such a fortunate mixture of different tempers and abilities as could scarcely be found, or even expected, a second time; two emperors without jealousy, two Cæsars without ambition and the same general interest invariably pursued by four independent princes. The abdication of Diocletian and Maximian was succeeded by eighteen years of discord and confusion. The empire was afflicted by five civil wars; and the remainder of the time was not so much a state of tranquillity as a suspension of arms between several hostile monarchs, who, viewing each other with an eye of fear and hatred, strove to increase their respective forces at the expense of their subjects.

For the first, and indeed for the last time, the Roman world was administered by six emperors. In the West, Constantine and Maxentius affected to reverence their father Maximian. In the East, Licinius and Maximin honoured with more real consideration their benefactor Galerius. The opposition of interest, and the memory of a recent war, divided the empire into two great hostile powers; but their mutual fears produced an apparent tranquillity, and even a feigned reconciliation, till the death of the elder princes, of Maximian, and more particularly of Galerius, gave a new direction to the views and passions of their surviving associates.

As soon as Diocletian and Maximian had resigned the purple, their station, according to the rules of the new constitution, was filled by the two Cæsars, Constantius and Galerius, who immediately assumed the title of Augustus. The honours of seniority and precedence were allowed to the former of those princes, and he continued under a new appellation to administer his ancient department of Gaul, Spain, and Britain. The British expedition, and an easy victory over the barbarians of Caledonia, were the last exploits of the reign of Constantius. He ended his life in the Imperial palace of York, fifteen months after he had received the title of Augustus, and almost fourteen years and a half after he had been promoted to the rank of Cæsar. His death was immediately succeeded by the elevation of Constantine.

The ambitious spirit of Galerius was scarcely reconciled to the disappointment of his views upon the Gallic provinces before the unexpected loss of Italy wounded his pride as well as power in a still more sensible part. The long absence of the emperors had filled Rome with discontent and indignation; and the people gradually discovered that the preference given to Nicomedia and Milan was not to be ascribed to the particular inclination of Diocletian, but to the permanent form of government which he had instituted. About that time the avarice of Galerius, or perhaps the exigencies of the state, had induced him to make a very strict and rigorous inquisition into the property of his subjects for the purpose of a general taxation, both on their lands and on their persons. A very minute survey appears to have been taken of their real estates; and, wherever there was the slightest suspicion of concealment, torture was very freely employed to obtain a sincere declaration of their personal wealth.

The conquest of Macedonia, as we have already observed, had delivered the Roman people from the weight of personal taxes. Though they had experienced every form of despotism, they had now enjoyed that exemption near five hundred years; nor could they patiently brook the insolence of an Illyrian peasant, who, from his distant residence in Asia, presumed to number Rome among the tributary cities of his empire. The rising fury of the people was encouraged by the authority, or at least the connivance, of the senate; and the feeble remains of the Prætorian guards, who had reason to apprehend their own dissolution, embraced so honourable a pretence and declared their readiness to draw their swords in the service of their oppressed country. It was the wish, and it soon became the hope, of every citizen that, after expelling from Italy their foreign tyrants, they should elect a prince who, by the place of his residence and by his maxims of government, might once more deserve the title of Roman emperor. The name, as well as the situation of Maxentius, determined in his favour the popular enthusiasm.

Maxentius was the son of the emperor Maximian, and he had married the daughter of Galerius. His birth and alliance seemed to offer him the fairest promise of succeeding to the empire; but his vices and incapacity procured him the same exclusion from the dignity of Cæsar which Constantine had deserved by a dangerous superiority of merit. Though the characters of Constantine and Maxentius had very little affinity with each other, their situation and interest were the same, and prudence seemed to require that they should unite their forces against the common enemy. Notwithstanding the superiority of his age and dignity, the indefatigable Maximian passed the Alps, and, courting a personal interview with the sovereign of Gaul, carried with him his daughter Fausta as the pledge of the new alliance. The marriage was celebrated at Arles with every circumstance of magnificence; and the ancient colleague of Diocletian, who again asserted his claim to the Western empire, conferred on his son-in-law and ally the title of Augustus. By consenting to receive that honour from Maximian, Constantine seemed to embrace the cause of Rome and of the senate; but his professions were ambiguous, and his assistance slow and ineffectual. He considered with attention the approaching contest between the masters of Italy and the emperor of the East.

The importance of the occasion called for the presence and abilities of Galerius. At the head of a powerful army collected from Illyricum and the East, he entered Italy, resolved to chastise the rebellious Romans; or, as he expressed his intentions in the furious language of a barbarian, to extirpate the senate and to destroy the people by the sword. But the skill of Maximian had concerted a prudent system of defence. The invader found every place hostile, fortified, and inaccessible; and though he forced his way as far as Narni, within sixty miles of Rome, his dominion in Italy was confined to the narrow limits of his camp.

Maxentius, who openly avowed his pretensions to the whole monarchy of the West, had already prepared a very considerable force to invade the Gallic provinces. Constantine no longer hesitated. He had deliberated with caution, he acted with vigour. He gave a private audience to the ambassadors who, in the name of the senate and people, conjured him to deliver Rome from a detested tyrant; and, without regarding the timid remonstrances of his council, he resolved to prevent the enemy, and to carry the war into the heart of Italy.

In the age of Constantine the peasants of the mountains were civilised and obedient subjects; the country was plentifully stocked with provisions, and the stupendous highways which the Romans had carried over the Alps opened several communications between Gaul and Italy. Constantine preferred the road of the Cottian Alps, or, as it is now called, of Mount Cenis, and led his troops with such active diligence, that he descended into the plain of Piedmont before the court of Maxentius had received any certain intelligence of his departure from the banks of the Rhine. The city of Susa, situated at the foot of Mount Cenis, was surrounded with walls and provided with a garrison sufficiently numerous to check the progress of an invader; but the impatience of Constantine's troops disdained the tedious forms of a siege. The same day that they appeared before Susa they applied fire to the gates and ladders to the walls; and mounting to the assault amidst a shower of stones and arrows, they entered the place sword in hand, and cut in pieces the greatest part of the garrison. The flames were extinguished by the care of Constantine, and the remains of Susa preserved from total destruction.

About forty miles from thence a more severe contest awaited him. A numerous army of Italians was assembled, under the lieutenants of Maxentius, in the plains of Turin. Its principal strength consisted in a species of heavy cavalry, which the Romans, since the decline of their discipline, had borrowed from the nations of the East. The horses, as well as the men, were clothed in complete armour, the joints of which were artfully adapted to the motions of their bodies. The aspect of this cavalry was formidable, their weight almost irresistible; and as, on this occasion, their generals had drawn them up in a compact column or wedge, with a sharp point, and with spreading flanks, they flattered themselves that they should easily break and trample down the army of Constantine.

They might, perhaps, have succeeded in their design, had not their experienced adversary embraced the same method of defence which in similar circumstances had been practised by Aurelian. The skilful evolutions of Constantine divided and baffled this massy column of cavalry. The troops of Maxentius fled in confusion towards Turin; and as the gates of the city were shut against them, very few escaped the sword of the victorious pursuers. By this important service Turin deserved to experience the clemency and even favour of the conqueror. He made his entry into the Imperial palace of Milan, and almost all the cities of Italy between the Alps and the Po not only acknowledged the power, but embraced with zeal the party of Constantine.

The virtues of Constantine were rendered more illustrious by the vices of Maxentius. Whilst the Gallic provinces enjoyed as much happiness as the condition of the times was capable of receiving, Italy and Africa groaned under the dominion of a tyrant as contemptible as he was odious. The zeal of flattery and faction has indeed too frequently sacrificed the reputation of the vanquished to the glory of their successful rivals; but even those writers who have revealed, with the most freedom and pleasure, the faults of Constantine, unanimously confess that Maxentius was cruel, rapacious, and profligate. He had the good fortune to suppress a slight rebellion in Africa. The governor and a few adherents had been guilty; the province suffered for their crime. The flourishing cities of Cirtha and Carthage, and the whole extent of that fertile country, were wasted by fire and sword. The abuse of victory was followed by the abuse of law and justice. A formidable army of sycophants and delators invaded Africa; the rich and the noble were easily convicted of a connection with the rebels; and those among them who experienced the emperor's clemency were punished only by the confiscation of their estates.

So signal a victory was celebrated by a magnificent triumph, and Maxentius exposed to the eyes of the people the spoils and captives of a Roman province. The state of the capital was no less deserving of compassion than that of Africa. The wealth of Rome supplied an inexhaustible fund for his vain and prodigal expenses, and the ministers of his revenue were skilled in the arts of rapine. It was under his reign that the method of exacting a *free gift* from the senators was first invented; and as the sum was insensibly increased, the pretences of levying it, a victory, a birth, a marriage, or an Imperial consulship, were proportionately multiplied.

Maxentius had imbibed the same implacable aversion to the senate which had characterised most of the former tyrants of Rome; nor was it possible for his ungrateful temper to forgive the generous fidelity which had raised him to the throne and supported him against all his enemies. The lives of the senators were exposed to his jealous suspicions, the dishonour of their wives and daughters heightened the gratification of his sensual passions. It may be presumed that an Imperial lover was seldom reduced to sigh in vain; but whenever persuasion proved ineffectual, he had recourse to violence; and there remains *one* memorable example of a noble matron who preserved her chastity by a voluntary death.

The soldiers were the only order of men whom he appeared to respect, or studied to please. He filled Rome and Italy with armed troops, connived at their tumults, suffered them with impunity to plunder, and even to massacre, the defenceless people; and indulging them in the same licentiousness which their emperor enjoyed, Maxentius often bestowed on his military favourites the splendid villa, or the beautiful wife, of a senator. Rome, which had so long regretted the absence, lamented, during the six years of his reign, the presence of her sovereign.

The celerity of Constantine's march has been compared to the rapid conquest of Italy by the first of the Cæsars; nor is the flattering parallel repugnant to the truth of history, since no more than fifty-eight days elapsed between the surrender of Verona and the final decision.

Constantine had always apprehended that the tyrant would consult the dictates of fear, and perhaps of prudence; and that, instead of risking his last hopes in a general engagement, he would shut himself up within the walls of Rome. It was with equal surprise and pleasure that, on his arrival at a place called Saxa Rubra, about nine miles from Rome, he discovered the army of Maxentius prepared to give him battle. Their long front filled a very spacious plain, and their deep array reached to the banks of the Tiber, which covered their rear, and forbade their retreat. We are informed, and we may believe, that Constantine disposed his troops with consummate skill, and that he chose for himself the post of honour and danger. Distinguished by the splendour of his arms, he charged in person the cavalry of his rival; and his irresistible attack determined the fortune of the day. Defeat of the two wings left the infantry without any protection on its flanks, and the undisciplined Italians fled without reluctance from the standard of a tyrant whom they had always hated, and whom they no longer feared.

The confusion became general, and the dismayed troops of Maxentius, pursued by an implacable enemy, rushed by thousands into the deep and rapid stream of the Tiber. The emperor himself attempted to escape back into the city over the Milvian bridge, but the crowds which pressed together through that narrow passage forced him into the river, where he was immediately drowned by the weight of his armour. Constantine thus achieved by his valour and ability the most splendid enterprise of his life.

The fame of Constantine has rendered posterity attentive to the most minute circumstances of his life and actions. The place of his birth, as well as the condition of his mother Helena, have been the subject not only of literary but of national disputes. Notwithstanding the recent tradition which assigns for her father a British king, we are obliged to confess that Helena was the daughter of an innkeeper; but at the same time we may defend the legality of her marriage against those who have represented her as the concubine of Constantius.

The great Constantine was most probably born at Naissus, in Dacia;

and it is not surprising that, in a family and province distinguished only by the profession of arms, the youth should discover very little inclination to improve his mind by the acquisition of knowledge. He was about eighteen years of age when his father was promoted to the rank of Cæsar; but that fortunate event was attended with his mother's divorce; and the splendour of an Imperial alliance reduced the son of Helena to a state of disgrace and humiliation. Instead of following Constantius in the West, he remained in the service of Diocletian, signalising his valour in the wars of Egypt and Persia, and gradually rose to the honourable station of a tribune of the first order.

The figure of Constantine was tall and majestic; he was dexterous in all his exercises, intrepid in war, affable in peace; in his whole conduct the active spirit of youth was tempered by habitual prudence; and while his mind was engrossed by ambition, he appeared cold and insensible to the allurements of pleasure.

The civil administration was sometimes interrupted by the military defence of the empire. The Goths, who in the time of Claudius and Aurelian had felt the weight of the Roman arms, respected the power of the empire even in the midst of its intestine divisions. But the strength of that warlike nation was now restored by a peace of near fifty years; a new generation had arisen, who no longer remembered the misfortunes of ancient days: the Sarmatians of the lake Mæotis followed the Gothic standard either as subjects or as allies, and their united force was poured upon the countries of Illyricum. Campona, Margus, and Bononia, appear to have been the scenes of several memorable sieges and battles; and though Constantine encountered a very obstinate resistance, he prevailed at length in the contest, and the Goths were compelled to purchase an ignominious retreat by restoring the booty and prisoners which they had taken. Nor was this advantage sufficient to satisfy the indignation of the emperor. He resolved to chastise as well as to repulse the insolent barbarians who had dared to invade the territories of Rome. At the head of his legions he passed the Danube, after repairing the bridge which had been constructed by Trajan, penetrated into the strongest recesses of Dacia, and, when he had inflicted a severe revenge, condescended to give peace to the suppliant Goths, on condition that, as often as they were required, they should supply his armies with a body of forty thousand soldiers.

Exploits like these were no doubt honourable to Constantine and beneficial to the state; but it may surely be questioned whether they can justify the exaggerated assertion of Eusebius, that ALL SCYTHIA, as far as the extremity of the North, divided as it was into so many names and nations of the most various and savage manners, had been added by his victorious arms to the Roman empire. Yet Constantine was almost perpetually in motion, to exercise the legions or to inspect the state of the provinces. Treves, Milan, Aquileia, Sirmium, Naissus, and Thessalonica were the occasional places of his residence till he founded a NEW ROME on the confines of Europe and Asia.

The motives, whether of pride or of policy, which first induced Diocletian to withdraw himself from the ancient seat of government had acquired additional weight by the example of his successors and the habits of forty years. Rome was insensibly confounded with the dependent kingdoms which had once acknowledged her supremacy; and the country of the Cæsars was viewed with cold indifference by a martial prince, born in the neighbourhood of the Danube, educated in the courts and armies of Asia, and invested with the purple by the legions of Britain. The Italians, who had received Constantine as their deliverer, submissively obeyed the edicts which he sometimes condescended to address to the senate and people of Rome; but they were seldom honoured with the presence of their new sovereign.

During the vigour of his age Constantine, according to the various exigencies of peace and war, moved with slow dignity or with active diligence along the frontiers of his extensive dominions; and was always prepared to take the field either against a foreign or a domestic enemy. But as he gradually reached the summit of prosperity and the decline of life, he began to meditate the design of fixing in a more permanent station the strength as well as majesty of the throne. In the choice of an advantageous situation he preferred the confines of Europe and Asia; to curb with a powerful arm the barbarians who dwelt between the Danube and the Tanais; to watch with an eye of jealousy the conduct of the Persian monarch, who indignantly supported the yoke of an ignominious treaty. With these views Diocletian had selected and embellished the residence of Nicomedia: but the memory of Diocletian was justly abhorred by the protector of the church; and Constantine was not insensible to the ambition of founding a city which might perpetuate the glory of his own name.

During the late operations of the war against Licinius he had sufficient opportunity to contemplate, both as a soldier and as a statesman, the incomparable position of Byzantium; and to observe how strongly it was guarded by nature against an hostile attack, whilst it was accessible on every side to the benefits of commercial intercourse. Many ages before Constantine, one of the most judicious historians of antiquity had described the advantages of a situation from whence a feeble colony of Greeks derived the command of the sea, and the honours of a flourishing and independent republic.

If we survey Byzantium in the extent which it acquired with the august name of Constantinople, the figure of the Imperial city may be represented under that of an unequal triangle. The obtuse point, which advances towards the east and the shores of Asia, meets and repels the waves of the Thracian Bosphorus. The northern side of the city is bounded by the harbour, and the southern is washed by the Propontis or Sea of Marmora. The basis of the triangle is opposed to the west, and terminates the continent of Europe. But the admirable form and division of the circumjacent land and water cannot, without a more ample explanation, be clearly or sufficiently understood.

The winding channel through which the waters of the Euxine flow with a rapid and incessant course towards the Mediterranean received the appellation of Bosphorus, a name not less celebrated in the history than in the fables of antiquity. A crowd of temples and of votive altars, profusely scattered along its steep and woody banks, attested the unskilfulness, the terrors, and the devotion of the Grecian navigators who, after the example of the Argonauts, explored the dangers of the inhospitable Euxine. On these banks tradition long preserved the memory of the palace of Phineus, infested by the obscene harpies;[1] and of the sylvan reign of Amycus, who defied the son of Leda to the combat of the Cestus.

The harbour of Constantinople, which may be considered as an arm of the Bosphorus, obtained, in a very remote period, the denomination of the *Golden Horn.* The curve which it describes might be compared to the horn of a stag, or as it should seem, with more propriety, to that of an ox. The epithet of *golden* was expressive of the riches which every wind wafted from the most distant countries into the secure and capacious port of Constantinople. The river Lycus, formed by the conflux of two little streams, pours into the harbour a perpetual supply of fresh water, which serves to cleanse the bottom and to invite the periodical shoals of fish to seek their retreat in that convenient recess. As the vicissitudes of tides are scarcely felt in those seas, the constant depth of the harbour allows goods to be landed on the quays without the assistance of boats; and it has been observed that, in many places, the largest vessels may rest their prows against the houses while their sterns are floating in the water. From the mouth of the Lycus to that of the harbour this arm of the Bosphorus is more than seven miles in length. The entrance is about five hundred yards broad, and a strong chain could be occasionally drawn across it to guard the port and city from the attack of an hostile navy.

Between the Bosphorus and the Hellespont, the shores of Europe and Asia receding on either side enclose the Sea of Marmora, which was known to the ancients by the denomination of Propontis. The navigation from the issue of the Bosphorus to the entrance of the Hellespont is about one hundred and twenty miles. Those who steer their westward course through the middle of the Propontis may at once descry the high lands of Thrace and Bithynia, and never lose sight of the lofty summit of Mount Olympus, covered with eternal snows. They leave on the left a deep gulf, at the bottom of which Nicomedia was seated, the Imperial residence of Diocletian; and they pass the small islands of Cyzicus and Proconnesus before they cast anchor at Gallipoli, where the sea, which separates Asia from Europe, is again contracted into a narrow channel.

The geographers who, with the most skilful accuracy, have surveyed the form and extent of the Hellespont, assign about sixty miles for the winding course, and about three miles for the ordinary breadth, of those celebrated straits. But the narrowest part of the channel is found to the

[1]There are very few conjectures so happy as that of Le Clerc (Bibliothèque Universelle, tom. i. p. 148), who supposes that the harpies were only locusts.

northward of the old Turkish castles, between the cities of Sestus and Abydus. It was here that the adventurous Leander braved the passage of the flood for the possession of his mistress. It was here likewise, in a place where the distance between the opposite banks cannot exceed five hundred paces, that Xerxes imposed a stupendous bridge of boats, for the purpose of transporting into Europe a hundred and seventy myriads of barbarians.

We are at present qualified to view the advantageous position of Constantinople, which appears to have been formed by nature for the centre and capital of a great monarchy. Situated in the forty-first degree of latitude, the Imperial city commanded, from her seven hills, the opposite shores of Europe and Asia; the climate was healthy and temperate, the soil fertile, the harbour secure and capacious, and the approach on the side of the continent was of small extent and easy defence. The Bosphorus and the Hellespont may be considered as the two gates of Constantinople, and the prince who possessed those important passages could always shut them against a naval enemy and open them to the fleets of commerce. The preservation of the eastern provinces may in some degree be ascribed to the policy of Constantine, as the barbarians of the Euxine, who in the preceding age had poured their armaments into the heart of the Mediterranean, soon desisted from the exercise of piracy and despaired of forcing this insurmountable barrier.

When the gates of the Hellespont and Bosphorus were shut, the capital still enjoyed within their spacious enclosure every production which could supply the wants or gratify the luxury of its numerous inhabitants. The sea-coasts of Thrace and Bithynia, which languish under the weight of Turkish oppression, still exhibit a rich prospect of vineyards, of gardens, and of plentiful harvests; and the Propontis has ever been renowned for an inexhaustible store of the most exquisite fish, that are taken in their stated seasons without skill, and almost without labour. But when the passages of the straits were thrown open for trade, they alternately admitted the natural and artificial riches of the North and South, of the Euxine and of the Mediterranean. Whatever rude commodities were collected in the forests of Germany and Scythia, as far as the sources of the Tanais and the Borysthenes; whatsoever was manufactured by the skill of Europe or Asia; the corn of Egypt, and the gems and spices of the farthest India, were brought by the varying winds into the port of Constantinople, which, for many ages, attracted the commerce of the ancient world.

The prospect of beauty, of safety, and of wealth united in a single spot was sufficient to justify the choice of Constantine. But as some decent mixture of prodigy and fable has, in every age, been supposed to reflect a becoming majesty on the origin of great cities, the emperor was desirous of ascribing his resolution not so much to the uncertain counsels of human policy as to the infallible and eternal decrees of divine wisdom. In one of his laws he has been careful to instruct posterity that, in obedience to the commands of God, he laid the everlasting foundations of Constantinople; and though he has not condescended to relate in what manner the celestial inspiration was communicated to his mind, the defect of his modest silence has been liberally supplied by the ingenuity of succeeding writers, who describe the nocturnal vision which appeared to the fancy of Constantine as he slept within the walls of Byzantium. The tutelar genius of the city, a venerable matron sinking under the weight of years and infirmities, was suddenly transformed into a blooming maid, whom his own hands adorned with all the symbols of Imperial greatness. The monarch awoke, interpreted the auspicious omen, and obeyed, without hesitation, the will of Heaven. The day which gave birth to a city or colony was celebrated by the Romans with such ceremonies as had been ordained by a generous superstition;[2] and though Constantine might omit some rites which savoured too strongly of their Pagan origin, yet he was anxious to leave a deep impression of hope and respect on the minds of the spectators. On foot, with a lance in his hand, the emperor himself led the solemn procession, and directed the line which was traced as the boundary of the destined capital, till the growing circumference was observed with astonishment by the assistants, who, at length, ventured to observe that he had already exceeded the most ample measure of a great city. "I shall still advance," replied Constantine, "till HE, the invisible guide who marches before me, thinks proper to stop."

In the actual state of the city, the palace and gardens of the Seraglio occupy the eastern promontory, the first of the seven hills, and cover about one hundred and fifty acres of our own measure. The seat of Turkish jealousy and despotism is erected on the foundations of a Grecian republic; but it may be supposed that the Byzantines were tempted by the conveniency of the harbour to extend their habitations on that side beyond the modern limits of the Seraglio.

The new walls of Constantine stretched from the port to the Propontis across the enlarged breadth of the triangle, at the distance of fifteen stadia from the ancient fortification, and with the city of Byzantium they enclosed five of the seven hills which, to the eyes of those who approach Constantinople, appear to rise above each other in beautiful order. About a century after the death of the founder, the new buildings, extending on one side up the harbour, and on the other along the Propontis, already covered the narrow ridge of the sixth and the broad summit of the seventh hill. The necessity of protecting those suburbs from the incessant inroads of the barbarians engaged the younger Theodosius to surround his capital with an adequate and permanent enclosure of walls.

From the eastern promontory to the golden gate, the extreme length of Constantinople was about three Roman miles, the circumference measured between ten and eleven, and the surface might be computed as equal to about two thousand English acres. It is impossible to justify the vain

[2]See Plutarch in Romul. [c. 11] tom. i. p. 49, edit. Bryan. Among other ceremonies, a large hole, which had been dug for that purpose, was filled up with handfuls of earth, which each of the settlers brought from the place of his birth, and thus adopted his new country.

and credulous exaggerations of modern travellers, who have sometimes stretched the limits of Constantinople over the adjacent villages of the European and even of the Asiatic coast. But the suburbs of Pera and Galata, though situate beyond the harbour, may deserve to be considered as a part of the city; and this addition may perhaps authorise the measure of a Byzantine historian, who assigns sixteen Greek (about fourteen Roman) miles for the circumference of his native city. Such an extent may seem not unworthy of an Imperial residence. Yet Constantinople must yield to Babylon and Thebes, to ancient Rome, to London, and even to Paris.

The master of the Roman world who aspired to erect an eternal monument of the glories of his reign could employ in the prosecution of that great work the wealth, the labour, and all that yet remained of the genius of obedient millions. Some estimate may be formed of the expense bestowed with Imperial liberality on the foundation of Constantinople by the allowance of about two million five hundred thousand pounds for the construction of the walls, the porticoes, and the aqueducts. The forests that overshadowed the shores of the Euxine, and the celebrated quarries of white marble in the little island of Proconnesus, supplied an inexhaustible stock of materials, ready to be conveyed, by the convenience of a short water-carriage, to the harbour of Byzantium. A multitude of labourers and artificers urged the conclusion of the work with incessant toil; but the impatience of Constantine soon discovered that, in the decline of the arts, the skill as well as numbers of his architects bore a very unequal proportion to the greatness of his designs. The magistrates of the most distant provinces were therefore directed to institute schools, to appoint professors, and, by the hopes of rewards and privileges, to engage in the study and practice of architecture a sufficient number of ingenious youths who had received a liberal education.

The buildings of the new city were executed by such artificers as the reign of Constantine could afford; but they were decorated by the hands of the most celebrated masters of the age of Pericles and Alexander. To revive the genius of Phidias and Lysippus surpassed indeed the power of a Roman emperor; but the immortal productions which they had bequeathed to posterity were exposed without defence to the rapacious vanity of a despot. By his commands the cities of Greece and Asia were despoiled of their most valuable ornaments. The trophies of memorable wars, the objects of religious veneration, the most finished statues of the gods and heroes, of the sages and poets of ancient times, contributed to the splendid triumph of Constantinople.

The populousness of his favoured city was the next and most serious object of the attention of its founder. In the dark ages which succeeded the translation of the empire, the remote and the immediate consequences of that memorable event were strangely confounded by the vanity of the Greeks and the credulity of the Latins. It was asserted and believed that all the noble families of Rome, the senate, and the equestrian order, with their innumerable attendants, had followed their emperor to the banks of the Propontis; that a spurious race of strangers and plebeians was left to possess the solitude of the ancient capital; and that the lands of Italy, long since converted into gardens, were at once deprived of cultivation and inhabitants. In the course of this history such exaggerations will be reduced to their just value; yet, since the growth of Constantinople cannot be ascribed to the general increase of mankind and of industry, it must be admitted that this artificial colony was raised at the expense of the ancient cities of the empire. Many opulent senators of Rome and of the eastern provinces were probably invited by Constantine to adopt for their country the fortunate spot which he had chosen for his own residence. The invitations of a master are scarcely to be distinguished from commands, and the liberality of the emperor obtained a ready and cheerful obedience. He bestowed on his favourites the palaces which he had built in the several quarters of the city, assigned them lands and pensions for the support of their dignity, and alienated the demesnes of Pontus and Asia to grant hereditary estates by the easy tenure of maintaining a house in the capital.

But these encouragements and obligations soon became superfluous, and were gradually abolished. Wherever the seat of government is fixed, a considerable part of the public revenue will be expended by the prince himself, by his ministers, by the officers of justice, and by the domestics of the palace. The most wealthy of the provincials will be attracted by the powerful motives of interest and duty, of amusement and curiosity. A third and more numerous class of inhabitants will insensibly be formed, of servants, of artificers, and of merchants, who derive their subsistence from their own labour, and from the wants or luxury of the superior ranks. In less than a century Constantinople disputed with Rome itself the pre-eminence of riches and numbers. The venerable parent still maintained the legal and acknowledged supremacy, due to her age, to her dignity, and to the remembrance of her former greatness.

At the festival of the dedication, an edict, engraved on a column of marble, bestowed the title of SECOND or NEW ROME on the city of Constantine. But the name of Constantinople has prevailed over that honourable epithet, and after the revolution of fourteen centuries still perpetuates the fame of its author.

The foundation of a new capital is naturally connected with the establishment of a new form of civil and military administration. The distinct view of the complicated system of policy introduced by Diocletian, improved by Constantine, and completed by his immediate successors, may not only amuse the fancy by the singular picture of a great empire but will tend to illustrate the secret and internal causes of its rapid decay. In the pursuit of any remarkable institution, we may be frequently led into the more early or the more recent times of the Roman history; but the proper limits of this inquiry will be included within a period of about one hundred and thirty years, from the accession of Constantine to the publication of the Theodosian code; from which, as well as from the *Notitia* of the East and West, we derive the most copious and authentic information of the state of the empire. This variety of objects will suspend, for some time, the course of the narrative; but the interruption will be censured only by those readers who are insensible to the importance of laws and manners, while they peruse, with eager curiosity, the transient intrigues of a court, or the accidental event of a battle.

The manly pride of the Romans, content with substantial power, had left to the vanity of the East the forms and ceremonies of ostentatious greatness. But when they lost even the semblance of those virtues which were derived from their ancient freedom, the simplicity of Roman manners was insensibly corrupted by the stately affectation of the courts of Asia. The patents of office were curiously emblazoned with such emblems as were best adapted to explain its nature and high dignity—the image or portrait of the reigning emperors; a triumphal car; the book of mandates placed on a table, covered with a rich carpet, and illuminated by four tapers; the allegorical figures of the provinces which they governed; or the appellations and standards of the troops whom they commanded. Some of these official ensigns were really exhibited in their hall of audience; others preceded their pompous march whenever they appeared in public; and every circumstance of their demeanour, their dress, their ornaments, and their train, was calculated to inspire a deep reverence for the representatives of supreme majesty. By a philosophic observer the system of the Roman government might have been mistaken for a splendid theatre, filled with players of every character and degree, who repeated the language, and imitated the passions, of their original model.

As long as the Roman consuls were the first magistrates of a free state, they derived their right to power from the choice of the people. As long as the emperors condescended to disguise the servitude which they imposed, the consuls were still elected by the real or apparent suffrage of the senate. From the reign of Diocletian even these vestiges of liberty were abolished, and the successful candidates, who were invested with the annual honours of the consulship, affected to deplore the humiliating condition of their predecessors. The Scipios and the Catos had been reduced to solicit the votes of plebeians, to pass through the tedious and expensive forms of a popular election, and to expose their dignity to the shame of a public refusal; while their own happier fate had reserved them for an age and government in which the rewards of virtue were assigned by the unerring wisdom of a gracious sovereign. In the epistles which the emperor addressed to the two consuls elect, it was declared that they were created by his sole authority. Their names and portraits, engraved on gilt tablets of ivory, were dispersed over the empire as presents to the provinces, the cities, the magistrates, the senate, and the people. Their solemn inauguration was performed at the place of the Imperial residence; and during a period of one hundred and twenty years Rome was constantly deprived of the presence of her ancient magistrates.

On the morning of the first of January the consuls assumed the ensigns of their dignity. Their dress was a robe of purple, embroidered in silk and gold, and sometimes ornamented with costly gems. On this solemn occasion they were attended by the most eminent officers of the state and army in the habit of senators; and the useless fasces, armed with the once formidable axes, were borne before them by the lictors. The procession moved from the palace to the Forum or principal square of the city, where the consuls ascended their tribunal, and seated themselves in the curule chairs, which were framed after the fashion of ancient times. They immediately exercised an act of jurisdiction, by the manumission of a slave who was brought before them for that purpose; and the ceremony was intended to represent the celebrated action of the elder Brutus, the author of liberty and of the consulship, when he admitted among his fellow-citizens the faithful Vindex, who had revealed the conspiracy of the Tarquins. The public festival was continued during several days in all the principal cities; in Rome, from custom; in Constantinople, from imitation; in Carthage, Antioch, and Alexandria, from the love of pleasure and the superfluity of wealth.

In the two capitals of the empire the annual games of the theatre, the circus, and the amphitheatre cost four thousand pounds of gold, (about) one hundred and sixty thousand pounds sterling; and if so heavy an expense surpassed the faculties or the inclination of the magistrates themselves, the sum was supplied from the Imperial treasury. As soon as the consuls had discharged these customary duties, they were at liberty to retire into the shade of private life, and to enjoy during the remainder of the year the undisturbed contemplation of their own greatness. They no longer presided in the national councils; they no longer executed the resolutions of peace or war. Their abilities (unless they were employed in more effective offices) were of little moment; and their names served only as the legal date of the year in which they had filled the chair of Marius and of Cicero. Yet it was still felt and acknowledged, in the last period of Roman servitude, that this empty name might be compared, and even preferred, to the possession of substantial power. The title of consul was still the most splendid object of ambition, the noblest reward of virtue and loyalty. The emperors themselves, who disdained the faint shadow of the republic, were conscious that they acquired an additional splendour and majesty as often as they assumed the annual honours of the consular dignity.

The proudest and most perfect separation which can be found in any age or country between the nobles and the people is perhaps that of the Patricians and the Plebeians, as it was established in the first age of the Roman republic. Wealth and honours, the offices of the state, and the ceremonies of religion, were almost exclusively possessed by the former; who, preserving the purity of their blood with the most insulting jealousy,[3] held their clients in a condition of specious vassalage. But these distinctions, so incompatible with the spirit of a free people, were removed, after a long

[3]Intermarriages between the Patricians and Plebeians were prohibited by the laws of the XII Tables; and the uniform operations of human nature may attest that the custom survived the law.

struggle, by the persevering efforts of the Tribunes. The most active and successful of the Plebeians accumulated wealth, aspired to honours, deserved triumphs, contracted alliances, and, after some generations, assumed the pride of ancient nobility. The Patrician families, on the other hand, whose original number was never recruited till the end of the commonwealth, either failed in the ordinary course of nature, or were extinguished in so many foreign and domestic wars, or, through a want of merit or fortune, insensibly mingled with the mass of the people. Very few remained who could derive their pure and genuine origin from the infancy of the city, or even from that of the republic, when Cæsar and Augustus, Claudius and Vespasian, created from the body of the senate a competent number of new Patrician families, in the hope of perpetuating an order which was still considered as honourable and sacred. But these artificial supplies (in which the reigning house was always included) were rapidly swept away by the rage of tyrants, by frequent revolutions, by the change of manners, and by the intermixture of nations. Little more was left when Constantine ascended the throne than a vague and imperfect tradition that the Patricians had once been the first of the Romans.

The fortunes of the Prætorian præfects were essentially different from those of the consuls and Patricians. The latter saw their ancient greatness evaporate in a vain title. The former, rising by degrees from the most humble condition, were invested with the civil and military administration of the Roman world. From the reign of Severus to that of Diocletian, the guards and the palace, the laws and the finances, the armies and the provinces, were entrusted to their superintending care; and, like the vizirs of the East, they held with one hand the seal, and with the other the standard, of the empire. The ambition of the præfects, always formidable, and sometimes fatal to the masters whom they served, was supported by the strength of the Prætorian bands; but, after those haughty troops had been weakened by Diocletian and finally suppressed by Constantine, the præfects, who survived their fall, were reduced without difficulty to the station of useful and obedient ministers. When they were no longer responsible for the safety of the emperor's person, they resigned the jurisdiction which they had hitherto claimed and exercised over all the departments of the palace. They were deprived by Constantine of all military command as soon as they had ceased to lead into the field, under their immediate orders, the flower of the Roman troops; and, at length, by a singular revolution, the captains of the guards were transformed into the civil magistrates of the provinces.

After the Prætorian præfects had been dismissed from all military command, the civil functions which they were ordained to exercise over so many subject nations were adequate to the ambition and abilities of the most consummate ministers. To their wisdom was committed the supreme administration of justice and of the finances, the two objects which, in a state of peace, comprehend almost all the respective duties of the sovereign and of the people; of the former, to protect the citizens who are obedient to the laws; of the latter, to contribute the share of their property which is required for the expenses of the state. The coin, the highways, the posts, the granaries, the manufactures, whatever could interest the public prosperity, was moderated by the authority of the Prætorian præfects. As the immediate representatives of the Imperial majesty, they were empowered to explain, to enforce, and on some occasions to modify, the general edicts by their discretionary proclamations. They watched over the conduct of the provincial governors, removed the negligent, and inflicted punishments on the guilty. From all the inferior jurisdictions an appeal in every matter of importance, either civil or criminal, might be brought before the tribunal of the præfect: but *his* sentence was final and absolute; and the emperors themselves refused to admit any complaints against the judgment or the integrity of a magistrate whom they honoured with such unbounded confidence. His appointments were suitable to his dignity; and, if avarice was his ruling passion, he enjoyed frequent opportunities of collecting a rich harvest of fees, of presents, and of perquisites. Though the emperors no longer dreaded the ambition of their præfects, they were attentive to counterbalance the power of this great office by the uncertainty and shortness of its duration.

As the spirit of jealousy and ostentation prevailed in the councils of the emperors, they proceeded with anxious diligence to divide the substance and to multiply the titles of power. The vast countries which the Roman conquerors had united under the same simple form of administration were imperceptibly crumbled into minute fragments, till at length the whole empire was distributed into one hundred and sixteen provinces, each of which supported an expensive and splendid establishment. Of these, three were governed by *proconsuls*, thirty-seven by *consulars*, five by *correctors*, and seventy-one by *presidents*. The appellations of these magistrates were different; they ranked in successive order, the ensigns of their dignity were curiously varied, and their situation, from accidental circumstances, might be more or less agreeable or advantageous. But they were all (excepting only the proconsuls) alike included in the class of *honourable* persons; and they were alike entrusted, during the pleasure of the prince, and under the authority of the præfects or their deputies, with the administration of justice and the finances in their respective districts.

The ponderous volumes of the Codes and Pandects would furnish ample materials for a minute inquiry into the system of provincial government, as in the space of six centuries it was improved by the wisdom of the Roman statesmen and lawyers. It may be sufficient for the historian to select two singular and salutary provisions, intended to restrain the abuse of authority.

1. For the preservation of peace and order, the governors of the provinces were armed with the sword of justice. They inflicted corporal punishments, and they exercised, in capital offences, the power of life and death. But they were not authorised to indulge the condemned criminal with the choice of his own execution or to pronounce a sentence of the mildest and most honourable kind of exile. These prerogatives were reserved to the præfects, who alone could impose the heavy fine of fifty pounds of gold: their vice-

gerents were confined to the trifling weight of a few ounces. This distinction, which seems to grant the larger while it denies the smaller degree of authority, was founded on a very rational motive. The smaller degree was infinitely more liable to abuse. The passions of a provincial magistrate might frequently provoke him into acts of oppression, which affected only the freedom or the fortunes of the subject; though, from a principle of prudence, perhaps of humanity, he might still be terrified by the guilt of innocent blood. It may likewise be considered that exile, considerable fines, or the choice of an easy death, relate more particularly to the rich and the noble; and the persons the most exposed to the avarice or resentment of a provincial magistrate were thus removed from his obscure persecution to the more august and impartial tribunal of the Prætorian præfect.

2. As it was reasonably apprehended that the integrity of the judge might be biassed, if his interest was concerned or his affections were engaged, the strictest regulations were established to exclude any person, without the special dispensation of the emperor, from the government of the province where he was born; and to prohibit the governor or his son from contracting marriage with a native or an inhabitant; or from purchasing slaves, lands, or houses within the extent of his jurisdiction.

Notwithstanding these rigorous precautions, the emperor Constantine, after a reign of twenty-five years, still deplores the venal and oppressive administration of justice, and expresses the warmest indignation that the audience of the judge, his despatch of business, his seasonable delays, and his final sentence, were publicly sold, either by himself or by the officers of his court. The continuance, and perhaps the impunity, of these crimes is attested by the repetition of impotent laws and ineffectual menaces.

All the civil magistrates were drawn from the profession of the law. The celebrated Institutes of Justinian are addressed to the youth of his dominions who had devoted themselves to the study of Roman jurisprudence; and the sovereign condescends to animate their diligence by the assurance that their skill and ability would in time be rewarded by an adequate share in the government of the republic. The rudiments of this lucrative science were taught in all the considerable cities of the East and West; but the most famous school was that of Berytus, on the coast of Phœnicia.

After a regular course of education, which lasted five years, the students dispersed themselves through the provinces in search of fortune and honours; nor could they want an inexhaustible supply of business in a great empire already corrupted by the multiplicity of laws, of arts, and of vices. The court of the Prætorian præfect of the East could alone furnish employment for one hundred and fifty advocates, sixty-four of whom were distinguished by peculiar privileges, and two were annually chosen with a salary of sixty pounds of gold to defend the causes of the treasury. The first experiment was made of their judicial talents by appointing them to act occasionally as assessors to the magistrates; from thence they were often raised to preside in the tribunals before which they had pleaded. They obtained the government of a province; and, by the aid of merit, of reputation, or of favour, they ascended, by successive steps, to the *illustrious* dignities of the state. In the practice of the bar these men had considered reason as the instrument of dispute; they interpreted the laws according to the dictates of private interest; and the same pernicious habits might still adhere to their characters in the public administration of the state.

In the system of policy introduced by Augustus, the governors, those at least of the Imperial provinces, were invested with the full powers of the sovereign himself. Ministers of peace and war, the distribution of rewards and punishments depended on them alone, and they successively appeared on their tribunal in the robes of civil magistracy, and in complete armour at the head of the Roman legions. The influence of the revenue, the authority of law, and the command of a military force, concurred to render their power supreme and absolute; and whenever they were tempted to violate their allegiance, the loyal province which they involved in their rebellion was scarcely sensible of any change in its political state. From the time of Commodus to the reign of Constantine, near one hundred governors might be enumerated who, with various success, erected the standard of revolt; and though the innocent were too often sacrificed, the guilty might sometimes be prevented by the suspicious cruelty of their master. To secure his throne and the public tranquillity from these formidable servants, Constantine resolved to divide the military from the civil administration.

About the same time that Constantine gave a legal sanction to the ecclesiastical order, he instituted in the Roman empire the nice balance of the civil and the military powers. The emulation, and sometimes the discord, which reigned between two professions of opposite interests and incompatible manners was productive of beneficial and of pernicious consequences. It was seldom to be expected that the general and the civil governor of a province should either conspire for the disturbance, or should unite for the service, of their country. While the one delayed to offer the assistance which the other disdained to solicit, the troops very frequently remained without orders or without supplies, the public safety was betrayed, and the defenceless subjects were left exposed to the fury of the barbarians. The divided administration formed by Constantine relaxed the vigour of the state, while it secured the tranquillity of the monarch.

The memory of Constantine has been deservedly censured for another innovation which corrupted military discipline, and prepared the ruin of the empire. The nineteen years which preceded his final victory over Licinius had been a period of licence and intestine war. The rivals who contended for the possession of the Roman world had withdrawn the greatest part of their forces from the guard of the general frontier; and the principal cities which formed the boundary of their respective dominions were filled with soldiers who considered their countrymen as their most implacable enemies. After the use of these internal garrisons had ceased with the civil war, the conqueror wanted either wisdom or firmness to revive the severe discipline of Diocletian, and to suppress a fatal indulgence which habit had endeared and almost confirmed to the military order. From the reign of Constantine a popular and even legal distinction was admitted between the *Palatines* and the *Borderers;* the troops of the court, as they were improperly styled, and the troops of the frontier. The former, elevated by the superiority of their pay and privileges, were permitted, except in the extraordinary emergencies of war, to occupy their tranquil stations in the heart of the provinces. The most flourishing cities were oppressed by the intolerable weight of quarters.

The soldiers insensibly forgot the virtues of their profession, and contracted only the vices of civil life. They were either degraded by the industry of mechanic trades, or enervated by the luxury of baths and theatres. They soon became careless of their martial exercises, curious in their diet and apparel, and while they inspired terror to the subjects of the empire, they trembled at the hostile approach of the barbarians.

The chain of fortifications which Diocletian and his colleagues had extended along the banks of the great rivers was no longer maintained with the same care, or defended with the same vigilance. The numbers which still remained under the name of the troops of the frontier might be sufficient for the ordinary defence. But their spirit was degraded by the humiliating reflection that *they,* who were exposed to the hardships and dangers of a perpetual warfare, were rewarded only with about two-thirds of the pay and emoluments which were lavished on the troops of the court. Even the bands or legions that were raised the nearest to the level of those unworthy favourites were in some measure disgraced by the title of honour which they were allowed to assume. It was in vain that Constantine repeated the most dreadful menaces of fire and sword against the Borderers who should dare to desert their colours, to connive at the inroads of the barbarians, or to participate in the spoil. The mischiefs which flow from injudicious counsels are seldom removed by the application of partial severities: and though succeeding princes laboured to restore the strength and numbers of the frontier garrisons, the empire, till the last moment of its dissolution, continued to languish under the mortal wound which had been so rashly or so weakly inflicted by the hand of Constantine.

The same timid policy, of dividing whatever is united, of reducing whatever is eminent, of dreading every active power, and of expecting that the most feeble will prove the most obedient, seems to pervade the institutions of several princes, and particularly those of Constantine. The martial pride of the legions, whose victorious camps had so often been the scene of rebellion, was nourished by the memory of their past exploits, and the consciousness of their actual strength. As long as they maintained their ancient establishment of six thousand men, they subsisted, under the reign of Diocletian, each of them singly, a visible and important object in the military history of the Roman empire. A few years afterwards these gigantic bodies were shrunk to a very diminutive size; and when *seven* legions, with some auxiliaries, defended the city of Amida against the Persians, the total garrison, with the inhabitants of both sexes, and the peasants of the deserted country, did not exceed the number of twenty thousand persons.

From this fact, and from similar examples, there is reason to believe that the constitution of the legionary troops, to which they partly owed their valour and discipline, was dissolved by Constantine; and that the bands of Roman infantry, which still assumed the same names and the same honours, consisted only of one thousand or fifteen hundred men. The conspiracy of so many separate detachments, each of which was awed by the sense of its own weakness, could easily be checked; and the successors of Constantine might indulge their love of ostentation by issuing their orders to one hundred and thirty-two legions, inscribed on the muster-roll of their numerous armies. The remainder of their troops was distributed into several hundred cohorts of infantry, and squadrons of cavalry. Their arms, and titles, and ensigns were calculated to inspire terror, and to display the variety of nations who marched under the Imperial standard. And not a vestige was left of that severe simplicity which, in the ages of freedom and victory, had distinguished the line of battle of a Roman army from the confused host of an Asiatic monarch.

A more particular enumeration, drawn from the *Notitia*, might exercise the diligence of an antiquary; but the historian will content himself with observing that the number of permanent stations or garrisons established on the frontiers of the empire amounted to five hundred and eighty-three; and that, under the successors of Constantine, the complete force of the military establishment was computed at six hundred and forty-five thousand soldiers. An effort so prodigious surpassed the wants of a more ancient and the faculties of a later period.

In the various states of society armies are recruited from very different motives. Barbarians are urged by their love of war; the citizens of a free republic may be prompted by a principle of duty; the subjects, or at least the nobles, of a monarchy are animated by a sentiment of honour; but the timid and luxurious inhabitants of a declining empire must be allured into the service by the hopes of profit, or compelled by the dread of punishment. The resources of the Roman treasury were exhausted by the increase of pay, by the repetition of donatives, and by the invention of new emoluments and indulgences, which, in the opinion of the provincial youth, might compensate the hardships and dangers of a military life. Yet, although the stature was lowered, although slaves, at least by a tacit connivance, were indiscriminately received into the ranks, the insurmountable difficulty of procuring a regular and adequate supply of volunteers obliged the emperors to adopt more effectual and coercive methods.

The lands bestowed on the veterans, as the free reward of their valour, were henceforwards granted under a condition which contains the first rudiments of the feudal tenures—that their sons, who succeeded to the inheritance, should devote themselves to the profession of arms as soon as they attained the age of manhood; and their cowardly refusal was punished by the loss of honour, of fortune, or even of life. But as the annual growth of the sons of the veterans bore a very small proportion to the demands of the service, levies of men were frequently required from the provinces, and every proprietor was obliged either to take up arms, or to procure a substitute, or to purchase his exemption by the payment of a heavy fine. The sum of forty-two pieces of gold, to which it was *reduced*, ascertains the exorbitant price of volunteers, and the reluctance with which the government admitted of this alternative. Such was the horror for the profession of a soldier which had affected the minds of the degenerate Romans that many of the youth of Italy and the provinces chose to cut off the fingers of their right hand to escape from being pressed into the service.

The introduction of barbarians into the Roman armies became every day more universal, more necessary, and more fatal. The most daring of the Scythians, of the Goths, and of the Germans, who delighted in war, and who found it more profitable to defend than to ravage the provinces, were enrolled not only in the auxiliaries of their respective nations, but in the legions themselves, and among the most distinguished of the Palatine troops. As they freely mingled with the subjects of the empire, they gradually learned to despise their manners and to imitate their arts. They abjured the implicit reverence which the pride of Rome had exacted from their ignorance, while they acquired the knowledge and possession of those advantages by which alone she supported her declining greatness. The barbarian soldiers who displayed any military talents were advanced, without exception, to the most important commands; and the names of the tribunes, of the counts and dukes, and of the generals themselves, betray a foreign origin which they no longer condescended to disguise. They were often entrusted with the conduct of a war against their countrymen; and though most of them preferred the ties of allegiance to those of blood, they did not always avoid the guilt, or at least the suspicion, of holding a treasonable correspondence with the enemy, of inviting his invasion, or of sparing his retreat.

The camps and the palace of the son of Constantine were governed by the powerful faction of the Franks, who preserved the strictest connection with each other and with their country, and who resented every personal affront as a national indignity. When the tyrant Caligula was suspected of an intention to invest a very extraordinary candidate with the consular robes, the sacrilegious profanation would have scarcely excited less astonishment if, instead of a horse, the noblest chieftain of Germany or Britain had been the object of his choice. The revolution of three centuries had produced so remarkable a change in the prejudices of the people, that, with the public approbation, Constantine showed his successors the example of bestowing the honours of the consulship on the barbarians who, by their merit and services, had deserved to be ranked among the first of the Romans.

But as these hardy veterans, who had been educated in the ignorance or contempt of the laws were incapable of exercising any civil offices, the powers of the human mind were contracted by the irreconcilable separation of talents as well as of professions. The accomplished citizens of the Greek and Roman republics, whose characters could adapt themselves to the bar, the senate, the camp, or the schools, had learned to write, to speak, and to act with the same spirit, and with equal abilities.

The perpetual intercourse between the court and the provinces was facilitated by the construction of roads and the institution of posts. But these beneficial establishments were accidentally connected with a pernicious and intolerable abuse. Two or three hundred *agents* or messengers were employed, under the jurisdiction of the master of the offices, to announce the names of the annual consuls, and the edicts or victories of the emperors. They insensibly assumed the licence of reporting whatever they could observe of the conduct either of magistrates or of private citizens; and were soon considered as the eyes of the monarch and the scourge of the people. Under the warm influence of a feeble reign they multiplied to the incredible number of ten thousand, disdained the mild though frequent admonitions of the laws, and exercised in the profitable management of the posts a rapacious and insolent oppression.

These official spies, who regularly corresponded with the palace, were encouraged, by favour and reward, anxiously to watch the progress of every treasonable design, from the faint and latent symptoms of disaffection, to the actual preparation of an open revolt. Their careless or criminal violation of truth and justice was covered by the consecrated mask of zeal; and they might securely aim their poisoned arrows at the breast either of the guilty or the innocent, who had provoked their resentment, or refused to purchase their silence. A faithful subject of Syria perhaps, or of Britain, was exposed to the danger, or at least to the dread, of being dragged in chains to the court of Milan or Constantinople, to defend his life and fortune against the malicious charge of these privileged informers. The ordinary administration was conducted by those methods which extreme necessity can alone palliate; and the defects of evidence were diligently supplied by the use of torture.

The deceitful and dangerous experiment of the criminal *quæstion*, as it is emphatically styled, was admitted, rather than approved in the jurisprudence of the Romans. They applied this sanguinary mode of examination only to servile bodies, whose sufferings were seldom weighed by those haughty republicans in the scale of justice or humanity; but they would never consent to violate the sacred person of a citizen till they possessed the clearest evidence of his guilt. The annals of tyranny, from the reign of Tiberius to that of Domitian, circumstantially relate the executions of many innocent victims; but, as long as the faintest remembrance was kept alive of the national freedom and honour, the last hours of a Roman were secure from the danger of ignominious torture. The conduct of the provincial magistrates was not, however, regulated by the practice of the city, or the strict maxims of the civilians. They found the use of torture established not only among the slaves of oriental despotism, but among the Macedonians, who obeyed a limited monarch; among the Rhodians, who flourished by the liberty of commerce; and even among the sage Athenians, who had asserted and adorned the dignity of human kind.

The acquiescence of the provincials encouraged their governors to acquire, or perhaps to usurp, a discretionary power of employing the rack, to extort from vagrants or plebeian criminals the confession of their guilt, till they insensibly proceeded to confound the distinctions of rank, and to disregard the privileges of Roman citizens. The apprehensions of the subjects urged them to solicit, and the interest of the sovereign engaged him to grant, a variety of special exemptions, which tacitly allowed, and even authorised, the general use of torture. They protected all persons of illustrious or honourable rank, bishops and their presbyters, professors of the liberal arts, soldiers and their families, municipal officers, and their posterity to the third generation, and all children under the age of puberty. But a fatal maxim was introduced into the new jurisprudence of the empire, that in the case of treason, which included every offence that the subtlety of lawyers could derive from an *hostile intention* towards the prince or republic, all privileges were suspended, and all conditions were reduced to the same ignominious level. As the safety of the emperor was avowedly preferred to every consideration of justice or humanity, the dignity of age and the tenderness of youth were alike exposed to the most cruel tortures; and the terrors of a malicious information, which might select them as the accomplices, or even as the witnesses, perhaps, of an imaginary crime, perpetually hung over the heads of the principal citizens of the Roman world.

These evils, however terrible they may appear, were confined to the smaller number of Roman subjects whose dangerous situation was in some degree compensated by the enjoyment of those advantages, either of nature or of fortune, which exposed them to the jealousy of the monarch. The obscure millions of a great empire have much less to dread from the cruelty than from the avarice of their masters; and *their* humble happiness is principally affected by the grievance of excessive taxes, which, gently pressing on the wealthy, descend with accelerated weight on the meaner and more indigent classes of society.

The whole landed property of the empire (without excepting the patrimonial estates of the monarch) was the object of ordinary taxation; and every new purchaser contracted the obligations of the former proprietor. An accurate *census*, or survey, was the only equitable mode of ascertaining the proportion which every citizen should be obliged to contribute for the public service; and from the well-known period of the indictions, there is reason to believe that this difficult and expensive operation was repeated at the regular distance of fifteen years.

The lands were measured by surveyors, who were sent into the provinces; their nature, whether arable or pasture, or vineyards or woods, was distinctly reported; and an estimate was made of their common value from the average produce of five years. The numbers of slaves and of cattle constituted an essential part of the report; an oath was administered to the proprietors which bound them to disclose the true state of their affairs; and their attempts to prevaricate, or elude the intention of the legislator, were severely watched, and punished as a capital crime, which included the double guilt of treason and sacrilege.

A large portion of the tribute was paid in money; and of the current coin of the empire, gold alone could be legally accepted. The remainder of the taxes, according to the proportions determined by the annual indiction, was furnished in a manner still more direct, and still more oppressive. According to the different nature of lands, their real produce in the various articles of wine or oil, corn or barley, wood or iron, was transported by the labour or at the expense of the provincials to the Imperial magazines, from whence they were occasionally distributed, for the use of the court, of the army, and of the two capitals, Rome and Constantinople. The commissioners of the revenue were so frequently obliged to make considerable purchases, that they were strictly prohibited from allowing any compensation, or from receiving in money the value of those supplies which were exacted in kind.

In the primitive simplicity of small communities this method may be well adapted to collect the almost voluntary offerings of the people; but it is at once susceptible of the utmost latitude and of the utmost strictness, which in a corrupt and absolute monarchy must introduce a perpetual contest between the power of oppression and the arts of fraud. The agriculture of the Roman provinces was insensibly ruined, and, in the progress of despotism, which tends to disappoint its own purpose, the emperors were obliged to derive some merit from the forgiveness of debts, or the remission of tributes, which their subjects were utterly incapable of paying.

According to the new division of Italy, the fertile and happy province of Campania, the scene of the early victories and of the delicious retirements of the citizens of Rome, extended between the sea and the Apennine from the Tiber to the Silarus. Within sixty years after the death of Constantine, and on the evidence of an actual survey, an exemption was granted in favour of three hundred and thirty thousand English acres of desert and uncultivated land, which amounted to one-eighth of the whole surface of the province. As the footsteps of the barbarians had not yet been seen in Italy, the cause of this amazing desolation, which is recorded in the laws, can be ascribed only to the administration of the Roman emperors.

Either from design or from accident, the mode of assessment seemed to unite the substance of a land-tax with the forms of a capitation. The returns which were sent of every province or district expressed the number of tributary subjects, and the amount of the public impositions. The latter of these sums was divided by the former; and the estimate, that such a province contained so many *capita*, or heads of tribute, and that each *head* was rated at such a price, was universally received, not only in the popular, but even in the legal computation. The value of a tributary head must have varied, according to many accidental, or at least fluctuating circumstances: but some knowledge has been preserved of a very curious fact, the more important since it relates to one of the richest provinces of the Roman empire, and which now flourishes as the most splendid of the European kingdoms. The rapacious ministers of Constantius had exhausted the wealth of Gaul, by exacting twenty-five pieces of gold for the annual tribute of every head. The humane policy of his successor reduced the capitation to seven pieces. A moderate proportion between these opposite extremes of extraordinary oppression and of transient indulgence may therefore be fixed at sixteen pieces of gold, or about nine pounds sterling, the common standard, perhaps, of the impositions of Gaul. But this calculation, or rather indeed the facts from whence it is deduced, cannot fail of suggesting two difficulties to a thinking mind, at once surprised by the *equality* and by the *enormity* of the capitation. An attempt to explain may perhaps reflect some light on the interesting subject of the finances of the declining empire.

In a country where personal freedom is the privilege of every subject, the whole mass of taxes, whether they are levied on property or on consumption, may be fairly divided among the whole body of the nation. But the far greater part of the lands of ancient Gaul, as well as of the other provinces of the Roman world, were cultivated by slaves, or by peasants, whose dependent condition was a less rigid servitude. In such a state the poor were maintained at the expense of the masters who enjoyed the fruits of their labour; and as the rolls of tribute were filled only with the names of those citizens who possessed the means of an honourable, or at least of a decent subsistence, the comparative smallness of their numbers explains and justifies the high rate of their capitation.

The truth of this assertion may be illustrated by the following example:—The Ædui, one of the most powerful and civilised tribes or *cities* of Gaul, occupied an extent of territory which now contains above five hundred thousand inhabitants, in the two eccesiastical dioceses of Autun and Nevers; and with the probable accession of those of Châlons and Maçon, the population would amount to eight hundred thousand souls. In the time of Constantine the territory of the Ædui afforded no more than twenty-five thousand *heads* of capitation, of whom seven thousand were discharged by that prince from the intolerable weight of tribute. A just analogy would seem to countenance the opinion of an ingenious historian, that the free and tributary citizens did not surpass the number of half a million; and if, in the ordinary administration of government, their annual payments may be computed at about four millions and a half of our money, it would appear that, although the share of each individual was four times as considerable, a fourth part only of the modern taxes of France was levied on the Imperial province of Gaul.

But this tax or capitation on the proprietors of land would have suffered a rich and numerous class of free citizens to escape. With the view of sharing that species of wealth which is derived from art or labour, and which exists in money or in merchandise, the emperors imposed a distinct and personal tribute on the trading part of their subjects. Some exemptions, very strictly confined both in time and place, were allowed to the proprietors who disposed of the produce of their own estates. Some indulgence was granted to the profession of the liberal arts; but every other branch of commercial industry was affected by the severity of the law. The honourable merchant of Alexandria, who imported the gems and spices of India for the use of the Western world; the usurer, who derived from the interest of money a silent and ignominious profit; the ingenious manufacturer, the diligent mechanic, and even the most obscure retailer of a sequestered village, were obliged to admit the officers of the revenue into the partnership of their gain; and the sovereign of the Roman empire, who tolerated the profession, consented to share the infamous salary of public prostitutes. As this general tax upon industry was collected every fourth year, it was styled the *Lustral Contribution:* and the historian Zosimus laments that the approach of the fatal period was announced by the tears and terrors of the citizens, who were often compelled by the impending scourge to embrace the most abhorred and unnatural methods of procuring the sum at which their poverty had been assessed.

A people elated by pride, or soured by discontent, is seldom qualified to form a just estimate of their actual situation. The subjects of Constantine were incapable of discerning the decline of genius and manly virtue, which so far degraded them below the dignity of their ancestors; but they could feel and lament the rage of tyranny, the relaxation of discipline, and the increase of taxes.

The impartial historian, who acknowledges the justice of their complaints, will observe some favourable circumstances which tended to alleviate the misery of their condition. The threatening tempest of barbarians, which so soon subverted the foundations of Roman greatness, was still repelled, or suspended, on the frontiers. The arts of luxury and literature were cultivated, and the elegant pleasures of society were enjoyed, by the inhabitants of a considerable portion of the globe. The forms, the pomp, and the expense of the civil administration contributed to restrain the irregular licence of the soldiers; and although the laws were violated by power, or perverted by subtlety, the sage principles of the Roman jurisprudence preserved a sense of order and equity unknown to the despotic governments of the East. The rights of mankind might derive some protection from religion and philosophy; and the name of freedom, which could no longer alarm, might sometimes admonish the successors of Augustus that they did not reign over a nation of slaves or barbarians.

CHAPTER XIII

The Motives, Progress, and Effects of the Conversion of Constantine—Legal Establishment of the Christian or Catholic Church

The public establishment of Christianity may be considered as one of the important domestic revolutions which excite the most lively curiosity, and afford the most valuable instruction. The victories and the civil policy of Constantine no longer influence the state of Europe; but a considerable portion of the globe still retains the impression which it received from the conversion of that monarch; and the ecclesiastical institutions of his reign are still connected, by an indissoluble chain, with the opinions, the passions, and the interests of the present generation.

In the consideration of a subject which may be examined with impartiality, but cannot be viewed with indifference, a difficulty immediately arises of a very unexpected nature—that of ascertaining the real and precise date of the conversion of Constantine. The eloquent Lactantius, in the midst of his court, seems impatient to proclaim to the world the glorious example of the sovereign of Gaul; who, in the first moments of his reign, acknowledged and adored the majesty of the true and only God. The learned Eusebius has ascribed the faith of Constantine to the miraculous sign which was displayed in the heavens whilst he meditated and prepared the Italian expedition. The historian Zosimus maliciously asserts that the emperor had imbrued his hands in the blood of his eldest son before he publicly renounced the gods of Rome and of his ancestors. The perplexity produced by these discordant authorities is derived from the behaviour of Constantine himself. According to the strictness of ecclesiastical language, the first of the *Christian* emperors was unworthy of that name till the moment of his death; since it was only during his last illness that he received, as a catechumen, the imposition of hands, and was afterwards admitted, by the initiatory rites of baptism, into the number of the faithful.

The Christianity of Constantine must be allowed in a much more vague and qualified sense; and the nicest accuracy is required in tracing the slow and almost imperceptible gradations by which the monarch declared himself the protector, and at length the proselyte, of the church. He artfully balanced the hopes and fears of his subjects, by publishing in the same year two edicts; the first of which enjoined the solemn observance of Sunday, and the second directed the regular consultation of the Auspices.

While this important revolution yet remained in suspense, the Christians and the Pagans watched the conduct of their sovereign with the same anxiety, but with very opposite sentiments. The former were prompted by every motive of zeal, as well as vanity, to exaggerate the marks of his favour and the evidences of his faith. The latter, till their just apprehensions were changed into despair and resentment, attempted to conceal from the world, and from themselves, that the gods of Rome could no longer reckon the emperor in the number of their votaries. The same passions and prejudices have engaged the partial writers of the times to connect the public profession of Christianity with the most glorious or the most ignominious era of the reign of Constantine.

Whatever symptoms of Christian piety might transpire in the discourses or actions of Constantine, he persevered till he was near forty years of age in the practice of the established religion. His liberality restored and enriched the temples of the gods; the medals which issued from his Imperial mint are impressed with the figures and attributes of Jupiter and Apollo, of Mars and Hercules; and his filial piety increased the council of Olympus by the solemn apotheosis of his father Constantius. The devotion of Constantine was more peculiarly directed to the genius of the Sun, the Apollo of Greek and Roman mythology; and he was pleased to be represented with the symbols of the God of Light and Poetry. But the example of his father instructed Constantine to esteem and to reward the merit of the Christians; and as long as Constantine exercised a limited sovereignty over the provinces of Gaul, his Christian subjects were protected by the authority, and perhaps by the laws, of a prince who wisely left to the gods the care of vindicating their own honour. If we may credit the assertion of Constantine himself, he had been an indignant spectator of the savage cruelties which were inflicted, by the hands of Roman soldiers, on those citizens whose religion was their only crime.

About five months after the conquest of Italy, the edict of Milan was received as a general and fundamental law of the Roman world. It was enacted that the places of worship, and public lands, which had been confiscated, should be restored to the church without dispute, without delay, and without expense: and this severe injunction was accompanied with a gracious promise, that, if any of the purchasers had paid a fair and adequate price, they should be indemnified from the Imperial treasury. The salutary regulations which guard the future tranquillity of the faithful are framed on the principles of enlarged and equal toleration; and such an equality must have been interpreted by a recent sect as an advantageous and honourable distinction.

The partial and increasing favour of Constantine may naturally be referred to the esteem which he entertained for the moral character of the Christians, and to a persuasion that the propagation of the Gospel would inculcate the practice of private and public virtue. Every principle which had once maintained the vigour and purity of Rome and Sparta was long since extinguished in a declining and despotic empire. But a prudent magistrate might observe with pleasure the progress of a religion which diffused among the people a pure, benevolent, and universal system of ethics, adapted to every duty and every condition of life, recommended as the will and reason of the supreme Deity, and enforced by the sanction of eternal rewards or punishments.

The passive and unresisting obedience which bows under the yoke of authority, or even of oppression, must have appeared in the eyes of an absolute monarch the most conspicuous and useful of the evangelic virtues. The primitive Christians derived the institution of civil government, not from the consent of the people, but from the decrees of Heaven. The reigning emperor, though he had usurped the sceptre by treason and murder, immediately assumed the sacred character of vicegerent of the Deity. To the Deity alone he was accountable for the abuse of his power; and his subjects were indissolubly bound by their oath of fidelity to a tyrant who had violated every law of nature and society. The humble Christians were sent into the world as sheep among wolves; and since they were not permitted to employ force even in the defence of their religion, they should be still more criminal if they were tempted to shed the blood of their fellow-creatures in disputing the vain privileges or the sordid possessions of this transitory life. Faithful to the doctrine of the apostle who in the reign of Nero had preached the duty of unconditional submission, the Christians of the three first centuries preserved their conscience pure and innocent of the guilt of secret conspiracy or open rebellion.

Perhaps the patience of the primitive church may be ascribed to its weakness as well as to its virtue. A sect of unwarlike Plebeians, without leaders, without arms, without fortifications, must have encountered inevitable destruction in a rash and fruitless resistance to the master of the Roman legions. But the Christians, when they deprecated the wrath of Diocletian, or solicited the favour of Constantine, could allege with truth and confidence that they held the principle of passive obedience, and that, in the space of three centuries, their conduct had always been conformable to their principles. They might add that the throne of the emperors would be established on a fixed and permanent basis if all their subjects, embracing the Christian doctrine, should learn to suffer and to obey.

The piety of Constantine was admitted as an unexceptionable proof of the justice of his arms; and his use of victory confirmed the opinion of the Christians that their hero was inspired and conducted by the Lord of Hosts. The conquest of Italy produced a general edict of toleration; and as soon as the defeat of Licinius had invested Constantine with the sole dominion of the Roman world, he immediately, by circular letters, exhorted all his subjects to imitate, without delay, the example of their sovereign, and to embrace the divine truth of Christianity.

The assurance that the elevation of Constantine was intimately connected with the designs of Providence instilled into the minds of the Christians two opinions, which, by very different means, assisted the accomplishment of the prophecy. Their warm and active loyalty exhausted in his favour every resource of human industry; and they confidently expected that their strenuous efforts would be seconded by some divine and miraculous aid. The enemies of Constantine have imputed to interested motives the alliance which he insensibly contracted with the Catholic church, and which apparently contributed to the success of his ambition. In the beginning of the fourth century the Christians still bore a very inadequate proportion to the inhabitants of the empire; but among a degenerate people, who viewed the change of masters with the indifference of slaves, the spirit and union of a religious party might assist the popular leader to whose service, from a principle of conscience, they had devoted their lives and fortunes.

Proselytes of the new faith must have multiplied in the court and army; the barbarians of Germany, who filled the ranks of the legions, were of a careless temper, which acquiesced without resistance in the religion of their commander; and when they passed the Alps it may fairly be presumed that a great number of the soldiers had already consecrated their swords to the service of Christ and of Constantine. The habits of mankind and the interest of religion gradually abated the horror of war and bloodshed which had so long prevailed among the Christians; and in the councils which were assembled under the gracious protection of Constantine the authority of the bishops was seasonably employed to ratify the obligation of the military oath, and to inflict the penalty of excommunication on those soldiers who threw away their arms during the peace of the church. While Constantine in his own dominions increased the number and zeal of his faithful adherents, he could depend on the support of a powerful faction in those provinces which were still possessed or usurped by his rivals.

The enthusiasm which inspired the troops, and perhaps the emperor himself, had sharpened their swords while it satisfied their conscience. They marched to battle with the full assurance that the same God who had formerly opened a passage to the Israelites through the waters of Jordan, and had thrown down the walls of Jericho at the sound of the trumpets of Joshua, would display his visible majesty and power in the victory of Constantine. The evidence of ecclesiastical history is prepared to affirm that their expectations were justified by the conspicuous miracle to which the conversion of the first Christian emperor has been almost unanimously ascribed. The real or imaginary cause of so important an event deserves and demands the attention of posterity; and I shall endeavour to form a just estimate of the famous vision of Constantine, by a distinct consideration of the *standard*, the *dream*, and the *celestial sign*.

I. An instrument of the tortures which were inflicted only on slaves and strangers became an object of horror in the eyes of a Roman citizen; and the ideas of guilt, of pain, and of ignominy, were closely united with the idea of the cross. The piety, rather than the humanity, of Constantine soon abolished in his dominions the punishment which the Saviour of mankind had condescended to suffer; but the emperor had already learned to despise the prejudices of his education and of his people, before he could erect in the midst of Rome his own statue, bearing a cross in its right hand. The same symbol sanctified the arms of the soldiers of Constantine; the cross glittered on their helmet, was engraved on their shields, was interwoven into their banners; and the consecrated emblems which adorned the person of the emperor himself were distinguished only by richer materials and more exquisite workmanship. But the principal standard which displayed the triumph of the cross was styled the *Labarum*, an obscure, though celebrated, name, which has been vainly derived from almost all the languages of the world. It is described as a long pike intersected by a transversal beam. The silken veil which hung down from the beam was curiously inwrought with the images of the reigning monarch and his children. The summit of the pike supported a crown of gold, which enclosed the mysterious monogram, at once expressive of the figure of the cross and the initial letters of the name of Christ.

The safety of the labarum was entrusted to fifty guards of approved valour and fidelity; their station was marked by honours and emoluments; and some fortunate accidents soon introduced an opinion that as long as the guards of the labarum were engaged in the execution of their office they were secure and invulnerable amidst the darts of the enemy. In the second civil war Licinius felt and dreaded the power of this consecrated banner, the sight of which in the distress of battle animated the soldiers of Constantine with an invincible enthusiasm, and scattered terror and dismay through the ranks of the adverse legions. There is still extant a medal of the emperor Constantius, where the standard of the labarum is accompanied with these memorable words, BY THIS SIGN THOU SHALT CONQUER.

II. In all occasions of danger or distress it was the practice of the primitive Christians to fortify their minds and bodies by the sign of the cross, which they used in all their ecclesiastical rites, in all the daily occurrences of life, as an infallible preservative against every species of spiritual or temporal evil. The authority of the church might alone have had sufficient weight to justify the devotion of Constantine, who, in the same prudent and gradual progress, acknowledged the truth and assumed the symbol of Christianity. But the testimony of a contemporary writer, who in a formal treatise has avenged the cause of religion, bestows on the piety of the emperor a more awful and sublime character. He affirms, with the most perfect confidence, that, in the night which preceded the last battle against Maxentius, Constantine was admonished in a dream to inscribe the shields of his soldiers with the *celestial sign of God*, the sacred monogram of the name of Christ; that he executed the commands of Heaven, and that his valour and obedience were rewarded by the decisive victory of the Milvian Bridge.

If the dream of Constantine is separately considered, it may be naturally explained either by the policy or the enthusiasm of the emperor. Whilst his anxiety for the approaching day, which must decide the fate of the empire, was suspended by a short and interrupted slumber, the venerable form of Christ, and the well-known symbol of his religion, might forcibly offer themselves to the active fancy of a prince who reverenced the name, and had perhaps secretly implored the power, of the God of the Christians. As readily might a consummate statesman indulge himself in the use of one of those military stratagems, one of those pious frauds, which Philip and Sertorius had employed with such art and effect. The præternatural origin of dreams was universally admitted by the nations of antiquity, and a considerable part of the Gallic army was already prepared to place their confidence in the salutary sign of the Christian religion.

III. The philosopher who with calm suspicion examines the dreams and omens, the miracles and prodigies, of profane or even of ecclesiastical history, will probably conclude that if the eyes of the spectators have sometimes been deceived by fraud, the understanding of the readers has much more frequently been insulted by fiction. Every event, or appearance, or accident, which seems to deviate from the ordinary course of nature, has been rashly ascribed to the immediate action of the Deity; and the astonished fancy of the multitude has sometimes given shape and colour, language and motion, to the fleeting but uncommon meteors of the air. The Christian fable of Eusebius, in the space of twenty-six years, might arise from the original dream. In one of the marches of Constantine he is reported to have seen with his own eyes the luminous trophy of the cross, placed above the meridian sun, and inscribed with the following words: By this conquer. This amazing object in the sky astonished the whole army, as well as the emperor himself, who was yet undetermined in the choice of a religion: but his astonishment was converted into faith by the vision of the ensuing night. Christ appeared before his eyes; and displaying the same celestial sign of the cross, he directed Constantine to frame a similar standard, and to march, with an assurance of victory, against Maxentius and all his enemies.

The protestant and philosophic readers of the present age will incline to believe that, in the account of his own conversion, Constantine attested a wilful falsehood by a solemn and deliberate perjury. They may not hesitate to pronounce that, in the choice of a religion, his mind was determined only by a sense of interest; and that (according to the expression of a profane poet) he used the altars of the church as a convenient footstool to the throne of the empire. A conclusion so harsh and so absolute is not, however, warranted by our knowledge of human nature, of Constantine, or of Christianity. In an age of religious fervour the most artful statesmen are observed to feel some part of the enthusiasm which they inspire; and the most orthodox saints assume the dangerous privilege of defending the cause of truth by the arms of deceit and falsehood. Personal interest is often the standard of our belief, as well as of our practice; and the same motives of temporal advantage which might influence the public conduct and professions of Constantine would insensibly dispose his mind to embrace a religion so propitious to his fame and fortunes. His vanity was gratified by the flattering assurance that *he* had been chosen by Heaven to reign over the earth: success had justified his divine title to the throne, and that title was founded on the truth of the Christian revelation.

As real virtue is sometimes excited by undeserved applause, the specious piety of Constantine, if at first it was only specious, might gradually, by the influence of praise, of habit, and of example, be matured into serious faith and fervent devotion. But whatever advantages might be derived from the acquisition of an Imperial proselyte, he was distinguished by the splendour of his purple, rather than by the superiority of wisdom or virtue, from the many thousands of his subjects who had embraced the doctrines of Christianity.

The awful mysteries of the Christian faith and worship were concealed from the eyes of strangers, and even of catechumens, with an affected secrecy which served to excite their wonder and curiosity. But the severe rules of discipline which the prudence of the bishops had instituted were relaxed by the same prudence in favour of an Imperial proselyte, whom it was so important to allure, by every gentle condescension, into the pale of the church; and Constantine was permitted, at least by a tacit dispensation, to enjoy *most* of the privileges, before he had contracted *any* of the obligations, of a Christian. Instead of retiring from the congregation when the voice of the deacon dismissed the profane multitude, he prayed with the faithful, disputed with the bishops, preached on the most sublime and intricate subjects of theology, celebrated with sacred rites the vigil of Easter, and publicly declared himself, not only a partaker, but, in some measure, a priest and hierophant of the Christian mysteries. Many years before his baptism and death Constantine had proclaimed to the world that neither his person nor his image should evermore be seen within the walls of an idolatrous temple; while he distributed through the provinces a variety of medals and pictures which represented the emperor in an humble and suppliant posture of Christian devotion.

The pride of Constantine, who refused the privileges of a catechumen, cannot easily be explained or excused; but the delay of his baptism may be justified by the maxims and the practice of ecclesiastical antiquity. The sacrament of baptism was regularly administered by the bishop himself, with his assistant clergy, in the cathedral church of the diocese, during the fifty days between the solemn festivals of Easter and Pentecost; and this holy term admitted a numerous band of infants and adult persons into the bosom of the church. The discretion of parents often suspended the baptism of their children till they could understand the obligations which they contracted: the severity of ancient bishops exacted from the new converts a novitiate of two or three years; and the catechumens themselves, from different motives of a temporal or a spiritual nature, were seldom impatient to assume the character of perfect and initiated Christians. The sacrament of baptism was supposed to contain a full and absolute expiation of sin; the soul was instantly restored to its original purity, and entitled to the promise of eternal salvation. Among the proselytes of Christianity there were many who judged it imprudent to precipitate a salutary rite which could not be repeated, to throw away an inestimable privilege which could never be recovered. By the delay of their baptism they could venture freely to indulge their passions in the enjoyment of this world, while they still retained in their own hands the means of a sure and easy absolution.

The gratitude of the church has exalted the virtues and excused the failings of a generous patron who seated Christianity on the throne of the Roman world; and the Greeks, who celebrate the festival of the Imperial saint, seldom mention the name of Constantine without adding the title of *equal to the Apostles*. Such a comparison, if it alludes to the character of those divine missionaries, must be imputed to the extravagance of impious flattery. But if the parallel is confined to the extent and number of their evangelic victories, the success of Constantine might perhaps equal that of the Apostles themselves. By the edicts of toleration he removed the temporal disadvantages which had hitherto retarded the progress of Christianity. The exact balance of the two religions continued but a moment; and the piercing eye of ambition and avarice soon discovered that the profession of Christianity might contribute to the interest of the present, as well as of a future life.

The hopes of wealth and honours, the example of an emperor, his exhortations, his irresistible smiles, diffused conviction among the venal and obsequious crowds which usually fill the apartments of a palace. The cities which signalised a forward zeal by the voluntary destruction of their temples were distinguished by municipal privileges and rewarded with popular donatives; and the new capital of the East gloried in the singular advantage that Constantinople was never profaned by the worship of idols. As the lower ranks of society are governed by imitation, the conversion of those who possessed any eminence of birth, of power, or of riches, was soon followed by dependent multitudes. The salvation of the common people was purchased at an easy rate, if it be true that, in one year, twelve thousand men were baptised at Rome, besides a proportionable number of women and children, and that a white garment, with twenty pieces of gold, had been promised by the emperor to every convert.

The powerful influence of Constantine was not circumscribed by the narrow limits of his life or of his dominions. War and commerce had spread the knowledge of the Gospel beyond the confines of the Roman provinces; and the barbarians, who had disdained an humble and proscribed sect, soon learned to esteem a religion which had been so lately embraced by the greatest monarch and the most civilised nation of the globe. The Goths and Germans who enlisted under the standard of Rome revered the cross which glittered at the head of the legions, and their fierce countrymen received at the same time the lessons of faith and of humanity. The kings of Iberia and Armenia worshipped the God of their protector; and their subjects, who have invariably preserved the name of Christians, soon formed a sacred and perpetual connection with their Roman brethren. The Christians of Persia were suspected, in time of war, of preferring their religion to their country; but as long as peace subsisted between the two empires, the persecuting spirit of the Magi was effectually restrained by the interposition of Constantine. The rays of the Gospel illuminated the coast of India, and Abyssinia still reveres the memory of Frumentius, who, in the time of Constantine, devoted his life to the conversion of those sequestered regions.

The irresistible power of the Roman emperors was displayed in the important and dangerous change of the national religion. The terrors of a military force silenced the faint and unsupported murmurs of the Pagans, and there was reason to expect that the cheerful submission of the Christian clergy, as well as people, would be the result of conscience and gratitude. It was long since established as a fundamental maxim of the Roman constitution that every rank of citizens was alike subject to the laws, and that the care of religion was the right as well as duty of the civil magistrate. Constantine and his successors could not easily persuade themselves that they had forfeited, by their conversion, any branch of the Imperial prerogatives, or that they were incapable of giving laws to a religion which they had protected and embraced. The emperors still continued to exercise a supreme jurisdiction over the ecclesiastical order; and the sixteenth book of the Theodosian code represents, under a variety of titles, the authority which they assumed in the government of the Catholic church.

But the distinction of the spiritual and temporal powers, which had never been imposed on the free spirit of Greece and Rome, was introduced and confirmed by the legal establishment of Christianity. The office of supreme pontiff, which, from the time of Numa to that of Augustus, had always been exercised by one of the most eminent of the senators, was at length united to the Imperial dignity. The first magistrate of the state, as often as he was prompted by superstition or policy, performed with his own hands the sacerdotal functions; nor was there any order of priests, either at Rome or in the provinces, who claimed a more sacred character among men, or a more intimate communication with the gods. But in the Christian church, which entrusts the service of the altar to a perpetual succession of consecrated ministers, the monarch, whose spiritual rank is less honourable than that of the meanest deacon, was seated below the rails of the sanctuary, and confounded with the rest of the faithful multitude. The emperor might be saluted as the father of his people, but he owed a filial duty and reverence to the fathers of the church. The same marks of respect which Constantine had paid to the persons of saints and confessors were soon exacted by the pride of the episcopal order, and a secret conflict between the civil and ecclesiastical jurisdictions embarrassed the operations of the Roman government.

The opposition or contempt of the civil power served to cement the discipline of the primitive church. The Christians had been obliged to elect their own magistrates, to raise and distribute a peculiar revenue, and to regulate the internal policy of their republic by a code of laws, which were ratified by the consent of the people and the practice of three hundred years. When Constantine embraced the faith of the Christians, he seemed to contract a perpetual alliance with a distinct and independent society; and the privileges granted or confirmed by that emperor, or by his successors, were accepted, not as the precarious favours of the court, but as the just and inalienable rights of the ecclesiastical order.

The Catholic church was administered by the spiritual and legal jurisdiction of eighteen hundred bishops; of whom one thousand were seated in the

Greek, and eight hundred in the Latin, provinces of the empire. The extent and boundaries of their respective dioceses had been variously and accidentally decided by the zeal and success of the first missionaries, by the wishes of the people, and by the propagation of the Gospel. Episcopal churches were closely planted along the banks of the Nile, on the sea-coast of Africa, in the proconsular Asia, and through the southern provinces of Italy. The bishops of Gaul and Spain, of Thrace and Pontus, reigned over an ample territory, and delegated their rural suffragans to execute the subordinate duties of the pastoral office. A Christian diocese might be spread over a province, or reduced to a village; but all the bishops possessed an equal and indelible character; they all derived the same powers and privileges from the Apostles, from the people, and from the laws. While the *civil* and *military* professions were separated by the policy of Constantine, a new and perpetual order of *ecclesiastical* ministers, always respectable, sometimes dangerous, was established in the church and state. The important review of their station and attributes may be distributed under the following heads: I. Popular election. II. Ordination of the clergy. III. Property. IV. Civil jurisdiction. V. Spiritual censures. VI. Exercise of public oratory. VII. Privilege of legislative assemblies.

I. The freedom of elections subsisted long after the legal establishment of Christianity, and the subjects of Rome enjoyed in the church the privilege which they had lost in the republic, of choosing the magistrates whom they were bound to obey. As soon as a bishop had closed his eyes, the metropolitan issued a commission to one of his suffragans to administer the vacant see, and prepare, within a limited time, the future election. The right of voting was vested in the inferior clergy, who were best qualified to judge of the merit of the candidates; in the senators or nobles of the city, all those who were distinguished by their rank or property; and finally in the whole body of the people, who on the appointed day flocked in multitudes from the most remote parts of the diocese, and sometimes silenced, by their tumultuous acclamations, the voice of reason and the laws of discipline.

The civil as well as ecclesiastical laws attempted to exclude the populace from this solemn and important transaction. The canons of ancient discipline, by requiring several episcopal qualifications of age, station, etc., restrained in some measure the indiscriminate caprice of the electors. The authority of the provincial bishops, who were assembled in the vacant church to consecrate the choice of the people, was interposed to moderate their passions and to correct their mistakes. The bishops could refuse to ordain an unworthy candidate, and the rage of contending factions sometimes accepted their impartial mediation. The submission or the resistance of the clergy and people, on various occasions, afforded different precedents, which were insensibly converted into positive laws and provincial customs: but it was everywhere admitted, as a fundamental maxim of religious policy, that no bishop could be imposed on an orthodox church without the consent of its members.

II. The religions of antiquity, which established a separate order of priests, dedicated a holy race, a tribe or family, to the perpetual service of the gods. But the Christian sanctuary was open to every ambitious candidate who aspired to its heavenly promises or temporal possessions. The office of priests, like that of soldiers or magistrates, was strenuously exercised by those men whose temper and abilities had prompted them to embrace the ecclesiastical profession, or who had been selected by a discerning bishop as the best qualified to promote the glory and interest of the church.

The whole body of the Catholic clergy, more numerous, perhaps, than the legions, was exempted by the emperors from all service, private or public, all municipal offices, and all personal taxes and contributions, which pressed on their fellow-citizens with intolerable weight; and the duties of their holy profession were accepted as a full discharge of their obligations to the republic. Each bishop acquired an absolute and indefeasible right to the perpetual obedience of the clerk whom he ordained; the clergy of each episcopal church, with its dependent parishes, formed a regular and permanent society; and the cathedrals of Constantinople and Carthage maintained their peculiar establishment of five hundred ecclesiastical ministers. Their ranks and numbers were insensibly multiplied by the superstition of the times, which introduced into the church the splendid ceremonies of a Jewish or Pagan temple; and a long train of priests, deacons, subdeacons, acolytes, exorcists, readers, singers, and doorkeepers contributed, in their respective stations, to swell the pomp and harmony of religious worship.

III. The edict of Milan secured the revenue as well as the peace of the church. The Christians not only recovered the lands and houses of which they had been stripped by the persecuting laws of Diocletian, but they acquired a perfect title to all the possessions which they had hitherto enjoyed by the connivance of the magistrate. As soon as Christianity became the religion of the emperor and the empire, the national clergy might claim a decent and honourable maintenance: and the payment of an annual tax might have delivered the people from the more oppressive tribute which superstition imposes on her votaries. But as the wants and expenses of the church increased with her prosperity, the ecclesiastical order was still supported and enriched by the voluntary oblations of the faithful. Eight years after the edict of Milan, Constantine granted to all his subjects the free and universal permission of bequeathing their fortunes to the holy Catholic church; and their devout liberality, which during their lives was checked by luxury or avarice, flowed with a profuse stream at the hour of their death.

The wealthy Christians were encouraged by the example of their sovereign. An absolute monarch, who is rich without patrimony, may be charitable without merit; and Constantine too easily believed that he should purchase the favour of Heaven if he maintained the idle at the expense of the industrious, and distributed among the saints the wealth of the republic. The liberality of Constantine increased in a just proportion to his faith and to his vices. He assigned in each city a regular allowance of corn to supply the fund of ecclesiastical charity, and the persons of both sexes who embraced the monastic life became the peculiar favourites of their sovereign.

The Christian temples of Antioch, Alexandria, Jerusalem, Constantinople, etc., displayed the ostentatious piety of a prince ambitious in a declining age to equal the perfect labours of antiquity. The form of these religious edifices was simple and oblong, though they might sometimes swell into the shape of a dome, and sometimes branch into the figure of a cross. The timbers were framed for the most part of cedars of Libanus; the roof was covered with tiles, perhaps of gilt brass; and the walls, the columns, the pavement, were incrusted with variegated marbles. The most precious ornaments of gold and silver, of silk and gems, were profusely dedicated to the service of the altar, and this specious magnificence was supported on the solid and perpetual basis of landed property.

In the space of two centuries, from the reign of Constantine to that of Justinian, the eighteen hundred churches of the empire were enriched by the frequent and unalienable gifts of the prince and people. An annual income of six hundred pounds sterling may be reasonably assigned to the bishops, who were placed at an equal distance between riches and poverty, but the standard of their wealth insensibly rose with the dignity and opulence of the cities which they governed. An authentic but imperfect rent-roll specifies some houses, shops, gardens, and farms, which belonged to the three *Basilicæ* of Rome–St. Peter, St. Paul, and St. John Lateran–in the provinces of Italy, Africa, and the East. They produce, besides a reserved rent of oil, linen, paper, aromatics, etc., a clear annual revenue of twenty-two thousand pieces of gold, or twelve thousand pounds sterling.

In the age of Constantine and Justinian the bishops no longer possessed, perhaps they no longer deserved, the unsuspecting confidence of their clergy and people. The ecclesiastical revenues of each diocese were divided into four parts, for the respective uses of the bishop himself, of his inferior clergy, of the poor, and of the public worship; and the abuse of this sacred trust was strictly and repeatedly checked. The patrimony of the church was still subject to all the public impositions of the state. The clergy of Rome, Alexandria, Thessalonica, etc., might solicit and obtain some partial exemptions; but the premature attempt of the great council of Rimini, which aspired to universal freedom, was successfully resisted by the son of Constantine.

IV. The Latin clergy, who erected their tribunal on the ruins of the civil and common law, have modestly accepted, as the gift of Constantine, the independent jurisdiction which was the fruit of time, of accident, and of their own industry. But the liberality of the Christian emperors had actually endowed them with some legal prerogatives which secured and dignified the sacerdotal character:

1. Under a despotic government, the bishops alone enjoyed and asserted the inestimable privilege of being tried only by their *peers;* and even in a capital accusation, a synod of their brethren were the sole judges of their guilt or innocence. Such a tribunal, unless it was inflamed by personal resentment or religious discord, might be favourable, or even partial, to the sacerdotal order: but Constantine was satisfied that secret impunity would

be less pernicious than public scandal, and the Nicene council was edified by his public declaration, that, if he surprised a bishop in the act of adultery, he should cast his Imperial mantle over the episcopal sinner.

2. The domestic jurisdiction of the bishops was at once a privilege and a restraint of the ecclesiastical order, whose civil causes were decently withdrawn from the cognisance of a secular judge. Their venial offences were not exposed to the shame of a public trial or punishment; and the gentle correction which the tenderness of youth may endure from its parents or instructors was inflicted by the temperate severity of the bishops. But if the clergy were guilty of any crime which could not be sufficiently expiated by their degradation from an honourable and beneficial profession, the Roman magistrate drew the sword of justice, without any regard to ecclesiastical immunities.

3. The arbitration of the bishops was ratified by a positive law; and the judges were instructed to execute, without appeal or delay, the episcopal decrees whose validity had hitherto depended on the consent of the parties. The conversion of the magistrates themselves, and of the whole empire, might gradually remove the fears and scruples of the Christians. But they still resorted to the tribunal of the bishops, whose abilities and integrity they esteemed; and the venerable Austin enjoyed the satisfaction of complaining that his spiritual functions were perpetually interrupted by the invidious labour of deciding the claim or the possession of silver and gold, of lands and cattle.

4. The ancient privilege of sanctuary was transferred to the Christian temples, and extended, by the liberal piety of the younger Theodosius, to the precincts of consecrated ground. The fugitive, and even guilty, suppliants were permitted to implore either the justice or the mercy of the Deity and his ministers. The rash violence of despotism was suspended by the mild interposition of the church, and the lives or fortunes of the most eminent subjects might be protected by the mediation of the bishop.

V. The bishop was the perpetual censor of the morals of his people. The discipline of penance was digested into a system of canonical jurisprudence, which accurately defined the duty of private or public confession, the rules of evidence, the degrees of guilt, and the measure of punishment. It was impossible to execute this spiritual censure, if the Christian pontiff who punished the obscure sins of the multitude respected the conspicuous vices and destructive crimes of the magistrate: but it was impossible to arraign the conduct of the magistrate without controlling the administration of civil government.

Some considerations of religion, or loyalty, or fear, protected the sacred persons of the emperors from the zeal or resentment of the bishops; but they boldly censured and excommunicated the subordinate tyrants who were not invested with the majesty of the purple. St. Athanasius excommunicated one of the ministers of Egypt, and the interdict which he pronounced of fire and water was solemnly transmitted to the churches of Cappadocia. Under the reign of the younger Theodosius, the polite and eloquent Synesius, one of the descendants of Hercules, filled the episcopal seat of Ptolemais, near the ruins of ancient Cyrene, and the philosophic bishop supported with dignity the character which he had assumed with reluctance. He vanquished the monster of Libya, the president Andronicus, who abused the authority of a venal office, invented new modes of rapine and torture, and aggravated the guilt of oppression by that of sacrilege. After a fruitless attempt to reclaim the haughty magistrate by mild and religious admonition, Synesius proceeds to inflict the last sentence of ecclesiastical justice, which devotes Andronicus, with his associates and their *families*, to the abhorrence of earth and heaven. The impenitent sinners, more cruel than Phalaris or Sennacherib, more destructive than war, pestilence, or a cloud of locusts, are deprived of the name and privileges of Christians, of the participation of the sacraments, and of the hope of Paradise. The bishop exhorts the clergy, the magistrates, and the people to renounce all society with the enemies of Christ, to exclude them from their houses and tables, and to refuse them the common offices of life, and the decent rites of burial. The church of Ptolemais, obscure and contemptible as she may appear, addresses this declaration to all her sister churches of the world; and the profane who reject her decrees will be involved in the guilt and punishment of Andronicus and his impious followers. These spiritual terrors were enforced by a dexterous application to the Byzantine court; the trembling president implored the mercy of the church, and the descendant of Hercules enjoyed the satisfaction of raising a prostrate tyrant from the ground. Such principles and such examples insensibly prepared the triumph of the Roman pontiffs, who have trampled on the necks of kings.

VI. Every popular government has experienced the effects of rude or artificial eloquence. The coldest nature is animated, the firmest reason is moved, by the rapid communication of the prevailing impulse; and each hearer is affected by his own passions and by those of the surrounding multitude. The ruin of civil liberty had silenced the demagogues of Athens and the tribunes of Rome; the custom of preaching, which seems to constitute a considerable part of Christian devotion, had not been introduced into the temples of antiquity; and the ears of monarchs were never invaded by the harsh sound of popular eloquence till the pulpits of the empire were filled with sacred orators, who possessed some advantages unknown to their profane predecessors.

The arguments and rhetoric of the tribune were instantly opposed, with equal arms, by skilful and resolute antagonists; and the cause of truth and reason might derive an accidental support from the conflict of hostile passions. The bishop, or some distinguished presbyter to whom he cautiously delegated the powers of preaching, harangued, without the danger of interruption or reply, a submissive multitude whose minds had been prepared and subdued by the awful ceremonies of religion. Such was the strict subordination of the Catholic church, that the same concerted sounds might issue at once from an hundred pulpits of Italy or Egypt, if they were *tuned* by the master-hand of the Roman or Alexandrian primate.

VII. The representatives of the Christian republic were regularly assembled in the spring and autumn of each year; and these synods diffused the spirit of ecclesiastical discipline and legislation through the hundred and twenty provinces of the Roman world. The archbishop or metropolitan was empowered by the laws to summon the suffragan bishops of his province; to revise their conduct, to vindicate their rights, to declare their faith, and to examine the merit of the candidates who were elected by the clergy and people to supply the vacancies of the episcopal college. The primates of Rome, Alexandria, Antioch, Carthage, and afterwards Constantinople, who exercised a more ample jurisdiction, convened the numerous assembly of their dependent bishops. But the convocation of great and extraordinary synods was the prerogative of the emperor alone. Whenever the emergencies of the church required this decisive measure, he despatched a peremptory summons to the bishops or the deputies of each province, with an order for the use of post-horses and a competent allowance for the expenses of their journey.

At an early period, when Constantine was the protector rather than the proselyte of Christianity, he referred the African controversy to the council of Arles, in which the bishops of York, of Treves, of Milan, and of Carthage, met as friends and brethren, to debate in their native tongue on the common interest of the Latin or Western church. Eleven years afterwards, a more numerous and celebrated assembly was convened at Nice in Bithynia, to extinguish, by their final sentence, the subtle disputes which had arisen in Egypt on the subject of the Trinity. Three hundred and eighteen bishops obeyed the summons. The ecclesiastics of every rank and sect and denomination have been computed at two thousand and forty-eight persons; the Greeks appeared in person; and the consent of the Latins was expressed by the legates of the Roman pontiff.

The session, which lasted about two months, was frequently honoured by the presence of the emperor. Leaving his guards at the door, he seated himself (with the permission of the council) on a low stool in the midst of the hall. Constantine listened with patience and spoke with modesty; and while he influenced the debates, he humbly professed that he was the minister, not the judge, of the successors of the Apostles, who had been established as priests and as gods upon earth. Such profound reverence of an absolute monarch towards a feeble and unarmed assembly of his own subjects can only be compared to the respect with which the senate had been treated by the Roman princes who adopted the policy of Augustus.

Within the space of fifty years, a philosophic spectator of the vicissitudes of human affairs might have contemplated Tacitus in the senate of Rome, and Constantine in the council of Nice. The fathers of the Capitol and those of the church had alike degenerated from the virtues of their founders; but as the bishops were more deeply rooted in the public opinion, they sustained their dignity with more decent pride, and sometimes opposed with a manly spirit the wishes of their sovereign.

CHAPTER XIV

Persecution of Heresy—The Arian Controversy—Toleration of Paganism

The grateful applause of the clergy has consecrated the memory of a prince who indulged their passions and promoted their interest. Constantine gave them security, wealth, honours, and revenge; and the support of the orthodox faith was considered as the most sacred and important duty of the civil magistrate. The edict of Milan, the great charter of toleration, had confirmed to each individual of the Roman world the privilege of choosing and professing his own religion. But this inestimable privilege was soon violated: with the knowledge of truth the emperor imbibed the maxims of persecution; and the sects which dissented from the Catholic church were afflicted and oppressed by the triumph of Christianity.

Constantine easily believed that the heretics who presumed to dispute *his* opinions or to oppose *his* commands were guilty of the most absurd and criminal obstinacy; and that a seasonable application of moderate severities might save those unhappy men from the danger of an everlasting condemnation. Not a moment was lost in excluding the ministers and teachers of the separated congregations from any share of the rewards and immunities which the emperor had so liberally bestowed on the orthodox clergy. But as the sectaries might still exist under the cloud of royal disgrace, the conquest of the East was immediately followed by an edict which announced their total destruction. After a preamble filled with passion and reproach, Constantine absolutely prohibits the assemblies of the heretics, and confiscates their public property to the use either of the revenue or of the Catholic church.

The sects against whom the Imperial severity was directed appear to have been the adherents of Paul of Samosata; the Montanists of Phrygia, who maintained an enthusiastic succession of prophecy; the Novatians, who sternly rejected the temporal efficacy of repentance; the Marcionites and Valentinians, under whose leading banners the various Gnostics of Asia and Egypt had insensibly rallied, and perhaps the Manichæans, who had recently imported from Persia a more artful composition of Oriental and Christian theology. The design of extirpating the name, or at least of restraining the progress of these odious heretics was prosecuted with vigour and effect. Some of the penal regulations were copied from the edicts of Diocletian; and this method of conversion was applauded by the same bishops who had felt the hand of oppression, and had pleaded for the rights of humanity.

Two immaterial circumstances may serve, however, to prove that the mind of Constantine was not entirely corrupted by the spirit of zeal and bigotry. Before he condemned the Manichæans and their kindred sects, he resolved to make an accurate inquiry into the nature of their religious principles. As if he distrusted the impartiality of his ecclesiastical counsellors, this delicate commission was entrusted to a civil magistrate, whose learning and moderation he justly esteemed, and of whose venal character he was probably ignorant. The emperor was soon convinced that he had too hastily proscribed the orthodox faith and the exemplary morals of the Novatians, who had dissented from the church in some articles of discipline which were not perhaps essential to salvation. By a particular edict he exempted them from the general penalties of the law; allowed them to build a church at Constantinople; respected the miracles of their saints; invited their bishop, Acesius, to the council of Nice; and gently ridiculed the narrow tenets of his sect by a familiar jest, which from the mouth of a sovereign must have been received with applause and gratitude.[1]

The complaints and mutual accusations which assailed the throne of Constantine, as soon as the death of Maxentius had submitted Africa to his victorious arms, were ill adapted to edify an imperfect proselyte. He learned with surprise that the provinces of that great country, from the confines of Cyrene to the Columns of Hercules, were distracted with religious discord. The source of the division was derived from a double election in the church of Carthage, the second in rank and opulence of the ecclesiastical thrones of the West.

But the schism of the Donatists was confined to Africa; the more diffusive mischief of the Trinitarian controversy successively penetrated into every part of the Christian world. The former was an accidental quarrel, occasioned by the abuse of freedom; the latter was a high and mysterious argument, derived from the abuse of philosophy.

The genius of Plato, informed by his own meditation or by the traditional knowledge of the priests of Egypt, had ventured to explore the mysterious nature of the Deity. When he had elevated his mind to the sublime contemplation of the first self-existent, necessary cause of the universe, the Athenian sage was incapable of conceiving *how* the simple unity of his essence could admit the infinite variety of distinct and successive ideas which compose the model of the intellectual world; *how* a Being purely incorporeal could execute that perfect model, and mould with a plastic hand the rude and independent chaos. The vain hope of extricating himself from these difficulties might induce Plato to consider the divine nature under the threefold modification—of the first cause, the reason, or *Logos,* and the soul or spirit of the universe. His poetical imagination sometimes fixed and animated these metaphysical abstractions; the three *archical* or original prin-

[1]Sozomen, 1. i. c. 22. Socrates, 1. i. c. 10. These historians have been suspected, but I think without reason, of an attachment to the Novatian doctrine. The emperor said to the bishop, "Acesius, take a ladder, and get up to heaven by yourself." Most of the Christian sects have, by turns, borrowed the ladder of Acesius.

ciples were represented in the Platonic system as three Gods, united with each other by a mysterious and ineffable generation; and the *Logos* was particularly considered under the more accessible character of the Son of an Eternal Father, and the Creator and Governor of the world. Such appear to have been the secret doctrines which were cautiously whispered in the gardens of the Academy; and which, according to the more recent disciples of Plato, could not be perfectly understood till after an assiduous study of thirty years.

The arms of the Macedonians diffused over Asia and Egypt the language and learning of Greece; and the theological system of Plato was taught, with less reserve, and perhaps with some improvements, in the celebrated school of Alexandria. A numerous colony of Jews had been invited, by the favour of the Ptolemies, to settle in their new capital. While the bulk of the nation practised the legal ceremonies, and pursued the lucrative occupations of commerce, a few Hebrews of a more liberal spirit devoted their lives to religious and philosophical contemplation. They cultivated with diligence, and embraced with ardour, the theological system of the Athenian sage. One hundred years before the birth of Christ, a philosophical treatise, which manifestly betrays the style and sentiments of the school of Plato, was produced by the Alexandrian Jews, and unanimously received as a genuine and valuable relic of the inspired Wisdom of Solomon. A similar union of the Mosaic faith and the Grecian philosophy distinguishes the works of Philo, which were composed, for the most part, under the reign of Augustus.

The eloquence of Plato, the name of Solomon, the authority of the school of Alexandria, and the consent of the Jews and Greeks, were insufficient to establish the truth of a mysterious doctrine, which might have been for ever confounded with the philosophical visions of the Academy, the Porch, and the Lyceum, if the name and divine attributes of the *Logos* had not been confirmed by the celestial pen of the last and most sublime of the Evangelists.[2] The divine sanction which the Apostle had bestowed on the fundamental principle of the theology of Plato encouraged the learned proselytes of the second and third centuries to admire and study the writings of the Athenian sage, who had thus marvellously anticipated one of the most surprising discoveries of the Christian revelation. The respectable name of Plato was used by the orthodox, and abused by the heretics, as the common support of truth and error: the authority of his skilful commentators and the science of dialectics were employed to justify the remote consequences of his opinions, and to supply the discreet silence of the inspired writers. The same subtle and profound questions concerning the nature, the generation, the distinction, and the equality of the three divine persons of the mysterious *Triad*, or *Trinity*, were agitated in the philosophical and in the Christian schools of Alexandria. But we may observe two essential and peculiar circumstances which discriminated the doctrines of the Catholic church from the opinions of the Platonic school.

[2]The Platonists admired the beginning of the Gospel of St. John, as containing an exact transcript of their own principles. Augustin. de Civitat.

I. A chosen society of philosophers, men of a liberal education and curious disposition, might silently meditate, and temperately discuss in the gardens of Athens or the library of Alexandria, the abstruse questions of metaphysical science. The lofty speculations, which neither convinced the understanding nor agitated the passions of the Platonists themselves, were carelessly overlooked by the idle, the busy, and even the studious part of mankind.

But after the *Logos* had been revealed as the sacred object of the faith, the hope, and the religious worship of the Christians, the mysterious system was embraced by a numerous and increasing multitude in every province of the Roman world. Those persons who, from their age, or sex, or occupations, were the least qualified to judge, who were the least exercised in the habits of abstract reasoning, aspired to contemplate the economy of the Divine Nature: and it is the boast of Tertullian that a Christian mechanic could readily answer such questions as had perplexed the wisest of the Grecian sages. These speculations, instead of being treated as the amusement of a vacant hour, became the most serious business of the present, and the most useful preparation for a future, life. A theology which it was incumbent to believe, which it was impious to doubt, and which it might be dangerous, and even fatal, to mistake, became the familiar topic of private meditation and popular discourse. The cold indifference of philosophy was inflamed by the fervent spirit of devotion; and even the metaphors of common language suggested the fallacious prejudices of sense and experience.

The Christians, who abhorred the gross and impure generation of the Greek mythology, were tempted to argue from the familiar analogy of the filial and paternal relations. The character of *Son* seemed to imply a perpetual subordination to the voluntary author of his existence; but as the act of generation, in the most spiritual and abstracted sense, must be supposed to transmit the properties of a common nature, they durst not presume to circumscribe the powers or the duration of the Son of an eternal and omnipotent Father. Fourscore years after the death of Christ, the Christians of Bithynia declared before the tribunal of Pliny that they invoked him as a god: and his divine honours have been perpetuated in every age and country, by the various sects who assume the name of his disciples.

Their tender reverence for the memory of Christ, and their horror for the profane worship of any created being, would have engaged them to assert the equal and absolute divinity of the *Logos*, if their rapid ascent towards the throne of heaven had not been imperceptibly checked by the apprehension of violating the unity and sole supremacy of the great Father of Christ, and of the Universe. The suspense and fluctuation produced in the minds of the Christians by these opposite tendencies may be observed in the writings of the theologians who flourished after the end of the apostolic age and before the origin of the Arian controversy.

II. The devotion of individuals was the first circumstance which distinguished the Christians from the Platonists: the second was the authority of the church. The disciples of philosophy asserted the rights of intellectual freedom, and their respect for the sentiments of their teachers was a liberal and voluntary tribute which they offered to superior reason. But the Christians formed a numerous and disciplined society; and the jurisdiction of their laws and magistrates was strictly exercised over the minds of the faithful. The loose wanderings of the imagination were gradually confined by creeds and confessions; the freedom of private judgment submitted to the public wisdom of synods; the authority of a theologian was determined by his ecclesiastical rank; and the episcopal successors of the Apostles inflicted the censures of the church on those who deviated from the orthodox belief.

After the edict of toleration had restored peace and leisure to the Christians, the Trinitarian controversy was revived in the ancient seat of Platonism, the learned, the opulent, the tumultuous city of Alexandria; and the flame of religious discord was rapidly communicated from the schools to the clergy, the people, the provinces, and the East. The abstruse question of the eternity of the *Logos* was agitated in ecclesiastic conferences and popular sermons; and the heterodox opinions of Arius were soon made public by his own zeal and by that of his adversaries. Synods in Palestine and Bithynia were opposed to the synods of Egypt. The attention of the prince and people was attracted by this theological dispute; and the decision, at the end of six years, was referred to the supreme authority of the general council of Nice.

The consubstantiality of the Father and the Son was established by the council of Nice, and has been unanimously received as a fundamental article of the Christian faith by the consent of the Greek, the Latin, the Oriental, and the Protestant churches. But if the same word had not served to stigmatise the heretics and to unite the Catholics, it would have been inadequate to the purpose of the majority by whom it was introduced into the orthodox creed. The intrepid Athanasius, the learned Gregory Nazianzen, and the other pillars of the church, who supported with ability and success the Nicene doctrine, ventured to illustrate their meaning by affirming that three men, as they belong to the same common species, are consubstantial or *homoousian* to each other. This pure and distinct equality was tempered, on the one hand, by the internal connection and spiritual penetration which indissolubly unites the divine persons; and, on the other, by the pre-eminence of the Father, which was acknowledged as far as it is compatible with the independence of the Son. Within these limits the almost invisible and tremulous ball of orthodoxy was allowed securely to vibrate. On either side, beyond this consecrated ground, the heretics and the dæmons lurked in ambush to surprise and devour the unhappy wanderer. But the authority of a general council inscribed on the banners of the orthodox party the mysterious characters of the word Homoousian, which essentially contributed, notwithstanding some obscure disputes, some nocturnal combats, to maintain and perpetuate the uniformity of faith, or at least of language.

One question which gradually arose from the Arian controversy served to produce and discriminate three sects who were united only by their common aversion to the Homoousian of the Nicene synod. The sect which asserted the doctrine of a *similar* substance was the most numerous, at least in the provinces of Asia; and when the leaders of both parties were assembled in the council of Seleucia, *their* opinion would have prevailed by a majority of one hundred and five to forty-three bishops. The Greek word which was chosen to express this mysterious resemblance bears so close an affinity to the orthodox symbol, that the profane of every age have derided the furious contests which the difference of a single diphthong excited between the Homoousians and the Homoiousians. As it frequently happens that the sounds and characters which approach the nearest to each other accidentally represent the most opposite ideas, the observation would be itself ridiculous, if it were possible to mark any real and sensible distinction between the doctrine of the Semi-Arians, as they were improperly styled, and that of the Catholics themselves.[3]

Such was the rise and progress, and such were the natural revolutions, of those theological disputes which disturbed the peace of Christianity under the reigns of Constantine and of his sons. But as those princes presumed to extend their despotism over the faith, as well as over the lives and fortunes of their subjects, the weight of their suffrage sometimes inclined the ecclesiastical balance: and the prerogatives of the King of Heaven were settled, or changed, or modified, in the cabinet of an earthly monarch.

The unhappy spirit of discord which pervaded the provinces of the East interrupted the triumph of Constantine; but the emperor continued for some time to view with cool and careless indifference the object of the dispute. As he was yet ignorant of the difficulty of appeasing the quarrels of theologians, he addressed to the contending parties a moderating epistle. He laments that the Christian people, who had the same God, the same religion, and the same worship, should be divided by such inconsiderable distinctions; and he seriously recommends to the clergy of Alexandria the example of the Greek philosophers, who could maintain their arguments without losing their temper, and assert their freedom without violating their friendship.

The indifference and contempt of the sovereign would have been, perhaps, the most effectual method of silencing the dispute, if the popular current had been less rapid and impetuous, and if Constantine himself, in the midst of faction and fanaticism, could have preserved the calm possession of his own mind. But his ecclesiastical ministers soon contrived to seduce the impartiality of the magistrate, and to awaken the zeal of the proselyte. He was provoked by the insults which had been offered to his statues; he was alarmed by the real as well as the imaginary magnitude of the spreading mischief; and he extinguished the hope of peace and toleration, from the moment that he assembled three hundred bishops within the walls of the same palace.

A Roman general whose religion might be still a subject of doubt, and

[3] I cannot forbear reminding the reader that the difference between the *Homoousian* and *Homoiousian* is almost invisible to the nicest theological eye.

whose mind had not been enlightened either by study or by inspiration, was indifferently qualified to discuss, in the Greek language, a metaphysical question, or an article of faith. But the credit of his favourite Osius, who appears to have presided in the council of Nice, might dispose the emperor in favour of the orthodox party; and a well-timed insinuation might exasperate him against their adversaries. The Nicene creed was ratified by Constantine; and his firm declaration, that those who resisted the divine judgment of the synod must prepare themselves for an immediate exile, annihilated the murmurs of a feeble opposition which, from seventeen, was almost instantly reduced to two, protesting bishops. The impious Arius was banished into one of the most remote provinces of Illyricum; his writings were condemned to the flames, and a capital punishment was denounced against those in whose possession they should be found.

As soon as the emperor was relieved from the terrors of the civil war, he devoted the leisure of his winter quarters at Arles, Milan, Sirmium, and Constantinople, to the amusement or toils of controversy: the sword of the magistrate, and even of the tyrant, was unsheathed, to enforce the reasons of the theologian; and as he opposed the orthodox faith of Nice, it is readily confessed that his incapacity and ignorance were equal to his presumption. The eunuchs, the women, and the bishops who governed the vain and feeble mind of the emperor had inspired him with an insuperable dislike to the Homoousian; but he alternately embraced and condemned the sentiments, he successively banished and recalled the leaders, of the Arian and Semi-Arian factions.

The sons of Constantine imitated, in the delay of their baptism, the example of their father. Like him, they presumed to pronounce their judgment on mysteries into which they had never been regularly initiated: and the fate of the Trinitarian controversy depended, in a great measure, on the sentiments of Constantius, who inherited the provinces of the East, and acquired the possession of the whole empire. But the triumph of Arianism had been preceded by the removal of the orthodox clergy, whom it was impossible either to intimidate or to corrupt; and the reign of Constantius was disgraced by the unjust and ineffectual persecution of the great Athanasius.

The immortal name of Athanasius will never be separated from the Catholic doctrine of the Trinity, to whose defence he consecrated every moment and every faculty of his being. Amidst the storms of persecution, the archbishop of Alexandria was patient of labour, jealous of fame, careless of safety. Five times was Athanasius expelled from his throne; twenty years he passed as an exile or a fugitive; and almost every province of the Roman empire was successively witness to his merit, and his sufferings in the cause of the Homoousian, which he considered as the sole pleasure and business, as the duty and as the glory of his life. In his youth the primate of Egypt resisted the great Constantine, who had repeatedly signified his will that Arius should be restored to the Catholic communion. Athanasius displayed a superiority of character and abilities which would have qualified him, far better than the degenerate sons of Constantine, for the government of a great monarchy.

The persecution of Athanasius and of so many respectable bishops, who suffered for the truth of their opinions, or at least for the integrity of their conscience, was a just subject of indignation and discontent to all Christians, except those who were blindly devoted to the Arian faction. The people regretted the loss of their faithful pastors, whose banishment was usually followed by the intrusion of a stranger into the episcopal chair, and loudly complained that the right of election was violated, and that they were condemned to obey a mercenary usurper, whose person was unknown and whose principles were suspected. The Catholics might prove to the world that they were not involved in the guilt and heresy of their ecclesiastical governor, by publicly testifying their dissent, or by totally separating themselves from his communion.

The first of these methods was invented at Antioch, and practised with such success that it was soon diffused over the Christian world. The doxology, or sacred hymn, which celebrates the *glory* of the Trinity, is susceptible of very nice, but material, inflections; and the substance of an orthodox or an heretical creed may be expressed by the difference of a disjunctive or a copulative particle. Alternate responses and a more regular psalmody were introduced into the public service by two devout and active laymen attached to the Nicene faith. Under their conduct a swarm of monks issued from the adjacent desert, bands of well-disciplined singers were stationed in the cathedral of Antioch, the Glory to the Father, AND the Son, AND the Holy Ghost was triumphantly chanted by a full chorus of voices.

The same zeal which inspired their songs prompted the more scrupulous members of the orthodox party to form separate assemblies, which were governed by the presbyters, till the death of their exiled bishop allowed the election and consecration of a new episcopal pastor. The revolutions of the court multiplied the number of pretenders, and the same city was often disputed, under the reign of Constantius, by two, or three, or even four bishops, who exercised their spiritual jurisdiction over their respective followers, and alternately lost and regained the temporal possessions of the church.

When Constantius visited Rome, he was assailed by the importunate solicitations of a people who had preserved, as the last remnant of their ancient freedom, the right of treating their sovereign with familiar insolence. The emperor consented that the two bishops, Liberius and Felix, should govern in peace their respective congregations. But the ideas of toleration were so repugnant to the practice, and even to the sentiments, of those times, that, when the answer of Constantius was publicly read in the Circus of Rome, so reasonable a project of accommodation was rejected with contempt and ridicule. The eager vehemence which animated the spectators on the decisive moment of a horse-race was now directed towards a different object, and the Circus resounded with the shout of thousands, who repeatedly exclaimed "One God, One Christ, One Bishop!"

The simple narrative of the intestine divisions which distracted the peace and dishonoured the triumph of the church, will confirm the remark of a Pagan historian, and justify the complaint of a venerable bishop. The experience of Ammianus had convinced him that the enmity of the Christians towards each other surpassed the fury of savage beasts against man; and Gregory Nazianzen most pathetically laments that the kingdom of heaven was converted by discord into the image of chaos, of a nocturnal tempest, and of hell itself. A modern writer would enumerate, among the causes of the decline of the empire, a law of Constantine by which the exercise of the Pagan worship was absolutely suppressed, and a considerable part of his subjects was left destitute of priests, of temples, and of any public religion. But a report that the ceremonies of Paganism were suppressed is formally contradicted by the emperor himself, who wisely assigns, as the principle of his moderation, the invincible force of habit, of prejudice, and of superstition. While Constantine designed to ruin the foundations, he seemed to reform the abuses, of the ancient religion. After the example of the wisest of his predecessors, he condemned, under the most rigorous penalties, the occult and impious arts of divination, which excited the vain hopes, and sometimes the criminal attempts, of those who were discontented with their present condition. An ignominious silence was imposed on the oracles, which had been publicly convicted of fraud and falsehood; the effeminate priests of the Nile were abolished; and Constantine discharged the duties of a Roman censor when he gave orders for the demolition of several temples of Phœnicia, in which every mode of prostitution was devoutly practised in the face of day, and to the honour of Venus.

The evidence of facts, and the monuments which are still extant of brass and marble, continue to prove the public exercise of the Pagan worship during the whole reign of the sons of Constantine. In the East as well as in the West, in cities as well as in the country, a great number of temples were respected, or at least were spared; and the devout multitude still enjoyed the luxury of sacrifices, of festivals, and of processions, by the permission, or by the connivance, of the civil government. The senate still presumed to consecrate, by solemn decrees, the *divine* memory of their sovereigns; and Constantine himself was associated, after death, to those gods whom he had renounced and insulted during his life. The title, the ensigns, the prerogatives, of SOVEREIGN PONTIFF, which had been instituted by Numa, and assumed by Augustus, were accepted, without hesitation, by seven Christian emperors, who were invested with a more absolute authority over the religion which they had deserted than over that which they professed.

Every motive of authority and fashion, of interest and reason, now militated on the side of Christianity; but two or three generations elapsed before their victorious influence was universally felt. The religion which had so long and so lately been established in the Roman empire was still revered by a numerous people, less attached indeed to speculative opinion than to ancient custom. The honours of the state and army were indifferently bestowed on all the subjects of Constantine and Constantius; and a considerable portion of knowledge and wealth and valours was still engaged in the service of Polytheism. The superstition of the senator and of the peasant, of the poet and the philosopher, was derived from very different causes, but they met with equal devotion in the temples of the gods. Their zeal was insensibly provoked by the insulting triumph of a proscribed sect; and their hopes were revived by the well-grounded confidence that the presumptive heir of the empire, a young and valiant hero, who had delivered Gaul from the arms of the barbarians, had secretly embraced the religion of his ancestors.

CHAPTER XV

Character of Constantine—Division of the Empire among His Three Sons—Civil War

The character of the prince who removed the seat of empire, and introduced such important changes into the civil and religious constitution of his country, has fixed the attention, and divided the opinions, of mankind. By the grateful zeal of the Christians the deliverer of the church has been decorated with every attribute of a hero, and even of a saint; while the discontent of the vanquished party has compared Constantine to the most abhorred of those tyrants who, by their vice and weakness, dishonoured the Imperial purple.

The same passions have, in some degree, been perpetuated to succeeding generations, and the character of Constantine is considered, even in the present age, as an object either of satire or of panegyric. By the impartial union of those defects which are confessed by his warmest admirers, and of those virtues which are acknowledged by his most implacable enemies, we might hope to delineate a just portrait of that extraordinary man, which the truth and candour of history should adopt without a blush. But it would soon appear that the vain attempt to blend such discordant colours, and to reconcile such inconsistent qualities, must produce a figure monstrous rather than human, unless it is viewed in its proper and distinct lights by a careful separation of the different periods of the reign of Constantine.

The person, as well as the mind, of Constantine had been enriched by nature with her choicest endowments. His stature was lofty, his countenance majestic, his deportment graceful; his strength and activity were displayed in every manly exercise, and, from his earliest youth to a very advanced season of life, he preserved the vigour of his constitution by a strict adherence to the domestic virtues of chastity and temperance. He delighted in the social intercourse of familar conversation; and though he might sometimes indulge his disposition to raillery with less reserve than was required by the severe dignity of his station, the courtesy and liberality of his manners gained the hearts of all who approached him. The sincerity of his friendship has been suspected; yet he showed, on some occasions, that he was not incapable of a warm and lasting attachment.

The disadvantage of an illiterate education had not prevented him from forming a just estimate of the value of learning; and the arts and sciences derived some encouragement from the munificent protection of Constantine. In the despatch of business his diligence was indefatigable; and the active powers of his mind were almost continually exercised in reading, writing, or meditating, in giving audience to ambassadors, and in examining the complaints of his subjects. Even those who censured the propriety of his measures were compelled to acknowledge that he possessed magnanimity to conceive, and patience to execute, the most arduous designs, without being checked either by the prejudices of education or by the clamours of the multitude.

In the field he infused his own intrepid spirit into the troops, whom he conducted with the talents of a consummate general; and to his abilities, rather than to his fortune, we may ascribe the signal victories which he obtained over the foreign and domestic foes of the republic.

He loved glory as the reward, perhaps as the motive, of his labours. The boundless ambition which, from the moment of his accepting the purple at York, appears as the ruling passion of his soul, may be justified by the dangers of his own situation, by the character of his rivals, by the consciousness of superior merit, and by the prospect that his success would enable him to restore peace and order to the distracted empire. In his civil wars against Maxentius and Licinius he had engaged on his side the inclinations of the people, who compared the undissembled vices of those tyrants with the spirit of wisdom and justice which seemed to direct the general tenor of the administration of Constantine.

In the life of Augustus we behold the tyrant of the republic converted almost by imperceptible degrees into the father of his country and of human kind. In that of Constantine we may contemplate a hero, who had so long inspired his subjects with love and his enemies with terror, degenerating into a cruel and dissolute monarch corrupted by his fortune, or raised by conquest above the necessity of dissimulation. The general peace which he maintained during the last fourteen years of his reign was a period of apparent splendour rather than of real prosperity; and the old age of Constantine was disgraced by the opposite yet reconcilable vices of rapaciousness and prodigality. A secret but universal decay was felt in every part of the public administration, and the emperor himself, though he still retained the obedience, gradually lost the esteem, of his subjects.

The dress and manners which, towards the decline of life, he chose to affect, served only to degrade him in the eyes of mankind. The Asiatic pomp which had been adopted by the pride of Diocletian assumed an air of softness and effeminacy in the person of Constantine. He is represented with false hair of various colours, laboriously arranged by the skilful artists of the times; a diadem of a new and more expensive fashion; a profusion of gems and pearls, of collars and bracelets; and a variegated flowing robe of silk, most curiously embroidered with flowers of gold. In such apparel, scarcely to be excused by the youth and folly of Elagabalus, we are at a loss to discover the wisdom of an aged monarch and the simplicity of a Roman veteran. A mind thus relaxed by prosperity and indulgence was incapable of rising to that magnanimity which disdains suspicion and dares to forgive. The deaths of Maximian and Licinius may perhaps be justified by the maxims of policy as they are taught in the schools of tyrants; but an impartial narrative of the executions, or rather murders, which sullied the declining age of Constantine, will suggest to our most candid thoughts the idea of a prince who could sacrifice, without reluctance, the laws of justice and the feelings of nature to the dictates either of his passions or of his interest.

Crispus, the eldest son of Constantine, and the presumptive heir of the empire, is represented by impartial historians as an amiable and accomplished youth. The care of his education, or at least of his studies, was entrusted to Lactantius, the most eloquent of the Christians, a preceptor admirably qualified to form the taste and to excite the virtues of his illustrious disciple. At the age of seventeen Crispus was invested with the title of Cæsar and the administration of the Gallic provinces, where the inroads of the Germans gave him an early occasion of signalising his military prowess.

In the civil war which broke out soon afterwards, the father and son divided their powers; and the names of Constantine and of Crispus were united in the joyful acclamations of their eastern subjects, who loudly proclaimed that the world had been subdued, and was now governed, by an emperor endowed with every virtue, and by his illustrious son, a prince beloved of Heaven, and the lively image of his father's perfections. The public favour, which seldom accompanies old age, diffused its lustre over the youth of Crispus. He deserved the esteem and he engaged the affections of the court, the army, and the people. The experienced merit of a reigning monarch is acknowledged by his subjects with reluctance, and frequently denied with partial and discontented murmurs; while, from the opening virtues of his successor, they fondly conceive the most unbounded hopes of private as well as public felicity.

This dangerous popularity soon excited the attention of Constantine, who, both as a father and as a king, was impatient of an equal. Instead of attempting to secure the allegiance of his son by the generous ties of confidence and gratitude, he resolved to prevent the mischiefs which might be apprehended from dissatisfied ambition. Crispus soon had reason to complain that, while his infant brother Constantius was sent with the title of Cæsar to reign over his peculiar department of the Gallic provinces, *he*, a prince of mature years, who had performed such recent and signal services, instead of being raised to the superior rank of Augustus, was confined almost a prisoner to his father's court, and exposed, without power or defence, to every calumny which the malice of his enemies could suggest.

Under such painful circumstances the royal youth might not always be able to compose his behaviour or suppress his discontent; and we may be assured that he was encompassed by a train of indiscreet or perfidious followers, who assiduously studied to inflame, and who were perhaps instructed to betray, the unguarded warmth of his resentment. An edict of Constantine, published about this time, manifestly indicates his real or affected suspicions that a secret conspiracy had been formed against his person and government. By all the allurements of honours and rewards he invites informers of every degree to accuse, without exception, his magistrates or ministers, his friends or his most intimate favourites, protesting, with a solemn asseveration, that he himself will listen to the charge, that he himself will revenge his injuries; and concluding with a prayer, which discovers some apprehension of danger, that the providence of the Supreme Being may still continue to protect the safety of the emperor and of the empire.

The informers who complied with so liberal an invitation were sufficiently versed in the arts of courts to select the friends and adherents of Crispus as the guilty persons; nor is there any reason to distrust the veracity of the emperor, who had promised an ample measure of revenge and punishment. The policy of Constantine maintained, however, the same appearances of regard and confidence towards a son whom he began to consider as his most irreconcilable enemy. Medals were struck with the customary vows for the long and auspicious reign of the young Cæsar; and as the people, who were not admitted into the secrets of the palace, still loved his virtues and respected his dignity, a poet who solicits his recall from exile adores with equal devotion the majesty of the father and that of the son.

The time was now arrived for celebrating the august ceremony of the twentieth year of the reign of Constantine, and the emperor, for that purpose, removed his court from Nicomedia to Rome, where the most splendid preparations had been made for his reception. Every eye and every tongue affected to express their sense of the general happiness, and the veil of ceremony and dissimulation was drawn for a while over the darkest designs of revenge and murder.

In the midst of the festival the unfortunate Crispus was apprehended by order of the emperor, who laid aside the tenderness of a father without assuming the equity of a judge. The examination was short and private; and as it was thought decent to conceal the fate of the young prince from the eyes of the Roman people, he was sent under a strong guard to Pola, in Istria, where, soon afterwards, he was put to death, either by the hand of the executioner or by the more gentle operation of poison.

The Cæsar Licinius, a youth of amiable manners, was involved in the ruin of Crispus, and the stern jealousy of Constantine was unmoved by the prayers and tears of his favourite sister, pleading for the life of a son whose rank was his only crime, and whose loss she did not long survive. The story of these unhappy princes, the nature and evidence of their guilt, the forms of their trial, and the circumstances of their death, were buried in mysterious obscurity; and the courtly bishop who has celebrated in an elaborate work the virtues and piety of his hero observes a prudent silence on the subject of these tragic events.

The innocence of Crispus was so universally acknowledged that the modern Greeks, who adore the memory of their founder, are reduced to palliate the guilt of an emperor which the common feelings of human nature forbade them to justify. They pretend that, as soon as the afflicted father discovered the falsehood of the accusation by which his credulity had been so fatally misled, he published to the world his repentance and remorse; that he mourned forty days, during which he abstained from the use of the bath and all the ordinary comforts of life; and that, for the lasting instruction of posterity, he erected a golden statue of Crispus, with this memorable inscription,—To MY SON, WHOM I UNJUSTLY CONDEMNED.

A tale so moral and so interesting would deserve to be supported by less exceptionable authority; but if we consult the more ancient and authentic writers, they will inform us that the repentance of Constantine was manifested only in acts of blood and revenge, and that he atoned for the murder of an innocent son by the execution, perhaps, of a guilty wife. They ascribe the misfortunes of Crispus to the arts of his stepmother Fausta, whose implacable hatred or whose disappointed love renewed in the palace of Constantine the ancient tragedy of Hippolytus and of Phædra. Like the daughter of Minos, the daughter of Maximian accused her son-in-law of an incestuous attempt on the chastity of his father's wife, and easily obtained, from the jealousy of the emperor, a sentence of death against a young prince whom she considered with reason as the most formidable rival of her own children. But Helena, the aged mother of Constantine, lamented and revenged the untimely fate of her grandson Crispus; nor was it long before a real or pretended discovery was made that Fausta herself entertained a criminal connection with a slave belonging to the Imperial stables. Her condemnation and punishment were the instant consequences of the charge, and the adulteress was suffocated by the steam of a bath, which, for that purpose, had been heated to an extraordinary degree. Notwithstanding the positive testimony of several writers of the Pagan as well as of the Christian religion, there may still remain some reason to believe, or at least to suspect, that Fausta escaped the blind and suspicious cruelty of her husband. The deaths of a son and of a nephew, with the execution of a great number of respectable and perhaps innocent friends who were involved in their fall, may be sufficient, however, to justify the discontent of the Roman people, and to explain the satirical verses affixed to the palace gate, comparing the splendid and bloody reigns of Constantine and Nero.

By the death of Crispus the inheritance of the empire seemed to devolve on the three sons of Fausta, who have been already mentioned under the names of Constantine, Constantius, and of Constans. These young princes were successively invested with the title of Cæsar, and the dates of their promotion may be referred to the tenth, the twentieth, and the thirtieth years of the reign of their father.

The whole empire was deeply interested in the education of these youths, the acknowledged successors of Constantine. The exercises of the body prepared them for the fatigues of war and the duties of active life. Those who occasionally mention the education or talents of Constantius allow that he excelled in the gymnastic arts of leaping and running; that he was a dexterous archer, a skilful horseman, and a master of all the different weapons used in the service either of the cavalry or of the infantry.

The same assiduous cultivation was bestowed, though not perhaps with equal success, to improve the minds of the sons and nephews of Constantine.

The most celebrated professors of the Christian faith, of the Grecian philosophy, and of the Roman jurisprudence, were invited by the liberality of the emperor, who reserved for himself the important task of instructing the royal youths in the science of government and the knowledge of mankind. But the genius of Constantine himself had been formed by adversity and experience. In the free intercourse of private life, and amidst the dangers of the court of Galerius, he had learned to command his own passions, to encounter those of his equals, and to depend for his present safety and future greatness on the prudence and firmness of his personal conduct. His destined successors had the misfortune of being born and educated in the Imperial purple. Incessantly surrounded with a train of flatterers, they passed their youth in the enjoyment of luxury and the expectation of a throne; nor would the dignity of their rank permit them to descend from that elevated station from whence the various characters of human nature appear to wear a smooth and uniform aspect. The pernicious tendency of the system introduced by Constantine was displayed in the feeble administration of his sons, who, by their vices and weakness, soon lost the esteem and affections of their people.

By chastising the pride of the Goths, and by accepting the homage of a suppliant nation, Constantine asserted the majesty of the Roman empire; and the ambassadors of Æthiopia, Persia, and the most remote countries of India, congratulated the peace and prosperity of his government. If he reckoned among the favours of fortune the death of his eldest son, of his nephew, and perhaps of his wife, he enjoyed an uninterrupted flow of private as well as public felicity till the thirtieth year of his reign; a period which none of his predecessors, since Augustus, had been permitted to celebrate. Constantine survived that solemn festival about ten months; and, at the mature age of sixty-four, after a short illness, he ended his memorable life at the palace of Aquyrion, in the suburbs of Nicomedia, whither he had retired for the benefit of the air, and with the hope of recruiting his exhausted strength by the use of the warm baths.

The excessive demonstrations of grief, or at least of mourning, surpassed whatever had been practised on any former occasion. Notwithstanding the claims of the senate and people of ancient Rome, the corpse of the deceased emperor, according to his last request, was transported to the city which was destined to preserve the name and memory of its founder. The body of Constantine, adorned with the vain symbols of greatness, the purple and diadem, was deposited on a golden bed in one of the apartments of the palace, which for that purpose had been splendidly furnished and illuminated. The forms of the court were strictly maintained. Every day, at the appointed hours, the principal officers of the state, the army, and the household, approaching the person of their sovereign with bended knees and a composed countenance, offered their respectful homage as seriously as if he had been still alive. From motives of policy, this theatrical representation was for some time continued; nor could flattery neglect the opportunity of remarking that Constantine alone, by the peculiar indulgence of Heaven, had reigned after his death.

But this reign could subsist only in empty pageantry; and it was soon discovered that the will of the most absolute monarch is seldom obeyed when his subjects have no longer anything to hope from his favour, or to dread from his resentment.

The voice of the dying emperor had recommended the care of his funeral to the piety of Constantius; and that prince, by the vicinity of his eastern station, could easily prevent the diligence of his brothers, who resided in their distant governments of Italy and Gaul. As soon as he had taken possession of the palace of Constantinople, his first care was to remove the apprehensions of his kinsmen, by a solemn oath which he pledged for their security. His next employment was to find some specious pretence which might release his conscience from the obligation of an imprudent promise. The arts of fraud were made subservient to the designs of cruelty; and a manifest forgery was attested by a person of the most sacred character. From the hands of the bishop of Nicomedia Constantius received a fatal scroll, affirmed to be the genuine testament of his father, in which the emperor expressed his suspicions that he had been poisoned by his brothers and conjured his sons to revenge his death, and to consult their own safety, by the punishment of the guilty.

Of so numerous a family, Gallus and Julian alone, the two youngest children of Julius Constantius, were saved from the hands of the assassins, till their rage, satiated with slaughter, had in some measure subsided. The massacre of the Flavian race was succeeded by a new division of the provinces, which was ratified in a personal interview of the three sons. Constantine, the eldest of the Cæsars, obtained, with a certain pre-eminence of rank, the possession of the new capital, which bore his own name and that of his father. Thrace and the countries of the East were allotted for the patrimony of Constantius; and Constans was acknowledged as the lawful sovereign of Italy, Africa, and the western Illyricum. When they first assumed the reins of government, the eldest of these princes was twenty-one, the second twenty, and the third only seventeen, years of age.

While the martial nations of Europe followed the standards of his brothers, Constantius, at the head of the effeminate troops of Asia, was left to sustain the weight of the Persian war. At the decease of Constantine, the throne of the East was filled by Sapor, son of Hormouz, or Hormisdas, and grandson of Narses, who, after the victory of Galerius, had humbly confessed the superiority of the Roman power. Although Sapor was in the thirtieth year of his long reign, he was still in the vigour of youth, as the date of his accession, by a very strange fatality, had preceded that of his birth. The wife of Hormouz remained pregnant at the time of her husband's death, and the uncertainty of the sex, as well as of the event, excited the ambitious hopes of the princes of the house of Sassan. The apprehensions of civil war were at length removed by the positive assurance of the

Magi that the widow of Hormouz had conceived, and would safely produce a son. Obedient to the voice of superstition, the Persians prepared, without delay, the ceremony of his coronation. A royal bed, on which the queen lay in state, was exhibited in the midst of the palace; the diadem was placed on the spot which might be supposed to conceal the future heir of Artaxerxes, and the prostrate satraps adored the majesty of their invisible and insensible sovereign.

The ambition of the Persian, to whom his enemies ascribe the virtues of a soldier and a statesman, was animated by the desire of revenging the disgrace of his fathers, and of wresting from the hands of the Romans the five provinces beyond the Tigris. The military fame of Constantine, and the real or apparent strength of his government, suspended the attack, and, while the hostile conduct of Sapor provoked the resentment, his artful negotiations amused the patience of the Imperial court. The death of Constantine was the signal of war, and the actual condition of the Syrian and Armenian frontier seemed to encourage the Persians by the prospect of a rich spoil and an easy conquest.

During the long period of the reign of Constantius the provinces of the East were afflicted by the calamities of the Persian war. The irregular incursions of the light troops alternately spread terror and devastation beyond the Tigris and beyond the Euphrates, from the gates of Ctesiphon to those of Antioch; and this active service was performed by the Arabs of the desert, who were divided in their interest and affections, some of their independent chiefs being enlisted in the party of Sapor, whilst others had engaged their doubtful fidelity to the emperor. The more grave and important operations of the war were conducted with equal vigour; and the armies of Rome and Persia encountered each other in nine bloody fields, in two of which Constantius himself commanded in person.

Whatever advantages might attend the arms of Sapor in the field, though nine repeated victories diffused among the nations the fame of his valour and conduct, he could not hope to succeed in the execution of his designs while the fortified towns of Mesopotamia remained in the possession of the Romans. The danger and difficulties of the Scythian war engaged him soon afterwards to conclude, or at least to observe, a truce with the Roman emperor, which was equally grateful to both princes, as Constantius himself, after the deaths of his two brothers, was involved, by the revolutions of the West, in a civil contest which required and seemed to exceed the most vigorous exertion of his undivided strength.

After the partition of the empire three years had scarcely elapsed before the sons of Constantine seemed impatient to convince mankind that they were incapable of contenting themselves with the dominions which they were unqualified to govern. The eldest of those princes soon complained that he was defrauded of his just proportion of the spoils of their murdered kinsmen; and though he might yield to the superior guilt and merit of Constantius, he exacted from Constans the cession of the African provinces. At the head of a tumultuary band, suited for rapine rather than for conquest, he suddenly broke into the dominions of Constans by the way of the Julian Alps.

The measures of Constans, who then resided in Dacia, were directed with more prudence and ability. On the news of his brother's invasion he detached a select and disciplined body of his Illyrian troops, proposing to follow them in person with the remainder of his forces. But the conduct of his lieutenants soon terminated the unnatural contest. By the artful appearances of flight, Constantine was betrayed into an ambuscade, which had been concealed in a wood, where the rash youth, with a few attendants, was surprised, surrounded, and slain. His body, after it had been found in the obscure stream of the Alsa, obtained the honours of an Imperial sepulchre, but his provinces transferred their allegiance to the conqueror, who, refusing to admit his elder brother Constantius to any share in these new acquisitions, maintained the undisputed possession of more than two-thirds of the Roman empire. The fate of Constans himself was delayed about ten years longer, and the revenge of his brother's death was reserved for the more ignoble hand of a domestic traitor.

The divided provinces of the empire were again united by the victory of Constantius; but as that feeble prince was destitute of personal merit either in peace or war; as he feared his generals, and distrusted his ministers, the emperor was persuaded to subscribe the condemnation of the unfortunate Gallus, and to add a new crime to the long list of unnatural murders which pollute the honour of the house of Constantine.

When the two nephews of Constantine, Gallus and Julian, were saved from the fury of the soldiers, the former was about twelve, and the latter about six years of age; and, as the eldest was thought to be of a sickly constitution, they obtained with the less difficulty a precarious and dependent life from the affected pity of Constantius, who was sensible that the execution of these helpless orphans would have been esteemed, by all mankind, an act of the most deliberate cruelty. Different cities of Ionia and Bithynia were assigned for the places of their exile and education; but as soon as their growing years excited the jealousy of the emperor, he judged it more prudent to secure those unhappy youths in the strong castle of Macellum, near Cæsarea.

The treatment which they experienced during a six years' confinement was partly such as they could hope from a careful guardian, and partly such as they might dread from a suspicious tyrant. Their prison was an ancient palace, the residence of the kings of Cappadocia; the situation was pleasant, the building stately, the enclosure spacious. They pursued their studies, and practised their exercises, under the tuition of the most skilful masters; and the numerous household appointed to attend, or rather to guard, the nephews of Constantine, was not unworthy of the dignity of their birth. But they could not disguise to themselves that they were deprived of fortune, of freedom, and of safety; secluded from the society of all whom they could trust or esteem, and condemned to pass their melancholy hours in the company of slaves devoted to the commands of a tyrant who had already injured them beyond the hope of reconciliation. At length Gallus, made Cæsar, was beheaded in prison like the vilest malefactor.

The writers the most indulgent to the memory of Gallus, and even Julian himself, though he wished to cast a veil over the frailties of his brother, are obliged to confess that the Cæsar was incapable of reigning. A temper naturally morose and violent, instead of being corrected, was soured by solitude and adversity; the remembrance of what he had endured disposed him to retaliation rather than to sympathy; and the ungoverned sallies of his rage were often fatal to those who approached his person, or were subject to his power.

But in the school of adversity Julian insensibly acquired the virtues of firmness and discretion. He most devoutly ascribes his miraculous deliverance to the protection of the gods, who had exempted his innocence from the sentence of destruction pronounced by their justice against the impious house of Constantine. As the most effectual instrument of their providence, he gratefully acknowledges the steady and generous friendship of the empress Eusebia, a woman of beauty and merit. By the intercession of his patroness Julian was admitted into the Imperial presence: he pleaded his cause with a decent freedom; he was heard with favour but advised to withdraw for a while into the neighbourhood of Milan, till the emperor thought proper to assign the city of Athens for the place of his honourable exile. As he had discovered from his earliest youth a propensity, or rather passion, for the language, the manners, the learning, and the religion of the Greeks, he obeyed with pleasure an order so agreeable to his wishes. Far from the tumult of arms and the treachery of courts, he spent six months amidst the groves of the Academy, in a free intercourse with the philosophers of the age, who studied to cultivate the genius, to encourage the vanity, and to inflame the devotion of their royal pupil.

CHAPTER XVI

Julian Is Declared Emperor by the Legions of Gaul—Administration of Julian

The distractions of civil war, and the irreparable loss which the Roman legions had sustained in the battle of Mursa, exposed the Illyrian provinces almost without defence to the light cavalry of the barbarians; and particularly to the inroads of the Quadi, a fierce and powerful nation, who seem to have exchanged the institutions of Germany for the arms and military arts of their Sarmatian allies. The garrisons of the frontier were insufficient to check their progress; and the indolent monarch was at length compelled to assemble, from the extremities of his dominions, the flower of the Palatine troops; to take the field in person; and to employ a whole campaign, with the preceding autumn and the ensuing spring, in the serious prosecution of the war.

The emperor passed the Danube on a bridge of boats, cut in pieces all that encountered his march, penetrated into the heart of the country of the Quadi, and severely retaliated the calamities which they had inflicted on the Roman province. The dismayed barbarians were soon reduced to sue for peace: they offered the restitution of his captive subjects as an atonement for the past, and the noblest hostages as a pledge of their future conduct.

The generous courtesy which was shown to the first among their chieftains who implored the clemency of Constantius encouraged the more timid, or the more obstinate, to imitate their example; and the Imperial camp was crowded with the princes and ambassadors of the most distant tribes, who occupied the plains of the Lesser Poland. While Constantius gave laws to the barbarians beyond the Danube, he distinguished with specious compassion the Sarmatian exiles, who had been expelled from their native country by the rebellion of their slaves.

The death of the late Cæsar had left Constantius invested with the sole command, and oppressed by the accumulated weight, of a mighty empire. Before the wounds of civil discord could be healed, the provinces of Gaul were overwhelmed by a deluge of barbarians. The Sarmatians no longer respected the barrier of the Danube. The impunity of rapine had increased the boldness and numbers of the wild Isaurians; those robbers descended from their craggy mountains to ravage the adjacent country, and had even presumed, though without success, to besiege the important city of Seleucia, which was defended by a garrison of three Roman legions.

Above all, the Persian monarch, elated by victory, again threatened the peace of Asia; and the presence of the emperor was indispensably required both in the West and in the East. For the first time Constantius sincerely acknowledged that his single strength was unequal to such an extent of care and dominion. It was resolved that Julian, after celebrating his nuptials with Helena, sister of Constantius, should be appointed, with the title of Cæsar, to reign over the countries beyond the Alps.

While the Roman emperor and the Persian monarch, at the distance of three thousand miles, defended their extreme limits against the barbarians of the Danube and of the Oxus, their intermediate frontier experienced the vicissitudes of a languid war and a precarious truce. Sapor, King of Kings, and Brother of the Sun and Moon (such were the lofty titles affected by oriental vanity), expressed his satisfaction that his brother, Constantius Cæsar, had been taught wisdom by adversity. As the lawful successor of Darius Hystaspes, Sapor asserted that the provinces of Armenia and Mesopotamia had been fraudulently extorted from his ancestors. He arrogantly threatened to take the field in the spring, and to support the justice of his cause by the strength of his invincible arms.

His ambassador was dismissed with the following answer: "Sapor should recollect that, if the Romans had sometimes been vanquished in battle, they had almost always been successful in the event of the war."

The defence of the East against the arms of Sapor required, and would have exercised, the abilities of the most consummate general; and it seemed fortunate for the state that it was the actual province of the brave Ursicinus, who alone deserved the confidence of the soldiers and people. In the hour of danger Ursicinus was removed from his station by intrigues; and the military command of the East was bestowed on Sabinian, a wealthy and subtle veteran, who had attained the infirmities, without acquiring the experience, of age. By a second order Ursicinus was again despatched to the frontier of Mesopotamia, and condemned to sustain the labours of a war, the honours of which had been transferred to his unworthy rival. Sabinian fixed his indolent station under the walls of Edessa; and while he amused himself with the idle parade of military exercise, and moved to the sound of flutes in the Pyrrhic dance, the public defence was abandoned to the boldness and diligence of the former general of the East. But whenever Ursicinus recommended any vigorous plan of operations; when he proposed, at the head of a light and active army, to wheel round the foot of the mountains, to intercept the convoys of the enemy, to harass the wide extent of the Persian lines, the timid and envious commander alleged that he was restrained by his positive orders from endangering the safety of the troops.

The pride of Constantius, and the ingenuity of his courtiers, were at a loss to discover any materials for panegyric in the events of the Persian war; while the glory of his cousin Julian, to whose military command he had entrusted the provinces of Gaul, was proclaimed to the world in the simple and concise narrative of his exploits.

In the blind fury of civil discord, Constantius had abandoned to the barbarians of Germany the countries of Gaul which still acknowledged the authority of his rival. A numerous swarm of Franks and Alemanni were invited to cross the Rhine by presents and promises, by the hopes of spoil, and by a perpetual grant of all the territories which they should be able to subdue. But the emperor, who for a temporary service had thus imprudently provoked the rapacious spirit of the barbarians, soon discovered and lamented the difficulty of dismissing these formidable allies, after they had tasted the richness of the Roman soil. Regardless of the nice distinction of loyalty and rebellion, these undisciplined robbers treated as their natural enemies all the subjects of the empire who possessed any property which they were desirous of acquiring. Forty-five flourishing cities, Tongres, Cologne, Trèves, Worms, Spires, Strasburg, etc., besides a far greater number of towns and villages, were pillaged, and for the most part reduced to ashes.

The barbarians of Germany, still faithful to the maxims of their ancestors, abhorred the confinement of walls, to which they applied the odious names of prisons and sepulchres; and, fixing their independent habitations on the banks of rivers, the Rhine, the Moselle, and the Meuse, they secured themselves against the danger of a surprise by a rude and hasty fortification of large trees, which were felled and thrown across the roads. The Alemanni were established in the modern countries of Alsace and Lorraine; the Franks occupied the island of the Batavians, together with an extensive district of Brabant, which may deserve to be considered as the original seat of their Gallic monarchy. From the sources to the mouth of the Rhine, the conquests of the Germans extended above forty miles to the west of that river, over a country peopled by colonies of their own name and nation; and the scene of their devastations was three times more extensive than that of their conquests. At a still greater distance the open towns of Gaul were deserted; and the inhabitants of the fortified cities, who trusted to their strength and vigilance, were obliged to content themselves with such supplies of corn as they could raise on the vacant land within the enclosure of their walls. The diminished legions, destitute of pay and provisions, of arms and discipline, trembled at the approach and even at the name of the barbarians.

Under these melancholy circumstances, an inexperienced youth was appointed to save and to govern the provinces of Gaul, or rather, as he expresses it himself, to exhibit the vain image of Imperial greatness. The retired scholastic education of Julian, in which he had been more conversant with books than with arms, with the dead than with the living, left him in profound ignorance of the practical arts of war and government; and when he awkwardly repeated some military exercise which it was necessary for him to learn, he exclaimed with a sigh, "O Plato, Plato, what a task for a philosopher!" Yet even this speculative philosophy, which men of business are too apt to despise, had filled the mind of Julian with the noblest precepts and the most shining examples; had animated him with the love of virtue, the desire of fame, and the contempt of death.

The habits of temperance recommended in the schools are still more essential in the severe discipline of a camp. The simple wants of nature regulated the measure of his food and sleep. Rejecting with disdain the delicacies provided for his table, he satisfied his appetite with the coarse and common fare which was allotted to the meanest soldiers. During the rigour of a Gallic winter he never suffered a fire in his bedchamber; and after a short and interrupted slumber, he frequently rose in the middle of the night from a carpet spread on the floor, to despatch any urgent business, to visit his rounds, or to steal a few moments for the prosecution of his favourite studies. The precepts of eloquence, which he had hitherto practised on fancied topics of declamation, were more usefully applied to excite or to assuage the passions of an armed multitude: and although Julian, from his early habits of conversation and literature, was more familiarly acquainted with the beauties of the Greek language, he had attained a competent knowledge of the Latin tongue.

Since Julian was not originally designed for the character of a legislator or a judge, it is probable that the civil jurisprudence of the Romans had not engaged any considerable share of his attention: but he derived from his philosophic studies an inflexible regard for justice, tempered by a disposition to clemency, the knowledge of the general principles of equity and evidence, and the faculty of patiently investigating the most intricate and tedious questions which could be proposed for his discussion. The measures of policy, and the operations of war, must submit to the various accidents of circumstance and character, and the unpractised student will often be perplexed in the application of the most perfect theory. But in the acquisition of this important science Julian was assisted by the active vigour of his own genius, as well as by the wisdom and experience of Sallust.

A tender regard for the peace and happiness of his subjects was the ruling principle which directed, or seemed to direct, the administration of Julian. He devoted the leisure of his winter-quarters to the offices of civil government; and affected to assume with more pleasure the character of a magistrate than that of a general. Before he took the field he devolved on the provincial governors most of the public and private causes which had been referred to his tribunal; but, on his return he carefully revised their proceedings, mitigated the rigour of the law, and pronounced a second judgment on the judges themselves. Superior to the last temptation of virtuous minds, an indiscreet and intemperate zeal for justice, he restrained with calmness and dignity the warmth of an advocate who prosecuted, for extortion, the president of the Narbonnese province. "Who will ever be found guilty," exclaimed the vehement Delphidius, "if it be enough to deny?" "And who," replied Julian, "will ever be innocent, if it is sufficient to affirm?"

In the general administration of peace and war, the interest of the sovereign is commonly the same as that of his people; but Constantius would have thought himself deeply injured if the virtues of Julian had defrauded him of any part of the tribute which he extorted from an oppressed and exhausted country. The Cæsar had rejected with abhorrence a mandate for the levy of an extraordinary tax; and the faithful picture of the public misery by which he had been obliged to justify his refusal offended the court of Constantius. We may enjoy the pleasure of reading the sentiments of Julian, as he expresses them with warmth and freedom in a letter to one of his most intimate friends. After stating his own conduct, he proceeds in the following terms:—"Was it possible for the disciple of Plato and Aristotle to act otherwise than I have done? Could I abandon the unhappy subjects entrusted to my care? Was I not called upon to defend them from the repeated injuries of these unfeeling robbers? A tribune who deserts his post is punished with death, and deprived of the honours of burial. With what justice could I pronounce *his* sentence, if, in the hour of danger, I myself neglected a duty far more sacred and far more important? God has placed me in this elevated post; his providence will guard and support me."

The precarious and dependent situation of Julian displayed his virtues and concealed his defects. The young hero who supported, in Gaul, the throne of Constantius was not permitted to reform the vices of the government; but he had courage to alleviate or to pity the distress of the people.

A very judicious plan of operations was adopted for the approaching campaign. Julian himself, at the head of the remains of the veteran bands, and of some new levies which he had been permitted to form, boldly penetrated into the centre of the German cantonments and carefully re-established the fortifications of Saverne, in an advantageous post which would either check the incursions or intercept the retreat of the enemy. At the same time Barbatio, general of the infantry, advanced from Milan with an army of thirty thousand men, and passing the mountains, prepared to throw a bridge over the Rhine in the neighbourhood of Basil. It was reasonable to expect that the Alemanni, pressed on either side by the Roman arms, would soon be forced to evacuate the provinces of Gaul, and to hasten to the defence of their native country.

But the hopes of the campaign were defeated by the incapacity, or the envy, or the secret instructions of Barbatio, who acted as if he had been the enemy of the Cæsar, and the secret ally of the barbarians. The negligence with which he permitted a troop of pillagers freely to pass, and to return, almost before the gates of his camp, may be imputed to his want of abilities; but the treasonable act of burning a number of boats, and a superfluous stock of provisions, which would have been of the most essential service to the army of Gaul, was an evidence of his hostile and criminal intentions. The Germans despised an enemy who appeared destitute either of power or of inclination to offend them; and the ignominious retreat of Barbatio deprived Julian of the expected support, and left him to extricate himself from a hazardous situation where he could neither remain with safety, nor retire with honour.

As soon as they were delivered from the fears of invasion, the Alemanni prepared to chastise the Roman youth who presumed to dispute the possession of that country which they claimed as their own by the right of conquest and of treaties. They employed three days, and as many nights, in transporting over the Rhine thirty-five thousand of the bravest warriors of the tribes of Germany. The confidence derived from the view of their own strength was increased by the intelligence which they received from a deserter, that the Cæsar, with a feeble army of thirteen thousand men, occupied a post about one-and-twenty miles from their camp of Strasburg. With this inadequate force Julian resolved to seek and to encounter the barbarian host. The conflict was obstinate and bloody. The Germans possessed the superiority of strength and stature, the Romans that of discipline and temper; and as the barbarians who served under the standard of the empire united the respective advantages of both parties, their strenuous efforts, guided by a skilful leader, at length determined the event of the day. The Romans lost four tribunes, and two hundred and forty-three soldiers, in this memorable battle of Strasburg, so glorious to the Cæsar, and so salutary to the afflicted provinces of Gaul. Six thousand of the Alemanni were slain in the field, without including those who were drowned in the Rhine, or transfixed with darts whilst they attempted to swim across the river.

After Julian had repulsed the Alemanni from the provinces of the Upper Rhine, he turned his arms against the Franks, who were seated nearer to the ocean, on the confines of Gaul and Germany; and who, from their numbers, and still more from their intrepid valour, had ever been esteemed the most formidable of the barbarians. Although they were strongly actuated by the allurements of rapine, they professed a disinterested love of war, which they considered as the supreme honour and felicity of human nature.

Julian suddenly pitched his camp near Tongres, while the enemy still supposed him in his winter-quarters of Paris, expecting the slow arrival of his convoys from Aquitain. Without allowing the Franks to unite or to deliberate, he skilfully spread his legions from Cologne to the ocean; and by the terror, as well as by the success of his arms, soon reduced the suppliant tribes to implore the clemency and to obey the commands of their conqueror.

As soon as the valour and conduct of Julian had secured an interval of peace, he applied himself to a work more congenial to his humane and philosophic temper. The cities of Gaul, which had suffered from the inroads of the barbarians, he diligently repaired; and seven important posts, between Mentz and the mouth of the Rhine, are particularly mentioned as having been rebuilt and fortified by the order of Julian. The vanquished Germans had submitted to the just but humiliating condition of preparing and conveying the necessary materials. The active zeal of Julian urged the prosecution of the work; and such was the spirit which he had diffused among the troops, that the auxiliaries themselves, waiving their exemption from any duties of fatigue, contended in the most servile labours with the diligence of the Roman soldiers.

It was incumbent on the Cæsar to provide for the subsistence as well as for the safety of the inhabitants and of the garrisons. The desertion of the former, and the mutiny of the latter, must have been the fatal and inevitable consequences of famine. The tillage of the provinces of Gaul had been interrupted by the calamities of war; but the scanty harvests of the continent were supplied, by his paternal care, from the plenty of the adjacent island. Six hundred large barques, framed in the forest of the Ardennes, made several voyages to the coast of Britain; and returning from thence, laden with corn, sailed up the Rhine, and distributed their cargoes to the several towns and fortresses along the banks of the river.

Unless he had been able to revive the martial spirit of the Romans, or to introduce the arts of industry and refinement among their savage enemies, he could not entertain any rational hopes of securing the public tranquillity, either by the peace or conquest of Germany. Yet the victories of Julian suspended for a short time the inroads of the barbarians, and delayed the ruin of the Western Empire.

His salutary influence restored the cities of Gaul, which had been so long exposed to the evils of civil discord, barbarian war, and domestic tyranny; and the spirit of industry was revived with the hopes of enjoyment. Agriculture, manufactures, and commerce again flourished under the protection of the laws; and the *curiæ*, or civil corporations, were again filled with useful and respectable members: the youth were no longer apprehensive of marriage, and married persons were no longer apprehensive of posterity; the public and private festivals were celebrated with customary pomp; and the frequent and secure intercourse of the provinces displayed the image of national prosperity. A mind like that of Julian must have felt the general happiness of which he was the author; but he viewed with peculiar satisfaction and complacency the city of Paris, the seat of his winter residence, and the object even of his partial affection. The licentiousness and corruption of Antioch recalled to the memory of Julian the severe and simple manners of his beloved Lutetia,[1] where the amusements of the theatre were unknown or despised. He indignantly contrasted the effeminate Syrians with the brave and honest simplicity of the Gauls.

While the Romans languished under the ignominious tyranny of eunuchs and bishops, the praises of Julian were repeated with transport in every part of the empire, except in the palace of Constantius. The barbarians of Germany had felt, and still dreaded, the arms of the young Cæsar; his soldiers were the companions of his victory; the grateful provincials enjoyed the blessings of his reign; but the favourites, who had opposed his elevation, were offended by his virtues; and they justly considered the friend of the people as the enemy of the court. As long as the fame of Julian was doubtful, the buffoons of the palace, who were skilled in the language of satire, tried the efficacy of those arts which they had so often

[1]Julian, in Misopogon, p. 340. Leucetia, or Lutetia, was the ancient name of the city which, according to the fashion of the fourth century, assumed the territorial appellation of *Parisii*.

practised with success. They easily discovered that his simplicity was not exempt from affectation: the ridiculous epithets of an hairy savage, of an ape invested with the purple, were applied to the dress and person of the philosophic warrior; and his modest despatches were stigmatised as the vain and elaborate fictions of a loquacious Greek, a speculative soldier, who had studied the art of war amidst the groves of the Academy.

The voice of malicious folly was at length silenced by the shouts of victory; the conqueror of the Franks and Alemanni could no longer be painted as an object of contempt; and the monarch himself was meanly ambitious of stealing from his lieutenant the honourable reward of his labours. In the letters crowned with laurel, which, according to ancient custom, were addressed to the provinces, the name of Julian was omitted. "Constantius had made his dispositions in person; *he* had signalised his valour in the foremost ranks; *his* military conduct had secured the victory; and the captive king of the barbarians was presented to *him* on the field of battle," from which he was at that time distant above forty days' journey.

The empress Eusebia had preserved, to the last moment of her life, the warm, and even jealous, affection which she had conceived for Julian; and her mild influence might have moderated the resentment of a prince who, since her death, was abandoned to his own passions. But the offended sovereign required that the presumptuous Cæsar should expressly renounce the appellation and rank of Augustus which he had accepted from the rebels; that he should descend to his former station of a limited and dependent minister; that he should vest the powers of the state and army in the hands of those officers who were appointed by the Imperial court. A part of the letter was afterwards read, in which the emperor arraigned the ingratitude of Julian, whom he had invested with the honours of the purple; whom he had educated with so much care and tenderness; whom he had preserved in his infancy, when he was left a helpless orphan. "An orphan!" interrupted Julian, who justified his cause by indulging his passions, "does the assassin of my family reproach me that I was left an orphan?"

As soon as Julian perceived that his moderate and respectful behaviour served only to irritate the pride of an implacable adversary, he boldly resolved to commit his life and fortune to the chance of a civil war. After this, Julian, who some weeks before had celebrated the Christian festival of the Epiphany, made a public declaration that he committed the care of his safety to the IMMORTAL GODS; and thus publicly renounced the religion as well as the friendship of Constantius.

The same troops which had taken up arms against Constantius, when he summoned them to leave Gaul, now declared with alacrity that they would follow Julian to the farthest extremities of Europe or Asia. The oath of fidelity was administered; and the soldiers, clashing their shields, and pointing their drawn swords to their throats, devoted themselves, with horrid imprecations, to the service of a leader whom they celebrated as the deliverer of Gaul and the conqueror of the Germans.

The hopes of Julian depended much less on the number of his troops than on the celerity of his motions. In the execution of a daring enterprise he availed himself of every precaution, as far as prudence could suggest; and where prudence could no longer accompany his steps, he trusted the event to valour and to fortune.

But the seasonable death of Constantius delivered the Roman empire from the calamities of civil war. The last of the sons of Constantine may be dismissed from the world with the remark that he inherited the defects, without the abilities, of his father. Before Constantius expired, he is said to have named Julian for his successor.

The throne of Julian, which the death of Constantius fixed on an independent basis, was the seat of reason, of virtue, and perhaps of vanity. He despised the honours, renounced the pleasures, and discharged with incessant diligence the duties of his exalted station: and there were few among his subjects who would have consented to relieve him from the weight of the diadem, had they been obliged to submit their time and their actions to the rigorous laws which their philosophic emperor imposed on himself. One of his most intimate friends, who had often shared the frugal simplicity of his table, has remarked that his light and sparing diet (which was usually of the vegetable kind) left his mind and body always free and active for the various and important business of an author, a pontiff, a magistrate, a general, and a prince.

In one and the same day he gave audience to several ambassadors, and wrote or dictated a great number of letters to his generals, his civil magistrates, his private friends, and the different cities of his dominions. He listened to the memorials which had been received, considered the subject of the petitions, and signified his intentions more rapidly than they could be taken in shorthand by the diligence of his secretaries. He possessed such flexibility of thought, and such firmness of attention, that he could employ his hand to write, his ear to listen, and his voice to dictate; and pursue at once three several trains of ideas without hesitation, and without error. While his ministers reposed, the prince flew with agility from one labour to another; and, after a hasty dinner, retired into his library till the public business which he had appointed for the evening summoned him to interrupt the prosecution of his studies. The supper of the emperor was still less substantial than the former meal; his sleep was never clouded by the fumes of indigestion; and, except in the short interval of a marriage which was the effect of policy rather than love, the chaste Julian never shared his bed with a female companion. He was soon awakened by the entrance of fresh secretaries, who had slept the preceding day; and his servants were obliged to wait alternately, while their indefatigable master allowed himself scarcely any other refreshment than the change of occupations.

The predecessors of Julian, his uncle, his brother, and his cousin, indulged their puerile taste for the games of the Circus, under the specious pretence of complying with the inclinations of the people; and they frequently remained the greatest part of the day as idle spectators, and as a part of the splendid spectacle, till the ordinary round of twenty-four races was completely finished. On solemn festivals, Julian, who felt and professed an unfashionable dislike to these frivolous amusements, condescended to appear in the Circus; and, after bestowing a careless glance on five or six of the races, he hastily withdrew with the impatience of a philosopher, who considered every moment as lost that was not devoted to the advantage of the public or the improvement of his own mind. By this avarice of time he seemed to protract the short duration of his reign; and, if the dates were less securely ascertained, we should refuse to believe that only sixteen months elapsed between the death of Constantius and the departure of his successor for the Persian war.

The reformation of the Imperial court was one of the first and most necessary acts of the government of Julian. Soon after his entrance into the palace of Constantinople he had occasion for the service of a barber. An officer, magnificently dressed, immediately presented himself. "It is a barber," exclaimed the prince, with affected surprise, "that I want, and not a receiver-general of the finances."

He questioned the man concerning the profits of his employment, and was informed that, besides a large salary and some valuable perquisites, he enjoyed a daily allowance for twenty servants and as many horses. A thousand barbers, a thousand cupbearers, a thousand cooks, were distributed in the several offices of luxury; the monarch who resigned to his subjects the superiority of merit and virtue was distinguished by the oppressive magnificence of his dress, his table, his buildings, and his train. The stately palaces erected by Constantine and his sons were decorated with many-coloured marbles and ornaments of massy gold. The most exquisite dainties were procured to gratify their pride rather than their taste; birds of the most distant climates, fish from the most remote seas, fruits out of their natural season, winter roses, and summer snows. The domestic crowd of the palace surpassed the expense of the legions.

The numerous army of spies, of agents, and informers, enlisted by Constantius to secure the repose of one man and to interrupt that of millions, was immediately disbanded by his generous successor. Julian was slow in his suspicions, and gentle in his punishments; and his contempt of treason was the result of judgment, of vanity, and of courage.

The generality of princes, if they were stripped of their purple and cast naked into the world, would immediately sink to the lowest rank of society, without a hope of emerging from their obscurity. But the personal merit of Julian was, in some measure, independent of his fortune. Whatever had been his choice of life, by the force of intrepid courage, lively wit, and intense application, he would have obtained, or at least he would have deserved, the highest honours of his profession, and Julian might have raised himself to the rank of minister or general of the state in which he was born a private citizen.

When we inspect with minute, or perhaps malevolent, attention the portrait of Julian, something seems wanting to the grace and perfection of the whole figure. His genius was less powerful and sublime than that of Cæsar, nor did he possess the consummate prudence of Augustus. The virtues of Trajan appear more steady and natural, and the philosophy of Marcus is more simple and consistent. Yet Julian sustained adversity with firmness, and prosperity with moderation. After an interval of one hundred and twenty years from the death of Alexander Severus, the Romans beheld an emperor who made no distinction between his duties and his pleasures, who laboured to relieve the distress and to revive the spirit of his subjects, and who endeavoured always to connect authority with merit, and happiness with virtue. Even faction, and religious faction, was constrained to acknowledge the superiority of his genius in peace as well as in war, and to confess, with a sigh, that the apostate Julian was a lover of his country, and that he deserved the empire of the world.

CHAPTER XVII

Julian Attempts to Restore and Reform the Pagan Worship—Jovian Saves the Roman Army by a Disgraceful Treaty

The character of apostate has injured the reputation of Julian; and the enthusiasm which clouded his virtues has exaggerated the real and apparent magnitude of his faults. A devout and sincere attachment for the gods of Athens and Rome constituted the ruling passion of Julian; the powers of an enlightened understanding were betrayed and corrupted by the influence of superstitious prejudice; and the phantoms which existed only in the mind of the emperor had a real and pernicious effect on the government of the empire. The vehement zeal of the Christians, who despised the worship, and overturned the altars, of those fabulous deities, engaged their votary in a state of irreconcilable hostility with a very numerous party of his subjects; and he was sometimes tempted, by the desire of victory or the shame of a repulse, to violate the laws of prudence, and even of justice.

The cause of his strange and fatal apostasy may be derived from the early period of his life when he was left an orphan in the hands of the murderers of his family. The names of Christ and of Constantius, the ideas of slavery and of religion, were soon associated in a youthful imagination. The dull and obstinate understanding of Gallus embraced with implicit zeal the doctrines of Christianity, which never influenced his conduct, or moderated his passions. The mild disposition of the younger brother was less repugnant to the precepts of the Gospel; and his active curiosity might have been gratified by a theological system which explains the mysterious essence of the Deity, and opens the boundless prospect of invisible and future worlds. But the independent spirit of Julian refused to yield the passive and unresisting obedience which was required, in the name of religion, by the haughty ministers of the church. Their speculative opinions were imposed as positive laws, and guarded by the terrors of eternal punishments; but while they prescribed the rigid formulary of the thoughts, the words, and the actions of the young prince, whilst they silenced his objections, and severely checked the freedom of his inquiries, they secretly provoked his impatient genius to disclaim the authority of his ecclesiastical guides. He was educated in the lesser Asia, amidst the scandals of the Arian controversy. The fierce contests of the Eastern bishops, the incessant alterations of their creeds, and the profane motives which appeared to actuate their conduct, insensibly strengthened the prejudice of Julian that they neither understood nor believed the religion for which they so fiercely contended.

The theological system of Julian appears to have contained the sublime and important principles of natural religion. But the disciple of Plato imprudently relapsed into the habits of vulgar superstition; and the popular and philosophic notion of the Deity seems to have been confounded in the practice, the writings, and even in the mind of Julian. The pious emperor acknowledged and adored the Eternal Cause of the universe, to whom he ascribed all the perfections of an infinite nature, invisible to the eyes and inaccessible to the understanding of feeble mortals. But Julian was secretly initiated at Ephesus, in the twentieth year of his age. His residence at Athens confirmed this unnatural alliance of philosophy and superstition. He obtained the privilege of a solemn initiation into the mysteries of Eleusis, which, amidst the general decay of the Grecian worship, still retained some vestiges of their primæval sanctity; and such was the zeal of Julian that he afterwards invited the Eleusinian pontiff to the court of Gaul, for the sole purpose of consummating, by mystic rites and sacrifices, the great work of his sanctification. As these ceremonies were performed in the depth of caverns and in the silence of the night, in the caverns of Ephesus and Eleusis the mind of Julian was penetrated with sincere, deep, and unalterable enthusiasm. From that moment he consecrated his life to the service of the gods; and while the occupations of war, of government, and of study seemed to claim the whole measure of his time, a stated portion of the hours of the night was invariably reserved for the exercise of private devotion. The temperance which adorned the severe manners of the soldier and the philosopher was connected with some strict and frivolous rules of religious abstinence; and it was in honour of Pan or Mercury, of Hecate or Isis, that Julian, on particular days, denied himself the use of some particular food, which might have been offensive to his tutelar deities.

The important secret of the apostasy of Julian was entrusted to the fidelity of the *initiated*, with whom he was united by the sacred ties of friendship and religion. The pleasing rumour was cautiously circulated among the adherents of the ancient worship; and his future greatness became the object of the hopes, the prayers, and the predictions of the Pagans in every province of the empire.

The dissimulation of Julian lasted above ten years, from his secret initiation at Ephesus to the beginning of the civil war; when he declared himself at once the implacable enemy of Christ and of Constantius. The Pagans, who were conscious of his fervent zeal, expected, perhaps with impatience, that the flames of persecution should be immediately kindled against the enemies of the gods; and that the ingenious malice of Julian would invent some cruel refinements of death and torture which had been unknown to the rude and inexperienced fury of his predecessors. But the hopes, as well as the fears, of the religious factions were apparently disappointed by the prudent humanity of a prince who was careful of his own fame, of the public peace, and of the rights of mankind. Instructed by history and reflection, Julian was persuaded that, if the diseases of the body may sometimes be cured by salutary violence, neither steel nor fire can eradicate the erroneous opinions of the mind. The reluctant victim may be dragged to the foot of the altar; but the heart still abhors and disclaims the sacrilegious act of the hand. Religious obstinacy is hardened and exasperated by oppression; and, as soon as the persecution subsides, those who have yielded are restored as penitents, and those who have resisted are honoured as saints and martyrs.

Julian surprised the world by an edict which was not unworthy of a statesman or a philosopher. He extended to all the inhabitants of the Roman world the benefits of a free and equal toleration; and the only hardship which he inflicted on the Christians was to deprive them of the power of tormenting their fellow-subjects, whom they stigmatised with the odious titles of idolaters and heretics. The Pagans received a gracious permission, or rather an express order, to open ALL their temples; and they were at once delivered from the oppressive laws and arbitrary vexations which they had sustained under the reign of Constantine and of his sons. At the same time, the bishops and clergy who had been banished by the Arian monarch were recalled from exile, and restored to their respective churches; the Donatists, the Novatians, the Macedonians, the Eunomians, and those who, with a more prosperous fortune, adhered to the doctrine of the council of Nice.

Julian, who understood and derided their theological disputes, invited to the palace the leaders of the hostile sects, that he might enjoy the agreeable spectacle of their furious encounters. The clamour of controversy sometimes provoked the emperor to exclaim, "Hear me! the Franks have heard me, and the Alemanni"; but he soon discovered that he was now engaged with more obstinate and implacable enemies; and though he exerted the powers of oratory to persuade them to live in concord, or at least in peace, he was perfectly satisfied, before he dismissed them from his presence, that he had nothing to dread from the union of the Christians.

As soon as he ascended the throne, he assumed, according to the custom of his predecessors, the character of supreme pontiff; not only as the most honourable title of Imperial greatness, but as a sacred and important office, the duties of which he was resolved to execute with pious diligence. As the business of the state prevented the emperor from joining every day in the public devotion of his subjects, he dedicated a domestic chapel to his tutelar deity the Sun; his gardens were filled with statues and altars of the gods; and each apartment of the palace displayed the appearance of a magnificent temple. Every morning he saluted the parent of light with a sacrifice; the blood of another victim was shed at the moment when the Sun sunk below the horizon; and the Moon, the Stars, and the Genii of the night received their respective and seasonable honours from the indefatigable devotion of Julian. On solemn festivals he regularly visited the temple of the god or goddess to whom the day was peculiarly consecrated, and endeavoured to excite the religion of the magistrates and people by the example of his own zeal.

Under the reign of a prince who practised the rigid maxims of economy, the expense of religious worship consumed a very large portion of the revenue; a constant supply of the scarcest and most beautiful birds was transported from distant climates, to bleed on the altars of the gods; an hundred oxen were frequently sacrificed by Julian on one and the same day; and it soon became a popular jest, that, if he should return with conquest from the Persian war, the breed of horned cattle must infallibly be extinguished.

But the genius and power of Julian were unequal to the enterprise of restoring a religion which was destitute of theological principles, of moral precepts, and of ecclesiastical discipline; which rapidly hastened to decay and dissolution, and was not susceptible of any solid or consistent reformation. The Imperial pontiff exhorts his inferior clergy: "The priest of the gods should never be seen in theatres or taverns. His conversation should be chaste, his diet temperate, his friends of honourable reputation; and if he sometimes visits the Forum or the Palace, he should appear only as the advocate of those who have vainly solicited either justice or mercy. His studies should be suited to the sanctity of his profession. Licentious tales, or comedies, or satires, must be banished from his library, which ought solely to consist of historical and philosophical writings; of history, which is founded in truth, and of philosophy, which is connected with religion. The impious opinions of the Epicureans and sceptics deserve his abhorrence and contempt; but he should diligently study the systems of Pythagoras, of Plato, and of the Stoics, which unanimously teach that there *are* gods; that the world is governed by their providence; that their goodness is the source of every temporal blessing; and that they have prepared for the human soul a future state of reward or punishment."

Julian beheld with envy the wise and humane regulations of the church; and he very frankly confessed his intention to deprive the Christians of the applause, as well as advantage, which they had acquired by the exclusive practice of charity and beneficence. But if these imaginary plans of reformation had been realised, the forced and imperfect copy would have been less beneficial to Paganism than honourable to Christianity. The Gentiles who peaceably followed the customs of their ancestors were rather surprised than pleased with the introduction of foreign manners; and, in the short period of his reign, Julian had frequent occasions to complain of the want of fervour of his own party.

As the army is the most forcible engine of absolute power, Julian applied himself with peculiar diligence to corrupt the religion of his troops, without whose hearty concurrence every measure must be dangerous and unsuccessful. The natural temper of soldiers made this conquest as easy as it was important. The legions of Gaul devoted themselves to the faith, as well as to the fortunes, of their victorious leader; and even before the death of Constantius, he had the satisfaction of announcing to his friends that they assisted, with fervent devotion and voracious appetite, at the sacrifices, which were repeatedly offered in his camp, of whole hecatombs of fat oxen.

The armies of the East, which had been trained under the standard of the cross and of Constantius, required a more artful and expensive mode of persuasion. On the days of solemn and public festivals the emperor received the homage, and rewarded the merit, of the troops. His throne of state was encircled with the military ensigns of Rome and the republic; the holy name of Christ was erased from the *Labarum;* and the symbols of war, of majesty, and of Pagan superstition were so dexterously blended that the faithful subject incurred the guilt of idolatry when he respectfully saluted the person or image of his sovereign. The soldiers passed successively in review, and each of them, before he received from the hand of Julian a liberal donative, proportioned to his rank and services, was required to cast a few grains of incense into the flame which burnt upon the altar.

While the devout monarch incessantly laboured to restore and propagate the religion of his ancestors, he embraced the extraordinary design of rebuilding the temple of Jerusalem. In a public epistle to the nation or community of the Jews dispersed through the provinces, he pities their misfortunes, condemns their oppressors, praises their constancy, declares himself their gracious protector, and expresses a pious hope that, after his return from the Persian war, he may be permitted to pay his grateful vows to the Almighty in his holy city of Jerusalem.

The emperor transferred to the pontiffs of his own religion the management of the liberal allowances from the public revenue which had been granted to the church by the piety of Constantine and his sons. The proud system of clerical honours and immunities, which had been constructed with so much art and labour, was levelled to the ground; the hopes of testamentary donations were intercepted by the rigour of the laws; and the priests of the Christian sect were confounded with the last and most ignominious class of the people.

A just and severe censure has been inflicted on the law which prohibited the Christians from teaching the arts of grammar and rhetoric. The edict of Julian appears to have included the physicians, and professors of all the liberal arts; and the emperor, who reserved to himself the approbation of the candidates, was authorised by the laws to corrupt, or to punish, the religious constancy of the most learned of the Christians. As soon as the resignation of the more obstinate teachers had established the unrivalled dominion of the Pagan sophists, Julian invited the rising generation to resort with freedom to the public schools, in a just confidence that their tender minds would receive the impressions of literature and idolatry. If the greatest part of the Christian youth should be deterred by their own scruples, or by those of their parents, from accepting this dangerous mode of instruction, they must, at the same time, relinquish the benefits of a liberal education. Julian had reason to expect that, in the space of a few years, the church would relapse into its primæval simplicity, and that the theologians who possessed an adequate share of the learning and eloquence of the age would be succeeded by a generation of blind and ignorant fanatics, incapable of defending the truth of their own principles, or of exposing the various follies of Polytheism.

It was undoubtedly the wish and the design of Julian to deprive the Christians of the advantages of wealth, of knowledge, and of power; but the injustice of excluding them from all offices of trust and profit seems to have been the result of his general policy, rather than the immediate consequence of any positive law. Superior merit might deserve and obtain some extraordinary exceptions; but the greater part of the Christian officers were gradually removed from their employments in the state, the army, and the provinces. The hopes of future candidates were extinguished by the declared partiality of a prince who maliciously reminded them that it was unlawful for a Christian to use the sword, either of justice or of war, and who studiously guarded the camp and the tribunals with the ensigns of idolatry. The powers of government were entrusted to the Pagans who professed an ardent zeal for the religion of their ancestors.

The most effectual instrument of oppression with which they were armed was the law that obliged the Christians to make full and ample satisfaction for the temples which they had destroyed under the preceding reign. The consecrated lands, which had increased the patrimony of the sovereign or of the clergy, were clearly defined, and easily restored. But on these lands, and on the ruins of Pagan superstition, the Christians had frequently erected their own religious edifices: and as it was necessary to remove the church before the temple could be rebuilt, the justice and piety of the emperor were applauded by one party, while the other deplored and execrated his sacrilegious violence.

Julian, who despised the Christians, honoured Athanasius with his sincere and peculiar hatred. The præfect of Egypt was awakened from lethargy by a severe reprimand: "Though you neglect," says Julian, "to write to me on any other subject, at least it is your duty to inform me of your conduct towards Athanasius, the enemy of the gods. My intentions have been long since communicated to you. I swear by the great Serapis, that unless, on the calends of December, Athanasius has departed from Alexandria, nay, from Egypt, the officers of your government shall pay a fine of one hundred pounds of gold. You know my temper: I am slow to condemn, but I am still slower to forgive." This epistle was enforced by a short postscript written with the emperor's own hand. "The contempt that is shown for all the gods fills me with grief and indignation. There is nothing that I should see, nothing that I should hear, with more pleasure, than the expulsion of Athanasius from all Egypt. The abominable wretch! Under my reign, the baptism of several Grecian ladies of the highest rank has been the effect of his persecutions."

The death of Athanasius was not *expressly* commanded; but the præfect of Egypt understood that it was safer for him to exceed than to neglect the orders of an irritated master. The archbishop prudently retired to the monasteries of the Desert; eluded, with his usual dexterity, the snares of the enemy; and lived to triumph over the ashes of a prince who, in words of formidable import, had declared his wish that the whole venom of the Galilæan school were contained in the single person of Athanasius.

The Christians considered Julian as a cruel and crafty tyrant, who suspended the execution of his revenge till he should return victorious from the Persian war. They expected that, as soon as he had triumphed over the foreign enemies of Rome, the amphitheatres would stream with the blood of hermits and bishops; and that the Christians who still persevered in the profession of the faith would be deprived of the common benefits of nature and society. It is impossible to determine how far the zeal of Julian would have prevailed over his good sense and humanity; but, if we seriously reflect on the strength and spirit of the church, we shall be convinced that, before the emperor could have extinguished the religion of Christ, he must have involved his country in the horrors of a civil war.

In the cool moments of reflection, Julian preferred the useful and benevolent virtues of Antoninus; but his ambitious spirit was inflamed by the glory of Alexander. He despised the trophies of a Gothic victory, and was satisfied that the rapacious barbarians of the Danube would be restrained from any future violation of the faith of treaties by the terror of his name and the additional fortifications with which he strengthened the Thracian and Illyrian frontiers. The successor of Cyrus and Artaxerxes was the only rival whom he deemed worthy of his arms, and he resolved, by the final conquest of Persia, to chastise the haughty nation which had so long resisted and insulted the majesty of Rome.

A formidable army was destined for this important service, and Julian, marching from Constantinople through the provinces of Asia Minor, arrived at Antioch about eight months after the death of his predecessor.

The church of Antioch was distracted by heresy and schism; but the Arians and the Athanasians were actuated by the same pious hatred of their common adversary. His subjects complained, with superstitious indignation, that famine had pursued the emperor's steps from Constantinople to Antioch, and the discontent of a hungry people was exasperated by the injudicious attempt to relieve their distress. The inclemency of the season had affected the harvests of Syria, and the price of bread in the markets of Antioch had naturally risen in proportion to the scarcity of corn. But the fair and reasonable proportion was soon violated by the rapacious arts of monopoly. In this unequal contest, in which the produce of the land is claimed by one party as his exclusive property, is used by another as a lucrative object of trade, and is required by a third for the daily and necessary support of life, all the profits of the intermediate agents are accumulated on the head of the defenceless consumers. The hardships of their situation were exaggerated and increased by their own impatience and anxiety, and the apprehension of a scarcity gradually produced the appearances of a famine. When the luxurious citizens of Antioch complained of the high price of poultry and fish, Julian publicly declared that a frugal city ought to be satisfied with a regular supply of wine, oil, and bread; but he acknowledged that it was the duty of a sovereign to provide for the subsistence of his people.

With this salutary view the emperor ventured on a very dangerous and doubtful step, of fixing, by legal authority, the value of corn. He enacted that, in a time of scarcity, it should be sold at a price which had seldom been known in the most plentiful years; and that his own example might strengthen his laws, he sent into the market four hundred and twenty-two thousand *modii*, or measures, which were drawn by his order from the granaries of Hierapolis, of Chalcis, and even of Egypt. The consequences might have been foreseen, and were soon felt. The Imperial wheat was purchased by the rich merchants; the proprietors of land or of corn withheld from the city the accustomed supply; and the small quantities that appeared in the market were secretly sold at an advanced and illegal price.

Julian still continued to applaud his own policy, treated the complaints of the people as a vain and ungrateful murmur, and convinced Antioch that he had inherited the obstinacy, though not the cruelty, of his brother Gallus. The remonstrances of the municipal senate served only to exasperate his inflexible mind. He was persuaded, perhaps with truth, that the senators of Antioch, who possessed lands or were concerned in trade, had themselves contributed to the calamities of their country.

The military dispositions of Julian were skilfully contrived to deceive the spies and to divert the attention of Sapor. The legions appeared to direct their march towards the Tigris. On a sudden they wheeled to the right and reached, on the third day, the banks of the Euphrates. From thence the emperor pursued his march, above ninety miles along the winding stream, till at length, about one month after his departure from Antioch, he discovered the towers of Circesium, the extreme limit of the Roman dominions.

The army of Julian, the most numerous that any of the Cæsars had ever led against Persia, consisted of sixty-five thousand effective and well-disciplined soldiers. The veteran bands of cavalry and infantry, of Romans and barbarians, had been selected from the different provinces, and a just preeminence of loyalty and valour was claimed by the hardy Gauls who guarded the throne and person of their beloved prince. A formidable body of Scythian auxiliaries had been transported from another climate, and almost from another world, to invade a distant country of whose name and situation they were ignorant. The love of rapine and war allured to the Imperial standard several tribes of Saracens, or roving Arabs, whose service Julian had commanded, while he sternly refused the payment of the accustomed subsidies.

The broad channel of the Euphrates was crowded by a fleet of eleven hundred ships, destined to attend the motions and to satisfy the wants of the Roman army. The military strength of the fleet was composed of fifty armed galleys, and these were accompanied by an equal number of flat-bottomed boats, which might occasionally be connected into the form of temporary bridges. The rest of the ships, partly constructed of timber and partly covered with raw hides, were laden with an almost inexhaustible supply of arms and engines, of utensils and provisions. The vigilant humanity of Julian had embarked a very large magazine of vinegar and biscuit for the use of the soldiers, but he prohibited the indulgence of wine, and rigorously stopped a long string of superfluous camels that attempted to follow the rear of the army.

The ordinary post of Julian was at the head of the centre column, but, as he preferred the duties of a general to the state of a monarch, he rapidly moved, with a small escort of light cavalry, to the front, the rear, the flanks, wherever his presence could animate or protect the march of the Roman army. The country which they traversed from the Chaboras to the cultivated lands of Assyria may be considered as a part of the desert of Arabia, a dry and barren waste, which could never be improved by the most powerful arts of human industry. Julian marched over the same ground which had been trod above seven hundred years before by the footsteps of the younger Cyrus, and which is described by one of the companions of his expedition, the sage and heroic Xenophon. "The country was a plain throughout, as even as the sea, and full of wormwood; and if any other kind of shrubs or reeds grew there, they had all an aromatic smell, but no trees could be seen. Bustards and ostriches, antelopes and wild asses, appeared to be the only inhabitants of the desert, and the fatigues of the march were alleviated by the amusements of the chase." The loose sand of the desert was frequently raised by the wind into clouds of dust, and a great number of soldiers of Julian, with their tents, were suddenly thrown to the ground by the violence of an unexpected hurricane.

The fertile province of Assyria, which stretched beyond the Tigris as far as the mountains of Media, extended about four hundred miles from the ancient wall of Macepracta to the territory of Basra, where the united streams of the Euphrates and Tigris discharge themselves into the Persian Gulf. The whole country might have claimed the peculiar name of Mesopotamia, as the two rivers, which are never more distant than fifty, approach, between Bagdad and Babylon, within twenty-five miles of each other. A multitude of artificial canals, dug without much labour in a soft and yielding soil, connected the rivers and intersected the plain of Assyria. The uses of these artificial canals were various and important. They served to discharge the superfluous waters from one river into the other at the season of their respective inundations. Subdividing themselves into smaller and smaller branches, they refreshed the dry lands and supplied the deficiency of rain. They facilitated the intercourse of peace and commerce, and, as the dams could be speedily broke down, they armed the despair of the Assyrians with the means of opposing a sudden deluge to the progress of an invading army.

To the soil and climate of Assyria nature had denied some of her choicest gifts—the vine, the olive, and the fig-tree; but the food which supports the life of man, and particularly wheat and barley, were produced with inexhaustible fertility, and the husbandman who committed his seed to the earth was frequently rewarded with an increase of two or even of three hundred. The face of the country was interspersed with groves of innumerable palm-trees, and the diligent natives celebrated, either in verse or prose, the three hundred and sixty uses to which the trunk, the branches, the leaves, the juice, and the fruit were skilfully applied. Several manufactures, especially those of leather and linen, employed the industry of a numerous people, and afforded valuable materials for foreign trade, which appears, however, to have been conducted by the hands of strangers.

Babylon had been converted into a royal park, but near the ruins of the ancient capital new cities had successively arisen, and the populousness of the country was displayed in the multitude of towns and villages, which were built of bricks dried in the sun and strongly cemented with bitumen, the natural and peculiar production of the Babylonian soil. While the successors of Cyrus reigned over Asia, the province of Assyria alone maintained, during a third part of the year, the luxurious plenty of the table and household of the Great King. Four considerable villages were assigned for the subsistence of his Indian dogs; eight hundred stallions and sixteen thousand mares were constantly kept, at the expense of the country, for the royal stables; and as the daily tribute which was paid to the satrap amounted to one English bushel of silver, we may compute the annual revenue of Assyria at more than twelve hundred thousand pounds sterling.

The fields of Assyria were devoted by Julian to the calamities of war; and the philosopher retaliated on a guiltless people the acts of rapine and cruelty which had been committed by their haughty master in the Roman provinces. The trembling Assyrians summoned the rivers to their assistance; and completed with their own hands the ruin of their country. The roads were rendered impracticable; a flood of waters was poured into the camp; and, during several days, the troops of Julian were obliged to contend with the most discouraging hardships. But every obstacle was surmounted by the perseverance of the legionaries, who were inured to toil as well as to danger, and who felt themselves animated by the spirit of their leader. The damage was gradually repaired; the waters were restored to their proper channels; while groves of palm-trees were cut down and placed along the broken parts of the road; and the army passed over the broad and deeper canals on bridges of floating rafts.

The neighbourhood of the capital of Persia was adorned with three stately palaces, laboriously enriched with every production that could gratify the luxury and pride of an Eastern monarch. The pleasant situation of the gardens along the banks of the Tigris was improved, according to the Persian taste, by the symmetry of flowers, fountains, and shady walks: and spacious parks were enclosed for the reception of the bears, lions, and wild boars, which were maintained at a considerable expense for the pleasure of the royal chase. The park-walls were broken down, the savage game was abandoned to the darts of the soldiers, and the palaces of Sapor were reduced to ashes by the command of the Roman emperor. Julian, on this occasion, showed himself ignorant or careless of the laws of civility, which the prudence and refinement of polished ages have established between hostile princes. Yet these wanton ravages need not excite in our breasts any vehement emotions of pity or resentment. A simple, naked statue, finished by the hand of a Grecian artist, is of more genuine value than all these rude and costly monuments of barbaric labour; and, if we are more deeply affected by the ruin of a palace than by the conflagration of a cottage, our humanity must have formed a very erroneous estimate of the miseries of human life.

Julian was an object of terror and hatred to the Persians; and the painters of that nation represented the invader of their country under the emblem of a furious lion, who vomited from his mouth a consuming fire. To his friends and soldiers the philosophic hero appeared in a more amiable light; and his virtues were never more conspicuously displayed than in the last and most active period of his life. He practised, without effort, and almost without merit, the habitual qualities of temperance and sobriety. According to the dictates of that artificial wisdom which assumes an absolute dominion over the mind and body, he sternly refused himself the indulgence of the most natural appetites. In the warm climate of Assyria, which solicited a luxurious people to the gratification of every sensual desire, a youthful conqueror preserved his chastity pure and inviolate: nor was Julian ever tempted, even by a motive of curiosity, to visit his female captives of exquisite beauty, who, instead of resisting his power, would have disputed with each other the honour of his embraces. With the same firmness that he resisted the allurements of love, he sustained the hardships of war. When the Romans marched through the flat and flooded country, their sovereign, on foot, at the head of his legions, shared their fatigues and animated their diligence. In every useful labour the hand of Julian was prompt and strenuous; and the Imperial purple was wet and dirty, as the coarse garment of the meanest soldier.

But the reduction, or even the siege, of the capital of Persia was still at a distance. Instead of confining his march to the banks of the Euphrates and Tigris, Julian resolved to imitate the adventurous spirit of Alexander, and boldly to advance into the inland provinces, till he forced his rival to contend with him, perhaps in the plains of Arbela, for the empire of Asia.

The extensive region that lies between the river Tigris and the mountains of Media was filled with villages and towns; and the fertile soil, for the most part, was in a very improved state of cultivation. Julian might expect that a conqueror who possessed the two forcible instruments of persuasion, steel and gold, would easily procure a plentiful subsistence from the fears or avarice of the natives. But on the approach of the Romans this rich and smiling prospect was instantly blasted. Wherever they moved, the inhabitants deserted the open villages and took shelter in the fortified towns; the cattle were driven away; the grass and ripe corn were consumed with fire; and, as soon as the flames had subsided which interrupted the march of Julian, he beheld the melancholy face of a smoking and naked desert. This desperate but effectual method of defence can only be executed by the enthusiasm of a people who prefer their independence to their property; or by the rigour of an arbitrary government, which consults the public safety without submitting to their inclinations the liberty of choice. On the present occasion the zeal and obedience of the Persians seconded the commands of Sapor; and the emperor was soon reduced to the scanty stock of provisions which continually wasted in his hands.

The hardy veterans accustomed to the cold climate of Gaul and Germany fainted under the sultry heat of an Assyrian summer; their vigour was exhausted by the incessant repetition of march and combat; and the progress of the army was suspended by the precautions of a slow and dangerous retreat in the presence of an active enemy.

As long as the Romans seemed to advance into the country, their march was observed and insulted from a distance by several bodies of Persian cavalry; who, showing themselves, sometimes in loose, and sometimes in closer order, faintly skirmished with the advanced guards. These detachments were, however, supported by a much greater force; and the heads of the columns were no sooner pointed towards the Tigris than a cloud of dust arose on the plain. The Romans, who now aspired only to the permission of a safe and speedy retreat, endeavoured to persuade themselves that this formidable appearance was occasioned by a troop of wild asses, or perhaps by the approach of some friendly Arabs.

They halted, pitched their tents, fortified their camp, passed the whole night in continual alarms; and discovered at the dawn of day that they were surrounded by an army of Persians.

Julian was foremost in every danger. His trembling guards reminded their fearless sovereign that he was without armour. As they exclaimed, a cloud of darts and arrows was discharged from the flying squadrons, and Julian fell senseless from his horse.

The welcome news of the death of Julian, which a deserter revealed to the camp of Sapor, inspired the desponding monarch with a sudden confidence of victory. The Roman commanders showed some disposition to adopt the salutary advice of an inferior officer, that they should act as they would have acted in the absence of the emperor; should exert their abilities to extricate the army from the present distress; and, if they were fortunate enough to reach the confines of Mesopotamia, should proceed with united and deliberate counsels in the election of a lawful sovereign. While they debated, a few voices saluted Jovian, who was no more than *first* of the domestics, with the names of Emperor and Augustus.

In this hopeless situation, the fainting spirits of the Romans were revived by the sound of peace. The transient presumption of Sapor had vanished: he observed, with serious concern, that, in the repetition of doubtful combats, he had lost his most faithful and intrepid nobles, his bravest troops, and the greatest part of his train of elephants.

Had Jovian been capable of executing a bold and prudent measure, he would have continued his march with unremitting diligence; instead, he accepted the humiliating conditions of peace. The five provinces beyond the Tigris, which had been ceded by the grandfather of Sapor, were restored to the Persian monarchy. Singara and the castle of the Moors, one of the strongest places of Mesopotamia, were likewise dismembered from the empire and the conqueror rigorously insisted that the Romans should for ever abandon the king and kingdom of Armenia.

As soon as the Romans had landed on the western bank of the Tigris they were delivered from the hostile pursuit of the barbarians; but in a laborious march of two hundred miles over the plains of Mesopotamia they endured the last extremities of thirst and hunger. They were obliged to traverse a sandy desert, which, in the extent of seventy miles, did not afford a single blade of sweet grass nor a single spring of fresh water, and the rest of the inhospitable waste was untrod by the footsteps either of friend or enemies. Whenever a small measure of flour could be discovered in the camp, twenty pounds weight were greedily purchased with ten pieces of gold, the beasts of burden were slaughtered and devoured, and the desert was strewed with the arms and baggage of the Roman soldiers.

The friends of Julian had confidently announced the success of his expedition. They entertained a fond persuasion that the temples of the gods would be enriched with the spoils of the East; that Persia would be reduced to the humble state of a tributary province, governed by the laws and magistrates of Rome; that the barbarians would adopt the dress, and manners, and language of their conquerors; and that the youth of Ecbatana and Susa would study the art of rhetoric under Grecian masters. The progress of the arms of Julian interrupted his communication with the empire, and, from the moment that he passed the Tigris, his affectionate subjects were ignorant of the fate and fortunes of their prince. Their contemplation of fancied triumphs was disturbed by the melancholy rumour of his death, and they persisted to doubt, after they could no longer deny, the truth of that fatal event. The messengers of Jovian promulgated the specious tale of a prudent and necessary peace; the voice of fame, louder and more sincere, revealed the disgrace of the emperor and the conditions of the ignominious treaty. The minds of the people were filled with astonishment and grief, with indignation and terror, when they were informed that the unworthy successor of Julian relinquished the five provinces. The inflexible spirit of the Roman senate had always disclaimed the unequal conditions which were extorted from the distress of her captive armies; and, if it were necessary to satisfy the national honour by delivering the guilty general into the hands of the barbarians, the greatest part of the subjects of Jovian would have cheerfully acquiesced in the precedent of ancient times.

But the emperor, whatever might be the limits of his constitutional authority, was the absolute master of the laws and arms of the state; and the same motives which had forced him to subscribe, now pressed him to execute the treaty of peace. He was impatient to secure an empire at the expense of a few provinces, and the respectable names of religion and honour concealed the personal fears and the ambition of Jovian. Sapor enjoyed the glory and the fruits of his victory; and this ignominious peace has justly been considered as a memorable era in the decline and fall of the Roman empire. The predecessors of Jovian had sometimes relinquished the dominion of distant and unprofitable provinces; but, since the foundation of the city, the genius of Rome, the god Terminus, who guarded the boundaries of the republic, had never retired before the sword of a victorious enemy.

CHAPTER XVIII

Division of the Eastern and Western Empires—Germany—Britain—Africa—The East—The Danube

The death of Julian had left the public affairs of the empire in a very doubtful and dangerous situation. The Roman army was saved by an inglorious, perhaps a necessary, treaty; and the first moments of peace were consecrated by the pious Jovian to restore the domestic tranquillity of the church and state. The indiscretion of his predecessor, instead of reconciling, had artfully fomented the religious war; and the balance which he affected to preserve between the hostile factions served only to perpetuate the contest by the vicissitudes of hope and fear, by the rival claims of ancient possession and actual favour. The Christians had forgotten the spirit of the Gospel, and the Pagans had imbibed the spirit of the church. In private families the sentiments of nature were extinguished by the blind fury of zeal and revenge; the majesty of the laws was violated or abused; the cities of the East were stained with blood; and the most implacable enemies of the Romans were in the bosom of their country.

Jovian was educated in the profession of Christianity; and as he marched from Nisibis to Antioch, the banner of the Cross, the Labarum of Constantine, which was again displayed at the head of the legions, announced to the people the faith of their new emperor. As soon as he ascended the throne he transmitted a circular epistle to all the governors of provinces, in which he confessed the divine truth and secured the legal establishment of the Christian religion. The insidious edicts of Julian were abolished, the ecclesiastical immunities were restored and enlarged, and Jovian condescended to lament that the distress of the times obliged him to diminish the measure of charitable distributions.

The Christians were unanimous in the loud and sincere applause which they bestowed on the pious successor of Julian; but they were still ignorant what creed or what synod he would choose for the standard of orthodoxy, and the peace of the church immediately revived those eager disputes which had been suspended during the season of persecution. The episcopal leaders of the contending sects, convinced from experience how much their fate would depend on the earliest impressions that were made on the mind of an untutored soldier, hastened to the court of Edessa, or Antioch. The highways of the East were crowded with Homoousian, and Arian, and Semi-Arian, and Eunomian bishops, who struggled to outstrip each other in the holy race. The moderation of Jovian, who recommended concord and charity, and referred the disputants to the sentence of a future council, was interpreted as a symptom of indifference; but his attachment to the Nicene Creed was at length discovered and declared by the reverence which he expressed for the *celestial* virtues of the great Athanasius.

The intrepid veteran of the faith, at the age of seventy, had issued from his retreat on the first intelligence of the tyrant's death. As soon as he had gained the confidence and secured the faith of the Christian emperor, he returned in triumph to his diocese, and continued, with mature counsels and undiminished vigour, to direct, ten years longer, the ecclesiastical government of Alexandria, Egypt, and the Catholic church.

The slightest force, when it is applied to assist and guide the natural descent of its object, operates with irresistible weight; and Jovian had the good fortune to embrace the religious opinions which were supported by the spirit of the times, and the zeal and numbers of the most powerful sect. Under his reign Christianity obtained an easy and lasting victory; and as soon as the smile of royal patronage was withdrawn, the genius of Paganism, which had been fondly raised and cherished by the arts of Julian, sank irrecoverably in the dust. In many cities the temples were shut or deserted; the philosophers who had abused their transient favour thought it prudent to shave their beards and disguise their profession; and the Christians rejoiced that they were now in a condition to forgive or to revenge the injuries which they had suffered under the preceding reign. The consternation of the Pagan world was dispelled by a wise and gracious edict of toleration, in which Jovian explicitly declared that, although he should severely punish the sacrilegious rites of magic, his subjects might exercise, with freedom and safety, the ceremonies of the ancient worship.

After the death of Jovian the throne of the Roman world remained ten days without a master. At length, when the hour was supposed to be propitious, Valentinian showed himself from a lofty tribunal; the judicious choice was applauded, and the new prince was solemnly invested with the diadem and the purple, amidst the acclamations of the troops, who were disposed in martial order round the tribunal. But when he stretched forth his hand to address the armed multitude, a busy whisper was accidentally started in the ranks, and insensibly swelled into a loud and imperious clamour that he should name, without delay, a colleague in the empire. Thirty days after his own elevation, he bestowed the title of Augustus on his brother Valens: and as the boldest patriots were convinced that their opposition, without being serviceable to their country, would be fatal to themselves, the declaration of his absolute will was received with silent submission.

Valentinian bestowed on his brother the rich præfecture of the *East*, from the Lower Danube to the confines of Persia; whilst he reserved for his immediate government the warlike præfectures of *Illyricum*, *Italy*, and *Gaul*, from the extremity of Greece to the Caledonian rampart and from the rampart of Caledonia to the foot of Mount Atlas.

We should turn with horror from the frequent executions which disgraced, both at Rome and Antioch, the reign of the two brothers. Valens was of a timid, and Valentinian of a choleric, disposition. An anxious regard to his personal safety was the ruling principle of the administration of Valens. In the condition of a subject, he had kissed, with trembling awe, the hand of the oppressor; and when he ascended the throne, he reasonably expected that the same fears which had subdued his own mind would secure the patient submission of his people. The favourites of Valens obtained by the privilege of rapine and confiscation the wealth which his economy would have refused. They urged, with persuasive eloquence, *that,* in all cases of treason, suspicion is equivalent to proof; *that* the power supposes the intention of mischief; *that* the intention is not less criminal than the act; and *that* a subject no longer deserves to live, if his life may threaten the safety, or disturb the repose, of his sovereign.

The judgment of Valentinian was sometimes deceived, and his confidence abused; but he would have silenced the informers with a contemptuous smile had they presumed to alarm his fortitude by the sound of danger. They praised his inflexible love of justice; and, in the pursuit of justice, the emperor was easily tempted to consider clemency as a weakness, and passion as a virtue. As long as he wrestled with his equals in the bold competition of an active and ambitious life, Valentinian was seldom injured, and never insulted, with impunity: if his prudence was arraigned, his spirit was applauded; and the proudest and most powerful generals were apprehensive of provoking the resentment of a fearless soldier. After he became master of the world, he unfortunately forgot that where no resistance can be made, no courage can be exerted; and instead of consulting the dictates of reason and magnanimity, he indulged the furious emotions of his temper, at a time when they were disgraceful to himself, and fatal to the defenceless objects of his displeasure. In the government of his household, or of his empire, slight, or even imaginary offences–a hasty word, a casual omission, an involuntary delay–were chastised by a sentence of immediate death. The expressions which issued the most readily from the mouth of the emperor of the West were, "Strike off his head;"–"Burn him alive;"–"Let him be beaten with clubs till he expires."

The arts of magic were equally condemned by the public opinion and by the laws of Rome, but, as they tended to gratify the most imperious passions of the heart of man, they were continually proscribed and continually practised. An imaginary cause is capable of producing the most serious and mischievous effects. The dark predictions of the death of an emperor or the success of a conspiracy were calculated only to stimulate the hopes of ambition and to dissolve the ties of fidelity, and the intentional guilt of magic was aggravated by the actual crimes of treason and sacrilege. Such vain terrors disturbed the peace of society and the happiness of individuals, and the harmless flame which insensibly melted a waxen image might derive a powerful and pernicious energy from the affrighted fancy of the person whom it was maliciously designed to represent. From the infusion of those herbs which were supposed to possess a supernatural influence it was an easy step to the use of more substantial poison.

As soon as the zeal of informers was encouraged by the ministers of Valens and Valentinian, they could not refuse to listen to another charge too frequently mingled in the scenes of domestic guilt, a charge of a softer and less malignant nature, for which the pious though excessive rigour of Constantine had recently decreed the punishment of death.

This deadly and incoherent mixture of treason and magic, of poison and adultery, afforded infinite gradations of guilt and innocence, of excuse and aggravation, which in these proceedings appear to have been confounded by the angry or corrupt passions of the judges. They easily discovered that the degree of their industry and discernment was estimated by the Imperial court according to the number of executions that were furnished from their respective tribunals. From the extremity of Italy and Asia the young and the aged were dragged in chains to the tribunals of Rome and Antioch. Senators, matrons, and philosophers expired in ignominious and cruel tortures. The soldiers who were appointed to guard the prisons declared, with a murmur of pity and indignation, that their numbers were insufficient to oppose the flight or resistance of the multitude of captives. The wealthiest families were ruined by fines and confiscations; the most innocent citizens trembled for their safety; and we may form some notion of the magnitude of the evil from the extravagant assertion of an ancient writer, that in the obnoxious provinces the prisoners, the exiles, and the fugitives formed the greatest part of the inhabitants.

But in the calmer moments of reflection, when the mind of Valens was not agitated by fear, or that of Valentinian by rage, the tyrant resumed the sentiments, or at least the conduct, of the father of his country. Both princes invariably retained, in the purple, the chaste and temperate simplicity which had adorned their private life; and under their reign the pleasures of the court never cost the people a blush or a sigh. They gradually reformed many of the abuses of the times of Constantius; judiciously adopted and improved the designs of Julian and his successor; and displayed a style and spirit of legislation which might inspire posterity with the most favourable opinion of their character and government. Tender regard for the welfare of his subjects prompted Valentinian to condemn the exposition of new-born infants, and to establish fourteen skilful physicians, with stipends and privileges, in the fourteen quarters of Rome. The good sense of an illiterate soldier founded an useful and liberal institution for the education of youth, and the support of declining science. It was his intention that the arts of rhetoric and grammar should be taught, in the Greek and Latin languages, in the metropolis of every province; and as the size and dignity of the school was usually proportioned to the importance of the city, the academies of Rome and Constantinople claimed a just and singular preëminence.

The fragments of the literary edicts of Valentinian imperfectly represent the school of Constantinople, which was gradually improved by subsequent regulations. That school consisted of thirty-one professors in different branches of learning: one philosopher and two lawyers; five sophists and ten grammarians for the Greek, and three orators and ten grammarians for the Latin tongue; besides seven scribes, or, as they were then styled, antiquarians, whose laborious pens supplied the public library with fair and correct copies of the classic writers.

The rule of conduct which was prescribed to the students is the more curious, as it affords the first outlines of the form and discipline of a modern university. It was required that they should bring proper certificates from the magistrates of their native province. Their names, professions, and places of abode were regularly entered in a public register. The studious youth were severely prohibited from wasting their time in feasts or in the theatre; and the term of their education was limited to the age of twenty. The præfect of the city was empowered to chastise the idle and refractory by stripes or expulsion; and he was directed to make an annual report to the master of the offices, that the knowledge and abilities of the scholars might be usefully applied to the public service.

Valentinian might reform the abuses of the fiscal administration; but he exacted, without scruple, a very large share of the private property, as he was convinced that the revenues which supported the luxury of individuals would be much more advantageously employed for the defence and improvement of the state.

But the most honourable circumstance of the character of Valentinian is the firm and temperate impartiality which he uniformly preserved in an age of religious contention. His strong sense, unenlightened, but uncorrupted, by study, declined, with respectful indifference, the subtle questions of theological debate. The government of the *Earth* claimed his vigilance, and satisfied his ambition; and while he remembered that he was the disciple of the church, he never forgot that he was the sovereign of the clergy. Under the reign of an apostate, he had signalised his zeal for the honour of Christianity: he allowed to his subjects the privilege which he had assumed for himself; and they might accept with gratitude and confidence the general toleration which was granted by a prince addicted to passion, but incapable of fear or of disguise. The Pagans, the Jews, and all the various sects which acknowledged the divine authority of Christ were protected by the laws from arbitrary power or popular insult; nor was any mode of worship prohibited by Valentinian, except those secret and criminal practices which abused the name of religion for the dark purposes of vice and disorder.

When the suffrage of the generals and of the army committed the sceptre of the Roman empire to the hands of Valentinian, his reputation in arms, his military skill and experience, and his rigid attachment to the forms as well as spirit of ancient discipline, were the principal motives of their judicious choice. As soon as the death of Julian had relieved the barbarians from the terror of his name, the most sanguine hopes of rapine and conquest excited the nations of the East, of the North, and of the South. Their inroads were often vexatious, and sometimes formidable; but, during the twelve years of the reign of Valentinian, his firmness and vigilance protected his own dominions.

Instead of aspiring to the conquest of Germany the wise monarch confined his attention to the important and laborious defence of the Gallic frontier against an enemy whose strength was renewed by a stream of daring volunteers, which incessantly flowed from the most distant tribes of the North. The banks of the Rhine, from its source to the straits of the ocean, were closely planted with strong castles and convenient towers; new works and new arms were invented by the ingenuity of a prince who was skilled in the mechanical arts; and his numerous levies of Roman and barbarian youth were severely trained in all the exercises of war. The progress of the work, which was sometimes opposed by modest representations and sometimes by hostile attempts, secured the tranquillity of Gaul during the nine subsequent years of the administration of Valentinian.

That prudent emperor, who diligently practised the wise maxims of Diocletian, was studious to foment and excite the intestine divisions of the tribes of Germany. About the middle of the fourth century, the countries, perhaps of Lusace and Thuringia, on either side of the Elbe, were occupied by the vague dominion of the BURGUNDIANS, a warlike and numerous people of the Vandal race. The disputed possession of some salt-pits engaged the Alemanni and the Burgundians in frequent contests: the latter were easily tempted by the secret solicitations and liberal offers of the emperor. An army of fourscore thousand Burgundians soon appeared on the banks of the Rhine, and impatiently required the support and subsidies which Valentinian had promised; but they were amused with excuses and delays, till at length, after a fruitless expectation, they were compelled to retire. The arms and fortifications of the Gallic frontier checked the fury of their just resentment; and their massacre of the captives served to embitter the hereditary feud of the Burgundians and the Alemanni. Perhaps it was the original design of Valentinian to intimidate rather than to destroy; as the balance of power would have been equally overturned by the extirpation of either of the German nations.

The land was covered by the fortifications of Valentinian; but the sea-coast of Gaul and Britain was exposed to the depredations of the Saxons. In the maps of Ptolemy that celebrated name faintly marks the narrow neck of the Cimbric peninsula, and three small islands towards the mouth of the Elbe. This contracted territory, the present duchy of Schleswig, or perhaps of Holstein, was incapable of pouring forth the inexhaustible swarms of Saxons who reigned over the ocean, who filled the British island with their language, their laws, and their colonies, and who so long defended the liberty of the North against the arms of Charlemagne. The situation of the native Saxons disposed them to embrace the hazardous professions of fishermen and pirates; and the success of their first adventures would naturally excite the emulation of their bravest countrymen, who were impatient of the gloomy solitude of their woods and mountains. Every tide might float down the Elbe whole fleets of canoes, filled with hardy and intrepid associates, who aspired to behold the unbounded prospect of the ocean, and to taste the wealth and luxury of unknown worlds. It should seem probable, however, that the most numerous auxiliaries of the Saxons were furnished by the nations who dwelt along the shores of the Baltic.

The various troops of pirates and adventurers who fought under the same standard were insensibly united in a permanent society, at first of rapine, and afterwards of government. A military confederation was gradually moulded into a national body by the gentle operation of marriage and consanguinity; and the adjacent tribes, who solicited the alliance, accepted the name and laws of the Saxons.

If the fact were not established by the most unquestionable evidence, we should appear to abuse the credulity of our readers by the description of the vessels in which the Saxon pirates ventured to sport in the waves of the German Ocean, the British Channel, and the Bay of Biscay. The keel of their large flat-bottomed boats was framed of light timber, but the sides and upper works consisted only of wicker, with a covering of strong hides. In the course of their slow and distant navigations they must always have been exposed to the danger, and very frequently to the misfortune, of shipwreck; and the naval annals of the Saxons were undoubtedly filled with the accounts of the losses which they sustained on the coasts of Britain and Gaul. But after they had acquired an accurate knowledge of the maritime provinces of the West they extended the scene of their depredations, and the most sequestered places had no reason to presume on their security.

Under the reign of Valentinian the maritime provinces of Gaul were afflicted by the Saxons: a military count was stationed for the defence of the sea-coast, or Armorican limit; and that officer, who found his strength or his abilities unequal to the task, implored the assistance of Severus, master-general of the infantry. The Saxons, surrounded and outnumbered, were forced to relinquish their spoil, and to yield a select band of their tall and robust youth to serve in the Imperial armies. They stipulated only a safe and honourable retreat; and the condition was readily granted by the Roman general, who meditated an act of perfidy, imprudent as it was inhuman, while a Saxon remained alive and in arms to revenge the fate of his countrymen. Some of the prisoners were saved from the edge of the sword to shed their blood in the amphitheatre; and the orator Symmachus complains that twenty-nine of those desperate savages, by strangling themselves with their own hands, had disappointed the amusement of the public. Yet the polite and philosophic citizens of Rome were impressed with the deepest horror when they were informed that the Saxons consecrated to the gods the tithe of their *human* spoil; and that they ascertained by lot the objects of the barbarous sacrifice.

The present age is satisfied with the simple and rational opinion that the islands of Great Britain and Ireland were gradually peopled from the adjacent continent of Gaul. From the coast of Kent to the extremity of Caithness and Ulster, the memory of a Celtic origin was distinctly preserved in the perpetual resemblance of language, of religion, and of manners. The Roman province was reduced to the state of civilised and peaceful servitude: the rights of savage freedom were contracted to the narrow limits of Caledonia. The inhabitants of that northern region were divided, as early as the reign of Constantine, between the two great tribes of the Scots and of the Picts, who have since experienced a very different fortune. The power, and almost the memory, of the Picts have been extinguished by their successful rivals; and the Scots, after maintaining for ages the dignity of an independent kingdom, have multiplied, by an equal and voluntary union, the honours of the English name.

The hand of nature had contributed to mark the ancient distinction of the Scots and Picts. The former were the men of the hills, and the latter those of the plain. The eastern coast of Caledonia may be considered as a level and fertile country, which, even in a rude state of tillage, was capable of producing a considerable quantity of corn; and the epithet of *cruitnich*, or wheat-eaters, expressed the contempt or envy of the carnivorous highlander. The cultivation of the earth might introduce a more accurate separation of property, and the habits of a sedentary life; but the love of arms and rapine was still the ruling passion of the Picts; and their warriors, who stripped themselves for a day of battle, were distinguished, in the eyes of the Romans, by the strange fashion of painting their naked bodies with gaudy colours and fantastic figures.

The two bold headlands of Caledonia almost touch the shores of a spacious island, which obtained, from its luxuriant vegetation, the epithet of *Green;* and has preserved, with a slight alteration, the name of Erin, or Ierne, or Ireland. It is *probable* that in some remote period of antiquity the fertile plains of Ulster received a colony of hungry Scots; and that the strangers of the North, who had dared to encounter the arms of the legions, spread their conquests over the savage and unwarlike natives of a solitary island. It is *certain* that, in the declining age of the Roman empire, Caledonia, Ireland, and the Isle of Man were inhabited by the Scots, and that the kindred tribes, who were often associated in military enterprise, were deeply affected by the various accidents of their mutual fortunes.

Their southern neighbours have felt, and perhaps exaggerated, the cruel depredations of the Scots and Picts; and a valiant tribe of Caledonia, the Attacotti, the enemies, and afterwards the soldiers, of Valentinian, are accused by an eye-witness of delighting in the taste of human flesh. When they hunted the woods for prey, it is said that they attacked the shepherd rather than his flock; and that they curiously selected the most delicate and brawny parts both of males and females, which they prepared for their horrid repasts. If in the neighbourhood of the commercial and literary town of Glasgow a race of cannibals really existed, we may contemplate in the period of the Scottish history the opposite extremes of savage and civilised life. Such reflections tend to enlarge the circle of our ideas, and to encourage the pleasing hope that New Zealand may produce in some future age the Hume of the Southern Hemisphere.

Every messenger who escaped across the British Channel conveyed the most melancholy and alarming tidings to the ears of Valentinian, and the emperor was soon informed that the two military commanders of the province had been surprised and cut off by the barbarians. Severus, count of the domestics, was hastily despatched, and as suddenly recalled, by the court of Trèves. After a long and serious consultation, the defence, or rather the recovery, of Britain was entrusted to the abilities of the brave Theodosius. In his march from Sandwich to London, Theodosius defeated several parties of the barbarians, released a multitude of captives, and, after distributing to his soldiers a small portion of the spoil, established the fame of disinterested justice by the restitution of the remainder to the rightful proprietors. The citizens of London, who had almost despaired of their safety, threw open their gates, and, as soon as Theodosius had obtained from the court of Trèves the important aid of a military lieutenant and a civil governor, he executed with wisdom and vigour the laborious task of the deliverance of Britain. In the important station of the Upper Danube, the conqueror of Britain checked and defeated the armies of the Alemanni, before he was chosen to suppress the revolt of Africa.

The military command of Africa had been long exercised by Count Romanus, and his abilities were not inadequate to his station; but as sordid interest was the sole motive of his conduct, he acted on most occasions as if he had been the enemy of the province, and the friend of the barbarians of the desert. The three flourishing cities of Oea, Leptis, and Sabrata, which, under the name of Tripoli, had long constituted a federal union, were obliged, for the first time, to shut their gates against a hostile invasion; several of their most honourable citizens were surprised and massacred, the villages and even the suburbs were pillaged, and the vines and fruit-trees of that rich territory were extirpated by the malicious savages of Gætulia. The unhappy provincials implored the protection of Romanus; but they soon found that their military governor was not less cruel and rapacious than the barbarians. As they were incapable of furnishing the four thousand camels and the exorbitant present which he required before he would march to the assistance of Tripoli, his demand was equivalent to a refusal.

At length, when the repetition of complaint had been justified by the repetition of public misfortunes, the notary Palladius was sent from the court of Trèves to examine the state of Africa and the conduct of Romanus. The rigid impartiality of Palladius was easily disarmed; he was tempted to reserve for himself a part of the public treasure which he brought with him for the payment of the troops, and, from the moment that he was conscious of his own guilt, he could no longer refuse to attest the innocence and merit of the count. Romanus, elated by impunity and irritated by resistance, was still continued in the military command, till the Africans were provoked, by his avarice, to join the rebellious standard of Firmus, the Moor. Firmus was subdued by the perseverance of Theodosius.

Africa had been lost by the vices of Romanus; it was restored by the virtues of Theodosius; and our curiosity may be usefully directed to the inquiry of the respective treatment which the two generals received from the Imperial court. The authority of Count Romanus had been suspended by the master-general of the cavalry, and he was committed to safe and honourable custody till the end of the war. His crimes were proved by the most authentic evidence, and the public expected, with some impatience, the decree of severe justice. But partial and powerful favour encouraged him to challenge his legal judges, to obtain repeated delays for the purpose of procuring a crowd of friendly witnesses, and, finally, to cover his guilty conduct by the additional guilt of fraud and forgery. About the same time the restorer of Britain and Africa, on a vague suspicion that his name and services were superior to the rank of a subject, was beheaded at Carthage.

The ignominious treaty which saved the army of Jovian had been faithfully executed on the side of the Romans; and as they had solemnly renounced the sovereignty and alliance of Armenia and Iberia, those tributary Kingdoms were exposed, without protection, to the arms of the Persian monarch. Yet, since the conversion of the Armenians and Iberians, those nations considered the Christians as the favourites, and the Magians as the adversaries, of the Supreme Being; the influence of the clergy over a superstitious people was uniformly exerted in the cause of Rome; and as long as the successors of Constantine disputed with those of Artaxerxes the sovereignty of the intermediate provinces, the religious connection always threw a decisive advantage into the scale of the empire.

A numerous and active party acknowledged Para, the son of Tiranus, as the lawful sovereign of Armenia, and his title to the throne was deeply rooted in the hereditary succession of five hundred years. By the unanimous consent of the Iberians, the country was equally divided between the rival princes; and Aspacuras, who owed his diadem to the choice of Sapor, was obliged to declare that his regard for his children, who were detained as hostages by the tyrant, was the only consideration which prevented him from openly renouncing the alliance of Persia. The emperor Valens, who respected the obligations of the treaty, and who was apprehensive of involving the East in a dangerous war, ventured, with slow and cautious measures, to support the Roman party in the kingdoms of Iberia and Armenia.

In the general picture of the affairs of the East under the reign of Valens, the adventures of Para form one of the most striking and singular objects. The noble youth, by the persuasion of his mother Olympias, had escaped through the Persian host that besieged Artogerassa, and implored the protection of the emperor of the East. By his timid councils, Para was alternately supported, and recalled, and restored, and betrayed. The hopes of the Armenians were sometimes raised by the presence of their natural sovereign, and the ministers of Valens were satisfied that they preserved the integrity of the public faith, if their vassal was not suffered to assume the diadem and title of King. But they soon repented of their own rashness. They were confounded by the reproaches and threats of the Persian monarch. They found reason to distrust the cruel and inconstant temper of Para himself, who sacrificed to the slightest suspicions the lives of his most faithful servants, and held a secret and disgraceful correspondence with the assassin of his father and the enemy of his country.

Under the specious pretence of consulting with the emperor on the subject of their common interest, Para was persuaded to descend from the mountains of Armenia, where his party was in arms, and to trust his independence and safety to the discretion of a perfidious court. The king of Armenia, for such he appeared in his own eyes and in those of his nation, was received with due honours by the governors of the provinces through which he passed; but when he arrived at Tarsus in Cilicia, his progress was stopped under various pretences, his motions were watched with respectful vigilance, and he gradually discovered that he was a prisoner in the hands of the Romans.

Para was invited to a Roman banquet, which had been prepared with all the pomp and sensuality of the East; the hall resounded with cheerful music, and the company was already heated with wine, when the count retired for an instant, drew his sword, and gave the signal of the murder. A robust and desperate barbarian instantly rushed on the king of Armenia, and though he bravely defended his life with the first weapon that chance offered to his hand, the table of the Imperial general was stained with the royal blood of a guest and an ally. Such were the weak and wicked maxims of the Roman administration, that, to attain a doubtful object of political interest, the laws of nations, and the sacred rights of hospitality were inhumanly violated in the face of the world.

During a peaceful interval of thirty years, the Romans secured their frontiers, and the Goths extended their dominions. The victories of the great Hermanric, king of the Ostrogoths, and the most noble of the race of the Amali, have been compared, by the enthusiasm of his countrymen, to the exploits of Alexander: with this singular, and almost incredible, difference, that the martial spirit of the Gothic hero, instead of being supported by the vigour of youth, was displayed with glory and success in the extreme period of human life, between the age of fourscore and one hundred and ten years. His dominions, which extended from the Danube to the Baltic, included the native seats, and the recent acquisitions, of the Goths; and he reigned over the greatest part of Germany and Scythia with the authority of a conqueror, and sometimes with the cruelty of a tyrant.

CHAPTER XIX

Manners of the Pastoral Nations—Progress of the Huns from China to Europe—Flight and Settlement of the Goths

In the second year of the reign of Valentinian and Valens, on the morning of the twenty-first day of July, the greatest part of the Roman world was shaken by a violent and destructive earthquake. The impression was communicated to the waters; the shores of the Mediterranean were left dry by the sudden retreat of the sea; great quantities of fish were caught with the hand; large vessels were stranded on the mud; and a curious spectator amused his eye, or rather his fancy, by contemplating the various appearance of valleys and mountains which had never, since the formation of the globe, been exposed to the sun. But the tide soon returned with the weight of an immense and irresistible deluge, which was severely felt on the coasts of Sicily, of Dalmatia, of Greece, and of Egypt; large boats were transported and lodged on the roofs of houses, or at the distance of two miles from the shore; the people, with their habitations, were swept away by the waters; and the city of Alexandria annually commemorated the fatal day on which fifty thousand persons had lost their lives in the inundation.

This calamity, the report of which was magnified from one province to another, astonished and terrified the subjects of Rome, and their affrighted imagination enlarged the real extent of a momentary evil. They recollected the preceding earthquakes, which had subverted the cities of Palestine and Bithynia; they considered these alarming strokes as the prelude only of still more dreadful calamities; and their fearful vanity was disposed to confound the symptoms of a declining empire and a sinking world.

The mischievous effects of an earthquake or deluge, a hurricane or the eruption of a volcano, bear a very inconsiderable proportion to the ordinary calamities of war, as they are now moderated by the prudence or humanity of the princes of Europe, who amuse their own leisure and exercise the courage of their subjects in the practice of the military art. But the laws and manners of modern nations protect the safety and freedom of the vanquished soldier; and the peaceful citizen has seldom reason to complain that his life or even his fortune is exposed to the rage of war. In the disastrous period of the fall of the Roman empire, which may justly be dated from the reign of Valens, the happiness and security of each individual were personally attacked, and the arts and labours of ages were rudely defaced by the barbarians of Scythia and Germany. The invasion of the Huns precipitated on the provinces of the West the Gothic nation, which advanced, in less than forty years, from the Danube to the Atlantic, and opened a way, by the success of their arms, to the inroads of so many hostile tribes more savage than themselves. The original principle of motion was concealed in the remote countries of the North, and the curious observation of the pastoral life of the Scythians or Tartars will illustrate the latent cause of these destructive emigrations.

The different characters that mark the civilised nations of the globe may be ascribed to the use and the abuse of reason, which so variously shapes and so artificially composes the manners and opinions of an European or a Chinese. But the operation of instinct is more sure and simple than that of reason; it is much easier to ascertain the appetites of a quadruped than the speculations of a philosopher; and the savage tribes of mankind, as they approach nearer to the condition of animals, preserve a stronger resemblance to themselves and to each other. The uniform stability of their manners is the natural consequence of the imperfection of their faculties. Reduced to a similar situation, their wants, their desires, their enjoyments still continue the same; and the influence of food or climate, which, in a more improved state of society, is suspended or subdued by so many moral causes, most powerfully contributes to form and to maintain the national character of barbarians.

In every age the immense plains of Scythia or Tartary have been inhabited by vagrant tribes of hunters and shepherds, whose indolence refuses to cultivate the earth, and whose restless spirit disdains the confinement of a sedentary life. In every age the Scythians and Tartars have been renowned for their invincible courage and rapid conquests. The thrones of Asia have been repeatedly overturned by the shepherds of the North, and their arms have spread terror and devastation over the most fertile and warlike countries of Europe. On this occasion, as well as on many others, the sober historian is forcibly awakened from a pleasing vision, and is compelled, with some reluctance, to confess that the pastoral manners which have been adorned with the fairest attributes of peace and innocence are much better adapted to the fierce and cruel habits of a military life.

In the ages of rustic and martial simplicity, a people of soldiers and husbandmen are dispersed over the face of an extensive and cultivated country; and some time must elapse before the warlike youth of Greece or Italy could be assembled under the same standard, either to defend their own confines, or to invade the territories of the adjacent tribes. The progress of manufactures and commerce insensibly collects a large multitude within the walls of a city; but these citizens are no longer soldiers, and the arts which adorn and improve the state of civil society corrupt the habits of the military life.

The pastoral manners of the Scythians seem to unite the different advantages of simplicity and refinement. The individuals of the same tribe are constantly assembled, but they are assembled in a camp, and the native spirit of these dauntless shepherds is animated by mutual support and emulation.

The memory of past events cannot long be preserved in the frequent and remote emigrations of illiterate barbarians. The modern Tartars are ignorant of the conquests of their ancestors; and our knowledge of the history of the Scythians is derived from their intercourse with the learned and civilised nations of the South—the Greeks, the Persians, and the Chinese.

The Huns, who under the reign of Valens threatened the empire of Rome, had been formidable, in a much earlier period, to the empire of China. Their ancient, perhaps their original, seat was an extensive, though dry and barren, tract of country immediately on the north side of the great wall. But the valour of the Huns had extended the narrow limits of their dominions. The course of their emigration soon carried them beyond the limits of the Chinese geography; but *we* are able to distinguish the two great divisions of these formidable exiles, which directed their march towards the Oxus and towards the Volga. The first of these colonies established their dominion in the fruitful and extensive plains on the eastern side of the Caspian, where they preserved the name of Huns. Their manners were softened, and even their features were insensibly improved, by the mildness of the climate and their long residence in a flourishing province, which might still retain a faint impression of the arts of Greece. The *white* Huns, a name which they derived from the change of their complexions, soon abandoned the pastoral life of Scythia. The vicinity of the Huns to the provinces of Persia involved them in frequent and bloody contests with the power of that monarchy. But they respected, in peace, the faith of treaties; in war, the dictates of humanity; and their memorable victory over Peroses, or Firuz, displayed the moderation as well as the valour of the barbarians.

The *second* division of their countrymen, the Huns who gradually advanced towards the northwest, were exercised by the hardships of a colder climate and a more laborious march. Necessity compelled them to exchange the silks of China for the furs of Siberia; the imperfect rudiments of civilised life were obliterated; and the native fierceness of the Huns was exasperated by their intercourse with the savage tribes, who were compared, with some propriety, to the wild beasts of the desert. Their independent spirit soon rejected the hereditary succession and their tumultuary council directed the public measures of the whole nation. As late as the thirteenth century their transient residence on the eastern banks of the Volga was attested by the name of Great Hungary.

The military power of the Huns and the Alani encountered each other with equal valour, but with unequal success. The Huns prevailed in the bloody contest; the king of the Alani was slain; and the remains of the vanquished nation were dispersed by the ordinary alternative of flight or submission. A colony of exiles found a secure refuge in the mountains of Caucasus, between the Euxine and the Caspian, where they still preserve their name and their independence. Another colony advanced, with more intrepid courage, towards the shores of the Baltic; associated themselves with the northern tribes of Germany; and shared the spoil of the Roman provinces of Gaul and Spain. But the greatest part of the nation of the Alani embraced the offers of an honourable and advantageous union; and the

Huns, who esteemed the valour of their less fortunate enemies, proceeded, with an increase of numbers and confidence, to invade the limits of the Gothic empire.

The great Hermanric, whose dominions extended from the Baltic to the Euxine, enjoyed, in the full maturity of age and reputation, the fruit of his victories, when he was alarmed by the formidable approach of an host of unknown enemies on whom his barbarous subjects might, without injustice, bestow the epithet of barbarians. The numbers, the strength, the rapid motions, and the implacable cruelty of the Huns were felt, and dreaded, and magnified by the astonished Goths, who beheld their fields and villages consumed with flames and deluged with indiscriminate slaughter. Against these enemies, Hermanric prepared to exert the united forces of the Gothic state; but he soon discovered that his vassal tribes, provoked by oppression, were much more inclined to second than to repel the invasion of the Huns. The Ostrogoths submitted to their fate: and the royal race of the Amali will hereafter be found among the subjects of the haughty Attila.

On the banks of the Dniester the prudent Athanaric, more attentive to his own than to the general safety, had fixed the camp of the Visigoths with the firm resolution of opposing the victorious barbarians, whom he thought it less advisable to provoke. The ordinary speed of the Huns was checked by the weight of baggage and the encumbrance of captives; but their military skill deceived and almost destroyed the army of Athanaric.

Valens had terminated the Gothic war with some appearance of defence of the Danube. He was informed that the North was agitated by a furious tempest; that the irruption of the Huns, an unknown and monstrous race of savages, had subverted the power of the Goths; and that the suppliant multitudes of that warlike nation, whose pride was now humbled in the dust, covered a space many miles along the banks of the river. With outstretched arms and pathetic lamentations they loudly deplored their past misfortunes and their present danger; acknowledged that their only hope of safety was in the clemency of the Roman government; and most solemnly protested that, if the gracious liberality of the emperor would permit them to cultivate the waste lands of Thrace, they should ever hold themselves bound, by the strongest obligations of duty and gratitude, to obey the laws and to guard the limits of the republic. These assurances were confirmed by the ambassadors of the Goths, who impatiently expected from the mouth of Valens an answer that must finally determine the fate of their unhappy countrymen.

The emperor of the East was no longer guided by the wisdom and authority of his elder brother, whose death happened towards the end of the preceding year; and as the distressful situation of the Goths required an instant and peremptory decision, he was deprived of the favourite resource of feeble and timid minds, who consider the use of the dilatory and ambiguous measures as the most admirable efforts of consummate prudence.

As long as the same passions and interests subsist among mankind, the questions of war and peace, of justice and policy, which were debated in the councils of antiquity, will frequently present themselves as the subject of modern deliberation. But the most experienced statesman of Europe has never been summoned to consider the propriety or the danger of admitting or rejecting an innumerable multitude of barbarians, who are driven by despair and hunger to solicit a settlement on the territories of a civilised nation. When that important proposition, so essentially connected with the public safety, was referred to the ministers of Valens, they were perplexed and divided; but they soon acquiesced in the flattering sentiment which seemed the most favourable to the pride, the indolence, and the avarice of their sovereign. The slaves, who were decorated with the titles of præfects and generals, dissembled or disregarded the terrors of this national emigration—so extremely different from the partial and accidental colonies which had been received on the extreme limits of the empire. But they applauded the liberality of fortune which had conducted, from the most distant countries of the globe, a numerous and invincible army of strangers to defend the throne of Valens, who might now add to the royal treasures the immense sums of gold supplied by the provincials to compensate their annual proportion of recruits.

The prayers of the Goths were granted, and their service was accepted by the Imperial court; and orders were immediately despatched by the civil and military governors of the Thracian diocese to make the necessary preparations for the passage and subsistence of a great people, till a proper and sufficient territory could be allotted for their future residence. The liberality of the emperor was accompanied, however, with two harsh and rigorous conditions, which prudence might justify on the side of the Romans, but which distress alone could extort from the indignant Goths. Before they passed the Danube they were required to deliver their arms, and it was insisted that their children should be taken from them and dispersed through the provinces of Asia, where they might be civilised by the arts of education, and serve as hostages to secure the fidelity of their parents.

A probable testimony has fixed the number of the Gothic warriors at two hundred thousand men; and if we can venture to add the just proportion of women, of children, and of slaves, the whole mass of people which composed this formidable emigration must have amounted to near a million of persons, of both sexes and of all ages.

The children of the Goths, those at least of a distinguished rank, were separated from the multitude. They were conducted without delay to the distant seats assigned for their residence and education; and as the numerous train of hostages or captives passed through the cities, their gay and splendid apparel, their robust and martial figure, excited the surprise and envy of the provincials. But the stipulation the most offensive to the Goths and the most important to the Romans was shamefully eluded. The barbarians, who considered their arms as the ensigns of honour and the pledges of safety, were disposed to offer a price which the lust or avarice of the Imperial officers was easily tempted to accept. To preserve their arms, the haughty warriors consented, with some reluctance, to prostitute their wives or their daughters; the charms of a beauteous maid, or a comely boy, secured the connivance of the inspectors, who sometimes cast an eye of covetousness on the fringed carpets and linen garments of their new allies, or who sacrificed their duty to the mean consideration of filling their farms with cattle and their houses with slaves. The Goths, with arms in their hands, were permitted to enter the boats; and when their strength was collected on the other side of the river, the immense camp which was spread over the plains and the hills of the Lower Mæsia assumed a threatening and even hostile aspect.

The leaders of the Ostrogoths appeared soon afterwards on the northern banks of the Danube, and immediately despatched their ambassadors to the court of Antioch to solicit, with the same professions of allegiance and gratitude, the same favour which had been granted to the suppliant Visigoths. The absolute refusal of Valens suspended their progress, and discovered the repentance, the suspicions, and the fears of the Imperial council.

An undisciplined and unsettled nation of barbarians required the firmest temper and the most dexterous management. The daily subsistence of near a million of extraordinary subjects could be supplied only by constant and skilful diligence, and might continually be interrupted by mistake or accident. The insolence or the indignation of the Goths, if they conceived themselves to be the objects either of fear or of contempt, might urge them to the most desperate extremities, and the fortune of the state seemed to depend on the prudence, as well as the integrity, of the generals of Valens. At this important crisis the military government of Thrace was exercised by Lupicinus and Maximus, in whose venal minds the slightest hope of private emolument outweighed every consideration of public advantage, and whose guilt was only alleviated by their incapacity of discerning the pernicious effects of their rash and criminal administration.

Instead of obeying the orders of their sovereign, and satisfying, with decent liberality, the demands of the Goths, they levied an ungenerous and oppressive tax on the wants of the hungry barbarians. The vilest food was sold at an extravagant price, and, in the room of wholesome and substantial provisions, the markets were filled with the flesh of dogs and of unclean animals who had died of disease. To obtain the valuable acquisition of a pound of bread, the Goths resigned the possession of an expensive though serviceable slave, and a small quantity of meat was greedily purchased with ten pounds of a precious but useless metal. When their property was exhausted, they continued this necessary traffic by the sale of their sons and daughters; and notwithstanding the love of freedom which animated every Gothic breast, they submitted to the humiliating maxim that it was better for their children to be maintained in a servile condition than to perish in a state of wretched and helpless independence.

The most lively resentment is excited by the tyranny of pretended benefactors, who sternly exact the debt of gratitude which they have cancelled by subsequent injuries. A spirit of discontent insensibly arose in the camp of the barbarians, who pleaded, without success, the merit of their patient and dutiful behaviour, and loudly complained of the inhospitable treatment which they had received from their new allies. They beheld around them the wealth and plenty of a fertile province, in the midst of which they suffered the intolerable hardships of artificial famine. But the means of relief, and even of revenge, were in their hands, since the rapaciousness of their tyrants had left to an injured people the possession and the use of arms. The clamours of a multitude, untaught to disguise their sentiments, announced the first symptoms of resistance, and alarmed the timid and guilty minds of Lupicinus and Maximus.

Those crafty ministers, who substituted the cunning of temporary expedients to the wise and salutary counsels of general policy, attempted to remove the Goths from their dangerous station on the frontiers of the empire, and to disperse them, in separate quarters of cantonment, through the interior provinces. As they were conscious how ill they had deserved the respect or confidence of the barbarians, they diligently collected from every side a military force that might urge the tardy and reluctant march of a people who had not yet renounced the title or the duties of Roman subjects. But the generals of Valens, while their attention was solely directed to the discontented Visigoths, imprudently disarmed the ships and the fortifications which constituted the defence of the Danube. By the help of such rafts and vessels as could be hastily procured, the leaders of the Ostrogoths transported, without opposition, their king and their army, and boldly fixed an hostile and independent camp on the territories of the empire.

Under the name of Judges, Alavivus and Fritigern were the leaders of the Visigoths in peace and war; and the authority which they derived from their birth was ratified by the free consent of the nation. In a season of tranquillity their power might have been equal as well as their rank; but, as soon as their countrymen were exasperated by hunger and oppression, the superior abilities of Fritigern assumed the military command which he was qualified to exercise for the public welfare. He restrained the impatient spirit of the Visigoths till the injuries and the insults of their tyrants should justify their resistance in the opinion of mankind: but he was not disposed to sacrifice any solid advantages for the empty praise of justice and moderation. Sensible of the benefits which would result from the union of the Gothic powers under the same standard, he secretly cultivated the friendship of the Ostrogoths; and while he professed an implicit obedience to the orders of the Roman generals, he proceeded by slow marches towards Marcianopolis, the capital of the Lower Mæsia, about seventy miles from the banks of the Danube.

On that fatal spot the flames of discord and mutual hatred burst forth into a dreadful conflagration. Lupicinus had invited the Gothic chiefs to a splendid entertainment; and their martial train remained under arms at the entrance of the palace. But the gates of the city were strictly guarded, and the barbarians were sternly excluded from the use of a plentiful market, to which they asserted their equal claim of subjects and allies. Their humble prayers were rejected with insolence and derision; and as their patience was now exhausted, the townsmen, the soldiers, and the Goths were soon involved in a conflict of passionate altercation and angry reproaches. A blow was imprudently given; a sword was hastily drawn; and the first blood that was spilt in this accidental quarrel became the signal of a long and destructive war.

The weak and guilty Lupicinus, who had dared to provoke, who had neglected to destroy, and who still presumed to despise his formidable enemy, marched against the Goths, at the head of such a military force as could be collected on this sudden emergency. The valour of the Goths was so ably directed by the genius of Fritigern that they broke, by a close and vigorous attack, the ranks of the Roman legions. "That successful day put an end to the distress of the barbarians and the security of the Romans; from that day the Goths, renouncing the precarious condition of strangers and exiles, assumed the character of citizens and masters, claimed an absolute dominion over the possessors of land, and held, in their own right, the northern provinces of the empire, which are bounded by the Danube." Such are the words of the Gothic historian, who celebrates, with rude eloquence, the glory of his countrymen.

But the dominion of the barbarians was exercised only for the purposes of rapine and destruction. As they had been deprived by the ministers of the emperor of the common benefits of nature and the fair intercourse of social life, they retaliated the injustice on the subjects of the empire; and the crimes of Lupicinus were expiated by the ruin of the peaceful husbandmen of Thrace, the conflagration of their villages, and the massacre or captivity of their innocent families. The report of the Gothic victory was soon diffused over the adjacent country; and while it filled the minds of the Romans with terror and dismay, their own hasty imprudence contributed to increase the forces of Fritigern and the calamities of the province.

Some time before the great emigration a numerous body of Goths, under the command of Suerid and Colias, had been received into the protection and service of the empire. They were encamped under the walls of Hadrianople: but the ministers of Valens were anxious to remove them beyond the Hellespont, at a distance from the dangerous temptation which might so easily be communicated by the neighbourhood and the success of their countrymen. The respectful submission with which they yielded to the order of their march might be considered as a proof of their fidelity; and their moderate request of a sufficient allowance of provisions and of a delay of only two days was expressed in the most dutiful terms. But the first magistrate of Hadrianople, incensed by some disorders which had been committed at his country-house, refused this indulgence; and arming against them the inhabitants and manufacturers of a populous city, he urged, with hostile threats, their instant departure. The barbarians stood silent and amazed, till they were exasperated by the insulting clamours and missile weapons of the populace: but when patience or contempt was fatigued, they crushed the undisciplined multitude, inflicted many a shameful wound on the backs of their flying enemies, and despoiled them of the splendid armour[1] which they were unworthy to bear.

The resemblance of their sufferings and their actions soon united this victorious detachment to the nation of the Visigoths; the troops of Colias and Suerid expected the approach of the great Fritigern, ranged themselves under his standard, and signalised their ardour in the siege of Hadrianople. But the resistance of the garrison informed the barbarians that in the attack of regular fortifications the efforts of unskilful courage are seldom effectual. Their general acknowledged his error, raised the siege, declared that "he was at peace with stone walls," and revenged his disappointment on the adjacent country. He accepted with pleasure the useful reinforcement of hardy workmen who laboured in the gold-mines of Thrace for the emolument and under the lash of an unfeeling master: and these new associates conducted the barbarians through the secret paths to the most sequestered places, which had been chosen to secure the inhabitants, the cattle, and the magazines of corn. With the assistance of such guides nothing could remain impervious or inaccessible: resistance was fatal; flight was impracticable; and the patient submission of helpless innocence seldom found mercy from the barbarian conqueror. In the course of these depredations a great number of the children of the Goths, who had been sold into captivity, were restored to the embraces of their afflicted parents. The children had suffered the most cruel indignities from the lustful or angry passions of their masters, and the same cruelties, the same indignities, were severely retaliated on the sons and daughters of the Romans.

The imprudence of Valens and his ministers had introduced into the heart of the empire a nation of enemies; but the Visigoths might even yet have been reconciled by the manly confession of past errors and the sincere performance of former engagements. These healing and temperate measures seemed to concur with the timorous disposition of the sovereign of the East: but on this occasion alone Valens was brave; and his unseasonable bravery was fatal to himself and to his subjects. He declared his intention of marching from Antioch to Constantinople, to subdue this dangerous rebellion; and, as he was not ignorant of the difficulties of the enterprise, he solicited the assistance of his nephew, the emperor Gratian, who commanded all the forces of the West. The veteran troops were hastily recalled from the defence of Armenia; that important frontier was abandoned to the discretion of Sapor. In a council of war, which was influenced by pride rather than by reason, it was resolved to seek and to encounter the barbarians, who lay encamped in the spacious and fertile meadows near the most southern of the six mouths of the Danube.

The legions of Armenia supported their fame in arms, but they were oppressed by the irresistible weight of the hostile multitude: the left wing of the Romans was thrown into disorder, and the field was strewed with

[1]An imperial manufacture of shields, etc., was established at Hadrianople; and the populace were headed by the *Fabricenses*, or workmen (Vales. ad Ammian. xxxi. 6).

their mangled carcasses. This partial defeat was balanced, however, by partial success; and when the two armies, at a late hour of the evening, retreated to their respective camps, neither of them could claim the honours or the effects of a decisive victory.

The progress of the Goths had been checked by the doubtful event of that bloody day; and the Imperial generals, whose army would have been consumed by the repetition of such a contest, embraced the more rational plan of destroying the barbarians by the wants and pressure of their own multitudes. They prepared to confine the Visigoths in the narrow angle of land between the Danube, the desert of Scythia, and the mountains of Hæmus, till their strength and spirit should be insensibly wasted by the inevitable operation of famine. The design was prosecuted with some conduct and success; the barbarians had almost exhausted their own magazines and the harvests of the country; and the diligence of Saturninus, the master-general of the cavalry, was employed to improve the strength and to contract the extent of the Roman fortifications. His labours were interrupted by the alarming intelligence that new swarms of barbarians had passed the unguarded Danube.

Fritigern had successfully appealed to the passions as well as to the interest of the chiefs of the Ostrogoths. But the most powerful auxiliaries of the Goths were drawn from the camp of those enemies who had expelled them from their native seats. The loose subordination and extensive possessions of the Huns and the Alani delayed the conquests and distracted the councils of that victorious people. Several of the hordes were allured by the liberal promises of Fritigern; and the rapid cavalry of Scythia added weight and energy to the steady and strenuous efforts of the Gothic infantry. The Sarmatians, who could never forgive the successor of Valentinian, enjoyed and increased the general confusion; and a seasonable irruption of the Alemanni into the provinces of Gaul engaged the attention and diverted the forces of the emperor of the West.

One of the most dangerous inconveniences of the introduction of the barbarians into the army and the palace was sensibly felt in their correspondence with their hostile countrymen, to whom they imprudently or maliciously revealed the weakness of the Roman empire. A soldier of the life-guards of Gratian was of the nation of the Alemanni, and of the tribe of the Lentienses, who dwelt beyond the lake of Constance. Some domestic business obliged him to request a leave of absence. In a short visit to his family and friends he was exposed to their curious inquiries, and the vanity of the loquacious soldier tempted him to display his intimate acquaintance with the secrets of the state and the designs of his master. The intelligence that Gratian was preparing to lead the military force of Gaul and of the West to the assistance of his uncle Valens, pointed out to the restless spirit of the Alemanni the moment and the mode of a successful invasion.

The enterprise of some light detachments, who in the month of February passed the Rhine upon the ice, was the prelude of a more important war. The boldest hopes of rapine, perhaps of conquest, outweighed the considerations of timid prudence or national faith. Every forest and every village poured forth a band of hardy adventurers; and the great army of the Alemanni, which on their approach was estimated at forty thousand men by the fears of the people, was afterwards magnified to the number of seventy thousand by the vain and credulous flattery of the Imperial court.

The legions which had been ordered to march into Pannonia were immediately recalled or detained for the defence of Gaul. The Alemanni, who long maintained their ground, were slaughtered with unrelenting fury: five thousand only of the barbarians escaped to the woods and mountains; and the glorious death of their king on the field of battle saved him from the reproaches of the people, who are always disposed to accuse the justice or policy of an unsuccessful war. At the age of nineteen the son of Valentinian seemed to possess the talents of peace and war; and his personal success against the Alemanni was interpreted as a sure presage of his Gothic triumphs.

While Gratian deserved and enjoyed the applause of his subjects, the ruin of Valens was precipitated by the deceitful arts of Fritigern and the prudent admonitions of the emperor of the West. The advantages of negotiating in the midst of war were perfectly understood by the general of the barbarians; and a Christian ecclesiastic was dispatched, as the holy minister of peace, to penetrate and to perplex the councils of the enemy. The misfortunes, as well as the provocations, of the Gothic nation were forcibly and truly described by their ambassador, who protested, in the name of Fritigern, that he was still disposed to lay down his arms, or to employ them only in the defence of the empire, if he could secure for his wandering countrymen a tranquil settlement on the waste lands of Thrace, and a sufficient allowance of corn and cattle. But he added, in a whisper of confidential friendship, that the exasperated barbarians were averse to these reasonable conditions; and that Fritigern was doubtful whether he could accomplish the conclusion of the treaty unless he found himself supported by the presence and terrors of an Imperial army.

About the same time, Count Richomer returned from the West to announce the defeat and submission of the Alemanni; to inform Valens that his nephew advanced by rapid marches at the head of the veteran and victorious legions of Gaul; and to request, in the name of Gratian and of the republic, that every dangerous and decisive measure might be suspended till the junction of the two emperors should ensure the success of the Gothic war. But the feeble sovereign of the East was actuated only by the fatal illusions of pride and jealousy. He disdained the importunate advice; he rejected the humiliating aid; he secretly compared the ignominious, at least the inglorious, period of his own reign with the fame of a beardless youth; and Valens rushed into the field to erect his imaginary trophy before the diligence of his colleague could usurp any share of the triumphs of the day.

On the 9th of August, a day which has deserved to be marked among the most inauspicious of the Roman calendar, the emperor Valens, leaving, under a strong guard, his baggage and military treasure, marched from Hadrianople to attack the Goths, who were encamped about twelve miles from the city. Valens and a great number of brave and distinguished officers perished in the battle of Hadrianople, which equalled in the actual loss, and far surpassed in the fatal consequences, the misfortune which Rome had formerly sustained in the fields of Cannæ. Above two-thirds of the Roman army were destroyed: and the darkness of the night was esteemed a very favourable circumstance, as it served to conceal the flight of the multitude.

The tide of the Gothic inundation rolled from the walls of Hadrianople to the suburbs of Constantinople. The barbarians were surprised with the splendid appearance of the capital of the East, the height and extent of the walls, the myriads of wealthy and affrighted citizens who crowded the ramparts, and the various prospect of the sea and land. While they gazed with hopeless desire on the inaccessible beauties of Constantinople, a sally was made from one of the gates by a party of Saracens, who had been fortunately engaged in the service of Valens. The cavalry of Scythia was forced to yield to the admirable swiftness and spirit of the Arabian horses; their riders were skilled in the evolutions of irregular war; and the Northern barbarians were astonished and dismayed by the inhuman ferocity of the barbarians of the South.

The Romans, who so coolly and so concisely mention the acts of *justice* which were exercised by the legions,[2] reserved their compassion and their eloquence for their own sufferings when the provinces were invaded and desolated by the arms of the successful barbarians. The vehement Jerom might justly deplore the calamities inflicted by the Goths and their barbarous allies on his native country of Pannonia, and the wide extent of the provinces from the walls of Constantinople, to the foot of the Julian Alps; the rapes, the massacres, the conflagrations, and, above all, the profanation of the churches that were turned into stables, and the contemptuous treatment of the relics of holy martyrs. But the saint is surely transported beyond the limits of nature and history when he affirms, "that in those desert countries nothing was left except the sky and the earth; that, after the destruction of the cities and the extirpation of the human race, the land was overgrown with thick forests and inextricable brambles; and that the universal desolation, announced by the prophet Zephaniah, was accomplished in the scarcity of the beasts, the birds, and even of the fish." Could it even be supposed that a large tract of country had been left without cultivation and without inhabitants, the consequences might not have been so fatal to the inferior productions of animated nature. The useful and feeble animals, which are nourished by the hand of man, might suffer and perish if they were deprived of his protection; but the beasts of the forest, his enemies or his victims, would multiply in the free and undisturbed possession of their

[2]Observe with how much indifference Cæsar relates, in the Commentaries of the Gallic war, *that* he put to death the whole senate of the Veneti, who had yielded to his mercy (iii. 16); *that* he laboured to extirpate the whole nation of the Eburones (vi. 43); *that* forty thousand persons were massacred at Bourges by the just revenge of his soldiers, who spared neither age nor sex (vii. 27), etc.

solitary domain. The various tribes that peopled the air or the waters are still less connected with the fate of the human species.

The emperor Gratian was far advanced on his march towards the plains of Hadrianople when he was informed that his impatient colleague had been slain in battle, and that two-thirds of the Roman army were exterminated by the sword of the victorious Goths. A formidable tempest of the barbarians of Germany seemed ready to burst over the provinces of Gaul, and the mind of Gratian was oppressed and distracted by the administration of the Western empire.

In this important crisis the government of the East and the conduct of the Gothic war required the undivided attention of a hero and a statesman. The great Theodosius, a name celebrated in history and dear to the Catholic church, was summoned to the Imperial court. He was the son of the elder Theodosius, a general whose exploits in Britain and Africa have formed one of the most splendid parts of the annals of Valentinian.

From the innocent, but humble, labours of his farm between Valladolid and Segovia, Theodosius was transported, in less than four months, to the throne of the Eastern empire: and the whole period of the history of the world will not perhaps afford a similar example of an elevation at the same time so pure and so honourable. What confidence must have been reposed in his integrity, since Gratian could trust that a pious son would forgive, for the sake of the republic, the murder of his father! What expectations must have been formed of his abilities, to encourage the hope that a single man could save, and restore, the empire of the East!

The thirty-four arsenals of the empire were plentifully stored with magazines of offensive and defensive arms; and the wealth of Asia might still have yielded an ample fund for the expenses of the war. But the effects which were produced by the battle of Hadrianople on the minds of the barbarians and of the Romans, extended the victory of the former, and the defeat of the latter, far beyond the limits of a single day. A Gothic chief was heard to declare, with insolent moderation, that, for his own part, he was fatigued with slaughter; but that he was astonished how a people who fled before him like a flock of sheep could still presume to dispute the possession of their treasures and provinces.

The same terrors which the name of the Huns had spread among the Gothic tribes were inspired, by the formidable name of the Goths, among the subjects and soldiers of the Roman empire. If Theodosius, hastily collecting his scattered forces, had led them into the field to encounter a victorious enemy, his army would have been vanquished by their own fears; and his rashness could not have been excused by the chance of success.

But the *great* Theodosius, an epithet which he honourably deserved on this momentous occasion, conducted himself as the firm and faithful guardian of the republic. He fixed his headquarters at Thessalonica, the capital of the Macedonian diocese; from whence he could watch the irregular motions of the barbarians, and direct the operations of his lieutenants, from the gates of Constantinople to the shores of the Hadriatic. The fortifications and garrisons of the cities were strengthened; and the troops, among whom a sense of order and discipline was revived, were insensibly emboldened by the confidence of their own safety. From these secure stations they were encouraged to make frequent sallies on the barbarians, who infested the adjacent country; and, as they were seldom allowed to engage, without some decisive superiority, either of ground or of numbers, their enterprises were, for the most part, successful; and they were soon convinced, by their own experience, of the possibility of vanquishing their *invincible* enemies.

The detachments of these separate garrisons were gradually united into small armies; the same cautious measures were pursued, according to an extensive and well-concerted plan of operations; the events of each day added strength and spirit to the Roman arms; and the artful diligence of the emperor, who circulated the most favourable reports of the success of the war, contributed to subdue the pride of the barbarians, and to animate the hopes and courage of his subjects.

The deliverance and peace of the Roman provinces was the work of prudence, rather than of valour: the prudence of Theodosius was seconded by fortune; and the emperor never failed to seize, and to improve, every favourable circumstance. As long as the superior genius of Fritigern preserved the union and directed the motions of the barbarians, their power was not inadequate to the conquest of a great empire. The death of that hero, the predecessor and master of the renowned Alaric, relieved an impatient multitude from the intolerable yoke of discipline and discretion. The barbarians, who had been restrained by his authority, abandoned themselves to the dictates of their passions; and their passions were seldom uniform or consistent. An army of conquerors was broken into many disorderly bands of savage robbers; and their blind and irregular fury was not less pernicious to themselves than to their enemies. Their mischievous disposition was shown in the destruction of every object which they wanted strength to remove, or taste to enjoy; and they often consumed, with improvident rage, the harvests, or the granaries, which soon afterwards became necessary for their own subsistence.

A spirit of discord arose among the independent tribes and nations, which had been united only by the bands of a loose and voluntary alliance. The troops of the Huns and the Alani would naturally upbraid the flight of the Goths, who were not disposed to use with moderation the advantages of their fortune: the ancient jealousy of the Ostrogoths and the Visigoths could not long be suspended; and the haughty chiefs still remembered the insults and injuries which they had reciprocally offered or sustained while the nation was seated in the countries beyond the Danube. The progress of domestic faction abated the more diffusive sentiment of national animosity; and the officers of Theodosius were instructed to purchase, with liberal gifts and promises, the retreat or service of the discontented party. The acquisition of Modar, a prince of the royal blood of the Amali, gave a bold and faithful champion to the cause of Rome. The illustrious deserter soon obtained the rank of master-general, with an important command; surprised an army of his countrymen, who were immersed in wine and sleep; and, after a cruel slaughter of the astonished Goths, returned with an immense spoil and four thousand waggons to the Imperial camp.

In the hands of a skilful politician the most different means may be successfully applied to the same ends; and the peace of the empire, which had been forwarded by the divisions, was accomplished by the re-union of the Gothic nation. Athanaric, who had been a patient spectator of these extraordinary events, was at length driven, by the chance of arms, from the dark recesses of the woods of Caucaland. He no longer hesitated to pass the Danube; and a very considerable part of the subjects of Fritigern, who already felt the inconveniences of anarchy, were easily persuaded to acknowledge for their king a Gothic Judge, whose birth they respected, and whose abilities they had frequently experienced. But age had chilled the daring spirit of Athanaric; and instead of leading his people to the field of battle and victory, he wisely listened to the fair proposal of an honourable and advantageous treaty.

Theodosius, who was acquainted with the merit and power of his new ally, condescended to meet him at the distance of several miles from Constantinople; and entertained him in the Imperial city with the confidence of a friend, and the magnificence of a monarch. The barbarian prince observed, with curious attention, the variety of objects which attracted his notice, and at last broke out into a sincere and passionate exclamation of wonder. "I now behold (said he) what I never could believe, the glories of this stupendous capital!" And as he cast his eyes around, he viewed and he admired the commanding situation of the city, the strength and beauty of the walls and public edifices, the capacious harbour crowded with innumerable vessels, the perpetual concourse of distant nations, and the arms and discipline of the troops. "Indeed (continued Athanaric), the emperor of the Romans is a god upon earth; and the presumptuous man who dares to lift his hand against him is guilty of his own blood." The Gothic king did not long enjoy this splendid and honourable reception; and, as temperance was not the virtue of his nation, it may justly be suspected that his mortal disease was contracted amidst the pleasures of the Imperial banquets. But the policy of Theodosius derived more solid benefit from the death than he could have expected from the most faithful services of his ally. The funeral of Athanaric was performed with solemn rites in the capital of the East; a stately monument was erected to his memory; and his whole army, won by the liberal courtesy and decent grief of Theodosius, enlisted under the standard of the Roman empire.

The submission of so great a body of the Visigoths was productive of the most salutary consequences; and the mixed influence of force, of reason, and of corruption, became every day more powerful and more extensive. Each independent chieftain hastened to obtain a separate treaty, from the apprehension that an obstinate delay might expose *him,* alone and unprotected, to the revenge or justice of the conqueror. The general, or rather the final, capitulation of the Goths, may be dated four years, one month, and twenty-five days, after the defeat and death of the emperor Valens.

The provinces of the Danube had been already relieved from the oppressive weight of the Ostrogoths. Their destructive course was pointed towards the West; but we must be satisfied with a very obscure and imperfect knowledge of their various adventures. The Ostrogoths impelled several of the German tribes on the provinces of Gaul; concluded, and soon violated, a treaty with the emperor Gratian; advanced into the unknown countries of the North; and, after an interval of more than four years, returned with accumulated force to the banks of the Lower Danube.

The ravages of war and tyranny had provided many large tracts of fertile but uncultivated land for the use of those barbarians who might not disdain the practice of agriculture. A numerous colony of the Visigoths was seated in Thrace: the remains of the Ostrogoths were planted in Phrygia and Lydia; their immediate wants were supplied by a distribution of corn and cattle; and their future industry was encouraged by an exemption from tribute during a certain term of years. The barbarians would have deserved to feel the cruel and perfidious policy of the Imperial court if they had suffered themselves to be dispersed through the provinces. They required and they obtained the sole possession of the villages and districts assigned for their residence; they still cherished and propagated their native manners and language; asserted, in the bosom of despotism, the freedom of their domestic government; and acknowledged the sovereignty of the emperor, without submitting to the inferior jurisdiction of the laws and magistrates of Rome. The hereditary chiefs of the tribes and families were still permitted to command their followers in peace and war; but the royal dignity was abolished, and the generals of the Goths were appointed and removed at the pleasure of the emperor.

An army of forty thousand Goths was maintained for the perpetual service of the empire of the East; and those haughty troops, who assumed the title of *Fœderati*, or allies, were distinguished by their gold collars, liberal pay, and licentious privileges. Their native courage was improved by the use of arms and the knowledge of discipline; and, while the republic was guarded or threatened by the doubtful sword of the barbarians, the last sparks of the military flame were finally extinguished in the minds of the Romans.

The barbarians still wore an angry and hostile aspect; but the experience of past times might encourage the hope that they would acquire the habits of industry and obedience; that their manners would be polished by time, education, and the influence of Christianity; and that their posterity would insensibly blend with the great body of the Roman people. Notwithstanding these specious arguments and these sanguine expectations, it was apparent to every discerning eye that the Goths would long remain the enemies, and might soon become the conquerors, of the Roman empire. Their rude and insolent behaviour expressed their contempt of the citizens and provincials, whom they insulted with impunity.

CHAPTER XX

Maximus—Administration of Theodosius—Final Destruction of Paganism

The fame of Gratian, before he had accomplished the twentieth year of his age, was equal to that of the most celebrated princes. His gentle and amiable disposition endeared him to his private friends, the graceful affability of his manners engaged the affection of the people; the men of letters, who enjoyed the liberality, acknowledged the taste and eloquence of their sovereign; his valour and dexterity in arms were equally applauded by the soldiers; and the clergy considered the humble piety of Gratian as the first and most useful of his virtues.

A more attentive view of the life of Gratian may perhaps suggest the true cause of the disappointment of the public hopes. His apparent virtues, instead of being the hardy productions of experience and adversity, were the premature and artificial fruits of a royal education. The anxious tenderness of his father was continually employed to bestow on him those advantages which he might perhaps esteem the more highly as he himself had been deprived of them, and the most skilful masters of every science and of every art had laboured to form the mind and body of the young prince. His preceptors gradually rose to the rank and consequence of ministers of state, and, as they wisely dissembled their secret authority, he seemed to act with firmness, with propriety, and with judgment on the most important occasions of his life and reign. But as soon as time and accident had removed those faithful counsellors from the throne, the emperor of the West insensibly descended to the level of his natural genius, abandoned the reins of government to the ambitious hands which were stretched forwards to grasp them, and amused his leisure with the most frivolous gratifications. A public sale of favour and injustice was instituted, both in the court and in the provinces, by the worthless delegates of his power.

Among the various arts which had exercised the youth of Gratian, he had applied himself, with singular inclination and success, to manage the horse, to draw the bow, and to dart the javelin; and these qualifications, which might be useful to a soldier, were prostituted to the viler purposes of hunting. Large parks were enclosed for the Imperial pleasures, and plentifully stocked with every species of wild beasts, and Gratian neglected the duties and even the dignity of his rank to consume whole days in the vain display of his dexterity and boldness in the chase. The pride and wish of the Roman emperor to excel in an art in which he might be surpassed by the meanest of his slaves reminded the numerous spectators of the examples of Nero and

Commodus; but the chaste and temperate Gratian was a stranger to their monstrous vices, and his hands were stained only with the blood of animals.

It is not very important to inquire from what causes the revolt of Britain was produced. The seeds of rebellion happened to fall on a soil which was supposed to be more fruitful than any other in tyrants and usurpers; the legions of that sequestered island had been long famous for a spirit of presumption and arrogance; and the name of Maximus was proclaimed by the tumultuary but unanimous voice both of the soldiers and of the provincials. The emperor, or the rebel, for his title was not yet ascertained by fortune, was a native of Spain, the countryman, the fellow-soldier, and the rival of Theodosius; the events of his life had long since fixed him in Britain, and I should not be unwilling to find some evidence for the marriage which he is said to have contracted with the daughter of a wealthy lord of Caernarvonshire.

From the moment that Maximus had violated his allegiance to his lawful sovereign, he could not hope to reign, or even to live, if he confined his moderate ambition within the narrow limits of Britain. He boldly and wisely invaded Gaul with a fleet and army which were long afterwards remembered as the emigration of a considerable part of the British nation. The emperor, in his peaceful residence of Paris, was alarmed by their hostile approach, and the darts which he idly wasted on lions and bears might have been employed more honourably against the rebels. But his feeble efforts announced his degenerate spirit and desperate situation, and deprived him of the resources which he still might have found in the support of his subjects and allies. The armies of Gaul, instead of opposing the march of Maximus, received him with joyful and loyal acclamations, and the shame of the desertion was transferred from the people to the prince. The troops whose station more immediately attached them to the service of the palace abandoned the standard of Gratian the first time that it was displayed in the neighbourhood of Paris. The emperor of the West fled towards Lyons with a train of only three hundred horse, and in the cities along the road, where he hoped to find a refuge, or at least a passage, he was taught by cruel experience that every gate is shut against the unfortunate.

The events of this revolution had passed in such rapid succession that it would have been impossible for Theodosius to march to the relief of his benefactor before he received the intelligence of his defeat and death. During the season of sincere grief or ostentatious mourning the Eastern emperor was interrupted by the arrival of the principal chamberlain of Maximus; and the choice of a venerable old man for an office which was usually exercised by eunuchs announced to the court of Constantinople the gravity and temperance of the British usurper. The ambassador condescended to justify or excuse the conduct of his master, and to protest, in specious language, that the murder of Gratian had been perpetrated, without his knowledge or consent, by the precipitate zeal of the soldiers. But he proceeded, in a firm and equal tone, to offer Theodosius the alternative of peace or war.

The assassin of Gratian had usurped, but he actually possessed, the most warlike provinces of the empire; the East was exhausted by the misfortunes, and even by the success, of the Gothic war; and it was seriously to be apprehended that, after the vital strength of the republic had been wasted in a doubtful and destructive contest, the feeble conqueror would remain an easy prey to the barbarians of the North. These weighty considerations engaged Theodosius to dissemble his resentment and to accept the alliance of the tyrant. But he stipulated that Maximus should content himself with the possession of the countries beyond the Alps. The brother of Gratian was confirmed and secured in the sovereignty of Italy, Africa, and the Western Illyricum.

Among the benefactors of the church, the fame of Constantine has been rivalled by the glory of Theodosius. As the emperor always fixed his eyes on the visible landmarks of orthodoxy which he had so prudently constituted, his religious opinions were never affected by the specious texts, the subtle arguments, and the ambiguous creeds of the Arian doctors. Once indeed he expressed a faint inclination to converse with the eloquent and learned Eunomius, who lived in retirement at a small distance from Constantinople. But the dangerous interview was prevented by the prayers of the empress Flacilla, who trembled for the salvation of her husband; and the mind of Theodosius was confirmed by a theological argument adapted to the rudest capacity. He had lately bestowed on his eldest son Arcadius the name and honours of Augustus, and the two princes were seated on a stately throne to receive the homage of their subjects. A bishop, Amphilochius of Iconium, approached the throne, and, after saluting with due reverence the person of his sovereign, he accosted the royal youth with the same familiar tenderness which he might have used towards a plebeian child. Provoked by this insolent behaviour, the monarch gave orders that the rustic priest should be instantly driven from his presence. But while the guards were forcing him to the door, the dexterous polemic had time to execute his design, by exclaiming, with a loud voice, "Such is the treatment, O emperor! which the King of heaven has prepared for those impious men who affect to worship the Father, but refuse to acknowledge the equal majesty of his divine Son." Theodosius immediately embraced the bishop of Iconium, and never forgot the important lesson which he received from this dramatic parable.

It was not enough that Theodosius had suppressed the insolent reign of Arianism, or that he had abundantly revenged the injuries which the Catholics sustained from the zeal of Constantius and Valens. The orthodox emperor considered every heretic as a rebel against the supreme powers of heaven and of earth; and each of those powers might exercise their peculiar jurisdiction over the soul and body of the guilty. The decrees of the council of Constantinople had ascertained the true standard of the faith; and the ecclesiastics who governed the conscience of Theodosius suggested the most effectual methods of persecution. In the space of fifteen years he promulgated at least fifteen severe edicts against the heretics, more especially against those who rejected the doctrine of the Trinity; and to deprive them of every hope of escape, he sternly enacted that, if any laws or rescripts should be alleged in their favour, the judges should consider them as the illegal productions either of fraud or forgery. The penal statutes were directed against the ministers, the assemblies, and the persons of the heretics; and the passions of the legislator were expressed in the language of declamation and invective. Every Roman might exercise the right of public accusation; but the office of *Inquisitors* of the Faith, a name so deservedly abhorred, was first instituted under the reign of Theodosius. Yet we are assured that the execution of his penal edicts was seldom enforced; and that the pious emperor appeared less desirous to punish than to reclaim or terrify his refractory subjects.

The theory of persecution was established by Theodosius, whose justice and piety have been applauded by the saints; but the practice of it, in the fullest extent, was reserved for his rival and colleague Maximus, the first among the Christian princes who shed the blood of his Christian subjects on account of their religious opinions. The cause of the Priscillianists, a recent sect of heretics who disturbed the provinces of Spain, was transferred, by appeal, from the synod of Bordeaux to the Imperial consistory of Trèves; and by the sentence of the Prætorian præfect, seven persons were tortured, condemned, and executed. The first of these was Priscillian himself, bishop of Avila, in Spain, who adorned the advantages of birth and fortune by the accomplishments of eloquence and learning. Two presbyters and two deacons accompanied their beloved master in his death, which they esteemed as a glorious martyrdom; and the number of religious victims was completed by the execution of Latronian, a poet, who rivalled the fame of the ancients; and of Euchrocia, a noble matron of Bordeaux, the widow of the orator Delphidius. It is with pleasure that we can observe the humane inconsistency of the most illustrious saints and bishops, Ambrose of Milan and Martin of Tours, who, on this occasion, asserted the cause of toleration. They pitied the unhappy men who had been executed at Trèves; they refused to hold communion with their episcopal murderers; and if Martin deviated from that generous resolution, his motives were laudable, and his repentance was exemplary. The bishops of Tours and Milan pronounced, without hesitation, the eternal damnation of heretics; but they were surprised and shocked by the bloody image of their temporal death, and the honest feelings of nature resisted the artificial prejudices of theology.

After the defeat and death of the tyrant of Gaul, the Roman world was in the possession of Theodosius. He derived from the choice of Gratian his honourable title to the provinces of the East; he had acquired the West by the right of conquest; and the three years which he spent in Italy were usefully employed to restore the authority of the laws and to correct the abuses which had prevailed with impunity under the usurpation of Maximus and the minority of Valentinian. The opinion, and perhaps the interest, of the public confirmed the division of the Eastern and Western empires; and the two royal youths, Arcadius and Honorius, who had already obtained the title of Augustus, were destined to fill the thrones of Constantinople and of Rome.

In the faithful picture of the virtues of Theodosius, his imperfections have not been dissembled; the acts of cruelty, and the habits of indolence, tarnished the glory of one of the greatest of the Roman princes. An historian perpetually adverse to the fame of Theodosius has exaggerated his vices and their pernicious effects; he boldly asserts that every rank of subjects imitated the effeminate manners of their sovereign; that every species of corruption polluted the course of public and private life; and that the feeble restraints of order and decency were insufficient to resist the progress of that degenerate spirit which sacrifices, without a blush, the consideration of duty and interest to the base indulgence of sloth and appetite.

If it can be affirmed, with any degree of truth, that the luxury of the Romans was more shameless and dissolute in the reign of Theodosius than in the age of Constantine, perhaps, or of Augustus, the alteration cannot be ascribed to any beneficial improvements which had gradually increased the stock of national riches. A long period of calamity or decay must have checked the industry and diminished the wealth of the people; and their profuse luxury must have been the result of that indolent despair which enjoys the present hour and declines the thoughts of futurity. The uncertain condition of their property discouraged the subjects of Theodosius from engaging in those useful and laborious undertakings which require an immediate expense, and promise a slow and distant advantage. The frequent examples of ruin and desolation tempted them not to spare the remains of a patrimony which might, every hour, become the prey of the rapacious Goth. And the mad prodigality which prevails in the confusion of a shipwreck or a siege may serve to explain the progress of luxury amidst the misfortunes and terrors of a sinking nation.

The effeminate luxury which infected the manners of courts and cities had instilled a secret and destructive poison into the camps of the legions. The heavy weapons of their ancestors, the short sword and the formidable *pilum,* which had subdued the world, insensibly dropped from their feeble hands. As the use of the shield is incompatible with that of the bow, they reluctantly marched into the field, condemned to suffer either the pain of wounds or the ignominy of flight, and always disposed to prefer the more shameful alternative. The cavalry of the Goths, the Huns, and the Alani, had felt the benefits and adopted the use of defensive armour; and, as they excelled in the management of missile weapons, they easily overwhelmed the naked and trembling legions, whose heads and breasts were exposed, without defence, to the arrows of the barbarians.

Paganism was still the constitutional religion of the senate. The hall or temple in which they assembled was adorned by the statue and altar of Victory; a majestic female standing on a globe, with flowing garments, expanded wings, and a crown of laurel in her outstretched hand. The senators were sworn on the altar of the goddess to observe the laws of the emperor and of the empire; and a solemn offering of wine and incense was the ordinary prelude of their public deliberations. The removal of this ancient monument was the only injury which Constantius had offered to the superstition of the Romans. The altar of Victory was again restored by Julian, tolerated by Valentinian, and once more banished from the senate by the zeal of Gratian. But the emperor yet spared the statues of the gods which were exposed to the public veneration: four hundred and twenty-four temples, or chapels, still remained to satisfy the devotion of the people, and in every quarter of Rome the delicacy of the Christians was offended by the fumes of idolatrous sacrifice.

But the Christians formed the least numerous party in the senate of Rome; and it was only by their absence that they could express their dissent from the legal, though profane, acts of a Pagan majority. In that assembly the dying embers of freedom were, for a moment, revived and inflamed by the breath of fanaticism. Four respectable deputations were successively voted to the Imperial court, to represent the grievances of the priesthood and the senate, and to solicit the restoration of the altar of Victory. The test of antiquity and success was applied with singular advantage to the religion of Numa; and ROME herself, the celestial genius that presided over the fates of the city, is introduced by the orator to plead her own cause before the tribunal of the emperors. "Most excellent princes," says the venerable matron, "fathers of your country! pity and respect my age, which has hitherto flowed in an uninterrupted course of piety. Since I do not repent, permit me to continue in the practice of my ancient rites. Since I am born free, allow me to enjoy my domestic institutions. This religion has reduced the world under my laws. These rites have repelled Hannibal from the city, and the Gauls from the Capitol. Were my grey hairs reserved for such intolerable disgrace? I am ignorant of the new system that I am required to adopt; but I am well assured that the correction of old age is always an ungrateful and ignominious office." The fears of the people supplied what the discretion of the orator had suppressed; and the calamities which afflicted or threatened the declining empire were unanimously imputed by the Pagans to the new religion of Christ and of Constantine.

In a full meeting of the senate the emperor proposed, according to the forms of the republic, the important question, whether the worship of Jupiter or that of Christ should be the religion of the Romans? The liberty of suffrages which he affected to allow was destroyed by the hopes and fears that his presence inspired; and the arbitrary exile of Symmachus was a recent admonition that it might be dangerous to oppose the wishes of the monarch. On a regular division of the senate, Jupiter was condemned and degraded by the sense of a very large majority.

The citizens who subsisted by their own industry, and the populace who were supported by the public liberality, filled the churches of the Lateran and Vatican with an incessant throng of devout proselytes. The decrees of the senate which proscribed the worship of idols, were ratified by the general consent of the Romans; the splendour of the Capitol was defaced, and the solitary temples were abandoned to ruin and contempt. A special commission was granted to the Prætorian præfect of the East, and afterwards to two officers of distinguished rank in the West, by which they were directed to shut the temples, to seize or destroy the instruments of idolatry, to abolish the privileges of the priests, and to confiscate the consecrated property for the benefit of the emperor, of the church, or of the army. Here the desolation might have stopped: and the naked edifices, which were no longer employed in the service of idolatry, might have been protected from the destructive rage of fanaticism. Many of those temples were the most splendid and beautiful monuments of Grecian architecture: and the emperor himself was interested not to deface the splendour of his own cities, or to diminish the value of his own possessions. Those stately edifices might be suffered to remain, as so many lasting trophies of the victory of Christ. In the decline of the arts, they might be usefully converted into magazines, manufactures, or places of public assembly: and perhaps, when the walls of the temple had been sufficiently purified by holy rites, the worship of the true Deity might be allowed to expiate the ancient guilt of idolatry. But as long as they subsisted, the Pagans fondly cherished the secret hope that an auspicious revolution, a second Julian, might again restore the altars of the gods: and the earnestness with which they addressed their unavailing prayers to the throne increased the zeal of the Christian reformers to extirpate, without mercy, the root of superstition.

A small number of temples was protected by the fears, the venality, the taste, or the prudence of the civil and ecclesiastical governors. The temple of the Celestial Venus at Carthage, whose sacred precincts formed a circumference of two miles, was judiciously converted into a Christian church; and a similar consecration has preserved inviolate the majestic dome of the Pantheon at Rome. But in almost every province of the Roman world, an army of fanatics, without authority and without discipline, invaded the peaceful inhabitants; and the ruin of the fairest structures of antiquity still displays the ravages of *those* barbarians who alone had time and inclination to execute such laborious destruction.

In this wide and various prospect of devastation, the spectator may distinguish the ruins of the temple of Serapis, at Alexandria. The valuable library of Alexandria was pillaged, and near twenty years afterwards the appearance of the empty shelves excited the regret and indignation of every spectator whose mind was not totally darkened by religious prejudice. The compositions of ancient genius, so many of which have irretrievably perished, might surely have been excepted from the wreck of idolatry, for the amusement and instruction of succeeding ages.

The temples of the Roman empire were deserted or destroyed; but the ingenious superstition of the Pagans still attempted to elude the laws of Theodosius, by which all sacrifices had been severely prohibited. The inhabitants of the country, whose conduct was less exposed to the eye of malicious curiosity, disguised their *religious* under the appearance of *convivial* meetings. On the days of solemn festivals they assembled in great numbers under the spreading shade of some consecrated trees; sheep and oxen were slaughtered and roasted; and this rural entertainment was sanctified by the use of incense and by the hymns which were sung in honour of the gods. But it was alleged that, as no part of the animal was made a burnt-offering, as no altar was provided to receive the blood, and as the previous oblation of salt cakes and the concluding ceremony of libations were carefully omitted, these festal meetings did not involve the guests in the guilt or penalty of an illegal sacrifice. Whatever might be the truth of the facts or the merit of the distinction, these vain pretences were swept away by the last edict of Theodosius, which inflicted a deadly wound on the superstition of the Pagans. This prohibitory law is expressed in the most absolute and comprehensive terms. "It is our will and pleasure," says the emperor, "that none of our subjects, whether magistrates or private citizens, however exalted or however humble may be their rank and condition, shall presume in any city or in any place to worship an inanimate idol by the sacrifice of a guiltless victim." The act of sacrificing and the practice of divination by the entrails of the victim are declared (without any regard to the object of the inquiry) a crime of high treason against the state, which can be expiated only by the death of the guilty. The rites of Pagan superstition which might seem less bloody and atrocious are abolished as highly injurious to the truth and honour of religion; luminaries, garlands, frankincense, and libations of wine are specially enumerated and condemned; and the harmless claims of the domestic genius, of the household gods, are included in this rigorous proscription. The use of any of these profane and illegal ceremonies subjects the offender to the forfeiture of the house or estate where they have been performed; and if he has artfully chosen the property of another for the scene of his impiety, he is compelled to discharge, without delay, a heavy fine of twenty-five pounds of gold, or more than one thousand pounds sterling.

In the cruel reigns of Decius and Diocletian Christianity had been proscribed, as a revolt from the ancient and hereditary religion of the empire; and the unjust suspicions which were entertained of a dark and dangerous faction were in some measure countenanced by the inseparable union and rapid conquests of the church. But the same excuses of fear and ignorance cannot be applied to the Christian emperors. The churches were filled with the increasing multitude of unworthy proselytes who conformed, from temporal motives, to the reigning religion; and whilst they devoutly imitated the postures and recited the prayers of the faithful, they satisfied their conscience by the silent and sincere invocation of the gods of antiquity. If the Pagans wanted patience to suffer, they wanted spirit to resist; and the disorderly opposition of the peasants of Syria and the populace of Alexandria was silenced by the name and authority of the emperor.

The profession of Christianity was not made an essential qualification for the enjoyment of the civil rights of society, nor were any peculiar hardships imposed on the sectaries who credulously received the fables of Ovid and obstinately rejected the miracles of the Gospel. The palace, the schools, the army, and the senate were filled with declared and devout Pagans; they obtained, without distinction, the civil and military honours of the empire. But the Imperial laws which prohibited the sacrifices and ceremonies of Paganism were rigidly executed; and every hour contributed to destroy the influence of a religion which was supported by custom rather than by argument. The generation that arose in the world after the promulgation of the Imperial laws was attracted within the pale of the Catholic church: and so rapid, yet so gentle, was the fall of Paganism, that only twenty-eight years after the death of Theodosius the faint and minute vestiges were no longer visible to the eye of the legislator.

The idols were crumbled into dust: and the mythology which had once been the creed of nations was so universally disbelieved, that it might be employed without scandal, or at least without suspicion, by Christian poets. Yet the vestiges of superstition were not absolutely obliterated, and the festival of the Lupercalia, whose origin had preceded the foundation of Rome, was still celebrated under the reign of Anthemius. The savage and simple rites were expressive of an early state of society before the invention of arts and agriculture. The rustic deities who presided over the toils and pleasures of the pastoral life, Pan, Faunus, and their train of satyrs, were such as the fancy of shepherds might create, sportive, petulant, and lascivious; whose power was limited, and whose malice was inoffensive. A goat was the offering the best adapted to their character and attributes; the flesh of the victim was roasted on willow spits; and the riotous youths, who crowded to the feast, ran naked about the fields, with leather thongs in their hands, communicating, as it was supposed, the blessing of fecundity to the women whom they touched. The altar of Pan was erected, perhaps by Evander the Arcadian, in a dark recess in the side of the Palatine hill, watered by a perpetual fountain, and shaded by a hanging grove. A tradition that, in the same place, Romulus and Remus were suckled by the wolf, rendered it still more sacred and venerable in the eyes of the Romans; and this sylvan spot was gradually surrounded by the stately edifices of the Forum.

After the conversion of the Imperial city, the Christians still continued, in the month of February, the annual celebration of the Lupercalia; to which they ascribed a secret and mysterious influence on the genial powers of the animal and vegetable world. The bishops of Rome were solicitous to abolish a profane custom so repugnant to the spirit of Christianity; but their zeal was not supported by the authority of the civil magistrate: the inveterate abuse subsisted till the end of the fifth century, and Pope Gelasius, who purified the capital from the last stain of idolatry, appeased, by a formal apology, the murmurs of the senate and people.

The ruin of the Pagan religion is described by the sophists as a dreadful and amazing prodigy, which covered the earth with darkness and restored the ancient dominion of chaos and of night. They relate in solemn and pathetic strains that the temples were converted into sepulchres, and that the holy places, which had been adorned by the statues of the gods, were basely polluted by the relics of Christian martyrs. "The monks" (a race of filthy animals, to whom Eunapius is tempted to refuse the name of men) "are the authors of the new worship, which, in the place of those deities who are conceived by the understanding, has substituted the meanest and most contemptible slaves. The heads, salted and pickled, of those infamous malefactors, who for the multitude of their crimes have suffered a just and ignominious death; their bodies, still marked by the impression of the lash and the scars of those tortures which were inflicted by the sentence of the magistrate; such" (continues Eunapius) "are the gods which the earth produces in our days; such are the martyrs, the supreme arbitrators of our prayers and petitions to the Deity, whose tombs are now consecrated as the objects of the veneration of the people." Without approving the malice, it is natural enough to share the surprise of the sophist, the spectator of a revolution which raised those obscure victims of the laws of Rome to the rank of celestial and invisible protectors of the Roman empire. The grateful respect of the Christians for the martyrs of the faith was exalted, by time and victory, into religious adoration; and the most illustrious of the saints and prophets were deservedly associated to the honours of the martyrs. In the age which followed the conversion of Constantine, the emperors, the consuls, and the generals of armies devoutly visited the sepulchres of a tentmaker and a fisherman.

The satisfactory experience that the relics of saints were more valuable than gold or precious stones stimulated the clergy to multiply the treasures of the church. Without much regard for truth or probability, they invented names for skeletons, and actions for names. The fame of the Apostles, and of the holy men who had imitated their virtues, was darkened by religious fiction. But the progress of superstition would have been much less rapid and victorious if the faith of the people had not been assisted by the seasonable aid of visions and miracles to ascertain the authenticity and virtue of the most suspicious relics. The confidence of petitioners was founded on the persuasion that the saints who reigned with Christ cast an eye of pity upon earth; that they were warmly interested in the prosperity of the Catholic church; and that the individuals who imitated the example of their faith and piety were the peculiar and favourite objects of their most tender regard. The imagination raised by a painful effort to the contemplation and worship of the Universal Cause eagerly embraced such inferior objects of adoration as were more proportioned to its gross conceptions and imperfect faculties. The sublime and simple theology of the primitive Christians was gradually corrupted: and the MONARCHY of heaven, already clouded by metaphysical subtleties, was degraded by the introduction of a popular mythology which tended to restore the reign of Polytheism.

As the objects of religion were gradually reduced to the standard of the imagination, the rites and ceremonies were introduced that seemed most powerfully to affect the senses of the vulgar. If, in the beginning of the fifth century, Tertullian or Lactantius had been suddenly raised from the dead, to assist at the festival of some popular saint or martyr, they would have gazed with astonishment and indignation on the profane spectacle which had succeeded to the pure and spiritual worship of a Christian congregation. As soon as the doors of the church were thrown open, they must have been offended by the smoke of incense, the perfume of flowers, and the glare of lamps and tapers, which diffused, at noon-day, a gaudy, superfluous, and, in their opinion, a sacrilegious light. If they approached the balustrade of the altar, they made their way through the prostrate crowd, consisting, for the most part, of strangers and pilgrims, who resorted to the city on the vigil of the feast; and who already felt the strong intoxication of fanaticism, and, perhaps, of wine. Their devout kisses were imprinted on the walls and pavement of the sacred edifice; and their fervent prayers were directed, whatever might be the language of their church, to the bones, the blood, or the ashes of the saint, which were usually concealed, by a linen or silken veil, from the eyes of the vulgar.

The Christians frequented the tombs of the martyrs, in the hope of obtaining, from their powerful intercession, every sort of spiritual, but more especially of temporal, blessings. They implored the preservation of their health, or the cure of their infirmities; the fruitfulness of their barren wives, or the safety and happiness of their children. Whenever they undertook any distant or dangerous journey, they requested that the holy martyrs would be their guides and protectors on the road; and if they returned without having experienced any misfortune, they again hastened to the tombs of the martyrs, to celebrate, with grateful thanksgivings, their obligations to the memory and relics of those heavenly patrons. The walls were hung round with symbols of the favours which they had received; eyes, and hands, and feet, of gold and silver: and edifying pictures, which could not long escape the abuse of indiscreet or idolatrous devotion, represented the image, the attributes, and the miracles of the tutelar saint. The same uniform original spirit of superstition might suggest, in the most distant ages and countries, the same methods of deceiving the credulity, and of affecting the senses of mankind: but it must ingenuously be confessed that the ministers of the church imitated the profane model which they were impatient to destroy. The most respectable bishops had persuaded themselves that the ignorant rustics would more cheerfully renounce the superstitions of Paganism, if they found some resemblance, some compensation, in the bosom of Christianity. The religion of Constantine achieved, in less than a century, the final conquest of the Roman empire: but the victors themselves were insensibly subdued by the arts of their vanquished rivals.

CHAPTER XXI

The Goths Plunder Greece—The Germans Overrun Gaul

The genius of Rome expired with Theodosius, the last of the successors of Augustus and Constantine who appeared in the field at the head of their armies, and whose authority was universally acknowledged throughout the whole extent of the empire. The memory of his virtues still continued, however, to protect the feeble and inexperienced youth of his two sons.

Arcadius appeared to reign over the provinces of Thrace, Asia Minor, Syria, and Egypt, from the Lower Danube to the confines of Persia and Æthiopia. His younger brother, Honorius, assumed, in the eleventh year of his age, the nominal government of Italy, Africa, Gaul, Spain, and Britain; and the troops which guarded the frontiers of his kingdom were opposed, on one side, to the Caledonians, and on the other to the Moors. The boundary in Europe was not very different from the line which now separates the Germans and the Turks; and the respective advantages of territory, riches, populousness, and military strength, were fairly balanced and compensated in this final and permanent division of the Roman empire.

At a time when the only hope of delaying the ruin of the Roman name depended on the firm union and reciprocal aid of all the nations to whom it had been gradually communicated, the subjects of Arcadius and Honorius were instructed, by their respective masters, to view each other in a foreign and even hostile light; to rejoice in their mutual calamities; and to embrace, as their faithful allies, the barbarians whom they excited to invade the territories of their countrymen. The natives of Italy affected to despise the servile and effeminate Greeks of Byzantium, who presumed to imitate the dress, and to usurp the dignity, of Roman senators; and the Greeks had not yet forgot the sentiments of hatred and contempt which their polished ancestors had so long entertained for the rude inhabitants of the West. The distinction of two governments, which soon produced the separation of two nations, will justify my design of suspending the series of the Byzantine history, to prosecute, without interruption, the disgraceful but memorable reign of Honorius.

The impartiality which Stilicho affected, as the common guardian of the royal brothers, engaged him to regulate the equal division of the arms, the jewels, and the magnificent wardrobe and furniture of the deceased emperor. But the most important object of the inheritance consisted of the numerous legions, cohorts, and squadrons, of Romans or barbarians, whom the event of the civil war had united under the standard of Theodosius. If Stilicho had endured the revolt of Africa, he would have betrayed the security of the capital, and the majesty of the Western emperor, to the capricious insolence of a Moorish rebel.

Gildo, the brother of the tyrant Firmus, had preserved and obtained, as the reward of his apparent fidelity, the immense patrimony which was forfeited by treason; long and meritorious service in the armies of Rome raised him to the dignity of a military count; the narrow policy of the court of Theodosius had adopted the mischievous expedient of supporting a legal government by the interest of a powerful family; and the brother of Firmus was invested with the command of Africa. His ambition soon usurped the administration of justice and of the finances, without account and without control; and he maintained, during a reign of twelve years, the possession of an office from which it was impossible to remove him without the danger of a civil war.

The subsistence of Rome depended on the harvests of Africa; and it was evident that a declaration of war would be the signal of famine. The præfect Symmachus, who presided in the deliberations of the senate, admonished the minister of his just apprehension that, as soon as the revengeful Moor should prohibit the exportation of corn, the tranquillity, and perhaps the safety, of the capital would be threatened by the hungry rage of a turbulent multitude. The prudence of Stilicho conceived, and executed without delay, the most effectual measure for the relief of the Roman people. A large and seasonable supply of corn, collected in the inland provinces of Gaul, was embarked on the rapid stream of the Rhone, and transported by an easy navigation from the Rhone to the Tiber. During the whole term of the African war, the granaries of Rome were continually filled, her dignity was vindicated from the humiliating dependence, and the minds of an immense people were quieted by the calm confidence of peace and plenty.

Gildo was prepared to resist the invasion with all the forces of Africa. By the liberality of his gifts and promises, he endeavoured to secure the doubtful allegiance of the Roman soldiers, whilst he attracted to his standard the distant tribes of Gætulia and Æthiopia. He proudly reviewed an army of seventy thousand men, and boasted, with the rash presumption which is the forerunner of disgrace, that his numerous cavalry would trample under their horses' feet, in a cloud of burning sand, the natives of the cold regions of Gaul and Germany. But the Moor who commanded the legions of Honorius was too well acquainted with the manners of the countrymen to entertain any serious apprehension of a naked and disorderly host of barbarians, whose left arm, instead of a shield, was protected only by a mantle; who were totally disarmed as soon as they had darted their javelin from their right hand; and whose horses had never been taught to bear the control, or to obey the guidance, of the bridle. He fixed his camp of five thousand veterans in the face of a superior enemy, and obtained the honours of an easy and almost bloodless victory.

But the son of Theodosius passed the slumber of his life a captive in his palace, a stranger in his country, and the patient, almost the indifferent, spectator of the ruin of the Western empire, which was repeatedly attacked, and finally subverted, by the arms of the barbarians. In the eventful history of a reign of twenty-eight years, it will seldom be necessary to mention the name of the emperor Honorius.

The great Theodosius died in the month of January; and before the end of the winter of the same year, the Gothic nation was in arms. The barbarian auxiliaries erected their independent standard, and boldly avowed the hostile designs which they had long cherished in their ferocious minds. Their countrymen, who had been condemned by the conditions of the last treaty to a life of tranquillity and labour, deserted their farms at the first sound of the trumpet, and eagerly resumed the weapons which they had reluctantly laid down. The barriers of the Danube were thrown open; the savage warriors of Scythia issued from their forests; and the uncommon severity of the winter allowed the poet to remark "that they rolled their ponderous waggons over the broad and icy back of the indignant river." The unhappy natives of the provinces to the south of the Danube submitted to the calamities which, in the course of twenty years, were almost grown familiar to their imagination; and the various troops of barbarians who gloried in the Gothic name were irregularly spread from the woody shores of Dalmatia to the walls of Constantinople. The Goths, instead of being impelled by the blind and headstrong passions of their chiefs, were now directed by the bold and artful genius of Alaric.

Theodosius had tarnished the glory of his reign by the elevation of Rufinus, an odious favourite, who in an age of civil and religious faction has deserved, from every party, the imputation of every crime. The death of the emperor confirmed the absolute authority of Rufinus over the person and dominions of Arcadius, a feeble youth, whom the imperious præfect considered as his pupil, rather than his sovereign.

The character of the civil and military officers on whom Rufinus had devolved the government of Greece confirmed the public suspicion that he had betrayed the ancient seat of freedom and learning to the Gothic invader. Alaric traversed, without resistance, the plains of Macedonia and Thessaly, as far as the foot of Mount Oeta, a steep and woody range of hills, almost impervious to his cavalry. They stretched from east to west, to the edge of the sea-shore; and left, between the precipice and the Malian Gulf, an interval of three hundred feet, which in some places was contracted to a road capable of admitting only a single carriage. In this narrow pass of Thermopylæ, where Leonidas and the three hundred Spartans had gloriously devoted their lives, the Goths might have been stopped or destroyed by a skilful general; and perhaps the view of that sacred spot might have kindled some sparks of military ardour in the breasts of the degenerate Greeks. The troops which had been posted to defend the straits of Thermopylæ retired, as they were directed, without attempting to disturb the secure and rapid passage of Alaric; and the fertile fields of

Phocis and Bœotia were instantly covered by a deluge of barbarians, who massacred the males of an age to bear arms, and drove away the beautiful females with the spoil and cattle of the flaming villages.

The travellers who visited Greece several years afterwards could easily discover the deep and bloody traces of the march of the Goths; and Thebes was less indebted for her preservation to the strength of her seven gates than to the eager haste of Alaric, who advanced to occupy the city of Athens and the important harbour of the Piræus. The same impatience urged him to prevent the delay and danger of a siege, by the offer of a capitulation; and as soon as the Athenians heard the voice of the Gothic herald, they were easily persuaded to deliver the greatest part of their wealth, as the ransom of the city of Minerva and its inhabitants. The treaty was ratified by solemn oaths, and observed with mutual fidelity. The Gothic prince, with a small and select train, was admitted within the walls; he indulged himself in the refreshment of the bath, accepted a splendid banquet which was provided by the magistrate, and affected to show that he was not ignorant of the manners of civilised nations. But the whole territory of Attica, from the promontory of Sunium to the town of Megara, was blasted by his baleful presence. Corinth, Argos, Sparta, yielded without resistance to the arms of the Goths; and the most fortunate of the inhabitants were saved by death from beholding the slavery of their families and the conflagration of their cities. The vases and statues were distributed among the barbarians, with more regard to the value of the materials than to the elegance of the workmanship; the female captives submitted to the laws of war; the enjoyment of beauty was the reward of valour; and the Greeks could not reasonably complain of an abuse which was justified by the example of the heroic times.

From Thermopylæ to Sparta the leader of the Goths pursued his victorious march without encountering any mortal antagonists; but one of the advocates of expiring Paganism has confidently asserted that the walls of Athens were guarded by the goddess Minerva, with her formidable Ægis, and by the angry phantom of Achilles, and that the conqueror was dismayed by the presence of the hostile deities of Greece. In an age of miracles it would perhaps be unjust to dispute the claim of the historian Zosimus to the common benefit, yet it cannot be dissembled that the mind of Alaric was ill prepared to receive, either in sleeping or waking visions, the impressions of Greek superstition. The songs of Homer and the fame of Achilles had probably never reached the ear of the illiterate *barbarian;* and the *Christian* faith, which he had devoutly embraced, taught him to despise the imaginary deities of Rome and Athens. The invasion of the Goths, instead of vindicating the honours, contributed, at least accidentally, to extirpate the last remains of Paganism; and the mysteries of Ceres, which had subsisted eighteen hundred years, did not survive the destruction of Eleusis and the calamities of Greece.

The last hope of a people who could no longer depend on their arms, their gods, or their sovereign, was placed in the powerful assistance of the general of the West; and Stilicho, who had not been permitted to repulse, advanced to chastise the invaders of Greece. A numerous fleet was equipped in the ports of Italy; and the troops, after a short and prosperous navigation over the Ionian Sea, were safely disembarked on the isthmus near the ruins of Corinth. The woody and mountainous country of Arcadia, the fabulous residence of Pan and the Dryads, became the scene of a long and doubtful conflict between two generals not unworthy of each other. The skill and perseverance of the Roman at length prevailed; and the Goths, after sustaining a considerable loss from disease and desertion, gradually retreated to the lofty mountain of Pholoe, near the sources of the Peneus, and on the frontiers of Elis—a sacred country, which had formerly been exempted from the calamities of war. The camp of the barbarians was immediately besieged; the waters of the river were diverted into another channel; and while they laboured under the intolerable pressure of thirst and hunger, a strong line of circumvallation was formed to prevent their escape. After these precautions Stilicho, too confident of victory, retired to enjoy his triumph in the theatrical games and lascivious dances of the Greeks; his soldiers, deserting their standards, spread themselves over the country of their allies, which they stripped of all that had been saved from the rapacious hands of the enemy.

Alaric appears to have seized the favourable moment to execute one of those hardy enterprises in which the abilities of a general are displayed with more genuine lustre than in the tumult of a day of battle. To extricate himself from the prison of Peloponnesus it was necessary that he should pierce the entrenchments which surrounded his camp; that he should perform a difficult and dangerous march of thirty miles, as far as the Gulf of Corinth; and that he should transport his troops, his captives, and his spoil, over an arm of the sea, which, in the narrow interval between Rhium and the opposite shore, is at least half a mile in breadth. The operations of Alaric must have been secret, prudent, and rapid, since the Roman general was confounded by the intelligence that the Goths, who had eluded his efforts, were in full possession of the important province of Epirus. This unfortunate delay allowed Alaric sufficient time to conclude the treaty which he secretly negotiated with the ministers of Constantinople. The apprehension of a civil war compelled Stilicho to retire, at the haughty mandate of his rivals, from the dominions of Arcadius; and he respected, in the enemy of Rome, the honourable character of the ally and servant of the emperor of the East.

An edict was published at Constantinople which declared the promotion of Alaric to the rank of master-general of the Eastern Illyricum. The Roman provincials, and the allies who had respected the faith of treaties, were justly indignant that the ruin of Greece and Epirus should be so liberally rewarded. The Gothic conqueror was received as a lawful magistrate in the cities which he had so lately besieged. The fathers whose sons he had massacred, the husbands whose wives he had violated, were subject to his authority; and the success of his rebellion encouraged the ambition of every leader of the foreign mercenaries. The use to which Alaric applied his new command distinguishes the firm and judicious character of his policy. He issued his orders to the four magazines and manufactures of offensive and defensive arms, Margus, Ratiaria, Naissus, and Thessalonica, to provide his troops with an extraordinary supply of shields, helmets, swords, and spears; the unhappy provincials were compelled to forge the instruments of their own destruction; and the barbarians removed the only defect which had sometimes disappointed the efforts of their courage.

The birth of Alaric, the glory of his past exploits, and confidence in his future designs, insensibly united the body of the nation under his victorious standards; and, with the unanimous consent of the barbarian chieftains, the master-general of Illyricum was elevated, according to ancient custom, on a shield, and solemnly proclaimed king of the Visigoths. Armed with this double power, seated on the verge of the two empires, he alternately sold his deceitful promises to the courts of Arcadius and Honorius, till he declared and executed his resolution of invading the dominions of the West. The provinces of Europe which belonged to the Eastern emperor were already exhausted, those of Asia were inaccessible, and the strength of Constantinople had resisted his attack. But he was tempted by the fame, the beauty, the wealth of Italy, which he had twice visited; and he secretly aspired to plant the Gothic standard on the walls of Rome, and to enrich his army with the accumulated spoils of three hundred triumphs.

The scarcity of facts, and the uncertainty of dates, oppose our attempts to describe the circumstances of the first invasion of Italy by the arms of Alaric. His march, perhaps from Thessalonica through the warlike and hostile country of Pannonia as far as the foot of the Julian Alps; his passage of those mountains, which were strongly guarded by troops and entrenchments; the siege of Aquileia, and the conquest of the provinces of Istria and Venetia, appear to have employed a considerable time.

Since the public and important events escape the diligence of the historian, he may amuse himself with contemplating for a moment the influence of the arms of Alaric on the fortunes of an husbandman of Verona. The *old man* who had passed his simple and innocent life in the neighbourhood of Verona, was a stranger to the quarrels both of kings and of bishops; *his* pleasures, his desires, his knowledge, were confined within the little circle of his paternal farm; and a staff supported his aged steps on the same ground where he had sported in his infancy. Yet even this humble and rustic felicity (which Claudian describes with so much truth and feeling) was still exposed to the undistinguishing rage of war. His trees, his old *contemporary* trees,[1] must blaze in the conflagration of the whole country; a detachment of Gothic cavalry might sweep away his cottage and

[1]Cowley's imitation of Claudian has some natural and happy strokes:

> A neighbouring wood born with himself he sees,
> And loves his old contemporary trees.

his family; and the power of Alaric could destroy this happiness, which he was not able either to taste or to bestow. "Fame," says the poet, "encircling with terror her gloomy wings, proclaimed the march of the barbarian army, and filled Italy with consternation."

The emperor Honorius was distinguished above his subjects by the pre-eminence of fear as well as of rank. The pride and luxury in which he was educated had not allowed him to suspect that there existed on the earth any power presumptuous enough to invade the repose of the successor of Augustus. The arts of flattery concealed the impending danger till Alaric approached the palace of Milan. But when the sound of war had awakened the young emperor, instead of flying to arms with the spirit, or even the rashness, of his age, he eagerly listened to those timid counsellors who proposed to convey his sacred person and his faithful attendants to some secure and distant station in the provinces of Gaul.

Stilicho issued his orders to the most remote troops of the West, to advance, by rapid marches, to the defence of Honorius and of Italy. The fortresses of the Rhine were abandoned; and the safety of Gaul was protected only by the faith of the Germans, and the ancient terror of the Roman name. Even the legion which had been stationed to guard the wall of Britain against the Caledonians of the North was hastily recalled. The prudence and vigour of Stilicho were conspicuous on this occasion, which revealed, at the same time, the weakness of the falling empire. The legions of Rome, which had long since languished in the gradual decay of discipline and courage, were exterminated by the Gothic and civil wars; and it was found impossible without exhausting and exposing the provinces, to assemble an army for the defence of Italy.

The loose discipline of the barbarians always exposed them to the danger of a surprise; but, instead of choosing the dissolute hours of riot and intemperance, Stilicho resolved to attack the *Christian* Goths whilst they were devoutly employed in celebrating the festival of Easter. The execution of the stratagem, or, as it was termed by the clergy, of the sacrilege, was entrusted to Saul, a barbarian and a Pagan, who had served, however, with distinguished reputation among the veteran generals of Theodosius. The camp of the Goths was thrown into confusion by the sudden and impetuous charge of the Imperial cavalry; but, in a few moments, the undaunted genius of their leader gave them an order and a field of battle; and, soon as they had recovered from their astonishment, the pious confidence that the God of the Christians would assert their cause added new strength to their native valour.

In the evening of the bloody day, the Goths retreated from the field of battle; the entrenchments of their camp were forced, and the scene of rapine and slaughter made some atonement for the calamities which they had inflicted on the subjects of the empire.

The character of the Gothic king is, indeed, branded with the reproachful epithets of pirate and robber, to which the conquerors of every age are so justly entitled; but the poet of Stilicho is compelled to acknowledge that Alaric possessed the invincible temper of mind which rises superior to every misfortune, and derives new resources from adversity. After the total defeat of his infantry, he escaped, or rather withdrew from the field of battle, with the greatest part of his cavalry entire and unbroken.

The citizens of Rome had been astonished by the approach of Alaric; and the diligence with which they laboured to restore the walls of the capital confessed their own fears, and the decline of the empire. After the retreat of the barbarians, Honorius was directed to accept the dutiful invitation of the senate, and to celebrate, in the Imperial city, the auspicious era of the Gothic victory, and of his sixth consulship. The suburbs and the streets, from the Milvian Bridge to the Palatine Mount, were filled by the Roman people, who in the space of an hundred years had only thrice been honoured with the presence of their sovereigns. While their eyes were fixed on the chariot where Stilicho was deservedly seated by the side of his royal pupil, they applauded the pomp of a triumph which was not stained, like that of Constantine or of Theodosius, with civil blood. The procession passed under a lofty arch, which had been purposely erected: but in less than seven years, the Gothic conquerors of Rome might read, if they were able to read, the superb inscription of that monument, which attested the total defeat and destruction of their nation.

The people were repeatedly gratified by the attention and courtesy of Honorius in the public games, which were celebrated on that occasion with a magnificence not unworthy of the spectator. As soon as the appointed number of chariot-races was concluded, the decoration of the Circus was suddenly changed; the hunting of wild beasts afforded a various and splendid entertainment; and the chase was succeeded by a military dance, which seems, in the lively description of Claudian, to present the image of a modern tournament.

In these games of Honorius, the inhuman combats of gladiators polluted for the last time the amphitheatre of Rome. The first Christian emperor may claim the honour of the first edict which condemned the art and amusement of shedding human blood; but this benevolent law expressed the wishes of the prince, without reforming an inveterate abuse which degraded a civilised nation below the condition of savage cannibals. Several hundred, perhaps several thousand, victims were annually slaughtered in the great cities of the empire; and the month of December, more peculiarly devoted to the combats of gladiators, still exhibited to the eyes of the Roman people a grateful spectacle of blood and cruelty. Amidst the general joy a Christian poet exhorted the emperor to extirpate, by his authority, the horrid custom which had so long resisted the voice of humanity and religion. The pathetic representations of Prudentius were less effectual than the generous boldness of Telemachus, an Asiatic monk, whose death was more useful to mankind than his life. The Romans were provoked by the interruption of their pleasures; and the rash monk, who had descended into the arena to separate the gladiators, was overwhelmed under a shower of stones. But the madness of the people soon subsided: they respected the memory of Telemachus, who had deserved the honours of martyrdom; and they submitted, without a murmur, to the laws of Honorius which abolished for ever the human sacrifices of the amphitheatre.

While Italy rejoiced in her deliverance from the Goths, a furious tempest was excited among the nations of Germany, who yielded to the irresistible impulse that appears to have been gradually communicated from the eastern extremity of the continent of Asia. The Chinese annals, as they have been interpreted by the learned industry of the present age, may be usefully applied to reveal the secret and remote causes of the fall of the Roman empire. The extensive territory to the north of the great wall was possessed after the flight of the Huns by the victorious Sienpi; who were sometimes broken into independent tribes, and sometimes re-united under a supreme chief; till at length, styling themselves *Topa*, or masters of the earth, they acquired a more solid consistence and a more formidable power. The Topa soon compelled the pastoral nations of the eastern desert to acknowledge the superiority of their arms; they invaded China in a period of weakness and intestine discord; and these fortunate Tartars, adopting the laws and manners of the vanquished people, founded an Imperial dynasty, which reigned near one hundred and sixty years over the northern provinces of the monarchy.

The chain of events is interrupted, or rather is concealed, as it passes from the Volga to the Vistula, through the dark interval which separates the extreme limits of the Chinese and of the Roman geography. Yet the temper of the barbarians, and the experience of successive emigrations, sufficiently declare that the Huns soon withdrew from the presence of an insulting victor. The countries towards the Euxine were already occupied by their kindred tribes; and their hasty flight, which they soon converted into a bold attack, would more naturally be directed towards the rich and level plains through which the Vistula gently flows into the Baltic Sea. The North must again have been alarmed and agitated by the invasion of the Huns; and the nations who retreated before them must have pressed with incumbent weight on the confines of Germany.

The inhabitants of those regions which the ancients have assigned to the Suevi, the Vandals, and the Burgundians, might embrace the resolution of abandoning to the fugitives of Sarmatia their woods and morasses, or at least of discharging their superfluous numbers on the provinces of the Roman empire. About four years after the victorious Toulun had assumed the title of Khan, another barbarian, the haughty Rhodogast, or Radagaisus, marched from the northern extremities of Germany almost to the gates of Rome, and left the remains of his army to achieve the destruction of the West. The Vandals, the Suevi, and the Burgundians, formed the strength of this mighty host; but the Alani, who had found an hospitable reception in their new seats, added their active cavalry to the heavy infantry of the Germans; and the Gothic adventurers crowded so eagerly to the standard of Radagaisus, that, by some historians, he has been styled the King of the Goths. Twelve thousand warriors, distinguished above the vulgar by their noble birth or their valiant deeds, glittered in the van; and the whole multitude, which was not less than two hundred thousand fighting men, might be increased, by the accession of women, of children, and of slaves, to the amount of four hundred thousand persons. This formidable emigration issued from the same coast of the Baltic which had poured forth the myriads of the Cimbri and Teutones to assault Rome and Italy in the vigour of the republic.

The correspondence of nations was in that age so imperfect and precarious, that the revolutions of the North might escape the knowledge of the court of Ravenna, till the dark cloud which was collected along the coast of the Baltic burst in thunder upon the banks of the Upper Danube. The safety of Rome was entrusted to the counsels and the sword of Stilicho; but such was the feeble and exhausted state of the empire, that it was impossible to restore the fortifications of the Danube, or to prevent by a vigorous effort the invasion of the Germans. The hopes of the vigilant minister of Honorius were confined to the defence of Italy. He once more abandoned the provinces, recalled the troops, pressed the new levies, which were rigorously exacted and pusillanimously eluded; employed the most efficacious means to arrest or allure the deserters; and offered the gift of freedom and of two pieces of gold to all the slaves who would enlist. By these efforts he painfully collected from the subjects of a great empire an army of thirty or forty thousand men, which, in the days of Scipio or Camillus, would have been instantly furnished by the free citizens of the territory of Rome. The thirty legions of Stilicho were reinforced by a large body of barbarian auxiliaries; the faithful Alani were personally attached to his service; and the troops of Huns and of Goths, who marched under the banners of their native princes Huldin and Sarus, were animated by interest and resentment to oppose the ambition of Radagaisus.

The king of the confederate Germans passed without resistance the Alps, the Po, and the Apennine; leaving on one hand the inaccessible palace of Honorius securely buried among the marshes of Ravenna, and, on the other, the camp of Stilicho, who had fixed his head-quarters at Ticinum, or Pavia, but who seems to have avoided a decisive battle till he had assembled his distant forces. Many cities of Italy were pillaged or destroyed; and the siege of Florence by Radagaisus is one of the earliest events in the history of that celebrated republic, whose firmness checked and delayed the unskilful fury of the barbarians.

The senate and people trembled at their approach within an hundred and eighty miles of Rome, and anxiously compared the danger which they had escaped with the new perils to which they were exposed. Alaric was a Christian and a soldier, the leader of a disciplined army; who understood the laws of war, who respected the sanctity of treaties, and who had familiarly conversed with the subjects of the empire in the same camps and the same churches. The savage Radagaisus was a stranger to the manners, the religion, and even the language of the civilised nations of the South. The fierceness of his temper was exasperated by cruel superstition; and it was universally believed that he had bound himself by a solemn vow to reduce the city into a heap of stones and ashes, and to sacrifice the most illustrious of the Roman senators on the altars of those gods who were appeased by human blood.

The public danger, which should have reconciled all domestic animosities, displayed the incurable madness of religious faction. The oppressed votaries of Jupiter and Mercury respected, in the implacable enemy of Rome, the character of a devout Pagan; loudly declared that they were more apprehensive of the sacrifices than of the arms of Radagaisus; and secretly rejoiced in the calamities of their country, which condemned the faith of their Christian adversaries.[2]

Florence was reduced to the last extremity; and the fainting courage of the citizens was supported only by the authority of St. Ambrose, who had communicated in a dream the promise of a speedy deliverance. On a sudden they beheld from their walls the banners of Stilicho.

Conscious that he commanded the *last* army of the republic, Stilicho would not expose it in the open field to the headstrong fury of the Germans. The method of surrounding the enemy with strong lines of circumvallation, which he had twice employed against the Gothic king, was repeated on a larger scale and with more considerable effect. The examples of Cæsar must have been familiar to the most illiterate of the Roman warriors; and the fortifications of Dyrrachium, which connected twenty-four castles by a perpetual ditch and rampart of fifteen miles, afforded the model of an entrenchment which might confine and starve the most numerous host of barbarians. The Roman troops had less degenerated from the industry than from the valour of their ancestors; and if the servile and laborious work offended the pride of the soldiers, Tuscany could supply many thousand peasants who would labour, though perhaps they would not fight, for the salvation of their native country. The imprisoned multitude of horses and men was gradually destroyed by famine rather than by the sword.

The fame of the victory, and more especially of the miracle, has encouraged a vain persuasion that the whole army, or rather nation, of Germans who migrated from the shores of the Baltic miserably perished under the walls of Florence. Such indeed was the fate of Radagaisus himself, of his brave and faithful companions, and of more than one-third of the various multitude of Suevi and Vandals, of Alani and Burgundians, who adhered to the standard of their general.

After the defeat of Radagaisus, two parts of the German host, which must have exceeded the number of one hundred thousand men, still remained in arms between the Apennine and the Alps, or between the Alps and the Danube. It is uncertain whether they attempted to revenge the death of their general; but their irregular fury was soon diverted by the prudence and firmness of Stilicho, who opposed their march and facilitated their retreat, who considered the safety of Rome and Italy as the great object of his care,

[2]Yet the Jupiter of Radagaisus, who worshipped Thor and Woden, was very different from the Olympic or Capitoline Jove. The accommodating temper of Polytheism might unite those various and remote deities; but the genuine Romans abhorred the human sacrifices of Gaul and Germany.

and who sacrificed with too much indifference the wealth and tranquillity of the distant provinces. The barbarians acquired, from the junction of some Pannonian deserters, the knowledge of the country and of the roads, and the invasion of Gaul, which Alaric had designed, was executed by the remains of the great army of Radagaisus.

Yet if they expected to derive any assistance from the tribes of Germany who inhabited the banks of the Rhine, their hopes were disappointed. The Alemanni preserved a state of inactive neutrality, and the Franks distinguished their zeal and courage in the defence of the empire. When the limits of Gaul and Germany were shaken by the northern emigration, the Franks bravely encountered the single force of the Vandals, who, regardless of the lessons of adversity, had again separated their troops from the standard of their barbarian allies. They paid the penalty of their rashness; and twenty thousand Vandals, with their king Godigisclus, were slain in the field of battle. The whole people must have been extirpated if the squadrons of the Alani, advancing to their relief, had not trampled down the infantry of the Franks, who, after an honourable resistance, were compelled to relinquish the unequal contest. The victorious confederates pursued their march, and on the last day of the year, in a season when the waters of the Rhine were most probably frozen, they entered without opposition the defenceless provinces of Gaul.

This memorable passage of the Suevi, the Vandals, the Alani, and the Burgundians, who never afterwards retreated, may be considered as the fall of the Roman empire in the countries beyond the Alps; and the barriers which had so long separated the savage and the civilised nations of the earth were from that fatal moment levelled with the ground.

CHAPTER XXII

Invasion of Italy by Alaric—Rome Is Pillaged by the Goths

While the peace of Germany was secured by the attachment of the Franks and the neutrality of the Alemanni, the subjects of Rome, unconscious of their approaching calamities, enjoyed the state of quiet and prosperity which had seldom blessed the frontiers of Gaul. Their flocks and herds were permitted to graze in the pastures of the barbarians; their huntsmen penetrated, without fear or danger, into the darkest recesses of the Hercynian wood. The banks of the Rhine were crowned, like those of the Tiber, with elegant houses and well-cultivated farms; and if a poet descended the river, he might express his doubt on which side was situated the territory of the Romans. This scene of peace and plenty was suddenly changed into a desert; and the prospect of the smoking ruins could alone distinguish the solitude of nature from the desolation of man. The flourishing city of Mentz was surprised and destroyed, and many thousand Christians were inhumanly massacred in the church. Worms perished after a long and obstinate siege; Strasburg, Spires, Rheims, Tournay, Arras, Amiens, experienced the cruel oppression of the German yoke; and the consuming flames of war spread from the banks of the Rhine over the greatest part of the seventeen provinces of Gaul. That rich and extensive country, as far as the ocean, the Alps, and the Pyrenees, was delivered to the barbarians, who drove before them in a promiscuous crowd the bishop, the senator, and the virgin, laden with the spoils of their houses and altars.

Adversity had exercised and displayed the genius of Alaric; he had deserved the esteem, and he soon accepted the friendship, of Stilicho himself. Renouncing the service of the emperor of the East, Alaric concluded, with the court of Ravenna, a treaty of peace and alliance, by which he was declared master-general of the Roman armies throughout the præfecture of Illyricum; as it was claimed, according to the true and ancient limits, by the minister of Honorius. The execution of the ambitious design, which was either stipulated or implied in the articles of the treaty, appears to have been suspended by the formidable irruption of Radagaisus.

The political and secret transactions of two statesmen who laboured to deceive each other and the world must for ever have been concealed in the impenetrable darkness of the cabinet, if the debates of a popular assembly had not thrown some rays of light on the correspondence of Alaric and Stilicho. The necessity of finding some artificial support for a government which, from a principle, not of moderation, but of weakness, was reduced to negotiate with its own subjects, had insensibly revived the authority of the Roman senate: and the minister of Honorius respectfully consulted the legislative council of the republic. Stilicho assembled the senate in the palace of the Cæsars; represented, in a studied oration, the actual state of affairs; proposed the demands of the Gothic king; and submitted to their consideration the choice of peace or war.

The senators, as if they had been suddenly awakened from a dream of four hundred years, appeared on this important occasion to be inspired by the courage, rather than by the wisdom, of their predecessors. They loudly declared, in regular speeches or in tumultuary acclamations, that it was unworthy of the majesty of Rome to purchase a precarious and disgraceful truce from a barbarian king; and that, in the judgment of a magnanimous people, the chance of ruin was always preferable to the certainty of dishonour. The minister, whose pacific intentions were seconded only by the voices of a few servile and venal followers, attempted to allay the general ferment, by an apology for his own conduct, and even for the demands of the Gothic prince. "The payment of a subsidy, which had excited the indignation of the Romans, ought not (such was the language of Stilicho) to be considered in the odious light either of a tribute or of a ransom, extorted by the menaces of a barbarian enemy. Alaric had faithfully asserted the just pretensions of the republic to the provinces which were usurped by the Greeks of Constantinople: he modestly required the fair and stipulated recompense of his services; and if he had desisted from the prosecution of his enterprise, he had obeyed, in his retreat, the peremptory, though private, letters of the emperor himself. These contradictory orders (he would not dissemble the errors of his own family) had been procured by the intercession of Serena. The tender piety of his wife had been too deeply affected by the discord of the royal brothers, the sons of her adopted father; and the sentiments of nature had too easily prevailed over the stern dictates of the public welfare."

These ostensible reasons, which faintly disguise the obscure intrigues of the palace of Ravenna, were supported by the authority of Stilicho; and obtained, after a warm debate, the reluctant approbation of the senate. The tumult of virtue and freedom subsided; and the sum of four thousand pounds of gold was granted, under the name of a subsidy, to secure the peace of Italy, and to conciliate the friendship of the king of the Goths. Lampadius alone, one of the most illustrious members of the assembly, still persisted in his dissent; exclaimed with a loud voice, "This is not a treaty of peace, but of servitude"; and escaped the danger of such bold opposition by immediately retiring to the sanctuary of a Christian church.

But the reign of Stilicho drew towards its end; and the proud minister might perceive the symptoms of his approaching disgrace. The services of Stilicho are great and manifest; his crimes, as they are vaguely stated in the language of flattery and hatred, are at least obscure and improbable. About four months after his death an edict was published, in the name of Honorius, to restore the free communication of the two empires, which had been so long interrupted by the *public enemy*. The minister, whose fame and fortune depended on the prosperity of the state, was accused of betraying Italy to the barbarians whom he repeatedly vanquished at Pollentia, at Verona, and before the walls of Florence.

The incapacity of a weak and distracted government may often assume the appearance and produce the effects of a treasonable correspondence with the public enemy. If Alaric himself had been introduced into the council of Ravenna, he would probably have advised the same measures which were actually pursued by the ministers of Honorius. The king of the Goths would have conspired, perhaps with some reluctance, to destroy the formidable adversary by whose arms, in Italy as well as in Greece, he had been twice overthrown. *Their* active and interested hatred laboriously accomplished the disgrace and ruin of the great Stilicho.

The Gothic prince would have subscribed with pleasure the edict which the fanaticism of Olympius dictated to the simple and devout emperor. Honorious excluded all persons who were adverse to the Catholic church from holding any office in the state; obstinately rejected the service of all those who dissented from his religion; and rashly disqualified many of his bravest and most skilful officers who adhered to the Pagan worship or who had imbibed the opinions of Arianism. These measures, so advantageous to an enemy, Alaric would have approved, and might perhaps have suggested; but it may seem doubtful whether the barbarian would have promoted his interest at the expense of the inhuman and absurd cruelty which was perpetrated by the direction, or at least with the connivance, of the Imperial ministers. The foreign auxiliaries who had been attached to the person of Stilicho lamented his death; but the desire of revenge was checked by a natural apprehension for the safety of their wives and children, who were detained as hostages in the strong cities of Italy, where they had likewise deposited their most valuable effects. At the same hour, and as if by a common signal, the cities of Italy were polluted by the same horrid scenes of universal massacre and pillage, which involved in promiscuous destruction the families and fortunes of the barbarians.

Exasperated by such an injury, which might have awakened the tamest and most servile spirit, they cast a look of indignation and hope towards the camp of Alaric, and unanimously swore to pursue with just and implacable war the perfidious nation that had so basely violated the laws of hospitality. By the imprudent conduct of the ministers of Honorius the republic lost the assistance, and deserved the enmity, of thirty thousand of her bravest soldiers; and the weight of that formidable army, which alone might have determined the event of the war, was transferred from the scale of the Romans into that of the Goths.

In the arts of negotiation, as well as in those of war, the Gothic king maintained his superior ascendant over an enemy whose seeming changes proceeded from the total want of counsel and design. From his camp on the confines of Italy Alaric attentively observed the revolutions of the palace, watched the progress of faction and discontent, disguised the hostile aspect of a barbarian invader, and assumed the more popular appearance of the friend and ally of the great Stilicho; to whose virtues, when they were no longer formidable, he could pay a just tribute of sincere praise and regret. The pressing invitation of the malcontents, who urged the king of the Goths to invade Italy, was enforced by a lively sense of his personal injuries; and he might speciously complain that the Imperial ministers still delayed and eluded the payment of the four thousand pounds of gold which had been granted by the Roman senate either to reward his services or to appease his fury. His decent firmness was supported by an artful moderation, which contributed to the success of his designs. He required a fair and reasonable satisfaction; but he gave the strongest assurances that, as soon as he had obtained it, he would immediately retire. He refused to trust the faith of the Romans, unless Aëtius and Jason, the sons of two great officers of state, were sent as hostages to his camp: but he offered to deliver in exchange several of the noblest youths of the Gothic nation.

The modesty of Alaric was interpreted by the ministers of Ravenna as a sure evidence of his weakness and fear. They disdained either to negotiate a treaty or to assemble an army; and with a rash confidence, derived only from their ignorance of the extreme danger, irretrievably wasted the decisive moments of peace and war. While they expected, in sullen silence, that the barbarians should evacuate the confines of Italy, Alaric, with bold and rapid marches, passed the Alps and the Po; hastily pillaged the cities of Aquileia, Altinum, Concordia, and Cremona, which yielded to his arms; increased his forces by the accession of thirty thousand auxiliaries; and, without meeting a single enemy in the field, advanced as far as the edge of the morass which protected the impregnable residence of the emperor of the West.

Instead of attempting the hopeless siege of Ravenna, the prudent leader of the Goths proceeded to Rimini, stretched his ravages along the sea-coast of the Hadriatic, and meditated the conquest of the ancient mistress of the world. An Italian hermit, whose zeal and sanctity were respected by the barbarians themselves, encountered the victorious monarch, and boldly denounced the indignation of Heaven against the oppressors of the earth: but the saint himself was confounded by the solemn asseveration of Alaric that he felt a secret and præternatural impulse, which directed, and even compelled, his march to the gates of Rome.

He felt that his genius and his fortune were equal to the most arduous enterprises; and the enthusiasm which he communicated to the Goths insensibly removed the popular and almost superstitious reverence of the nations for the majesty of the Roman name. His troops, animated by the hopes of spoil, followed the course of the Flaminian way, occupied the unguarded passes of the Apennine, descended into the rich plains of Umbria; and, as they lay encamped on the banks of the Clitumnus, might wantonly slaughter and devour the milk-white oxen which had been so long reserved for the use of Roman triumphs. A lofty situation and a seasonable tempest of thunder and lightning preserved the little city of Narni: but the king of the

Goths, despising the ignoble prey, still advanced with unabated vigour; and after he had passed through the stately arches, adorned with the spoils of barbaric victories, he pitched his camp under the walls of Rome.

During a period of six hundred and nineteen years the seat of empire had never been violated by the presence of a foreign enemy. From the time of the Punic war the uninterrupted succession of senators had preserved the name and image of the republic; and the degenerate subjects of Honorius ambitiously derived their descent from the heroes who had repulsed the arms of Hannibal and subdued the nations of the earth. The vanity of the rich, who desired to be noble, was gratified by these lofty pretensions. Encouraged by the applause of their parasites, they easily imposed on the credulity of the vulgar; and were countenanced in some measure by the custom of adopting the name of their patron, which had always prevailed among the freedmen and clients of illustrious families.

Most of those families, however, attacked by so many causes of external violence or internal decay, were gradually extirpated: and it would be more reasonable to seek for a lineal descent of twenty generations among the mountains of the Alps or in the peaceful solitude of Apulia, than on the theatre of Rome, the seat of fortune, of danger, and of perpetual revolutions. Under each successive reign and from every province of the empire a crowd of hardy adventurers, rising to eminence by their talents or their vices, usurped the wealth, the honours, and the palaces of Rome; and oppressed or protected the poor and humble remains of consular families, who were ignorant, perhaps, of the glory of their ancestors.

From the reign of Diocletian to the final extinction of the Western empire the Anician name shone with a lustre which was not eclipsed in the public estimation by the majesty of the Imperial purple. The several branches to whom it was communicated united, by marriage or inheritance, the wealth and titles of the Annian, the Petronian, and the Olybrian houses; and in each generation the number of consulships was multiplied by an hereditary claim. The Anician family excelled in faith and in riches: they were the first of the Roman senate who embraced Christianity. Their ample patrimony was increased by the industry of Probus, the chief of the Anician family, who shared with Gratian the honours of the consulship, and exercised four times the high office of Prætorian præfect. His immense estates were scattered over the wide extent of the Roman world; and though the public might suspect or disapprove the methods by which they had been acquired, the generosity and magnificence of that fortunate statesman deserved the gratitude of his clients and the admiration of strangers.

"The marbles of the Anician palace," were used as a proverbial expression of opulence and splendour; but the nobles and senators of Rome aspired in due gradation to imitate that illustrious family. The accurate description of the city, which was composed in the Theodosian age, enumerates one thousand seven hundred and eighty *houses*, the residence of wealthy and honourable citizens. Many of these stately mansions might almost excuse the exaggeration of the poet—that Rome contained a multitude of palaces, and that each palace was equal to a city, since it included within its own precincts everything which could be subservient either to use or luxury: markets, hippodromes, temples, fountains, baths, porticos, shady groves, and artificial aviaries.

The historian Olympiodorus, who represents the state of Rome when it was besieged by the Goths, continues to observe that several of the richest senators received from their estates an annual income of four thousand pounds of gold, above one hundred and sixty thousand pounds sterling; without computing the stated provision of corn and wine, which, had they been sold, might have equalled in value one-third of the money. Compared to this immoderate wealth, an ordinary revenue of a thousand or fifteen hundred pounds of gold might be considered as no more than adequate to the dignity of the senatorian rank, which required many expenses of a public and ostentatious kind. Several examples are recorded in the age of Honorius of vain and popular nobles who celebrated the year of their prætorship by a festival which lasted seven days and cost above one hundred thousand pounds sterling.

The estates of the Roman senators, which so far exceed the proportion of modern wealth, were not confined to the limits of Italy. Their possessions extended far beyond the Ionian and Ægean seas to the most distant provinces: the city of Nicopolis, which Augustus had founded as an eternal monument of the Actian victory, was the property of the devout Paula; and it is observed by Seneca, that the rivers which had divided hostile nations now flowed through the lands of private citizens.

According to their temper and circumstances, the estates of the Romans were either cultivated by the labour of their slaves, or granted, for a certain and stipulated rent, to the industrious farmer. The economical writers of antiquity strenuously recommend the former method wherever it may be practicable; but if the object should be removed by its distance or magnitude from the immediate eye of the master, they prefer the active care of an old hereditary tenant, attached to the soil and interested in the produce, to the mercenary administration of a negligent, perhaps an unfaithful, steward.

The opulent nobles of an immense capital, who were never excited by the pursuit of military glory, and seldom engaged in the occupations of civil government, naturally resigned their leisure to the business and amusements of private life. At Rome commerce was always held in contempt; but the senators, from the first age of the republic, increased their patrimony and multiplied their clients by the lucrative practice of usury, and the obsolete laws were eluded or violated by the mutual inclinations and interest of both parties. A considerable mass of treasure must always have existed at Rome, either in the current coin of the empire, or in the form of gold and silver plate; and there were many sideboards in the time of Pliny which contained more solid silver than had been transported by Scipio from vanquished Carthage.

The greater part of the nobles, who dissipated their fortunes in profuse luxury, found themselves poor in the midst of wealth, and idle in a constant round of dissipation. Their desires were continually gratified by the labour of a thousand hands; of the numerous train of their domestic slaves, who were actuated by the fear of punishment; and of the various professions of artificers and merchants, who were more powerfully impelled by the hopes of gain. The ancients were destitute of many of the conveniences of life which have been invented or improved by the progress of industry; and the plenty of glass and linen has diffused more real comforts among the modern nations of Europe than the senators of Rome could derive from all the refinements of pompous or sensual luxury.

Their luxury and their manners have been the subject of minute and laborious disquisition; but as such inquiries would divert me too long from the design of the present work, I shall produce an authentic state of Rome and its inhabitants which is more peculiarly applicable to the period of the Gothic invasion. Ammianus Marcellinus, who prudently chose the capital of the empire as the residence the best adapted to the historian of his own times, has mixed with the narrative of public events a lively representation of the scenes with which he was familiarly conversant. The judicious reader will not always approve the asperity of censure, the choice of circumstances, or the style of expression; he will perhaps detect the latent prejudices and personal resentments which soured the temper of Ammianus himself; but he will surely observe, with philosophic curiosity, the interesting and original picture of the manners of Rome.

"The greatness of Rome (such is the language of the historian) was founded on the rare and almost incredible alliance of virtue and of fortune. The long period of her infancy was employed in a laborious struggle against the tribes of Italy, the neighbours and enemies of the rising city. In the strength and ardour of youth she sustained the storms of war, carried her victorious arms beyond the seas and the mountains, and brought home triumphal laurels from every country of the globe. At length, verging towards old age, and sometimes conquering by the terror only of her name, she sought the blessings of ease and tranquillity. The VENERABLE CITY, which had trampled on the necks of the fiercest nations, and established a system of laws, the perpetual guardians of justice and freedom, was content, like a wise and wealthy parent, to devolve on the Cæsars, her favourite sons, the care of governing her ample patrimony. A secure and profound peace, such as had been once enjoyed in the reign of Numa, succeeded to the tumults of a republic; while Rome was still adored as the queen of the earth, and the subject nations still reverenced the name of the people and the majesty of the senate.

"But this native splendour (continues Ammianus) is degraded and sullied by the conduct of some nobles, who, unmindful of their own dignity and of that of their country, assume an unbounded licence of vice and folly. They contend with each other in the empty vanity of titles and surnames, and curiously select or invent the most lofty and sonorous appellations—Reburrus or Fabunius, Pagonius or Tarrasius—which may impress the ears of the vulgar with astonishment and respect. From a vain ambition of perpetuating their memory, they affect to multiply their likeness in statues of bronze and marble; nor are they satisfied unless those statues are covered with plates of gold; an honourable distinction, first granted to Acilius the consul, after he had subdued by his arms and counsels the power of king Antiochus.

"The ostentation of displaying, of magnifying perhaps, the rent-roll of the estates which they possess in all the provinces, from the rising to the setting sun, provokes the just resentment of every man who recollects that their poor and invincible ancestors were not distinguished from the meanest of the soldiers by the delicacy of their food or the splendour of their apparel. But the modern nobles measure their rank and consequence according to the loftiness of their chariots, and the weighty magnificence of their dress. Their long robes of silk and purple float in the wind; and as they are agitated, by art or accident, they occasionally discover the under garments, the rich tunics, embroidered with the figures of various animals. Followed by a train of fifty servants, and tearing up the pavement, they move along the streets with the same impetuous speed as if they travelled with post-horses; and the example of the senators is boldly imitated by the matrons and ladies, whose covered carriages are continually driving round the immense space of the city and suburbs.

"Whenever these persons of high distinction condescend to visit the public baths, they assume, on their entrance, a tone of loud and insolent command, and appropriate to their own use the conveniences which were designed for the Roman people. If, in these places of mixed and general resort, they meet any of the infamous ministers of their pleasures, they express their affection by a tender embrace, while they proudly decline the salutations of their fellow-citizens, who are not permitted to aspire above the honour of kissing their hands or their knees. As soon as they have indulged themselves in the refreshment of the bath, they resume their rings and the other ensigns of their dignity, select from their private wardrobe of the finest linen, such as might suffice for a dozen persons, the garments the most agreeable to their fancy, and maintain till their departure the same haughty demeanour, which perhaps might have been excused in the great Marcellus after the conquest of Syracuse.

"Sometimes indeed these heroes undertake more arduous achievements: they visit their estates in Italy, and procure themselves, by the toil of servile hands, the amusements of the chase. If at any time, but more especially on a hot day, they have courage to sail in their painted galleys from the Lucrine lake to their elegant villas on the sea-coast of Puteoli and Caieta, they compare their own expeditions to the marches of Cæsar and Alexander. Yet should a fly presume to settle on the silken folds of their gilded umbrellas, should a sunbeam penetrate through some unguarded and imperceptible chink, they deplore their intolerable hardships, and lament in affected language that they were not born in the land of the Cimmerians, the regions of eternal darkness.

"In these journeys into the country the whole body of the household marches with their master. In the same manner as the cavalry and infantry, the heavy and the light armed troops, the advanced guard and the rear, are marshalled by the skill of their military leaders, so the domestic officers, who bear a rod as an ensign of authority, distribute and arrange the numerous train of slaves and attendants. The baggage and wardrobe move in the front, and are immediately followed by a multitude of cooks and inferior ministers employed in the service of the kitchens and of the table. The main body is composed of a promiscuous crowd of slaves, increased by the accidental concourse of idle or dependent plebeians. The rear is closed by the favourite band of eunuchs, distributed from age to youth, according to the order of seniority. Their numbers and their deformity excite the horror of the indignant spectators, who are ready to execrate the memory of Semiramis for the cruel art which she invented of frustrating the purposes of nature, and of blasting in the bud the hopes of future generations.

"In the exercise of domestic jurisdiction the nobles of Rome express an exquisite sensibility for any personal injury, and a contemptuous indifference for the rest of the human species. When they have called for warm water, if a slave has been tardy in his obedience, he is instantly chastised with three hundred lashes; should the same slave commit a wilful murder, the master will mildly observe that he is a worthless fellow, but that if he repeats the offence he shall not escape punishment.

"Hospitality was formerly the virtue of the Romans; and every stranger who could plead either merit or misfortune was relieved or rewarded by their generosity. At present, if a foreigner, perhaps of no contemptible rank, is introduced to one of the proud and wealthy senators, he is welcomed indeed in the first audience with such warm professions and such kind inquiries, that he retires enchanted with the affability of his illustrious friend, and full of regret that he had so long delayed his journey to Rome, the native seat of manners as well as of empire. Secure of a favorable reception, he repeats his visit the ensuing day, and is mortified by the discovery that his person, his name, and his country are already forgotten. If he still has resolution to persevere, he is gradually numbered in the train of dependents, and obtains the permission to pay his assiduous and unprofitable court to a haughty patron, incapable of gratitude or friendship, who scarcely deigns to remark his presence, his departure, or his return.

"Whenever the rich prepare a solemn and popular entertainment, whenever they celebrate with profuse and pernicious luxury their private banquets, the choice of the guests is the subject of anxious deliberation. The modest, the sober, and the learned are seldom preferred; and the nomenclators, who are commonly swayed by interested motives, have the address to insert in the list of invitations the obscure names of the most worthless of mankind. But the frequent and familiar companions of the great are those parasites who practise the most useful of all arts, the art of flattery; who eagerly applaud each word and every action of their immortal patron; gaze with rapture on his marble columns and variegated pavements, and strenuously praise the pomp and elegance which he is taught to consider as a part of his personal merit. At the Roman tables the birds, the *squirrels*, or the fish, which appear of an uncommon size, are contemplated with curious attention; a pair of scales is accurately applied to ascertain their real weight; and, while the more rational guests are disgusted by the vain and tedious repetition, notaries are summoned to attest by an authentic record the truth of such a marvellous event.

"Another method of introduction into the houses and society of the great is derived from the profession of gaming, or, as it is more politely styled, of play. The confederates are united by a strict and indissoluble bond of friendship, or rather of conspiracy; a superior degree of skill in the *Tesserarian* art (which may be interpreted the game of dice and tables) is a sure road to wealth and reputation. A master of that sublime science, who in a supper or assembly is placed below a magistrate, displays in his countenance the surprise and indignation which Cato might be supposed to feel when he was refused the prætorship by the votes of a capricious people.

"The acquisition of knowledge seldom engages the curiosity of the nobles, who abhor the fatigue and disdain the advantages of study; and the only books which they peruse are the Satires of Juvenal, and the verbose and fabulous histories of Marius Maximus. The libraries which they have inherited from their fathers are secluded, like dreary sepulchres, from the light of day. But the costly instruments of the theatre, flutes, and enormous lyres, and hydraulic organs, are constructed for their use; and the harmony of vocal and instrumental music is incessantly repeated in the palaces of Rome. In those palaces sound is preferred to sense, and the care of the body to that of the mind.

"It is allowed as a salutary maxim, that the light and frivolous suspicion of a contagious malady is of sufficient weight to excuse the visits of the most intimate friends; and even the servants who are despatched to make the decent inquiries are not suffered to return home till they have undergone the ceremony of a previous ablution. Yet this selfish and unmanly delicacy occasionally yields to the more imperious passion of avarice. The prospect of gain will urge a rich and gouty senator as far as Spoleto; every sentiment of arrogance and dignity is subdued by the hopes of an inheritance, or even of a legacy; and a wealthy childless citizen is the most powerful of the Romans. The art of obtaining the signature of a favourable testament, and sometimes of hastening the moment of its execution, is perfectly understood; and it has happened that in the same house, though in different apartments, a husband and a wife, with the laudable design of overreaching each other, have summoned their respective lawyers, to declare at the same time their mutual but contradictory intentions.

"The distress which follows and chastises extravagant luxury often reduces the great to the use of the most humiliating expedients. When they desire to borrow, they employ the base and supplicating style of the slave in the comedy; but when they are called upon to pay, they assume the royal and tragic declamation of the grandsons of Hercules. If the demand is repeated, they readily procure some trusty sycophant, instructed to maintain a charge of poison, or magic, against the insolent creditor, who is seldom released from prison till he has signed a discharge of the whole debt. These vices, which degrade the moral character of the Romans, are mixed with a puerile superstition that disgraces their understanding. They listen with confidence to the predictions of haruspices, who pretend to read in the entrails of victims the signs of future greatness and prosperity; and there are many who do not presume either to bathe or to die, or to appear in public, till they have diligently consulted, according to the rules of astrology, the situation of Mercury and the aspect of the moon. It is singular enough that this vain credulity may often be discovered among the profane sceptics who impiously doubt or deny the existence of a celestial power."

In populous cities, which are the seat of commerce and manufactures, the middle ranks of inhabitants, who derive their subsistence from the dexterity or labour of their hands, are commonly the most prolific, the most useful, and, in that sense, the most respectable part of the community. But the plebeians of Rome, who disdained such sedentary and servile arts, had been oppressed from the earliest times by the weight of debt and usury; and the husbandman, during the term of his military service, was obliged to abandon the cultivation of his farm. The lands of Italy, which had been originally divided among the families of free and indigent proprietors, were insensibly purchased or usurped by the avarice of the nobles; and in the age which preceded the fall of the republic, it was computed that only two thousand citizens were possessed of any independent substance.

As long as the people bestowed by their suffrages the honours of the state, the command of the legions, and the administration of wealthy provinces, their conscious pride alleviated in some measure the hardships of poverty; and their wants were seasonably supplied by the ambitious liberality of the candidates, who aspired to secure a venal majority in the thirty-five tribes, or the hundred and ninety-three centuries, of Rome. But when the prodigal commons had imprudently alienated not only the *use*, but the *inheritance*, of power, they sank, under the reign of the Cæsars, into a vile and wretched populace, which must, in a few generations, have been totally extinguished, if it had not been continually recruited by the manumission of slaves and the influx of strangers.

As early as the time of Hadrian it was the just complaint of the ingenuous natives that the capital had attracted the vices of the universe and the manners of the most opposite nations. The intemperance of the Gauls, the cunning and levity of the Greeks, the savage obstinacy of the Egyptians and Jews, the servile temper of the Asiatics, and the dissolute, effeminate prostitution of the Syrians, were mingled in the various multitude which, under the proud and false denomination of Romans, presumed to despise their fellow-subjects, and even their sovereigns, who dwelt beyond the precincts of the ETERNAL CITY.[1]

[1]Seneca, when he proposes to comfort his mother (Consolat. ad Helv. c. 6) by the reflection that a great part of mankind were in a state of exile, reminds her how few of the inhabitants of Rome were born in the city.

Yet the name of that city was still pronounced with respect: the frequent and capricious tumults of its inhabitants were indulged with impunity; and the successors of Constantine, instead of crushing the last remains of the democracy by the strong arm of military power, embraced the mild policy of Augustus, and studied to relieve the poverty and to amuse the idleness of an innumerable people.

I. For the convenience of the lazy plebeians, the monthly distributions of corn were converted into a daily allowance of bread; a great number of ovens were constructed and maintained at the public expense; and at the appointed hour, each citizen, who was furnished with a ticket, ascended the flight of steps which had been assigned to his peculiar quarter or division, and received, either as a gift or at a very low price, a loaf of bread of the weight of three pounds for the use of his family.

II. The forests of Lucania, whose acorns fattened large droves of wild hogs, afforded, as a species of tribute, a plentiful supply of cheap and wholesome meat. During five months of the year a regular allowance of bacon was distributed to the poorer citizens; and the annual consumption of the capital, at a time when it was much declined from its former lustre, was ascertained, by an edict of Valentinian the Third, at three millions six hundred and twenty-eight thousand pounds.

III. In the manners of antiquity the use of oil was indispensable for the lamp as well as for the bath, and the annual tax which was imposed on Africa for the benefit of Rome amounted to the weight of three millions of pounds, to the measure, perhaps, of three hundred thousand English gallons.

IV. The anxiety of Augustus to provide the metropolis with sufficient plenty of corn was not extended beyond that necessary article of human subsistence; and when the popular clamour accused the dearness and scarcity of wine, a proclamation was issued by the grave reformer to remind his subjects that no man could reasonably complain of thirst, since the aqueducts of Agrippa had introduced into the city so many copious streams of pure and salubrious water. This rigid sobriety was insensibly relaxed; and the use of wine was allowed on very easy and liberal terms. The administration of the public cellars was delegated to a magistrate of honourable rank; and a considerable part of the vintage of Campania was reserved for the fortunate inhabitants of Rome.

The stupendous aqueducts, so justly celebrated by the praises of Augustus himself, replenished the *Thermæ*, or baths, which had been constructed in every part of the city with Imperial magnificence. The baths of Antoninus Caracalla, which were open, at stated hours, for the indiscriminate service of the senators and the people, contained above sixteen hundred seats of marble; and more than three thousand were reckoned in the baths of Diocletian. The walls of the lofty apartments were covered with curious mosaics, that imitated the art of the pencil in the elegance of design and the variety of colours. The Egyptian granite was beautifully encrusted with the precious green marble of Numidia; the perpetual stream of hot water was poured into the capacious basins through so many wide mouths of bright and massy silver; and the meanest Roman could purchase, with a small copper coin, the daily enjoyment of a scene of pomp and luxury which might excite the envy of the kings of Asia. From these stately palaces issued a swarm of dirty and ragged plebeians, without shoes and without a mantle; who loitered away whole days in the street or Forum to hear news and to hold disputes; who dissipated in extravagant gaming the miserable pittance of their wives and children; and spent the hours of the night in obscure taverns and brothels in the indulgence of gross and vulgar sensuality.

But the most lively and splendid amusement of the idle multitude depended on the frequent exhibition of public games and spectacles. The piety of Christian princes had suppressed the inhuman combats of gladiators; but the Roman people still considered the Circus as their home, their temple, and the seat of the republic. The impatient crowd rushed at the dawn of day to secure their places, and there were many who passed a sleepless and anxious night in the adjacent porticos. From the morning to the evening, careless of the sun or of the rain, the spectators, who sometimes amounted to the number of four hundred thousand, remained in eager attention; their eyes fixed on the horses and charioteers, their minds agitated with hope and fear for the success of the *colours* which they espoused; and the happiness of Rome appeared to hang on the event of a race. The same immoderate ardour inspired their clamours and their applause as often as they were entertained with the hunting of wild beasts and the various modes of theatrical representation. The vast and magnificent theatres of Rome were filled by three thousand female dancers, and by three thousand singers, with the masters of the respective choruses. Such was the popular favour which they enjoyed, that, in a time of scarcity, when all strangers were banished from the city, the merit of contributing to the public pleasures exempted *them* from a law which was strictly executed against the professors of the liberal arts.

It is said that the foolish curiosity of Elagabalus attempted to discover, from the quantity of spiders' webs, the number of the inhabitants of Rome. The most diligent researches have collected only the following circumstances to illustrate the question of the populousness of ancient Rome:

I. When the capital of the empire was besieged by the Goths, the circuit of the walls was accurately measured by Ammonius, the mathematician, who found it equal to twenty-one miles. It should not be forgotten that the form of the city was almost that of a circle, the geometrical figure which is known to contain the largest space within any given circumference.

II. The architect Vitruvius, who flourished in the Augustan age, and whose evidence, on this occasion, has peculiar weight and authority, observes that the innumerable habitations of the Roman people would have spread themselves far beyond the narrow limits of the city; and that the want of ground, which was probably contracted on every side by gardens and villas, suggested the common, though inconvenient, practice of raising the houses to a considerable height in the air. But the loftiness of these buildings, which often consisted of hasty work and insufficient materials, was the cause of frequent and fatal accidents; and it was repeatedly enacted by Augustus, as well as by Nero, that the height of private edifices within the walls of Rome should not exceed the measure of seventy feet from the ground.

III. Juvenal laments, as it should seem from his own experience, the hardships of the poorer citizens, to whom he addresses the salutary advice of emigrating, without delay, from the smoke of Rome, since they might purchase in the little towns of Italy a cheerful, commodious dwelling at the same price which they annually paid for a dark and miserable lodging. House-rent was therefore immoderately dear: the rich acquired, at an enormous expense, the ground, which they covered with palaces and gardens; but the body of the Roman people was crowded into a narrow space; and the different floors and apartments of the same house were divided, as it is still the custom of Paris and other cities, among several families of plebeians.

IV. The total number of houses in the fourteen regions of the city is accurately stated in the description of Rome composed under the reign of Theodosius, and they amount to forty-eight thousand three hundred and eighty-two. The two classes of *domus* and of *insulæ,* into which they are divided, include all the habitations of the capital, of every rank and condition, from the marble palace of the Anicii, with a numerous establishment of freedmen and slaves, to the lofty and narrow lodging-house where the poet Codrus and his wife were permitted to hire a wretched garret immediately under the tiles. If we adopt the same average which, under similar circumstances, has been found applicable to Paris, and indifferently allow about twenty-five persons for each house, of every degree, we may fairly estimate the inhabitants of Rome at twelve hundred thousand: a number which cannot be thought excessive for the capital of a mighty empire, though it exceeds the populousness of the greatest cities of modern Europe.

Such was the state of Rome under the reign of Honorius, at the time when the Gothic army formed the siege, or rather the blockade, of the city. By a skilful disposition of his numerous forces, who impatiently watched the moment of an assault, Alaric encompassed the walls, commanded the twelve principal gates, intercepted all communication with the adjacent country, and vigilantly guarded the navigation of the Tiber, from which the Romans derived the surest and most plentiful supply of provisions.

The first emotions of the nobles and of the people were those of surprise and indignation, that a vile barbarian should dare to insult the capital of the world. That unfortunate city gradually experienced the distress of scarcity, and at length the horrid calamities of famine. The daily allowance of three pounds of bread was reduced to one-half, to one-third, to nothing; and the price of corn still continued to rise in a rapid and extravagant proportion. The poorer citizens, who were unable to purchase the necessaries of life, solicited the precarious charity of the rich; and for a while the public misery was alleviated by the humanity of Læta, the widow of the emperor Gratian, who had fixed her residence at Rome, and consecrated to the use of the indigent the princely revenue which she annually received from the grateful successors of her husband.

But these private and temporary donatives were insufficient to appease the hunger of a numerous people; and the progress of famine invaded the marble palaces of the senators themselves. The persons of both sexes, who had been educated in the enjoyment of ease and luxury, discovered how little is requisite to supply the demands of nature; and lavished their unavailing treasures of gold and silver to obtain the coarse and scanty sustenance which they would formerly have rejected with disdain. The food the most repugnant to sense or imagination, the aliments the most unwholesome and pernicious to the constitution, were eagerly devoured, and fiercely disputed, by the rage of hunger.

A dark suspicion was entertained that some desperate wretches fed on the bodies of their fellow-creatures whom they had secretly murdered; and even mothers (such was the horrid conflict of the two most powerful instincts implanted by nature in the human breast), even mothers are said to have tasted the flesh of their slaughtered infants! Many thousands of the inhabitants of Rome expired in their houses, or in the streets, for want of sustenance; and as the public sepulchres without the walls were in the power of the enemy, the stench which arose from so many putrid and unburied carcasses infected the air; and the miseries of famine were succeeded and aggravated by the contagion of a pestilential disease.

The assurances of speedy and effectual relief, which were repeatedly transmitted from the court of Ravenna, supported for some time the fainting resolution of the Romans; at length the despair of any human aid tempted them to accept the offers of a præternatural deliverance. Pompeianus, præfect of the city, had been persuaded, by the art or fanaticism of some Tuscan diviners, that, by the mysterious force of spells and sacrifices, they could extract the lightning from the clouds, and point those celestial fires against the camp of the barbarians. The important secret was communicated to Innocent, the bishop of Rome; and the successor of St. Peter is accused, perhaps without foundation, of preferring the safety of the republic to the rigid severity of the Christian worship. But when the question was agitated in the senate, when it was proposed as an essential condition that those sacrifices should be performed in the Capitol, by the authority and in the presence of the magistrates, the majority of that respectable assembly, apprehensive either of the Divine or of the Imperial displeasure, refused to join in an act which appeared almost equivalent to the public restoration of Paganism.

The last resource of the Romans was in the clemency, or at least in the moderation, of the king of the Goths. The senate, who in this emergency assumed the supreme powers of government, appointed two ambassadors to negotiate with the enemy. This important trust was delegated to Basilius, a senator of Spanish extraction, and already conspicuous in the administration of provinces; and to John, the first tribune of the notaries, who was peculiarly qualified, by his dexterity in business, as well as by his former intimacy with the Gothic prince. When they were introduced into his presence, they declared, perhaps in a more lofty style than became their abject condition, that the Romans were resolved to maintain their dignity, either in peace or war; and that, if Alaric refused them a fair and honourable capitulation, he might sound his trumpets, and prepare to give battle to an innumerable people, exercised in arms and animated by despair.

"The thicker the hay, the easier it is mowed," was the concise reply of the barbarian; and this rustic metaphor was accompanied by a loud and insulting laugh, expressive of his contempt for the menaces of an unwarlike populace, enervated by luxury before they were emaciated by famine. He then condescended to fix the ransom which he would accept as the price of his retreat from the walls of Rome: *all* the gold and silver in the city, whether it were the property of the state, or of individuals; *all* the rich and precious movables; and *all* the slaves who could prove their title to the name of *barbarians*. The ministers of the senate presumed to ask, in a modest and suppliant tone, "If such, O king! are your demands, what do you intend to leave us?" "YOUR LIVES," replied the haughty conqueror: they trembled and retired.

Yet before they retired, a short suspension of arms was granted, which allowed some time for a more temperate negotiation. The stern features of Alaric were insensibly relaxed; he abated much of the rigour of his terms; and at length consented to raise the siege on the immediate payment of five thousand pounds of gold, of thirty thousand pounds of silver, of four thousand robes of silk, of three thousand pieces of fine scarlet cloth, and of three thousand pounds weight of pepper. But the public treasury was exhausted; the annual rents of the great estates in Italy and the provinces were intercepted by the calamities of war; the gold and gems had been exchanged, during the famine, for the vilest sustenance; the hoards of secret wealth were still concealed by the obstinacy of avarice; and some remains of consecrated spoils afforded the only resource that could avert the impending ruin of the city.

As soon as the Romans had satisfied the rapacious demands of Alaric, they were restored, in some measure, to the enjoyment of peace and plenty. Several of the gates were cautiously opened; the importation of provisions from the river and the adjacent country was no longer obstructed by the Goths; the citizens resorted in crowds to the free market which was held during three days in the suburbs; and while the merchants who undertook this gainful trade made a considerable profit, the future subsistence of the city was secured by the ample magazines which were deposited in the public and private granaries. A more regular discipline than could have been expected was maintained in the camp of Alaric; and the wise barbarian justified his regard for the faith of treaties by the just severity with which he chastised a party of licentious Goths who had insulted some Roman citizens on the road to Ostia.

His army, enriched by the contributions of the capital, slowly advanced into the fair and fruitful province of Tuscany, where he proposed to establish his winter-quarters; and the Gothic standard became the refuge of forty thousand barbarian slaves, who had broke their chains, and aspired, under the command of their great deliverer, to revenge the injuries and the disgrace of their cruel servitude. About the same time he received a more honourable reinforcement of Goths and Huns, whom Adolphus, the brother of his wife, had conducted, at his pressing invitation, from the banks of the Danube to those of the Tiber, and who had cut their way, with some difficulty and loss, through the superior numbers of the Imperial troops. A victorious leader, who united the daring spirit of a barbarian with the art and discipline of a Roman general, was at the head of an hundred thousand fighting men; and Italy pronounced with terror and respect the formidable name of Alaric.

At the distance of fourteen centuries we may be satisfied with relating the military exploits of the conquerors of Rome, without presuming to investigate the motives of their political conduct. In the midst of his apparent prosperity, Alaric was conscious, perhaps, of some secret weakness, some internal defect; or perhaps the moderation which he displayed was intended only to deceive and disarm the easy credulity of the ministers of Honorius. The king of the Goths repeatedly declared that it was his desire to be considered as the friend of peace and of the Romans. Three senators, at his earnest request, were sent ambassadors to the court of Ravenna, to solicit the exchange of hostages and the conclusion of the treaty; and the proposals which he more clearly expressed during the course of the negotiations could only inspire a doubt of his sincerity, as they might seem inadequate to the state of his fortune. The barbarian still aspired to the rank of master-general of the armies of the West; he stipulated an annual subsidy of corn and money; and he chose the provinces of Dalmatia, Noricum, and Venetia for the seat of his new kingdom, which would have commanded the important communication between Italy and the Danube. If these modest terms should be rejected, Alaric showed a disposition to relinquish his pecuniary demands, and even to content himself with the possession of Noricum; an exhausted and impoverished country, perpetually exposed to the inroads of the barbarians of Germany.

But the hopes of peace were disappointed by the weak obstinacy, or interested views, of the minister Olympius. Without listening to the salutary remonstrances of the senate, he dismissed their ambassadors under the conduct of a military escort, too numerous for a retinue of honour, and too feeble for an army of defence. Six thousand Dalmatians, the flower of the Imperial legions, were ordered to march from Ravenna to Rome, through an open country which was occupied by the formidable myriads of the barbarians. These brave legionaries, encompassed and betrayed, fell a sacrifice to ministerial folly; their general, Valens, with an hundred soldiers, escaped from the field of battle; and one of the ambassadors, who could no longer claim the protection of the law of nations, was obliged to purchase his freedom with a ransom of thirty thousand pieces of gold. Yet Alaric, instead of resenting this act of impotent hostility, immediately renewed his proposals of peace; and the second embassy of the Roman senate, which derived weight and dignity from the presence of Innocent, bishop of the city, was guarded from the dangers of the road by a detachment of Gothic soldiers.

But the court and councils of Honorius still remained a scene of weakness and distraction, of corruption and anarchy. The emperor was persuaded to assume a lofty tone of inflexible dignity, such as neither his situation nor his character could enable him to support; and a letter, signed with the name of Honorius, was despatched to the Prætorian præfect, granting him a free permission to dispose of the public money, but sternly refusing to prostitute the military honours of Rome to the proud demands of a barbarian. This letter was imprudently communicated to Alaric himself; and the Goth, who in the whole transaction had behaved with temper and decency, expressed in the most outrageous language his lively sense of the insult so wantonly offered to his person and to his nation.

The conference of Rimini was hastily interrupted; the principal officers of the state and army were obliged to swear that, without listening in *any* circumstances to *any* conditions of peace, they would still persevere in perpetual and implacable war against the enemy of the republic. This rash engagement opposed an insuperable bar to all future negotiation. The ministers of Honorius were heard to declare that, if they had only invoked the name of the Deity, they would consult the public safety, and trust their souls to the mercy of Heaven: but they had sworn by the sacred head of the emperor himself; they had touched in solemn ceremony that august seat of majesty and wisdom; and the violation of their oath would expose them to the temporal penalties of sacrilege and rebellion.

Olympius might have continued to insult the just resentment of a people who loudly accused him as the author of the public calamities, but his power was undermined by the secret intrigues of the palace. The favourite eunuchs transferred the government of Honorius and the empire to Jovius, the Prætorian præfect—an unworthy servant, who did not atone by the merit of personal attachment for the errors and misfortunes of his administration. The exile, or escape, of the guilty Olympius reserved him for more vicissitudes of fortune: he experienced the adventures of an obscure and wandering life; he again rose to power; he fell a second time into disgrace; his ears were cut off—he expired under the lash—and his ignominious death afforded a grateful spectacle to the friends of Stilicho.

After the removal of Olympius, whose character was deeply tainted with religious fanaticism, the Pagans and heretics were delivered from the impolitic proscription which excluded them from the dignities of the state. The brave Gennerid, a soldier of barbarian origin, who still adhered to the worship of his ancestors, had been obliged to lay aside the military belt; and though he was repeatedly assured by the emperor himself that laws were not made for persons of his rank or merit, he refused to accept any partial dispensation, and persevered in honourable disgrace till he had extorted a general act of justice from the distress of the Roman government. The conduct of Gennerid in the important station to which he was promoted or restored, of master-general of Dalmatia, Pannonia, Noricum, and Rhætia, seemed to revive the discipline and spirit of the republic. From a life of idleness and want his troops were soon habituated to severe exercise and plentiful subsistence, and his private generosity often supplied the rewards which were denied by the avarice or poverty of the court of Ravenna. The valour of Gennerid, formidable to the adjacent barbarians, was the firmest bulwark of the Illyrian frontier; and his vigilant care assisted the empire with a reinforcement of ten thousand Huns.

While the emperor and his court enjoyed with sullen pride the security of the marshes and fortifications of Ravenna, they abandoned Rome, almost without defence, to the resentment of Alaric. Yet such was the moderation which he still preserved, or affected, that as he moved with his army along the Flaminian way he successively despatched the bishops of the towns of Italy to reiterate his offers of peace, and to conjure the emperor that he would save the city and its inhabitants from hostile fire and the sword of the barbarians.

These impending calamities were averted, not indeed by the wisdom of Honorius, but by the prudence or humanity of the Gothic king, who employed a milder though not less effectual method of conquest. Instead of assaulting the capital he successfully directed his efforts against the *Port* of Ostia, one of the boldest and most stupendous works of Roman magnificence.

The accidents to which the precarious subsistence of the city was continually exposed in a winter navigation and an open road had suggested to the genius of the first Cæsar the useful design which was executed under the reign of Claudius. The artificial moles which formed the narrow entrance advanced far into the sea, and firmly repelled the fury of the waves, while the largest vessels securely rode at anchor within three deep and capacious basins which received the northern branch of the Tiber about two miles from the ancient colony of Ostia. The Roman *Port* insensibly swelled to the size of an episcopal city, where the corn of Africa was deposited in spacious granaries for the use of the capital.

As soon as Alaric was in possession of that important place he summoned the city to surrender at discretion; and his demands were enforced by the positive declaration that a refusal, or even a delay, should be instantly followed by the destruction of the magazines on which the life of the Roman people depended. The clamours of that people and the terror of famine subdued the pride of the senate; they listened without reluctance to the proposal of placing a new emperor on the throne of the unworthy Honorius; and the suffrage of the Gothic conqueror bestowed the purple on Attalus, præfect of the city. The grateful monarch immediately acknowledged his protector as master-general of the armies of the West; Adolphus, with the rank of count of the domestics, obtained the custody of the person of

Attalus; and the two hostile nations seemed to be united in the closest bands of friendship and alliance.

The gates of the city were thrown open, and the new emperor of the Romans, encompassed on every side by the Gothic arms, was conducted in tumultuous procession to the palace of Augustus and Trajan. After he had distributed the civil and military dignities among his favourites and followers, Attalus convened an assembly of the senate, before whom, in a formal and florid speech, he asserted his resolution of restoring the majesty of the republic, and of uniting to the empire the provinces of Egypt and the East which had once acknowledged the sovereignty of Rome. Such extravagant promises inspired every reasonable citizen with a just contempt for the character of an unwarlike usurper, whose elevation was the deepest and most ignominious wound which the republic had yet sustained from the insolence of the barbarians. But the populace, with their usual levity, applauded the change of masters.

At the head of a formidable army, Alaric conducted his royal captive almost to the gates of Ravenna; and a solemn embassy of the principal ministers–of Jovius the Prætorian præfect, of Valens, master of the cavalry and infantry, of the quæstor Potamius, and of Julian, the first of the notaries –was introduced with martial pomp into the Gothic camp. In the name of their sovereign they consented to acknowledge the lawful election of his competitor, and to divide the provinces of Italy and the West between the two emperors. Their proposals were rejected with disdain; and the refusal was aggravated by the insulting clemency of Attalus, who condescended to promise that if Honorius would instantly resign the purple he should be permitted to pass the remainder of his life in the peaceful exile of some remote island.

The favourable intelligence which was received from Africa suddenly changed the opinions of men and the state of public affairs. The troops and officers whom Attalus had sent into that province were defeated and slain, and the active zeal of Heraclian maintained his own allegiance and that of his people. The faithful count of Africa transmitted a large sum of money, which fixed the attachment of the Imperial guards; and his vigilance in preventing the exportation of corn and oil introduced famine, tumult and discontent into the walls of Rome. In a large plain near Rimini, and in the presence of an innumerable multitude of Romans and barbarians, the wretched Attalus was publicly despoiled of the diadem and purple; and those ensigns of royalty were sent by Alaric as the pledge of peace and friendship to the son of Theodosius.

The degradation of Attalus removed the only real obstacle to the conclusion of the peace, and Alaric advanced within three miles of Ravenna. His indignation was kindled by a herald who publicly declared that the guilt of Alaric had for ever excluded him from the friendship and alliance of the emperor.

The crime and folly of the court of Ravenna was expiated a third time by the calamities of Rome. The king of the Goths, who no longer dissembled his appetite for plunder and revenge, appeared in arms under the walls of the capital; and the trembling senate, without any hopes of relief, prepared by a desperate resistance to delay the ruin of their country. But they were unable to guard against the secret conspiracy of their slaves and domestics, who either from birth or interest were attached to the cause of the enemy. At the hour of midnight the Salarian gate was silently opened, and the inhabitants were awakened by the tremendous sound of the Gothic trumpet. Eleven hundred and sixty-three years after the foundation of Rome, the Imperial city, which had subdued and civilised so considerable a part of mankind, was delivered to the licentious fury of the tribes of Germany and Scythia.

The proclamation of Alaric, when he forced his entrance into a vanquished city, discovered some regard for the laws of humanity and religion. He encouraged his troops boldly to seize the rewards of valour, and to enrich themselves with the spoils of a wealthy and effeminate people; but he exhorted them at the same time to spare the lives of the unresisting citizens, and to respect the churches of the Apostles St. Peter and St. Paul as holy and inviolable sanctuaries. Amidst the horrors of a nocturnal tumult several of the Christian Goths displayed the fervour of a recent conversion; and some instances of their uncommon piety and moderation are related, and perhaps adorned, by the zeal of ecclesiastical writers.[2] While the barbarians roamed through the city in quest of prey, the humble dwelling of an aged virgin, who had devoted her life to the service of the altar, was forced open by one of the powerful Goths. He immediately demanded, though in civil language, all the gold and silver in her possession, and was astonished at the readiness with which she conducted him to a splendid hoard of massy plate of the richest materials and the most curious workmanship. The barbarian viewed with wonder and delight this valuable acquisition, till he was interrupted by a serious admonition, addressed to him in the following words: "These," said she, "are the consecrated vessels belonging to St. Peter: if you presume to touch them, the sacrilegious deed will remain on your conscience. For my part, I dare not keep what I am unable to defend." The Gothic captain, struck with reverential awe, despatched a messenger to inform the king of the treasure which he had discovered, and received a peremptory order from Alaric, that all the consecrated plate and ornaments should be transported, without damage or delay, to the church of the Apostle. From the extremity, perhaps, of the Quirinal hill to the distant quarter of the Vatican, a numerous detachment of Goths, marching in order of battle through the principal streets, protected with glittering arms the long train of their devout companions who bore aloft on their heads the sacred vessels of gold and silver, and the martial shouts of the barbarians were mingled with the sound of religious psalmody. From all the adjacent houses a crowd of Christians hastened to join this edifying procession, and a multitude of fugitives, without distinction of age

[2]Orosius (l. vii. c. 39, p. 573–576) applauds the piety of the Christian Goths without seeming to perceive that the greatest part of them were Arian heretics.

or rank, or even of sect, had the good fortune to escape to the secure and hospitable sanctuary of the Vatican. The learned work concerning the *City of God* was professedly composed by St. Augustin, to justify the ways of Providence in the destruction of the Roman greatness.[8]

In the sack of Rome some rare and extraordinary examples of barbarian virtue have been deservedly applauded. But the holy precincts of the Vatican and the apostolic churches could receive a very small proportion of the Roman people: many thousand warriors, more especially of the Huns who served under the standard of Alaric, were strangers to the name, or at least to the faith, of Christ, and we may suspect, without any breach of charity or candour, that in the hour of savage licence, when every passion was inflamed and every restraint was removed, the precepts of the Gospel seldom influenced the behaviour of the Gothic Christians. The writers the best disposed to exaggerate their clemency have freely confessed that a cruel slaughter was made of the Romans, and that the streets of the city were filled with dead bodies which remained without burial during the general consternation. The despair of the citizens was sometimes converted into fury; and whenever the barbarians were provoked by opposition, they extended the promiscuous massacre to the feeble, the innocent, and the helpless. The private revenge of forty thousand slaves was exercised without pity or remorse; and the ignominious lashes which they had formerly received were washed away in the blood of the guilty or obnoxious families.

In the pillage of Rome a just preference was given to gold and jewels, which contain the greatest value in the smallest compass and weight; but, after these portable riches had been removed by the more diligent robbers, the palaces of Rome were rudely stripped of their splendid and costly furniture. The sideboards of massy plate, and the variegated wardrobes of silk and purple, were irregularly piled in the waggons that always followed the march of a Gothic army. The most exquisite works of art were roughly handled or wantonly destroyed: many a statue was melted for the sake of the precious materials; and many a vase, in the division of the spoil, was shivered into fragments by the stroke of a battle-axe. The acquisition of riches served only to stimulate the avarice of the rapacious barbarians, who proceeded by threats, by blows, and by tortures, to force from their prisoners the confession of hidden treasure. Visible splendour and expense were alleged as the proof of a plentiful fortune; the appearance of poverty was imputed to a parsimonious disposition; and the obstinacy of some misers, who endured the most cruel torments before they would discover the secret object of their affection, was fatal to many unhappy wretches, who expired under the lash for refusing to reveal their imaginary treasures.

The edifices of Rome, though the damage has been much exaggerated, received some injury from the violence of the Goths. At their entrance

[8]According to Isidore, Alaric himself was heard to say that he waged war with the Romans, and not with the Apostles. Such was the style of the seventh century; two hundred years before, the fame and merit had been ascribed, not to the Apostles, but to Christ.

through the Salarian gate they fired the adjacent houses to guide their march and to distract the attention of the citizens; the flames, which encountered no obstacle in the disorder of the night, consumed many private and public buildings, and the ruins of the palace of Sallust remained in the age of Justinian a stately monument of the Gothic conflagration. Yet a contemporary historian has observed that fire could scarcely consume the enormous beams of solid brass, and that the strength of man was insufficient to subvert the foundations of ancient structures. Some truth may possibly be concealed in his devout assertion, that the wrath of Heaven supplied the imperfections of hostile rage, and that the proud Forum of Rome, decorated with the statues of so many gods and heroes, was levelled in the dust by the stroke of lightning.

Whatever might be the numbers of equestrian or plebeian rank who perished in the massacre of Rome, it is confidently affirmed that only one senator lost his life by the sword of the enemy. But it was not easy to compute the multitudes who, from an honourable station and a prosperous fortune, were suddenly reduced to the miserable condition of captives and exiles. As the barbarians had more occasion for money than for slaves, they fixed at a moderate price the redemption of their indigent prisoners; and the ransom was often paid by the benevolence of their friends or the charity of strangers. The captives, who were regularly sold, either in open market or by private contract, would have legally regained their native freedom, which it was impossible for a citizen to lose or to alienate. But as it was soon discovered that the vindication of their liberty would endanger their lives, and that the Goths, unless they were tempted to sell, might be provoked to murder their useless prisoners, the civil jurisprudence had been already qualified by a wise regulation, that they should be obliged to serve the moderate term of five years, till they had discharged by their labour the price of their redemption.

The nations who invaded the Roman empire had driven before them, into Italy, whole troops of hungry and affrighted provincials, less apprehensive of servitude than of famine. The calamities of Rome and Italy dispersed the inhabitants to the most lonely, the most secure, the most distant places of refuge. While the Gothic cavalry spread terror and desolation along the sea-coast of Campania and Tuscany, the little island of Igilium, separated by a narrow channel from the Argentarian promontory, repulsed, or eluded, their hostile attempts; and at so small a distance from Rome, great numbers of citizens were securely concealed in the thick woods of that sequestered spot.

The ample patrimonies which many senatorian families possessed in Africa invited them, if they had time and prudence to escape from the ruin of their country, to embrace the shelter of that hospitable province. The most illustrious of these fugitives was the noble and pious Proba, the widow of the præfect Petronius. After the death of her husband, the most powerful subject of Rome, she had remained at the head of the Anician family, and successively supplied, from her private fortune, the expense of the consulships of her three sons. When the city was besieged and taken by the Goths, Proba supported with Christian resignation the loss of immense riches; embarked in a small vessel, from whence she beheld, at sea, the flames of her burning palace; and fled with her daughter Læta, and her grand-daughter, the celebrated virgin Demetrias, to the coast of Africa. The benevolent profusion with which the matron distributed the fruits or the price of her estates contributed to alleviate the misfortunes of exile and captivity. But even the family of Proba herself was not exempt from the rapacious oppression of Count Heraclian, who basely sold, in matrimonial prostitution, the noblest maidens of Rome to the lust or avarice of the Syrian merchants. The Italian fugitives were dispersed through the provinces, along the coast of Egypt and Asia, as far as Constantinople and Jerusalem; and the village of Bethlehem, the solitary residence of St. Jerom and his female converts, was crowned with illustrious beggars, of either sex and every age, who excited the public compassion by the remembrance of their past fortune. This awful catastrophe of Rome filled the astonished empire with grief and terror. So interesting a contrast of greatness and ruin disposed the fond credulity of the people to deplore, and even to exaggerate, the afflictions of the queen of cities. The clergy, who applied to recent events the lofty metaphors of Oriental prophecy, were sometimes tempted to confound the destruction of the capital and the dissolution of the globe.

The retreat of the victorious Goths, who evacuated Rome on the sixth day, might be the result of prudence, but it was not surely the effect of fear. At the head of an army encumbered with rich and weighty spoils, their intrepid leader advanced along the Appian Way into the southern provinces of Italy.

The prosperity which Italy had attained in the auspicious age of the Antonines had gradually declined with the decline of the empire. The fruits of a long peace perished under the rude grasp of the barbarians; and they themselves were incapable of tasting the more elegant refinements of luxury which had been prepared for the use of the soft and polished Italians. Each soldier, however, claimed an ample portion of the substantial plenty, the corn and cattle, oil and wine, that was daily collected and consumed, in the Gothic camp; and the principal warriors insulted the villas and gardens, once inhabited by Lucullus and Cicero, along the beauteous coast of Campania. Their trembling captives, the sons and daughters of Roman senators, presented, in goblets of gold and gems, large draughts of Falernian wine to the haughty victors, who stretched their huge limbs under the shade of plane-trees.

Whether fame, or conquest, or riches were the object of Alaric, he pursued that object with an indefatigable ardour which could neither be quelled by adversity nor satiated by success. No sooner had he reached the extreme land of Italy than he was attracted by the neighbouring prospect of a fertile and peaceful island. Yet even the possession of Sicily he considered only as an intermediate step to the important expedition which he already meditated against the continent of Africa.

The straits of Rhegium and Messina are twelve miles in length, and in the narrowest passage about one mile and a half broad; and the fabulous monsters of the deep, the rocks of Scylla and the whirlpool of Charybdis, could terrify none but the most timid and unskilled mariners. Yet as soon as the first division of the Goths had embarked, a sudden tempest arose, which sunk or scattered many of the transports; their courage was daunted by the terrors of a new element; and the whole design was defeated by the premature death of Alaric, which fixed, after a short illness, the fatal term of his conquests. The ferocious character of the barbarians was displayed in the funeral of a hero whose valour and fortune they celebrated with mournful applause. By the labour of a captive multitude they forcibly diverted the course of the Busentinus, a small river that washes the walls of Consentia. The royal sepulchre, adorned with the splendid spoils and trophies of Rome, was constructed in the vacant bed; the waters were then restored to their natural channel; and the secret spot where the remains of Alaric had been deposited was for ever concealed by the inhuman massacre of the prisoners who had been employed to execute the work.

The personal animosities and hereditary feuds of the barbarians were suspended by the strong necessity of their affairs; and the brave Adolphus, the brother-in-law of the deceased monarch, was unanimously elected to succeed to his throne. The character and political system of the new king of the Goths may be best understood from his own conversation with an illustrious citizen of Narbonne, who afterwards, in a pilgrimage to the Holy Land, related it to St. Jerom, in the presence of the historian Orosius. "In the full confidence of valour and victory, I once aspired (said Adolphus) to change the face of the universe; to obliterate the name of Rome; to erect on its ruins the dominion of the Goths; and to acquire, like Augustus, the immortal fame of the founder of a new empire. By repeated experiments I was gradually convinced that laws are essentially necessary to maintain and regulate a well-constituted state; and that the fierce untractable humour of the Goths was incapable of bearing the salutary yoke of laws and civil government. From that moment I proposed to myself a different object of glory and ambition; and it is now my sincere wish that the gratitude of future ages should acknowledge the merit of a stranger, who employed the sword of the Goths, not to subvert, but to restore and maintain, the prosperity of the Roman empire."

With these pacific views the successor of Alaric suspended the operations of war, and seriously negotiated with the Imperial court a treaty of friendship and alliance. It was the interest of the ministers of Honorius, who were now released from the obligation of their extravagant oath, to deliver Italy from the intolerable weight of the Gothic powers; and they readily accepted their service against the tyrants and barbarians who infested the provinces beyond the Alps. Adolphus, assuming the character of a Roman general, directed his march from the extremity of Campania to the southern provinces of Gaul. His troops, either by force or agreement, immediately occupied the cities of Narbonne, Toulouse, and Bordeaux; and though they were repulsed by Count Boniface from the walls of Marseilles, they soon extended their quarters from the Mediterranean to the ocean.

The professions of Adolphus were probably sincere, and his attachment to the cause of the republic was secured by the ascendant which a Roman princess had acquired over the heart and understanding of the barbarian king. Placidia, the daughter of the great Theodosius, submitted without reluctance to the desires of the conqueror, a young and valiant prince, who yielded to Alaric in loftiness of stature, but who excelled in the more attractive qualities of grace and beauty. The marriage of Adolphus and Placidia was consummated before the Goths retired from Italy; and the solemn, perhaps the anniversary, day of their nuptials was afterwards celebrated in the house of Ingenuus, one of the most illustrious citizens of Narbonne in Gaul. The bride, attired and adorned like a Roman empress, was placed on a throne of state; and the king of the Goths, who assumed on this occasion the Roman habit, contented himself with a less honourable seat by her side. The nuptial gift, which, according to the custom of his nation, was offered to Placidia, consisted of the rare and magnificent spoils of her country.

The hundred basins of gold and gems presented to Placidia at her nuptial feast formed an inconsiderable portion of the Gothic treasury. When that treasury, after the conquest of Spain, was plundered by the Arabs, they admired a table of considerable size, of one single piece of solid emerald, encircled with three rows of fine pearls, supported by three hundred and sixty-five feet of gems and massy gold.

After the deliverance of Italy from the oppression of the Goths, some secret counsellor was permitted, amidst the factions of the palace, to heal the wounds of that afflicted country. A decent and respectful attention was paid to the restoration of the capital; the citizens were encouraged to rebuild the edifices which had been destroyed or damaged by hostile fire; and extraordinary supplies of corn were imported from the coast of Africa. The crowds that so lately fled before the sword of the barbarians were soon recalled by the hopes of plenty and pleasure; and Albinus, præfect of Rome, informed the court, with some anxiety and surprise, that in a single day he had taken an account of the arrival of fourteen thousand strangers. In less than seven years the vestiges of the Gothic invasion were almost obliterated, and the city appeared to resume its former splendour and tranquillity. The venerable matron replaced her crown of laurel, which had been ruffled by the storms of war, and was still amused in the last moment of her decay with the prophecies of revenge, of victory, and of eternal dominion.

CHAPTER XXIII

Gaul and Spain Occupied by the Barbarians—Independence of Britain—Conquest of Africa by the Vandals

At a time when it was universally confessed that almost every man in the empire was superior in personal merit to the princes whom the accident of their birth had seated on the throne, a rapid succession of usurpers, regardless of the fate of their predecessors, still continued to arise. This mischief was peculiarly felt in the provinces of Spain and Gaul.

The situation of Spain, separated on all sides from the enemies of Rome, by the sea, by the mountains, and by intermediate provinces, had secured the long tranquillity of that remote and sequestered country; and we may observe, as a sure symptom of domestic happiness, that, in a period of four hundred years, Spain furnished very few materials to the history of the Roman empire. The footsteps of the barbarians, who in the reign of Gallienus had penetrated beyond the Pyrenees, were soon obliterated by the return of peace; and in the fourth century of the Christian era, the cities of Emerita or Merida, of Corduba, Seville, Bracara, and Tarragona, were numbered with the most illustrious of the Roman world. The various plenty of the animal, the vegetable, and the mineral kingdoms, was improved and manufactured by the skill of an industrious people; and the peculiar advantages of naval stores contributed to support an extensive and profitable trade. The arts and sciences flourished under the protection of the emperors; and if the character of the Spaniards was enfeebled by peace and servitude, the hostile approach of the Germans, who had spread terror and desolation from the Rhine to the Pyrenees, seemed to rekindle some sparks of military ardour.

As long as the defence of the mountains was entrusted to the hardy and faithful militia of the country, they successfully repelled the frequent attempts of the barbarians. But no sooner had the national troops been compelled to resign their post to the Honorian bands in the service of Constantine, than the gates of Spain were treacherously betrayed to the public enemy, about ten months before the sack of Rome by the Goths. The consciousness of guilt, and the thirst of rapine, prompted the mercenary guards of the Pyrenees to desert their station; to invite the arms of the Suevi, the Vandals, and the Alani; and to swell the torrent which was poured with irresistible violence from the frontiers of Gaul to the sea of Africa.

The misfortunes of Spain may be described in the language of its most eloquent historian, who has concisely expressed the passionate, and perhaps exaggerated, declamations of contemporary writers. "The irruption of these nations was followed by the most dreadful calamities: as the barbarians exercised their indiscriminate cruelty on the fortunes of the Romans and the Spaniards, and ravaged with equal fury the cities and the open country. The progress of famine reduced the miserable inhabitants to feed on the flesh of their fellow-creatures; and even the wild beasts, who multiplied, without control, in the desert, were exasperated by the taste of blood and the impatience of hunger boldly to attack and devour their human prey.

"Pestilence soon appeared, the inseparable companion of famine; a large proportion of the people was swept away; and the groans of the dying excited only the envy of their surviving friends. At length the barbarians satiated with carnage and rapine, and afflicted by the contagious evils which they themselves had introduced, fixed their permanent seats in the depopulated country. The ancient Gallicia, whose limits included the kingdom of Old Castille, was divided between the Suevi and the Vandals; the Alani were scattered over the provinces of Carthagena and Lusitania, from the Mediterranean to the Atlantic Ocean; and the fruitful territory of Bætica was allotted to the Silingi, another branch of the Vandalic nation. After regulating this partition, the conquerors contracted with their new subjects some reciprocal engagements of protection and obedience: the lands were again cultivated; and the towns and villages were again occupied by a captive people. The greatest part of the Spaniards was even disposed to prefer this new condition of poverty and barbarism to the severe oppressions of the Roman government; yet there were many who still asserted their native freedom, and who refused, more especially in the mountains of Gallicia, to submit to the barbarian yoke."

In the last years of the reign of Honorius, the GOTHS, the BURGUNDIANS and the FRANKS, obtained a permanent seat and dominion in the provinces of Gaul. The liberal grant of the usurper Jovinus to his Burgundian allies was confirmed by the lawful emperor; the lands of the First, or Upper Germany were ceded to those formidable barbarians; and they gradually occupied, either by conquest or treaty, the two provinces which still retain with the titles of *Duchy* and of *County*, the national appellation of Burgundy. The Franks, the valiant and faithful allies of the Roman republic, were soon tempted to imitate the invaders whom they had so bravely resisted. Trèves, the capital of Gaul, was pillaged by their lawless bands; and the humble colony which they so long maintained in the district of Toxandria, in Brabant, insensibly multiplied along the banks of the Meuse and Scheld, till their independent power filled the whole extent of the Second, or Lower, Germany.

The ruin of the opulent provinces of Gaul may be dated from the establishment of these barbarians, whose alliance was dangerous and oppressive, and who were capriciously impelled, by interest or passion, to violate the public peace. A heavy and partial ransom was imposed on the surviving provincials who had escaped the calamities of war; the fairest and most fertile lands were assigned to the rapacious strangers, for the use of their families, their slaves, and their cattle; and the trembling natives relinquished with a sigh the inheritance of their fathers. Yet the odious name of conquerors was softened into the mild and friendly appellation of the *guests* of the Romans; and the barbarians of Gaul, more especially the Goths, repeatedly declared that they were bound to the people by the ties of hospitality, and to the emperor by the duty of allegiance and military service. The title of Honorius and his successors, their laws and their civil magistrates, were still respected in the provinces of Gaul, of which they had resigned the possession to the barbarian allies; and the kings, who exercised a supreme and independent authority over their native subjects, ambitiously solicited the more honourable rank of master-generals of the Imperial armies. Such was the involuntary reverence which the Roman name still impressed on the minds of those warriors who had borne away in triumph the spoils of the Capitol.

Whilst Italy was ravaged by the Goths, and a succession of feeble tyrants oppressed the provinces beyond the Alps, the British island separated itself from the body of the Roman empire. The regular forces which guarded that remote province had been gradually withdrawn; and Britain was abandoned, without defence, to the Saxon pirates and the savages of Ireland and Caledonia. The Britons, reduced to this extremity, no longer relied on the tardy and doubtful aid of a declining monarchy. They assembled in arms, repelled the invaders, and rejoiced in the important discovery of their own strength.

This revolution dissolved the artificial fabric of civil and military government; and the independent country, during a period of forty years, till the descent of the Saxons, was ruled by the authority of the clergy, the nobles, and the municipal towns. Zosimus, who alone has preserved the memory of this singular transaction, very accurately observes that the letters of Honorius were addressed to the *cities* of Britain.

Under the protection of the Romans, ninety-two considerable towns had arisen in the several parts of that great province; and, among these, thirty-three cities were distinguished above the rest by their superior privileges and importance. Each of these cities, as in all the other provinces of the empire, formed a legal corporation, for the purpose of regulating their domestic policy; and the powers of municipal government were distributed among annual magistrates, a select senate, and the assembly of the people, according to the original model of the Roman constitution. The management of a common revenue, the exercise of civil and criminal jurisdiction, and the habits of public counsel and command, were inherent to these petty republics; and when they asserted their independence, the youth of the city, and of the adjacent districts, would naturally range themselves under the standard of the magistrate.

But the desire of obtaining the advantages, and of escaping the burthens, of political society, is a perpetual and inexhaustible source of discord; nor can it reasonably be presumed that the restoration of British freedom was exempt from tumult and faction. The pre-eminence of birth and fortune must have been frequently violated by bold and popular citizens; and the haughty nobles, who complained that they were become the subjects of their own servants, would sometimes regret the reign of an arbitrary monarch.

The jurisdiction of each city over the adjacent country was supported by the patrimonial influence of the principal senators; and the smaller towns, the villages, and the proprietors of land, consulted their own safety by adhering to the shelter of these rising republics. The sphere of their attraction was proportioned to the respective degrees of their wealth and populousness; but the hereditary lords of ample possessions, who were not oppressed by the neighbourhood of any powerful city, aspired to the rank of independent princes, and boldly exercised the rights of peace and war. The gardens and villas, which exhibited some faint imitation of Italian elegance, would soon be converted into strong castles, the refuge, in time of danger, of the adjacent country; the produce of the land was applied to purchase arms and horses, to maintain a military force of slaves, of peasants, and of licentious followers; and the chieftain might assume, within his own domain, the powers of a civil magistrate. Several of these British chiefs might be the genuine posterity of ancient kings; and many more would be tempted to adopt this honourable genealogy, and to vindicate their hereditary claims, which had been suspended by the usurpation of the Cæsars. Their situation and their hopes would dispose them to affect the dress, the language, and the customs of their ancestors.

If the *princes* of Britain relapsed into barbarism, while the *cities* studiously preserved the laws and manners of Rome, the whole island must have been gradually divided by the distinction of two national parties; again broken into a thousand subdivisions of war and faction by the various provocations of interest and resentment. The public strength, instead of being united against a foreign enemy, was consumed in obscure and intestine quarrels; and the personal merit which had placed a successful leader at the head of his equals might enable him to subdue the freedom of some neighbouring cities, and to claim a rank among the *tyrants* who infested Britain after the dissolution of the Roman government.

The British church might be composed of thirty or forty bishops, with an adequate proportion of the inferior clergy; and the want of riches (for they seem to have been poor) would compel them to deserve the public esteem by a decent and exemplary behaviour. The interest, as well as the temper, of the clergy, was favourable to the peace and union of their distracted country: those salutary lessons might be frequently inculcated in their popular discourses; and the episcopal synods were the only councils that could pretend to the weight and authority of a national assembly. In such councils, where the princes and magistrates sat promiscuously with the bishops, the important affairs of the state, as well as of the church, might be freely debated, differences reconciled, alliances formed, contributions imposed, wise resolutions often concerted, and sometimes executed; and there is reason to believe, that, in moments of extreme danger, a *Pendragon*, or Dictator, was elected by the general consent of the Britons.

It is somewhat remarkable, or rather it is extremely natural, that the revolt of Britain and Armorica should have introduced an appearance of liberty into the obedient provinces of Gaul. In a solemn edict, filled with the strongest assurances of that paternal affection which princes so often express, and so seldom feel, the emperor Honorius promulgated his intention of convening an annual assembly of the *seven provinces:* a name peculiarly appropriated to Aquitain and the ancient Narbonnese, which had long since exchanged their Celtic rudeness for the useful and elegant arts of Italy. Arles, the seat of government and commerce, was appointed for the place of the assembly, which regularly continued twenty-eight days, from the fifteenth of August to the thirteenth of September of every year. It consisted of the Prætorian præfect of the Gauls; of seven provincial governors, one consular, and six presidents; of the magistrates, and perhaps the bishops, of about sixty cities; and of a competent, though indefinite, number of the most honourable and opulent *possessors* of land, who might justly be considered as the representatives of their country. They were empowered to interpret and communicate the laws of their sovereign; to expose the grievances and wishes of their constituents; to moderate the excessive or unequal weight of taxes; and to deliberate on every subject of local or national importance that could tend to the restoration of the peace and prosperity of the seven provinces.

If such an institution, which gave the people an interest in their own government, had been universally established by Trajan or the Antonines, the seeds of public wisdom and virtue might have been cherished and propagated in the empire of Rome. The privileges of the subject would have secured the throne of the monarch; the abuses of an arbitrary administration might have been prevented, in some degree, or corrected, by the interposition of these representative assemblies; and the country would have been defended against a foreign enemy by the arms of natives and freemen. Under the mild and generous influence of liberty, the Roman empire might have remained invincible and immortal; or if its excessive magnitude, and the instability of human affairs, had opposed such perpetual continuance, its vital and constituent members might have separately preserved their vigour and independence.

But in the decline of the empire, when every principle of health and life had been exhausted, the tardy application of this partial remedy was incapable of producing any important or salutary effects. The emperor Honorius expresses his surprise that he must compel the reluctant provinces to accept a privilege which they should ardently have solicited. A fine of three, or even five, pounds of gold was imposed on the absent representatives, who seem to have declined this imaginary gift of a free constitution, as the last and most cruel insult of their oppressors.

The division of the Roman world between the sons of Theodosius marks the final establishment of the empire of the East, which, from the reign of Arcadius to the taking of Constantinople by the Turks, subsisted one thousand and fifty-eight years in a state of premature and perpetual decay.

The sovereign of that empire assumed and obstinately retained the vain, and at length fictitious, title of Emperor of the ROMANS; and the hereditary appellations of CÆSAR and AUGUSTUS continued to declare that he was the legitimate successor of the first of men, who had reigned over the first of nations.

The palace of Constantinople rivalled, and perhaps excelled, the magnificence of Persia; and the eloquent sermons of St. Chrysostom celebrate, while they condemn, the pompous luxury of the reign of Arcadius. "The emperor," says he, "wears on his head either a diadem or a crown of gold, decorated with precious stones of inestimable value. These ornaments and his purple garments are reserved for his sacred person alone; and his robes of silk are embroidered with the figures of golden dragons. His throne is of massy gold. Whenever he appears in public he is surrounded by his courtiers, his guards, and his attendants. Their spears, their shields, their cuirasses, the bridles and trappings of their horses, have either the substance or the appearance of gold; and the large splendid boss in the midst of their shield is encircled with smaller bosses, which represent the shape of the human eye. The two mules that draw the chariot of the monarch are perfectly white, and shining all over with gold. The chariot itself, of pure and solid gold, attracts the admiration of the spectators, who contemplate the purple curtains, the snowy carpet, the size of the precious stones, and the resplendent plates of gold, that glitter as they are agitated by the motion of the carriage. The Imperial pictures are white, on a blue ground; the emperor appears seated on his throne, with his arms, his horses, and his guards beside him; and his vanquished enemies in chains at his feet."

The successors of Constantine established their perpetual residence in the royal city which he had erected on the verge of Europe and Asia. Inaccessible to the menaces of their enemies, and perhaps to the complaints of their people, they received with each wind the tributary productions of every climate; while the impregnable strength of their capital continued for ages to defy the hostile attempts of the barbarians. Their dominions were bounded by the Hadriatic and the Tigris; and the whole interval of twenty-five days' navigation, which separated the extreme cold of Scythia from the torrid zone of Æthiopia, was comprehended within the limits of the empire of the East. The populous countries of that empire were the seat of art and learning, of luxury and wealth; and the inhabitants, who had assumed the language and manners of Greeks, styled themselves, with some appearance of truth, the most enlightened and civilised portion of the human species. The form of government was a pure and simple monarchy; the name of the ROMAN REPUBLIC, which so long preserved a faint tradition of freedom, was confined to the Latin provinces; and the princes of Constantinople measured their greatness by the servile obedience of their people. They were ignorant how much this passive disposition enervates and degrades every faculty of the mind. The subjects who had resigned their will to the absolute commands of a master were equally incapable of guarding their lives and fortunes gainst the assaults of the barbarians or of defending their reason from the errors of superstition.

The first events of the reign of Arcadius and Honorius are so intimately connected that the rebellion of the Goths and the fall of Rufinus have lready claimed a place in the history of the West. Eutropius, one of the principal eunuchs of the palace of Constantinople, succeeded the haughty minister Rufinus, whose ruin he had accomplished and whose vices he soon imitated. Every order of the state bowed to the new favourite; and their ame and obsequious submission encouraged him to insult the laws, and, what is still more difficult and dangerous, the manners of his country. As ong as he despoiled the oppressors who had enriched themselves with the plunder of the people, Eutropius might gratify his covetous disposition without much envy or injustice: but the progress of his rapine soon invaded the wealth which had been acquired by lawful inheritance or laudable industry. The usual methods of extortion were practised and improved; and Claudian has sketched a lively and original picture of the public auction of the state: "This infamous broker of the empire appreciates and divides the Roman provinces from Mount Hæmus to the Tigris. One man, at the expense of his villa, is made proconsul of Asia; a second purchases Syria with his wife's jewels; and a third laments that he has exchanged his paternal estate for the government of Bithynia. In the antechamber of Eutropius a large tablet is exposed to public view, which marks the respective prices of the provinces. The different value of Pontus, of Galatia, of Lydia is accurately distinguished. Lycia may be obtained for so many thousand pieces of gold; but the opulence of Phrygia will require a more considerable sum. The eunuch wishes to obliterate by the general disgrace his personal ignominy; and as he has been sold himself, he is desirous of selling the rest of mankind. In the eager contention, the balance, which contains the fate and fortunes of the province, often trembles on the beam; and till one of the scales is inclined by a superior weight, the mind of the impartial judge remains in anxious suspense. Such" (continues the indignant poet) "are the fruits of Roman valour, of the defeat of Antiochus, and of the triumph of Pompey."

This venal prostitution of public honours secured the impunity of *future* crimes; but the riches which Eutropius derived from confiscation were *already* stained with injustice, since it was decent to accuse and to condemn the proprietors of the wealth which he was impatient to confiscate. Some noble blood was shed by the hand of the executioner; and the most inhospitable extremities of the empire were filled with innocent and illustrious exiles.

The public hatred and the despair of individuals continually threatened, or seemed to threaten, the personal safety of Eutropius, as well as of the numerous adherents who were attached to his fortune and had been promoted by his venal favour. For their mutual defence he contrived the safeguard of a law which violated every principle of humanity and justice: "It is enacted, in the name and by the authority of Arcadius, that all those who shall conspire, either with subjects or with strangers, against the lives of any of the persons whom the emperor considers as the members of his own body, shall be punished with death and confiscation." This species of fictitious and metaphorical treason is extended to protect not only the *illustrious* officers of the state and army who are admitted into the sacred consistory, but likewise the principal domestics of the palace, the senators of Constantinople, the military commanders, and the civil magistrates of the provinces: a vague and indefinite list, which, under the successors of Constantine, included an obscure and numerous train of subordinate ministers.

This extreme severity might perhaps be justified, had it been only directed to secure the representatives of the sovereign from any actual violence in the execution of their office. But the whole body of Imperial dependents claimed a privilege, or rather impunity, which screened them in the loosest moments of their lives from the hasty, perhaps the justifiable, resentment of their fellow-citizens: and, by a strange perversion of the laws, the same degree of guilt and punishment was applied to a private quarrel and to a deliberate conspiracy against the emperor and the empire. The edict of Arcadius most positively and most absurdly declares that in such cases of treason, *thoughts* and *actions* ought to be punished with equal severity; that the knowledge of a mischievous intention, unless it be instantly revealed, becomes equally criminal with the intention itself; and that those rash men who shall presume to solicit the pardon of traitors shall themselves be branded with public and perpetual infamy.

"With regard to the sons of the traitors" (continues the emperor), "although they ought to share the punishment, since they will probably imitate the guilt of their parents, yet, by the special effect of our Imperial lenity, we grant them their lives; but, at the same time, we declare them incapable of inheriting, either on the father's or on the mother's side, or of receiving any gift or legacy from the testament either of kinsmen or of strangers. Stigmatised with hereditary infamy, excluded from the hopes of honours or fortune, let them endure the pangs of poverty and contempt till they shall consider life as a calamity and death as a comfort and relief."

In such words, so well adapted to insult the feelings of mankind, did the emperor, or rather his favourite eunuch, applaud the moderation of a law which transferred the same unjust and inhuman penalties to the children of all those who had seconded or who had not disclosed these fictitious conspiracies. Some of the noblest regulations of Roman jurisprudence have been suffered to expire; but this edict, a convenient and forcible engine of ministerial tyranny, was carefully inserted in the codes of Theodosius and Justinian; and the same maxims have been revived in modern ages to protect the electors of Germany and the cardinals of the church of Rome.

During a long and disgraceful reign of twenty-eight years, Honorius, emperor of the West, was separated from the friendship of his brother, and afterwards of his nephew, who reigned over the East; and Constantinople beheld, with apparent indifference and secret joy, the calamities of Rome.

After the retreat of the Goths the authority of Honorius had obtained a precarious establishment in Spain, except only in the province of Gallicia, where the Suevi and the Vandals had fortified their camps in mutual discord and hostile independence. The Vandals prevailed, and their adversaries were besieged in the Nervasian hills, between Leon and Oviedo, till the approach of Count Asterius compelled, or rather provoked, the victorious barbarians to remove the scene of the war to the plains of Bætica. The rapid progress of the Vandals soon required a more effectual opposition, and the master-general Castinus marched against them with a numerous army of Romans and Goths. Vanquished in battle by an inferior enemy, Castinus fled with dishonour to Tarragona; and this memorable defeat, which has been represented as the punishment, was most probably the effect of his rash presumption.

Seville and Carthagena became the reward, or rather the prey, of the ferocious conquerors; and the vessels which they found in the harbour of Carthagena might easily transport them to the isles of Majorca and Minorca, where the Spanish fugitives, as in a secure recess, had vainly concealed their families and their fortunes. The experience of navigation, and perhaps the prospect of Africa, encouraged the Vandals to accept the invitation which they received from Count Boniface, and the death of Gonderic served only to forward and animate the bold enterprise. In the room of a prince not conspicuous for any superior powers of the mind or body, they acquired his bastard brother, the terrible Genseric; a name which in the destruction of the Roman empire has reserved an equal rank with the names of Alaric and Attila.

The king of the Vandals is described to have been of a middle stature, with a lameness in one leg, which he had contracted by an accidental fall from his horse. His slow and cautious speech seldom declared the deep purposes of his soul: he disdained to imitate the luxury of the vanquished, but he indulged the sterner passions of anger and revenge. The ambition of Genseric was without bounds and without scruples, and the warrior could dexterously employ the dark engines of policy to solicit the allies who might be useful to his success, or to scatter among his enemies the seeds of hatred and contention. Almost in the moment of his departure he was informed that Hermanric, king of the Suevi, had presumed to ravage the Spanish territories which he was resolved to abandon. Impatient of the insult, Genseric pursued the hasty retreat of the Suevi as far as Merida, precipitated the king and his army into the river Anas, and calmly returned to the sea-shore to embark his victorious troops. The vessels which transported the Vandals over the modern Straits of Gibraltar, a channel only twelve miles in breadth, were furnished by the Spaniards, who anxiously wished their departure, and by the African general, who had implored their formidable assistance.

Our fancy, so long accustomed to exaggerate and multiply the martial swarms of barbarians that seemed to issue from the North, will perhaps be surprised by the account of the army which Genseric mustered on the coast of Mauritania. The Vandals, who in twenty years had penetrated from the

Elbe to Mount Atlas, were united under the command of their warlike king; and he reigned with equal authority over the Alani, who had passed within the term of human life from the cold of Scythia to the excessive heat of an African climate. The hopes of the bold enterprise had excited many brave adventurers of the Gothic nation, and many desperate provincials were tempted to repair their fortunes by the same means which had occasioned their ruin. Yet this various multitude amounted only to fifty thousand effective men; and though Genseric artfully magnified his apparent strength by appointing eighty *chiliarchs*, or commanders of thousands, the fallacious increase of old men, of children, and of slaves, would scarcely have swelled his army to the number of fourscore thousand persons.

But his own dexterity and the discontents of Africa soon fortified the Vandal powers by the accession of numerous and active allies. The parts of Mauritania which border on the great desert and the Atlantic Ocean were filled with a fierce and untractable race of men, whose savage temper had been exasperated rather than reclaimed by their dread of the Roman arms. The wandering Moors, as they gradually ventured to approach the sea-shore and the camp of the Vandals, must have viewed with terror and astonishment the dress, the armour, the martial pride and discipline of the unknown strangers who had landed on their coast; and the fair complexions of the blue-eyed warriors of Germany formed a very singular contrast with the swarthy or olive hue which is derived from the neighbourhood of the torrid zone. After the first difficulties had in some measure been removed which arose from the mutual ignorance of their respective language, the Moors, regardless of any future consequence, embraced the alliance of the enemies of Rome, and a crowd of naked savages rushed from the woods and valleys of Mount Atlas, to satiate their revenge on the polished tyrants who had injuriously expelled them from the native sovereignty of the land.

The persecution of the Donatists was an event not less favourable to the designs of Genseric. Seventeen years before he landed in Africa, a public conference was held at Carthage by the order of the magistrate. The Catholics were satisfied that, after the invincible reasons which they had alleged, the obstinacy of the schismatics must be inexcusable and voluntary, and the emperor Honorius was persuaded to inflict the most rigorous penalties on a faction which had so long abused his patience and clemency. Three hundred bishops, with many thousands of the inferior clergy, were torn from their churches, stripped of their ecclesiastical possessions, banished to the islands, and proscribed by the laws, if they presumed to conceal themselves in the provinces of Africa. Their numerous congregations, both in cities and in the country, were deprived of the rights of citizens and of the exercise of religious worship. A regular scale of fines, from ten to two hundred pounds of silver, was curiously ascertained, according to the distinctions of rank and fortune, to punish the crime of assisting at schismatic conventicle; and if the fine had been levied five times without subduing the obstinacy of the offender, his future punishment was referred to the discretion of the Imperial court.

By these severities, which obtained the warmest approbation of St. Augustin, great numbers of Donatists were reconciled to the Catholic church; but the fanatics who still persevered in their opposition were provoked to madness and despair; the distracted country was filled with tumult and bloodshed; the armed troops of Circumcellions alternately pointed their rage against themselves or against their adversaries; and the calendar of martyrs received on both sides a considerable augmentation. Under these circumstances Genseric, a Christian, but an enemy of the orthodox communion, showed himself to the Donatists as a powerful deliverer, from whom they might reasonably expect the repeal of the odious and oppressive edicts of the Roman emperors.[1]

The conquest of Africa was facilitated by the active zeal or the secret favour of a domestic faction; the wanton outrages against the churches and the clergy, of which the Vandals are accused, may be fairly imputed to the fanaticism of their allies; and the intolerant spirit which disgraced the triumph of Christianity contributed to the loss of the most important province of the West. The victorious barbarians insulted the open country; and Carthage, Cirta, and Hippo Regius, were the only cities that appeared to rise above the general inundation.

The long and narrow tract of the African coast was filled with frequent monuments of Roman art and magnificence; and the respective degrees of improvement might be accurately measured by the distance from Carthage and the Mediterranean. A simple reflection will impress every thinking mind with the clearest idea of fertility and cultivation: the country was extremely populous; the inhabitants reserved a liberal subsistence for their own use; and the annual exportation, particularly of wheat, was so regular and plentiful, that Africa deserved the name of the common granary of Rome and of mankind.

On a sudden the seven fruitful provinces, from Tangier to Tripoli, were overwhelmed by the invasion of the Vandals, whose destructive rage has perhaps been exaggerated by popular animosity, religious zeal, and extravagant declamation. War in its fairest form implies a perpetual violation of humanity and justice; and the hostilities of barbarians are inflamed by the fierce and lawless spirit which incessantly disturbs their peaceful and domestic society. The Vandals, where they found resistance, seldom gave quarter; and the deaths of the valiant countrymen were expiated by the ruin of the cities under whose walls they had fallen. Careless of the distinction of age, or sex, or rank, they employed every species of indignity and torture to force from the captives a discovery of their hidden wealth. The stern policy of Genseric justified his frequent examples of military execution: he was not always the master of his own passions or of those of his followers; and the calamities of war were aggravated by the licentiousness of the Moors and the fanaticism of the Donatists. Yet I shall not easily be persuaded that

[1]According to St. Augustin and Theodoret, the Donatists were inclined to the principles, or at least to the party, of the Arians, which Genseric supported. Tillemont, Mém. Ecclés. tom. vi. p. 68.

it was the common practice of the Vandals to extirpate the olives and other fruit trees of a country where they intended to settle: nor can I believe that it was a usual stratagem to slaughter great numbers of their prisoners before the walls of a besieged city, for the sole purpose of infecting the air and producing a pestilence, of which they themselves must have been the first victims.

Perhaps by the ignorance of the Vandals, the siege of Hippo was protracted above fourteen months: the sea was continually open; and when the adjacent country had been exhausted by irregular rapine, the besiegers themselves were compelled by famine to relinquish their enterprise. The importance and danger of Africa were deeply felt by the regent of the West. Placidia implored the assistance of her Eastern ally; and the Italian fleet and army were reinforced from Constantinople with a powerful armament. As soon as the force of the two empires was united under the command of Boniface, he boldly marched against the Vandals; and the loss of a second battle irretrievably decided the fate of Africa. He embarked with the precipitation of despair, and the people of Hippo were permitted, with their families and effects, to occupy the vacant place of the soldiers, the greatest part of whom were either slain or made prisoners by the Vandals.

It might naturally be expected that the Vandals would achieve without resistance or delay the conquest of Africa. Eight years however elapsed from the evacuation of Hippo to the reduction of Carthage. In the midst of that interval the ambitious Genseric, in the full tide of apparent prosperity, negotiated a treaty of peace, by which he gave his son Hunneric for an hostage, and consented to leave the Western emperor in the undisturbed possession of the three Mauritanias.

This moderation, which cannot be imputed to the justice, must be ascribed to the policy of the conqueror. His throne was encompassed with domestic enemies, who accused the baseness of his birth, and asserted the legitimate claims of his nephews, the sons of Gonderic. Those nephews, indeed, he sacrificed to his safety, and their mother, the widow of the deceased king, was precipitated by his order into the river Ampsaga. But the public discontent burst forth in dangerous and frequent conspiracies; and the warlike tyrant is supposed to have shed more Vandal blood by the hand of the executioner than in the field of battle. The convulsions of Africa, which had favoured his attack, opposed the firm establishment of his power; and the various seditions of the Moors and Germans, the Donatists and Catholics, continually disturbed or threatened the unsettled reign of the conqueror. As he advanced towards Carthage he was forced to withdraw his troops from the Western provinces; the sea-coast was exposed to the naval enterprises of the Romans of Spain and Italy; and, in the heart of Numidia, the strong inland city of Cirta still persisted in obstinate independence.

These difficulties were gradually subdued by the spirit, the perseverance, and the cruelty of Genseric, who alternately applied the arts of peace and war to the establishment of his African kingdom. He subscribed a solemn treaty, with the hope of deriving some advantage from the term of its continuance and the moment of its violation. The vigilance of his enemies was relaxed by the protestations of friendship which concealed his hostile approach; and Carthage was at length surprised by the Vandals, five hundred and eighty-five years after the destruction of the city and republic by the younger Scipio.

A new city had arisen from its ruins, with the title of a colony; and though Carthage might yield to the royal prerogatives of Constantinople, and perhaps to the trade of Alexandria, or the splendour of Antioch, she still maintained the second rank in the West; as the *Rome* (if we may use the style of contemporaries) of the African world. That wealthy and opulent metropolis displayed, in a dependent condition, the image of a flourishing republic. Carthage contained the manufactures, the arms, and the treasures of the six provinces. A regular subordination of civil honours gradually ascended from the procurators of the streets and quarters of the city to the tribunal of the supreme magistrate, who, with the title of proconsul, represented the state and dignity of a consul of ancient Rome. Schools and *gymnasia* were instituted for the education of the African youth; and the liberal arts and manners, grammar, rhetoric, and philosophy, were publicly taught in the Greek and Latin languages. The buildings of Carthage were uniform and magnificent: a shady grove was planted in the midst of the capital; the *new* port, a secure and capacious harbour, was subservient to the commercial industry of citizens and strangers; and the splendid games of the Circus and theatre were exhibited almost in the presence of the barbarians.

The reputation of the Carthaginians was not equal to that of their country, and the habits of trade and the abuse of luxury had corrupted their manners. The king of the Vandals severely reformed the vices of a voluptuous people; and the ancient, noble, ingenuous freedom of Carthage was reduced by Genseric into a state of ignominious servitude. An edict was promulgated, which enjoined all persons, without fraud or delay, to deliver their gold, silver, jewels, and valuable furniture or apparel to the royal officers; and the attempt to secrete any part of their patrimony was inexorably punished with death and torture as an act of treason against the state. The lands of the proconsular province, which formed the immediate district of Carthage, were accurately measured and divided among the barbarians.

It was natural enough that Genseric should hate those whom he had injured: the nobility and senators of Carthage were exposed to his jealousy and resentment; and all those who refused the ignominious terms which their honour and religion forbade them to accept were compelled by the Arian tyrant to embrace the condition of perpetual banishment. Rome, Italy, and the provinces of the East, were filled with a crowd of exiles, of fugitives and of ingenuous captives, who solicited the public compassion.

The memorable fable of the Seven Sleepers corresponds with the conquest of Africa by the Vandals. When the emperor Decius persecuted the Christians, seven noble youths of Ephesus concealed themselves in a spacious cavern in the side of an adjacent mountain where they were doomed to perish by the tyrant, who gave orders that the entrance should be firmly secured with a pile of huge stones. They immediately fell into a deep slumber, which was miraculously prolonged, without injuring the powers of life, during a period of one hundred and eighty-seven years. At the end of that time, the slaves of Adolius, to whom the inheritance of the mountain had descended, removed the stone, to supply materials for some rustic edifice: the light of the sun darted into the cavern, and the Seven Sleepers were permitted to awake. After a slumber, as they thought of a few hours, they were pressed by the calls of hunger; and resolved that Jamblichus, one of their number, should secretly return to the city to purchase bread for the use of his companions. The youth (if we may still employ that appellation) could no longer recognise the once familiar aspect of his native country; and his surprise was increased by the appearance of a large cross, triumphantly erected over the principal gate of Ephesus. His singular dress and obsolete language confounded the baker, to whom he offered an ancient medal of Decius as the current coin of the empire; and Jamblichus, on the suspicion of a secret treasure, was dragged before the judge. Their mutual inquiries produced the amazing discovery that two centuries were almost elapsed since Jamblichus and his friends had escaped from the rage of a Pagan tyrant. The bishop of Ephesus, the clergy, the magistrates, the people, and, as it is said, the emperor Theodosius himself, hastened to visit the cavern of the Seven Sleepers; who bestowed their benediction, related their story, and at the same instant peaceably expired. The origin of this marvellous fable cannot be ascribed to the pious fraud and credulity of the *modern* Greeks, since the authentic tradition may be traced within half a century of the supposed miracle.

But if the interval between two memorable eras could be instantly annihilated; if it were possible, after a momentary slumber of two hundred years, to display the *new* world to the eyes of a spectator who still retained a lively and recent impression of the *old*, his surprise and his reflections would furnish the pleasing subject of a philosophical romance. The scene could not be more advantageously placed than in the two centuries which elapsed between the reigns of Decius and of Theodosius the Younger. During this period the seat of government had been transported from Rome to a new city on the banks of the Thracian Bosphorus and the abuse of military spirit had been suppressed by an artificial system of tame and ceremonious servitude. The throne of the persecuting Decius was filled by a succession of Christian and orthodox princes, who had extirpated the fabulous gods of antiquity: and the public devotion of the age was impatient to exalt the saints and martyrs of the Catholic church on the altars of Diana and Hercules. The union of the Roman empire was dissolved; its genius was humbled in the dust; and armies of unknown barbarians, issuing from the frozen regions of the North, had established their victorious reign over the fairest provinces of Europe and Africa.

CHAPTER XXIV

The Character, Conquests, and Courts of Attila, King of the Huns

The western world was oppressed by the Goths and Vandals, who fled before the Huns; but the achievements of the Huns themselves were not adequate to their power and prosperity. Their victorious hordes spread from the Volga to the Danube; but the public force was exhausted by the discord of independent chieftains; their valour was idly consumed in obscure and predatory excursions; and they often degraded their national dignity, by condescending, for the hopes of spoil, to enlist under the banners of their fugitive enemies. In the reign of Attila the Huns again became the terrors of the world. That formidable barbarian alternately insulted and invaded the East and the West and urged the rapid downfall of the Roman empire.

In the tide of emigration which impetuously rolled from the confines of China to those of Germany, the most powerful and populous tribes may commonly be found on the verge of the Roman provinces. The accumulated weight was sustained for a while by artificial barriers; and the easy condescension of the emperors invited, without satisfying, the insolent demands of the barbarians, who had acquired an eager appetite for the luxuries of civilised life. Some ecclesiastical historians have destroyed the barbarians with lightning and pestilence, but Theodosius was reduced to the more humble expedient of stipulating an annual payment of three hundred and fifty pounds of gold, and of disguising this dishonourable tribute by the title of general, which the king of the Huns condescended to accept.

The kings of the Huns dictated the conditions of peace, and each condition was an insult on the majesty of the empire. Besides the freedom of a safe and plentiful market on the banks of the Danube, they required that the annual contribution should be augmented from three hundred and fifty to seven hundred pounds of gold; that a fine or ransom, of eight pieces of gold, should be paid for every Roman captive who had escaped from his barbarian master; that the emperor should renounce all treaties and engagements with the enemies of the Huns; and that all the fugitives who had taken refuge in the court or provinces of Theodosius should be delivered to the justice of their offended sovereign.

Attila, the son of Mundzuk, deduced his noble, perhaps his regal, descent from the ancient Huns, who had formerly contended with the monarchs of China. His features, according to the observation of a Gothic historian, bore the stamp of his national origin; and the portrait of Attila exhibits the genuine deformity of a modern Calmuck; a large head, a swarthy complexion, small deep-seated eyes, a flat nose, a few hairs in the place of a beard, broad shoulders, and a short square body, of nervous strength, though of a disproportioned form. The haughty step and demeanour of the king of the Huns expressed the consciousness of his superiority above the rest of mankind; and he had a custom of fiercely rolling his eyes, as if he wished to enjoy the terror which he inspired. Yet this savage hero was not inaccessible to pity; his suppliant enemies might confide in the assurance of peace or pardon; and Attila was considered by his subjects as a just and indulgent master. He delighted in war; but, after he had ascended the throne in a mature age, his head, rather than his hand, achieved the conquest of the North; and the fame of an adventurous soldier was usefully exchanged for that of a prudent and successful general.

The religious arts of Attila were not less skilfully adapted to the character of his age and country. It was natural enough that the Scythians should adore, with peculiar devotion, the god of war; but as they were incapable of forming either an abstract idea or a corporeal representation, they worshipped their tutelar deity under the symbol of an iron cimeter. One of the shepherds of the Huns perceived that a heifer, who was grazing, had wounded herself in the foot, and curiously followed the track of the blood, till he discovered, among the long grass, the point of an ancient sword, which he dug out of the ground, and presented to Attila. That magnanimous, or rather that artful, prince accepted, with pious gratitude, this celestial favour; and, as the rightful possessor of the *sword of Mars*, asserted his divine and indefeasible claim to the dominion of the earth. If the rites of Scythia were practised on this solemn occasion, a lofty altar, or rather pile of faggots, three hundred yards in length and in breadth, was raised in a spacious plain; and the sword of Mars was placed erect on the summit of this rustic altar, which was annually consecrated by the blood of sheep, horses, and of the hundredth captive. Whether human sacrifices formed any part of the worship of Attila, or whether he propitiated the god of war with the victims which he continually offered in the field of battle, the favourite of Mars soon acquired a sacred character, which rendered his conquests more easy and more permanent; and the barbarian princes confessed, in the language of devotion or flattery, that they could not presume to gaze with a steady eye on the divine majesty of the king of the Huns.

If a line of separation were drawn between the civilised and the savage climates of the globe, between the inhabitants of cities, who cultivated the earth, and the hunters and shepherds, who dwelt in tents, Attila might aspire to the title of supreme and sole monarch of the barbarians. He alone, among the conquerors of ancient and modern times, united the two mighty kingdoms of Germany and Scythia; and those vague appellations, when they are applied to his reign, may be understood with an ample latitude.

Thuringia, which stretched beyond its actual limits as far as the Danube, was in the number of his provinces; he interposed, with the weight of a powerful neighbour, in the domestic affairs of the Franks; and one of his lieutenants chastised, and almost exterminated, the Burgundians of the Rhine. He subdued the islands of the ocean, the kingdoms of Scandinavia, encompassed and divided by the waters of the Baltic; and the Huns might derive a tribute of furs from that northern region, which has been protected from all other conquerors by the severity of the climate and the courage of the natives. Towards the East, it is difficult to circumscribe the dominion of Attila over the Scythian deserts; yet we may be assured that he reigned on the banks of the Volga; that the king of the Huns was dreaded, not only as a warrior, but as a magician; that he insulted and vanquished the khan of the formidable Geougen; and that he sent ambassadors to negotiate an equal alliance with the empire of China.

In the proud review of the nations who acknowledged the sovereignty of Attila, and who never entertained, during his lifetime, the thought of a revolt, the Gepidæ and the Ostrogoths were distinguished by their numbers, their bravery, and the personal merit of their chiefs. The renowned Ardaric, king of the Gepidæ, was the faithful and sagacious counsellor of the monarch, who esteemed his intrepid genius, whilst he loved the mild and discreet virtues of the noble Walamir, king of the Ostrogoths. The crowd of vulgar kings, the leaders of so many martial tribes, who served under the standard of Attila, were ranged in the submissive order of guards and domestics round the person of their master. They watched his nod; they trembled at his frown; and at the first signal of his will, they executed, without murmur or hesitation, his stern and absolute commands. In time of peace, the dependent princes, with their national troops, attended the royal camp in regular succession; but when Attila collected his military force he was able to bring into the field an army of five, or, according to another account, of seven hundred thousand barbarians.

The ambassadors of the Huns might awaken the attention of Theodosius, by reminding him that they were his neighbours both in Europe and Asia; since they touched the Danube on one hand, and reached with the other as far as the Tanais. In the reign of his father Arcadius, a band of adventurous Huns had ravaged the provinces of the East, from whence they brought away rich spoils and innumerable captives. They advanced, by a secret path, along the shores of the Caspian Sea; traversed the snowy mountains of Armenia; passed the Tigris, the Euphrates, and the Halys; recruited their weary cavalry with the generous breed of Cappadocian horses; occupied the hilly country of Cilicia; and disturbed the festal songs and dances of the citizens of Antioch. Egypt trembled at their approach; and the monks and pilgrims of the Holy Land prepared to escape their fury by a speedy embarkation. The memory of this invasion was still recent in the minds of the Orientals. The subjects of Attila might execute, with superior forces, the design which these adventurers had so boldly attempted; and it soon became the subject of anxious conjecture whether the tempest would fall on the dominions of Rome or of Persia.

In the free conversation of the Imperial ambassadors, who discussed, at the court of Attila, the character and designs of their formidable enemy, the ministers of Constantinople expressed their hope that his strength might be diverted and employed in a long and doubtful contest with the princes of the house of Sassan. The more sagacious Italians admonished their Eastern brethren of the folly and danger of such a hope; and convinced them, *that* the Medes and Persians were incapable of resisting the arms of the Huns; and *that* the easy and important acquisition would exalt the pride, as well as power, of the conqueror. Instead of contenting himself with a moderate contribution and a military title, which equalled him only to the generals of Theodosius, Attila would proceed to impose a disgraceful and intolerable yoke on the necks of the prostrate and captive Romans, who would then be encompassed on all sides by the empire of the Huns.

While the powers of Europe and Asia were solicitous to avert the impending danger, the alliance of Attila maintained the Vandals in the possession of Africa. An enterprise had been concerted between the courts of Ravenna and Constantinople for the recovery of that valuable province; and the ports of Sicily were already filled with the military and naval forces of Theodosius. But the subtle Genseric, who spread his negotiations round the world, prevented their designs, by exciting the king of the Huns to invade the Eastern empire; and a trifling incident soon became the motive, or pretence, of a destructive war. The Illyrian frontier was covered by a line of castles and fortresses; and though the greatest part of them consisted only of a single tower, with a small garrison, they were commonly sufficient to repel, or to intercept, the inroads of an enemy who was ignorant of the art, and impatient of the delay, of a regular siege. But these slight obstacles were instantly swept away by the inundation of the Huns. They destroyed, with fire and sword, the populous cities of Sirmium and Singidunum, of Ratiaria and Marcianopolis, of Naissus and Sardica; where every circumstance in the discipline of the people and the construction of the buildings had been gradually adapted to the sole purpose of defence. The whole breadth of Europe, as it extends above five hundred miles from the Euxine to the Hadriatic, was at once invaded, and occupied, and desolated, by the myriads of barbarians whom Attila led into the field.

The public danger and distress could not provoke Theodosius to interrupt his amusements and devotion, or to appear in person at the head of the Roman legions. But the troops which had been sent against Genseric were hastily recalled from Sicily; the garrisons, on the side of Persia, were exhausted; and a military force was collected in Europe, formidable by their arms and numbers, if the generals had understood the science of command, and their soldiers the duty of obedience. The armies of the Eastern empire were vanquished in three successive engagements; and the progress of Attila may be traced by the fields of battle. The two former, on the banks of the Utus, and under the walls of Marcianopolis, were fought in the extensive plains between the Danube and Mount Hæmus. As the Romans were pressed by a victorious enemy, they gradually, and unskilfully, retired towards the Chersonesus of Thrace; and that narrow peninsula, the last extremity of the land, was marked by their third and irreparable defeat. By the destruction of this army, Attila acquired the indisputable possession of the field.

From the Hellespont to Thermopylæ and the suburbs of Constantinople he ravaged, without resistance and without mercy, the provinces of Thrace and Macedonia. Heraclea and Hadrianople might, perhaps, escape this dreadful irruption of the Huns; but the words the most expressive of total extirpation and erasure are applied to the calamities which they inflicted on seventy cities of the Eastern empire. Theodosius, his court, and the unwarlike people, were protected by the walls of Constantinople; but those walls had been shaken by a recent earthquake, and the fall of fifty-eight towers had opened a large and tremendous breach. The damage indeed was speedily repaired; but this accident was aggravated by a superstitious fear that Heaven itself had delivered the Imperial city to the shepherds of Scythia, who were strangers to the laws, the language, and the religion of the Romans.

The Huns of Attila may without injustice be compared to the Moguls and Tartars before their primitive manners were changed by religion and luxury; and the evidence of Oriental history may reflect some light on the short and imperfect annals of Rome. After the Moguls had subdued the northern provinces of China, it was seriously proposed, not in the hour of victory and passion, but in calm deliberate council, to exterminate all the inhabitants of that populous country, that the vacant land might be converted to the pasture of cattle.

It may be affirmed that the Huns depopulated the provinces of the empire by the number of Roman subjects whom they led away into captivity. In the hands of a wise legislator such an industrious colony might have contributed to diffuse through the deserts of Scythia the rudiments of the useful and ornamental arts; but these captives, who had been taken in war, were accidentally dispersed among the hordes that obeyed the empire of Attila. The estimate of their respective value was formed by the simple judgment of unenlightened and unprejudiced barbarians.

The perpetual intercourse of the Huns and the Goths had communicated the familiar knowledge of the two national dialects; and the barbarians were ambitious of conversing in Latin, the military idiom even of the Eastern empire. But they disdained the language and the sciences of the Greeks; and the vain sophist or grave philosopher who had enjoyed the flattering applause of the schools was mortified to find that his robust servant was a captive of more value and importance than himself. The mechanic arts were encouraged and esteemed, as they tended to satisfy the wants of the Huns. An architect in the service of Onegesius, one of the favourites of Attila, was employed to construct a bath: but this work was a rare example of private luxury; and the trades of the smith, the carpenter, the armourer, were much more adapted to supply a wandering people with the useful instruments of peace and war. But the merit of the physician was received with universal favour and respect: the barbarians, who despised death, might be apprehensive of disease; and the haughty conqueror trembled in the presence of a captive to whom he ascribed perhaps an imaginary power of prolonging or preserving his life.

The Huns might be provoked to insult the misery of their slaves, over whom they exercised a despotic command; but their manners were not susceptible of a refined system of oppression, and the efforts of courage and diligence were often recompensed by the gift of freedom. The historian Priscus, whose embassy is a source of curious instruction, was accosted in the camp of Attila by a stranger who saluted him in the Greek language, but whose dress and figure displayed the appearance of a wealthy Scythian. In the siege of Viminiacum he had lost, according to his own account, his fortune and liberty: he became the slave of Onegesius; but his faithful services against the Romans and the Acatzires had gradually raised him to the rank of the native Huns, to whom he was attached by the domestic pledges of a new wife and several children. The spoils of war had restored and improved his private property; he was admitted to the table of his former lord; and the apostate Greek blessed the hour of his captivity, since it had been the introduction to a happy and independent state. The freedman of Onegesius exposed, in true and lively colours, the vices of a declining empire of which he had so long been the victim; the cruel absurdity of the Roman princes, unable to protect their subjects against the public enemy, unwilling to trust them with arms for their own defence; the intolerable weight of taxes, rendered still more oppressive by the intricate or arbitrary modes of collection; the obscurity of numerous and contradictory laws; the tedious and expensive forms of judicial proceedings; the partial administration of justice; and the universal corruption which increased the influence of the rich and aggravated the misfortunes of the poor.

The timid or selfish policy of the Western Romans had abandoned the Eastern empire to the Huns. The loss of armies and the want of discipline or virtue were not supplied by the personal character of the monarch. Theodosius might still affect the style as well as the title of *Invincible Augustus*, but he was reduced to solicit the clemency of Attila who imperiously dictated these harsh and humiliating conditions of peace:

I. The emperor of the East resigned, by an express or tacit convention, an extensive and important territory which stretched along the southern banks of the Danube, from Singidunum, or Belgrade, as far as Novæ, in the diocese of Thrace. The breadth was defined by the vague computation of fifteen days' journey; but, from the proposal of Attila to remove the situation of the national market, it soon appeared that he comprehended the ruined city of Naissus within the limits of his dominions.

II. The king of the Huns required and obtained that his tribute or subsidy should be augmented from seven hundred pounds of gold to the annual sum of two thousand one hundred; and he stipulated the immediate payment of six thousand pounds of gold to defray the expenses, or to expiate the guilt, of the war. One might imagine that such a demand, which scarcely equalled the measure of private wealth, would have been readily discharged by the opulent empire of the East; and the public distress affords a remarkable proof of the impoverished, or at least of the disorderly, state of the finances. A large proportion of the taxes extorted from the people was detained and intercepted in their passage through the foulest channels to the treasury of Constantinople. The revenue was dissipated by Theodosius and his favourites in wasteful and profuse luxury, which was disguised by the names of Imperial magnificence or Christian charity. The immediate supplies had been exhausted by the unforeseen necessity of military preparations. A personal contribution, rigorously but capriciously imposed on the members of the senatorian order, was the only expedient that could disarm without loss of time the impatient avarice of Attila: and the poverty of the nobles compelled them to adopt the scandalous resource of exposing to public auction the jewels of their wives and the hereditary ornaments of their palaces.

III. The king of the Huns appears to have established as a principle of national jurisprudence, that he could never lose the property which he had once acquired in the persons who had yielded either a voluntary or reluctant submission to his authority. From this principle he concluded, and the conclusions of Attila were irrevocable laws, that the Huns who had been taken prisoners in war should be released without delay and without ransom; that every Roman captive who had presumed to escape should purchase his right to freedom at the price of twelve pieces of gold; and that all the barbarians who had deserted the standard of Attila should be restored without any promise or stipulation of pardon. In the execution of this cruel and ignominious treaty the Imperial officers were forced to massacre several loyal and noble deserters who refused to devote themselves to certain death.

It would have been strange indeed if Theodosius had purchased, by the loss of honour, a secure and solid tranquillity, or if his tameness had not invited the repetition of injuries. The Byzantine court was insulted by five or six successive embassies; and the ministers of Attila were uniformly instructed to press the tardy or imperfect execution of the last treaty; to produce the names of fugitives and deserters who were still protected by the empire; and to declare, with seeming moderation, that, unless their sovereign obtained complete and immediate satisfaction, it would be impossible for him, were it even his wish, to check the resentment of his warlike tribes. Besides the motive of pride and interest which might prompt the king of the Huns to continue this train of negotiation, he was influenced by the less honourable view of enriching his favourites at the expense of his enemies.

Attila weighed, with suspicious pride, the character and station of the Imperial envoys; but he condescended to promise that he would advance as far as Sardica to receive any minister who had been invested with the consular dignity. The council of Theodosius eluded this proposal by representing the desolate and ruined condition of Sardica; and even ventured to insinuate that every officer of the army or household was qualified to treat with the most powerful princes of Scythia. Maximin, a respectable courtier, whose abilities had been long exercised in civil and military employments, accepted with reluctance the troublesome, and perhaps dangerous, commission; but the secret of the embassy, a fatal and guilty secret, was entrusted only to the interpreter Vigilius.

The palace of Attila, which surpassed all other houses in his dominions, was built entirely of wood, and covered an ample space of ground. The outward enclosure was a lofty wall, or palisade, of smooth square timber, intersected with high towers, but intended rather for ornament than defence. This wall, which seems to have encircled the declivity of a hill, comprehended a great variety of wooden edifices, adapted to the uses of royalty. A separate house was assigned to each of the numerous wives of Attila; and, instead of the rigid and illiberal confinement imposed by Asiatic jealousy, they politely admitted the Roman ambassadors to their presence, their table, and even to the freedom of an innocent embrace. When Maximin offered his presents to Cerca the principal queen, he admired the singular architecture of her mansion, the height of the round columns, the size and beauty of the wood, which was curiously shaped or turned, or polished or carved; and his attentive eye was able to discover some taste in the ornaments, and some regularity in the proportions.

After passing through the guards who watched before the gate, the ambassadors were introduced into the private apartment of Cerca. The wife of Attila received their visit sitting, or rather lying, on a soft couch; the floor was covered with a carpet; the domestics formed a circle round the queen; and her damsels, seated on the ground, were employed in working the variegated embroidery which adorned the dress of the barbaric warriors. The Huns were ambitious of displaying those riches which were the fruit and evidence of their victories; the trappings of their horses, their swords, and even their shoes, were studded with gold and precious stones; and their tables were profusely spread with plates, and goblets, and vases of gold and silver, which had been fashioned by the labour of Grecian artists. The monarch alone assumed the superior pride of still adhering to the simplicity of his Scythian ancestors. The dress of Attila, his arms, and the furniture of his horse, were plain, without ornament, and of a single colour. The royal table was served in wooden cups and platters; flesh was his only food; and the conqueror of the North never tasted the luxury of bread.

When Attila first gave audience to the Roman ambassadors on the banks of the Danube, his tent was encompassed with a formidable guard. The monarch himself was seated in a wooden chair. His stern countenance, angry gestures, and impatient tone astonished the firmness of Maximin; but Vigilius had more reason to tremble.

The barbarians condescended, by producing an accurate list, to expose the bold falsehood of Vigilius, who had affirmed that no more than seventeen deserters could be found. But he arrogantly declared that he apprehended only the disgrace of contending with his fugitive slaves. "For what fortress" (added Attila), "what city, in the wide extent of the Roman empire, can hope to exist, secure and impregnable, if it is our pleasure that it should be erased from the earth?"

During his residence at the seat of empire his hours were not wasted in the idle retirement of a seraglio; and the king of the Huns could maintain his superior dignity without concealing his person from the public view. He frequently assembled his council, and gave audience to the ambassadors of the nations; and his people might appeal to the supreme tribunal, which he held at stated times, and, according to the Eastern custom, before the principal gate of his wooden palace. The Romans, both of the East and of the West, were twice invited to the banquet where Attila feasted with the princes and nobles of Scythia. Maximin and his colleagues were stopped on the threshold, till they had made a devout libation to the health and prosperity of the king of the Huns; and were conducted, after this ceremony, to their respective seats in a spacious hall. The royal table and couch, covered with carpets and fine linen, was raised by several steps in the midst of the hall; and a son, an uncle, or perhaps a favourite king, were admitted to share the simple and homely repast of Attila. Two lines of small tables, each of which contained three or four guests, were ranged in order on either hand; the right was esteemed the most honourable, but the Romans ingenuously confess that they were placed on the left; and that Beric, an unknown chieftain, most probably of the Gothic race, preceded the representatives of Theodosius and Valentinian.

The barbarian monarch received from his cupbearer a goblet filled with wine, and courteously drank to the health of the most distinguished guest, who rose from his seat and expressed, in the same manner, his loyal and respectful vows. This ceremony was successively performed for all, or at least for the illustrious persons of the assembly; and a considerable time must have been consumed, since it was thrice repeated as each course or service was placed on the table. But the wine still remained after the meat had been removed; and the Huns continued to indulge their intemperance long after the sober and decent ambassadors of the two empires had withdrawn themselves from the nocturnal banquet.

But the Roman ambassador was ignorant of the treacherous design which had been concealed under the mask of the public faith. The surprise and satisfaction of the Hun ambassador Edecon, when he contemplated the splendour of Constantinople, had encouraged the interpreter Vigilius to procure for him a secret interview with the eunuch Chrysaphius, who governed the emperor and the empire. After some previous conversation, and a mutual oath of secrecy, the eunuch ventured to propose the death of Attila, as an important service by which Edecon might deserve a liberal share of the wealth and luxury which he admired. The ambassador of the Huns listened to the tempting offer; and professed, with apparent zeal, his ability, as well as readiness, to execute the bloody deed: the design was communicated to the master of the offices, and the devout Theodosius consented to the assassination of his invincible enemy. But this perfidious conspiracy was defeated by the dissimulation, or the repentance, of Edecon; and though he might exaggerate his inward abhorrence for the treason which he seemed to approve, he dexterously assumed the merit of an early and voluntary confession.

If we *now* review the embassy of Maximin and the behaviour of Attila, we must applaud the barbarian, who respected the laws of hospitality, and generously entertained and dismissed the minister of a prince who had conspired against his life.

The emperor Theodosius did not long survive the most humiliating circumstance of an inglorious life. As he was riding or hunting in the neighbourhood of Constantinople, he was thrown from his horse into the river Lycus. His sister Pulcheria, whose authority had been controlled both in civil and ecclesiastical affairs by the pernicious influence of the eunuchs, was unanimously proclaimed empress of the East; and the Romans, for the first time, submitted to a female reign.

Amidst the general acclamations of the clergy and people, the empress did not forget the prejudice and disadvantage to which her sex was exposed; and she wisely resolved to prevent their murmurs by the choice of a colleague who would always respect the superior rank and virgin chastity of his wife. She gave her hand to Marcian, a senator, about sixty years of age, and the nominal husband of Pulcheria was solemnly invested with the Imperial purple.

It was the opinion of Marcian, that war should be avoided as long as it is possible to preserve a secure and honourable peace; but it was likewise his opinion that peace cannot be honourable or secure, if the sovereign betrays a pusillanimous aversion to war. This temperate courage dictated his reply to the demands of Attila, who insolently pressed the payment of the annual tribute. The emperor signified to the barbarians that they must no longer insult the majesty of Rome by the mention of a tribute; that he was disposed to reward, with becoming liberality, the faithful friendship of his allies; but that, if they presumed to violate the public peace, they should feel that he possessed troops, and arms, and resolution, to repel their attacks.

The same language, even in the camp of the Huns, was used by his ambassador Apollonius, whose bold refusal to deliver the presents, till he had been admitted to a personal interview, displayed a sense of dignity, and a contempt of danger, which Attila was not prepared to expect from the degenerate Romans. He threatened to chastise the rash successor of Theodosius; but he hesitated whether he should first direct his invincible arms against the Eastern or the Western empire. While mankind awaited his decision with awful suspense, he sent an equal defiance to the courts of Ravenna and Constantinople; and his ministers saluted the two emperors with the same haughty declaration. "Attila, *my* lord, and *thy* lord, commands thee to provide a palace for his immediate reception."

But as the barbarian despised, or affected to despise, the Romans of the East, whom he had so often vanquished, he soon declared his resolution of suspending the easy conquest till he had achieved a more glorious and important enterprise. In the memorable invasions of Gaul and Italy, the Huns were naturally attracted by the wealth and fertility of those provinces; but the particular motives and provocations of Attila can only be explained by the state of the Western empire under the reign of Valentinian, or, to speak more correctly, under the administration of Aëtius.

The Gothic historian ingenuously confesses that Aëtius was born for the salvation of the Roman republic; and the following portrait, though it is drawn in the fairest colours, must be allowed to contain a much larger proportion of truth than of flattery. "His mother was a wealthy and noble Italian, and his father Gaudentius, who held a distinguished rank in the province of Scythia, gradually rose from the station of a military *domestic* to the dignity of master of the cavalry. Their son, who was enrolled almost in his infancy in the guards, was given as a hostage, first to Alaric, and afterwards to the Huns; and he successively obtained the civil and military honours of the palace, for which he was equally qualified by superior merit. The graceful figure of Aëtius was not above the middle stature; but his manly limbs were admirably formed for strength, beauty, and agility; and he excelled in the martial exercises of managing a horse, drawing a bow, and darting the javelin. He could patiently endure the want of food or of sleep; and his mind and body were alike capable of the most laborious efforts. He possessed the genuine courage that can despise not only dangers, but injuries: and it was impossible either to corrupt, or deceive, or intimidate the firm integrity of his soul." The barbarians, who had seated themselves in the Western provinces, were insensibly taught to respect the faith and valour of the patrician Aëtius. He soothed their passions, consulted their prejudices, balanced their interest, and checked their ambition. A seasonable treaty which he concluded with Genseric protected Italy from the depredations of the Vandals; the independent Britons implored and acknowledged his salutary aid; the Imperial authority was restored and maintained in Gaul and Spain; and he compelled the Franks and the Suevi, whom he had vanquished in the field, to become the useful confederates of the republic.

From a principle of interest, as well as gratitude, Aëtius assiduously cultivated the alliance of the Huns. While he resided in their tents as an hostage or an exile, he had familiarly conversed with Attila himself, the nephew of his benefactor; and the two famous antagonists appear to have been connected by a personal and military friendship, which they afterwards confirmed by mutual gifts, frequent embassies, and the education of Carpilio, the son of Aëtius, in the camp of Attila.

The kingdom established by the Visigoths in the southern provinces of Gaul had gradually acquired strength and maturity; and the conduct of those ambitious barbarians, either in peace or war, engaged the perpetual vigilance of Aëtius. After the death of Wallia, the Gothic sceptre devolved to Theodoric, the son of the great Alaric; and his prosperous reign of more than thirty years over a turbulent people may be allowed to prove that his prudence was supported by uncommon vigour, both of mind and body. Impatient of his narrow limits, Theodoric aspired to the possession of Arles, the wealthy seat of government and commerce; but the city was saved by the timely approach of Aëtius; and the Gothic king, who had raised the siege with some loss and disgrace, was persuaded, for an adequate subsidy, to divert the martial valour of his subjects in a Spanish war. Yet Theodoric still watched, and eagerly seized, the favourable moment of renewing his hostile attempts. The Goths besieged Narbonne, while the Belgic provinces were invaded by the Burgundians; and the public safety was threatened on every side by the apparent union of the enemies of Rome. Theodoric, king of the Visigoths, appears to have deserved the love of his subjects, the confidence of his allies, and the esteem of mankind.

The Franks, whose monarchy was still confined to the neighbourhood of the Lower Rhine, had wisely established the right of hereditary succession in the noble family of the Merovingians. These princes were elevated on a buckler, the symbol of military command; and the royal fashion of long hair was the ensign of their birth and dignity. Their flaxen locks, which they combed and dressed with singular care, hung down in flowing ringlets on their back and shoulders; while the rest of the nation were obliged, either by law or custom, to shave the hinder part of their head, to comb their hair over the forehead, and to content themselves with the ornament of two small whiskers. The lofty stature of the Franks and their blue eyes denoted a Germanic origin; their close apparel accurately expressed the figure of their limbs; a weighty sword was suspended from a broad belt; their bodies were protected by a large shield: and these warlike barbarians were trained from their earliest youth to run, to leap, to swim; to dart the javelin or battle-axe with unerring aim; to advance without hesitation against a superior enemy; and to maintain, either in life or death, the invincible reputation of their ancestors.

The three capitals, Mentz, Trèves, and Cologne, experienced the effects of hostile cruelty and avarice. The distress of Cologne was prolonged by the perpetual dominion of the same barbarians who evacuated the ruins of Trèves, and Trèves, which in the space of forty years had been four times besieged and pillaged, was disposed to lose the memory of her afflictions in the vain amusements of the circus.

When Attila declared his resolution of supporting the cause of his allies the Vandals and the Franks, at the same time, and almost in the spirit of romantic chivalry, the savage monarch professed himself the lover and the champion of the princess Honoria. The sister of Valentinian was educated in the palace of Ravenna; and as her marriage might be productive of some danger to the state, she was raised, by the title of *Augusta*, above the hopes of the most presumptuous subject. But the fair Honoria had no sooner attained the sixteenth year of her age than she detested the importunate greatness which must for ever exclude her from the comforts of honourable love: in the midst of vain and unsatisfactory pomp Honoria sighed, yielded to the impulse of nature, and threw herself into the arms of her chamberlain Eugenius. Her guilt and shame (such is the absurd language of imperious man) were soon betrayed by the appearances of pregnancy: but the disgrace of the royal family was published to the world by the imprudence of the empress Placidia, who dismissed her daughter, after a strict and shameful confinement, to a remote exile at Constantinople.

The unhappy princess passed twelve or fourteen years in the irksome society of the sisters of Theodosius and their chosen virgins, to whose *crown* Honoria could no longer aspire, and whose monastic assiduity of prayer, fasting, and vigils she reluctantly imitated. Her impatience of long and hopeless celibacy urged her to embrace a strange and desperate resolution. The name of Attila was familiar and formidable at Constantinople, and his frequent embassies entertained a perpetual intercourse between his camp and the Imperial palace. In the pursuit of love, or rather of revenge, the daughter of Placidia sacrificed every duty and every prejudice, and offered to deliver her person into the arms of a barbarian of whose language she was ignorant, whose figure was scarcely human, and whose religion and manners she abhorred. By the ministry of a faithful eunuch she transmitted to Attila a ring, the pledge of her affection, and earnestly conjured him to claim her as a lawful spouse to whom he had been secretly betrothed.

These indecent advances were received, however, with coldness and disdain; and the king of the Huns continued to multiply the number of his wives till his love was awakened by the more forcible passions of ambition and avarice. The invasion of Gaul was preceded and justified by a formal demand of the princess Honoria, with a just and equal share of the Imperial patrimony. His predecessors, the ancient Tanjous, had often addressed in the same hostile and peremptory manner the daughters of China; and the pretensions of Attila were not less offensive to the majesty of Rome. A firm but temperate refusal was communicated to his ambassadors. The right of female succession, though it might derive a specious argument from the recent examples of Placidia and Pulcheria, was strenuously denied, and the indissoluble engagements of Honoria were opposed to the claims of her Scythian lover. On the discovery of her connection with the king of the Huns, the guilty princess had been sent away, as an object of horror, from Constantinople to Italy: her life was spared, but the ceremony of her marriage was performed with some obscure and nominal husband before she was immured in a perpetual prison, to bewail those crimes and misfortunes which Honoria might have escaped had she not been born the daughter of an emperor.

The kings and nations of Germany and Scythia, from the Volga perhaps to the Danube, obeyed the warlike summons of Attila. From the royal village in the plains of Hungary his standard moved towards the West, and after a march of seven or eight hundred miles he reached the conflux of the Rhine and the Neckar, where he was joined by the Franks. A troop of light barbarians who roamed in quest of plunder might choose the winter for the convenience of passing the river on the ice, but the innumerable cavalry of the Huns required such plenty of forage and provisions as could be procured only in a milder season; the Hercynian forest supplied materials for a bridge of boats, and the hostile myriads were poured with resistless violence into the Belgic provinces. The consternation of Gaul was universal, and the various fortunes of its cities have been adorned by tradition with martyrdoms and miracles. Troyes was saved by the merits of St. Lupus; St. Servatius was removed from the world that he might not behold the ruin of Tongres; and the prayers of St. Genevieve diverted the march of Attila from the neighbourhood of Paris. But as the greatest part of the Gallic cities were alike destitute of saints and soldiers, they were besieged and stormed by the Huns, who practised, in the example of Metz, their customary maxims of war. They involved in a promiscuous massacre the priests who served at the altar and the infants who, in the hour of danger, had been providently baptised by the bishop; the flourishing city was delivered to the flames, and a solitary chapel of St. Stephen marked the place where it formerly stood. From the Rhine and the Moselle, Attila advanced into the heart of Gaul, crossed the Seine at Auxerre, and after a long and laborious march fixed his camp under the walls of Orleans.

The facility with which Attila had penetrated into the heart of Gaul may be ascribed to his insidious policy as well as to the terror of his arms. His public declarations were skilfully mitigated by his private assurances; he alternately soothed and threatened the Romans and the Goths; and the courts of Ravenna and Toulouse, mutually suspicious of each other's intentions, beheld with supine indifference the approach of their common enemy. Aëtius was the sole guardian of the public safety; but his wisest measures were embarrassed by a faction which infested the Imperial palace: the youth of Italy trembled at the sound of the trumpet; and the barbarians, who from fear or affection were inclined to the cause of Attila, awaited with doubtful and venal faith the event of the war. The patrician passed the Alps at the head of some troops whose strength and numbers scarcely deserved the name of an army. But on his arrival at Arles or Lyons he was confounded by the intelligence that the Visigoths, refusing to embrace the defence of Gaul, had determined to expect within their own territories the formidable invader whom they professed to despise.

The senator Avitus, who after the honourable exercise of the Prætorian præfecture had retired to his estate in Auvergne, was persuaded to accept the important embassy, which he executed with ability and success. He represented to Theodoric that an ambitious conqueror who aspired to the dominion of the earth could be resisted only by the firm and unanimous alliance of the powers whom he laboured to oppress. The lively eloquence of Avitus inflamed the Gothic warriors by the description of the injuries which their ancestors had suffered from the Huns, whose implacable fury still pursued them from the Danube to the foot of the Pyrenees. He strenuously urged that it was the duty of every Christian to save from sacrilegious violation the churches of God and the relics of the saints; that it was the interest of every barbarian who had acquired a settlement in Gaul to defend the fields and vineyards, which were cultivated for his use, against the desolation of the Scythian shepherds. Theodoric yielded to the evidence of truth, adopted the measure at once the most prudent and the most honourable, and declared that as the faithful ally of Aëtius and the Romans he was ready to expose his life and kingdom for the common safety of Gaul.

The Visigoths, who at that time were in the mature vigour of their fame and power, obeyed with alacrity the signal of war, prepared their arms and horses, and assembled under the standard of their aged king, who was resolved, with his two eldest sons, Torismond and Theodoric, to command in person his numerous and valiant people. The example of the Goths determined several tribes or nations that seemed to fluctuate between the Huns and the Romans. The indefatigable diligence of the patrician gradually collected the troops of Gaul and Germany, who had formerly acknowledged themselves the subjects or soldiers of the republic, but who now claimed the rewards of voluntary service and the rank of independent allies; the Læti, the Armoricans, the Breones, the Saxons, the Burgundians, the Sarmatians or Alani, the Ripuarians, and the Franks who followed Meroveus as their lawful prince. Such was the various army which, under the conduct of Aëtius and Theodoric, advanced by rapid marches to relieve Orleans, and to give battle to the innumerable host of Attila.

On their approach the king of the Huns immediately raised the siege, and sounded a retreat to recall the foremost of his troops from the pillage of a city which they had already entered. The valour of Attila was always guided by his prudence; and as he foresaw the fatal consequences of a defeat in the heart of Gaul, he repassed the Seine, and expected the enemy in the plains of Châlons, whose smooth and level surface was adapted to the operations of his Scythian cavalry.

The nations from the Volga to the Atlantic were assembled on the plain of Châlons; but many of these nations had been divided by faction, or conquest, or emigration; and the appearance of similar arms and ensigns, which threatened each other, presented the image of a civil war.

After the mutual and repeated discharge of missile weapons, in which the archers of Scythia might signalise their superior dexterity, the cavalry and infantry of the two armies were furiously mingled in closer combat. The Huns, who fought under the eyes of their king, pierced through the feeble and doubtful centre of the allies, separated their wings from each other, and wheeling, with a rapid effort, to the left, directed their whole force against the Visigoths. As Theodoric rode along the ranks to animate his troops, he received a mortal stroke from the javelin of a noble Ostrogoth.

Attila already exulted in the confidence of victory, when the valiant

Torismond descended from the hills. The Visigoths, who had been thrown into confusion by the flight, or defection, of the Alani, gradually restored their order of battle; and the Huns were undoubtedly vanquished, since Attila was compelled to retreat. He had exposed his person with the rashness of a private soldier; but the intrepid troops of the centre had pushed forwards beyond the rest of the line; their attack was faintly supported; their flanks were unguarded; and the conquerors of Scythia and Germany were saved by the approach of the night from a total defeat. They retired within the circle of waggons that fortified their camp; and the dismounted squadrons prepared themselves for a defence to which neither their arms nor their temper were adapted. The event was doubtful: but Attila had secured a last and honourable resource. The saddles and rich furniture of the cavalry were collected by his order into a funeral pile; and the magnanimous barbarian had resolved, if his entrenchments should be forced, to rush headlong into the flames, and to deprive his enemies of the glory which they might have acquired by the death or captivity of Attila.

But his enemies had passed the night in equal disorder and anxiety. Aëtius himself, separated from his allies, ignorant of their victory, and anxious for their fate, encountered and escaped the hostile troops that were scattered over the plains of Châlons; and at length reached the camp of the Goths, which he could only fortify with a slight rampart of shields till the dawn of day. The Imperial general was soon satisfied of the defeat of Attila, who still remained inactive within his entrenchments; and when he contemplated the bloody scene, he observed, with secret satisfaction, that the loss had principally fallen on the barbarians. The body of Theodoric, pierced with honourable wounds, was discovered under a heap of the slain: his subjects bewailed the death of their king and father; but their tears were mingled with songs and acclamations, and his funeral rites were performed in the face of a vanquished enemy. The Goths, clashing their arms, elevated on a buckler his eldest son Torismond, to whom they justly ascribed the glory of their success; and the new king accepted the obligation of revenge as a sacred portion of his paternal inheritance.

Yet the Goths themselves were astonished by the fierce and undaunted aspect of their formidable antagonist; and their historian has compared Attila to a lion encompassed in his den and threatening his hunters with redoubled fury. The kings and nations who might have deserted his standard in the hour of distress were made sensible that the displeasure of their monarch was the most imminent and inevitable danger. All his instruments of martial music incessantly sounded a loud and animating strain of defiance; and the foremost troops, who advanced to the assault, were checked or destroyed by showers of arrows from every side of the entrenchments. It was determined in a general council of war to besiege the king of the Huns in his camp, to intercept his provisions, and to reduce him to the alternative of a disgraceful treaty or an unequal combat. But the impatience of the barbarians soon disdained these cautious and dilatory measures: and the mature policy of Aëtius was apprehensive that, after the extirpation of the Huns, the republic would be oppressed by the pride and power of the Gothic nation. The patrician exerted the superior ascendant of authority and reason to calm the passions which the son of Theodoric considered as a duty; represented, with seeming affection and real truth, the dangers of absence and delay; and persuaded Torismond to disappoint, by his speedy return, the ambitious designs of his brothers, who might occupy the throne and treasures of Toulouse.

After the departure of the Goths, and the separation of the allied army, Attila was surprised at the vast silence that reigned over the plains of Châlons: the suspicion of some hostile stratagem detained him several days within the circle of his waggons, and his retreat beyond the Rhine confessed the last victory which was achieved in the name of the Western empire. Meroveus and his Franks, observing a prudent distance, and magnifying the opinion of their strength by the numerous fires which they kindled every night, continued to follow the rear of the Huns till they reached the confines of Thuringia. The Thuringians served in the army of Attila: they traversed, both in their march and in their return, the territories of the Franks; and it was perhaps in this war that they exercised the cruelties which, about fourscore years afterwards, were revenged by the son of Clovis. They massacred their hostages, as well as their captives: two hundred young maidens were tortured with exquisite and unrelenting rage; their bodies were torn asunder by wild horses, or their bones were crushed under the weight of rolling waggons; and their unburied limbs were abandoned on the public roads as a prey to dogs and vultures. Such were those savage ancestors whose imaginary virtues have sometimes excited the praise and envy of civilised ages!

Neither the spirit, nor the forces, nor the reputation of Attila were impaired by the failure of the Gallic expedition. In the ensuing spring he repeated his demand of the princess Honoria, invaded Italy, and besieged Aquileia with an innumerable host of barbarians. The walls of Aquileia were assaulted by a formidable train of battering rams, movable turrets, and engines that threw stones, darts, and fire; and the monarch of the Huns employed the forcible impulse of hope, fear, emulation, and interest, to subvert the only barrier which delayed the conquest of Italy. Aquileia was at that period one of the richest, the most populous, and the strongest of the maritime cities of the Hadriatic coast; and the succeeding generation could scarcely discover the ruins of Aquileia. After this dreadful chastisement, Attila pursued his march; and as he passed, the cities of Altinum, Concordia, and Padua were reduced into heaps of stones and ashes. The inland towns, Vicenza, Verona, and Bergamo, were exposed to the rapacious cruelty of the Huns. Milan and Pavia submitted, without resistance, to the loss of their wealth; and applauded the unusual clemency which preserved from the flames the public as well as private buildings, and spared the lives of the captive multitude. The popular traditions of Comum, Turin, or Modena may justly be suspected; yet they concur with more authentic evidence to prove that Attila spread his ravages over the rich plains of modern

Lombardy, which are divided by the Po, and bounded by the Alps and Apennine.

When he took possession of the royal palace of Milan, he was surprised and offended at the sight of a picture which represented the Cæsars seated on their throne, and the princes of Scythia prostrate at their feet. The revenge which Attila inflicted on this monument of Roman vanity was harmless and ingenious. He commanded a painter to reverse the figures and the attitudes; and the emperors were delineated on the same canvas approaching in a suppliant posture to empty their bags of tributary gold before the throne of the Scythian monarch.

It is a saying worthy of the ferocious pride of Attila, that the grass never grew on the spot where his horse had trod. Yet the savage destroyer undesignedly laid the foundations of a republic which revived, in the feudal state of Europe, the art and spirit of a commercial industry. The celebrated name of Venice, or Venetia, was formerly diffused over a large and fertile province of Italy, from the confines of Pannonia to the river Addua, and from the Po to the Rhætian and Julian Alps. Before the irruption of the barbarians, fifty Venetian cities flourished in peace and prosperity: Aquileia was placed in the most conspicuous station: but the ancient dignity of Padua was supported by agriculture and manufactures; and the property of five hundred citizens, who were entitled to the equestrian rank, must have amounted, at the strictest computation, to one million seven hundred thousand pounds. Many families of Aquileia, Padua, and the adjacent towns, who fled from the sword of the Huns, found a safe, though obscure, refuge in the neighbouring islands. At the extremity of the Gulf, where the Hadriatic feebly imitates the tides of the ocean, near an hundred small islands are separated by shallow water from the continent, and protected from the waves by several long slips of land, which admit the entrance of vessels through some secret and narrow channels. Till the middle of the fifth century these remote and sequestered spots remained without cultivation, with few inhabitants, and almost without a name. But the manners of the Venetian fugitives, their arts and their government, were gradually formed by their new situation.

The Italians, who had long since renounced the exercise of arms, were surprised, after forty years' peace, by the approach of a formidable barbarian, whom they abhorred as the enemy of their religion as well as of their republic. Amidst the general consternation, Aëtius alone was incapable of fear; but it was impossible that he should achieve alone and unassisted any military exploits worthy of his former renown. The barbarians who had defended Gaul refused to march to the relief of Italy; and the succours promised by the Eastern emperor were distant and doubtful. Since Aëtius, at the head of his domestic troops, still maintained the field, and harassed or retarded the march of Attila, he never showed himself more truly great than at the time when his conduct was blamed by an ignorant and ungrateful people. If the mind of Valentinian had been susceptible of any generous sentiments, he would have chosen such a general for his example and his guide. But the timid grandson of Theodosius, instead of sharing the dangers, escaped from the sound, of war; and his hasty retreat from Ravenna to Rome, from an impregnable fortress to an open capital, betrayed his secret intention of abandoning Italy as soon as the danger should approach his Imperial person.

This shameful abdication was suspended, however, by the spirit of doubt and delay which commonly adheres to pusillanimous counsels, and sometimes corrects their pernicious tendency. The Western emperor, with the senate and people of Rome, embraced the more salutary resolution of deprecating, by a solemn and suppliant embassy, the wrath of Attila. This important commission was accepted by Avienus, who, from his birth and riches, his consular dignity, the numerous train of his clients, and his personal abilities, held the first rank in the Roman senate. The specious and artful character of Avienus was admirably qualified to conduct a negotiation either of public or private interest: his colleague Trigetius had exercised the Prætorian præfecture of Italy; and Leo, bishop of Rome, consented to expose his life for the safety of his flock.

The Roman ambassadors were introduced to the tent of Attila, as he lay encamped at the place where the slow-winding Mincius is lost in the foaming waves of the lake Benacus, and trampled, with his Scythian cavalry, the farms of Catullus and Virgil. The barbarian monarch listened with favourable, and even respectful, attention; and the deliverance of Italy was purchased by the immense ransom or dowry of the princess Honoria.

When Attila declared his resolution of carrying his victorious arms to the gates of Rome, he was admonished by his friends, as well as by his enemies, that Alaric had not long survived the conquest of the eternal city. His mind, superior to real danger, was assaulted by imaginary terrors; nor could he escape the influence of superstition, which had so often been subservient to his designs.

Before the king of the Huns evacuated Italy, he threatened to return more dreadful, and more implacable, if his bride, the princess Honoria, were not delivered to his ambassadors within the term stipulated by the treaty. Yet, in the meanwhile, Attila relieved his tender anxiety, by adding a beautiful maid, whose name was Ildico, to the list of his innumerable wives. Their marriage was celebrated with barbaric pomp and festivity, at his wooden palace beyond the Danube; and the monarch, oppressed with wine and sleep, retired at a late hour from the banquet to the nuptial bed. His attendants continued to respect his pleasures or his repose the greatest part of the ensuing day, till the unusual silence alarmed their fears and suspicions; and, after attempting to awaken Attila by loud and repeated cries, they at length broke into the royal apartment. They found the trembling bride sitting by the bedside, hiding her face with her veil, and lamenting her own danger, as well as the death of the king, who had expired during the night.[1]

[1]The report of her *guilt* reached Constantinople, where it obtained a very different name; and Marcellinus observes, that the tyrant of Europe was slain in the night by the hand and the knife of a woman.

The remains of Attila were enclosed within three coffins of gold, of silver, and of iron, and privately buried in the night: the spoils of nations were thrown into his grave; the captives who had opened the ground were inhumanly massacred; and the same Huns, who had indulged such excessive grief, feasted, with dissolute and intemperate mirth, about the recent sepulchre of their king. After his death the boldest chieftains aspired to the rank of kings; the most powerful kings refused to acknowledge a superior; and the numerous sons whom so many various mothers bore to the deceased monarch divided and disputed like a private inheritance the sovereign command of the nations of Germany and Scythia. They were soon overwhelmed by a torrent of new barbarians, who followed the same road which their own ancestors had formerly discovered. The *Geougen*, or Avares, whose residence is assigned by the Greek writers to the shores of the ocean, impelled the adjacent tribes; till at length the Igours of the North, issuing from the cold Siberian regions which produce the most valuable furs, spread themselves over the desert as far as the Borysthenes and the Caspian gates, and finally extinguished the empire of the Huns.

Such an event might contribute to the safety of the Eastern empire under the reign of a prince who conciliated the friendship, without forfeiting the esteem, of the barbarians. But the emperor of the West, the feeble and dissolute Valentinian, who had reached his thirty-fifth year without attaining the age of reason or courage, abused this apparent security to undermine the foundations of his own throne by the murder of the patrician Aëtius. From the instinct of a base and jealous mind, he hated the man who was universally celebrated as the terror of the barbarians and the support of the republic. The fame of Aëtius, his wealth and dignity, the numerous and martial train of barbarian followers, his powerful dependents who filled the civil offices of the state, and the hopes of his son Gaudentius, who was already contracted to Eudoxia, the emperor's daughter, had raised him above the rank of a subject. The ambitious designs, of which he was secretly accused, excited the fears as well as the resentment of Valentinian. Aëtius himself, supported by the consciousness of his merit, his services, and perhaps his innocence, seems to have maintained a haughty and indiscreet behaviour. Whilst he urged, perhaps with intemperate vehemence, the marriage of his son, Valentinian, drawing his sword—the first sword he had ever drawn—plunged it in the breast of a general who had saved his empire. The emperor was confounded by the honest reply of a Roman whose approbation he had not disdained to solicit. "I am ignorant, sir, of your motives or provocations; I only know that you have acted like a man who cuts off his right hand with his left."

The luxury of Rome seems to have attracted the long and frequent visits of Valentinian, who was consequently more despised at Rome than in any other part of his dominions. Valentinian, who supposed that every human breast was devoid like his own of friendship and gratitude, had imprudently admitted among his guards several domestics and followers of Aëtius. Two of these, of barbarian race, were persuaded to execute a sacred and honourable duty by punishing with death the assassin of their patron; and their intrepid courage did not long expect a favourable moment. Whilst Valentinian amused himself in the field of Mars with the spectacle of some military sports, they suddenly rushed upon him with drawn weapons, despatched the guilty Heraclius, and stabbed the emperor to the heart, without the least opposition from his numerous train, who seemed to rejoice in the tyrant's death.

As early as the time of Cicero and Varro it was the opinion of the Roman augurs that the *twelve vultures* which Romulus had seen represented the *twelve centuries* assigned for the fatal period of his city. This prophecy, disregarded perhaps in the season of health and prosperity, inspired the people with gloomy apprehensions when the twelfth century, clouded with disgrace and misfortune, was almost elapsed;[2] and even posterity must acknowledge with some surprise that the arbitrary interpretation of an accidental or fabulous circumstance has been seriously verified in the downfall of the Western empire. But its fall was announced by a clearer omen than the flight of vultures: the Roman government appeared every day less formidable to its enemies, more odious and oppressive to its subjects. The taxes were multiplied with the public distress; economy was neglected in proportion as it became necessary; and the injustice of the rich shifted the unequal burden from themselves to the people, whom they defrauded of the *indulgences* that might sometimes have alleviated their misery. The severe inquisition, which confiscated their goods and tortured their persons, compelled the subjects of Valentinian to prefer the more simple tyranny of the barbarians, to fly to the woods and mountains, or to embrace the vile and abject condition of mercenary servants. They abjured and abhorred the name of Roman citizens, which had formerly excited the ambition of mankind. If all the barbarian conquerors had been annihilated in the same hour, their total destruction would not have restored the empire of the West: and if Rome still survived, she survived the loss of freedom, of virtue, and of honour.

[2]According to Varro, the twelfth century would expire A.D. 447.

CHAPTER XXV

Sack of Rome by Genseric, King of the Vandals—Total Extinction of the Western Empire—Odoacer, the First Barbarian King of Italy

The loss or desolation of the provinces from the Ocean to the Alps impaired the glory and greatness of Rome: her internal prosperity was irretrievably destroyed by the separation of Africa. The rapacious Vandals confiscated the patrimonial estates of the senators, and intercepted the regular subsidies which relieved the poverty and encouraged the idleness of the plebeians. The distress of the Romans was soon aggravated by an unexpected attack; and the province, so long cultivated for their use by industrious and obedient subjects, was armed against them by an ambitious barbarian.

The Vandals and Alani, who followed the successful standard of Genseric, had acquired a rich and fertile territory, which stretched along the coast above ninety days' journey from Tangier to Tripoli; but their narrow limits were pressed and confined, on either side, by the sandy desert and the Mediterranean. The discovery and conquest of the Black nations, that might dwell beneath the torrid zone, could not tempt the rational ambition of Genseric; but he cast his eyes towards the sea; he resolved to create a naval power, and his bold resolution was executed with steady and active perseverance. The woods of Mount Atlas afforded an inexhaustible nursery of timber; his new subjects were skilled in the arts of navigation and shipbuilding; he animated his daring Vandals to embrace a mode of warfare which would render every maritime country accessible to their arms; the Moors and Africans were allured by the hopes of plunder; and, after an interval of six centuries, the fleets that issued from the port of Carthage again claimed the empire of the Mediterranean. The success of the Vandals, the conquest of Sicily, the sack of Palermo, and the frequent descents on the coast of Lucania, awakened and alarmed the mother of Valentinian and the sister of Theodosius. Alliances were formed; and armaments, expensive and ineffectual, were prepared for the destruction of the common enemy, who reserved his courage to encounter those dangers which his policy could not prevent or elude. The designs of the Roman government were repeatedly baffled by his artful delays, ambiguous promises, and apparent concessions; and the interposition of his formidable confederate, the king of the Huns, recalled the emperors from the conquest of Africa to the care of their domestic safety. The revolutions of the palace, which left the Western empire without a defender and without a lawful prince, dispelled the apprehensions and stimulated the avarice of Genseric. He immediately equipped a numerous fleet of Vandals and Moors, and cast anchor at the mouth of the Tiber, about three months after the death of Valentinian and the elevation of Maximus to the Imperial throne.

The private life of the senator Petronius Maximus was often alleged as a rare example of human felicity. His birth was noble and illustrious, since he descended from the Anician family; his dignity was supported by an adequate patrimony in land and money; and these advantages of fortune were accompanied with liberal arts and decent manners, which adorn or imitate the inestimable gifts of genius and virtue. The luxury of his palace and table was hospitable and elegant. Whenever Maximus appeared in public, he was surrounded by a train of grateful and obsequious clients; and it is possible that among these clients he might deserve and possess some real friend. His merit was rewarded by the favour of the prince and senate: he thrice exercised the office of Prætorian præfect of Italy; he was twice invested with the consulship, and he obtained the rank of patrician. But whatever abilities Maximus might have shown in a subordinate station, he was found incapable of administering an empire: and though he might easily have been informed of the naval preparations which were made on the opposite shores of Africa, he expected with supine indifference the approach of the enemy, without adopting any measures of defence, of negotiation, or of a timely retreat. When the Vandals disembarked at the mouth of the Tiber, the emperor was suddenly roused from his lethargy by the clamours of a trembling and exasperated multitude. The only hope which presented itself to his astonished mind was that of a precipitate flight, and he exhorted the senators to imitate the example of their prince. But no sooner did Maximus appear in the streets than he was assaulted by a shower of stones: a Roman or a Burgundian soldier claimed the honour of the first wound; his mangled body was ignominiously cast into the Tiber.

On the third day after the tumult, Genseric boldly advanced from the port of Ostia to the gates of the defenceless city. Instead of a sally of the Roman youth, there issued from the gates an unarmed and venerable procession of the bishop at the head of his clergy. The fearless spirit of Leo, his authority and eloquence, *again* mitigated the fierceness of a barbarian conqueror: the king of the Vandals promised to spare the unresisting multitude, to protect the buildings from fire, and to exempt the captives from torture; and although such orders were neither seriously given, nor strictly obeyed, the mediation of Leo was glorious to himself, and in some degree beneficial to his country. But Rome and its inhabitants were delivered to the licentiousness of the Vandals and Moors, whose blind passions revenged the injuries of Carthage. The pillage lasted fourteen days and nights; and all that yet remained of public or private wealth, of sacred or profane treasure, was diligently transported to the vessels of Genseric.

Among the spoils, the splendid relics of two temples, or rather of two religions, exhibited a memorable example of the vicissitudes of human and divine things. Since the abolition of Paganism, the Capitol had been violated and abandoned; yet the statues of the gods and heroes were still respected, and the curious roof of gilt bronze was reserved for the rapacious hands of Genseric. The holy instruments of the Jewish worship, the gold table, and the gold candlestick with seven branches, originally framed according to the particular instructions of God himself, and which were placed in the sanctuary of his temple, had been ostentatiously displayed to the Roman people in the triumph of Titus. They were afterwards deposited in the temple of Peace; and at the end of four hundred years, the spoils of Jerusalem were transferred from Rome to Carthage, by a barbarian who derived his origin from the shores of the Baltic. These ancient monuments might attract the notice of curiosity as well as of avarice. But the Christian churches, enriched and adorned by the prevailing superstition of the times, afforded more plentiful materials for sacrilege; and the pious liberality of Pope Leo, who melted six silver vases, the gift of Constantine, each of an hundred pounds weight, is an evidence of the damage which he attempted to repair. In the forty-five years that had elapsed since the Gothic invasion, the pomp and luxury of Rome were in some measure restored; and it was difficult either to escape, or to satisfy, the avarice of a conqueror who possessed leisure to collect, and ships to transport, the wealth of the capital. The Imperial ornaments of the palace, the magnificent furniture and wardrobe, the sideboards of massy plate, were accumulated with disorderly rapine: the gold and silver amounted to several thousand talents; yet even the brass and copper were laboriously removed. Many thousand Romans of both sexes, chosen for some useful or agreeable qualifications, reluctantly embarked on board the fleet of Genseric; and their distress was aggravated by the unfeeling barbarians, who, in the division of the booty, separated the wives from their husbands, and the children from their parents. The charity of Deogratias, bishop of Carthage, was their only consolation and support. He generously sold the gold and silver plate of the church to purchase the freedom of some, to alleviate the slavery of others, and to assist the wants and infirmities of a captive multitude, whose health was impaired by the hardships which they had suffered in the passage from Italy to Africa. By his order, two spacious churches were converted into hospitals: the sick were distributed in convenient beds, and liberally supplied with food and medicines; and the aged prelate repeated his visits both in the day and night, with an assiduity that surpassed his strength.

The deaths of Aëtius and Valentinian had relaxed the ties which held the barbarians of Gaul in peace and subordination. The sea-coast was infested by the Saxons; the Alemanni and the Franks advanced from the Rhine to the Seine; and the ambition of the Goths seemed to meditate more extensive and permanent conquests. But the fate of Gaul depended on the Visigoths; and the Roman general Avitus, less attentive to his dignity than to the public interest, did not disdain to visit Toulouse in the character of an ambassador. He was received with courteous hospitality by Theodoric, the king of the Goths; but while Avitus laid the foundations of a solid alliance with that powerful nation, he was astonished by the intelligence that the emperor Maximus was slain, and that Rome had been pillaged by the Vandals. A vacant throne, which he might ascend without guilt or danger, tempted his ambition: and the Visigoths were easily persuaded to support his claim by their irresistible suffrage. The season was now approaching in which the annual assembly of the seven provinces was held at Arles; their deliberations might perhaps be influenced by the presence of Theodoric and his martial brothers; but their choice would naturally incline to the most illustrious of their countrymen. Avitus, after a decent resistance, accepted the Imperial diadem from the representatives of Gaul; and his election was ratified by the acclamations of the barbarians and provincials. The formal consent of Marcian, emperor of the East, was solicited and obtained; but the senate, Rome, and Italy, though humbled by their recent calamities, submitted with a secret murmur to the presumption of the Gallic usurper. The Romans were not inclined either to excuse his faults or to acknowledge his virtues. The several parts of the empire became every day more alienated from each other; and the stranger of Gaul was the object of popular hatred and contempt.

The successor of Avitus presents the welcome discovery of a great and heroic character, such as sometimes arises, in a degenerate age, to vindicate the honour of the human species. The emperor Majorian has deserved the praises of his contemporaries and of posterity.

The private and public actions of Majorian are very imperfectly known: but his laws, remarkable for an original cast of thought and expression, faithfully represent the character of a sovereign who loved his people, who sympathised in their distress, who had studied the causes of the decline of the empire, and who was capable of applying (as far as such reformation was practicable) judicious and effectual remedies to the public disorders.

The spectator who casts a mournful view over the ruins of ancient Rome is tempted to accuse the memory of the Goths and Vandals for the mischief which they had neither leisure, nor power, nor perhaps inclination, to perpetrate. The tempest of war might strike some lofty turrets to the ground; but the destruction which undermined the foundations of those massy fabrics was prosecuted, slowly and silently, during a period of ten centuries; and the motives of interest, that afterwards operated without shame or control, were severely checked by the taste and spirit of the emperor Majorian.

The decay of the city had gradually impaired the value of the public works. The Circus and theatres might still excite, but they seldom gratified, the desires of the people: the temples which had escaped the zeal of the Christians were no longer inhabited either by gods or men; the diminished crowds of the Romans were lost in the immense space of their baths and porticoes; and the stately libraries and halls of justice became useless to an indolent generation whose repose was seldom disturbed either by study or business. The monuments of consular or Imperial greatness were no longer revered as the immortal glory of the capital: they were only esteemed as an inexhaustible mine of materials, cheaper, and more convenient, than the distant quarry. Specious petitions were continually addressed to the easy magistrates of Rome which stated the want of stones or bricks for some necessary service: the fairest forms of architecture were rudely defaced for the sake of some paltry or pretended repairs; and the degenerate Romans, who converted the spoil to their own emolument, demolished, with sacrilegious hands, the labours of their ancestors.

While the emperor Majorian assiduously laboured to restore the happiness and virtue of the Romans, he encountered the arms of Genseric, from his character and situation their most formidable enemy. A fleet of Vandals and Moors landed at the mouth of the Liris or Garigliano; but the Imperial troops surprised and attacked the disorderly barbarians, who were encumbered with the spoils of Campania; they were chased with slaughter to their ships, and their leader, the king's brother-in-law, was found in the number of the slain. Such vigilance might announce the character of the new reign, but the strictest vigilance and the most numerous forces were insufficient to protect the long-extended coast of Italy from the depredations of a naval war.

The public opinion had imposed a nobler and more arduous task on the genius of Majorian. Rome expected from him alone the restitution of Africa, and the design which he formed of attacking the Vandals in their new settlements was the result of bold and judicious policy. If the intrepid emperor could have infused his own spirit into the youth of Italy, if he could have revived in the field of Mars the manly exercises in which he had always surpassed his equals, he might have marched against Genseric at the head of a *Roman* army. Such a reformation of national manners might be embraced by the rising generation; but it is the misfortune of those princes who laboriously sustain a declining monarchy, that, to obtain some immediate advantage, or to avert some impending danger, they are forced to countenance, and even to multiply, the most pernicious abuses. Majorian, like the weakest of his predecessors, was reduced to the disgraceful expedient of substituting barbarian auxiliaries in the place of his unwarlike subjects: and his superior abilities could only be displayed in the vigour and dexterity with which he wielded a dangerous instrument, so apt to recoil on the hand that used it.

Besides the confederates who were already engaged in the service of the empire, the fame of his liberality and valour attracted the nations of the Danube, the Borysthenes, and perhaps of the Tanais. Many thousands of the bravest subjects of Attila, the Gepidæ, the Ostrogoths, the Rugians, the Burgundians, the Suevi, the Alani, assembled in the plains of Liguria, and their formidable strength was balanced by their mutual animosities. They passed the Alps in a severe winter. The emperor led the way on foot and in complete armour, sounding with his long staff the depth of the ice or snow, and encouraging the Scythians, who complained of the extreme cold, by the cheerful assurance that they should be satisfied with the heat of Africa. The citizens of Lyons had presumed to shut their gates: they soon implored, and experienced, the clemency of Majorian. He vanquished Theodoric in the field, and admitted to his friendship and alliance a king whom he had found not unworthy of his arms. The beneficial though precarious reunion of the greatest part of Gaul and Spain was the effect of persuasion as well as of force; and the independent Bagaudæ, who had escaped or resisted the oppression of former reigns, were disposed to confide in the virtues of Majorian. His camp was filled with barbarian allies; his throne was supported by the zeal of an affectionate people; but the emperor had foreseen that it was impossible without a maritime power to achieve the conquest of Africa.

The woods of the Apennine were felled; the arsenals and manufactures of Ravenna and Misenum were restored; Italy and Gaul vied with each other in liberal contributions to the public service; and the Imperial navy of three hundred large galleys, with an adequate proportion of transports and smaller vessels, was collected in the secure and capacious harbour of Carthagena in Spain. The intrepid countenance of Majorian animated his troops with a confidence of victory; and if we might credit the historian Procopius, his courage sometimes hurried him beyond the bounds of prudence. Anxious to explore with his own eyes the state of the Vandals, he ventured, after disguising the colour of his hair, to visit Carthage in the character of his own ambassador: and Genseric was afterwards mortified by the discovery that he had entertained and dismissed the emperor of the Romans. Such an anecdote may be rejected as an improbable fiction, but it is a fiction which would not have been imagined unless in the life of a hero.

Without the help of a personal interview, Genseric was sufficiently acquainted with the genius and designs of his adversary. He practised his customary arts of fraud and delay, but he practised them without success. His applications for peace became each hour more submissive, and perhaps more sincere; but the inflexible Majorian had adopted the ancient maxim that Rome could not be safe as long as Carthage existed in a hostile state. The king of the Vandals distrusted the valour of his native subjects, who were enervated by the luxury of the South; he suspected the fidelity of the vanquished people, who abhorred him as an Arian tyrant; and the desperate measure which he executed of reducing Mauritania into a desert could not defeat the operations of the Roman emperor, who was at liberty to land his troops on any part of the African coast. But Genseric was saved from impending and inevitable ruin by the treachery of some powerful subjects, envious or apprehensive of their master's success. Guided by their secret intelligence, he surprised the unguarded fleet in the bay of Carthagena: many of the ships were sunk, or taken, or burnt; and the preparations of three years were destroyed in a single day.

After this event the behaviour of the two antagonists showed them superior to their fortune. The Vandal, instead of being elated by this accidental victory, immediately renewed his solicitations for peace. The emperor of the West, who was capable of forming great designs and of supporting heavy disappointments, consented to a treaty, or rather to a suspension of arms, in the full assurance that before he could restore his navy he should be supplied with provocations to justify a second war. Majorian returned to Italy to prosecute his labours for the public happiness; and as he was conscious of his own integrity, he might long remain ignorant of the dark conspiracy which threatened his throne and his life. The recent misfortune of Carthagena sullied the glory which had dazzled the eyes of the multitude: almost every description of civil and military officers were exasperated against the Reformer, since they all derived some advantage from the abuses which he endeavoured to suppress; and the patrician Ricimer impelled the inconstant passions of the barbarians against a prince whom he esteemed and hated. The virtues of Majorian could not protect him from the impetuous sedition which broke out in the camp near Tortona at the foot of the Alps. He was compelled to abdicate the Imperial purple; five days after his abdication it was reported that he died of a dysentery. The Vandals repeatedly visited the coasts of Spain, Liguria, Tuscany, Campania, Lucania, Bruttium, Apulia, Calabria, Venetia, Dalmatia, Epirus, Greece, and Sicily: they were tempted to subdue the island of Sardinia, so advantageously placed in the centre of the Mediterranean; and their arms spread desolation or terror from the Columns of Hercules to the mouth of the Nile. As they were more ambitious of spoil than of glory, they seldom attacked any fortified cities, or engaged any regular troops in the open field. But the celerity of their motions enabled them almost at the same time to threaten and to attack the most distant objects which attracted their desires; and as they always embarked a sufficient number of horses, they had no sooner landed than they swept the dismayed country with a body of light cavalry. Yet, notwithstanding the example of their king, the native Vandals and Alani insensibly declined this toilsome and perilous warfare; the hardy generation of the first conquerors was almost extinguished, and their sons, who were born in Africa, enjoyed the delicious baths and gardens which had been acquired by the valour of their fathers. Their place was readily supplied by a various multitude of Moors and Romans, of captives and outlaws.

The Italians, destitute of a naval force, which alone was capable of protecting their coasts, implored the aid of the more fortunate nations of the East, who had formerly acknowledged in peace and war the supremacy of Rome. But the perpetual division of the two empires had alienated their interest and their inclinations; the faith of a recent treaty was alleged; and the Western Romans, instead of arms and ships, could only obtain the assistance of a cold and ineffectual mediation. Italy submitted, as the price and security of the alliance, to accept a master from the choice of the emperor of the East.

Since the death of the younger Theodosius, the domestic repose of Constantinople had never been interrupted by war or faction. But the powers of the Eastern empire were strenuously exerted to deliver Italy and the Mediterranean from the Vandals; and Genseric, who had so long oppressed both the land and sea, was threatened from every side with a formidable invasion.

The fleet that sailed from Constantinople to Carthage consisted of eleven hundred and thirteen ships, and the number of soldiers and mariners exceeded one hundred thousand men. Basiliscus, the brother of the empress Verina, was entrusted with this important command. His sister, the wife of the emperor Leo, had exaggerated the merit of his former exploits against the Scythians. But the discovery of his guilt, or incapacity, was reserved for the African war.

Experience has shown that the success of an invader most commonly depends on the vigour and celerity of his operations. The strength and sharpness of the first impression are blunted by delay; the health and spirit of the troops insensibly languish in a distant climate; the naval and military force, a mighty effort which perhaps can never be repeated, is silently consumed; and every hour that is wasted in negotiation accustoms the enemy to contemplate and examine those hostile terrors which, on their first appearance, he deemed irresistible. The formidable navy of Basiliscus pursued its prosperous navigation from the Thracian Bosphorus to the coast of Africa. He landed his troops at Cape Bona, or the promontory of Mercury, about forty miles from Carthage. The army of Heraclius, and the fleet of Marcellinus, either joined or seconded the Imperial lieutenant; and the Vandals who opposed his progress by sea or land were successively vanquished. If Basiliscus had seized the moment of consternation, and boldly advanced to the capital, Carthage must have surrendered, and the kingdom of the Vandals was extinguished.

Genseric beheld the danger with firmness, and eluded it with his veteran dexterity. He protested, in the most respectful language, that he was ready to submit his person and his dominions to the will of the emperor; but he requested a truce of five days to regulate the terms of his submission; and it was universally believed that his secret liberality contributed to the success of this public negotiation. Instead of obstinately refusing whatever indulgence his enemy so earnestly solicited, the guilty, or the credulous, Basiliscus consented to the fatal truce; and his imprudent security seemed to proclaim that he already considered himself as the conqueror of Africa. During this short interval the wind became favourable to the designs of Genseric. He manned his largest ships of war with the bravest of the Moors and Vandals; and they towed after them many large barks filled with combustible materials. In the obscurity of the night, these destructive vessels were impelled against the unguarded and unsuspecting fleet of the Romans, who were awakened by the sense of their instant danger. Their close and crowded order assisted the progress of the fire, which was communicated with rapid and irresistible violence; and the noise of the wind, the crackling of the flames, the dissonant cries of the soldiers and mariners, who could neither command nor obey, increased the horror of the nocturnal tumult. Whilst they laboured to extricate themselves from the fire-ships, and to save at least a part of the navy, the galleys of Genseric assaulted them with temperate and disciplined valour; and many of the Romans, who escaped the fury of the flames, were destroyed or taken by the victorious Vandals.

After the failure of this great expedition, Genseric again became the tyrant of the sea: the coasts of Italy, Greece, and Asia, were again exposed to his revenge and avarice; Tripoli and Sardinia returned to his obedience; he added Sicily to the number of his provinces; and, before he died, in the fulness of years and of glory, he beheld the final extinction of the empire of the West.

During his long and active reign the African monarch had studiously cultivated the friendship of the barbarians of Europe, whose arms he might employ in a seasonable and effectual diversion against the two empires. After the death of Attila he renewed his alliance with the Visigoths of Gaul.

One of the last acts of jurisdiction which the Roman senate exercised over their subjects of Gaul was the trial and condemnation of Arvandus, the Prætorian præfect. Sidonius, who rejoices that he lived under a reign in which he might pity and assist a state-criminal, has expressed, with tenderness and freedom, the faults of his indiscreet and unfortunate friend. From the perils which he had escaped, Arvandus imbibed confidence rather than wisdom; and such was the various, though uniform, imprudence of his behaviour, that his prosperity must appear much more surprising than his downfall. The second præfecture, which he obtained within the term of five years, abolished the merit and popularity of his preceding administration. His easy temper was corrupted by flattery and exasperated by opposition; he was forced to satisfy his importunate creditors with the spoils of the province; his capricious insolence offended the nobles of Gaul; and he sunk under the weight of the public hatred. The mandate of his disgrace summoned him to justify his conduct before the senate; and he passed the sea of Tuscany with a favourable wind, the presage, as he vainly imagined, of his future fortunes. A decent respect was still observed for the *Præfectorian* rank; and on his arrival at Rome Arvandus was committed to the hospitality, rather than to the custody, of Flavius Asellus, the count of the sacred largesses, who resided in the Capitol. He was eagerly pursued by his accusers, the four deputies of Gaul, who were all distinguished by their birth, their dignities, or their eloquence. In the name of a great province, and according to the forms of Roman jurisprudence, they instituted a civil and criminal action, requiring such restitution as might compensate the losses of individuals, and such punishment as might satisfy the justice of the state. Their charges of corrupt oppression were numerous and weighty; but they placed their secret dependence on a letter which they had intercepted, and which they could prove, by the evidence of his secretary, to have been dictated by Arvandus himself. The author of this letter seemed to dissuade the king of the Goths from a peace with the *Greek* emperor: he suggested the attack of the Britons on the Loire; and he recommended a division of Gaul, according to the law of nations, between the Visigoths and the Burgundians. These pernicious schemes, which a friend could only palliate by the reproaches of vanity and indiscretion, were susceptible of a treasonable interpretation; and the deputies had artfully resolved not to produce their most formidable weapons till the decisive moment of the contest. But their intentions were discovered by the zeal of Sidonius. He immediately apprised the unsuspecting criminal of his danger; and sincerely lamented, without any mixture of anger, the haughty presumption of Arvandus, who rejected, and even resented, the salutary advice of his friends.

Ignorant of his real situation, Arvandus showed himself in the Capitol in the white robe of a candidate, accepted indiscriminate salutations and offers of service, examined the shops of the merchants, the silks, and gems, sometimes with the indifference of a spectator and sometimes with the attention of a purchaser; and complained of the times, of the senate, of the prince, and of the delays of justice. His complaints were soon removed. An early day was fixed for his trial; and Arvandus appeared, with his accusers, before a numerous assembly of the Roman senate. The mournful garb which they affected excited the compassion of the judges, who were scandalised by the gay and splendid dress of their adversary: and when the præfect Arvandus, with the first of the Gallic deputies, were directed to take their places on the senatorial benches, the same contrast of pride and modesty was observed in their behaviour. In this memorable judgment, which presented a lively image of the old republic, the Gauls exposed, with force and freedom, the grievances of the province; and as soon as the minds of the audience were sufficiently inflamed, they recited the fatal epistle. The obstinacy of Arvandus was founded on the strange supposition that a subject could not be convicted of treason, unless he had actually conspired to assume the purple. As the paper was read, he repeatedly, and with a loud voice, acknowledged it for his genuine composition; and his astonishment was equal to his dismay when the unanimous voice of the senate declared him guilty of a capital offence. By their decree he was degraded from the rank of a præfect to the obscure condition of a plebeian, and ignominiously dragged by servile hands to the public prison. After a fortnight's adjournment the senate was again convened to pronounce the sentence of his death: but while he expected, in the island of Æsculapius, the expiration of the thirty days allowed by an ancient law to the vilest malefactors, his friends interposed, the emperor Anthemius relented, and the præfect of Gaul obtained the milder punishment of exile and confiscation. The faults of Arvandus might deserve compassion; but the impunity of Seronatus accused the justice of the republic, till he was condemned and executed on the complaint of the people of Auvergne. That flagitious minister, the Catiline of his age and country, held a secret correspondence with the Visigoths to betray the province which he oppressed: his industry was continually exercised in the discovery of new taxes and obsolete offences; and his extravagant vices would have inspired contempt if they had not excited fear and abhorrence.

The nations who had asserted their independence after the death of Attila were established, by the right of possession or conquest, in the boundless countries to the north of the Danube; or in the Roman provinces between the river and the Alps. But the bravest of their youth enlisted in the army of *confederates*, who formed the defence and the terror of Italy; and in this promiscuous multitude, the names of the Heruli, the Sciri, the Alani, the Turcilingi, and the Rugians, appear to have predominated. The example of these warriors was imitated by Orestes, the son of Tatullus, and the father of the last Roman emperor of the West.

The troops had been long accustomed to reverence the character and authority of Orestes, who affected their manners, conversed with them in their own language, and was intimately connected with their national chieftains by long habits of familiarity and friendship. At his solicitation they rose in arms against the obscure Greek who presumed to claim their obedience; and when Orestes, from some secret motive, declined the purple, they consented, with the same facility, to acknowledge his son Augustulus as the emperor of the West. But Orestes discovered, before the end of the first year, that the lessons of perjury and ingratitude which a rebel must inculcate will be retorted against himself, and that the precarious sovereign of Italy was only permitted to choose whether he would be the slave or the victim of his barbarian mercenaries. The dangerous alliance of these strangers had oppressed and insulted the last remains of Roman freedom and dignity. At each revolution their pay and privileges were augmented; but their insolence increased in a still more extravagant degree; they envied the fortune of their brethren in Gaul, Spain, and Africa, whose victorious arms had acquired an independent and perpetual inheritance; and they insisted on their peremptory demand that a *third* part of the lands of Italy should be immediately divided among them. Orestes, with a spirit which, in another situation, might be entitled to our esteem, chose rather to encounter the rage of an armed multitude than to subscribe the ruin of an innocent people. He rejected the audacious demand; and his refusal was favourable to the ambition of Odoacer, a bold barbarian, who assured his fellow-soldiers that, if they dared to associate under his command, they might soon extort the justice which had been denied to their dutiful petitions.

The confederates of Italy would not have elected him for their general unless the exploits of Odoacer had established a high opinion of his courage and capacity. Their military acclamations saluted him with the title of king; but he abstained during his whole reign from the use of the purple and diadem, lest he should offend those princes whose subjects, by their accidental mixture, had formed the victorious army which time and policy might insensibly unite into a great nation.

Royalty was familiar to the barbarians, and the submissive people of Italy was prepared to obey, without a murmur, the authority which he should condescend to exercise as the vice-gerent of the emperor of the West. But Odoacer had resolved to abolish that useless and expensive office; and such is the weight of antique prejudice, that it required some boldness and penetration to discover the extreme facility of the enterprise. The unfortunate Augustulus was made the instrument of his own disgrace; he signified his resignation to the senate; and that assembly, in their last act of obedience to a Roman prince, still affected the spirit of freedom and the forms of the constitution. An epistle was addressed, by their unanimous decree, to the emperor Zeno, the son-in-law and successor of Leo, who had lately been restored, after a short rebellion, to the Byzantine throne. They solemnly "disclaim the necessity, or even the wish, of continuing any longer the Imperial succession in Italy; since, in their opinion, the majesty of a sole monarch is sufficient to pervade and protect, at the same time, both the East and the West. In their own name, and in the name of the people, they consent that the seat of universal empire shall be transferred from Rome to Constantinople; and they basely renounce the right of choosing their master, the only vestige that yet remained of the authority which had given laws to the world. The republic (they repeat that name without a blush) might safely confide in the civil and military virtues of Odoacer; and they humbly request that the emperor would invest him with the title of Patrician, and the administration of the *diocese* of Italy." The deputies of the senate were received at Constantinople with some mark of displeasure and indignation: and when they were admitted to the audience of Zeno, he sternly reproached them with their treatment of the two emperors, Anthemius and Nepos, whom the East had successively granted to the prayers of Italy. "The first (continued he) you have murdered; the second you have expelled: but the second is still alive, and whilst he lives he is your lawful sovereign." But the prudent Zeno soon deserted the hopeless cause of his abdicated colleague. His vanity was gratified by the title of sole emperor, and by the statues erected to his honour in the several quarters of Rome; he entertained a friendly, though ambiguous, correspondence with the *patrician* Odoacer; and he gratefully accepted the Imperial ensigns, the sacred ornaments of the throne and palace, which the barbarian was not unwilling to remove from the sight of the people.

In the space of twenty years since the death of Valentinian, nine emperors had successively disappeared; and the son of Orestes, a youth recommended only by his beauty, would be the least entitled to the notice of posterity, if his reign, which was marked by the extinction of the Roman empire in the West, did not leave a memorable era in the history of mankind.[1] The patrician Orestes had married the daughter of Count *Romulus*, of Petovio in Noricum: the name of *Augustus*, notwithstanding the jealousy of power, was known at Aquileia as a familiar surname; and the appellations of the two great founders, of the city and of the monarchy, were thus strangely united in the last of their successors. The son of Orestes assumed and disgraced the names of Romulus Augustus; but the first was corrupted into Momyllus by the Greeks, and the second has been changed by the Latins into the contemptible diminutive Augustulus. The life of this inoffensive youth was spared by the generous clemency of Odoacer; who dismissed

[1]The precise year in which the Western empire was extinguished is not positively ascertained. The vulgar era of A.D. 476 *appears* to have the sanction of authentic chronicles. But the two dates assigned by Jornandes (c. 46, p. 680) would delay that great event to the year 479; and though M. de Buat has overlooked *his* evidence, he produces (tom. viii. pp. 261–288) many collateral circumstances in support of the same opinion.

him, with his whole family, from the Imperial palace, fixed his annual allowance at six thousand pieces of gold, and assigned the castle of Lucullus, in Campania, for the place of his exile or retirement.

Odoacer was the first barbarian who reigned in Italy, over a people who had once asserted their just superiority above the rest of mankind. The disgrace of the Romans still excites our respectful compassion, and we fondly sympathise with the imaginary grief and indignation of their degenerate posterity. But the calamities of Italy had gradually subdued the proud consciousness of freedom and glory. In the age of Roman virtue the provinces were subject to the arms, and the citizens to the laws, of the republic, till those laws were subverted by civil discord, and both the city and the provinces became the servile property of a tyrant. The forms of the constitution, which alleviated or disguised their abject slavery, were abolished by time and violence; the Italians alternately lamented the presence or the absence of the sovereigns whom they detested or despised; and the succession of five centuries inflicted the various evils of military licence, capricious despotism, and elaborate oppression. During the same period, the barbarians had emerged from obscurity and contempt, and the warriors of Germany and Scythia were introduced into the provinces, as the servants, the allies, and at length the masters, of the Romans, whom they insulted or protected. The hatred of the people was suppressed by fear; they respected the spirit and splendour of the martial chiefs who were invested with the honours of the empire; and the fate of Rome had long depended on the sword of those formidable strangers.

The king of Italy was not unworthy of the high station to which his valour and fortune had exalted him: his savage manners were polished by the habits of conversation; and he respected, though a conqueror and a barbarian, the institutions, and even the prejudices, of his subjects. After an interval of seven years, Odoacer restored the consulship of the West. For himself, he modestly, or proudly, declined an honour which was still accepted by the emperors of the East; but the curule chair was successively filled by eleven of the most illustrious senators. The laws of the emperors were strictly enforced, and the civil administration of Italy was still exercised by the Prætorian præfect and his subordinate officers. Odoacer devolved on the Roman magistrates the odious and oppressive task of collecting the public revenue; but he reserved for himself the merit of seasonable and popular indulgence. Italy was protected by the arms of its conqueror; and its frontiers were respected by the barbarians of Gaul and Germany, who had so long insulted the feeble race of Theodosius. Odoacer passed the Hadriatic, to chastise the assassins of the emperor Nepos, and to acquire the maritime province of Dalmatia. He passed the Alps, to rescue the remains of Noricum from Fava, or Feletheus, king of the Rugians, who held his residence beyond the Danube. The king was vanquished in battle, and led away prisoner; a numerous colony of captives and subjects was transplanted into Italy; and Rome, after a long period of defeat and disgrace, might claim the triumph of her barbarian master.

Notwithstanding the prudence and success of Odoacer, his kingdom exhibited the sad prospect of misery and desolation. Since the age of Tiberius, the decay of agriculture had been felt in Italy; and it was a just subject of complaint that the life of the Roman people depended on the accidents of the winds and waves. In the division and the decline of the empire, the tributary harvests of Egypt and Africa were withdrawn; the numbers of the inhabitants continually diminished with the means of subsistence; and the country was exhausted by the irretrievable losses of war, famine, and pestilence. St. Ambrose has deplored the ruin of a populous district, which had been once adorned with the flourishing cities of Bologna, Modena, Rhegium, and Placentia. Pope Gelasius was a subject of Odoacer; and he affirms, with strong exaggeration, that in Æmilia, Tuscany, and the adjacent provinces, the human species was almost extirpated. The plebeians of Rome, who were fed by the hand of their master, perished or disappeared as soon as his liberality was suppressed; the decline of the arts reduced the industrious mechanic to idleness and want; and the senators, who might support with patience the ruin of their country, bewailed their private loss of wealth and luxury. One third of those ample estates, to which the ruin of Italy is originally imputed, was extorted for the use of the conquerors. Injuries were aggravated by insults; the sense of actual sufferings was embittered by the fear of more dreadful evils; and as new lands were allotted to new swarms of barbarians, each senator was apprehensive lest the arbitrary surveyors should approach his favourite villa, or his most profitable farm.

CHAPTER XXVI

Establishment of the French Monarchy in Gaul—The Visigoths of Spain—Conquest of Britain by the Saxons—Conversion of the Barbarians

The Gauls, who impatiently supported the Roman yoke, received a memorable lesson from one of the lieutenants of Vespasian: "The protection of the republic has delivered Gaul from internal discord and foreign invasions. By the loss of national independence you have acquired the name and privileges of Roman citizens. You enjoy, in common with ourselves, the permanent benefits of civil government; and your remote situation is less exposed to the accidental mischiefs of tyranny. Instead of exercising the rights of conquest, we have been contented to impose such tributes as are requisite for your own preservation. Peace cannot be secured without armies, and armies must be supported at the expense of the people. It is for your sake, not for our own, that we guard the barrier of the Rhine against the ferocious Germans, who have so often attempted, and who will always desire, to exchange the solitude of their woods and morasses for the wealth and fertility of Gaul. The fall of Rome would be fatal to the provinces, and you would be buried in the ruins of that mighty fabric which has been raised by the valour and wisdom of eight hundred years. Your imaginary freedom would be insulted and oppressed by a savage master, and the expulsion of the Romans would be succeeded by the eternal hostilities of the barbarian conquerors."

This salutary advice was accepted, and this strange prediction was accomplished. In the space of four hundred years the hardy Gauls, who had encountered the arms of Cæsar, were imperceptibly melted into the general mass of citizens and subjects: the Western empire was dissolved; and the Germans who had passed the Rhine fiercely contended for the possession of Gaul, and excited the contempt or abhorrence of its peaceful and polished inhabitants. With that conscious pride which the pre-eminence of knowledge and luxury seldom fails to inspire, they derided the hairy and gigantic savages of the North; their rustic manners, dissonant joy, voracious appetite, and their horrid appearance, equally disgusting to the sight and to the smell. The liberal studies were still cultivated in the schools of Autun and Bordeaux, and the language of Cicero and Virgil was familiar to the Gallic youth. Their ears were astonished by the harsh and unknown sounds of the Germanic dialect, and they ingeniously lamented that the trembling muses fled from the harmony of a Burgundian lyre. The Gauls were endowed with all the advantages of art and nature, but, as they wanted courage to defend them, they were justly condemned to obey, and even to flatter, the victorious barbarians by whose clemency they held their precarious fortunes and their lives.

As soon as Odoacer had extinguished the Western empire, he sought the friendship of the most powerful of the barbarians. The new sovereign of Italy resigned to Euric, king of the Visigoths, all the Roman conquests beyond the Alps, as far as the Rhine and the Ocean, and the senate might confirm this liberal gift with some ostentation of power, and without any real loss of revenue or dominion. The lawful pretensions of Euric were justified by ambition and success, and the Gothic nation might aspire under his command to the monarchy of Spain and Gaul. Arles and Marseilles surrendered to his arms: he oppressed the freedom of Auvergne, and the bishop condescended to purchase his recall from exile by a tribute of just but reluctant praise. Sidonius waited before the gates of the palace among a crowd of ambassadors and suppliants, and their various business at the court of Bordeaux attested the power and the renown of the king of the Visigoths. The Heruli of the distant ocean, who painted their naked bodies with its cærulean colour, implored his protection; and the Saxons respected the maritime provinces of a prince who was destitute of any naval force. The tall Burgundians submitted to his authority; nor did he restore the captive Franks till he had imposed on that fierce nation the terms of an unequal peace. The Vandals of Africa cultivated his useful friendship, and the Ostrogoths of Pannonia were supported by his powerful aid against the oppression of the neighbouring Huns. The North (such are the lofty strains of the poet) was agitated or appeased by the nod of Euric, the great king of Persia consulted the oracle of the West, and the aged god of the Tiber was protected by the swelling genius of the Garonne. The fortune of nations has often depended on accidents; and France may ascribe her greatness to the premature death of the Gothic king at a time when his son Alaric was a helpless infant, and his adversary Clovis an ambitious and valiant youth.

While Childeric, the father of Clovis, lived an exile in Germany, he was hospitably entertained by the queen as well as by the king of the Thuringians. After his restoration Bafina escaped from her husband's bed to the arms of her lover, freely declaring that, if she had known a man wiser, stronger, or more beautiful than Childeric, that man should have been the object of her preference. Clovis was the offspring of this voluntary union, and when he was no more than fifteen years of age he succeeded, by his father's death, to the command of the Salian tribe. The narrow limits of his kingdom were confined to the island of the Batavians, with the ancient dioceses of Tournay and Arras; and at the baptism of Clovis the number of his warriors could not exceed five thousand. The kindred tribes of the Franks who had seated themselves along the Belgic rivers, the Scheldt, the Meuse, the Moselle, and the Rhine, were governed by their independent kings of the Merovingian race—the equals, the allies, and sometimes the enemies, of the Salic prince. But the Germans, who obeyed in peace the hereditary jurisdiction of their chiefs, were free to follow the standard of a popular and victorious general; and the superior merit of Clovis attracted the respect and allegiance of the national confederacy. When he first took the field, he had neither gold and silver in his coffers, nor wine and corn in his magazines; but he imitated the example of Cæsar, who in the same country had acquired wealth by the sword, and purchased soldiers with the fruits of conquest. After each successful battle or expedition the spoils were accumulated in one common mass; every warrior received his proportionable share, and the royal prerogative submitted to the equal regulations of military law.

The untamed spirit of the barbarians was taught to acknowledge the advantages of regular discipline. At the annual review of the month of March their arms were diligently inspected, and when they traversed a peaceful territory they were prohibited from touching a blade of grass. The justice of Clovis was inexorable, and his careless or disobedient soldiers were punished with instant death. It would be superfluous to praise the valour of a Frank, but the valour of Clovis was directed by cool and consummate prudence. In all his transactions with mankind he calculated the weight of interest, of passion, and of opinion; and his measures were sometimes adapted to the sanguinary manners of the Germans, and sometimes moderated by the milder genius of Rome and Christianity. He was intercepted in the career of victory, since he died in the forty-fifth year of his age: but he had already accomplished, in a reign of thirty years, the establishment of the French monarchy in Gaul.

Till the thirtieth year of his age Clovis continued to worship the gods of his ancestors. His disbelief, or rather disregard of Christianity, might encourage him to pillage with less remorse the churches of an hostile territory: but his subjects of Gaul enjoyed the free exercise of religious worship, and the bishops entertained a more favourable hope of the idolater than of the heretics. The Merovingian prince had contracted a fortunate alliance with the fair Clotilda, the niece of the king of Burgundy, who in the midst of an Arian court was educated in the profession of the Catholic faith. It was her interest as well as her duty to achieve the conversion of a Pagan husband; and Clovis insensibly listened to the voice of love and religion. He consented (perhaps such terms had been previously stipulated) to the baptism of his eldest son; and though the sudden death of the infant excited some superstitious fears, he was persuaded a second time to repeat the dangerous experiment. In the distress of the battle of Tolbiac, Clovis loudly invoked the God of Clotilda and the Christians; and victory disposed him to hear with respectful gratitude the eloquent Remigius, bishop of Rheims, who forcibly displayed the temporal and spiritual advantages of his conversion. The king declared himself satisfied of the truth of the Catholic faith; and the political reasons which might have suspended his public profession were removed by the devout or loyal acclamations of the Franks, who showed themselves alike prepared to follow their heroic leader to the field of battle or to the baptismal font. The important ceremony was performed in the cathedral of Rheims with every circumstance of magnificence and solemnity that could impress an awful sense of religion on the minds of its rude proselytes.

The new Constantine was immediately baptised with three thousand of his warlike subjects, and their example was imitated by the remainder of the *gentle barbarians*, who, in obedience to the victorious prelate, adored the cross which they had burnt, and burnt the idols which they had formerly adored. The mind of Clovis was susceptible of transient fervour: he was exasperated by the pathetic tale of the passion and death of Christ; and instead of weighing the salutary consequences of that mysterious sacrifice, he exclaimed with indiscreet fury, "Had I been present at the head of my valiant Franks, I would have revenged his injuries."

But the savage conqueror of Gaul was incapable of examining the proofs of a religion which depends on the laborious investigation of historic evidence and speculative theology. He was still more incapable of feeling the mild influence of the Gospel, which persuades and purifies the heart of a genuine convert. His ambitious reign was a perpetual violation of moral and Christian duties: his hands were stained with blood in peace as well as in war; and, as soon as Clovis had dismissed a synod of the Gallician church, he calmly assassinated *all* the princes of the Merovingian race.

Yet the king of the Franks might sincerely worship the Christian God as a Being more excellent and powerful than his national deities; and the signal deliverance and victory of Tolbiac encouraged Clovis to confide in the future protection of the Lord of Hosts. Martin, the most popular of the saints, had filled the Western world with the fame of those miracles which were incessantly performed at his holy sepulchre of Tours. His visible or invisible aid promoted the cause of a liberal and orthodox prince; and the profane remark of Clovis himself, that St. Martin was an expensive friend, need not be interpreted as the symptom of any permanent or rational scepticism. But earth as well as heaven rejoiced in the conversion of the Franks. On the memorable day when Clovis ascended from the baptismal font, he alone in the Christian world deserved the name and prerogatives of a Catholic king. The emperor Anastasius entertained some dangerous errors concerning the nature of the divine incarnation; and the barbarians of Italy, Africa, Spain, and Gaul were involved in the Arian heresy. The eldest, or rather the only son of the church, was acknowledged by the clergy as their lawful sovereign or glorious deliverer; and the arms of Clovis were strenuously supported by the zeal and favour of the Catholic faction.

Under the Roman empire the wealth and jurisdiction of the bishops, their sacred character and perpetual office, their numerous dependents, popular eloquence, and provincial assemblies, had rendered them always respectable, and sometimes dangerous. Their influence was augmented with the progress of superstition; and the establishment of the French monarchy may, in some degree, be ascribed to the firm alliance of an hundred prelates, who reigned in the discontented or independent cities of Gaul.

The reduction of the northern provinces of Gaul, instead of being decided by the chance of a single battle, appears to have been slowly effected by the gradual operation of war and treaty; and Clovis acquired each object of his ambition by such efforts or such concessions as were adequate to its real value.

The first victory of Clovis had insulted the honour of the Goths. They viewed his rapid progress with jealousy and terror; and the youthful fame of Alaric was oppressed by the more potent genius of his rival. Some disputes inevitably arose on the edge of their contiguous dominions; and after the delays of fruitless negotiation a personal interview of the two kings was proposed and accepted. This conference of Clovis and Alaric was held in a small island of the Loire, near Amboise. They embraced, familiarly conversed, and feasted together; and separated with the warmest professions of peace and brotherly love. But their apparent confidence concealed a dark suspicion of hostile and treacherous designs; and their mutual complaints solicited, eluded, and disclaimed a final arbitration. At Paris, which he already considered as his royal seat, Clovis declared to an assembly of the princes and warriors the pretence and the motive of a Gothic war. "It grieves me to see that the Arians still possess the fairest portion of Gaul. Let us march against them with the aid of God; and, having vanquished the heretics, we will possess and divide their fertile provinces." The Franks, who were inspired by hereditary valour and recent zeal, applauded the generous design of their monarch; expressed their resolution to conquer or die, since death and conquest would be equally profitable; and solemnly protested that they would never shave their beards till victory should absolve them from that inconvenient vow.

After the success of the Gothic war, Clovis accepted the honours of the Roman consulship. On the solemn day, the monarch of Gaul, placing a diadem on his head, was invested, in the church of St. Martin, with a purple and mantle. From thence he proceeded on horseback to the cathedral of Tours; and, as he passed through the streets, profusely scattered, with his own hand, a donative of gold and silver to the joyful multitude, who incessantly repeated their acclamations of *Consul* and *Augustus.*

The actual or legal authority of Clovis could not receive any new accessions from the consular dignity. It was a name, a shadow, an empty pageant; and if the conqueror had been instructed to claim the ancient prerogatives of that high office, they must have expired with the period of its annual duration. But the Romans were disposed to revere, in the person of their master, that antique title which the emperors condescended to assume: the barbarian himself seemed to contract a sacred obligation to respect the majesty of the republic; and the successors of Theodosius, by soliciting his friendship, tacitly forgave, and almost ratified, the usurpation of Gaul.

The Franks, or French, are the only people of Europe who can deduce a perpetual succession from the conquerors of the Western empire. But their conquest of Gaul was followed by ten centuries of anarchy and ignorance. On the revival of learning, the students who had been formed in the schools of Athens and Rome disdained their barbarian ancestors; and a long period elapsed before patient labour could provide the requisite materials to satisfy, or rather to excite, the curiosity of more enlightened times.

The rudest, or the most servile, condition of human society, is regulated however by some fixed and general rules. When Tacitus surveyed the primitive simplicity of the Germans, he discovered some permanent maxims, or customs, of public and private life, which were preserved by faithful tradition till the introduction of the art of writing, and of the Latin tongue. Before the election of the Merovingian kings, the most powerful tribe, or nation, of the Franks, appointed four venerable chieftains to compose the *Salic* laws; and their labours were examined and approved in three successive assemblies of the people. The same care was extended to their vassals; and the rude institutions of the *Alemanni* and *Bavarians* were diligently compiled and ratified by the supreme authority of the Merovingian kings. The *Visigoths* and *Burgundians*, whose conquests in Gaul preceded those of the Franks, showed less impatience to attain one of the principal benefits of civilised society. Euric was the first of the Gothic princes who expressed in writing the manners and customs of his people; and the composition of the Burgundian laws was a measure of policy rather than of justice, to alleviate the yoke and regain the affections of their Gallic subjects. Thus, by a singular coincidence, the Germans framed their artless institutions at a time when the elaborate system of Roman jurisprudence was finally consummated. In the Salic laws, and the Pandects of Justinian, we may compare the first rudiments, and the full maturity, of civil wisdom; and whatever prejudices may be suggested in favour of barbarism, our calmer reflections will ascribe to the Romans the superior advantages, not only of science and reason, but of humanity and justice.

Yet the laws of the barbarians were adapted to their wants and desires, their occupations and their capacity; and they all contributed to preserve the peace, and promote the improvements, of the society for whose use they were originally established. The Merovingians, instead of imposing a uniform rule of conduct on their various subjects, permitted each people, and each family, of their empire freely to enjoy their domestic institutions; nor were the Romans excluded from the common benefits of this legal toleration. The children embraced the *law* of their parents, the wife that of her husband, the freedman that of his patron; and in all causes where the parties were of different nations, the plaintiff or accuser was obliged to follow the tribunal of the defendant, who may always plead a judicial presumption of right or innocence. A more ample latitude was allowed, if every citizen, in the presence of the judge, might declare the law under which he desired to live, and the national society to which he chose to belong. Such an indulgence would abolish the partial distinctions of victory: and the Roman provincials might patiently acquiesce in the hardships of their condition, since it depended on themselves to assume the privilege, if they dared to assert the character, of free and warlike barbarians.

When justice inexorably requires the death of a murderer, each private citizen is fortified by the assurance that the laws, the magistrate, and the whole community, are the guardians of his personal safety. But in the loose society of the Germans, revenge was always honourable, and often meritorious: the independent warrior chastised, or vindicated, with his own hand, the injuries which he had offered or received; and he had only to dread the resentment of the sons and kinsmen of the enemy whom he had sacrificed to his selfish or angry passions. The magistrate, conscious of his weakness, interposed, not to punish, but to reconcile; and he was satisfied if he could persuade or compel the contending parties to pay and to accept the moderate fine which had been ascertained as the price of blood. The fierce spirit of the Franks would have opposed a more rigorous sentence; the same fierceness despised these ineffectual restraints; and, when their simple manners had been corrupted by the wealth of Gaul, the public peace was continually violated by acts of hasty or deliberate guilt.

In every just government the same penalty is inflicted, or at least is imposed, for the murder of a peasant or a prince. But the national inequality established by the Franks in their criminal proceedings was the last insult and abuse of conquest. In the calm moments of legislation they solemnly pronounced that the life of a Roman was of smaller value than that of a barbarian. The *Antrustion*, a name expressive of the most illustrious birth or dignity among the Franks, was appreciated at the sum of six hundred pieces of gold; while the noble provincial, who was admitted to the king's table, might be legally murdered at the expense of three hundred pieces. Two hundred were deemed sufficient for a Frank of ordinary condition; but the meaner Romans were exposed to disgrace and danger by a trifling compensation of one hundred, or even fifty, pieces of gold. Had these laws been regulated by any principle of equity or reason, the public protection should have supplied, in just proportion, the want of personal strength. But the legislator had weighed in the scale, not of justice, but of policy, the loss of a soldier against that of a slave: the head of an insolent and rapacious barbarian was guarded by a heavy fine; and the slightest aid was afforded to the most defenceless subjects.

Trials by single combat gradually obtained superior credit and authority among a warlike people who could not believe that a brave man deserved to suffer, or that a coward deserved to live. Both in civil and criminal proceedings, the plaintiff, or accuser, the defendant, or even the witness, were exposed to mortal challenge from the antagonist who was destitute of legal proofs; and it was incumbent on them either to desert their cause or publicly to maintain their honour in the lists of battle. They fought either on foot or on horseback, according to the custom of their nation; and the decision of the sword or lance was ratified by the sanction of Heaven, of the judge, and of the people. This sanguinary law was introduced into Gaul by the Burgundians; and their legislator Gundobald condescended to answer the complaints and objections of his subject Avitus. "Is it not true," said the king of Burgundy to the bishop, "that the event of national wars and private combats is directed by the judgment of God; and that his providence awards the victory to the juster cause?" By such prevailing arguments, the absurd and cruel practice of judicial duels, which had been peculiar to some tribes of Germany, was propagated and established in all the monarchies of Europe, from Sicily to the Baltic.

According to the maxims of ancient war, the conqueror became the lawful master of the enemy whom he had subdued and spared: and the fruitful cause of personal slavery, which had been almost suppressed by the peaceful sovereignty of Rome, was again revived and multiplied by the perpetual hostilities of the independent barbarians. The Goth, the Burgundian, or the Frank who returned from a successful expedition dragged after him a long train of sheep, of oxen, and of human captives, whom he treated with the same brutal contempt. The youths of an elegant form and ingenuous aspect were set apart for the domestic service; a doubtful situation, which alternately exposed them to the favourable or cruel impulse of passion. The useful mechanics and servants (smiths, carpenters, tailors, shoemakers, cooks, gardeners, dyers, and workmen in gold and silver, etc.) employed their skill for the use or profit of their master. But the Roman captives who were destitute of art, but capable of labour, were condemned, without regard to their former rank, to tend the cattle and cultivate the lands of the barbarians.

From the reign of Clovis, during five successive centuries, the laws and manners of Gaul uniformly tended to promote the increase, and to confirm the duration, of personal servitude. Time and violence almost obliterated the intermediate ranks of society, and left an obscure and narrow interval between the noble and the slave. This arbitrary and recent division has been transformed by pride and prejudice into a *national* distinction, universally established by the arms and the laws of the Merovingians. The nobles, who claimed their genuine or fabulous descent from the independent and victorious Franks, have asserted and abused the indefeasible right of conquest over a prostrate crowd of slaves and plebeians, to whom they imputed the imaginary disgrace of a Gallic or Roman extraction.

The general state and revolutions of *France*, a name which was imposed by the conquerors, may be illustrated by the particular example of a province. Auvergne had formerly maintained a just pre-eminence among the independent states and cities of Gaul. The brave and numerous inhabitants displayed a singular trophy—the sword of Cæsar himself, which he had lost when he was repulsed before the walls of Gergovia. As the common offspring of Troy, they claimed a fraternal alliance with the Romans; and if each province had imitated the courage and loyalty of Auvergne, the fall of the Western empire might have been prevented or delayed.

But the Franks of Austrasia soon yielded to the persuasive eloquence of their king. "Follow me," said Theodoric, "into Auvergne; I will lead you into a province where you may acquire gold, silver, slaves, cattle, and precious apparel, to the full extent of your wishes. I repeat my promise;

I give you the people and their wealth as your prey; and you may transport them at pleasure into your own country." By the execution of this promise Theodoric justly forfeited the allegiance of a people whom he devoted to destruction. His troops, reinforced by the fiercest barbarians of Germany, spread desolation over the fruitful face of Auvergne.

Before the Austrasian army retreated from Auvergne, Theodoric exacted some pledges of the future loyalty of a people whose just hatred could be restrained only by their fear. A select band of noble youths, the sons of the principal senators, was delivered to the conqueror as the hostages of the faith of Childebert and of their countrymen. On the first rumour of war or conspiracy these guiltless youths were reduced to a state of servitude.

But a discontented Roman might freely aspire or descend to the title and character of a barbarian. The honours of the state were accessible to his ambition: the education and temper of the Romans more peculiarly qualified them for the offices of civil government; and as soon as emulation had rekindled their military ardour, they were permitted to march in the ranks, or even at the head, of the victorious Germans.

However, the fierce and illiterate barbarians were excluded, during several generations, from the dignities, and even from the orders, of the church. The clergy of Gaul consisted almost entirely of native provincials; the haughty Franks fell prostrate at the feet of their subjects who were dignified with the episcopal character; and the power and riches which had been lost in war were insensibly recovered by superstition.

The Franks, after they mingled with their Gallic subjects, might have imparted the most valuable of human gifts, a spirit and system of constitutional liberty. Under a king, hereditary but limited, the chiefs and counsellors might have debated at Paris in the palace of the Cæsars: the adjacent field, where the emperors reviewed their mercenary legions, would have admitted the legislative assembly of freemen and warriors; and the rude model which had been sketched in the woods of Germany might have been polished and improved by the civil wisdom of the Romans. But the careless barbarians, secure of their personal independence, disdained the labour of government: the annual assemblies of the month of March were silently abolished, and the nation was separated and almost dissolved by the conquest of Gaul. The monarchy was left without any regular establishment of justice, of arms, or of revenue.

As long as the Visigoths were satisfied with the rude customs of their ancestors, they indulged their subjects of Aquitain and Spain in the enjoyment of the Roman law. Their gradual improvement in arts, in policy, and at length in religion, encouraged them to imitate and to supersede these foreign institutions, and to compose a code of civil and criminal jurisprudence for the use of a great and united people. The same obligations and the same privileges were communicated to the nations of the Spanish monarchy; and the conquerors, insensibly renouncing the Teutonic idiom, submitted to the restraints of equity, and exalted the Romans to the participation of freedom.

While the kingdoms of the Franks and Visigoths were established in Gaul and Spain, the Saxons achieved the conquest of Britain, the third great diocese of the præfecture of the West.

About forty years after the dissolution of the Roman government Vortigern appears to have obtained the supreme, though precarious, command of the princes and cities of Britain. That unfortunate monarch has been almost unanimously condemned for the weak and mischievous policy of inviting a formidable stranger to repel the vexatious inroads of a domestic foe. His ambassadors are despatched by the gravest historians to the coast of Germany: they address a pathetic oration to the general assembly of the Saxons, and those warlike barbarians resolve to assist with a fleet and army the suppliants of a distant and unknown island. If Britain had indeed been unknown to the Saxons, the measure of its calamities would have been less complete. But the strength of the Roman government could not always guard the maritime province against the pirates of Germany: the independent and divided states were exposed to their attacks, and the Saxons might sometimes join the Scots and the Picts in a tacit or express confederacy of rapine and destruction. Vortigern could only balance the various perils which assaulted on every side his throne and his people; and his policy may deserve either praise or excuse if he preferred the alliance of *those* barbarians whose naval power rendered them the most dangerous enemies, and the most serviceable allies. Hengist and Horsa, as they ranged along the eastern coast with three ships, were engaged by the promise of an ample stipend to embrace the defence of Britain, and their intrepid valour soon delivered the country from the Caledonian invaders.

The Isle of Thanet, a secure and fertile district, was allotted for the residence of these German auxiliaries, and they were supplied according to the treaty with a plentiful allowance of clothing and provisions. This favourable reception encouraged five thousand warriors to embark with their families in seventeen vessels, and the infant power of Hengist was fortified by this strong and seasonable reinforcement. The crafty barbarian suggested to Vortigern the obvious advantage of fixing, in the neighbourhood of the Picts, a colony of faithful allies: a third fleet, of forty ships, under the command of his son and nephew, sailed from Germany, ravaged the Orkneys, and disembarked a new army on the coast of Northumberland or Lothian, at the opposite extremity of the devoted land. It was easy to foresee, but it was impossible to prevent, the impending evils. The two nations were soon divided and exasperated by mutual jealousies. The Saxons magnified all that they had done and suffered in the cause of an ungrateful people; while the Britons regretted the liberal rewards which could not satisfy the avarice of those haughty mercenaries. The causes of fear and hatred were inflamed into an irreconcilable quarrel. The Saxons flew to arms; and if they perpetrated a treacherous massacre during the security of a feast, they destroyed the reciprocal confidence which sustains the intercourse of peace and war.

Hengist, who boldly aspired to the conquest of Britain, exhorted his countrymen to embrace the glorious opportunity: he painted in lively colours the fertility of the soil, the wealth of the cities, the pusillanimous temper of the natives, and the convenient situation of a spacious solitary island, accessible on all sides to the Saxon fleets. While the continent of Europe and Africa yielded, without resistance, to the barbarians, the British island, alone and unaided, maintained a long, vigorous, though an unsuccessful, struggle, against the formidable pirates who, almost at the same instant, assaulted the northern, the eastern, and the southern coasts. The cities, which had been fortified with skill, were defended with resolution; the advantages of ground, hills, forests, and morasses, were diligently improved by the inhabitants; the conquest of each district was purchased with blood; and the defeats of the Saxons are strongly attested by the discreet silence of their annalist.

Seven independent thrones, the Saxon Heptarchy, were founded by the conquerors; and seven families, one of which has been continued, by female succession, to our present sovereign, derived their equal and sacred lineage from Woden, the god of war. It has been pretended that this republic of kings was moderated by a general council and a supreme magistrate. But such an artificial scheme of policy is repugnant to the rude and turbulent spirit of the Saxons: their laws are silent, and their imperfect annals afford only a dark and bloody prospect of intestine discord.

After a war of an hundred years the independent Britons still occupied the whole extent of the western coast, from the wall of Antoninus to the extreme promontory of Cornwall; and the principal cities of the inland country still opposed the arms of the barbarians. Resistance became more languid, as the number and boldness of the assailants continually increased. Winning their way by slow and painful efforts, the Saxons, the Angles, and their various confederates, advanced from the North, from the East, and from the South, till their victorious banners were united in the centre of the island. Beyond the Severn the Britons still asserted their national freedom, which survived the heptarchy, and even the monarchy, of the Saxons. The bravest warriors, who preferred exile to slavery, found a secure refuge in the mountains of Wales: the reluctant submission of Cornwall was delayed for some ages; and a band of fugitives acquired a settlement in Gaul, by their own valour, or the liberality of the Merovingian kings.

But every British name is effaced by the illustrious name of ARTHUR, the hereditary prince of the Silures, in South Wales, and the elective king or general of the nation. According to the most rational account, he defeated, in twelve successive battles, the Angles of the North and the Saxons of the West; but the declining age of the hero was embittered by popular ingratitude and domestic misfortunes.

Resistance, if it cannot avert, must increase the miseries of conquest; and conquest has never appeared more dreadful and destructive than in the hands of the Saxons, who hated the valour of their enemies, disdained the faith of treaties, and violated, without remorse, the most sacred objects of the Christian worship. The fields of battle might be traced, almost in every district, by monuments of bones; the fragments of falling towers were stained with blood; the last of the Britons, without distinction of age or sex, was massacred, in the ruins of Anderida; and the repetition of such calamities was frequent and familiar under the Saxon Heptarchy.

The arts and religion, the laws and language, which the Romans had so carefully planted in Britain, were extirpated by their barbarous successors. After the destruction of the principal churches, the bishops who had declined the crown of martyrdom retired with the holy relics into Wales and Armorica; the remains of their flocks were left destitute of any spiritual food; the practice, and even the remembrance, of Christianity were abolished; and the British clergy might obtain some comfort from the damnation of the idolatrous strangers. The kings of France maintained the privileges of their Roman subjects; but the ferocious Saxons trampled on the laws of Rome and of the emperors. The proceedings of civil and criminal jurisdiction, the titles of honour, the forms of office, the ranks of society, and even the domestic rights of marriage, testament, and inheritance, were finally suppressed; and the indiscriminate crowd of noble and plebeian slaves was governed by the traditionary customs which had been coarsely framed for the shepherds and pirates of Germany. The language of science, of business, and of conversation, which had been introduced by the Romans, was lost in the general desolation.

The kingdom of Sussex, which spread from the sea to the Thames, contained seven thousand families: twelve hundred were ascribed to the Isle of Wight; and, if we multiply this vague computation, it may seem probable that England was cultivated by a million of servants, or *villeins*, who were attached to the estates of their arbitrary landlords. The indigent barbarians were often tempted to sell their children or themselves into perpetual, and even foreign, bondage; yet the special exemptions which were granted to *national* slaves sufficiently declare that they were much less numerous than the strangers and captives who had lost their liberty, or changed their masters, by the accidents of war. When time and religion had mitigated the fierce spirit of the Anglo-Saxons, the laws encouraged the frequent practice of manumission; and their subjects, of Welsh or Cambrian extraction, assumed the respectable station of inferior freemen, possessed of lands, and entitled to the rights of civil society. Such gentle treatment might secure the allegiance of a fierce people, who had been recently subdued on the confines of Wales and Cornwall. The sage Ina, the legislator of Wessex, united the two nations in the bands of domestic alliance; and four British lords of Somersetshire may be honourably distinguished in the court of a Saxon monarch.

The independent Britons appear to have relapsed into the state of original barbarism from whence they had been imperfectly reclaimed. Separated by their enemies from the rest of mankind, they soon became an object of scandal and abhorrence to the Catholic world. Christianity was still professed in the mountains of Wales; but the rude schismatics, in the *form* of the clerical tonsure, and in the *day* of the celebration of Easter, obstinately resisted the imperious mandates of the Roman pontiffs. The use of the Latin language was insensibly abolished, and the Britons were deprived of the arts and learning which Italy communicated to her Saxon proselytes.

By the revolution of Britain the limits of science as well as of empire were contracted. The dark cloud which had been cleared by the Phœnician discoveries, and finally dispelled by the arms of Cæsar, again settled on the shores of the Atlantic, and a Roman province was again lost among the fabulous Islands of the Ocean. Seven independent kingdoms were agitated by perpetual discord; and the *British world* was seldom connected, either in peace or war, with the nations of the continent.

I have now accomplished the laborious narrative of the decline and fall of the Roman empire, from the fortunate age of Trajan and the Antonines to its total extinction in the West, about five centuries after the Christian era. At that unhappy period the Saxons fiercely struggled with the natives for the possession of Britain: Gaul and Spain were divided between the powerful monarchies of the Franks and Visigoths and the dependent kingdoms of the Suevi and Burgundians: Africa was exposed to the cruel persecution of the Vandals and the savage insults of the Moors: Rome and Italy, as far as the banks of the Danube, were afflicted by an army of barbarian mercenaries, whose lawless tyranny was succeeded by the reign of Theodoric the Ostrogoth. All the subjects of the empire, who, by the use of the Latin language, more particularly deserved the name and privileges of Romans, were oppressed by the disgrace and calamities of foreign conquest; and the victorious nations of Germany established a new system of manners and government in the western countries of Europe.

The indissoluble connection of civil and ecclesiastical affairs has compelled and encouraged me to relate the progress, the persecutions, the establishment, the divisions, the final triumph, and the gradual corruption of Christianity. I have purposely delayed consideration of a religious event interesting in the study of human nature and important in the decline and fall of the Roman empire, conversion of the northern barbarians.

The progress of Christianity has been marked by two glorious and decisive victories: over the learned and luxurious citizens of the Roman empire; and over the warlike barbarians of Scythia and Germany, who subverted the empire and embraced the religion of the Romans. The Goths were the foremost of these savage proselytes; and the nation was indebted for its conversion to a countryman, or at least to a subject, worthy to be ranked among the inventors of useful arts who have deserved the remembrance and gratitude of posterity. A great number of Roman provincials had been led away into captivity by the Gothic bands who ravaged Asia in the time of Gallienus; and of these captives many were Christians, and several belonged to the ecclesiastical order. Those involuntary missionaries, dispersed as slaves in the villages of Dacia, successively laboured for the salvation of their masters. The seeds which they planted of the evangelic doctrine were gradually propagated; and before the end of a century the pious work was achieved by the labours of Ulphilas, whose ancestors had been transported beyond the Danube from a small town of Cappadocia.

Ulphilas, the bishop and apostle of the Goths, acquired their love and reverence by his blameless life and indefatigable zeal; and they received with implicit confidence the doctrines of truth and virtue which he preached and practised. He executed the arduous task of translating the Scriptures into their native tongue, a dialect of the German or Teutonic language; but he prudently suppressed the four books of Kings, as they might tend to irritate the fierce and sanguinary spirit of the barbarians. The rude, imperfect idiom of soldiers and shepherds, so ill qualified to communicate any spiritual ideas, was improved and modulated by his genius; and Ulphilas, before he could frame his version, was obliged to compose a new alphabet of twenty-four letters, four of which he invented to express the peculiar sounds that were unknown to the Greek and Latin pronunciation.

But the prosperous state of the Gothic church was soon afflicted by war and intestine discord, and the chieftains were divided by religion as well as by interest. Fritigern, the friend of the Romans, became the proselyte of Ulphilas, while the haughty soul of Athanaric disdained the yoke of the empire and of the Gospel. The faith of the new converts was tried by the persecution which he excited. A waggon bearing aloft the shapeless image of Thor, perhaps, or of Woden, was conducted in solemn procession through the streets of the camp, and the rebels who refused to worship the god of their fathers were immediately burnt with their tents and families. The character of Ulphilas recommended him to the esteem of the Eastern court, where he twice appeared as the minister of peace; he pleaded the cause of the distressed Goths, who implored the protection of Valens; and the name of *Moses* was applied to this spiritual guide, who conducted his people through the deep waters of the Danube to the Land of Promise. The devout shepherds, who were attached to his person and tractable to his voice, acquiesced in their settlement at the foot of the Mæsian mountains, in a country of woodlands and pastures, which supported their flocks and herds, and enabled them to purchase the corn and wine of the more plentiful provinces. These harmless barbarians multiplied in obscure peace and the profession of Christianity.

Their fiercer brethren, the formidable Visigoths, universally adopted the religion of the Romans, with whom they maintained a perpetual intercourse of war, of friendship, or of conquest. In their long and victorious march from the Danube to the Atlantic Ocean they converted their allies; they educated the rising generation; and the devotion which reigned in the camp of Alaric, or the court of Toulouse, might edify or disgrace the palaces of Rome and Constantinople. During the same period Christianity was embraced by almost all the barbarians who established their kingdoms on the ruins of the Western empire; the Burgundians in Gaul, the Suevi in Spain, the Vandals in Africa, the Ostrogoths in Pannonia, and the various bands of mercenaries that raised Odoacer to the throne of Italy. The Franks and the Saxons still persevered in the errors of Paganism; but the Franks obtained the monarchy of Gaul by their submission to the example of Clovis; and the Saxon conquerors of Britain were reclaimed from their savage superstition by the missionaries of Rome. These barbarian proselytes displayed an ardent and successful zeal in the propagation of the faith. The Merovingian kings and their successors, Charlemagne and the Othos, extended by their laws and victories the dominion of the cross. England produced the apostle of Germany; and the evangelic light was gradually diffused from the neighbourhood of the Rhine to the nations of the Elbe, the Vistula, and the Baltic.

The different motives which influenced the reason or the passions of the barbarian converts cannot easily be ascertained. They were often capricious and accidental; a dream, an omen, the report of a miracle, the example of some priest or hero, the charms of a believing wife, and, above all, the fortunate event of a prayer or vow which, in a moment of danger, they had addressed to the God of the Christians. The early prejudices of education were insensibly erased by the habits of frequent and familiar society; the moral precepts of the Gospel were protected by the extravagant virtues of the monks; and a spiritual theology was supported by the visible power of relics and the pomp of religious worship. But the rational and ingenious mode of persuasion which a Saxon bishop suggested to a popular saint might sometimes be employed by the missionaries who laboured for the conversion of infidels. "Admit," says the sagacious disputant, "whatever they are pleased to assert of the fabulous and carnal genealogy of their gods and goddesses, who are propagated from each other. From this principle deduce their imperfect nature and human infirmities, the assurance they were *born*, and the probability that they will *die*. At what time, by what means, from what cause, were the eldest of the gods or goddesses produced? Do they still continue, or have they ceased, to propagate? If they have ceased, summon your antagonist to declare the reason of this strange alteration. If they still continue, the number of the gods must become infinite; and shall we not risk, by the indiscreet worship of some impotent deity, to excite the resentment of his jealous superior? The visible heavens and earth, the whole system of the universe, which may be conceived by the mind, is it created or eternal? If created, how or where could the gods themselves exist before the creation? If eternal, how could they assume the empire of an independent and pre-existing world? Urge these arguments with temper and moderation; insinuate, at seasonable intervals, the truth and beauty of the Christian revelation; and endeavour to make the unbelievers ashamed without making them angry."

This metaphysical reasoning, too refined perhaps for the barbarians of Germany, was fortified by the grosser weight of authority and popular consent. The advantage of temporal prosperity had deserted the Pagan cause and passed over to the service of Christianity. The Romans themselves, the most powerful and enlightened nation of the globe, had renounced their ancient superstition; and if the ruin of their empire seemed to accuse the efficacy of the new faith, the disgrace was already retrieved by the conversion of the victorious Goths. The valiant and fortunate barbarians who subdued the provinces of the West successively received and reflected the same edifying example. Before the age of Charlemagne, the Christian nations of Europe might exult in the exclusive possession of the temperate climates, of the fertile lands which produced corn, wine, and oil; while the savage idolaters and their helpless idols were confined to the extremities of the earth, the dark and frozen regions of the North.

Christianity, which opened the gates of Heaven to the barbarians, introduced an important change in their moral and political condition. They received, at the same time, the use of letters, so essential to a religion whose doctrines are contained in a sacred book; and while they studied the divine truth, their minds were insensibly enlarged by the distant view of history, of nature, of the arts, and of society. The version of the Scriptures into their native tongue, which had facilitated their conversion, must excite, among their clergy, some curiosity to read the original text, to understand the sacred liturgy of the church, and to examine, in the writings of the fathers, the chain of ecclesiastical tradition. These spiritual gifts were preserved in the Greek and Latin languages, which concealed the inestimable monuments of ancient learning. The immortal productions of Virgil, Cicero, and Livy, which were accessible to the Christian barbarians, maintained a silent intercourse between the reign of Augustus and the times of Clovis and Charlemagne. The emulation of mankind was encouraged by the remembrance of a more perfect state; and the flame of science was secretly kept alive, to warm and enlighten the mature age of the Western world.

In the most corrupt state of Christianity the barbarians might learn justice from the *law*, and mercy from the *gospel;* and if the knowledge of their duty was insufficient to guide their actions or to regulate their passions, they were sometimes restrained by conscience, and frequently punished by remorse. But the direct authority of religion was less effectual than the holy communion which united them with their Christian brethren in spiritual friendship. The influence of these sentiments contributed to secure their fidelity in the service or the alliance of the Romans, to alleviate the horrors of war, to moderate the insolence of conquest, and to preserve, in the downfall of the empire, a permanent respect for the name and institutions of Rome. In the days of Paganism the priests of Gaul and Germany reigned over the people, and controlled the jurisdiction of the magistrates; and the zealous proselytes transferred an equal, or more ample, measure of devout obedience to the pontiffs of the Christian faith. The sacred character of the bishops was supported by their temporal possessions; they obtained an honourable seat in the legislative assemblies of soldiers and freemen; and it was their interest, as well as their duty, to mollify by peaceful counsels the fierce spirit of the barbarians. The perpetual correspondence of the Latin clergy, the frequent pilgrimages to Rome and Jerusalem, and the growing authority of the popes, cemented the union of the Christian republic, and gradually produced the similar manners and common jurisprudence which have distinguished from the rest of mankind the independent, and even hostile, nations of modern Europe.

But the operation of these causes was checked and retarded by the unfortunate accident which infused a deadly poison into the cup of salvation. Whatever might be the early sentiments of Ulphilas, his connections with the empire and the church were formed during the reign of Arianism. The apostle of the Goths subscribed the creed of Rimini; professed with freedom, and perhaps with sincerity, that the Son was not equal or consubstantial to the FATHER; communicated these errors to the clergy and people; and infected the barbaric world with an heresy which the great Theodosius proscribed and extinguished among the Romans. The temper and understanding of the new proselytes were not adapted to metaphysical subtleties; but they strenuously maintained what they had piously received as the pure and genuine doctrines of Christianity. The advantage of preaching and expounding the Scriptures in the Teutonic language promoted the apostolic labours of Ulphilas and his successors; and they ordained a competent number of bishops and presbyters for the instruction of the kindred tribes. The Ostrogoths, the Burgundians, the Suevi, and the Vandals, who had listened to the eloquence of the Latin clergy, preferred the more intelligible lessons of their domestic teachers; and Arianism was adopted as the national faith of the warlike converts who were seated on the ruins of the Western empire. This irreconcilable difference of religion was a perpetual source of jealousy and hatred; and the reproach of *Barbarian* was embittered by the more odious epithet of *Heretic*.

The heroes of the North, who had submitted with some reluctance to believe that all their ancestors were in hell, were astonished and exasperated to learn that they themselves had only changed the mode of their eternal condemnation. Instead of the smooth applause which Christian kings are accustomed to expect from their loyal prelates, the orthodox bishops and their clergy were in a state of opposition to the Arian courts; and their indiscreet opposition frequently became criminal, and might sometimes be dangerous. The pulpit, that safe and sacred organ of sedition, resounded with the names of Pharaoh and Holofernes; the public discontent was inflamed by the hope or promise of a glorious deliverance; and the seditious saints were tempted to promote the accomplishment of their own predictions.

Notwithstanding these provocations, the Catholics of Gaul, Spain, and Italy enjoyed, under the reign of the Arians, the free and peaceful exercise of their religion. Their haughty masters respected the zeal of a numerous people, resolved to die at the foot of their altars, and the example of their devout constancy was admired and imitated by the barbarians themselves. The conquerors evaded the disgraceful reproach or confession of fear by attributing their toleration to the liberal motives of reason and humanity;

and while they affected the language, they imperceptibly imbibed the spirit, of genuine Christianity.

The Vandals and the Ostrogoths persevered in the profession of Arianism till the final ruin of the kingdoms which they had founded in Africa and Italy. The barbarians of Gaul submitted to the orthodox dominion of the Franks; and Spain was restored to the Catholic church by the voluntary conversion of the Visigoths.

The first missionaries who preached the Gospel to the barbarians appealed to the evidence of reason, and claimed the benefit of toleration. But no sooner had they established their spiritual dominion than they exhorted the Christian kings to extirpate, without mercy, the remains of Roman or barbaric superstition. The successors of Clovis inflicted one hundred lashes on the peasants who refused to destroy their idols; the crime of sacrificing to the demons was punished by the Anglo-Saxon laws with the heavier penalties of imprisonment and confiscation; and even the wise Alfred adopted, as an indispensable duty, the extreme rigour of the Mosaic institutions. But the punishment and the crime were gradually abolished among a Christian people; the theological disputes of the schools were suspended by propitious ignorance; and the intolerant spirit which could find neither idolaters nor heretics, was reduced to the persecution of the Jews.

That exiled nation had founded some synagogues in the cities of Gaul; but Spain, since the time of Hadrian, was filled with their numerous colonies. The wealth which they accumulated by trade and the management of the finances invited the pious avarice of their masters; and they might be oppressed without danger, as they had lost the use, and even the remembrance, of arms. Sisebut, a Gothic king who reigned in the beginning of the seventh century, proceeded at once to the last extremes of persecution. Ninety thousand Jews were compelled to receive the sacrament of baptism; the fortunes of the obstinate infidels were confiscated, their bodies were tortured, and it seems doubtful whether they were permitted to abandon their native country. The excessive zeal of the Catholic king was moderated even by the clergy of Spain, who solemnly pronounced an inconsistent sentence: *that* the sacraments should not be forcibly imposed; but *that* the Jews who had been baptised should be constrained, for the honour of the church, to persevere in the external practice of a religion which they disbelieved and detested. Their frequent relapses provoked one of the successors of Sisebut to banish the whole nation from his dominions; and a council of Toledo published a decree that every Gothic king should swear to maintain this salutary edict. But the tyrants were unwilling to dismiss the victims whom they delighted to torture, or to deprive themselves of the industrious slaves over whom they might exercise a lucrative oppression. The Jews still continued in Spain, under the weight of the civil and ecclesiastical laws which in the same country have been faithfully transcribed in the Code of the Inquisition.

Even the religious toleration which Theodoric had the glory of introducing into the Christian world was painful and offensive to the orthodox zeal of the Italians. They respected the armed heresy of the Goths; but their pious rage was safely pointed against the rich and defenceless Jews, who had formed their establishments at Naples, Rome, Ravenna, Milan, and Genoa, for the benefit of trade and under the sanction of the laws. Their persons were insulted, their effects were pillaged, and their synagogues were burnt by the mad populace of Ravenna and Rome, inflamed, as it should seem, by the most frivolous or extravagant pretences. The government which could neglect would have deserved such an outrage. A legal inquiry was instantly directed; and as the authors of the tumult had escaped in the crowd, the whole community was condemned to repair the damage, and the obstinate bigots, who refused their contributions, were whipped through the streets by the hand of the executioner. This simple act of justice exasperated the discontent of the Catholics, who applauded the merit and patience of these holy confessors. Three hundred pulpits deplored the persecution of the church; and if the chapel of St. Stephen at Verona was demolished by the command of Theodoric, it is probable that some miracle hostile to his name and dignity had been performed on that sacred theatre.

Theodoric, king of the Ostrogoths, a hero alike excellent in the arts of war and of government, restored an age of peace and prosperity, and his name still excites and deserves the attention of mankind.

As the patron of the republic, it was the interest and duty of the Gothic king to cultivate the affections of the senate and people. The nobles of Rome were flattered by sonorous epithets and formal professions of respect, which had been more justly applied to the merit and authority of their ancestors. The people enjoyed, without fear or danger, the three blessings of a capital, order, plenty, and public amusements. A visible diminution of their numbers may be found even in the measure of liberality; yet Apulia, Calabria, and Sicily poured their tribute of corn into the granaries of Rome; an allowance of bread and meat was distributed to the indigent citizens; and every office was deemed honourable which was consecrated to the care of their health and happiness. The public games, such as a Greek ambassador might politely applaud, exhibited a faint and feeble copy of the magnificence of the Cæsars: yet the musical, the gymnastic, and the pantomime arts, had not totally sunk in oblivion; the wild beasts of Africa still exercised in the amphitheatre the courage and dexterity of the hunters; and the indulgent Goth either patiently tolerated or gently restrained the blue and green factions, whose contests so often filled the Circus with clamour, and even with blood.

In the seventh year of his peaceful reign, Theodoric visited the old capital of the world; the senate and people advanced in solemn procession to salute a second Trajan, a new Valentinian; and he nobly supported that character, by the assurance of a just and legal government, in a discourse which he was not afraid to pronounce in public and to inscribe on a tablet of brass. Rome, in this august ceremony, shot a last ray of declining glory; and a saint, the spectator of this pompous scene, could only hope, in his pious fancy, that it was excelled by the celestial splendour of the New Jerusalem.

During a residence of six months, the fame, the person, and the courteous demeanour of the Gothic king excited the admiration of the Romans, and he contemplated, with equal curiosity and surprise, the monuments that remained of their ancient greatness. He imprinted the footsteps of a conqueror on the Capitoline hill, and frankly confessed that each day he viewed with fresh wonder the forum of Trajan and his lofty column. The theatre of Pompey appeared, even in its decay, as a huge mountain, artificially hollowed and polished, and adorned by human industry; and he vaguely computed that a river of gold must have been drained to erect the colossal amphitheatre of Titus.

From the mouths of fourteen aqueducts a pure and copious stream was diffused into every part of the city; among these the Claudian water, which arose at the distance of thirty-eight miles in the Sabine mountains, was conveyed along a gentle though constant declivity of solid arches, till it descended on the summit of the Aventine hill. The long and spacious vaults which had been constructed for the purpose of common sewers subsisted after twelve centuries in their pristine strength; and these subterraneous channels have been preferred to all the visible wonders of Rome. The Gothic kings, so injuriously accused of the ruin of antiquity, were anxious to preserve the monuments of the nation whom they had subdued. The royal edicts were framed to prevent the abuses, the neglect, or the depredations of the citizens themselves; and a professed architect, the annual sum of two hundred pounds of gold, twenty-five thousand tiles, and the receipt of customs from the Lucrine port, were assigned for the ordinary repairs of the walls and public edifices. A similar care was extended to the statues of metal or marble of men or animals. The spirit of the horses which have given a modern name to the Quirinal was applauded by the barbarians; the brazen elephants of the *Via sacra* were diligently restored; the famous heifer of Myron deceived the cattle, as they were driven through the forum of peace; and an officer was created to protect those works of art, which Theodoric considered as the noblest ornament of his kingdom.

After the example of the last emperors, Theodoric preferred the residence of Ravenna, where he cultivated an orchard with his own hands. As often as the peace of his kingdom was threatened (for it was never invaded) by the barbarians, he removed his court to Verona on the northern frontier, and the image of his palace, still extant on a coin, represents the oldest and most authentic model of Gothic architecture. These two capitals, as well as Pavia, Spoleto, Naples, and the rest of the Italian cities, acquired under his reign the useful or splendid decorations of churches, aqueducts, baths, porticoes, and palaces.

But the happiness of the subject was more truly conspicuous in the busy scene of labour and luxury, in the rapid increase and bold enjoyment of national wealth. From the shades of Tibur and Præneste, the Roman senators still retired in the winter season to the warm sun and salubrious springs of Baiæ; and their villas, which advanced on solid moles into the bay of Naples, commanded the various prospect of the sky, the earth, and the water. On the eastern side of the Hadriatic a new Campania was formed in the fair and fruitful province of Istria, which communicated with the palace of Ravenna by an easy navigation of one hundred miles. The rich productions of Lucania and the adjacent provinces were exchanged at the Marcilian fountain, in a populous fair annually dedicated to trade, intemperance, and superstition. In the solitude of Comum, which had once been animated by the mild genius of Pliny, a transparent basin above sixty miles in length still reflected the rural seats which encompassed the margin of the Larian lake; and the gradual ascent of the hills was covered by a triple plantation of olives, of vines, and of chestnut-trees.

Agriculture revived under the shadow of peace, and the number of husbandmen was multiplied by the redemption of captives. The iron-mines of Dalmatia, a gold-mine in Bruttium, were carefully explored, and the Pomptine marshes, as well as those of Spoleto, were drained and cultivated by private undertakers, whose distant reward must depend on the continuance of the public prosperity. Whenever the seasons were less propitious, the doubtful precautions of forming magazines of corn, fixing the price, and prohibiting the exportation, attested at least the benevolence of the state; but such was the extraordinary plenty which an industrious people produced from a grateful soil, that a gallon of wine was sometimes sold in Italy for less than three farthings, and a quarter of wheat at about five shillings and sixpence. A country possessed of so many valuable objects of exchange soon attracted the merchants of the world, whose beneficial traffic was encouraged and protected by the liberal spirit of Theodoric. The free intercourse of the provinces by land and water was restored and extended; the city gates were never shut either by day or by night; and the common saying, that a purse of gold might be safely left in the fields, was expressive of the conscious security of the inhabitants.

A difference of religion is always pernicious and often fatal to the harmony of the prince and people: the Gothic conqueror had been educated in the profession of Arianism, and Italy was devoutly attached to the Nicene faith. But the persuasion of Theodoric was not infected by zeal: and he piously adhered to the heresy of his fathers, without condescending to balance the subtile arguments of theological metaphysics. Satisfied with the private toleration of his Arian sectaries, he justly conceived himself to be the guardian of the public worship, and his external reverence for a superstition which he despised may have nourished in his mind the salutary indifference of a statesman or philosopher. The Catholics of his dominions acknowledged, perhaps with reluctance, the peace of the church; their clergy, according to the degrees of rank or merit, were honourably entertained in the palace of Theodoric; he esteemed the living sanctity of Cæsarius and Epiphanius, the orthodox bishops of Arles and Pavia; and presented a decent offering on the tomb of St. Peter, without any scrupulous inquiry into the creed of the Apostle.

CHAPTER XXVII

Reign of Justinian—Trade and Manufacture of Silk—Church of St. Sophia—Abolition of the Schools of Athens and the Consulship of Rome

After rome herself had been stripped of the Imperial purple, the princes of Constantinople assumed the sole and sacred sceptre of the monarchy; demanded, as their rightful inheritance, the provinces which had been subdued by the consuls or possessed by the Cæsars; and feebly aspired to deliver their faithful subjects of the West from the usurpation of heretics and barbarians. The execution of this splendid design was in some degree reserved for Justinian. During the five first years of his reign he reluctantly waged a costly and unprofitable war against the Persians, till his pride submitted to his ambition, and he purchased, at the price of four hundred and forty thousand pounds sterling, the benefit of a precarious truce, which, in the language of both nations, was dignified with the appellation of the *endless* peace. The safety of the East enabled the emperor to employ his forces against the Vandals.

The preparations for the African war were not unworthy of the last contest between Rome and Carthage. The pride and flower of the army consisted of the guards of Belisarius, who, according to the pernicious indulgence of the times, devoted themselves, by a particular oath of fidelity, to the service of their patrons. Their strength and stature, for which they had been curiously selected, the goodness of their horses and armour, and the assiduous practice of all the exercises of war, enabled them to act whatever their courage might prompt; and their courage was exalted by the social honour of their rank, and the personal ambition of favour and fortune.

Procopius defends the soldiers of his own time against the morose critics who confined that respectable name to the heavy-armed warriors of antiquity, and maliciously observed that the word *archer* is introduced by Homer as a term of contempt. "Such contempt might perhaps be due to the naked youths who appeared on foot in the fields of Troy, and, lurking behind a tombstone, or the shield of a friend, drew the bowstring to their breast, and dismissed a feeble and lifeless arrow. But our archers (pursues the historian) are mounted on horses, which they manage with admirable skill; their head and shoulders are protected by a casque or buckler; they wear greaves of iron on their legs, and their bodies are guarded by a coat of mail. On their right side hangs a quiver, a sword on their left, and their hand is accustomed to wield a lance or javelin in closer combat. Their bows are strong and weighty; they shoot in every possible direction, advancing, retreating, to the front, to the rear, or to either flank; and as they are taught to draw the bowstring not to the breast, but to the right ear, firm indeed must be the armour that can resist the rapid violence of their shaft."

Five hundred transports, navigated by twenty thousand mariners of Egypt, Cilicia, and Ionia, were collected in the harbour of Constantinople. The smallest of these vessels may be computed at thirty, the largest at five hundred, tons; and the fair average will supply an allowance, liberal, but not profuse, of about one hundred thousand tons, for the reception of thirty-five thousand soldiers and sailors, of five thousand horses, of arms, engines, and military stores, and of a sufficient stock of water and provisions for a voyage, perhaps, of three months. The proud galleys which in former ages swept the Mediterranean with so many hundred oars had long since disappeared; and the fleet of Justinian was escorted only by ninety-two light brigantines, covered from the missile weapons of the enemy, and rowed by two thousand of the brave and robust youth of Constantinople.

Twenty-two generals are named, most of whom were afterwards distinguished in the wars of Africa and Italy; but the supreme command, both by land and sea, was delegated to Belisarius alone. From Carthage he despatched his principal lieutenant to inform the emperor that in the space of three months he had achieved the conquest of Africa.

Belisarius spoke the language of truth. The Vandals yielded, the neighbourhood of Carthage submitted to his presence, and the more distant provinces were successively subdued by the report of his victory. Tripoli was confirmed in her voluntary allegiance; Sardinia and Corsica surrendered and the isles of Majorca, Minorca, and Yvica consented to remain an humble appendage of the African kingdom. Cæsarea, a royal city, which in looser geography may be confounded with the modern Algiers, was situate thirty days' march to the westward of Carthage; by land the road was infested by the Moors, but the sea was open, and the Romans were now masters of the sea.

The Goths, both of Italy and Spain, insensible of their approaching danger, beheld with indifference, and even with joy, the rapid downfall of the Vandals. After the failure of the royal line, the sceptre of Spain was disputed by a civil war. The weaker candidate solicited the protection of Justinian, and ambitiously subscribed a treaty of alliance which deeply wounded the independence and happiness of his country. Several cities, both on the ocean and the Mediterranean, were ceded to the Roman troops, who afterwards refused to evacuate those pledges, as it should seem, either of safety or payment; and as they were fortified by perpetual supplies from Africa, they maintained their impregnable stations for the mischievous purpose of inflaming the civil and religious factions of the barbarians. Seventy years elapsed before this painful thorn could be extirpated from the bosom of the monarchy; and as long as the emperors retained any share of these remote and useless possessions, their vanity might number Spain in the list of their provinces, and the successors of Alaric in the rank of their vassals.

The error of the Goths who reigned in Italy was less excusable than that of their Spanish brethren, and their punishment was still more immediate and terrible. In Italy, as well as in Africa, the guilt of a usurper appeared to justify the arms of Justinian. Steering the same course as in his former expedition, Belisarius cast anchor before Catana, in Sicily, to survey the strength of the island, and to decide whether he should attempt the conquest or peaceably pursue his voyage for the African coast. He found a fruitful land and a friendly people. Notwithstanding the decay of agriculture, Sicily still supplied the granaries of Rome; the farmers were graciously exempted from the oppression of military quarters; and the Goths, who trusted the defence of the island to the inhabitants, had some reason to complain that their confidence was ungratefully betrayed. Instead of soliciting and expecting the aid of the king of Italy, they yielded to the first summons a cheerful obedience; and this province, the first fruits of the Punic wars, was again, after a long separation, united to the Roman empire.

The Goths consented to retreat in the presence of a victorious enemy, to delay till the next spring the operations of offensive war, to summon their scattered forces, to relinquish their distant possessions, and to trust even Rome itself to the faith of its inhabitants. A feeble garrison might have seconded the zeal, though it was incapable of opposing the wishes, of the Romans. But a momentary enthusiasm of religion and patriotism was kindled in their minds. They furiously exclaimed that the apostolic throne should no longer be profaned by the triumph or toleration of Arianism; that the tombs of the Cæsars should no longer be trampled by the savages of the North; and, without reflecting that Italy must sink into a province of Constantinople, they fondly hailed the restoration of a Roman emperor as a new era of freedom and prosperity. The deputies of the pope and clergy, of the senate and people, invited the lieutenant of Justinian to accept their voluntary allegiance, and to enter the city, whose gates would be thrown open for his reception.

As soon as Belisarius had fortified his new conquests, Naples and Cumæ, he advanced about twenty miles to the banks of the Vulturnus, contemplated the decayed grandeur of Capua, and halted at the separation of the Latin and Appian ways. The work of the censor, after the incessant use of nine centuries, still preserved its primæval beauty, and not a flaw could be discovered in the large polished stones of which that solid though narrow road was so firmly compacted. Belisarius, however, preferred the Latin way, which, at a distance from the sea and the marshes, skirted in a space of one hundred and twenty miles along the foot of the mountains. His enemies had disappeared: when he made his entrance through the Asinarian gate the garrison departed without molestation along the Flaminian way; the city, after sixty years' servitude, was delivered from the yoke of the barbarians; and the Gothic chief, himself a trophy of the victory, was sent with the keys of Rome to the throne of the emperor Justinian.

The first days, which coincided with the old Saturnalia, were devoted to mutual congratulations and the public joy; and the Catholics prepared to celebrate without a rival the approaching festival of the nativity of Christ. The epistle of Belisarius to the emperor announced his victory. "According to your commands, we have entered the dominions of the Goths, and reduced to your obedience Sicily, Campania, and the city of Rome."

The whole nation of the Ostrogoths was almost entirely consumed in the siege of Rome. If any credit be due to an intelligent spectator, one-third at least of their enormous host was destroyed in frequent and bloody combats under the walls of the city. The bad fame and pernicious qualities of the summer air might already be imputed to the decay of agriculture and population, and the evils of famine and pestilence were aggravated by their own licentiousness and the unfriendly disposition of the country.

When Justinian first meditated the conquest of Italy, he sent ambassadors to the kings of the Franks, and adjured them, by the common ties of alliance and religion, to join in the holy enterprise against the Arians. The Goths, as their wants were more urgent, employed a more effectual mode of persuasion, and vainly strove, by the gift of lands and money, to purchase the friendship, or at least the neutrality, of a light and perfidious nation. But the arms of Belisarius and the revolt of the Italians had no sooner shaken the Gothic monarchy, than Theodebert of Austrasia, the most powerful and warlike of the Merovingian kings, was persuaded to succour their distress by an indirect and seasonable aid.

Italy trembled at the march of the Franks, and both the Gothic prince and the Roman general, alike ignorant of their designs, solicited with hope and terror the friendship of these dangerous allies. Till he had secured the passage of the Po on the bridge of Pavia, the grandson of Clovis dissembled his intentions, which he at length declared by assaulting, almost at the same instant, the hostile camps of the Romans and Goths. Instead of uniting their arms, they fled with equal precipitation, and the fertile though desolate provinces of Liguria and Æmilia were abandoned to a licentious host of barbarians. If it were not a melancholy truth that the first and most cruel sufferings must be the lot of the innocent and helpless, history might exult in the misery of the conquerors, who, in the midst of riches, were left destitute of bread or wine, reduced to drink the waters of the Po, and to feed on the flesh of distempered cattle. The dysentery swept away one-third of their army, and the clamours of his subjects, who were impatient to pass the Alps, disposed Theodebert to listen with respect to the mild exhortations of Belisarius. The memory of this inglorious and destructive warfare was perpetuated on the medals of Gaul, and Justinian, without unsheathing his sword, assumed the title of conqueror of the Franks.

The submission of the capital was imitated in the towns and villages of Italy which had not been subdued or even visited by the Romans; and the independent Goths, who remained in arms at Pavia and Verona, were ambitious only to become the subjects of Belisarius. But his inflexible loyalty rejected, except as the substitute of Justinian, their oaths of allegiance.

The Eastern empire, after Rome was barbarous, still embraced the nations whom she had conquered beyond the Hadriatic, and as far as the frontiers of Æthiopia and Persia. Justinian reigned over sixty-four provinces and nine hundred and thirty-five cities; his dominions were blessed by nature with the advantages of soil, situation, and climate, and the improvements of human art had been perpetually diffused along the coast of the Mediterranean and the banks of the Nile from ancient Troy to the Egyptian Thebes. Abraham had been relieved by the well-known plenty of Egypt; the same country, a small and populous tract, was still capable of exporting each year two hundred and sixty thousand quarters of wheat for the use of Constantinople; and the capital of Justinian was supplied with the manufactures of Sidon fifteen centuries after they had been celebrated in the poems of Homer. The annual powers of vegetation, instead of being exhausted by two thousand harvests, were renewed and invigorated by skilful husbandry, rich manure, and seasonable repose. The breed of domestic animals was infinitely multiplied. Plantations, buildings, and the instruments of labour and luxury, which are more durable than the term of human life, were accumulated by the care of successive generations. Tradition preserved, and experience simplified, the humble practice of the arts; society was enriched by the division of labour and the facility of exchange; and every Roman was lodged, clothed, and subsisted by the industry of a thousand hands. The invention of the loom and distaff has been piously ascribed to the gods. In every age a variety of animal and vegetable productions, hair, skins, wool, flax, cotton, and at length *silk*, have been skilfully manufactured to hide or adorn the human body; they were stained with an infusion of permanent colours, and the pencil was successfully employed to improve the labours of the loom. In the choice of those colours which imitate the beauties of nature, the freedom of taste and fashion was indulged; but the deep purple which the Phœnicians extracted from a shell-fish was restrained to the sacred person and palace of the emperor, and the penalties of treason were denounced against the ambitious subjects who dared to usurp the prerogative of the throne.

I need not explain that *silk* is originally spun from the bowels of a caterpillar, and that it composes the golden tomb from whence a worm emerges in the form of a butterfly. Till the reign of Justinian, the silkworms who feed on the leaves of the white mulberry-tree were confined to China; those of the pine, the oak, and the ash were common in the forests both of Asia and Europe; but as their education is more difficult, and their produce more uncertain, they were generally neglected, except in the little island of Ceos, near the coast of Attica. A thin gauze was procured from their webs, and this Cean manufacture, the invention of a woman, for female use, was long admired both in the East and at Rome. Whatever suspicions may be raised by the garments of the Medes and Assyrians, Virgil is the most ancient writer who expressly mentions the soft wool which was combed from the trees of the Seres or Chinese; and this natural error, less marvellous than the truth, was slowly corrected by the knowledge of a valuable insect, the first artificer of the luxury of nations.

That rare and elegant luxury was censured, in the reign of Tiberius, by the gravest of the Romans; and Pliny, in affected though forcible language, has condemned the thirst of gain, which explored the last confines of the earth for the pernicious purpose of exposing to the public eye naked draperies and transparent matrons. A dress which showed the turn of the limbs and colour of the skin might gratify vanity or provoke desire; the silks which had been closely woven in China were sometimes unravelled by the Phœnician women, and the precious materials were multiplied by a looser texture, and the intermixture of linen threads. Two hundred years after the age of Pliny the use of pure or even of mixed silks was confined to the female sex, till the opulent citizens of Rome and the provinces were insensibly familiarised with the example of Elagabalus, the first who, by this effeminate habit, had sullied the dignity of an emperor and a man. Aurelian complained that a pound of silk was sold at Rome for twelve ounces of gold; but the supply increased with the demand, and the price diminished with the supply. If accident or monopoly sometimes raised the value even above the standard of Aurelian, the manufacturers of Tyre and Berytus were sometimes compelled, by the operation of the same causes, to content themselves with a ninth part of that extravagant rate. A law was thought necessary to discriminate the dress of comedians from that of senators, and of the silk exported from its native country the far greater part was consumed by the subjects of Justinian. They were still more intimately acquainted with a shell-fish of the Mediterranean, surnamed the silkworm of the sea. The fine wool or hair by which the mother-of-pearl affixes itself to the rock is now manufactured for curiosity rather than use; a robe obtained from the same singular materials was the gift of the Roman emperor to the satraps of Armenia.

A valuable merchandise of small bulk is capable of defraying the expense of land-carriage, and the caravans traversed the whole latitude of Asia in two hundred and forty-three days from the Chinese ocean to the sea-coast of Syria. Silk was immediately delivered to the Romans by the Persian merchants who frequented the fairs of Armenia and Nisibis; but this trade, which in the intervals of truce was oppressed by avarice and jealousy, was totally interrupted by the long wars of the rival monarchies. The Great King might proudly number Sogdiana, and even *Serica*, among the provinces of his empire, but his real dominion was bounded by the Oxus, and his useful intercourse with the Sogdoites, beyond the river, depended on the pleasure of their conquerors, the white Huns and the Turks, who successively reigned over that industrious people. Yet the most savage dominion has not extirpated the seeds of agriculture and commerce in a region which is celebrated as one of the four gardens of Asia; the cities of Samarcand and Bochara are advantageously seated for the exchange of its various productions, and their merchants purchased from the Chinese the raw or manufactured silk which they transported into Persia for the use of the Roman empire. In the vain capital of China the Sogdian caravans were entertained as the suppliant embassies of tributary kingdoms, and, if they returned in safety, the bold adventure was rewarded with exorbitant gain.

But the difficult and perilous march from Samarcand to the first town of Shensi could not be performed in less than sixty, eighty, or one hundred days; as soon as they had passed the Jaxartes they entered the desert, and the wandering hordes, unless they are restrained by armies and garrisons, have always considered the citizen and the traveller as the objects of lawful rapine. To escape the Tartar robbers and the tyrants of Persia, the silk-caravans explored a more southern road: they traversed the mountains of Thibet, descended the streams of the Ganges or the Indus, and patiently expected, in the ports of Guzerat and Malabar, the annual fleets of the West. But the dangers of the desert were found less intolerable than toil, hunger, and the loss of time; the attempt was seldom renewed, and the only European who has passed that unfrequented way applauds his own diligence that, in nine months after his departure from Pekin, he reached the mouth of the Indus.

The ocean, however, was open to the free communication of mankind. From the great river to the tropic of Cancer the provinces of China were subdued and civilised by the emperors of the North; they were filled about the time of the Christian era with cities and men, mulberry-trees and their precious inhabitants; and if the Chinese, with the knowledge of the compass, had possessed the genius of the Greeks or Phœnicians, they might have spread their discoveries over the southern hemisphere. I am not qualified to examine, and I am not disposed to believe, their distant voyages to the Persian Gulf or the Cape of Good Hope; but their ancestors might equal the labours and success of the present race, and the sphere of their navigation might extend from the isles of Japan to the straits of Malacca, the Pillars, if we may apply that name, of an Oriental Hercules. Without losing sight of land, they might sail along the coast to the extreme promontory of Achin, which is annually visited by ten or twelve ships laden with the productions, the manufactures, and even the artificers of China; the island of Sumatra and the opposite peninsula are faintly delineated as the regions of gold and silver, and the trading cities named in the geography of Ptolemy may indicate that this wealth was not solely derived from the mines.

The direct interval between Sumatra and Ceylon is about three hundred leagues; the Chinese and Indian navigators were conducted by the flight of birds and periodical winds, and the ocean might be securely traversed in square-built ships, which, instead of iron, were sewed together with the strong thread of the cocoanut. Ceylon, Serendib, or Taprobana was divided between two hostile princes, one of whom possessed the mountains, the elephants, and the luminous carbuncle, and the other enjoyed the more solid riches of domestic industry, foreign trade, and the capacious harbour of Trinquemale, which received and dismissed the fleets of the East and West. In this hospitable isle, at an equal distance (as it was computed) from their respective countries, the silk-merchants of China, who had collected in their voyages aloes, cloves, nutmeg, and sandal-wood, maintained a free and beneficial commerce with the inhabitants of the Persian Gulf. The subjects of the Great King exalted, without a rival, his power and magnificence;

and the Roman, who confounded their vanity by comparing his paltry coin with a gold medal of the emperor Anastasius, had sailed to Ceylon, in an Æthiopian ship, as a simple passenger.

As silk became of indispensable use, the emperor Justinian saw with concern that the Persians had occupied by land and sea the monopoly of this important supply, and that the wealth of his subjects was continually drained by a nation of enemies and idolaters. An active government would have restored the trade of Egypt and the navigation of the Red Sea, which had decayed with the prosperity of the empire; and the Roman vessels might have sailed for the purchase of silk to the ports of Ceylon, of Malacca, or even of China. Justinian embraced a more humble expedient, and solicited the aid of his Christian allies, the Æthiopians of Abyssinia, who had recently acquired the arts of navigation, the spirit of trade, and the seaport of Adulis, still decorated with the trophies of a Grecian conqueror. Along the African coast they penetrated to the equator in search of gold, emeralds, and aromatics; but they wisely declined an unequal competition, in which they must be always prevented by the vicinity of the Persians to the markets of India: and the emperor submitted to the disappointment till his wishes were gratified by an unexpected event. The Gospel had been preached to the Indians: a bishop already governed the Christians of St. Thomas on the pepper-coast of Malabar; a church was planted in Ceylon, and the missionaries pursued the footsteps of commerce to the extremities of Asia.

Two Persian monks had long resided in China, perhaps in the royal city of Nankin, the seat of a monarch addicted to foreign superstitions, and who actually received an embassy from the isle of Ceylon. Amidst their pious occupations they viewed with a curious eye the common dress of the Chinese, the manufactures of silk, and the myriads of silkworms, whose education (either on trees or in houses) had once been considered as the labour of queens. They soon discovered that it was impracticable to transport the short-lived insect, but that in the eggs a numerous progeny might be preserved and multiplied in a distant climate. Religion or interest had more power over the Persian monks than the love of their country: after a long journey they arrived at Constantinople, imparted their project to the emperor, and were liberally encouraged by the gifts and promises of Justinian. To the historians of that prince a campaign at the foot of Mount Caucasus has seemed more deserving of a minute relation than the labours of these missionaries of commerce, who again entered China, deceived a jealous people by concealing the eggs of the silkworm in a hollow cane, and returned in triumph with the spoils of the East. Under their direction the eggs were hatched at the proper season by the artificial heat of dung; the worms were fed with mulberry-leaves; they lived and laboured in a foreign climate; a sufficient number of butterflies was saved to propagate the race, and trees were planted to supply the nourishment of the rising generations. I am not insensible of the benefits of elegant luxury; yet I reflect with some pain that if the importers of silk had introduced the art of printing, already practised by the Chinese, the comedies of Menander and the entire decads of Livy would have been perpetuated in the editions of the sixth century. A larger view of the globe might at least have promoted the improvement of speculative science; but the Christian geography was forcibly extracted from texts of Scripture, and the study of nature was the surest symptom of an unbelieving mind. The orthodox faith confined the habitable world to *one* temperate zone, and represented the earth as an oblong surface, four hundred days' journey in length, two hundred in breadth, encompassed by the ocean and covered by the solid crystal of the firmament.

In the exercise of supreme power, the first act of Justinian was to divide it with the woman whom he loved, the famous Theodora, whose strange elevation cannot be applauded as the triumph of female virtue. The usual honours which the severity of Roman manners had allowed to the wives of princes could not satisfy either the ambition of Theodora or the fondness of Justinian. He seated her on the throne as an equal and independent colleague in the sovereignty of the empire, and an oath of allegiance was imposed on the governors of the provinces in the joint names of Justinian and Theodora. The Eastern world fell prostrate; the prostitute who, in the presence of innumerable spectators, had polluted the theatre of Constantinople, was adored as a queen in the same city, by grave magistrates, orthodox bishops, victorious generals, and captive monarchs.

Those who believe that the female mind is totally depraved by the loss of chastity will eagerly listen to all the invectives of private envy or popular resentment, which have dissembled the virtues of Theodora, and exaggerated her vices. The name of Theodora was introduced, with equal honour, in all the pious and charitable foundations of Justinian; and the most benevolent institution of his reign may be ascribed to the sympathy of the empress for her less fortunate sisters, who had been seduced or compelled to embrace the trade of prostitution.

The subjects of Justinian were dissatisfied with the times and with the government. Europe was overrun by the barbarians and Asia by the monks: the poverty of the West discouraged the trade and manufactures of the East: the produce of labour was consumed by the unprofitable servants of the church, the state, and the army; and a rapid decrease was felt in the fixed and circulating capitals which constitute the national wealth. The public distress had been alleviated by the economy of Anastasius, and that prudent emperor accumulated an immense treasure while he delivered his people from the most odious or oppressive taxes. Their gratitude universally applauded the abolition of the *gold of affliction*, a personal tribute on the industry of the poor.

The *edifices* of Justinian were cemented with the blood and treasure of his people; but those stately structures appeared to announce the prosperity of the empire, and actually displayed the skill of their architects. Both the theory and practice of the arts which depend on mathematical science and mechanical power were cultivated under the patronage of the emperors. His favourite architects submitted their designs and difficulties to Justinian, and discreetly confessed how much their laborious meditations were surpassed by the intuitive knowledge or celestial inspiration of an emperor whose views were always directed to the benefit of his people, the glory of his reign, and the salvation of his soul.

The principal church, which was dedicated by the founder of Constantinople to Saint Sophia, or the eternal wisdom, had been twice destroyed by fire. The ruins were cleared away, a more spacious plan was described, and, as it required the consent of some proprietors of ground, they obtained the most exorbitant terms from the eager desires and timorous conscience of the monarch. Anthemius formed the design, and his genius directed the hands of ten thousand workmen, whose payment in pieces of fine silver was never delayed beyond the evening. The emperor himself, clad in a linen tunic, surveyed each day their rapid progress, and encouraged their diligence by his familiarity, his zeal, and his rewards. The new cathedral of St. Sophia was consecrated by the patriarch, five years, eleven months, and ten days from the first foundation; and in the midst of the solemn festival Justinian exclaimed with devout vanity, "Glory be to God, who hath thought me worthy to accomplish so great a work; I have vanquished thee, O Solomon!"

But the pride of the Roman Solomon, before twenty years had elapsed, was humbled by an earthquake, which overthrew the eastern part of the dome. Its splendour was again restored by the perseverance of the same prince; and in the thirty-sixth year of his reign Justinian celebrated the second dedication of a temple which remains, after twelve centuries, a stately monument of his fame. The architecture of St. Sophia, which is now converted into the principal mosque, has been imitated by the Turkish sultans, and that venerable pile continues to excite the fond admiration of the Greeks, and the more rational curiosity of European travellers. The eye of the spectator is disappointed by an irregular prospect of half-domes and shelving roofs: the western front, the principal approach, is destitute of simplicity and magnificence; and the scale of dimensions has been much surpassed by several of the Latin cathedrals. But the architect who first erected an *aërial* cupola is entitled to the praise of bold design and skilful execution. The dome of St. Sophia, illuminated by four-and-twenty windows, is formed with so small a curve, that the depth is equal only to one-sixth of its diameter; the measure of that diameter is one hundred and fifteen feet, and the lofty centre, where a crescent has supplanted the cross, rises to the perpendicular height of one hundred and eighty feet above the pavement. The circle which encompasses the dome lightly reposes on four strong arches, and their weight is firmly supported by four massy piles, whose strength is assisted on the northern and southern sides by four columns of Egyptian granite.

A Greek cross, inscribed in a quadrangle, represents the form of the edifice; the exact breadth is two hundred and forty-three feet, and two hundred and sixty-nine may be assigned for the extreme length, from the sanctuary in the east to the nine western doors which open into the vestibule, and from thence into the *narthex* or exterior portico. That portico was the humble station of the penitents. The nave or body of the church was filled by the congregation of the faithful; but the two sexes were prudently distinguished, and the upper and lower galleries were allotted for the more private devotion of the women. Beyond the northern and southern piles, a balustrade, terminated on either side by the thrones of the emperor and the patriarch, divided the nave from the choir; and the space, as far as the steps of the altar, was occupied by the clergy and singers. The altar itself, a name which insensibly became familiar to Christian ears, was placed in the eastern recess, artificially built in the form of a demicylinder; and this sanctuary communicated by several doors with the sacristy, the vestry, the baptistery, and the contiguous buildings, subservient either to the pomp of worship, or the private use of the ecclesiastical ministers.

The memory of past calamities inspired Justinian with a wise resolution that no wood, except for the doors, should be admitted into the new edifice; and the choice of the materials was applied to the strength, the lightness, or the splendour of the respective parts. The solid piles which sustained the cupola were composed of huge blocks of freestone, hewn into squares and triangles, fortified by circles of iron, and firmly cemented by the infusion of lead and quicklime; but the weight of the cupola was diminished by the levity of its substance, which consists either of pumice-stone that floats in the water, or of bricks, from the isle of Rhodes, five times less ponderous than the ordinary sort. The whole frame of the edifice was constructed of brick; but those base materials were concealed by a crust of marble; and the inside of St. Sophia, the cupola, the two larger and the six smaller semidomes, the walls, the hundred columns, and the pavement, delight even the eyes of barbarians with a rich and variegated picture.

A poet who beheld the primitive lustre of St. Sophia, enumerates the colours, the shades, and the spots of ten or twelve marbles, jaspers, and porphyries, which nature had profusely diversified, and which were blended and contrasted as it were by a skilful painter. The triumph of Christ was adorned with the last spoils of Paganism, but the greater part of these costly stones was extracted from the quarries of Asia Minor, the isles and continent of Greece, Egypt, Africa, and Gaul. Eight columns of porphyry, which Aurelian had placed in the Temple of the Sun, were offered by the piety of a Roman matron; eight others of green marble were presented by the ambitious zeal of the magistrates of Ephesus: both are admirable by their size and beauty, but every order of architecture disclaims their fantastic capitals. A variety of ornaments and figures was curiously expressed in mosaic; and the images of Christ, of the Virgin, of saints, and of angels, which have been defaced by Turkish fanaticism, were dangerously exposed to the superstition of the Greeks. According to the sanctity of each object, the precious metals were distributed in thin leaves or in solid masses. The balustrade of the choir, the capitals of the pillars, the ornaments of the doors and galleries, were of gilt bronze. The spectator was dazzled by the glittering aspect of the cupola. The sanctuary contained forty thousand pound weight of silver, and the holy vases and vestments of the altar were of the purest gold, enriched with inestimable gems.

So minute a description of an edifice which time has respected may attest the truth and excuse the relation of the innumerable works, both in the capital and provinces, which Justinian constructed on a smaller scale and less durable foundations. In Constantinople alone, and the adjacent suburbs, he dedicated twenty-five churches to the honour of Christ, the Virgin, and the saints. Almost every saint in the calendar acquired the honours of a temple—almost every city of the empire obtained the solid advantages of bridges, hospitals, and aqueducts; but the severe liberality of the monarch disdained to indulge his subjects in the popular luxury of baths and theatres.

A material difference may be observed in the games of antiquity: the most eminent of the Greeks were actors, the Romans were merely spectators. The Olympic stadium was open to wealth, merit, and ambition; and if the candidates could depend on their personal skill and activity, they might pursue the footsteps of Diomede and Menelaus, and conduct their own horses in the rapid career. Ten, twenty, forty chariots, were allowed to start at the same instant; a crown of leaves was the reward of the victor, and his fame, with that of his family and country, was chanted in lyric strains more durable than monuments of brass and marble. But a senator, or even a citizen, conscious of his dignity, would have blushed to expose his person or his horses in the circus of Rome. The games were exhibited at the expense of the republic, the magistrates, or the emperors; but the reins were abandoned to servile hands; and if the profits of a favourite charioteer sometimes exceeded those of an advocate, they must be considered as the effects of popular extravagance, and the high wages of a disgraceful profession.

The race, in its first institution, was a simple contest of two chariots, whose drivers were distinguished by *white* and *red* liveries: two additional colours, a light *green* and a cærulean *blue*, were afterwards introduced; and, as the races were repeated twenty-five times, one hundred chariots contributed in the same day to the pomp of the circus. The four *factions* soon acquired a legal establishment and a mysterious origin, and their fanciful colours were derived from the various appearances of nature in the four seasons of the year; the red dog-star of summer, the snows of winter, the deep shades of autumn, and the cheerful verdure of the spring. Another interpretation preferred the elements to the seasons, and the struggle of the green and blue was supposed to represent the conflict of the earth and sea. Their respective victories announced either a plentiful harvest or a prosperous navigation, and the hostility of the husbandmen and mariners was somewhat less absurd than the blind ardour of the Roman people, who devoted their lives and fortunes to the colour which they had espoused. Such folly was disdained and indulged by the wisest princes; but the names of Caligula, Nero, Vitellius, Verus, Commodus, Caracalla, and Elagabalus, were enrolled in the blue or green factions of the circus: they frequented their stables, applauded their favourites, chastised their antagonists, and deserved the esteem of the populace by the natural or affected imitation of their manners. The bloody and tumultuous contest continued to disturb the public festivity till the last age of the spectacles of Rome; and Theodoric, from a motive of justice or affection, interposed his authority to protect the greens against the violence of a consul and a patrician who were passionately addicted to the blue faction of the circus.

Constantinople adopted the follies, though not the virtues, of ancient Rome; and the same factions which had agitated the circus raged with redoubled fury in the hippodrome. Under the reign of Anastasius, this popular frenzy was inflamed by religious zeal; and the greens, who had treacherously concealed stones and daggers under baskets of fruit, massacred at a solemn festival three thousand of their blue adversaries. From the capital this pestilence was diffused into the provinces and cities of the East, and the sportive distinction of two colours produced two strong and irreconcilable factions, which shook the foundations of a feeble government. The popular dissensions, founded on the most serious interest or holy pretence, have scarcely equalled the obstinacy of this wanton discord, which invaded the peace of families, divided friends and brothers, and tempted the female sex, though seldom seen in the circus, to espouse the inclinations of their lovers, or to contradict the wishes of their husbands. Every law, either human or divine, was trampled under foot; and as long as the party was successful, its deluded followers appeared careless of private distress or public calamity. The licence, without the freedom, of democracy, was revived at Antioch and Constantinople, and the support of a faction became necessary to every candidate for civil or ecclesiastical honours. A secret attachment to the family or sect of Anastasius was imputed to the greens; the blues were zealously devoted to the cause of orthodoxy and Justinian.

The first edict of Justinian, which was often repeated and sometimes executed, announced his firm resolution to support the innocent, and to chastise the guilty, of every denomination and *colour*. Yet the balance of justice was still inclined in favour of the blue faction.

A sedition, which almost laid Constantinople in ashes, was excited by the mutual hatred and momentary reconciliation of the two factions. In the fifth year of his reign Justinian celebrated the festival of the ides of January: the games were incessantly disturbed by the clamorous discontent of the greens; till the twenty-second race the emperor maintained his silent gravity; at length, yielding to his impatience, he condescended to hold, in abrupt sentences, and by the voice of a crier, the most singular dialogue that ever passed between a prince and his subjects. Their first complaints were respectful and modest; they accused the subordinate ministers of oppression, and proclaimed their wishes for the long life and victory of the emperor. "Be patient and attentive, ye insolent railers!" exclaimed Justinian; "be mute, ye Jews, Samaritans, and Manichæans!" The greens still attempted to awaken his compassion. "We are poor, we are innocent, we are injured, we dare not pass through the streets: a general persecution is exercised against our name and colour. Let us die, O emperor! but let us die by your command, and for your service!" But the repetition of partial and passionate invectives degraded, in their eyes, the majesty of the purple; they renounced allegiance to the prince who refused justice to his people, lamented that the father of Justinian had been born, and branded his son with the opprobrious names of a homicide, an ass, and a perjured tyrant. "Do you despise your lives?" cried the indignant monarch.

The blues rose with fury from their seats, their hostile clamours thundered in the hippodrome, and their adversaries, deserting the unequal contest, spread terror and despair through the streets of Constantinople. At this dangerous moment, seven notorious assassins of both factions, who had been condemned by the præfect, were carried round the city, and afterwards transported to the place of execution in the suburb of Pera. Four were immediately beheaded; a fifth was hanged; but, when the same punishment was inflicted on the remaining two, the rope broke, they fell alive to the ground, the populace applauded their escape, and the monks of St. Conon, issuing from the neighbouring convent, conveyed them in a boat to the sanctuary of the church. As one of these criminals was of the blue, and the other of the green, livery, the two factions were equally provoked by the cruelty of their oppressor or the ingratitude of their patron, and a short truce was concluded till they had delivered their prisoners and satisfied their revenge. The palace of the præfect, who withstood the seditious torrent, was instantly burnt, his officers and guards were massacred, the prisons were forced open, and freedom was restored to those who could only use it for the public destruction. A military force which had been dispatched to the aid of the civil magistrate was fiercely encountered by an armed multitude, whose numbers and boldness continually increased: and the Heruli, the wildest barbarians in the service of the empire, overturned the priests and their relics, which, from a pious motive, had been rashly interposed to separate the bloody conflict. The tumult was exasperated by this sacrilege; the people fought with enthusiasm in the cause of God; the women, from the roofs and windows, showered stones on the heads of the soldiers, who darted firebrands against the houses; and the various flames, which had been kindled by the hands of citizens and strangers, spread without control over the face of the city. The conflagration involved the cathedral of St. Sophia, the baths of Zeuxippus, a part of the palace from the first entrance to the altar of Mars, and the long portico from the palace to the forum of Constantine: a large hospital, with the sick patients, was consumed; many churches and stately edifices were destroyed; and an immense treasure of gold and silver was either melted or lost. From such scenes of horror and distress the wise and wealthy citizens escaped over the Bosphorus to the Asiatic side, and during five days Constantinople was abandoned to the factions, whose watchword, NIKA, *vanquish!* has given a name to this memorable sedition.

The fortifications of Europe and Asia were multiplied by Justinian; but the repetition of those timid and fruitless precautions exposes, to a philosophic eye, the debility of the empire. From Belgrade to the Euxine, from the conflux of the Save to the mouth of the Danube, a chain of above four-score fortified places was extended along the banks of the great river. Single watch-towers were changed into spacious citadels; vacant walls, which the engineers contracted or enlarged according to the nature of the ground, were filled with colonies or garrisons; a strong fortress defended the ruins of Trajan's bridge; and several military stations affected to spread beyond the Danube the pride of the Roman name. But that name was divested of its terrors; the barbarians, in their annual inroads, passed and contemptuously repassed before these useless bulwarks; and the inhabitants of the frontier, instead of reposing under the shadow of the general defence, were compelled to guard with incessant vigilance their separate habitations.

Yet some generations elapsed before their minds were reduced to the level of slavery. The populous villages of Mount Taurus were filled with horsemen and archers; they resisted the imposition of tributes, but they recruited the armies of Justinian; and his civil magistrates, the proconsul of Cappadocia, the count of Isauria, and the prætors of Lycaonia and Pisidia, were invested with military power.

If we extend our view from the tropic to the mouth of the Tanais, we may observe, on one hand, the precautions of Justinian to curb the savages of Æthiopia, and, on the other, the long walls which he constructed in Crimæa for the protection of his friendly Goths, a colony of three thousand shepherds and warriors. From that peninsula to Trebizond the eastern curve of the Euxine was secured by forts, by alliance, or by religion. Trebizond, in after times the seat of a romantic empire, was indebted to the liberality of Justinian for a church, an aqueduct, and a castle, whose ditches are hewn in the solid rock. From that maritime city a frontier line of five hundred miles may be drawn to the fortress of Circesium, the last Roman station on the Euphrates.

Without insisting on places less important, the fortifications of Dara may represent the military architecture of the age. The city was surrounded with two walls, and the interval between them, of fifty paces, afforded a retreat to the cattle of the besieged. The inner wall was a monument of strength and beauty: it measured sixty feet from the ground, and the height of the towers was one hundred feet; the loopholes, from whence an enemy might be annoyed with missile weapons, were small, but numerous; the soldiers were planted along the rampart, under the shelter of double galleries; and a third platform, spacious and secure, was raised on the summit of the towers. The exterior wall appears to have been less lofty, but more solid, and each tower was protected by a quadrangular bulwark. A hard rocky soil resisted the tools of the miners, and on the south-east, where the ground was more tractable, their approach was retarded by a new work, which advanced in the shape of a half-moon. The double and treble ditches were filled with a stream of water, and in the management of the river the most skilful labour was employed to supply the inhabitants, to distress the besiegers, and to prevent the mischiefs of a natural or artificial inundation. Dara continued more than sixty years to fulfil the wishes of its founders and to provoke the jealousy of the Persians, who incessantly complained that this impregnable fortress had been constructed in manifest violation of the treaty of peace between the two empires.

Justinian suppressed the schools of Athens and the consulship of Rome, which had given so many sages and heroes to mankind. Both these institutions had long since degenerated from their primitive glory, yet some reproach may be justly inflicted on the avarice and jealousy of a prince by whose hand such venerable ruins were destroyed.

Athens, after her Persian triumphs, adopted the philosophy of Ionia, and the rhetoric of Sicily; and these studies became the patrimony of a city whose inhabitants, about thirty thousand males, condensed, within the period of a single life, the genius of ages and millions. Our sense of the dignity of human nature is exalted by the simple recollection that Isocrates was the companion of Plato and Xenophon; that he assisted, perhaps with the historian Thucydides, at the first representations of the Œdipus of Sophocles and the Iphigenia of Euripides; and that his pupils Æschines and Demosthenes contended for the crown of patriotism in the presence of Aristotle, the master of Theophrastus, who taught at Athens with the founders of the Stoic and Epicurean sects. The ingenuous youth of Attica enjoyed the benefits of their domestic education, which was communicated without envy to the rival cities. Two thousand disciples heard the lessons of Theophrastus; the schools of rhetoric must have been still more populous than those of philosophy; and a rapid succession of students diffused the fame of their teachers as far as the utmost limits of the Grecian language and name. Those limits were enlarged by the victories of Alexander; the arts of Athens survived her freedom and dominion; and the Greek colonies which the Macedonians planted in Egypt, and scattered over Asia, undertook long and frequent pilgrimages to worship the Muses in their favourite temple on the banks of the Ilissus. The Latin conquerors respectfully listened to the instructions of their subjects and captives; the names of Cicero and Horace were enrolled in the schools of Athens; and after the perfect settlement of the Roman empire, the natives of Italy, of Africa, and of Britain, conversed in the groves of the Academy with their fellow-students of the East.

The studies of philosophy and eloquence are congenial to a popular state, which encourages the freedom of inquiry, and submits only to the force of persuasion. In the republics of Greece and Rome the art of speaking was the powerful engine of patriotism or ambition; and the schools of rhetoric poured forth a colony of statesmen and legislators. When the liberty of public debate was suppressed, the orator, in the honourable profession of an advocate, might plead the cause of innocence and justice; he might abuse his talents in the more profitable trade of panegyric; and the same precepts continued to dictate the fanciful declamations of the sophist, and the chaster beauties of historical composition. The systems which professed to unfold the nature of God, of man, and of the universe, entertained the curiosity of the philosophic student; and according to the temper of his mind, he might doubt with the Sceptics, or decide with the Stoics, sublimely speculate with

Plato, or severely argue with Aristotle. The pride of the adverse sects had fixed an unattainable term of moral happiness and perfection: but the race was glorious and salutary; the disciples of Zeno, and even those of Epicurus, were taught both to act and to suffer; and the death of Petronius was not less effectual than that of Seneca to humble a tyrant by the discovery of his impotence.

The light of science could not indeed be confined within the walls of Athens. Her incomparable writers address themselves to the human race; the living masters emigrated to Italy and Asia; Berytus, in later times, was devoted to the study of the law; astronomy and physic were cultivated in the museum of Alexandria; but the Attic schools of rhetoric and philosophy maintained their superior reputation from the Peloponnesian war to the reign of Justinian. Athens, though situate in a barren soil, possessed a pure air, a free navigation, and the monuments of ancient art. That sacred retirement was seldom disturbed by the business of trade or government; and the last of the Athenians were distinguished by their lively wit, the purity of their taste and language, their social manners, and some traces, at least in discourse, of the magnanimity of their fathers. In the suburbs of the city, the *Academy* of the Platonists, the *Lyceum* of the Peripatetics, the *Portico* of the Stoics, and the *Garden* of the Epicureans, were planted with trees and decorated with statues; and the philosophers, instead of being immured in a cloister, delivered their instructions in spacious and pleasant walks, which at different hours were consecrated to the exercises of the mind and body. The genius of the founders still lived in those venerable seats; the ambition of succeeding to the masters of human reason excited a generous emulation; and the merit of the candidates was determined, on each vacancy, by the free voices of an enlightened people. The Athenian professors were paid by their disciples: according to their mutual wants and abilities, the price appears to have varied from a mina to a talent; and Isocrates himself, who derides the avarice of the sophists, required, in his school of rhetoric, about thirty pounds from each of his hundred pupils. The wages of industry are just and honourable, yet the same Isocrates shed tears at the first receipt of a stipend: the Stoic might blush when he was hired to preach the contempt of money; and I should be sorry to discover that Aristotle or Plato so far degenerated from the example of Socrates as to exchange knowledge for gold. But some property of lands and houses was settled, by the permission of the laws, and the legacies of deceased friends, on the philosophic chairs of Athens. Epicurus bequeathed to his disciples the gardens which he had purchased for eighty minæ or two hundred and fifty pounds, with a fund sufficient for their frugal subsistence and monthly festivals; and the patrimony of Plato afforded an annual rent, which, in eight centuries, was gradually increased from three to one thousand pieces of gold. The schools of Athens were protected by the wisest and most virtuous of the Roman princes. The library, which Hadrian founded, was placed in a portico adorned with pictures, statues, and a roof of alabaster, and supported by one hundred columns of Phrygian marble. The public salaries were assigned by the generous spirit of the Antonines; and each professor, of politics, of rhetoric, of the Platonic, the Peripatetic, the Stoic, and the Epicurean philosophy, received an annual stipend of ten thousand drachmæ, or more than three hundred pounds sterling.

After the death of Marcus, these liberal donations, and the privileges attached to the *thrones* of science, were abolished and revived, diminished and enlarged; but some vestige of royal bounty may be found under the successors of Constantine; and their arbitrary choice of an unworthy candidate might tempt the philosophers of Athens to regret the days of independence and poverty. It is remarkable that the impartial favour of the Antonines was bestowed on the four adverse sects of philosophy which they considered as equally useful, or at least as equally innocent. Socrates had formerly been the glory and the reproach of his country; and the first lessons of Epicurus so strangely scandalised the pious ears of the Athenians, that by his exile, and that of his antagonists, they silenced all vain disputes concerning the nature of the gods. But in the ensuing year they recalled the hasty decree, restored the liberty of the schools, and were convinced by the experience of ages that the moral character of philosophers is not affected by the diversity of their theological speculations.

The Gothic arms were less fatal to the schools of Athens than the establishment of a new religion, whose ministers superseded the exercise of reason, resolved every question by an article of faith, and condemned the infidel or sceptic to eternal flame. In many a volume of laborious controversy they exposed the weakness of the understanding and the corruption of the heart, insulted human nature in the sages of antiquity, and proscribed the spirit of philosophical inquiry, so repugnant to the doctrine, or at least to the temper, of a humble believer. The surviving sect of the Platonists, alone in the midst of a Christian world, indulged a secret rancour against the government of the church and state whose severity was still suspended over their heads. The edict of Justinian imposed a perpetual silence on the schools of Athens, and excited the grief and indignation of the few remaining votaries of Grecian science and superstition.

Seven friends and philosophers, Diogenes and Hermias, Eulalius and Priscian, Damascius, Isidore, and Simplicius, who dissented from the religion of their sovereign, embraced the resolution of seeking in a foreign land the freedom which was denied in their native country. They had heard, and they credulously believed, that the republic of Plato was realised in the despotic government of Persia, and that a patriot king reigned over the happiest and most virtuous of nations. They were soon astonished by the natural discovery that Persia resembled the other countries of the globe; that Chosroes, who affected the name of a philosopher, was vain, cruel, and ambitious; that bigotry, and a spirit of intolerance, prevailed among the Magi; that the nobles were haughty, the courtiers servile, and the magistrates unjust; that the guilty sometimes escaped, and that the innocent were often oppressed. The disappointment of the philosophers provoked them to overlook the real virtues of the Persians; and they were scandalised, more deeply perhaps than became their profession, with the plurality of wives and concubines, the incestuous marriages, and the custom of exposing dead bodies to the dogs and vultures, instead of hiding them in the earth, or consuming them with fire. Their repentance was expressed by a precipitate return, and they loudly declared that they had rather die on the borders of the empire than enjoy the wealth and favour of the barbarian. From this journey, however, they derived a benefit which reflects the purest lustre on the character of Chosroes. He required that the seven sages who had visited the court of Persia should be exempted from the penal laws which Justinian enacted against his Pagan subjects; and this privilege, expressly stipulated in a treaty of peace, was guarded by the vigilance of a powerful mediator. Simplicius and his companions terminate the long list of Grecian philosophers, who may be justly praised, notwithstanding their defects, as the wisest and most virtuous of their contemporaries. The writings of Simplicius are now extant. His physical and metaphysical commentaries on Aristotle have passed away with the fashion of the times; but his moral interpretation of Epictetus is preserved in the library of nations, as a classic book.

About the same time that Pythagoras first invented the appellation of philosopher, liberty and the consulship were founded at Rome by the elder Brutus. The revolutions of the consular office, which may be viewed in the successive lights of a substance, a shadow, and a name, have been occasionally mentioned in the present history. The first magistrates of the republic had been chosen by the people, to exercise, in the senate and in the camp, the powers of peace and war which were afterwards translated to the emperors. But the tradition of ancient dignity was long revered by the Romans and barbarians. A Gothic historian applauds the consulship of Theodoric as the height of all temporal glory and greatness; the king of Italy himself congratulates those annual favourites of fortune who, without the cares, enjoyed the splendour of the throne; and at the end of a thousand years two consuls were created by the sovereigns of Rome and Constantinople for the sole purpose of giving a date to the year and a festival to the people. But the expenses of this festival, in which the wealthy and the vain aspired to surpass their predecessors, insensibly arose to the enormous sum of fourscore thousand pounds; the wisest senators declined a useless honour which involved the certain ruin of their families, and to this reluctance I should impute the frequent chasms in the last age of the consular *Fasti.* The predecessors of Justinian had assisted from the public treasures the dignity of the less opulent candidates; the avarice of that prince preferred the cheaper and more convenient method of advice and regulation. Seven *processions* or spectacles were the number to which his edict confined the horse and chariot races, the athletic sports, the music and pantomimes of the theatre, and the hunting of wild beasts; and small pieces of silver were discreetly substituted to the gold medals which had always excited tumult and drunkenness when they were scattered with a profuse hand among the populace.

Notwithstanding these precautions and his own example, the succession of consuls finally ceased in the thirteenth year of Justinian, whose despotic temper might be gratified by the silent extinction of a title which admonished the Romans of their ancient freedom. Yet the annual consulship still lived in the minds of the people; they fondly expected its speedy restoration; they applauded the gracious condescension of successive princes, by whom it was assumed in the first year of their reign; and three centuries elapsed, after the death of Justinian, before that obsolete dignity, which had been suppressed by custom, could be abolished by law. The imperfect mode of distinguishing each year by the name of a magistrate was usefully supplied by the date of a permanent era: the creation of the world, according to the Septuagint version, was adopted by the Greeks; and the Latins, since the age of Charlemagne, have computed their time from the birth of Christ.

CHAPTER XXVIII

ROMAN JURISPRUDENCE—THE TWELVE TABLES—THE LAWS OF THE PEOPLE—DECREES OF THE SENATE—EDICTS OF THE EMPERORS

EXPERIENCE AND CHRISTIANITY refuted the superstitious hope that Rome was founded by the gods to reign for ever over the nations of the earth. But the proud claim of perpetual and indefeasible dominion, which her soldiers could no longer maintain, was firmly asserted by her statesmen and lawyers, whose opinions have been sometimes revived and propagated in the modern schools of jurisprudence.

The primitive government of Rome was composed with some political skill of an elective king, a council of nobles, and a general assembly of the people. War and religion were administered by the supreme magistrate, and he alone proposed the laws which were debated in the senate, and finally ratified or rejected by a majority of votes in the thirty *curiæ* or parishes of the city. Romulus, Numa, and Servius Tullius are celebrated as the most ancient legislators; and each of them claims his peculiar part in the threefold division of jurisprudence. The laws of marriage, the education of children, and the authority of parents, which may seem to draw their origin from *nature* itself, are ascribed to the untutored wisdom of Romulus. The law of *nations* and of religious worship, which Numa introduced, was derived from his nocturnal converse with the nymph Egeria. The *civil* law is attributed to the experience of Servius; he balanced the rights and fortunes of the seven classes of citizens, and guarded by fifty new regulations the observance of contracts and the punishment of crimes. The state, which he had inclined towards a democracy, was changed by the last Tarquin into lawless despotism; and when the kingly office was abolished, the patricians engrossed the benefits of freedom. The royal laws became odious or obsolete, the mysterious deposit was silently preserved by the priests and nobles, and at the end of sixty years the citizens of Rome still complained that they were ruled by the arbitrary sentence of the magistrates. Yet the positive institutions of the kings had blended themselves with the public and private manners of the city; some fragments of that venerable jurisprudence were compiled by the diligence of antiquarians, and above twenty texts still speak the rudeness of the Pelasgic idiom of the Latins.

I shall not repeat the well-known story of the Decemvirs, who sullied by their actions the honour of inscribing on brass, or wood, or ivory, the TWELVE TABLES of the Roman laws. They were dictated by the rigid and jealous spirit of an aristocracy which had yielded with reluctance to the just demands of the people. But the substance of the Twelve Tables was adapted to the state of the city, and the Romans had emerged from barbarism, since they were capable of studying and embracing the institutions of their more enlightened neighbours. A wise Ephesian was driven by envy from his native country: before he could reach the shores of Latium, he had observed the various forms of human nature and civil society; he imparted his knowledge to the legislators of Rome, and a statue was erected in the forum to the perpetual memory of Hermodorus.

The names and divisions of the copper money, the sole coin of the infant state, were of Dorian origin; the harvests of Campania and Sicily relieved the wants of a people whose agriculture was often interrupted by war and faction; and since the trade was established, the deputies who sailed from the Tiber might return from the same harbours with a more precious cargo of political wisdom. The colonies of Great Greece had transported and improved the arts of their mother-country. Cumæ and Rhegium, Crotona and Tarentum, Agrigentum and Syracuse, were in the rank of the most flourishing cities. The disciples of Pythagoras applied philosophy to the use of government, the unwritten laws of Charondas accepted the aid of poetry and music, and Zaleucus framed the republic of the Locrians, which stood without alteration above two hundred years. From a similar motive of national pride, both Livy and Dionysius are willing to believe that the deputies of Rome visited Athens under the wise and splendid administration of Pericles, and the laws of Solon were transfused into the Twelve Tables. If such an embassy had indeed been received from the barbarians of Hesperia, the Roman name would have been familiar to the Greeks before the reign of Alexander, and the faintest evidence would have been explored and celebrated by the curiosity of succeeding times. But the Athenian monuments are silent, nor will it seem credible that the patricians should undertake a long and perilous navigation to copy the purest model of a democracy. In the comparison of the tables of Solon with those of the Decemvirs, some casual resemblance may be found; some rules which nature and reason have revealed to every society; some proofs of a common descent from Egypt or Phœnicia. But in all the great lines of public and private jurisprudence the legislators of Rome and Athens appear to be strangers or adverse to each other.

Whatever might be the origin or the merit of the Twelve Tables, they obtained among the Romans that blind and partial reverence which the lawyers of every country delight to bestow on their municipal institutions. The study is recommended by Cicero as equally pleasant and instructive. "They amuse the mind by the remembrance of old words, and the portrait of ancient manners; they inculcate the soundest principles of government and morals; and I am not afraid to affirm that the brief composition of the Decemvirs surpasses in genuine value the libraries of Grecian philosophy. How admirable," says Tully, with honest or affected prejudice, "is the wisdom of our ancestors! We alone are the masters of civil prudence, and our superiority is the more conspicuous if we deign to cast our eyes on the rude nd almost ridiculous jurisprudence of Draco, of Solon, and of Lycurgus." The Twelve Tables were committed to the memory of the young and the neditation of the old; they were transcribed and illustrated with learned liligence: they escaped the flames of the Gauls, they subsisted in the age of ustinian, and their subsequent loss has been imperfectly restored by the abours of modern critics. But although these venerable monuments were considered as the rule of right and the fountain of justice, they were overvhelmed by the weight and variety of new laws which, at the end of five enturies, became a grievance more intolerable than the vices of the city. Three thousand brass plates, the acts of the senate and people, were deposted in the Capitol; and some of the acts, as the Julian law against extortion, urpassed the number of a hundred chapters. The Decemvirs had neglected o import the sanction of Zaleucus, which so long maintained the integrity f his republic. A Locrian who proposed any new law stood forth in the ssembly of the people with a cord around his neck, and if the law was ejected the innovator was instantly strangled.

The Decemvirs had been named, and their tables were approved, by an ssembly of the *centuries*, in which riches preponderated against numbers. To the first class of Romans, the proprietors of one hundred thousand ounds of copper, ninety-eight votes were assigned, and only ninety-five vere left for the six inferior classes, distributed according to their substance y the artful policy of Servius. But the tribunes soon established a more pecious and popular maxim, that every citizen has an equal right to enact he laws which he is bound to obey. Instead of the *centuries*, they convened he *tribes;* and the patricians, after an impotent struggle, submitted to the lecrees of an assembly in which their votes were confounded with those of he meanest plebeians. Yet as long as the tribes successively passed over arrow *bridges*, and gave their voices aloud, the conduct of each citizen was xposed to the eyes and ears of his friends and countrymen. The insolvent lebtor consulted the wishes of his creditor, the client would have blushed to ppose the views of his patron, the general was followed by his veterans, nd the aspect of a grave magistrate was a living lesson to the multitude. A new method of secret ballot abolished the influence of fear and shame, f honour and interest; and the abuse of freedom accelerated the progress of narchy and despotism. The Romans had aspired to be equal, they were evelled by the equality of servitude, and the dictates of Augustus were atiently ratified by the formal consent of the tribes or centuries. Once, nd once only, he experienced a sincere and strenuous opposition. His ubjects had resigned all political liberty; they defended the freedom of lomestic life. A law which enforced the obligation and strengthened the onds of marriage was clamorously rejected; Propertius, in the arms of Delia, applauded the victory of licentious love; and the project of reform vas suspended till a new and more tractable generation had arisen in the vorld.

Such an example was not necessary to instruct a prudent usurper of the nischief of popular assemblies; and their abolition, which Augustus had silently prepared, was accomplished without resistance, and almost withou notice, on the accession of his successor. Sixty thousand plebeian legislators whom numbers made formidable and poverty secure, were supplanted by six hundred senators, who held their honours, their fortunes, and their live by the clemency of the emperor. The loss of executive power was alleviate by the gift of legislative authority; and Ulpian might assert, after the prac tice of two hundred years, that the decrees of the senate obtained the forc and validity of laws. In the times of freedom the resolves of the people ha often been dictated by the passion or error of the moment: the Cornelian Pompeian, and Julian laws were adapted by a single hand to the prevailin disorders; but the senate, under the reign of the Cæsars, was composed o magistrates and lawyers, and in questions of private jurisprudence the integ rity of their judgment was seldom perverted by fear or interest.

The silence or ambiguity of the laws was supplied by the occasiona EDICTS of those magistrates who were invested with the *honours* of the state This ancient prerogative of the Roman kings was transferred in their respec tive offices to the consuls and dictators, the censors and prætors; and similar right was assumed by the tribunes of the people, the ædiles, and th proconsuls. At Rome, and in the provinces, the duties of the subject and th intentions of the governor were proclaimed; and the civil jurisprudence wa reformed by the annual edicts of the supreme judge, the prætor of the city As soon as he ascended his tribunal, he announced by the voice of the crier and afterwards inscribed on a white wall, the rules which he proposed t follow in the decision of doubtful cases, and the relief which his equity would afford from the precise rigour of ancient statutes. A principle o discretion more congenial to monarchy was introduced into the republic the art of respecting the name and eluding the efficacy of the laws wa improved by successive prætors; subtleties and fictions were invented t defeat the plainest meaning of the Decemvirs; and where the end was salu tary, the means were frequently absurd. The secret or probable wish of th dead was suffered to prevail over the order of succession and the forms o testaments; and the claimant, who was excluded from the character of heir accepted with equal pleasure from an indulgent prætor the possession of th goods of his late kinsman or benefactor. In the redress of private wrongs compensations and fines were substituted to the obsolete rigour of th Twelve Tables; time and space were annihilated by fanciful suppositions and the plea of youth, or fraud, or violence, annulled the obligation o excused the performance of an inconvenient contract. A jurisdiction thu vague and arbitrary was exposed to the most dangerous abuse; the substance as well as the form of justice, were often sacrificed to the prejudices o virtue, the bias of laudable affection, and the grosser seductions of interes or resentment. But the errors or vices of each prætor expired with hi annual office; such maxims alone as had been approved by reason an practice were copied by succeeding judges; the rule of proceeding wa defined by the solution of new cases; and the temptations of injustice wer removed by the Cornelian law, which compelled the prætor of the year t adhere to the letter and spirit of his first proclamation. It was reserved for the curiosity and learning of Hadrian to accomplish the design which had been conceived by the genius of Cæsar; and the prætorship of Salvius Julian, an eminent lawyer, was immortalised by the composition of the PERPETUAL EDICT. This well-digested code was ratified by the emperor and the senate; the long divorce of law and equity was at length reconciled; and, instead of the Twelve Tables, the Perpetual Edict was fixed as the invariable standard of civil jurisprudence.

From Augustus to Trajan, the modest Cæsars were content to promulgate their edicts in the various characters of a Roman magistrate; and in the decrees of the senate the *epistles* and *orations* of the prince were respectfully inserted. Hadrian appears to have been the first who assumed without disguise the plenitude of legislative power. And this innovation, so agreeable to his active mind, was countenanced by the patience of the times and his long absence from the seat of government. The same policy was embraced by succeeding monarchs, and, according to the harsh metaphor of Tertullian, "the gloomy and intricate forest of ancient laws was cleared away by the axe of royal mandates and *constitutions*." During four centuries, from Hadrian to Justinian, the public and private jurisprudence was moulded by the will of the sovereign, and few institutions, either human or divine, were permitted to stand on their former basis.

The origin of Imperial legislation was concealed by the darkness of ages and the terrors of armed despotism; and a double fiction was propagated by the servility, or perhaps the ignorance, of the civilians who basked in the sunshine of the Roman and Byzantine courts. 1. To the prayer of the ancient Cæsars the people or the senate had sometimes granted a personal exemption from the obligation and penalty of particular statutes, and each indulgence was an act of jurisdiction exercised by the republic over the first of her citizens. His humble privilege was at length transformed into the prerogative of a tyrant; and the Latin expression of "released from the laws" was supposed to exalt the emperor above *all* human restraints, and to leave his conscience and reason as the sacred measure of his conduct. 2. A similar dependence was implied in the decrees of the senate, which in every reign defined the titles and powers of an elective magistrate.

But it was not before the ideas and even the language of the Romans had been corrupted that a *royal* law, and an irrevocable gift of the people, were created by the fancy of Ulpian, or more probably of Tribonian himself; and the origin of Imperial power, though false in fact and slavish in its consequence, was supported on a principle of freedom and justice. "The pleasure of the emperor has the vigour and effect of law, since the Roman people, by the royal law, have transferred to their prince the full extent of their own power and sovereignty." The will of a single man, of a child, perhaps, was allowed to prevail over the wisdom of ages and the inclinations of millions, and the degenerate Greeks were proud to declare that in his hands alone the arbitrary exercise of legislation could be safely deposited. "What interest or passion," exclaims Theophilus in the court of Justinian, "can reach the calm and sublime elevation of the monarch? he is already master of the lives and fortunes of his subjects, and those who have incurred his displeasure are already numbered with the dead."

Disdaining the language of flattery, the historian may confess that in questions of private jurisprudence the absolute sovereign of a great empire can seldom be influenced by any personal considerations. Virtue, or even reason, will suggest to his impartial mind that he is the guardian of peace and equity, and that the interest of society is inseparably connected with his own. Under the weakest and most vicious reign, the seat of justice was filled by the wisdom and integrity of Papinian and Ulpian, and the purest materials of the Code and Pandects are inscribed with the names of Caracalla and his ministers. The tyrant of Rome was sometimes the benefactor of the provinces. A dagger terminated the crimes of Domitian; but the prudence of Nerva confirmed his acts, which, in the joy of their deliverance, had been rescinded by an indignant senate. Yet in the *rescripts*, replies to the consultations of the magistrates, the wisest of princes might be deceived by a partial exposition of the case. And this abuse, which placed their hasty decisions on the same level with mature and deliberate acts of legislation, was ineffectually condemned by the sense and example of Trajan.

The *rescripts* of the emperor, his *grants* and *decrees*, his *edicts* and *pragmatic sanctions*, were subscribed in purple ink, and transmitted to the provinces as general or special laws, which the magistrates were bound to execute and the people to obey. But as their number continually multiplied, the rule of obedience became each day more doubtful and obscure, till the will of the sovereign was fixed and ascertained in the Gregorian, the Hermogenian, and the Theodosian codes. The two first, of which some fragments have escaped, were framed by two private lawyers to preserve the constitutions of the Pagan emperors from Hadrian to Constantine. The third, which is still extant, was digested in sixteen books by the order of the younger Theodosius to consecrate the laws of the Christian princes from Constantine to his own reign. But the three codes obtained an equal authority in the tribunals, and any act which was not included in the sacred deposit might be disregarded by the judge as spurious or obsolete.

Among savage nations the want of letters is imperfectly supplied by the use of visible signs, which awaken attention and perpetuate the remembrance of any public or private transaction. The jurisprudence of the first Romans exhibited the scenes of a pantomime; the words were adapted to the gestures, and the slightest error or neglect in the *forms* of proceeding was sufficient to annul the *substance* of the fairest claim. The communion of the marriage-life was denoted by the necessary elements of fire and water; and the divorced wife resigned the bunch of keys, by the delivery of which she had been invested with the government of the family. The manumission of a son or a slave was performed by turning him round with a gentle blow on the cheek; a work was prohibited by the casting of a stone; prescription was interrupted by the breaking of a branch; the clenched fist was the symbol of a pledge or deposit; the right hand was the gift of faith and confidence. The indenture of covenants was a broken straw; weights and scales were introduced into every payment; and the heir who accepted a testament was sometimes obliged to snap his fingers, to cast away his garments, and to leap and dance with real or affected transport. If a citizen pursued any stolen goods into a neighbour's house, he concealed his nakedness with a linen towel, and hid his face with a mask or basin, lest he should encounter the eyes of a virgin or a matron. In a civil action, the plaintiff touched the ear of his witness, seized his reluctant adversary by the neck, and implored, in solemn lamentation, the aid of his fellow-citizens. The two competitors grasped each other's hand as if they stood prepared for combat before the tribunal of the prætor; he commanded them to produce the object of the dispute; they went, they returned with measured steps, and a clod of earth was cast at his feet to represent the field for which they contended. This occult science of the words and actions of law was the inheritance of the pontiffs and patricians. Like the Chaldæan astrologers, they announced to their clients the days of business and repose; these important trifles were interwoven with the religion of Numa, and after the publication of the Twelve Tables the Roman people was still enslaved by the ignorance of judicial proceedings. The treachery of some plebeian officers at length revealed the profitable mystery; in a more enlightened age the legal actions were derided and observed, and the same antiquity which sanctified the practice, obliterated the use and meaning, of this primitive language.

A more liberal art was cultivated, however, by the sages of Rome, who, in a stricter sense, may be considered as the authors of the civil law. The alteration of the idiom and manners of the Romans rendered the style of the Twelve Tables less familiar to each rising generation, and the doubtful passages were imperfectly explained by the study of legal antiquarians. To define the ambiguities, to circumscribe the latitude, to apply the principles, to extend the consequences, to reconcile the real or apparent contradictions, was a much nobler and more important task; and the province of legislation was silently invaded by the expounders of ancient statutes. Their subtle interpretations concurred with the equity of the prætor to reform the tyranny of the darker ages; however strange or intricate the means, it was the aim of artificial jurisprudence to restore the simple dictates of nature and reason, and the skill of private citizens was usefully employed to undermine the public institutions of their country.

The revolution of almost one thousand years, from the Twelve Tables to the reign of Justinian, may be divided into three periods almost equal in duration, and distinguished from each other by the mode of instruction and the character of the civilians. Pride and ignorance contributed, during the first period, to confine within narrow limits the science of the Roman law. On the public days of market or assembly the masters of the art were seen walking in the forum, ready to impart the needful advice to the meanest of their fellow-citizens, from whose votes, on a future occasion, they might solicit a grateful return. As their years and honours increased, they seated themselves at home on a chair or throne, to expect, with patient gravity, the visits of their clients, who at the dawn of day, from the town and country, began to thunder at their door. The duties of social life and the incidents of judicial proceeding were the ordinary subject of these consultations, and the verbal or written opinion of the *juris-consults* was framed according to the rules of prudence and law. The youths of their own order and family were permitted to listen; their children enjoyed the benefit of more private lessons, and the Mucian race was long renowned for the hereditary knowledge of the civil law. The second period, the learned and splendid age of jurisprudence, may be extended from the birth of Cicero to the reign of Severus Alexander. A system was formed, schools were instituted, books were composed, and both the living and the dead became subservient to the instruction of the student. The *tripartite* of Ælius Pætus, surnamed Catus, or the Cunning, was preserved as the oldest work of jurisprudence. Cato the Censor derived some additional fame from his legal studies and those of his son; the kindred appellation of Mucius Scævola was illustrated by three sages of the law, but the perfection of the science was ascribed to Servius Sulpicius, their disciple, and the friend of Tully; and the long succession, which shone with equal lustre under the republic and under the Cæsars, is finally closed by the respectable characters of Papinian, of Paul, and of Ulpian. Their names, and the various titles of their productions, have been minutely preserved, and the example of Labeo may suggest some idea of their diligence and fecundity. That eminent lawyer of the Augustan age divided the year between the city and country, between business and composition, and four hundred books are enumerated as the fruit of his retirement. Of the collections of his rival Capito, the two hundred and fifty-ninth book is expressly quoted, and few teachers could deliver their opinions in less than a century of volumes. In the third period, between the reigns of Alexander and Justinian, the oracles of jurisprudence were almost mute. The measure of curiosity had been filled; the throne was occupied by tyrants and barbarians; the active spirits were diverted by religious disputes; and the professors of Rome, Constantinople, and Berytus, were humbly content to repeat the lessons of their more enlightened predecessors. From the slow advances and rapid decay of these legal studies, it may be inferred that they require a state of peace and refinement. From the multitude of voluminous civilians who fill the intermediate space, it is evident that such studies may be pursued, and such works may be performed, with a common share of judgment, experience, and industry. The genius of Cicero and Virgil was more sensibly felt, as each revolving age had been found incapable of producing a similar or a second; but the most eminent teachers of the law were assured of leaving disciples equal or superior to themselves in merit and reputation.

The jurisprudence which had been grossly adapted to the wants of the first Romans was polished and improved in the seventh century of the city by the alliance of Grecian philosophy. The Scævolas had been taught by use and experience; but Servius Sulpicius was the first civilian who established his art on a certain and general theory. For the discernment of truth and falsehood he applied, as an infallible rule, the logic of Aristotle and the

Stoics, reduced particular cases to general principles, and diffused over the shapeless mass the light of order and eloquence. Cicero, his contemporary and friend, declined the reputation of a professed lawyer; but the jurisprudence of his country was adorned by his incomparable genius, which converts into gold every object that it touches. After the example of Plato, he composed a republic; and, for the use of his republic, a treatise of laws, in which he labours to deduce from a celestial origin the wisdom and justice of the Roman constitution. The whole universe, according to his sublime hypothesis, forms one immense commonwealth: gods and men, who participate of the same essence, are members of the same community; reason prescribes the law of nature and nations; and all positive institutions, however modified by accident or custom, are drawn from the rule of right, which the Deity has inscribed on every virtuous mind. From these philosophical mysteries he mildly excludes the sceptics who refuse to believe, and the epicureans who are unwilling to act. The latter disdain the care of the republic: he advises them to slumber in their shady gardens. But he humbly entreats that the new Academy would be silent, since her bold objections would too soon destroy the fair and well-ordered structure of his lofty system. Plato, Aristotle, and Zeno he represents as the only teachers who arm and instruct a citizen for the duties of social life. Of these, the armour of the Stoics was found to be of the firmest temper; and it was chiefly worn, both for use and ornament, in the schools of jurisprudence. From the Portico the Roman civilians learned to live, to reason, and to die: but they imbibed in some degree the prejudices of the sect; the love of paradox, the pertinacious habits of dispute, and a minute attachment to words and verbal distinctions. The superiority of *form* to *matter* was introduced to ascertain the right of property: and the equality of crimes is countenanced by an opinion of Trebatius, that he who touches the ear touches the whole body; and that he who steals from a heap of corn or a hogshead of wine, is guilty of the entire theft.

Arms, eloquence, and the study of the civil law promoted a citizen to the honours of the Roman state; and the three professions were sometimes more conspicuous by their union in the same character. In the composition of the edict a learned prætor gave a sanction and preference to his private sentiments; the opinion of a censor or a consul was entertained with respect; and a doubtful interpretation of the laws might be supported by the virtues or triumphs of the civilian. The patrician arts were long protected by the veil of mystery; and in more enlightened times the freedom of inquiry established the general principles of jurisprudence. Subtle and intricate cases were elucidated by the disputes of the forum; rules, axioms, and definitions were admitted as the genuine dictates of reason; and the consent of the legal professors was interwoven into the practice of the tribunals. But these interpreters could neither enact nor execute the laws of the republic; and the judges might disregard the authority of the Scævolas themselves, which was often overthrown by the eloquence or sophistry of an ingenious pleader.

Augustus and Tiberius were the first to adopt, as a useful engine, the science of the civilians; and their servile labours accommodated the old system to the spirit and views of despotism. Under the fair pretence of securing the dignity of the art, the privilege of subscribing legal and valid opinions was confined to the sages of senatorian or equestrian rank, who had been previously approved by the judgment of the prince; and this monopoly prevailed till Hadrian restored the freedom of the profession to every citizen conscious of his abilities and knowledge. The discretion of the prætor was now governed by the lessons of his teachers; the judges were enjoined to obey the comment as well as the text of the law; and the use of codicils was a memorable innovation, which Augustus ratified by the advice of the civilians.

The most absolute mandate could only require that the judges should agree with the civilians, if the civilians agreed among themselves. But positive institutions are often the result of custom and prejudice; laws and language are ambiguous and arbitrary; where reason is incapable of pronouncing, the love of argument is inflamed by the envy of rivals, the vanity of masters, the blind attachment of their disciples; and the Roman jurisprudence was divided by the once famous sects of the *Proculians* and *Sabinians.* Two sages of the law, Ateius Capito and Antistius Labeo, adorned the peace of the Augustan age: the former distinguished by the favour of his sovereign; the latter more illustrious by his contempt of that favour, and his stern though harmless opposition to the tyrant of Rome. Their legal studies were influenced by the various colours of their temper and principles. Labeo was attached to the form of the old republic; his rival embraced the more profitable substance of the rising monarchy. But the disposition of a courtier is tame and submissive; and Capito seldom presumed to deviate from the sentiments, or at least from the words, of his predecessors; while the bold republican pursued his independent ideas without fear of paradox or innovations. The freedom of Labeo was enslaved, however, by the rigour of his own conclusions, and he decided, according to the letter of the law, the same questions which his indulgent competitor resolved with a latitude of equity more suitable to the common sense and feelings of mankind. If a fair exchange had been substituted to the payment of money, Capito still considered the transaction as a legal sale; and he consulted nature for the age of puberty, without confining his definition to the precise period of twelve or fourteen years. This opposition of sentiments was propagated in the writings and lessons of the two founders; the schools of Capito and Labeo maintained their inveterate conflict from the age of Augustus to that of Hadrian.

The Institutes of Justinian are divided into four books: they proceed, with no contemptible method, from I. *Persons,* to, II. *Things,* and from things to, III. *Actions;* and the article IV., of *Private Wrongs,* is terminated by the principles of *Criminal Law.*

I. The distinction of ranks and *persons* is the firmest basis of a mixed, limited government. The first Cæsars had scrupulously guarded the distinction of *ingenuous* and *servile* birth, which was decided by the condition of the mother; and the candour of the laws was satisfied if *her* freedom could be ascertained, during a single moment, between the conception and the delivery. The slaves who were liberated by a generous master immediately entered into the middle class of *libertines* or freedmen; but they could never be enfranchised from the duties of obedience and gratitude: whatever were the fruits of their industry, their patron and his family inherited the third part; or even the whole of their fortune if they died without children and without a testament.

The law of nature instructs most animals to cherish and educate their infant progeny. The law of reason inculcates to the human species the returns of filial piety. But the exclusive, absolute, and perpetual dominion of the father over his children is peculiar to the Roman jurisprudence, and seems to be coeval with the foundation of the city. The paternal power was instituted or confirmed by Romulus himself; and, after the practice of three centuries, it was inscribed on the fourth table of the Decemvirs. In the forum, the senate, or the camp, the adult son of a Roman citizen enjoyed the public and private rights of a *person:* in his father's house he was a mere *thing;* confounded by the laws with the movables, the cattle, and the slaves, whom the capricious master might alienate or destroy without being responsible to any earthly tribunal. The hand which bestowed the daily sustenance might resume the voluntary gift, and whatever was acquired by the labour or fortune of the son was immediately lost in the property of the father. His stolen goods (his oxen or his children) might be recovered by the same action of theft; and if either had been guilty of a trespass, it was in his own option to compensate the damage, or resign to the injured party the obnoxious animal. At the call of indigence or avarice, the master of a family could dispose of his children or his slaves. But the condition of the slave was far more advantageous, since he regained, by the first manumission, his alienated freedom: the son was again restored to his unnatural father; he might be condemned to servitude a second and a third time, and it was not till after the third sale and deliverance that he was enfranchised from the domestic power which had been so repeatedly abused. According to his discretion, a father might chastise the real or imaginary faults of his children by stripes, by imprisonment, by exile, by sending them to the country to work in chains among the meanest of his servants. The majesty of a parent was armed with the power of life and death; and the examples of such bloody executions, which were sometimes praised and never punished, may be traced in the annals of Rome, beyond the times of Pompey and Augustus. Neither age, nor rank, nor the consular office, nor the honours of a triumph, could exempt the most illustrious citizen from the bonds of filial subjection: his own descendants were included in the family of their common ancestor; and the claims of adoption were not less sacred or less rigorous than those of nature. Without fear, though not without danger of abuse, the Roman legislators had reposed an unbounded confidence in the sentiments of paternal love; and the oppression was tempered by the assurance that each generation must succeed in its turn to the awful dignity of parent and master.

The first limitation of paternal power is ascribed to the justice and humanity of Numa; and the maid who, with *his* father's consent, had espoused a freeman, was protected from the disgrace of becoming the wife of a slave. In the first ages, when the city was pressed and often famished by her Latin and Tuscan neighbours, the sale of children might be a frequent practice; but as a Roman could not legally purchase the liberty of his fellow-citizen, the market must gradually fail, and the trade would be destroyed by the conquests of the republic. An imperfect right of property was at length communicated to sons; and the threefold distinction of *profectitious, adventitious*, and *professional* was ascertained by the jurisprudence of the Code and Pandects. Of all that proceeded from the father he imparted only the use, and reserved the absolute dominion; yet, if his goods were sold, the filial portion was excepted, by a favourable interpretation, from the demands of the creditors. In whatever accrued by marriage, gift, or collateral succession, the property was secured to the son; but the father, unless he had been specially excluded, enjoyed the usufruct during his life. As a just and prudent reward of military virtue, the spoils of the enemy were acquired, possessed, and bequeathed by the soldier alone; and the fair analogy was extended to the emoluments of any liberal profession, the salary of public service, and the sacred liberality of the emperor or the empress. The life of a citizen was less exposed than his fortune to the abuse of paternal power. Yet his life might be adverse to the interest or passions of an unworthy father: the same crimes that flowed from the corruption, were more sensibly felt by the humanity of the Augustan age; and the cruel Erixo, who whipped his son till he expired, was saved by the emperor from the just fury of the multitude. The Roman father, from the licence of servile dominion, was reduced to the gravity and moderation of a judge. The presence and opinion of Augustus confirmed the sentence of exile pronounced against an intentional child murderer by the tribunal of Arius. Hadrian transported to an island the jealous parent, who, like a robber, had seized the opportunity of hunting to assassinate a youth, the incestuous lover of his stepmother. A private jurisdiction is repugnant to the spirit of monarchy; the parent was again reduced from a judge to an accuser; and the magistrates were enjoined by Severus Alexander to hear his complaints and execute his sentence. He could no longer take the life of a son without incurring the guilt and punishment of murder; and the penalties of murder, from which he had been excepted by the Pompeian law, were finally inflicted by the justice of Constantine. The same protection was due to every period of existence; and reason must applaud the humanity of Paulus for imputing the crime of murder to the father who strangles, or starves, or abandons his new-born infant, or exposes him in a public place to find the mercy which he himself had denied. But the exposition of children was the prevailing and stubborn vice of antiquity: it was sometimes prescribed, often permitted, almost always practised with impunity by the nations who never entertained the Roman ideas of paternal power; and the dramatic poets, who appeal to the human heart, represent with indifference a popular custom which was palliated by the motives of economy and compassion. If the father could subdue his own feelings, he might escape, though not the censure, at least the chastisement, of the laws; and the Roman empire was stained with the blood of infants, till such murders were included by Valentinian and his colleagues in the letter and spirit of the Cornelian law. The lessons of jurisprudence and Christianity had been insufficient to eradicate this inhuman practice, till their gentle influence was fortified by the terrors of capital punishment.

Experience has proved that savages are the tyrants of the female sex, and that the condition of women is usually softened by the refinements of social life. In the hope of a robust progeny, Lycurgus had delayed the season of marriage: it was fixed by Numa at the tender age of twelve years, that the Roman husband might educate to his will a pure and obedient virgin. According to the custom of antiquity, he bought his bride of her parents, and she fulfilled the *coemption* by purchasing, with three pieces of copper, a just introduction to his house and household deities. A sacrifice of fruits was offered by the pontiffs in the presence of ten witnesses; the contracting parties were seated on the same sheepskin; they tasted a salt cake of *far*, or rice; and this *confarreation*, which denoted the ancient food of Italy, served as an emblem of their mystic union of mind and body. But this union on the side of the woman was rigorous and unequal; and she renounced the name and worship of her father's house, to embrace a new servitude, decorated only by the title of adoption: a fiction of the law, neither rational nor elegant, bestowed on the mother of a family (her proper appellation) the strange characters of sister to her own children and of daughter to her husband or master, who was invested with the plenitude of paternal power. By his judgment or caprice her behaviour was approved, or censured, or chastised; he exercised the jurisdiction of life and death; and it was allowed that in the cases of adultery or drunkenness the sentence might be properly inflicted. She acquired and inherited for the sole profit of her lord; and so clearly was woman defined, not as a *person*, but as a *thing*, that, if the original title were deficient, she might be claimed, like other movables, by the *use* and possession of an entire year. The inclination of the Roman husband discharged or withheld the conjugal debt, so scrupulously exacted by the Athenian and Jewish laws: but as polygamy was unknown, he could never admit to his bed a fairer or more favoured partner.

After the Punic triumphs the matrons of Rome aspired to the common benefits of a free and opulent republic; their wishes were gratified by the indulgence of fathers and lovers, and their ambition was unsuccessfully resisted by the gravity of Cato the Censor. They declined the solemnities of the old nuptials, defeated the annual prescription by an absence of three days, and, without losing their name or independence, subscribed the liberal and definite terms of a marriage contract. Of their private fortunes, they communicated the use and secured the property: the estates of a wife could neither be alienated nor mortgaged by a prodigal husband; their mutual gifts were prohibited by the jealousy of the laws; and the misconduct of either party might afford, under another name, a future subject for an action of theft. To this loose and voluntary compact religious and civil rites were no longer essential, and between persons of a similar rank the apparent community of life was allowed as sufficient evidence of their nuptials. The dignity of marriage was restored by the Christians, who derived all spiritual grace from the prayers of the faithful and the benediction of the priest or bishop. The origin, validity, and duties of the holy institution were regulated by the tradition of the synagogue, the precepts of the Gospel, and the canons of general or provincial synods; and the conscience of the Christians was awed by the decrees and censures of their ecclesiastical rulers. Yet the magistrates of Justinian were not subject to the authority of the church; the emperor consulted the unbelieving civilians of antiquity; and the choice of matrimonial laws in the Code and Pandects is directed by the earthly motives of justice, policy, and the natural freedom of both sexes.

Besides the agreement of the parties, the essence of every rational contract, the Roman marriage required the previous approbation of the parents. A father might be forced by some recent laws to supply the wants of a mature daughter, but even his insanity was not generally allowed to supersede the necessity of his consent. The causes of the dissolution of matrimony have varied among the Romans; but the most solemn sacrament, the confarreation itself, might always be done away by rites of a contrary tendency. In the first ages the father of a family might sell his children, and his wife was reckoned in the number of his children: the domestic judge might pronounce the death of the offender, or his mercy might expel her from his bed and house; but the slavery of the wretched female was hopeless and perpetual, unless he asserted for his own convenience the manly prerogative of divorce. The warmest applause has been lavished on the virtue of the Romans, who abstained from the exercise of this tempting privilege above five hundred years; but the same fact evinces the unequal terms of a connection in which the slave was unable to renounce her tyrant, and the tyrant was unwilling to relinquish his slave. When the Roman matrons became the equal and voluntary companions of their lords, a new jurisprudence was introduced, that marriage, like other partnerships, might be dissolved by the abdication of one of the associates. In three centuries of prosperity and corruption, this principle was enlarged to frequent practice and pernicious abuse. Passion, interest, or caprice suggested daily motives for the dissolution of marriage; a word, a sign, a message, a letter, the mandate of a freedman, declared the separation; the most tender of human connections was degraded to a transient society of profit or pleasure. According to the various conditions of life, both sexes alternately felt the disgrace and injury: an inconstant spouse transferred her wealth to a new family, abandoning a numerous, perhaps a spurious, progeny to the paternal authority and care of her late husband; a beautiful virgin might be dismissed to the world, old, indigent, and friendless; but the reluctance of the Romans, when they were pressed to marriage by Augustus, sufficiently marks that the prevailing institutions were least favourable to the males.[1]

[1]Jerom saw at Rome a triumphant husband bury his twenty-first wife, who had interred twenty-two of his less sturdy predecessors (Opp. tom. i. p. 90, ad

Insufficient remedies followed with distant and tardy steps the rapid rogress of the evil. The ancient worship of the Romans afforded a peculiar oddess to hear and reconcile the complaints of a married life; but her pithet of *Viriplaca*, the appeaser of husbands, too clearly indicates on which ide submission and repentance were always expected. Every act of a citizen vas subject to the judgment of the *censors;* the first who used the privilege f divorce assigned at their command the motives of his conduct; and a enator was expelled for dismissing his virgin spouse without the knowledge r advice of his friends. Whenever an action was instituted for the recovery f a marriage-portion, the *prætor*, as the guardian of equity, examined the ause and the characters, and gently inclined the scale in favour of the uiltless and injured party. Augustus, who united the powers of both agistrates, adopted their different modes of repressing or chastising the cence of divorce. The presence of seven Roman witnesses was required for ie validity of this solemn and deliberate act: if any adequate provocation ad been given by the husband, instead of the delay of two years, he was ompelled to refund immediately or in the space of six months; but if he ould arraign the manners of his wife, her guilt or levity was expiated by ie loss of the sixth or eighth part of her marriage-portion. The Christian rinces were the first who specified the just causes of a private divorce; eir institutions, from Constantine to Justinian, appear to fluctuate between ie custom of the empire and the wishes of the church.

In the most rigorous laws a wife was condemned to support a gamester, drunkard, or a libertine, unless he were guilty of homicide, poison, or icrilege; in which cases the marriage, as it should seem, might have been issolved by the hand of the executioner. But the sacred right of the husand was invariably maintained to deliver his name and family from he isgrace of adultery; the list of *mortal* sins, either male or female, was irtailed and enlarged by successive regulations, and the obstacles of incurable impotence, long absence, and monastic profession, were allowed to escind the matrimonial obligation. Whoever transgressed the permission of ie law was subject to various and heavy penalties. The woman was stripped f her wealth and ornaments, without excepting the bodkin of her hair; if ie man introduced a new bride into his bed, *her* fortune might be lawfully ized by the vengeance of his exiled wife. Forfeiture was sometimes comuted to a fine; the fine was sometimes aggravated by transportation to an land, or imprisonment in a monastery; the injured party was released from ie bonds of marriage, but the offender, during life or a term of years, was sabled from the repetition of nuptials.

The freedom of love and marriage was restrained among the Romans by itural and civil impediments. An instinct, almost innate and universal, pears to prohibit the incestuous commerce of parents and children in the finite series of ascending and descending generations. Concerning the blique and collateral branches nature is indifferent, reason mute, and cus-

erontiam). But the ten husbands in a month of the poet Martial is an extravagant perbole (l. vi. epigram 7).

tom various and arbitrary. In Egypt the marriage of brothers and sisters wa admitted without scruple or exception: a Spartan might espouse the daugh ter of his father; an Athenian, that of his mother; and the nuptials of a uncle with his niece were applauded at Athens as a happy union of th dearest relations. The profane lawgivers of Rome were never tempted b interest or superstition to multiply the forbidden degrees; but they inflex ibly condemned the marriage of sisters and brothers, hesitated whether firs cousins should be touched by the same interdict, revered the parental char acter of aunts and uncles, and treated affinity and adoption as a just imita tion of the ties of blood. According to the proud maxims of the republic, legal marriage could only be contracted by free citizens; an honourable, a least an ingenuous, birth was required for the spouse of a senator: but th blood of kings could never mingle in legitimate nuptials with the blood of Roman; and the name of Stranger degraded Cleopatra and Berenice to liv the *concubines* of Mark Antony and Titus. This appellation, indeed, s injurious to the majesty, cannot without indulgence be applied to the man ners, of these Oriental queens. A concubine, in the strict sense of th civilians, was a woman of servile or plebeian extraction, the sole and faithfu companion of a Roman citizen, who continued in a state of celibacy. He modest station, below the honours of a wife, above the infamy of a prost tute, was acknowledged and approved by the laws: from the age of August to the tenth century the use of this secondary marriage prevailed both i the West and East; and the humble virtues of a concubine were often pre ferred to the pomp and insolence of a noble matron. In this connection th two Antonines, the best of princes and of men, enjoyed the comforts o domestic love; the example was imitated by many citizens impatient o celibacy, but regardful of their families. If at any time they desired t legitimate their natural children, the conversion was instantly performed b the celebration of their nuptials with a partner whose fruitfulness ar fidelity they had already tried. By this epithet of *natural* the offspring o the concubine were distinguished from the spurious brood of adultery, pro titution, and incest; and these natural children alone were capable of su ceeding to a sixth part of the inheritance of their reputed father. Accordi to the rigour of law, bastards were entitled only to the name and conditi of their mother, from whom they might derive the character of a slave, stranger, or a citizen. The outcasts of every family were adopted, witho reproach, as the children of the state.

The relation of guardian and ward, or, in Roman words, of *tutor* a *pupil,* which covers so many titles of the Institutes and Pandects, is of a ve simple and uniform nature. The person and property of an orphan mu always be trusted to the custody of some discreet friend. If the deceas father had not signified his choice, the *agnats,* or paternal kindred of t nearest degree, were compelled to act as the natural guardians: the Athenia were apprehensive of exposing the infant to the power of those most inte ested in his death; but an axiom of Roman jurisprudence has pronounc that the charge of tutelage should constantly attend the emolument of su cession. If the choice of the father and the line of consanguinity afforded no efficient guardian, the failure was supplied by the nomination of the prætor of the city or the president of the province; but the person whom they named to this *public* office might be legally excused by insanity or blindness, by ignorance or inability, by previous enmity or adverse interest, by the number of children or guardianships with which he was already burthened, and by the immunities which were granted to the useful labours of magistrates, lawyers, physicians, and professors. Till the infant could speak and think, he was represented by the tutor, whose authority was finally determined by the age of puberty. Without his consent, no act of the pupil could bind himself to his own prejudice, though it might oblige others for his personal benefit. It is needless to observe that the tutor often gave security, and always rendered an account; and that the want of diligence or integrity exposed him to a civil and almost criminal action for the violation of his sacred trust. The age of puberty had been rashly fixed by the civilians at fourteen; but, as the faculties of the mind ripen more slowly than those of the body, a *curator* was interposed to guard the fortunes of a Roman youth from his own inexperience and headstrong passions. Such a trustee had been first instituted by the prætor to save the family from the blind havoc of a prodigal or madman; and the minor was compelled by the laws to solicit the same protection to give validity to his acts till he accomplished the full period of twenty-five years. Women were condemned to the perpetual tutelage of parents, husbands, or guardians; a sex created to please and obey was never supposed to have attained the age of reason and experience. Such at least was the stern and haughty spirit of the ancient law.

II. The original right of property can only be justified by the accident or merit of prior occupancy; and on this foundation it is wisely established by the philosophy of the civilians. The savage who hollows a tree, inserts a sharp stone into a wooden handle, or applies a string to an elastic branch, becomes in a state of nature the just proprietor of the canoe, the bow, or the hatchet. The materials were common to all; the new form, the produce of his time and simple industry, belongs solely to himself. His hungry brethren cannot, without a sense of their own injustice, extort from the hunter the game of the forest overtaken or slain by his personal strength and dexterity. If his provident care preserves and multiplies the tame animals, whose nature is tractable to the arts of education, he acquires a perpetual title to the use and service of their numerous progeny, which derives its existence from him alone. If he encloses and cultivates a field for their sustenance and his own, a barren waste is converted into a fertile soil; the seed, the manure, the labour, create a new value, and the rewards of harvest are painfully earned by the fatigues of the revolving year. In the successive states of society, the hunter, the shepherd, the husbandman, may defend their possessions by two reasons which forcibly appeal to the feelings of the human mind: that whatever they enjoy is the fruit of their own industry; and that every man who envies their felicity may purchase similar acquisitions by the exercise of similar diligence. Such, in truth, may be the freedom and plenty of a small colony cast on a fruitful island. But the colony multiplies, while the space still continues the same; the common rights, the equal inheritance of mankind, are engrossed by the bold and crafty; each field and forest is circumscribed by the landmarks of a jealous master; and it is the peculiar praise of the Roman jurisprudence that it asserts the claim of the first occupant to the wild animals of the earth, the air, and the waters. In the progress from primitive equity to final injustice, the steps are silent, the shades are almost imperceptible, and the absolute monopoly is guarded by positive laws and artificial reason. The active, insatiate principle of self-love can alone supply the arts of life and the wages of industry; and as soon as civil government and exclusive property have been introduced, they become necessary to the existence of the human race.

Except in the singular institutions of Sparta, the wisest legislators have disapproved an agrarian law as a false and dangerous innovation. Among the Romans, the enormous disproportion of wealth surmounted the ideal restraints of a doubtful tradition and an obsolete statute—a tradition that the poorest follower of Romulus had been endowed with the perpetual inheritance of two *jugera;* a statute which confined the richest citizen to the measure of five hundred jugera, or three hundred and twelve acres of land. The original territory of Rome consisted only of some miles of wood and meadow along the banks of the Tiber; and domestic exchange could add nothing to the national stock. But the goods of an alien or enemy were lawfully exposed to the first hostile occupier; the city was enriched by the profitable trade of war; and the blood of her sons was the only price that was paid for the Volscian sheep, the slaves of Britain, or the gems and gold of Asiatic kingdoms. In the language of ancient jurisprudence, which was corrupted and forgotten before the age of Justinian, these spoils were distinguished by the name of *manceps* or *mancipium*, taken with the hand; and whenever they were sold or *emancipated*, the purchaser required some assurance that they had been the property of an enemy, and not of a fellow-citizen. A citizen could only forfeit his rights by apparent dereliction, and such dereliction of a valuable interest could not easily be presumed. Yet, according to the Twelve Tables, a prescription of one year for movables, and of two years for immovables, abolished the claim of the ancient master, if the actual possessor had acquired them by a fair transaction from the person whom he believed to be the lawful proprietor.

The personal title of the first proprietor must be determined by his death; but the possession, without any appearance of change, is peaceably continued in his children, the associates of his toil, and the partners of his wealth. This natural inheritance has been protected by the legislators of every climate and age, and the father is encouraged to persevere in slow and distant improvements, by the tender hope that a long posterity will enjoy the fruits of his labour. The *principle* of hereditary succession is universal; but the *order* has been variously established by convenience or caprice, by the spirit of national institutions, or by some partial example which was originally decided by fraud or violence. The jurisprudence of the Romans appears to have deviated from the equality of nature much less than the Jewish, the Athenian, or the English institutions. On the death of a citizen, all his descendants, unless they were already freed from his paternal power, were called to the inheritance of his possessions. The insolent prerogative of primogeniture was unknown; the two sexes were placed on a just level; all the sons and daughters were entitled to an equal portion of the patrimonial estate; and if any of the sons had been intercepted by a premature death, his person was represented, and his share was divided, by his surviving children.

On the failure of the direct line, the right of succession must diverge to the collateral branches. The degrees of kindred are numbered by the civilians, ascending from the last possessor to a common parent, and descending from the common parent to the next heir: my father stands in the first degree, my brother in the second, his children in the third, and the remainder of the series may be conceived by fancy, or pictured in a genealogical table. In this computation a distinction was made, essential to the laws and even the constitution of Rome: the *agnats*, or persons connected by a line of males, were called, as they stood in the nearest degree, to an equal partition; but a female was incapable of transmitting any legal claims; and the *cognats* of every rank, without excepting the dear relation of a mother and a son, were disinherited by the Twelve Tables, as strangers and aliens. Among the Romans a *gens* or lineage was united by a common *name* and domestic rites; the various *cognomens* or *surnames* of Scipio or Marcellus distinguished from each other the subordinate branches or families of the Cornelian or Claudian race: the default of the *agnats* of the same surname was supplied by the larger denomination of *gentiles;* and the vigilance of the laws maintained, in the same name, the perpetual descent of religion and property. A similar principle dictated the Voconian law, which abolished the right of female inheritance. As long as virgins were given or sold in marriage, the adoption of the wife extinguished the hopes of the daughter. But the equal succession of independent matrons supported their pride and luxury, and might transport into a foreign house the riches of their fathers. While the maxims of Cato were revered, they tended to perpetuate in each family a just and virtuous mediocrity: till female blandishments insensibly triumphed, and every salutary restraint was lost in the dissolute greatness of the republic. The rigour of the Decemvirs was tempered by the equity of the prætors. Their edicts restored emancipated and posthumous children to the rights of nature; and upon the failure of the *agnats,* they preferred the blood of the *cognats* to the name of the gentiles, whose title and character were insensibly covered with oblivion. The reciprocal inheritance of mothers and sons was established in the Tertullian and Orphitian decrees by the humanity of the senate.

The order of succession is regulated by nature, or at least by the general and permanent reason of the lawgiver; but this order is frequently violated by the arbitrary and partial *wills*, which prolong the dominion of the testator beyond the grave. In the simple state of society this last use or abuse of the right of property is seldom indulged; it was introduced at Athens by the laws of Solon, and the private testaments of the father of a family are authorised by the Twelve Tables. Before the time of the Decemvirs, a Roman citizen exposed his wishes and motives to the assembly of the thirty curiæ or parishes, and the general law of inheritance was suspended by an occasional act of the legislature. After the permission of the Decemvirs, each private lawgiver promulgated his verbal or written testament in the presence of five citizens, who represented the five classes of the Roman people; a sixth witness attested their concurrence; a seventh weighed the copper money, which was paid by an imaginary purchaser, and the estate was emancipated by a fictitious sale and immediate release. This singular ceremony, which excited the wonder of the Greeks, was still practised in the age of Severus; but the prætors had already approved a more simple testament, for which they required the seals and signatures of seven witnesses, free from all legal exception, and purposely summoned for the execution of that important act. A domestic monarch, who reigned over the lives and fortunes of his children, might distribute their respective shares according to the degrees of their merit or his affection; his arbitrary displeasure chastised an unworthy son by the loss of his inheritance, and the mortifying preference of a stranger. But the experience of unnatural parents recommended some limitations of their testamentary powers. A son, or, by the laws of Justinian, even a daughter, could no longer be disinherited by their silence: they were compelled to name the criminal, and to specify the offence; and the justice of the emperor enumerated the sole causes that could justify such a violation of the first principles of nature and society. Unless a legitimate portion, a fourth part, had been reserved for the children, they were entitled to institute an action or complaint of *inofficious* testament—to suppose that their father's understanding was impaired by sickness or age, and respectfully to appeal from his rigorous sentence to the deliberate wisdom of the magistrate. In the Roman jurisprudence an essential distinction was admitted between the inheritance and the legacies. The heirs who succeeded to the entire unity, or to any of the twelve fractions of the substance of the testator, represented his civil and religious character, asserted his rights, fulfilled his obligations, and discharged the gifts of friendship or liberality which his last will had bequeathed under the name of legacies. But as the imprudence or prodigality of a dying man might exhaust the inheritance, and leave only risk and labour to his successor, he was empowered to retain the *Falcidian* portion; to deduct, before the payment of the legacies, a clear fourth for his own emolument. A reasonable time was allowed to examine the proportion between the debts and the estate, to decide whether he should accept or refuse the testament; and if he used the benefit of an inventory, the demands of the creditors could not exceed the valuation of the effects. The last will of a citizen might be altered during his life, or rescinded after his death: the persons whom he named might die before him, or reject the inheritance, or be exposed to some legal disqualification. In the contemplation of these events, he was permitted to substitute second and third heirs, to replace each other according to the order of the testament; and the incapacity of a madman or an infant to bequeath his property might be supplied by a similar substitution. But the power of the testator expired with the acceptance of the testament: each Roman of mature age and discretion acquired the absolute dominion of his inheritance, and the simplicity of the civil law was never clouded by the long and intricate entails which confine the happiness and freedom of unborn generations.

A stranger of Greece or Africa might be the friend or benefactor of a childless Roman, but none except a fellow-citizen could act as his heir. The Voconian law, which abolished female succession, restrained the legacy or inheritance of a woman to the sum of one hundred thousand sesterces; and an only daughter was condemned almost as an alien in her father's house. The zeal of friendship and parental affection suggested a liberal artifice: a qualified citizen was named in the testament, with a prayer or injunction that he would restore the inheritance to the person for whom it was truly intended. Various was the conduct of the trustees in this painful situation; they had sworn to observe the laws of their country, but honour prompted them to violate their oath; and, if they preferred their interest under the mask of patriotism, they forfeited the esteem of every virtuous mind. The declaration of Augustus relieved their doubts, gave a legal sanction to confidential testaments and codicils, and gently unravelled the forms and restraints of the republican jurisprudence. But as the new practice of trusts degenerated into some abuse, the trustee was enabled, by the Trebellian and Pegasian decrees, to reserve one fourth of the estate, or to transfer on the head of the real heir all the debts and actions of the succession. The interpretation of testaments was strict and literal; but the language of *trusts* and codicils was delivered from the minute and technical accuracy of the civilians.

III. The general duties of mankind are imposed by their public and private relations, but their specific *obligations* to each other can only be the effect of, 1, a promise; 2, a benefit; or 3, an injury; and when these obligations are ratified by law, the interested party may compel the performance by a judicial *action.* On this principle the civilians of every country have erected a similar jurisprudence, the fair conclusion of universal reason and justice.

1. The goddess of *faith* (of human and social faith) was worshipped, not only in her temples, but in the lives of the Romans; and if that nation was deficient in the more amiable qualities of benevolence and generosity, they astonished the Greeks by their sincere and simple performance of the most burdensome engagements. Yet among the same people, according to the rigid maxims of the patricians and Decemvirs, a *naked pact*, a promise, or even an oath, did not create any civil obligation, unless it was confirmed by the legal form of a *stipulation.* Whatever might be the etymology of the Latin word, it conveyed the idea of a firm and irrevocable contract, which was always expressed in the mode of a question and answer. Do

you promise to pay me one hundred pieces of gold? was the solemn interrogation of Seius. I do promise—was the reply of Sempronius. The friends of Sempronius, who answered for his ability and inclination, might be separately sued at the option of Seius; and the benefit of partition, or order of reciprocal actions, insensibly deviated from the strict theory of stipulation. The most cautious and deliberate consent was justly required to sustain the validity of a gratuitous promise, and the citizen who might have obtained a legal security incurred the suspicion of fraud, and paid the forfeit of his neglect. But the ingenuity of the civilians successfully laboured to convert simple engagements into the form of solemn stipulations. The prætors, as the guardians of social faith, admitted every rational evidence of a voluntary and deliberate act, which in their tribunal produced an equitable obligation, and for which they gave an action and a remedy.

2. The obligations of the second class, as they were contracted by the delivery of a thing, are marked by the civilians with the epithet of real. A grateful return is due to the author of a benefit; and whoever is entrusted with the property of another has bound himself to the sacred duty of restitution. In the case of a friendly loan, the merit of generosity is on the side of the lender only; in a deposit, on the side of the receiver; but in a *pledge*, and the rest of the selfish commerce of ordinary life, the benefit is compensated by an equivalent, and the obligation to restore is variously modified by the nature of the transaction. The Latin language very happily expresses the fundamental difference between the *commodatum* and the *mutuum*, which our poverty is reduced to confound under the vague and common appellation of a loan. In the former, the borrower was obliged to restore the same individual thing with which he had been *accommodated* for the temporary supply of his wants; in the latter, it was destined for his use and consumption, and he discharged this *mutual* engagement by substituting the same specific value according to a just estimation of number, of weight, and of measure. In the contract of *sale*, the absolute dominion is transferred to the purchaser, and he repays the benefit with an adequate sum of gold or silver, the price and universal standard of all earthly possessions. The obligation of another contract, that of *location*, is of a more complicated kind. Lands or houses, labour or talents, may be hired for a definite term; at the expiration of the time, the thing itself must be restored to the owner with an additional reward for the beneficial occupation and employment. In these lucrative contracts, to which may be added those of partnership and commissions, the civilians sometimes imagine the delivery of the object, and sometimes presume the consent of the parties. The substantial pledge has been refined into the invisible rights of a mortgage or *hypotheca;* and the agreement of sale for a certain price imputes, from that moment, the chances of gain or loss to the account of the purchaser. It may be fairly supposed that every man will obey the dictates of his interest; and if he accepts the benefit, he is obliged to sustain the expense, of the transaction. In this boundless

subject, the historian will observe the *location* of land and money, the rent of the one and the interest of the other, as they materially affect the prosperity of agriculture and commerce. The landlord was often obliged to advance the stock and instruments of husbandry, and to content himself with a partition of the fruits. If the feeble tenant was oppressed by accident, contagion, or hostile violence, he claimed a proportionable relief from the equity of the laws: five years were the customary term, and no solid or costly improvements could be expected from a farmer who, at each moment, might be ejected by the sale of the estate. Usury, the inveterate grievance of the city, had been discouraged by the Twelve Tables, and abolished by the clamours of the people. It was revived by their wants and idleness, tolerated by the discretion of the prætors, and finally determined by the Code of Justinian.

3. A Roman pursued and recovered his stolen goods by a civil action of theft; they might pass through a succession of pure and innocent hands, but nothing less than a prescription of thirty years could extinguish his original claim. They were restored by the sentence of the prætor, and the injury was compensated by double, or three-fold, or even quadruple damages, as the deed had been perpetrated by secret fraud or open rapine, as the robber had been surprised in the fact or detected by a subsequent research. The Aquilian law defended the living property of a citizen, his slaves and cattle, from the stroke of malice or negligence: the highest price was allowed that could be ascribed to the domestic animal at any moment of the year preceding his death; a similar latitude of thirty days was granted on the destruction of any other valuable effects. A personal injury is blunted or sharpened by the manners of the times and the sensibility of the individual: the pain or the disgrace of a word or blow cannot easily be appreciated by a pecuniary equivalent. The rude jurisprudence of the Decemvirs had confounded all hasty insults, which did not amount to the fracture of a limb, by condemning the aggressor to the common penalty of twenty-five *asses*. But the same denomination of money was reduced, in three centuries, from a pound to the weight of half an ounce; and the insolence of a wealthy Roman indulged himself in the cheap amusement of breaking and satisfying the law of the Twelve Tables. Veratius ran through the streets striking on the face the inoffensive passengers, and his attendant pursebearer immediately silenced their clamours by the legal tender of twenty-five pieces of copper, about the value of one shilling.

The execution of the Alban dictator, who was dismembered by eight horses, is represented by Livy as the first and last instance of Roman cruelty in the punishment of the most atrocious crimes. But this act of justice or revenge was inflicted on a foreign enemy in the heat of victory, and at the command of a single man. The Twelve Tables afford a more decisive proof of the national spirit, since they were framed by the wisest of the senate and accepted by the free voices of the people; yet these laws, like the statutes of Draco, are written in characters of blood. They approve the inhuman and unequal principle of retaliation; and the forfeit of an eye for an eye, a tooth for a tooth, a limb for a limb, is rigorously exacted, unless the offender can redeem his pardon by a fine of three hundred pounds of copper. The Decemvirs distributed with much liberality the slighter chastisements of flagellation and servitude; and nine crimes of a very different complexion are adjudged worthy of death. 1. Any act of *treason* against the state, or of correspondence with the public enemy. The mode of execution was painful and ignominious: the head of the degenerate Roman was shrouded in a veil, his hands were tied behind his back, and, after he had been scourged by the lictor, he was suspended in the midst of the forum on a cross, or inauspicious tree. 2. Nocturnal meetings in the city, whatever might be the pretence–of pleasure, or religion, or the public good. 3. The murder of a citizen; for which the common feelings of mankind demand the blood of the murderer. Poison is still more odious than the sword or dagger; and we are surprised to discover, in two flagitious events, how early such subtle wickedness had infected the simplicity of the republic and the chaste virtues of the Roman matrons. The parricide, who violated the duties of nature and gratitude, was cast into the river or the sea, enclosed in a sack; and a cock, a viper, a dog, and a monkey, were successively added as the most suitable companions. Italy produces no monkeys; but the want could never be felt till the middle of the sixth century first revealed the guilt of a parricide. 4. The malice of an *incendiary*. After the previous ceremony of whipping, he himself was delivered to the flames; and in this example alone our reason is tempted to applaud the justice of retaliation. 5. *Judicial perjury*. The corrupt or malicious witness was thrown headlong from the Tarpeian rock to expiate his falsehood, which was rendered still more fatal by the severity of the penal laws and the deficiency of written evidence. 6. The corruption of a judge, who accepted bribes to pronounce an iniquitous sentence. 7. Libels and satires, whose rude strains sometimes disturbed the peace of an illiterate city. The author was beaten with clubs, a worthy chastisement; but it is not certain that he was left to expire under the blows of the executioner. 8. The nocturnal mischief of damaging or destroying a neighbour's corn. The criminal was suspended as a grateful victim to Ceres. But the sylvan deities were less implacable, and the extirpation of a more valuable tree was compensated by the moderate fine of twenty-five pounds of copper. 9. Magical incantations; which had power, in the opinion of the Latian shepherds, to exhaust the strength of an enemy, to extinguish his life, and to remove from their seats his deep-rooted plantations. The cruelty of the Twelve Tables against insolvent debtors still remains to be told. After the judicial proof or confession of the debt, thirty days of grace were allowed before a Roman was delivered into the power of his fellow-citizen. In this private prison twelve ounces of rice were his daily food; he might be bound with a chain of fifteen pounds weight; and his misery was thrice exposed in the marketplace, to solicit the compassion of his friends and countrymen. At the expiration of sixty days the debt was discharged by the loss of liberty or life; the insolvent debtor was either put to death or sold in foreign slavery beyond the Tiber: but, if several creditors were alike obstinate and unrelenting, they might legally dismember his body, and satiate their revenge by this horrid partition. The advocates for this savage law have insisted that it must strongly operate in deterring idleness and fraud from contracting debts which they were unable to discharge; but experience would dissipate this salutary terror, by proving that no creditor could be found to exact this unprofitable penalty of life or limb. As the manners of Rome were insensibly polished, the criminal code of the Decemvirs was abolished by the humanity of accusers, witnesses, and judges; and impunity became the consequence of immoderate rigour. The Porcian and Valerian laws prohibited the magistrates from inflicting on a free citizen any capital, or even corporal, punishment; and the obsolete statutes of blood were artfully, and perhaps truly, ascribed to the spirit, not of patrician, but of regal, tyranny.

IV. In the absence of penal laws and the insufficiency of civil actions, the peace and justice of the city were imperfectly maintained by the private jurisdiction of the citizens. The malefactors who replenish our gaols are the outcasts of society, and the crimes for which they suffer may be commonly ascribed to ignorance, poverty, and brutal appetite. For the perpetration of similar enormities, a vile plebeian might claim and abuse the sacred character of a member of the republic; but on the proof or suspicion of guilt the slave or the stranger was nailed to a cross, and this strict and summary justice might be exercised without restraint over the greatest part of the populace of Rome. Each family contained a domestic tribunal, which was not confined, like that of the prætor, to the cognisance of external actions: virtuous principles and habits were inculcated by the discipline of education, and the Roman father was accountable to the state for the manners of his children, since he disposed without appeal of their life, their liberty, and their inheritance. In some pressing emergencies, the citizen was authorised to avenge his private or public wrongs. The consent of the Jewish, the Athenian, and the Roman laws, approved the slaughter of the nocturnal thief; though in open daylight a robber could not be slain without some previous evidence of danger and complaint. Whoever surprised an adulterer in his nuptial bed might freely exercise his revenge; the most bloody or wanton outrage was excused by the provocation; nor was it before the reign of Augustus that the husband was reduced to weigh the rank of the offender, or that the parent was condemned to sacrifice his daughter with her guilty seducer. After the expulsion of the kings, the ambitious Roman who should dare to assume their title or imitate their tyranny was devoted to the infernal gods: each of his fellow-citizens was armed with the sword of justice; and the act of Brutus, however repugnant to gratitude or prudence, had been already sanctified by the judgment of his country. The barbarous practice of wearing arms in the midst of peace, and the bloody maxims of honour, were unknown to the Romans; and during the two purest ages, from the establishment of equal freedom to the end of the Punic wars, the city was never disturbed by sedition, and rarely polluted with atrocious crimes. The failure of penal laws was more sensibly felt when every vice was inflamed by faction at home and dominion abroad. In the time of Cicero each private citizen enjoyed the privilege of anarchy—each minister of the republic was exalted to the temptations of regal power, and their virtues are entitled to the warmest praise as the spontaneous fruits of nature or philosophy. After a triennial indulgence of lust, rapine, and cruelty, Verres, the tyrant of Sicily, could only be sued for the pecuniary restitution of three hundred thousand pounds sterling; and such was the temper of the laws, the judges, and perhaps the accuser himself, that, on refunding a thirteenth part of his plunder, Verres could retire to an easy and luxurious exile.

The first imperfect attempt to restore the proportion of crimes and punishments was made by the dictator Sylla, who, in the midst of his sanguinary triumph, aspired to restrain the licence rather than to oppress the liberty of the Romans. He gloried in the arbitrary proscription of four thousand seven hundred citizens. But, in the character of a legislator, he respected the prejudices of the times; and instead of pronouncing a sentence of death against the robber or assassin, the general who betrayed an army or the magistrate who ruined a province, Sylla was content to aggravate the pecuniary damages by the penalty of exile, or, in more constitutional language, by the interdiction of fire and water. The Cornelian, and afterwards the Pompeian and Julian laws, introduced a new system of criminal jurisprudence; and the emperors, from Augustus to Justinian, disguised their increasing rigour under the names of the original authors. But the invention and frequent use of *extraordinary pains* proceeded from the desire to extend and conceal the progress of despotism. In the condemnation of illustrious Romans, the senate was always prepared to confound, at the will of their masters, the judicial and legislative powers. It was the duty of the governors to maintain the peace of their province by the arbitrary and rigid administration of justice; the freedom of the city evaporated in the extent of empire, and the Spanish malefactor who claimed the privilege of a Roman was elevated by the command of Galba on a fairer and more lofty cross. Occasional rescripts issued from the throne to decide the questions which, by their novelty or importance, appeared to surpass the authority and discernment of a proconsul. Transportation and beheading were reserved for honourable persons; meaner criminals were either hanged, or burnt, or buried in the mines, or exposed to the wild beasts of the amphitheatre. Armed robbers were pursued and extirpated as the enemies of society; the driving away horses or cattle was made a capital offence; but simple theft was uniformly considered as a mere civil and private injury. The degrees of guilt and the modes of punishment were too often determined by the discretion of the rulers, and the subject was left in ignorance of the legal danger which he might incur by every action of his life.

A sin, a vice, a crime, are the objects of theology, ethics, and jurisprudence. Whenever their judgments agree, they corroborate each other; but as often as they differ, a prudent legislator appreciates the guilt and punishment according to the measure of social injury. On this principle the most daring attack on the life and property of a private citizen is judged less atrocious than the crime of treason or rebellion, which invades the *majesty* of the republic: the obsequious civilians unanimously pronounced that the republic is contained in the person of its chief, and the edge of the Julian law was sharpened by the incessant diligence of the emperors. The licentious commerce of the sexes may be tolerated as an impulse of nature, or forbidden as a source of disorder and corruption; but the fame, the fortunes, the family of the husband, are seriously injured by the adultery of the wife. The wisdom of Augustus, after curbing the freedom of revenge, applied to this domestic offence the animadversion of the laws; and the guilty parties, after the payment of heavy forfeitures and fines, were condemned to long or perpetual exile in two separate islands. Religion pronounces an equal censure against the infidelity of the husband, but, as it is not accompanied by the same civil effects, the wife was never permitted to vindicate her wrongs; and the distinction of simple or double adultery, so familiar and so important in the canon law, is unknown to the jurisprudence of the Code and Pandects.

The primitive Romans were infected by the example of the Etruscans and Greeks; and the Scatinian law, which had been extorted by an act of violence, was insensibly abolished by the lapse of time and the multitude of criminals. By this law the rape, perhaps the seduction, of an ingenuous youth was compensated as a personal injury by the poor damages of ten thousand sesterces, or four-score pounds; the ravisher might be slain by the resistance or revenge of chastity. But the practice of vice was not discouraged by the severity of opinion, nor was the licentious lover exposed to the same dishonour which he impressed on the male or female partner of his guilt. From Catullus to Juvenal, the poets accuse and celebrate the degeneracy of the times; and the reformation of manners was feebly attempted by the reason and authority of the civilians.

A new spirit of legislation, respectable even in its error, arose in the empire with the religion of Constantine. The laws of Moses were received as the divine original of justice, and the Christian princes adapted their penal statutes to the degrees of moral and religious turpitude. Adultery was first declared to be a capital offence: the frailty of the sexes was assimilated to poison or assassination, to sorcery or parricide; the same penalties were inflicted on the passive and active guilt of pæderasty; and all criminals, of free or servile condition, were either drowned, or beheaded, or cast alive into the avenging flames.

The free citizens of Athens and Rome enjoyed in all criminal cases the invaluable privilege of being tried by their country. 1. The administration of justice is the most ancient office of a prince: it was exercised by the Roman kings, and abused by Tarquin, who alone, without law or council, pronounced his arbitrary judgments. The first consuls succeeded to this regal prerogative; but the sacred right of appeal soon abolished the jurisdiction of the magistrates, and all public causes were decided by the supreme tribunal of the people. But a wild democracy, superior to the forms, too often disdains the essential principles, of justice; the pride of despotism was envenomed by plebeian envy; and the heroes of Athens might sometimes applaud the happiness of the Persian, whose fate depended on the caprice of a *single* tyrant. Some salutary restraints, imposed by the people on their own passions, were at once the cause and effect of the gravity and temperance of the Romans. The right of accusation was confined to the magistrates. A vote of the thirty-five tribes could inflict a fine; but the cognisance of all capital crimes was reserved by a fundamental law to the assembly of the centuries, in which the weight of influence and property was sure to preponderate. Repeated proclamations and adjournments were interposed, to allow time for prejudice and resentment to subside; the whole proceeding might be annulled by a seasonable omen or the opposition of a tribune, and such popular trials were commonly less formidable to innocence than they were favourable to guilt. But this union of the judicial and legislative powers left it doubtful whether the accused party was pardoned or acquitted; and, in the defence of an illustrious client, the orators of Rome and Athens address their arguments to the policy and benevolence, as well as to the justice, of their sovereign. 2. The task of convening the citizens for the trial of each offender became more difficult, as the citizens and the offenders continually multiplied, and the ready expedient was adopted of delegating the jurisdiction of the people to the ordinary magistrates or to extraordinary *inquisitors*. In the first ages these questions were rare and occasional. In the beginning of the seventh century of Rome they were made perpetual: four prætors were annually empowered to sit in judgment on the state offences of treason, extortion, peculation, and bribery; and Sylla added new prætors and new questions for those crimes which more directly injure the safety of individuals. By these *inquisitors* the trial was prepared and directed; but they could only pronounce the sentence of the majority of *judges*, who, with some truth and more prejudice, have been compared to the English juries. To discharge this important though burdensome office, an annual list of ancient and respectable citizens was formed by the prætor. After many constitutional struggles, they were chosen in equal numbers from the senate, the equestrian order, and the people; four hundred and fifty were appointed for single questions, and the various rolls or *decuries* of judges must have contained the names of some thousand Romans, who represented the judicial authority of the state. In each particular cause a sufficient number was drawn from the urn; their integrity was guarded by an oath; the mode of ballot secured their independence; the suspicion of partiality was removed by the mutual challenges of the accuser and defendant; and the judges of Milo, by the retrenchment of fifteen on each side, were reduced to fifty-one voices or tablets, of acquittal, of condemnation, or of favourable doubt. 3. In his civil jurisdiction the prætor of the city was truly a judge, and almost a legislator; but, as soon as he had prescribed the action of law, he often referred to a delegate the determination of the fact. With the increase of legal proceedings, the tribunal of the centumvirs, in which he presided, acquired more weight and reputation. But whether he acted alone or with the advice of his council, the most absolute powers might be trusted to a magistrate who was annually chosen by the votes of the people. The rules and precautions of freedom have required some explanation; the order of despotism is simple and inanimate. Before the age of Justinian, or perhaps of Diocletian, the decuries of Roman judges had sunk to an empty title; the humble advice of the assessors might be accepted or despised; and in each tribunal the civil and criminal jurisdiction was administered by a single magistrate, who was raised and disgraced by the will of the emperor.

A Roman accused of any capital crime might prevent the sentence of the law by voluntary exile or death. Till his guilt had been legally proved, his innocence was presumed and his person was free; till the votes of the last *century* had been counted and declared, he might peaceably secede to any of the allied cities of Italy, or Greece, or Asia. His fame and fortunes were preserved, at least to his children, by this civil death; and he might still be happy in every rational and sensual enjoyment, if a mind accustomed to the ambitious tumult of Rome could support the uniformity and silence of Rhodes or Athens. A bolder effort was required to escape from the tyranny of the Cæsars; but this effort was rendered familiar by the maxims of the Stoics, the example of the bravest Romans, and the legal encouragements of suicide. The bodies of condemned criminals were exposed to public ignominy, and their children, a more serious evil, were reduced to poverty by the confiscation of their fortunes. But, if the victims of Tiberius and Nero anticipated the decree of the prince or senate, their courage and despatch were recompensed by the applause of the public, the decent honours of burial, and the validity of their testaments. The exquisite avarice and cruelty of Domitian appears to have deprived the unfortunate of this last consolation, and it was still denied even by the clemency of the Antonines. A voluntary death, which, in the case of a capital offence, intervened between the accusation and the sentence, was admitted as a confession of guilt, and the spoils of the deceased were seized by the inhuman claims of the treasury.

The penal statutes form a very small proportion of the sixty-two books of the Code and Pandects, and in all judicial proceedings the life or death of a citizen is determined with less caution and delay than the most ordinary question of covenant or inheritance. This singular distinction, though something may be allowed for the urgent necessity of defending the peace of society, is derived from the nature of criminal and civil jurisprudence. Our duties to the state are simple and uniform; the law by which he is condemned is inscribed not only on brass or marble, but on the conscience of the offender, and his guilt is commonly proved by the testimony of a single fact. But our relations to each other are various and infinite; our obligations are created, annulled, and modified by injuries, benefits, and promises; and the interpretation of voluntary contracts and testaments, which are often dictated by fraud or ignorance, affords a long and laborious exercise to the sagacity of the judge. The business of life is multiplied by the extent of commerce and dominion, and the residence of the parties in the distant provinces of an empire is productive of doubt, delay, and inevitable appeals from the local to the supreme magistrate.

CHAPTER XXIX

Causes of Decay and Destruction—Conclusion of the Whole Work

The rise of a city which swelled into an empire may deserve, as a singular prodigy, the reflection of a philosophic mind. But the decline of Rome was the natural and inevitable effect of immoderate greatness. Prosperity ripened the principle of decay; the causes of destruction multiplied with the extent of conquest; and as soon as time or accident had removed the artificial supports, the stupendous fabric yielded to the pressure of its own weight. The story of its ruin is simple and obvious; and instead of inquiring *why* the Roman empire was destroyed, we should rather be surprised that it had subsisted so long. The victorious legions, who, in distant wars, acquired the vices of strangers and mercenaries, first oppressed the freedom of the republic, and afterwards violated the majesty of the purple. The emperors, anxious for their personal safety and the public peace, were reduced to the base expedient of corrupting the discipline which rendered them alike formidable to their sovereign and to the enemy; the vigour of the military government was relaxed and finally dissolved by the partial institutions of Constantine; and the Roman world was overwhelmed by a deluge of barbarians.

The decay of Rome has been frequently ascribed to the translation of the seat of empire; but this history has already shown that the powers of Government were *divided* rather than *removed.* The throne of Constantinople was erected in the East; while the West was still possessed by a series of emperors who held their residence in Italy, and claimed their equal inheritance of the legions and provinces. This dangerous novelty impaired the strength and fomented the vices of a double reign: the instruments of an oppressive and arbitrary system were multiplied; and a vain emulation of luxury, not of merit, was introduced and supported between the degenerate successors of Theodosius. Extreme distress, which unites the virtue of a free people, embitters the factions of a declining monarchy. The hostile favourites of Arcadius and Honorius betrayed the republic to its common enemies; and the Byzantine court beheld with indifference, perhaps with pleasure, the disgrace of Rome, the misfortunes of Italy, and the loss of the West. Under the succeeding reigns the alliance of the two empires was restored; but the aid of the Oriental Romans was tardy, doubtful, and ineffectual; and the national schism of the Greeks and Latins was enlarged by the perpetual difference of language and manners, of interests, and even of religion. Yet the salutary event approved in some measure the judgment of Constantine. During a long period of decay his impregnable city repelled the victorious armies of barbarians, protected the wealth of Asia, and commanded, both in peace and war, the important straits which connect the Euxine and Mediterranean seas. The foundation of Constantinople more essentially contributed to the preservation of the East than to the ruin of the West.

As the happiness of a *future* life is the great object of religion, we may hear without surprise or scandal that the introduction, or at least the abuse of Christianity, had some influence on the decline and fall of the Roman empire. The clergy successfully preached the doctrines of patience and pusillanimity; the active virtues of society were discouraged; and the last remains of military spirit were buried in the cloister. Faith, zeal, curiosity, and more earthly passions of malice and ambition, kindled the flame of theological discord; the church, and even the state, were distracted by religious factions, whose conflicts were sometimes bloody and always implacable; the attention of the emperors was diverted from camps to synods; the Roman world was oppressed by a new species of tyranny; and the persecuted sects became the secret enemies of their country. Yet the bishops, from eighteen hundred pulpits, inculcated the duty of passive obedience to a lawful and orthodox sovereign; their frequent assemblies and perpetual correspondence maintained the communion of distant churches; and the benevolent temper of the Gospel was strengthened by the spiritual alliance of the Catholics. Religious precepts are easily obeyed which indulge and sanctify the natural inclinations of their votaries; but the pure and genuine influence of Christianity may be traced in its beneficial, though imperfect, effects on the barbarian proselytes of the North. If the decline of the Roman empire was hastened by the conversion of Constantine, his victorious religion broke the violence of the fall, and mollified the ferocious temper of the conquerors.

This awful revolution may be usefully applied to the instruction of the present age. It is the duty of a patriot to prefer and promote the exclusive interest and glory of his native country: but a philosopher may be permitted to enlarge his views, and to consider Europe as one great republic, whose various inhabitants have attained almost the same level of politeness and cultivation. The balance of power will continue to fluctuate, and the prosperity of our own or the neighbouring kingdoms may be alternately exalted or depressed; but these partial events cannot essentially injure our general state of happiness, the system of arts, and laws, and manners, which so advantageously distinguish, above the rest of mankind, the Europeans and their colonies. The savage nations of the globe are the common enemies of civilised society; and we may inquire, with anxious curiosity, whether Europe is still threatened with a repetition of those calamities which formerly oppressed the arms and institutions of Rome. Perhaps the same reflections will illustrate the fall of that mighty empire, and explain the probable causes of our actual security.

I. The Romans were ignorant of the extent of their dangers and the number of their enemies. Beyond the Rhine and Danube the northern countries of Europe and Asia were filled with innumerable tribes of hunters and shepherds, poor, voracious, and turbulent; bold in arms, and impatient to ravish the fruits of industry. The barbarian world was agitated by the rapid impulse of war; and the peace of Gaul or Italy was shaken by the distant revolutions of China. The Huns, who fled before a victorious enemy, directed their march towards the West; and the torrent was swelled by the gradual accession of captives and allies. The flying tribes who yielded to the Huns assumed in *their* turn the spirit of conquest; the endless column of barbarians pressed on the Roman empire with accumulated weight; and, if the foremost were destroyed, the vacant space was instantly replenished by new assailants.

Such formidable emigrations no longer issue from the North; and the long repose, which has been imputed to the decrease of population, is the happy consequence of the progress of arts and agriculture. Instead of some rude villages thinly scattered among its woods and morasses, Germany now produces a list of two thousand three hundred walled towns: the Christian kingdoms of Denmark, Sweden, and Poland have been successively established; and the Hanse merchants, with the Teutonic knights, have extended their colonies along the coast of the Baltic as far as the Gulf of Finland.

From the Gulf of Finland to the Eastern Ocean, Russia now assumes the form of a powerful and civilised empire. The plough, the loom, and the forge are introduced on the banks of the Volga, the Oby, and the Lena; and the fiercest of the Tartar hordes have been taught to tremble and obey. The reign of independent barbarism is now contracted to a narrow span; and the remnant of Calmucks or Uzbecks, whose forces may be almost numbered, cannot seriously excite the apprehensions of the great republic of Europe.

Yet this apparent security should not tempt us to forget that new enemies and unknown dangers may *possibly* arise from some obscure people, scarcely visible in the map of the world. The Arabs or Saracens, who spread their conquests from India to Spain, had languished in poverty and contempt till Mahomet breathed into those savage bodies the soul of enthusiasm.

II. The empire of Rome was firmly established by the singular and perfect coalition of its members. The subject nations, resigning the hope and even the wish of independence, embraced the character of Roman citizens; and the provinces of the West were reluctantly torn by the barbarians from the bosom of their mother country. But this union was purchased by the loss of national freedom and military spirit; and the servile provinces, destitute of life and motion, expected their safety from the mercenary troops and governors who were directed by the orders of a distant court. The happiness of an hundred millions depended on the personal merit of one or two men, perhaps children, whose minds were corrupted by education, luxury, and despotic power. The deepest wounds were inflicted on the empire during the minorities of the sons and grandsons of Theodosius; and, after those incapable princes seemed to attain the age of manhood, they abandoned the church to the bishops, the state to the eunuchs, and the provinces to the barbarians.

Europe is now divided into twelve powerful, though unequal kingdoms, three respectable commonwealths, and a variety of smaller, though independent states: the chances of royal and ministerial talent are multiplied, at least, with the number of its rulers; and a Julian, or Semiramis, may reign in the North, while Arcadius and Honorius again slumber on the thrones of the South. The abuses of tyranny are restrained by the mutual influence of fear and shame; republics have acquired order and stability; monarchies have imbibed the principles of freedom, or, at least, of moderation; and some sense of honour and justice is introduced into the most defective constitutions by the general manners of the times. In peace, the progress of knowledge and industry is accelerated by the emulation of so many active rivals: in war, the European forces are exercised by temperate and undecisive contests. If a savage conqueror should issue from the deserts of Tartary, he must repeatedly vanquish the robust peasants of Russia, the numerous armies of Germany, the gallant nobles of France, and the intrepid freemen of Britain; who, perhaps, might confederate for their common defence. Should the victorious barbarians carry slavery and desolation as far as the Atlantic Ocean, ten thousand vessels would transport beyond their pursuit the remains of civilised society; and Europe would revive and flourish in the American world, which is already filled with her colonies and institutions.

III. Cold, poverty, and a life of danger and fatigue fortify the strength and courage of barbarians. In every age they have oppressed the polite and peaceful nations of China, India, and Persia, who neglected, and still neglect, to counterbalance these natural powers by the resources of military art. The warlike states of antiquity, Greece, Macedonia, and Rome, educated a race of soldiers; exercised their bodies, disciplined their courage, multiplied their forces by regular evolutions, and converted the iron which they possessed into strong and serviceable weapons. But this superiority insensibly declined with their laws and manners: and the feeble policy of Constantine and his successors armed and instructed, for the ruin of the empire, the rude valour of the barbarian mercenaries. The military art has been changed by the invention of gunpowder, which enables man to command the two most powerful agents of nature, air and fire. Mathematics, chemistry, mechanics, architecture, have been applied to the service of war; and the adverse parties oppose to each other the most elaborate modes of attack and of defence. Historians may indignantly observe that the preparations of a siege would found and maintain a flourishing colony; yet we cannot be displeased that the subversion of a city should be a work of cost and difficulty; or that an industrious people should be protected by those arts which survive and supply the decay of military virtue. Cannon and fortifications now form an impregnable barrier against the Tartar horse; and

Europe is secure from any future irruption of barbarians; since, before they can conquer, they must cease to be barbarous. Their gradual advances in the science of war would always be accompanied, as we may learn from the example of Russia, with a proportionable improvement in the arts of peace and civil policy; and they themselves must deserve a place among the polished nations whom they subdue.

Should these speculations be found doubtful or fallacious, there still remains a more humble source of comfort and hope. The discoveries of ancient and modern navigators, and the domestic history or tradition of the most enlightened nations, represent the *human savage* naked both in mind and body, and destitute of laws, of arts, of ideas, and almost of language. From this abject condition, perhaps the primitive and universal state of man, he has gradually arisen to command the animals, to fertilise the earth, to traverse the ocean, and to measure the heavens. His progress in the improvement and exercise of his mental and corporeal faculties has been irregular and various; infinitely slow in the beginning, and increasing by degrees with redoubled velocity: ages of laborious ascent have been followed by a moment of rapid downfall; and the several climates of the globe have felt the vicissitudes of light and darkness. Yet the experience of four thousand years should enlarge our hopes and diminish our apprehensions: we cannot determine to what height the human species may aspire in their advance towards perfection; but it may safely be presumed that no people, unless the face of nature is changed, will relapse into their original barbarism.

The improvements of society may be viewed under a threefold aspect. 1. The poet or philosopher illustrates his age and country by the efforts of a *single* mind; but these superior powers of reason or fancy are rare and spontaneous productions; and the genius of Homer, or Cicero, or Newton, would excite less admiration if they could be created by the will of a prince or the lessons of a preceptor. 2. The benefits of law and policy, of trade and manufactures, of arts and sciences, are more solid and permanent; and *many* individuals may be qualified, by education and discipline, to promote, in their respective stations, the interest of the community. But this general order is the effect of skill and labour; and the complex machinery may be decayed by time, or injured by violence. 3. Fortunately for mankind, the more useful, or, at least, more necessary arts, can be performed without superior talents or national subordination; without powers of *one*, or the union of *many*. Each village, each family, each individual, must always possess both ability and inclination to perpetuate the use of fire and of metals; the propagation and service of domestic animals; the methods of hunting and fishing; the rudiments of navigation; the imperfect cultivation of corn or other nutritive grain; and the simple practice of the mechanic trades. Private genius and public industry may be extirpated, but these hardy plants survive the tempest, and strike an everlasting root into the most unfavourable soil. The splendid days of Augustus and Trajan were eclipsed by a cloud of ignorance; and the barbarians subverted the laws and palaces of Rome. But the scythe, the invention or emblem of Saturn, still continued annually to mow the harvests of Italy; and the human feasts of the Læstrigons have never been renewed on the coast of Campania.

Since the first discovery of the arts, war, commerce, and religious zeal have diffused among the savages of the Old and New World these inestimable gifts: they have been successively propagated; they can never be lost. We may therefore acquiesce in the pleasing conclusion that every age of the world has increased and still increases the real wealth, the happiness, the knowledge, and perhaps the virtue, of the human race.

In the last days of Pope Eugenius the Fourth, two of his servants, the learned Poggius and a friend, ascended the Capitoline hill, reposed themselves among the ruins of columns and temples, and viewed from that commanding spot the wide and various prospect of desolation. The place and the object gave ample scope for moralising on the vicissitudes of fortune, which spares neither man nor the proudest of his works, which buries empires and cities in a common grave; and it was agreed that, in proportion to her former greatness, the fall of Rome was the more awful and deplorable. "Her primeval state, such as she might appear in a remote age, when Evander entertained the stranger of Troy, has been delineated by the fancy of Virgil. This Tarpeian rock was then a savage and solitary thicket: in the time of the poet it was crowned with the golden roofs of a temple; the temple is overthrown, the gold has been pillaged, the wheel of fortune has accomplished her revolution, and the sacred ground is again disfigured with thorns and brambles. The hill of the Capitol, on which we sit, was formerly the head of the Roman empire, the citadel of the earth, the terror of kings; illustrated by the footsteps of so many triumphs, enriched with the spoils and tributes of so many nations. This spectacle of the world, how is it fallen! how changed! how defaced! the path of victory is obliterated by vines, and the benches of the senators are concealed by a dunghill. Cast your eyes on the Palatine hill, and seek among the shapeless and enormous fragments the marble theatre, the obelisks, the colossal statues, the porticoes of Nero's palace: survey the other hills of the city, the vacant space is interrupted only by ruins and gardens. The forum of the Roman people, where they assembled to enact their laws and elect their magistrates, is now enclosed for the cultivation of potherbs, or thrown open for the reception of swine and buffaloes. The public and private edifices, that were founded for eternity, lie prostrate, naked, and broken, like the limbs of a mighty giant; and the ruin is the more visible, from the stupendous relics that have survived the injuries of time and fortune."

These relics are minutely described by Poggius, one of the first who raised his eyes from the monuments of legendary to those of classic superstition. 1. Besides a bridge, an arch, a sepulchre, and the pyramid of Cestius, he could discern, of the age of the republic, a double row of vaults in the salt-office of the Capitol, which were inscribed with the name and munificence of Catulus. 2. Eleven temples were visible in some degree, from the perfect form of the Pantheon to the three arches and a marble column of the temple of Peace, which Vespasian erected after the civil wars and the Jewish triumph. 3. Of the number, which he rashly defines, of seven *thermœ*, or public baths, none were sufficiently entire to represent the use and distribution of the several baths; but those of Diocletian and Antoninus Caracalla still retained the titles of the founders, and astonished the curious spectator, who, in observing their solidity and extent, the variety of marbles, the size and multitude of the columns, compared the labour and expense with the use and importance. Of the baths of Constantine, of Alexander, of Domitian, or rather of Titus, some vestige might yet be found. 4. The triumphal arches of Titus, Severus, and Constantine, were entire, both the structure and the inscriptions: a falling fragment was honoured with the name of Trajan; and two arches, then extant, in the Flaminian way, have been ascribed to the base memory of Faustina and Gallienus. 5. After the wonder of the Coliseum, Poggius might have overlooked a small amphitheatre of brick, most probably for the use of the prætorian camp: the theatres of Marcellus and Pompey were occupied in a great measure by public and private buildings; and in the Circus, Agonalis and Maximus, little more than the situation and the form could be investigated. 6. The columns of Trajan and Antonine were still erect; but the Egyptian obelisks were broken or buried. A people of gods and heroes, the workmanship of art, was reduced to one equestrian figure of gilt brass and to five marble statues, of which the most conspicuous were the two horses of Phidias and Praxiteles. 7. The two mausoleums or sepulchres of Augustus and Hadrian could not totally be lost; but the former was only visible as a mound of earth, and the latter, the castle of St. Angelo, had acquired the name and appearance of a modern fortress. With the addition of some separate and nameless columns, such were the remains of the ancient city; for the marks of a more recent structure might be detected in the walls, which formed a circumference of ten miles, included three hundred and seventy-nine turrets, and opened into the country by thirteen gates.

This melancholy picture was drawn above nine hundred years after the fall of the Western empire, and even of the Gothic kingdom of Italy. A long period of distress and anarchy, in which empire, and arts, and riches had migrated from the banks of the Tiber, was incapable of restoring or adorning the city; and, as all that is human must retrograde if it do not advance, every successive age must have hastened the ruin of the work of antiquity. While the Roman edifices were still entire, the first blows, however weighty and impetuous, were resisted by the solidity of the mass and the harmony of the parts; but the slightest touch would precipitate the fragments of arches and columns that already nodded to their fall.

After a diligent inquiry I can discern four principal causes of the ruin of Rome, which continued to operate in a period of more than a thousand years. I. The injuries of time and nature. II. The hostile attacks of the barbarians and Christians. III. The use and abuse of the materials. And, IV. The domestic quarrels of the Romans.

I. The art of man is able to construct monuments far more permanent than the narrow span of his own existence: yet these monuments, like himself, are perishable and frail; and in the boundless annals of time his life and his labours must equally be measured as a fleeting moment. Of a simple and solid edifice it is not easy however to circumscribe the duration. As the wonders of ancient days, the pyramids attracted the curiosity of the ancients: a hundred generations, the leaves of autumn, have dropped into the grave; and after the fall of the Pharaohs and Ptolemies, the Cæsars and caliphs, the same pyramids stand erect and unshaken above the floods of the Nile. A complex figure of various and minute parts is more accessible to injury and decay; and the silent lapse of time is often accelerated by hurricanes and earthquakes, by fires and inundations. The air and earth have doubtless been shaken; and the lofty turrets of Rome have tottered from their foundations; but the seven hills do not appear to be placed on the great cavities of the globe; nor has the city, in any age, been exposed to the convulsions of nature, which, in the climate of Antioch, Lisbon, or Lima, have crumbled in a few moments the works of ages into dust. Fire is the most powerful agent of life and death: the rapid mischief may be kindled and propagated by the industry or negligence of mankind; and every period of the Roman annals is marked by the repetition of similar calamities. A memorable conflagration, the guilt or misfortune of Nero's reign, continued, though with unequal fury, either six or nine days. Innumerable buildings, crowded in close and crooked streets, supplied perpetual fuel for the flames; and when they ceased, four only of the fourteen regions were left entire; three were totally destroyed, and seven were deformed by the relics of smoking and lacerated edifices. In the full meridian of empire the metropolis arose with fresh beauty from her ashes; yet the memory of the old deplored their irreparable losses, the arts of Greece, the trophies of victory, the monuments of primitive or fabulous antiquity. In the days of distress and anarchy every wound is mortal, every fall irretrievable; nor can the damage be restored either by the public care of government, or the activity of private interest. Yet two causes may be alleged which render the calamity of fire more destructive to a flourishing than a decayed city. 1. The more combustible materials of brick, timber, and metals, are first melted or consumed; but the flames may play without injury or effect on the naked walls and massy arches that have been despoiled of their ornaments. 2. It is among the common and plebeian habitations that a mischievous spark is most easily blown to a conflagration; but as soon as they are devoured, the greater edifices which have resisted or escaped are left as so many islands in a state of solitude and safety.

From her situation, Rome is exposed to the danger of frequent inundations. Without excepting the Tiber, the rivers that descend from either side of the Apennine have a short and irregular course; a shallow stream in the summer heats; an impetuous torrent when it is swelled in the spring or winter, by the fall of rain and the melting of the snows. When the current is repelled from the sea by adverse winds, when the ordinary bed is inadequate to the weight of waters, they rise above the banks, and overspread, without limits or control, the plains and cities of the adjacent country. Soon after the triumph of the first Punic war the Tiber was increased by unusual rains; and the inundation, surpassing all former measure of time and place, destroyed all the buildings that were situate below the hills of Rome. According to the variety of ground, the same mischief was produced by different means; and the edifices were either swept away by the sudden impulse, or dissolved and undermined by the long continuance, of the flood.

Under the reign of Augustus the same calamity was renewed: the lawless river overturned the palaces and temples on its banks; and, after the labours of the emperor in cleansing and widening the bed that was encumbered with ruins, the vigilance of his successors was exercised by similar dangers and designs. The project of diverting into new channels the Tiber itself, or some of the dependent streams, was long opposed by superstition and local interests; nor did the use compensate the toil and cost of the tardy and imperfect execution. The servitude of rivers is the noblest and most important victory which man has obtained over the licentiousness of nature; and if such were the ravages of the Tiber under a firm and active government, what could oppose, or who can enumerate, the injuries of the city after the fall of the Western empire? A remedy was at length produced by the evil itself: the accumulation of rubbish and the earth that has been washed down from the hills is supposed to have elevated the plain of Rome fourteen or fifteen feet, perhaps, above the ancient level; and the modern city is less accessible to the attacks of the river.

II. The crowd of writers of every nation, who impute the destruction of the Roman monuments to the Goths and the Christians, have neglected to inquire how far they were animated by a hostile principle, and how far they possessed the means and the leisure to satiate their enmity. The shepherds of Scythia and Germany had been educated in the armies of the empire, whose discipline they acquired, and whose weakness they invaded: with the familiar use of the Latin tongue they had learned to reverence the name and titles of Rome; and, though incapable of emulating, they were more inclined to admire than to abolish the arts and studies of a brighter period. In the transient possession of a rich and unresisting capital, the soldiers of Alaric and Genseric were stimulated by the passions of a victorious army; amidst the wanton indulgence of lust or cruelty, portable wealth was the object of their search: nor could they derive either pride or pleasure from the unprofitable reflection that they had battered to the ground the works of the consuls and Cæsars. Their moments were indeed precious: the Goths evacuated Rome on the sixth, the Vandals on the fifteenth day; and, though it be far more difficult to build than to destroy, their hasty assault would have made a slight impression on the solid piles of antiquity. We may remember that both Alaric and Genseric affected to spare the buildings of the city; that they subsisted in strength and beauty under the auspicious government of Theodoric.

It is probable that a portion of guilt or merit may be imputed with justice to the Roman proselytes. Yet their abhorrence was confined to the monuments of heathen superstition; and the civil structures that were dedicated to the business or pleasure of society might be preserved without injury or scandal. The change of religion was accomplished, not by a popular tumult, but by the decrees of the emperors, of the senate, and of time. Of the Christian hierarchy, the bishops of Rome were commonly the most prudent and least fanatic; nor can any positive charge be opposed to the meritorious act of saving and converting the majestic structure of the Pantheon.

III. The value of any object that supplies the wants or pleasures of mankind is compounded of its substance and its form, of the materials and the manufacture. Its price must depend on the number of persons by whom it may be acquired and used; on the extent of the market; and consequently on the ease or difficulty of remote exportation, according to the nature of the commodity, its local situation, and the temporary circumstances of the world. The barbarian conquerors of Rome usurped in a moment the toil and treasure of successive ages; but, except the luxuries of immediate consumption, they must view without desire all that could not be removed from the city in the Gothic waggons or the fleet of the Vandals. Gold and silver were the first objects of their avarice; as in every country, and in the smallest compass, they represent the most ample command of the industry and possessions of mankind. A vase or a statue of those precious metals might tempt the vanity of some barbarian chief; but the grosser multitude, regardless of the form, was tenacious only of the substance; and the melted ingots might be readily divided and stamped into the current coin of the empire. The less active or less fortunate robbers were reduced to the baser plunder of brass, lead, iron, and copper: whatever had escaped the Goths and Vandals was pillaged by the Greek tyrants; and the emperor Constans, in his rapacious visit, stripped the bronze tiles from the roof of the Pantheon. The edifices of Rome might be considered as a vast and various mine; the first labour of extracting the materials was already performed; the metals were purified and cast; the marbles were hewn and polished; and after foreign and domestic rapine had been satiated, the remains of the city, could a purchaser have been found, were still venal. The monuments of antiquity had been left naked of their precious ornaments; but the Romans would demolish with their own hands the arches and walls, if the hope of profit could surpass the cost of the labour and exportation.

The Romans, alone and unenvied, might have applied to their private or public use the remaining structures of antiquity, if in their present form and situation they had not been useless in a great measure to the city and its inhabitants. The walls still described the old circumference, but the city had descended from the seven hills into the Campus Martius; and some of the noblest monuments which had braved the injuries of time were left in a desert far remote from the habitations of mankind. The palaces of the senators were no longer adapted to the manners or fortunes of their indigent successors: the use of baths and porticoes was forgotten: in the sixth century the games of the theatre, amphitheatre, and circus had been interrupted: some temples were devoted to the prevailing worship; but the Christian churches preferred the holy figure of the cross.

IV. I have reserved for the last the most potent and forcible cause of destruction, the domestic hostilities of the Romans themselves. Under the dominion of the Greek and French emperors the peace of the city was disturbed by accidental, though frequent, seditions: it is from the decline of the latter, from the beginning of the tenth century, that we may date the licentiousness of private war, which violated with impunity the laws of the Code and the Gospel, without respecting the majesty of the absent sovereign, or the presence and person of the vicar of Christ. In a dark period of five hundred years Rome was perpetually afflicted by the sanguinary quarrels of the nobles and the people, the Guelphs and Ghibellines, the Colonna and Ursini; and the factions of Italy alternately exercised a blind and thoughtless vengeance on their adversaries, whose houses and castles they razed to the ground. In comparing the *days* of foreign with the *ages* of domestic hostility, we must pronounce that the latter have been far more ruinous to the city; and our opinion is confirmed by the evidence of Petrarch. "Behold," says the laureate, "the relics of Rome, the image of her pristine greatness! neither time nor the barbarian can boast the merit of this stupendous destruction: it was perpetrated by her own citizens, by the most illustrious of her sons; and your ancestors (he writes to a noble Annibaldi) have done with the battering-ram what the Punic hero could not accomplish with the sword." The influence of the two last principles of decay must in some degree be multiplied by each other; since the houses and towers which were subverted by civil war required a new and perpetual supply from the monuments of antiquity.

These general observations may be separately applied to the amphitheatre of Titus, which has obtained the name of the COLISEUM, either from its magnitude, or from Nero's colossal statue: an edifice, had it been left to time and nature, which might perhaps have claimed an eternal duration. The curious antiquaries who have computed the numbers and seats are disposed to believe that above the upper row of stone steps the amphitheatre was encircled and elevated with several stages of wooden galleries, which were repeatedly consumed by fire, and restored by the emperors. Whatever was precious, or portable, or profane, the statues of gods and heroes, and the costly ornaments of sculpture, which were cast in brass, or overspread with leaves of silver and gold, became the first prey of conquest or fanaticism, of the avarice of the barbarians or the Christians. In the massy stones of the Coliseum many holes are discerned; and the two most probable conjectures represent the various accidents of its decay. These stones were connected by solid links of brass or iron, nor had the eye of rapine overlooked the value of the baser metals; the vacant space was converted into a fair or market; the artisans of the Coliseum are mentioned in an ancient survey; and the chasms were perforated or enlarged to receive the poles that supported the shops or tents of the mechanic trades.

Reduced to its naked majesty, the Flavian amphitheatre was contemplated with awe and admiration by the pilgrims of the North; and their rude enthusiasm broke forth in a sublime proverbial expression, which is recorded in the eighth century, in the fragments of the venerable Bede: "As long as the Coliseum stands, Rome shall stand; when the Coliseum falls, Rome will fall; when Rome falls, the world will fall."

THE EMPERORS OF ROME

	Date of Accession		*Date of Accession*
Augustus	B.C. 27	Gordian III	(*also* A.D. 238)
Tiberius	A.D. 14	Philip	A.D. 244
Caligula	A.D. 37	Decius	A.D. 249
Claudius	A.D. 41	Gallus	A.D. 251
Nero	A.D. 54	Aemilianus	A.D. 253
Galba		Valerian	A.D. 260
Otho	A.D. 68	Gallienus	
Vitellius		Claudius	A.D. 268
Vespasian	A.D. 69	Quintillus	A.D. 270
Titus	A.D. 79	Aurelian	
Domitian	A.D. 81	Tacitus	A.D. 275
Nerva	A.D. 96	Probus	A.D. 276
Trajan	A.D. 98	Carus	A.D. 282
Hadrian	A.D. 117	Carinus	A.D. 283
Antoninus Pius	A.D. 138	Numerian	
Marcus Aurelius	A.D. 161	Diocletian	A.D. 284
Commodus	A.D. 180	(with Maximian, from A.D. 286)	
Pertinax		Constantius Galerius	A.D. 305
Didius Julianus	A.D. 193	Licinus	A.D. 311
Septimus Severus		Constantine I	
Caracalla	A.D. 211	Constantine I	A.D. 324
Macrinus	A.D. 217	Constantine II	
Elagabalus	A.D. 218	Constantius II	A.D. 337
Alexander Severus	A.D. 222	Constans	
Maximinus	A.D. 235	Constantius II	A.D. 350
The two Gordianii	A.D. 238	Julian	A.D. 361
Pupienus and Balbinus		Jovian	A.D. 363

Division of the Empire

West		*East*	
Valentinian I	A.D. 364	Valens	
Gratian, Valentinian II	A.D. 375		
Valentinian II	A.D. 383	Theodosius I	A.D. 379

East and West

Theodosius I A.D. 392

West		*East*	
Honorius	A.D. 395	Arcadius	
Valentinian III	A.D. 423	Theodosius II	A.D. 408
Maximus	A.D. 455	Marcian	A.D. 450
Avitus	A.D. 455		
Marjorian	A.D. 457	Leo I	A.D. 457
Severus	A.D. 461		
Anthemius	A.D. 467		
Olybrius	A.D. 472		
Glycerius	A.D. 473		
Julius Nepos	A.D. 474	Leo II	A.D. 474
Romulus Augustulus	A.D. 475		